T0223455

Lecture Notes in Computer Science   **9415**

Commenced Publication in 1973
Founding and Former Series Editors:
Gerhard Goos, Juris Hartmanis, and Jan van Leeuwen

More information about this series at http://www.springer.com/series/7409

Christophe Debruyne · Hervé Panetto
Robert Meersman · Tharam Dillon
Georg Weichhart · Yuan An
Claudio Agostino Ardagna (Eds.)

On the Move to Meaningful Internet Systems: OTM 2015 Conferences

Confederated International Conferences:
CoopIS, ODBASE, and C&TC 2015
Rhodes, Greece, October 26–30, 2015
Proceedings

 Springer

Editors

Christophe Debruyne
Trinity College Dublin
Dublin 2
Ireland

Hervé Panetto
University of Lorraine
Vandoeuvre-les-Nancy Cedex
France

Robert Meersman
TU Graz
Graz
Austria

Tharam Dillon
La Trobe University
Melbourne
Australia

Georg Weichhart
PROFACTOR GmbH
Steyr-Gleink
Austria

Yuan An
Drexel University
Philadelphia, PA
USA

Claudio Agostino Ardagna
Università degli Studi di Milano
Crema
Italy

ISSN 0302-9743   ISSN 1611-3349   (electronic)
Lecture Notes in Computer Science
ISBN 978-3-319-26147-8   ISBN 978-3-319-26148-5   (eBook)
DOI 10.1007/978-3-319-26148-5

Library of Congress Control Number: 2015953246

LNCS Sublibrary: SL3 – Information Systems and Applications, incl. Internet/Web, and HCI

Springer International Publishing AG Switzerland is part of Springer Science+Business Media
(www.springer.com)

General Co-Chairs' Message for OnTheMove 2015, Rhodes, Greece

The OnTheMove 2015 event held during October 26–30, in Rhodes, Greece, further consolidated the importance of this series of annual conferences that was started in 2002 in Irvine, California. It then moved to Catania, Sicily, in 2003, to Cyprus in 2004 and 2005, Montpellier in 2006, Vilamoura in 2007 and 2009, in 2008 to Monterrey, Mexico, to Heraklion, Crete, in 2010 and 2011, Rome in 2012, Graz in 2013, and Amantea, Italy, in 2014. This prime event continues to attract a diverse and relevant selection of today's research worldwide on the scientific concepts underlying new computing paradigms, which of necessity must be distributed, heterogeneous, and supporting an environment of resources that are autonomous yet must meaningfully cooperate. Indeed, as such large, complex, and networked intelligent information systems become the focus and norm for computing, there continues to be an acute and even increasing need to address the implied software, system, and enterprise issues and discuss them face to face in an integrated forum that covers methodological, semantic, theoretical, and application issues as well. As we all realize, e-mail, the Internet, and even video conferences on their own are not optimal or even sufficient for effective and efficient scientific exchange.

The OnTheMove (OTM) Federated Conference series was created precisely to cover the scientific exchange needs of the communities that work in the broad yet closely connected fundamental technological spectrum of Web-based distributed computing. The OTM program every year covers data and Web semantics, distributed objects, Web services, databases, information systems, enterprise workflow and collaboration, ubiquity, interoperability, mobility, as well as grid and high-performance computing.

OTM does *not* consider itself a so-called multi-conference event but instead is proud to give meaning to the "federated" aspect in its full title[1]: It aspires to be a primary scientific meeting place where all aspects of research and development of Internet- and intranet-based systems in organizations and for e-business are discussed in a scientifically motivated way, in a forum of loosely interconnected workshops and conferences. This year's 14th edition of the OTM Federated Conferences event therefore once more provided an opportunity for researchers and practitioners to understand, discuss, and publish these developments within the broader context of distributed, ubiquitous computing. To further promote synergy and coherence, the main conferences of OTM 2015 were conceived against a background of three interlocking global themes:

- Trusted Cloud Computing Infrastructures Emphasizing Security and Privacy
- Technology and Methodology for Data and Knowledge Resources on the (Semantic) Web

---

[1] On The Move Towards Meaningful Internet Systems and Ubiquitous Computing – Federated Conferences and Workshops

- Deployment of Collaborative and Social Computing for and in an Enterprise Context

Originally the federative structure of OTM was formed by the co-location of three related, complementary, and successful main conference series: DOA (Distributed Objects and Applications, held since 1999), covering the relevant infrastructure-enabling technologies, ODBASE (Ontologies, DataBases and Applications of SEmantics, since 2002), covering Web semantics, XML databases, and ontologies, and of course CoopIS (Cooperative Information Systems, held since 1993), which studies the application of these technologies in an enterprise context through, e.g., workflow systems and knowledge management. In the 2011 edition, security issues, originally started as topics of the IS workshop in OTM 2006, became the focus of DOA as secure virtual infrastructures, further broadened to cover aspects of trust and privacy in so-called cloud-based systems. As this latter aspect came to dominate agendas in this and overlapping research communities, we decided in 2014 to rename the event as the Cloud and Trusted Computing (C&TC) conference, and to organize and launch it in a workshop format to define future editions.

Both main conferences specifically seek high-quality contributions of a more mature nature and encourage researchers to treat their respective topics within a framework that simultaneously incorporates (a) theory, (b) conceptual design and development, (c) methodology and pragmatics, and (d) application in particular case studies and industrial solutions.

As in previous years, we again solicited and selected additional quality workshop proposals to complement the more mature and "archival" nature of the main conferences. Our workshops are intended to serve as "incubators" for emergent research results in selected areas related, or becoming related, to the general domain of Web-based distributed computing. This year the difficult and time-consuming job of selecting and coordinating the workshops was brought to a successful end by Ioana Ciuciu, and we were very glad to see that some of our earlier successful workshops (EI2N, META4eS, ISDE, INBAST, MSC) re-appeared in 2015, in some cases in alliance with other older or newly emerging workshops. The new Fact-Based Modeling (FBM) workshop succeeded and expanded the scope of the successful ORM workshop. The Industry Case Studies Program, started in 2011 under the leadership of Hervé Panetto and OMG's Richard Mark Soley, further gained momentum and visibility in its fifth edition this year.

The OTM registration format ("one workshop or conference buys all workshops or conferences") actively intends to promote synergy between related areas in the field of distributed computing and to stimulate workshop audiences to productively mingle with each other and, optionally, with those of the main conferences. In particular EI2N continues to create and exploit a visible cross-pollination with CoopIS.

We were happy to see that also in 2015 the number of quality submissions for the OnTheMove Academy (OTMA) stabilized for the fourth consecutive year. OTMA implements our unique, actively coached and therefore very time- and effort-intensive formula to bring PhD students together, and aims to carry our "vision for the future" in research in the areas covered by OTM. Its 2015 edition was organized and managed by a dedicated team of collaborators and faculty, Peter Spyns, Maria-Esther Vidal, Anja Metzner, and Alfred Holl, inspired as always by the OTMA Dean, Erich Neuhold.

In the OTM Academy, PhD research proposals are submitted by students for peer review; selected submissions and their approaches are to be presented by the students in front of a wider audience at the conference, and are independently and extensively analyzed and discussed in front of this audience by a panel of senior professors. One will readily appreciate the resources invested in this by OTM and especially the OTMA faculty!

As the three main conferences and the associated workshops all share the distributed aspects of modern computing systems, they experience the application pull created by the Internet and by the so-called Semantic Web, in particular developments of big data, increased importance of security issues, and the globalization of mobile-based technologies. For ODBASE 2015, the focus continued to be the knowledge bases and methods required for enabling the use of formal semantics in Web-based databases and information systems. For CoopIS 2015, the focus as before was on the interaction of such technologies and methods with business process issues, such as occur in networked organizations and enterprises. These subject areas overlap in a scientifically natural and fascinating fashion and many submissions in fact also covered and exploited the mutual impact among them. For our C&TC 2015 event, its primary emphasis was again squarely put on the virtual and security aspects of Web-based computing in the broadest sense. As with the earlier OTM editions, the organizers wanted to stimulate this cross-pollination by a program of famous keynote speakers from academia and industry around the chosen themes and shared by all OTM component events. We are quite proud to list for this year:

- Michele Bezzi
- Eva Kühn
- John Mylopoulos
- Sjir Nijssen

The general downturn in submissions observed in recent years for almost all conferences in computer science and IT is also affecting OTM, but we were still fortunate to receive a total of 130 submissions for the three main conferences and 86 submissions in total for the workshops. Not only may we indeed again claim success in attracting a representative volume of scientific papers, many from the USA and Asia, but these numbers of course allowed the respective Program Committees to again compose a high-quality cross-section of current research in the areas covered by OTM. Acceptance rates vary but the aim was to stay consistently at about one accepted full paper for two to three submitted (nearly one in four for CoopIS), yet as always these rates are subordinated to professional peer assessment of proper scientific quality. As usual we have separated the proceedings into two volumes with their own titles, one for the main conferences and one for the workshops and posters, and we are again most grateful to the Springer LNCS team in Heidelberg for their professional support, suggestions, and meticulous collaboration in producing the files and indexes ready for downloading on the USB sticks.

The reviewing process by the respective OTM Program Committees was performed to professional quality standards: Each paper review in the main conferences was assigned to at least three referees, with arbitrated e-mail discussions in the case of strongly diverging evaluations. It may be worthwhile to emphasize once more that it is an explicit OTM policy that all conference Program Committees and Chairs make their selections in a completely sovereign manner, autonomous and independent from any OTM organizational considerations. As in recent years, proceedings in paper form are now only available to be ordered separately.

The General Chairs are once more especially grateful to the many people directly or indirectly involved in the set-up of these federated conferences. Not everyone realizes the large number of persons that need to be involved, and the huge amount of work, commitment, and in the uncertain economic and funding climate of 2015 certainly also financial risk that is entailed by the organization of an event like OTM. Apart from the persons in their aforementioned roles, we therefore wish to thank in particular explicitly our main conference Program Committee Chairs:

- CoopIS 2015: Georg Weichhart, with Heiko Ludwig and Michael Rosemann
- ODBASE 2015: Yuan An, with Min Song and Markus Strohmaier
- C&TC 2015: Claudio Ardagna, with Meiko Jensen

And similarly we thank the Program Committee (Co-)Chairs of the 2015 ICSP, OTMA, and Workshops (in their order of appearance on the website): Peter Spyns, Maria-Esther Vidal, Arne J. Berre, Gregoris Mentzas, Nadia Abchiche-Mimouni, Alexis Aubry, Fenareti Lampathaki, Eduardo Rocha Loures, Milan Zdravkovic, Peter Bollen, Hans Mulder, Maurice Nijssen, Miguel Ángel Rodríguez-García, Rafael Valencia García, Thomas Moser, Ricardo Colomo Palacios, Alok Mishra, Deepti Mishra, Jürgen Münch, Ioana Ciuciu, Christophe Debruyne, Anna Fensel, Maria Chiara Caschera, Fernando Ferri, Patrizia Grifoni, Arianna D'Ulizia, Mustafa Jarrar, António Lucas Soares, Cristovão Sousa.

Together with their many Program Committee members, they performed a superb and professional job in managing the difficult yet existential process of peer review and selection of the best papers from the harvest of submissions. We all also owe a significant debt of gratitude to our supremely competent and experienced Conference Secretariat and technical support staff in Guadalajara, Brussels, and Dublin, respectively, Daniel Meersman, Jan Demey, and Christophe Debruyne.

The General Conference and Workshop Co-Chairs also thankfully acknowledge the academic freedom, logistic support, and facilities they enjoy from their respective institutions — Technical University of Graz, Austria; Université de Lorraine, Nancy, France; Latrobe University, Melbourne, Australia; and Babes-Bolyai University, Cluj, Romania — without which such a project quite simply would not be feasible. We do hope that the results of this federated scientific enterprise contribute to your research and your place in the scientific network. We look forward to seeing you at next year's event!

September 2015

Robert Meersman
Hervé Panetto
Tharam Dillon
Ernesto Damiani
Ioana Ciuciu

Organization

OTM (On The Move) is a federated event involving a series of major international conferences and workshops. These proceedings contain the papers presented at the OTM 2015 Federated conferences, consisting of CoopIS 2015 (Co-operative Information Systems), ODBASE 2015 (Ontologies, Databases, and Applications of Semantics), and C&TC 2015 (Cloud and Trusted Computing).

Executive Committee

General Co-Chairs

Robert Meersman   TU Graz, Austria
Hervé Panetto   University of Lorraine, France
Ernesto Damiani   Politecnico di Milano, Italy

OnTheMove Academy Dean

Erich Neuhold   University of Vienna, Austria

Industry Case Studies Program Chairs

Hervé Panetto   University of Lorraine, France

CoopIS 2015 PC Co-Chairs

Georg Weichhart   University of Linz, Austria
Heiko Ludwig   IBM Almaden Research Center, USA

ODBASE 2015 PC Co-Chairs

Yuan An   Drexel University, USA
Min Song   Yonsei University, Korea
Markus Strohmaier   University of Koblenz-Landau, Germany

C&TC 2015 PC Co-Chairs

Claudio Ardagna   University of Milan, Italy
Meiko Jensen   University of South Denmark, Denmark

Logistics Team

Daniel Meersman

CoopIS 2015 Program Committee

Hamideh Afsarmanesh
Marco Aiello
Joonsoo Bae
Zohra Bellahsene
Frédérick Benaben
Djamal Benslimane
Gash Bhullar
Nacer Boudjlida
Luis M. Camarinha-Matos
Massimo Canducci
Carlos Cetina
Martine Collard
Carlo Combi
Alfredo Cuzzocrea
Antonio De Nicola
Claudia Diamantini
Schahram Dustdar
Johann Eder
Rik Eshuis
Peter Forbrig
Jose Luis Garrido
Paolo Giorgini
Ted Goranson
Paul Grefen
Wided Guédria
Giancarlo Guizzardi
Mohand-Said Hacid
Christian Huemer
Stefan Jablonski
Frank-Walter Jäkel
Epaminondas Kapetanios
Stephan Kassel
Rania Khalaf
Hiroyuki Kitagawa
Matthias Klusch
Benjamin Knoke
Julius Köpke
Akhil Kumar
Lea Kutvonen
Ulrike Lechner
Fenglin Li
Lin Liu
Sanjay K. Madrias

Tiziana Margaria
Maristella Matera
Heinrich Mayr
Massimo Mecella
Jan Mendling
John Miller
Michele Missikoff
Mohamed Mohamed
Arturo Molina
Jörg Müller
Yannick Naudet
Alex Norta
Selmin Nurcan
Andreas Opdahl
Gerlad Oster
Oscar Pastor
Vicente Pelechano
Barbara Pernici
Erik Proper
Jolita Ralyté
Lakshmish Ramaswamy
Manfred Reichert
Stefanie Rinderle-Ma
David Carlos Romero Diaz
Antonio Ruiz Cortés
Shazia Sadiq
Ralf Schenkel
Simon Schlosser
Werner Schmidt
Christian Stary
Jianwen Su
Xiaoping Sun
Francesco Taglino
François B. Vernadat
Maria Esther Vidal
Barbara Weber
Lijie Wen
Mathias Weske
Hongji Yang
Eric Yu
Martin Zelm
Min Zhou

ODBASE 2015 Program Committee

Jesús M. Almendros-Jimenez
Marie-Aude Aufaure
Payam Barnaghi
Zohra Bellahsene
Ladjel Bellatreche
Sonia Bergamaschi
Devis Bianchini
Said Bleik
Francesco Buccafurri
Andrea Cali
Sunil Choenni
Philippe Cudre-Mauroux
Alfredo Cuzzocrea
Christophe Debruyne
Claudia Diamantini
Alicia Diaz
Dejing Dou
Bilel Elayeb
Walid Gaaloul
Giorgos Giannopoulos
Michael Granitzer
Sergio Greco
Giancarlo Guizzardi
Mohand-Said Hacid
Allel Hadjali
Harry Halpin
Takahiro Hara
Laura Hollink
Irena Holubová
Muhammad Intizar Ali
Prateek Jain
Amit Joshi
Jaewoo Kang
Selma Khouri

Christian Kop
Manolis Koubarakis
Rajasekar Krishnamurthy
Steffen Lamparter
Wookey Lee
Young-Koo Lee
Jinsoo Lee
Mengchi Liu
Frederick Maier
Eduardo Mena
Ginés Moreno
Bernd Neumayr
Natalya F. Noy
Esko Nuutila
Csongor Nyulas
Declan O'Sullivan
Matteo Palmonari
Dimitris Plexousakis
Ivana Podnar Zarko
Geert Poels
Antonella Poggi
Alexandra Poulovassilis
José Rodríguez
Satya Sahoo
Kai-Uwe Sattler
Michael Schrefl
Timos Sellis
Angelo Spognardi
Srinath Srinivasa
Yannis Stavrakas
Domenico Ursino
Yanghua Xiao

C&TC 2015 Program Committee

Marco Anisetti
Vijay Atluri
Narayanaswamy Balakrishnan
Endre Bangerter
Michele Bezzi
Bud Brugger

Marco Casassa Mont
David Chadwick
Henry Chan
Alfredo Cuzzocrea
Ernesto Damiani
Stefan Dessloch

Francesco Di Cerbo
Scharam Dustdar
Stefanos Gritzalis
Nils Gruschka
Marit Hansen
Ching Hsien Hsu
Patrick Hung
Martin Jaatun
Florian Kerschbaum
Ryan Ko

Zhiqiang Lin
Luigi Lo Iacono
Gregorio Martinez
Hadi Otrok
Smriti R. Ramakrishnan
Damien Sauveron
Jorg Schwenk
Russell Sears
Bhavani Thuraisingham
Luca Viganò

OnTheMove 2015 Keynotes

Data Semantics in the Days of Big Data

John Mylopoulos

University of Trento, Italy

Short Bio

John Mylopoulos holds a professor emeritus position at the Universities of Trento and Toronto. He earned a PhD degree from Princeton University in 1970 and joined the Department of Computer Science at the University of Toronto that year. His research interests include conceptual modelling, requirements engineering, data semantics, and knowledge management. Mylopoulos is a fellow of the Association for the Advancement of Artificial Intelligence (AAAI) and the Royal Society of Canada (Academy of Sciences). He has served as program/general chair of international conferences in artificial intelligence, databases and software engineering, including IJCAI (1991), Requirements Engineering (1997), and VLDB (2004). Mylopoulos is the recipient of an advanced grant from the European Research Council for a project titled "Lucretius: Foundations for Software Evolution."

Talk

"Data Semantics in the Days of Big Data"

In the good old days, the semantics of data was defined in terms of entities and relationships. For example, a tuple (widget:w#123, price: €10, date: 1970.07.30) in the SALES relation meant something like "widget w#123 was sold for €10 on July 30, 1970." This simple view of semantics no longer applies in the days of big data, where gigabytes of data are pouring in every day and the intended meaning is defined in terms of strategic objectives such as, "We want to grow our sales by 2% over three years," or tactical ones such as, "We want to grow sales for our clothing products by 2.5% over the next quarter in Lombardia." We review some of the elements of this new perspective on data and present some of the analysis techniques that are emerging along with big data technologies.

Reusable Coordination Components: A Silver Bullet for Reliable Development of Cooperative Information Systems?

Eva Kühn

TU Wien, Austria

Short Bio

Eva Kühn graduated as an engineer of computer sciences, with a PhD, habilitation, and professor position at TU Wien. Heinz-Zemanek Research Award for PhD work on "Multi Database Systems". She received a Kurt-Gödel Research Grant from the Austrian Government for a sabbatical at the Indiana Center for Databases at Purdue University, USA. She has several international publications and teaching experience in the areas of methods and tools for software development, software engineering, coordination languages, software integration, parallel and distributed programming, heterogeneous transaction processing, and space-based computing. Eva has been project coordinator of nationally (FWF, FFG, AT) and internationally (EU Commission) funded research projects as well as projects with industry. She has international software patents for research work on a new "Coordination System," and seven years of experience as Chief Technological Officer (CTO) of an Austrian spin-off company for software development. She has served as conference chair, program committee member, organizer, and coordinator of international conferences. She is a member of the Governing Board of the Austrian and European UNIX systems user group, of the ISO Working Group for the standardization of Prolog, of the Senate of the Christian Doppler Forschungsgesellschaft (CDG), and of the Science and Research Council of the Federal State of Salzburg.

Talk

"Reusable Coordination Components: A Silver Bullet for Reliable Development of Cooperative Information Systems?"

Today's emerging trends such as factory of the future, big data, Internet of Things, intelligent traffic solutions, cyber-physical systems, wireless sensor networks, and smart home/city/grid raise major new challenges on software development. They are characterized by high concurrency, distribution, and dynamics as well as huge numbers of heterogeneous devices, resources, and users that must collaborate in a reliable way. The management of all interactions and dependencies between the participants is a complex task posing massive coordination and integration problems. Must these be solved for each new application from scratch?

An alternative approach would be to identify similarities in their communication and synchronization behavior, to design corresponding "reusable patterns" with the help of a suitable and flexible coordination model, and finally to realize the patterns in the form of software components that run on a suitable middleware platform. In this keynote we discuss state-of-the-art coordination models and middleware systems to achieve this goal. The sharing of coordination components among different use cases on different platforms, reaching from energy-aware micro-controller platforms to enterprise server systems, is demonstrated by means of real-life scenarios from different domains. The vision is to compose advanced cooperative information systems from proven, configurable, reusable "coordination components," thus reducing software development risks and costs.

Durable Modeling and Ever-Changing Implementation Technologies

Sjir Nijssen

PNA Group, Netherlands

Short Bio

Dr. Sjir Nijssen is an emeritus professor and has been CTO at PNA in The Netherlands (www.pna-group.com) for the last 25 years. Dr. Nijssen first experienced the essential steps of working with facts in 1959 and 1960 while serving as a draft officer in the Royal Dutch Air Force, where at that time there was careful observation of planes of friends and enemies by boys on towers in the field, and girls plotting the information by the boys in one of the seven areas of The Netherlands, over telephone lines on a large table in atomic-free bunkers. The contents of the tables of the seven areas was verbalized by girls sitting at the next higher level and were then plotted by girls in the central command on a table covering the entire Netherlands. That information was used by the officers to direct interceptor planes. This was a world with very clear protocols on how to observe, how to formulate the facts, how to convert the facts into another representation of the facts on a land map table, verbalizing the information of the local tables into facts and transmitting these facts to the girls plotting the information read on the central table. Dr. Nijssen started with fact-based business communication modeling in the early 1970s, at Control Data's European headquarters in Brussels. Since then it has been more than his full-time occupation. It was there that NIAM (Natural language Information Analysis Method), a fact-based protocol to develop a conceptual schema and notation, was conceived. Prof. Robert Meersman was one of the pillars of the 22-person research lab at Control Data, from 1970 to 1982. From 1983, Dr. Nijssen held a position as professor of Computer Science for seven years at the University of Queensland in Australia. In 1989 he founded the company PNA, exclusively dedicated to delivering durable and tested business requirements, conceptual modeling, consulting, and educational services fully based on fact orientation. PNA currently employs about 30 people. Dr. Nijssen can be reached directly at `sjir.nijssen@pna-group.com`.

Talk

"Durable Modeling and Ever-Changing Implementation Technologies"

In the relative short history of information technology we have seen substantial improvements. However, between the wishes of the users and the implemented services there is still in many cases an enormous gap. And the problem of very substantial cost overruns in the development of these services is still a serious challenge in too many cases. Today we aim to fill this gap between the requirements and the running services with what is called a durable model. The road toward a durable model has been a long one and an overview will be given since the 1960s. During the 1970s and 1980s the term conceptual model was used to refer to a durable model, with many contributions from the IFIP WG 2.6 conferences and the landmark publication of the ISO Technical Report TR9007 in 1987, "Concepts and Terminology for the Conceptual Schema and the Information Base." Thereafter we discuss how durable modeling has evolved and been misused by various factions in the research and business world.

Since 2012 a co-creation has been established in The Netherlands consisting of government service organizations, universities, and innovative companies with the aim of developing an engineering protocol on how to "transform" laws, regulations, and policies into a durable model. The aim is to develop a national protocol that will be offered to all government departments and all other organizations in The Netherlands. Of course it will be offered to the world. We discuss the scientific foundation of this protocol, called CogniLex, as well as its practical version and report on experiences obtained so far. To the best of our knowledge, this is the most extensive protocol currently available. The skills of protocolled observation and transformation into facts, transforming the facts into another representation mode adequate for a specific purpose, and transforming the other representation mode back into verbalized facts are vital parts of any testing protocol, called ex-ante in Terra Legis. We demonstrate how certain legal domain protocol essentials like Hohfeld can be modeled in fact-based modeling, a durable modeling approach. We also demonstrate how fact-based modeling has been used to detect the needed extensions to the famous work of Hohfeld. If time permits, the transformation of such a durable model into UML, ER, OWL, SBVR, and DMN will be discussed.

From (Security) Research to Innovation

Michele Bezzi

Sap Labs, France

Short Bio

Michele Bezzi is Research Manager at SAP Product Security Research. He heads a group of researchers investigating applied research and innovative security solutions, addressing topics such as security tools for development, intrusion detection systems, and software security analysis.

He received his Master of Physics degree from the University of Florence in 1994 and his PhD in Physics from the University of Bologna in 1998. He has over 15 years' experience in industrial research in SONY, Accenture, and SAP. He has supervised several European projects, and has published more than 50 scientific papers in various research areas: security, privacy, pervasive computing, neural networks, evolutionary models, and complex systems.

Talk

"From (Security) Research to Innovation"

I present some concrete examples of research projects, and show how these research results have been used in SAP products and processes.

The security research team addresses different topics such as security tools for development, intrusion detection systems, and software security analysis. For example, in recent years, we prototyped an application level intrusion detection software, now released as a product — SAP Enterprise Threat Detection (ETD) — able to detect attacks, in real time, on complex software landscape. We also devise tools to support developers in secure development, allowing, for example, security testing during the code writing phase, as well as innovative tools for security governance. In this talk, starting from these examples, I also discuss challenges and opportunities in transferring research results to industrial products or processes.

Contents

Cooperative Information Systems 2015 (CoopIS) 2015

CoopIS 2015 PC Co-Chairs' Message

CoopIS in the Cloud

Collaborative Autonomic Management of Distributed Component-Based
Applications.. 3
    Nabila Belhaj, Imen Ben Lahmar, Mohamed Mohamed,
    and Djamel Belaïd

An Efficient Optimization Algorithm of Autonomic Managers
in Service-Based Applications................................. 19
    Leila Hadded, Faouzi Ben Charrada, and Samir Tata

TrustedMR: A Trusted MapReduce System Based on Tamper
Resistance Hardware....................................... 38
    Quoc-Cuong To, Benjamin Nguyen, and Philippe Pucheral

Social Networking Applications of CoopIS

Similarity and Trust to Form Groups in Online Social Networks........... 57
    Pasquale De Meo, Fabrizio Messina, Giuseppe Pappalardo,
    Domenico Rosaci, and Giuseppe M.L. Sarnè

Supporting Peer Help in Collaborative Learning Environments:
A Discussion Based on Two Case Studies........................ 76
    Luana Müller, Letícia Lopes Leite, and Milene Selbach Silveira

Finding Collective Decisions: Change Negotiation in Collaborative
Business Processes 90
    Walid Fdhila, Conrad Indiono, Stefanie Rinderle-Ma,
    and Rudolf Vetschera

Real-Time Relevance Matching of News and Tweets.................. 109
    Sei Onishi, Yuto Yamaguchi, and Hiroyuki Kitagawa

Information and Knowledge Quality in CoopIS

Context-Aware Process Injection: Enhancing Process Flexibility by Late
Extension of Process Instances 127
    Nicolas Mundbrod, Gregor Grambow, Jens Kolb, and Manfred Reichert

A Multi-view Learning Approach to the Discovery of Deviant
Process Instances 146
   Alfredo Cuzzocrea, Francesco Folino, Massimo Guarascio,
   and Luigi Pontieri

A Genetic Algorithm for Automatic Business Process Test Case Selection . . . 166
   Kristof Böhmer and Stefanie Rinderle-Ma

Discovering BPMN Models with Sub-Processes
and Multi-Instance Markers 185
   Yuquan Wang, Lijie Wen, Zhiqiang Yan, Bo Sun, and Jianmin Wang

Information and Knowledge Quality in CoopIS

Information Quality in Dynamic Networked Business Process Management . . . 202
   Mohammad R. Rasouli, Rik Eshuis, Jos J.M. Trienekens, Rob J. Kusters,
   and Paul W.P.J. Grefen

Utilizing the Hive Mind – How to Manage Knowledge in Fully
Distributed Environments.................................. 219
   Thomas Bach, Muhammad Adnan Tariq, Christian Mayer,
   and Kurt Rothermel

∂u∂u Multi-Tenanted Framework: Distributed Near Duplicate Detection
for Big Data... 237
   Pradeeban Kathiravelu, Helena Galhardas, and Luís Veiga

Multilevel Mapping of Ecosystem Descriptions: Short Paper 257
   Matt Selway, Markus Stumptner, Wolfgang Mayer, Andreas Jordan,
   Georg Grossmann, and Michael Schrefl

Interoperability of CoopIS

Determining the Quality of Product Data Integration 267
   Julian Tiedeken, Thomas Bauer, Joachim Herbst, and Manfred Reichert

Inference Control in Data Integration Systems 285
   Mokhtar Sellami, Mohand-Said Hacid,
   and Mohamed Mohsen Gammoudi

Integrated Process Oriented Requirements Management 303
   Nikolaus Wintrich, Patrick Gering, and Malte Meissner

Various Aspects of CoopIS

Supporting Structural Consistency Checking in Adaptive
Case Management... 311
    Christoph Czepa, Huy Tran, Uwe Zdun, Stefanie Rinderle-Ma,
    Thanh Tran Thi Kim, Erhard Weiss, and Christoph Ruhsam

A Probabilistic Unified Framework for Event Abstraction and Process
Detection from Log Data..................................... 320
    Bettina Fazzinga, Sergio Flesca, Filippo Furfaro, Elio Masciari,
    and Luigi Pontieri

Property Hypergraphs as an Attributed Predicate RDF................. 329
    Dewi W. Wardani and Josef Küng

Rewinding and Repeating Scientific Choreographies 337
    Andreas Weiß, Vasilios Andrikopoulos, Michael Hahn,
    and Dimka Karastoyanova

Enabling DevOps Collaboration and Continuous Delivery Using Diverse
Application Environments 348
    Johannes Wettinger, Vasilios Andrikopoulos, and Frank Leymann

Ontologies, DataBases, and Applications of Semantics (ODBASE) 2015

ODBASE 2015 PC Co-Chairs' Message

Ontology-based Information Modeling and Extraction

COBieOWL, an OWL Ontology Based on COBie Standard............. 361
    Tarcisio M. Farias, Ana Roxin, and Christophe Nicolle

A Semantic Graph Model...................................... 378
    Liu Chen, Ting Yu, and Mengchi Liu

An Approach for Ontology Population Based on Information Extraction
Techniques: Application to Cultural Heritage (Short Paper) 397
    Riyadh Benammar, Alain Trémeau, and Pierre Maret

Semantic Modeling, Matching, and Querying Over Linked Open Data

Matchmaking Public Procurement Linked Open Data 405
    Jindřich Mynarz, Vojtěch Svátek, and Tommaso Di Noia

Preference Queries with Ceteris Paribus Semantics for Linked Data........ 423
    Jessica Rosati, Tommaso Di Noia, Thomas Lukasiewicz,
    Renato De Leone, and Andrea Maurino

Semantic Support for Processing Web Services and Social Networks

Modeling and Retrieving Linked RESTful APIs: A Graph
Database Approach   443
  Sahar Aljalbout, Omar Boucelma, and Sana Sellami

Crowdsourcing for Web Service Discovery   451
  Fatma Slaimi, Sana Sellami, Omar Boucelma, and Ahlem Ben Hassine

Web Services Discovery Based on Semantic Tag   465
  Sana Sellami and Hanane Becha

A Model for Identifying Misinformation in Online Social Networks   473
  Sotirios Antoniadis, Iouliana Litou, and Vana Kalogeraki

Semantic Data Processing and Access in Emerging Domains

Traceability of Tightly Coupled Phases of Semantic Data
Warehouse Design   483
  Selma Khouri and Ladjel Bellatreche

Aggregation Operators in Geospatial Queries for Open Street Map   501
  Jesús M. Almendros-Jiménez, Antonio Becerra-Terón,
  and Manuel Torres

Provalets: OSGi-based Prova Agents for Rule-Based Data Access   519
  Adrian Paschke

Ontology Matching and Alignment

Light-Weight Cross-Lingual Ontology Matching with LYAM++   527
  Abdel Nasser Tigrine, Zohra Bellahsene, and Konstantin Todorov

ABOM and ADOM: Arabic Datasets for the Ontology Alignment
Evaluation Campaign.   545
  Abderrahmane Khiat, Gayo Diallo, Beyza Yaman,
  Ernesto Jiménez-Ruiz, and Moussa Benaissa

Cloud and Trusted Computing 2015 (C&TC) 2015

C&TC 2015 PC Co-Chairs' Message

All You Need is Trust – An Analysis of Trust Measures Communicated
by Cloud Providers   557
  Julian Gantner, Lukas Demetz, and Ronald Maier

Modelling the Live Migration Time of Virtual Machines   575
Kateryna Rybina, Waltenegus Dargie, Subramanya Umashankar,
and Alexander Schill

CloudIDEA: A Malware Defense Architecture for Cloud Data Centers   594
Andreas Fischer, Thomas Kittel, Bojan Kolosnjaji, Tamas K. Lengyel,
Waseem Mandarawi, Hermann de Meer, Tilo Müller, Mykola Protsenko,
Hans P. Reiser, Benjamin Taubmann, and Eva Weishäupl

S-Test: A Framework for Services Testing   612
Nabil El Ioini

Design and Implementation of a Trust Service for the Cloud   620
Julien Lacroix and Omar Boucelma

Security Aspects of de-Materialized Local Public Administration Processes. . . .   639
Giancarlo Ballauco, Paolo Ceravolo, Ernesto Damiani, Fulvio Frati,
and Francesco Zavatarelli

Monitoring-Based Certification of Cloud Service Security   644
Maria Krotsiani, George Spanoudakis, and Christos Kloukinas

Balancing Trust and Risk in Access Control.   660
Alessandro Armando, Michele Bezzi, Francesco Di Cerbo,
and Nadia Metoui

Author Index   677

Cooperative Information Systems 2015 (CoopIS) 2015

CoopIS 2015 PC Co-Chairs' Message

The 23rd International Conference on Cooperative Information System is the latest event of a conference series that has established itself as a major forum for exchanging emerging ideas and latest research findings on collaboration technologies and their impact on organizations and all involved stakeholders. Cooperative Information Systems (CIS) facilitate the cooperation between individuals, organizations, smart devices, and systems of systems. In an increasingly hyper-connected world, CIS technologies provide flexible, scalable and intelligent services far beyond the boundaries of corporations and increasingly are explored as part of global user communities and digitally empowered citizens.

The technologies discussed in these proceedings include Computer Supported Cooperative Work (CSCW), Web-based and Cloud-based systems, business process management, and associated software architectures. CoopIS, however, does not only focus on the computer sciences aspect, but takes a broader information systems point of view.

Thanks to the large number of high-quality submissions we were able to compile a very strong program. The selection process was highly competitive. In total, we received 86 submissions, out of which the international program committee members selected 16 as full papers for presentation and publication (18.6% acceptance rate). In addition, 7 submissions have been accepted as short-papers to be included in the proceedings (26.7% acceptance rate including short papers).

We are thankful to all who made CoopIS 2015 possible. CoopIS 2015 – and its predecessors – is part of the OnTheMove (OTM) federated conferences organized by Robert Meersman and his team. We would like to thank the 85 program committee members who have reviewed submissions in a timely manner, providing valuable and constructive feedback (and their expertise) to the authors. Finally, we would like to thank the most important group of contributors, the authors and presenters who make CoopIS such a thriving scientific event.

September 2015

Heiko Ludwig
Michael Rosemann
Georg Weichhart

Collaborative Autonomic Management
of Distributed Component-Based Applications

Nabila Belhaj[1]([✉]), Imen Ben Lahmar[2], Mohamed Mohamed[3],
and Djamel Belaïd[1]

[1] Institut MINES-TELECOM, TELECOM SudParis,
UMR CNRS SAMOVAR, Evry, France
{nabila.belhaj,djamel.belaid}@telecom-sudparis.eu
[2] ReDCAD-Research Unit, Higher Institute of
Computer Science and Multimedia of Sfax, Sfax, Tunisia
imen.benlahmar@redcad.org
[3] IBM Research, Almaden Research Center, San Jose, CA, USA
mmohamed@us.ibm.com

Abstract. Executing component-based applications in dynamic distributed environments requires autonomic management to cope with the changes of these environments. However, using a centralized Autonomic Manager (AM) for monitoring and adaptation of a large number of distributed components is a non trivial task. Therefore, we argue for a distributed management by using an AM for each component. These distributed managers should collaborate to avoid conflicting decisions that may entail the application's failure. Towards this objective, we propose a collaborative autonomic management of component-based applications in distributed environments. An application is considered as a composite of atomic or composite components. Each component or composite is managed by its AM that holds local strategies for its reconfiguration. An AM is able to collaborate with other managers in different hierarchical levels for the self-management of the whole application. We show the utility of our approach through a use case in the context of Cloud computing.

Keywords: Component-based applications · Autonomic management · Container · Collaboration

1 Introduction

Distributed environments are characterized by their heterogeneity in terms of resources and services. They host resources having mutual interactions and providing different services. In these environments, applications are executed collaboratively by integrating various services provided by various resources. One particular paradigm that allows to build applications upon a set of services is the Service-Oriented Architecture (SOA) [17] that defines applications as an assembly of services. These services are provided by components implementing the

© Springer International Publishing Switzerland 2015
C. Debruyne et al. (Eds.): OTM 2015 Conferences, LNCS 9415, pp. 3–18, 2015.
DOI: 10.1007/978-3-319-26148-5_1

functional business of these services. Hence, a component-based application is represented by a composite of components requiring and/or providing services from/to one another.

Due to the dynamic of the distributed environments, executing component-based applications is a challenging task. In fact, the resources of a distributed environment may exhibit highly dynamic conditions in terms of their availability, load, efficiency, etc. Therefore, it becomes inevitable to enforce the autonomy of component-based applications with Autonomic Computing management.

The introduction of Autonomic Computing implies the usage of an Autonomic Manager (AM) implementing an autonomic loop (MAPE-K) that allows managing a set of resources [8]. This loop consists of collecting monitoring data, analyzing them and generating reconfiguration strategies. In distributed environments, the main role of AM is to adapt the associated resources not just to their internal dynamic behavior but also to the dynamic changes of their environment.

However, managing a distributed application by using a centralized AM is not a trivial task as it can be the source of bottlenecks. Therefore in this paper, we argue for a distributed management. This implies that each component of a distributed application will be managed by its own AM that holds local analysis rules and reconfiguration strategies. Nonetheless, different or mismatched decisions taken by AMs of the application's components may potentially generate corrupted results. This may end up with the failure of the reconfiguration of the whole application. This challenge motivates the need for designing an AM to dynamically reconfigure a component and also to collaborate with other AMs for the management of the whole application.

Towards this challenge, several research work have proposed solutions to the problem of the self-management of distributed applications. Given the existing work, few attempts propose solutions for the management of component-based applications in distributed environments [2],[4],[5]. Moreover, the existing collaborative autonomic loops focus mainly on the collaboration between resources in different levels (e.g., between IaaS, PaaS and SaaS layers in the Cloud context[15],[5]). To our knowledge, none of the existing work deals for example with the collaboration between AMs in the same level.

Therefore, we propose in this paper an autonomic container that implements the different functionalities of a classical AM and enhances them with collaboration capabilities. This container is responsible for the self-management of a component. It is also able to collaborate with other containers in different hierarchical levels for the management of the whole composite application. The purpose of this container is to discharge the applications developers from the burden of the management tasks and let them focus on the business of their applications.

The remainder of this paper is structured as follows. Section 2 describes the structure of our proposed autonomic container and details the covered loops and the supported collaborations. Through a use case in Section 3, we explain how the containers manage some adaptation contexts in Cloud environments. In Section 4 and 5, we give some implementation details and evaluation results.

Section 6 provides an overview of existing related work. Finally, we conclude the paper and give some perspectives in Section 7.

2   Autonomic Container for the Management of Component-Based Applications

In this section, we present a hierarchical description of a distributed component-based application. Then, we describe the structure of our proposed autonomic container and the collaborations that it supports.

2.1   Architectural Description of Component-Based Applications

A component-based application is represented by a composite of components as illustrated in Figure 1(a). A composite consists of an assembly of heterogeneous components, which offer services and require services from other components. A component of the application may be itself a composite implying that it hosts components providing functionalities fulfilling its business logic.

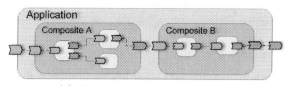

(a) Component-based application

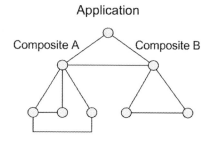

(b) Application components hierarchy

Fig. 1. Hierarchical organization of a component-based application

As shown in Figure 1(b), a composite of an application may be represented by a hierarchy of components. While, the root of the hierarchy represents the application's composite, its nodes (i.e., children) represent either atomic components or composites of components. We distinguish two relationships between the nodes of this hierarchical representation: vertical or horizontal relationships. The horizontal relationship represents the functional binding between offered and required services of an application's components. However, the vertical relationship is set between a composite (i.e., parent) and its components (i.e., children).

2.2   Structure of the Autonomic Container

Since the application is defined as an assembly of components, we propose to encapsulate each component into its own container for its self-management. This component is called a Managed component. The container consists of an assembly of components allowing the functionalities of Monitoring, Analysis, Planning, Execution and Knowledge supplied by a classical autonomic control loop. The separation of these functionalities among different components allows an isolated replacement or removal of components which ensures more flexibility and reusability to the container.

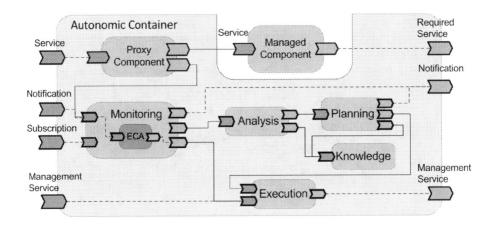

Fig. 2. Architecture of the autonomic container

We introduce our autonomic container in Figure 2 that shows its included components and their interactions. For a Managed component, this container proposes and requires functional as well as non-functional services. As the Managed components of an application maintain business interactions between them, the autonomic container promotes a Managed component's provided/required services as its functional services. Whereas, non-functional services are those concerning autonomic management facilities and collaboration capabilities. The container proposes non-functional services of Notification, Subscription and Management. It also requires Notification and Management Services. In the following we explain further the functionalities of the involved components and their interactions.

The Proxy Component: is included into the autonomic container for monitoring needs. It acts like an intermediary component that supervises the Managed component exchanges. The Proxy provides the same services initially provided by the Managed component. Whenever a remote component invokes these services, the Proxy intercepts the call to extract monitoring data then forwards it (i.e., the call) to the Managed component. Extracted data is sent to the Monitoring component and are about the service call, the execution time and the change of properties values [14].

The Monitoring Component: is responsible of receiving notifications (as events) from the Proxy component and from remote containers. Accordingly, it provides a (callback) service of Notification. Furthermore, it offers a Subscription service to enable subscriptions to specific notifications for interested components. This allows subscribers to be notified with the monitored data they are interested in. This component embeds an ECA (Event Condition Action) component that is described in Section 2.3.

The Knowledge Component: is essential to hold information employed by the other MAPE components to perform their functionalities. This component contains a full description of the Managed component (i.e., identifier, proposed and required services, embedded components, used implementation, monitored and reconfigurable properties, etc.). Each time an adaptation occurs, the Knowledge provides the possibility to establish a historical memory about any modification brought to the Managed component. It is then enriched progressively and continuously. The Knowledge component contains also rules descriptions defining adaptation situations. In addition, it maintains descriptions of the elementary Management Services offered by the Execution component.

The Analysis Component: is used to analyze monitoring data and determine whether an event matches an adaptation context or not. The Analysis gauges the current situation by comparing it against some rules described within the Knowledge. When an adaptation context is confirmed, the Analysis generates an alert (as an event) to the Planning component.

The Planning Component: is in charge of producing adaptation plans. Once this component receives an alert from the Analysis component, it generates an orchestrated workflow of adaptation actions. The adaptation plan can be modeled by making use of existing workflow languages such as BPEL (Business Process Execution Language) [16] or BPMN 2.0 (Business Process Model and Notation) [18]. The generated adaptation plan represents an orchestrated invocation of elementary Management Services (i.e., management actions) described within the Knowledge component and provided by the Execution components.

The Execution Component: is responsible of executing the adaptation plan. It provides two services of Management and Adaptation as shown in Figure 3. The Management Service is provided through a facade component (i.e., Management component) by some basic management components among them we can cite: (a)The LifeCycle component that enables the creation, the activation, the deactivation and the destruction of a component; (b)the Binding component that permits the management of functional dependencies of a component; (c)the Adapter component that allows the insertion and removal of adapters components in the container [3]; (d)the Parametric component that has the ability to adjust the values of the reconfigurable properties of the Managed component.

The adaptation plan represents the implementation of the Adaptation component. Once the Planning component invokes the Adaptation service of the Execution component, the Adaptation component is instantiated with its given implementation to execute the adaptation actions. Executing an adaptation plan may entail the invocation of the Local Management Service for a local adaptation or the Management Services of remote Execution components for remote adaptations.

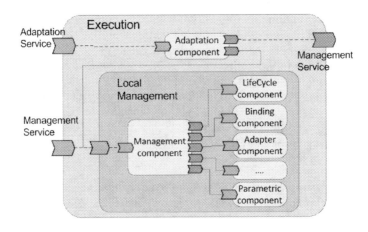

Fig. 3. Structure of the Execution component

2.3   Covered Autonomic Loops

Our work aims also at optimizing the activity of the MAPE-K loop. Seeking to fulfill this objective, our autonomic container performs two types of autonomic loops: reactive and deliberative autonomic loops. A reactive loop is a simple and rapid adaptation, in contrast, a deliberative loop is an adaptation that needs relatively long time processing compared to a reactive one. In the following, we detail these two types of loops.

Reactive Autonomic Loop: is inspired from the unconscious reflexes of the human being in emergency situations. For instance, when sensory neurons take inputs from the skin in a dangerous situation (e.g. burn, stepping on a sharp object, etc.), motor neurons related to the area are stimulated to promptly lift up the concerned limb out of the danger before the brain can consciously realize it [11]. The connections of such involuntary reflexes are orchestrated at the spinal cord level and do not reach the brain. This human autonomic loop is called the Reflex Arc which engages basic, simple and low-level functions. Our autonomic container is endowed with such a reactive autonomic loop which is responsible of instantaneous adaptations of the Managed component. Instead of forwarding the events to the Analysis as it usually happens in a common MAPE-K loop, the Monitoring component performs the context adaptation itself immediately.

Each time the Monitoring component captures an event from the Proxy or remote components, it forwards it to its encapsulated ECA (Event-Condition-Action) component (see Figure 2). In case an event entry is confirmed, the ECA component checks if the conditions match, then invokes the corresponding actions on the Execution component. The actions represent the elementary Management Services proposed by the Execution component. This reactive autonomic loop is represented only by the Monitoring and the Execution components. Our approach allows the avoidance of unnecessary processing by the Analysis and Planning components to optimize the activity of a regular autonomic loop.

Deliberative Autonomic Loop: is inspired from high-level brain functions which involve more complex data processing. Reasoning and data treatments may be performed over a longer period compared to a reactive adaptation. The deliberative loop is employed when the captured event needs more processing. Actually, in case the ECA component do not find a match for the captured event, the latter is forwarded to the Analysis component to reason on it. The reasoning process implies consulting the Knowledge component to detect an adaptation context if any. The Analysis triggers an alert to the Planning component that also refers to the Knowledge to produce adaptation actions. Finally, these actions are invoked on the Execution component to be carried out.

When an adaptation plan brings local adjustments to the Managed component, we call it intra-container adaptation. Nevertheless, when the adaptation plan requires a collaborative execution by several containers, we name it inter-containers adaptation. In this case, a distinction of two collaboration aspects is made: horizontal and vertical inter-containers collaboration.

Horizontal Inter-containers Collaboration. The generated adaptation plan is carried out by autonomic containers whose Managed components act upon their business interdependencies. These containers belong to the same hierarchical level. Once a container generates an adaptation plan involving another container, the execution of the plan entails the invocation of the Management Services of both containers through their Execution components.

Vertical Inter-containers Collaboration. The adaptation plan is run by collaborating containers that reside in different hierarchical levels. For instance, if the Planning component of a container has no ability to generate an adaptation plan, it notifies the upper level container (i.e, parent) about the situation. And since the parent container has a wider view of the system compared to its child and is better placed for planning decisions. The parent examines the situation and attempts to produce a suitable adaptation plan. The parent container executes the plan by invoking the Management Service of its child and eventually other Management Services of other involved containers.

3   Use Case Study

In order to validate our proposal, we realized an application that allows users to purchase products on the Internet. We represent the application by a set of distributed components that expose and require services. As shown in Figure 4, the application allows a user to consult products on an on-line catalog that brings products information from multiple inventories. The user has the ability to add products to a cart and then validate it. A cart validation triggers the creation of an order. The user can carry out its order which renders logging to its account mandatory in order to retrieve its personal information (e.g., invoicing and shipping address). The order's and personal user's information are used for the payment and interactions with remote banking components. Once the payment is validated by the user's bank, a confirmation mail is sent to the user's e-mail address, resuming details of the order and payment.

The distributed application components are deployed on different PaaS instances. To simplify the realization of the use case, we deployed the different components among two PaaS instances. One instance of CloudFoundry PaaS and one instance of OpenShift. These two instances are deployed in our local cluster. In order to interact seamlessly with these PaaS instances we used a generic API that we developed previously and that allows to interact with PaaS providers in a generic way [19]. In the following we present the scenarios that we performed to show the utility of our approach.

3.1   Reactive Loop Scenario

In order to illustrate the reactive loop activity, we consider the Mailer component. Once the container of the Mailer component notices that the Mailer is not responding, it restarts it. Restarting the Mailer consists on sending a REST query to the PaaS manager asking the restart of this component. The PaaS manager will handle this task and keep the same identifier and endpoint of the component to maintain the consistency of the application.

3.2   Deliberative Loop: Horizontal Collaboration Scenario

To show the utility of the horizontal collaboration, we consider two components of the same hierarchical level: the Catalog and the Inventory 1. Let us suppose that the container of the Inventory 1 detects bandwidth congestion impacting its functional interactions with the Catalog. The container of the Inventory 1 diagnoses the problem and decides to insert a compression adapter [3] in order to compress

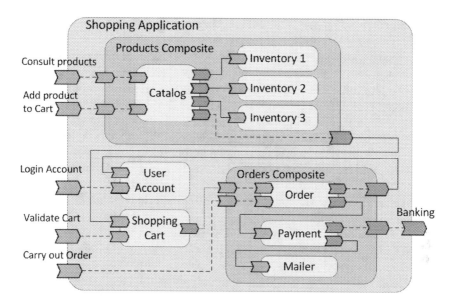

Fig. 4. Component-based description of a shopping application

the messages sent to the Catalog component. This decision will impact the Catalog component that needs to use an adapter to decompress the received messages. This decision implies also the modification of the bindings to make the exchanged messages go through the adapters first. These management actions are executed collaboratively between both containers of the Inventory 1 and the Catalog.

3.3 Deliberative Loop: Vertical Collaboration Scenario

To highlight the usage of the vertical collaboration, we consider the Catalog component and the Products composite having a child-parent relationship. Since the Catalog is heavily requested by the users in sales season, this component is overloaded. The container related to this component notifies its parent about the overload. The parent container decides to instantiate another Catalog, add a load balancer for traffic load balancing between the two Catalog components and then modify the bindings. This adaptation involves an architectural modification about the Products composite which can solely be handled by a container of a parent composite that disposes of a wider view of the system. The parent composite uses its Execution component to send a scale up query to the PaaS through our generic API. The PaaS manager will then add a new instance and place a load balancer having the same endpoint as the original Catalog component.

4   Implementation

In this section, we present the different aspects of our implementation.

We implemented our components using the Service Component Architecture (SCA) standard [9]. SCA provides a programming model for building applications based on SOA. The main idea behind SCA is to describe distributed applications as composites of a set of components. One of the main features of SCA is its independence of particular technology, protocol, and implementation. This allows the designer to conceive applications using available components despite their heterogeneous implementations (JAVA, BPEL, C, etc.). Henceforward, the choice of using SCA will allow an easy integration of existing off-the-shelf solutions despite their heterogeneity. In our solution we have implemented the MAPE-K as separate components to allow more flexibility on adding or removing new facilities. The Monitoring component is eventually implemented as a composite that contains the needed facilities to enable autonomic management as described in Section 2.2. The Analysis and Planning components are two abstract SCA components. Since the analysis and planning are domain specific tasks, we used Mixin mechanism to customize and instantiate these components. The Mixin mechanism allows to extend a given class with new functionalities when needed without reinventing all the component.

In our use case, almost all the implemented components are in JAVA, and since the Mixin mechanism is not a native functionality for JAVA, we used mixin4j framework [1]. This framework allows to create Java Mixins by the use of annotations. To this end, it is possible to define the classes to be extended as abstract classes annotated with *"@MixinBase"* annotation. It is to say that this abstract class will be extended using Mixins. To create the Mixin itself, it is necessary to create an interface for this Mixin. Then, the *@MixinType* annotation is used to say that this interface represents a Mixin. The implementation of the interface must be specified following the *@MixinType* annotation. Consequently, the framework allows to instantiate new classes from the abstract classes annotated with *@MixinBase* mixed with implementations of the interfaces annotated with *@MixinType*. We used this framework to define our Mixins. We annotated our Analysis and Planning components with *@MixinBase* to be able to extend them later with specific behaviors. Then, we defined all the interfaces of our Mixins and annotated them with *@MixinType*. Moreover, we implemented the different Mixins containing the needed functionalities for analysis and planning aspects related to our use case. In our implementation, the *Analysis and Planning Components* are generic. They are implemented as abstract Mixin Base. Using mixin4j, we mixed them with the *RuleSet* and the *PlanSet* Mixins that specifically implement the two MixinType interfaces *AnalysisRuleInterface* and *PlanInterface*. These Mixins will describe exactly how to analyze received events and how to generate the adaptation plan.

The proxy component that we use for monitoring purposes is dynamically byte-code generated. For this required byte-code level manipulation we used the

---

[1] http://hg.berniecode.com/java-mixins

Java reflection API and the open source software JAVA programming ASSISTant (Javassist) library [2]. The Java reflection API provides classes and interfaces for obtaining reflective information about classes and objects. Javassist is a class library for editing Java byte-codes; it enables Java programs to define a new class and to modify a class file when the Java Virtual Machine (JVM) loads it.

It is worthy to note that in our implementation, the Planning component generates an adaptation plan as a BPEL workflow that is supported by almost all the SCA engines. This BPEL is sent to the Execution component to use it as an implementation of the Adaptation component. The Execution component benefits also from the existing services offered by PaaS providers. This component can use other Management Services when available, since it is able to host components managing SaaS, PaaS or IaaS resources [13]. Basically, for the vertical collaboration scenario, the container needs to scale up or down the Catalog component. Instead of reinventing this functionality, we needed just to map it to a REST query to the PaaS provider. For REST queries we used Restlet framework[3]. Restlet is an easy framework that allows to add REST mechanisms. After adding the needed libraries, one needs just to add the Restlet annotations to implement the different REST actions (i.e., POST, GET, PUT and DELETE). Moreover, in order to cover different PaaS providers offering the same functionalities, we used COAPS API [19]. COAPS is a generic API that allows to seamlessly interact with heterogeneous PaaS providers in a generic manner.

5   Evaluation

According to [6], the evaluation of autonomic management could be based on stability, accuracy, settling time, overshoot. In our evaluation we will focus just on accuracy and settling time. Accuracy shows whether the system's state converges to its desired state when applying an adaptation. While the settling time is the time needed to apply the adaptation and takes the system to its desired state.

Referring back to the horizontal collaboration scenario in Section 3.2, we proposed to inject a compression and decompression adapters to transfer the messages over a lower bandwidth between the Inventory 1 and Catalog components. In order to measure the settling time for this adaptation, we measured the time required for the deployment of these adapters. In fact, each adapter consists of a generated proxy component and an extra-functional compression or decompression component [1]. Through the evaluation results, we deduce that the time required for the generation of the byte-code of a proxy component has more impact on the time needed for the deployment of an adapter. Indeed, the generation of a proxy includes the time for loading interfaces classes from a disk memory and the time of byte-code class generation.

For this, we have varied the number of interfaces and methods for the implementation of a proxy component to measure the time required for its generation.

---

[2] http://www.csg.is.titech.ac.jp/~chiba/javassist
[3] http://restlet.org/

Then, we aggregated the result to the time required for the instantiation of the adapter's components to calculate its deployment time.

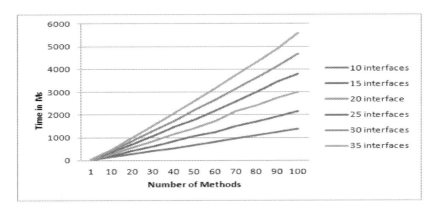

Fig. 5. Deployment of a compression adapter by varying the number of interfaces and methods of its proxy component

We deduce from Figure 5 that the growth slope of the deployment of an adapter is largely small when its proxy component implements 10 interfaces and 40 methods, than the deployment time for an adapter whose its proxy implements 30 interfaces. This proves that the number of interfaces influences more than the number of the methods on the time required for the generation of a proxy's byte code. Nonetheless, the deployment of an adapter does not take much time that is in order of few seconds.

To evaluate the accuracy of our application with the performed adaptation, we need to show that the introduction of the adapters enhances the behavior of the application in the specific situation (i.e., low bandwidth). Accordingly, we measured the time required for the transfer of big messages by using these adapters. For this, we varied the compression rate of voluminous messages (5Mo) and the data flows to observe the improvement rate as shown in Figure 6. This later represents the ratio between the time required for a transfer of a big message using adapters and the time measured without using these adapters.

As shown in Figure 6, integrating a compression and decompression adapters between the Catalog and Inventory 1 conserves the accuracy of the application allowing the fast transfer of messages if the data flow is under 7.5 Mb/s. Using these adapters will decrease the transfer time of these messages.

6   Related Work

During the last years, there have been different research work aiming at endowing distributed systems resources with self-management capabilities. Some of them tried to address the collaboration of autonomic loops in the Cloud and in

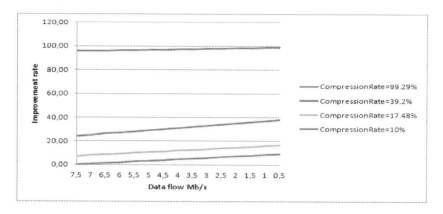

Fig. 6. Improvement rates calculated for the integration of compression and decompression adapters between Inventory 1 and Catalog components

distributed environments. The foregoing gives an overview of the cited work as well as a brief discussion spinning around the taken approaches.

The work presented in [15] addresses SLA violations in the Cloud by improving the response time of a web server. Authors organize the AMs in a hierarchical manner where upper level AMs have more authority over those of lower levels. An AM of a lower level keeps allocating resources (i.e., Memory, CPU, Maximum number of clients) to its web server to enhance its response time. If no more allocations are possible, the AM requests another AM belonging to the upper level for further allocations. These AMs collaborate by exchanging predefined messages between Cloud layers by means of an interface named *"ManagedObjects"* provided by each AM. This interface encapsulates properties, metrics and associated actions of the managed objects. However, this work presents some limitations. The exchanged messages are managed by a single broker between each two Cloud layers which represents a potential source of bottlenecks. Moreover, this approach does not take into consideration a possible horizontal collaboration among AMs. In addition, the solution seems to be SLA-specific which makes it hardly applicable to other management issues.

In [5], the authors propose a framework for the coordination of multiple AMs in the Cloud. They introduce two types of AMs: AAM (Application AM) that is used to manage an application in SaaS layer. IAM (Infrastructure AM) that is employed to administrate resource allocation in IaaS layer. At SaaS level, an AAM is associated to each application, whereas a single IAM operates for the overall IaaS resources. Each AAM maintains a local and private knowledge while the IAM holds a global and shared knowledge. AAMs can bring changes to the shared knowledge by means of a synchronization protocol. This protocol attributes a token to sychronize the AMs' access to the global knowledge critical sections to avoid concurrency and render available the knowledge to both SaaS and IaaS resources. An event-based coordination protocol is also proposed through which AMs coordinate their actions. Nevertheless, the exchanged messages are handeled by a single broker over all the framework. Furthermore, the management of IaaS resources relies on a unique IAM, consequently, greater load may alter its activity, especially collaborating with all the AAMs of the system. Another limitation lies in the fact that AAMs do not collaborate horizontally.

In their work [6], authors explore the possibility of making use of control theory principles to build self-managing computing systems. They describe a layered hierarchy in which a controller (i.e., higher level manager) is placed on top of new or existing components. Lower level managers are treated like resources by higher ones. Driven by the need to ease research in autonomic computing, they introduce DTAC, a deployable testbed enriched with pluggable components (e.g., control algorithms, sensors, effectors). Authors proposed the SASO properties (Stability, Accuracy, Settling time and Overshoot) of control systems to evaluate an autonomic computing system after an adaptation occurs. However, their research area is merely focused on self-management features. Meanwhile, they do not propose any collaboration between AMs, instead, they suppose that this aspect is processed recursively from a higher to a lower level.

Another approach is introduced in [7] based on synchronized languages and discrete control synthesis. In their paper, Gueye et al introduce a framework where autonomic components coordinate in a hierarchical structure. Their solution consists in using the BZR reactive language [10] to program AMs into nodes. Within a node, the behavior of an AM is modeled as a finite state machine (i.e., automaton). The behavior of an AM is controlled through controlling its states' transition. Moreover, the authors gather all the AMs behaviors in the system into one single and final node (i.e., final controller). The coordination policy is specified as a behavioral contract and associated to the final controller that is finally placed on top of the hierarchy. The rest of lower level AMs become sensors or actuators. Nonetheless, this approach leaves the system with a centralized management node gathering all the AMs behaviors which turns out to be source of trouble in case it experiences overload or outage.

Authors in [12] introduce collaborating knowledge planes in distributed environments. A neighborhood of knowledge planes improves its intelligence by sharing the strategies they acquire by means of a self-organization algorithm. This capability aims at helping AMs to have non-conflicting strategies at their disposal and then, gain a unified view of the system. Moreover, they propose a self-adaptation algorithm to allow a knowledge plane acquiring new strategies when the system encounters unknown situations for which no policy is already predefined. The newly acquired strategies are examined to decide whether they can be kept or not. The knowledge planes collaborate among a given neighborhood in contrast with our architecture where the collaboration relies on the containers' services of the application's components.

Our solution consists in proposing a generic and flexible autonomic container that frees developers from the overwhelming management tasks. We enhance the traditional behavior of the encapsulated MAPE-K components with new features of management and vertical and horizontal collaboration. In fact, no significant work targeting horizontal collaboration was noticed. Not to mention that the majority of the stated work was focused only on the vertical collaboration [15],[5],[7]. Nonetheless, neglected interactions between AMs belonging to the same hierarchical level is definitely source of mismatches. The majority of the stated work did not conduct research in optimizing an autonomic loop activity [15],[5],[7],[6]. In this direction, we proposed to enhance the behavior of a MAPE-K loop by addressing the cases of reactive adaptations in order to avoid unnecessary analysis and planning.

7   Conclusion

In this paper, we introduced a generic and flexible autonomic container that aims at endowing component-based applications with autonomic management facilities and collaboration capabilities. Herein, we gave descriptions of the different generic components that constitute the MAPE-K loop offered by our container, their provided services and the possible collaborations between containers. Besides, in our solution we propose to enhance the classical MAPE-K loop by introducing the reactive and deliberative autonomic loops. For the evaluation of our approach, we realized a shopping application use case and we started performing some evaluation focused on the horizontal collaboration scenario between containers. We are investigating machine learning techniques in order to support predictive analysis and learning strategies planning. We also intend to investigate autonomic management and collaboration among containers in pervasive and Cloud environments.

References

1. Ben Lahmar, I., Belaïd, D.: Developing adapters for structural adaptation of component-based applications. In: 22nd IEEE International Conference on Enabling Technologies: Infrastructures for Collaborative Enterprises, pp. 92–97. IEEE Computer Society, Hammamet, June 2013
2. Ben Lahmar, I., Belaïd, D.: An autonomic container for the management of component-based applications in pervasive environments. In: 11th IEEE International Conference on Autonomic and Trusted Computing, Bali, Indonesia, pp. 548–555, December 2014
3. Ben Lahmar, I., Belaïd, D., Mukhtar, H.: A Pattern-based Adaptation for Abstract Applications in Pervasive Environments. International Journal On Advances in Software, 367–377 (2011)
4. Carlston, M., Chapman, M., Heneveld, A., Hinkelman, A., Johnston-Watt, S., Karmarkar, A., Kunze, T., Malhotra, T., Mischkinsky, J., Otto, A., Pandey, V., Pilz, G., Song, Z., Yendluri, P.: Cloud Application Management for Platforms Version 1.1. Tech. rep., November 2014. http://docs.oasis-open.org/camp/camp-spec/v1.1/cs01/camp-spec-v1.1-cs01.pdf
5. De Oliveira, J.F.A., Ledoux, T., Sharrock, R.: A framework for the coordination of multiple autonomic managers in cloud environments. In: 7th IEEE International Conference on Self-Adaptive and Self-Organizing Systems, SASO, pp. 179–188, September 2013

6. Diao, Y., Hellerstein, J.L., Parekh, S., Griffith, R., Kaiser, G., Phung, D.: A control theory foundation for self-managing computing systems. In: 12th IEEE International Conference and Workshops on the Engineering of Computer-Based Systems, pp. 441–448, April 2005

7. Gueye, S.M.K., de Palma, N., Rutten, E.: Component-based autonomic managers for coordination control. In: De Nicola, R., Julien, C. (eds.) COORDINATION 2013. LNCS, vol. 7890, pp. 75–89. Springer, Heidelberg (2013)

8. IBM: An Architectural Blueprint for Autonomic Computing. Tech. rep., June 2005. http://www-03.ibm.com/autonomic/pdfs/AC%20Blueprint%20White%20Paper%20V7.pdf

9. IBM: An Introduction to Creating Service Component Architecture Applications in Rational Application Developer Version 8.0. IBM Corporation 2010, September 2010

10. INRIA-Institute: Heptagon/BZR Manual, October 2013. http://bzr.inria.fr/pub/bzr-manual.pdf

11. Lalanda, P., McCann, J.A., Diaconescu, A.: Autonomic Computing - Principles, Design and Implementation. Undergraduate Topics in Computer Science. Springer London (2013)

12. Mbaye, M., Krief, F.: A collaborative knowledge plane for autonomic networks. In: Autonomic Communication, pp. 69–92. Springer US (2009)

13. Mohamed, M., Amziani, M., Belaïd, D., Tata, S., Melliti, T.: An Autonomic Approach to Manage Elasticity of Business Processes in the Cloud. Future Generation Computer Systems **50**, 49–61 (2014)

14. Mohamed, M., Belaïd, D., Tata, S.: Adding monitoring and reconfiguration facilities for service-based applications in the cloud. In: 27th IEEE International Conference on Advanced Information Networking and Applications, AINA, pp. 756–763, March 2013

15. Mola, O., Bauer, M.: Collaborative policy-based autonomic management: in a hierarchical model. In: 7th International Conference on Network and Service Management, CNSM, pp. 1–5, October 2011

16. OASIS: Web Services Business Process Execution Language Version 2.0. Tech. rep., April 2007. http://docs.oasis-open.org/wsbpel/2.0/OS/wsbpel-v2.0-OS.pdf

17. OASIS: Reference Architecture Foundation for Service Oriented Architecture Version 1.0. Tech. rep., December 2012. http://docs.oasis-open.org/soa-rm/soa-ra/v1.0/cs01/soa-ra-v1.0-cs01.pdf

18. OMG: Business Process Model and Notation (BPMN) Version 2.0. Tech. rep., January 2011. http://www.omg.org/spec/BPMN/2.0

19. Sellami, M., Yangui, S., Mohamed, M., Tata, S.: PaaS-independent provisioning and management of applications in the cloud. In: 6th IEEE International Conference on Cloud Computing (CLOUD), Santa Clara Marriott, CA, USA, pp. 693–700, June 2013

An Efficient Optimization Algorithm of Autonomic Managers in Service-Based Applications

Leila Hadded[1]([✉]), Faouzi Ben Charrada[1], and Samir Tata[2]

[1] Faculty of Science of Tunis, URAPAD,
University of Tunis El Manar, 2092 Tunis, Tunisia
hadded.leila@gmail.com, f.charrada@gnet.tn
[2] Institut Mines-Telecom, Telecom SudParis, UMR CNRS Samovar, Evry, France
Samir.Tata@mines-telecom.fr

Abstract. Cloud Computing is an emerging paradigm in Information Technologies that enables the delivery of infrastructure, software and platform resources as services. It is an environment with automatic service provisioning and management. In these last years autonomic management of Cloud services is receiving an increasing attention. Meanwhile, optimization of autonomic managers remains not well explored. In fact, almost all the existing solutions on autonomic computing have been interested in modeling and implementing of autonomic environments without paying attention on optimization. In this paper, we propose a new efficient algorithm to optimize autonomic managers for the management of service-based applications. Our algorithm allows to determine the minimum number of autonomic managers and to assign them to services that compose managed service-based applications. The realized experiments proves that our approach is efficient and adapted to service-based applications that can be not only described as architecture-based but also as behavior-based compositions of services.

Keywords: Cloud computing · Autonomic managers · Service-based applications · Optimization

1 Introduction

Cloud computing is a new computing paradigm that refers to a model for enabling convenient, on demand network access to a shared pool of configurable computing resources (e.g. servers, storage, applications and services). These resource can be rapidly provisioned and released with minimal management effort or service provider interaction [13]. In this paradigm, there are basically three levels for Cloud services' provision, which are Infrastructure as a Service (IaaS), Platform as a Service (PaaS), and Software as a Service (SaaS). At this later level, the effort is made to model, develop, deploy and manage applications and components/services that compose them. These applications

C. Debruyne et al. (Eds.): OTM 2015 Conferences, LNCS 9415, pp. 19–37, 2015.
DOI: 10.1007/978-3-319-26148-5_2

are also known as service-based applications (SBAs). Their service composition can be architecture-based (e.g. described in Service Component Architecture [12] or UML component diagram [4]) or behavior-based (e.g. described in Business Process Execution Language [11] (BPEL) or Business Process Model and Notation [16] (BPMN)).

Over the last years, autonomic computing got an increasing attention. It has been widely used in Cloud computing for dynamically adapting Cloud resources and service to changes in Cloud environments. Indeed, it aims at managing Cloud resources with minimal human intervention. Autonomic management usually relies on a MAPE-K (Monitor, Analyze, Plan, Execute and Knowledge) loop. This loop consists in collecting monitoring data from Cloud resources, analyzing them and producing series of planned changes to be executed on managed Cloud resources.

Managing SBAs according to principals of autonomic management, consists in determining and assigning MAPE-K loops to services that compose managed SBAs. To do that, two naive solutions can be considered. The first one consists in assigning one MAPE-K loop to a managed SBA. The second one consists in assigning one MAPE-K loop to each service of the managed SBA. It is obvious that the later solution is resource consuming while the former one may cause a bottleneck in managing SBAs. Consequently, it is of interest to optimize MAPE-K loopse consumption by minimizing the number of them while avoiding management bottlenecks.

When we visited the existing works on autonomic management and optimization of Cloud resources, we found out that they are not suitable to the considered problem of this paper. Indeed, on one hand, existing works on autonomic computing have been interested in modeling and implementing of autonomic environments without paying any attention to optimization. On the other hand optimization approaches are not adequate since they consider a number of resources known in advance.

In our previous works we have been interested in modeling, deployment and management of SBAs in Cloud environment [14,23]. In this paper, we are interested in the optimization of number of autonomic managers (i.e. autonomic control loops) for SBAs. We propose a new algorithm consists of two steps. In the first step we determine all sets of services of a given SBA that can be run in parallel, which aims at determining the lower bound of the number of MAPE-K loops. In the second step, MAPE-K loops are determined, based on results from step one, and assigned to services of the managed SBA.

The rest of this paper is organized as follows. In Section 2, we present some preliminary notions on autonomic computing and we represent SBAs as graphs. Our proposed efficient algorithm for MAPE-K loops optimization is presented in Section 3. Experiments conducted on realistic data are detailed in Section 4. In Section 5, we present the state of art. Finally, we conclude the paper and we give directions for future works in Section 6.

2   Autonomic Management of Service-Based Applications

In this section, we present the background of our work, in which we aim at optimizing autonomic managers for the management of SBAs. We start with defining MAPE-K loop, then, we define service-based applications. After that, we show how these applications are represented as graphs. Finally, we present the problem of optimizing autonomic managers in SBAs.

2.1   The MAPE-K Control Loop

To achieve autonomic computing, IBM has suggested a reference model for autonomic control loops [1], which is called the MAPE-K (Monitor, Analyze, Plan, Execute, Knowledge) loop as depicted in Fig. 1.

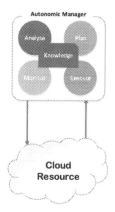

Fig. 1. Autonomic loop for a Cloud resource

This loop consists on harvesting monitoring data, analyzing them and generating reconfiguration actions to correct violations (self-healing and self-protecting) or to target a new state of the system (self-configuring and self-optimizing).

2.2   Service-Based Application

SBAs consists in composing a set of services using appropriate service composition specifications that can be architecture-based or behavior-based like. In the following we define these two types of compositions.

A SBA composed using an architecture-based composition can be described as a set of linked components. A component provides one or more services. It may consume one or several references, which are services provided by other components. As an example, we consider the online store example illustrated in Fig. 2 using a SCA assembly view. In the following sections, we use to this example in order to explain our concepts and motivate our work.

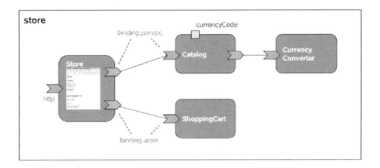

Fig. 2. Example of an on-line store (source [20])

The example is a composition of four services. The Store service provides the interface of the on-line store. The Catalog service which the Store service can ask for catalog items provides the item prices. The CurrencyConverter service does the currency conversion for the Catalog service. The ShoppingCart service is used to include items chosen from the Catalog service.

A SBA composed using a behavior-based specification can be described as a structured process which consists of a set of process nodes and transitions between them. A process node can be service, Or-Join, Or-Split, And-Split or And-Join. Fig. 3 depicts a BPMN business process of an online purchasing process of a clothing store.

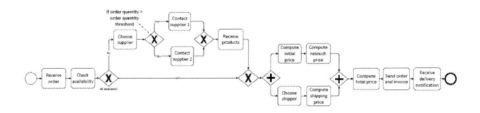

Fig. 3. Example of a SBA application modelled as a process

The customer sends a purchase order request with details about the required products and the needed quantity. Upon receipt of customer order, the seller checks product availability. If some of the products are not in stock, the alternative branch ordering from suppliers is executed. When all products are available, the choice of a shipper and the calculation of the initial price of the order are launched. Afterwards, the shipping price and the retouch price are computed simultaneously. The total price is then computed in order to send invoice and deliver the order. Finally, a notification is received from the shipper assuring that the order is already delivered.

The above-presented two types of compositions can be represented by graphs that we present in the following section.

2.3 SBA Graphs

The semantics of a graph that represents a SBA (called SBA graph) is described as follows. If s_1 and s_2 are nodes of graph and s_1 is connected to s_2 then the execution of s_2 follows the execution of s_1 or s_1 runs and references the services of s_2 during its execution. For instance, the later semantics reflects architecture-based compositions (e.g. SCA specification) while the former reflects behavior-based compositions (e.g. BPMN specification). Based on the above considerations, we can model a SBA like the one presented in Fig. 3 as a directed graph. Services, Or-Split, Or-Join, And-Split and And-Join nodes will be represented by graph nodes and connections/transitions between services will be represented by edges. Nodes are identified by an ID (a number).

Definition 1 (SBA graph). *A SBA graph is a 3 tuple $\langle S, E, v \rangle$ where:*

- *S is a set of services, Or-Split, Or-Join, And-Split and And-Join nodes composing the considered application (when the application is architecture-based S does not contain Or-Join, Or-Split, And-Split and And-Join nodes);*
- *$E \subseteq S \times S$ is the vertex connection set;*
- *v is the initial vertex of the graph.*

Fig. 4 represents the SBA graph of the SBA of Fig. 2 (v=Store).

Fig. 4. The SBA graph of the on-line store

According to the semantics presented above, if the composition is behavior-based the execution of *Catalog* and *ShoppingCart* services are performed in parallel. Indeed, when the *Store* service is finished, *Catalog* and *ShoppingCart* services will be launched in parallel. Nevertheless, if the composition is architecture-based they may be run in sequence or in parallel. In fact, the *Store* service may reference both *Catalog* and *ShoppingCart* services in parallel or in sequence. We say in this later case that *Catalog* and *ShoppingCart* services may run in parallel.

2.4 Problem Statement

In this paper we present an approach for optimizing autonomic managers for the management of SBAs. Let's consider the example of Fig. 4 that presents a

SBA composed of four services. To determine the number of MAPE-K loops that can be assigned to the four services, two naive solutions can be considered. The first one, represented by Figure 5-(a), consists in considering one MAPE-K loop assigned to the four services that compose the managed SBA. The second solution, represented by Figure 5-(b), consists in considering four MAPE-K loops so that each one is assigned to one service. It is obvious that the later solution is resource consuming while the former one may cause a bottleneck in the management. It is, consequently, of interest to optimize MAPE-K loops consumption while avoiding management bottlenecks.

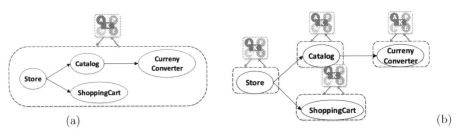

Fig. 5. Two naive solutions can be considered, (a) one MAPE-K loop assigned to the four services, (b) one MAPE-K loop assigned to each service

A solution, that can make a tradeoff between MAPE-K loops consumption, on one hand, and avoiding management bottleneck, on the other hand, would consist in considering two MAPE-K loops, one dedicated to *Store* and *Shopping-Cart* services and one dedicated to *Catalog* and *Currency Converter* services. This later solutions minimize the number of used MAPE-K loops while not assigning one MAPE-K loop to more than one running service at a time.

Based on the above-mentioned illustrations, we can state the problem we tackle in this paper. Given a SBA graph, our objective is to determine the minimum number of MAPE-K loops needed to manage its services with the following requirement and assumption. Two services running in parallel should be provided with two different MAPE-K loops for their management to avoid the bottleneck problem. Two services that may run in parallel are considered running in parallel. This later assumption allows us to consider both types of composition semantics and cover different situations of service compositions whatever they are architecture-based or behavior-based.

3   Algorithm for an Efficient Optimization of MAPE-K Loops in SBAs

3.1   Approach Overview

In this section, we propose an algorithm for the optimization of autonomic managers (MAPE-K loops) in SBAs. This algorithm is based on four procedures called *Predecessor*, *LowerBound*, *ServiceRelatedParallelSets* and *AutonomicLoopsAssignement*. The *Predecessor* procedure consists in determining for each service the number of its predecessors. *This procedure is used when the application is behavior-based* where a service begins execution only when all its predecessors have finished execution. The *LowerBound* procedure consists in determining a set of sets of services that satisfy the following property. Services that belong to one set can be run in parallel. The *ServiceRelatedParallelSets* procedure consists in determining for each service the set of services that can be run in parallel with it. *AutonomicLoopsAssignement* consists in assigning to each service a MAPE-K loop which is different from loops that are already assigned to services to be run in parallel with it. In the following we present these four above-mentioned procedures.

3.2 *Predecessor* Procedure

The *Predecessor* procedure, presented in Algorithm 1, takes as input a SBA graph. It returns an array containing for each service the number of its predecessors. Initially, the number of predecessors of each service is equal to zero (see Algorithm 1, lines 1-3). For each service s, the number of its predecessors is incremented by 1 if there is a service s successor of s_i (see lines 4-6).

Algorithm 1. Predecessor procedure

Require: $\langle S, E, v \rangle$: SBA graph
Ensure: *Predecessors*: array containing for each service the number of its
    predecessors
1: **for all** $s \in S$ **do**
2:    *Predecessors*[ID of s] $\leftarrow$ 0;
3: **end for**
4: **for all** $(s_i, s) \in E$ **do**
5:    *Predecessors*[ID of s] $\leftarrow$ *Predecessors*[ID of s] $+ 1$;
6: **end for**

3.3 *LowerBound* Procedure

The *LowerBound* procedure, presented in Algorithm 2, takes as input a SBA graph and an array containing for each service the number of its predecessors. It returns a set of sets of services that can be run in parallel and the maximum cardinality of its elements which constitutes a lower bound number of MAPE-K loops. The initial vertex of the SBA graph v is assigned to an initial set (see Algorithm 2, line 1). The *LowerBound* procedure is to be executed while the current set of services that can be run in parallel is not empty and is not a subset of a set that is already made in a previous iteration (see line 24). The current set of services composed of services, which are successors of services of the previous set where all its predecessor services are already treated in the previous sets (see lines 10-11). Otherwise, the number of predecessors is decremented by 1 (see line 13). If the current set is not already made in a previous iteration, then it is added to the set of sets (see lines 18-19). The lower bound number is possibly updated (see lines 20-22). This number is the maximum number of services that can be run in parallel. When the application is architecture-based the current set of services is composed of services, which are successors of services of the previous set (doesn't exist a test to check for each service s_j that all its predecessors are treated (see line 10)).

Algorithm 2. LowerBound procedure

Require: $\langle S, E, v \rangle$: SBA graph
Require: $Predecessors$: array containing for each service the number of its
       predecessors
Ensure: $ParallelSets$: set of sets of services that can be run in parallel
Ensure: lbn: the lower bound number

  1: $CurrentParallelSet \leftarrow \{v\}$;
  2: $ParallelSets \leftarrow \{CurrentParallelSet\}$;
  3: $lbn \leftarrow 1$;
  4: **repeat**
  5:    $PreviousParallelSet \leftarrow CurrentParallelSet$;
  6:    $CurrentParallelSet \leftarrow \emptyset$;
  7:    **for all** $s_i \in PreviousParallelSet$ **do**
  8:      **for all** $s_j \in S$ **do**
  9:        **if** $(s_i, s_j) \in E$ **then**
10:          **if** $Predecessors[ID\ of\ s_j] = 1$ **then**
11:            $CurrentParallelSet \leftarrow CurrentParallelSet \cup \{s_j\}$;
12:          **else**
13:            $Predecessors[ID\ of\ s_j] \leftarrow Predecessors[ID\ of\ s_j] - 1$;
14:          **end if**
15:        **end if**
16:      **end for**
17:    **end for**
18:    **if** $\nexists\ set\ s.t.(set \in ParallelSets$ **and** $CurrentParallelSet \subseteq set)$ **then**
19:      $ParallelSets \leftarrow ParallelSets \cup CurrentParallelSet$;
20:      **if** $|CurrentParallelSet| > lbn$ **then**
21:        $lbn \leftarrow |CurrentParallelSet|$;
22:      **end if**
23:    **end if**
24: **until** $(CurrentParallelSet =$
    $\emptyset$ **or** $\exists\ set\ s.t.(set \in ParallelSets$ **and** $CurrentParallelSet \subseteq set))$

The needed MAPE-K loops for a given SBA graph may be greater than the lower bound number. To give an example of such situation let's consider the example of Fig. 6 when the application is architecture-based as depicted in Section 2.3 if s_1 and s_2 are nodes of graph and s_1 is connected to s_2 then s_1 runs and references the services of s_2 during its execution.

Applied to this later example, the *LowerBound* procedure produces the following results:

- $ParallelSets$: $\{\{s_1\}, \{s_2, s_3\}, \{s_4, s_5\}, \{s_5, s_6\}, \{s_6, s_3\}, \{s_3, s_5\}\}$
- $lbn= 2$

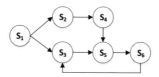

Fig. 6. Example of a SBA graph of a SCA-based Application

With respect to the semantics of applications specified in SCA, First, s_5 and s_6 may run in parallel. Second, s_6 and s_3 may run in parallel. Third, s_3 and s_5 may run in parallel. To satisfy these requirements, on one hand, and to assign different MAPE-K loops for services running in parallel, on the other hand, it is obvious that the number of needed MAPE-K loops for this example is equal to 3, while the lower bound number is equal to 2. Therefore, we need additional computing based the result of the *LowerBound* procedure to determine the number of needed MAPE-K loops for a given SBA and their assignment. This is the objective of the following algorithms.

3.4 *ServiceRelatedParallelSets* Procedure

The *ServiceRelatedParallelSets* procedure, presented in Algorithm 3, takes as input a SBA graph and a set of sets of services that can be run in parallel. It returns for each services s the set of services which can be run in parallel with it. This set is the union of all sets that belong to *ParallelSets* and that contain s (see Algorithm 3, lines 5-9).

Algorithm 3. ServiceRelatedParallelSets procedure

Require: $\langle S, E, v \rangle$: SBA graph
Require: *ParallelSets*: set of sets of services that can be run in parallel
Ensure: *ServiceRelatedParallelSets* : array of $< serviceIndex, serviceSet >$
1: $i \leftarrow 1$;
2: **for all** $s \in S$ **do**
3:     $ServiceRelatedParallelSets[i].serviceIndex \leftarrow ID$ of s;
4:     $ServiceRelatedParallelSets[i].serviceSet \leftarrow \emptyset$;
5:     **for all** $set \in ParallelSets$ **do**
6:         **if** $s \in set$ **then**
7:             ServiceRelatedParallelSets[i].serviceSet $\leftarrow$
               ServiceRelatedParallelSets[i] $\cup (set - \{s\})$;
8:         **end if**
9:     **end for**
10:     $i \leftarrow i + 1$;
11: **end for**

3.5 *AutonomicLoopsAssignement* Procedure

The *AutonomicLoopsAssignement* procedure, presented in Algorithm 4, takes as input a SBA graph and an array containing for each service the set of services that can be run in parallel with it. It returns an array containing for each service the MAPE-K loop assigned to it and the number of MAPE-K loops used for the managed SBA represented by the input SBA graph. *AutonomicLoops* is an array that will contain for each service s, the number of the MAPE-K loop assigned to it. Initially, the elements of this array are equal to zero, which means that loops are not yet assigned to services (see Algorithm 4, lines 1-3). MAPE-K loops assignment begins with the service whose related parallel set has the biggest cardinality. Consequently, the array *ServiceRelatedParallelSets* is sorted in decreasing order according to the cardinality of sets of its elements (see line 4). For each service s (see lines 6-14), the variable *currentLoop* is initialized with the value 1. This is a tentative to assign the loop number 1 to the s (see line 7). If this *currentLoop* isn't already assigned to a service that belongs to the set of services that can be run in parallel with s, then *currentLoop* is assigned to s (see line 10). Otherwise, *currentLoop* is incremented by 1. This is done to try assigning the next loop to s (see line 12). This computing is repeated until assigning a loop to s (see line 14). The number of autonomic loops needed to manage the given SBA is then computed (see lines 15-17).

Algorithm 4. AutonomicLoopsAssignement procedure

Require: $\langle S, E, v \rangle$: SBA graph
Require: *ServiceRelatedParallelSets* : array of $< serviceIndex, serviceSet >$
Ensure: *AutonomicLoops*: array containing for each service the MAPE-K loop assigned to it
Ensure: *numberAutonomicLoops*: number of MAPE-K loops
 1: **for all** $i \in \{1, 2, \dots |S|\}$ **do**
 2:     $AutonomicLoops[i] \leftarrow 0$;
 3: **end for**
 4: sortDecreasingOrderOfCardinalityOfSets(*ServiceRelatedParallelSets*);
 5: $numberAutonomicLoops \leftarrow 0$;
 6: **for all** $i \in \{1, 2, \dots |S|\}$ **do**
 7:     $currentLoop \leftarrow 1$;
 8:     **repeat**
 9:         **if** $\nexists$ s s.t. ($s \in ServiceRelatedParallelSets[i].serviceSet$
            and $AutonomicLoops[ID \ of \ s] = currentAutonomicLoop$) **then**
10:             AutonomicLoops[ServiceRelatedParallelSets[i].serviceIndex]$\leftarrow$
                currentLoop;
11:         **else**
12:             $currentLoop \leftarrow currentLoop + 1$;
13:         **end if**
14:     **until** $\nexists$ s s.t. ($s \in ServiceRelatedParallelSets[i].serviceSet$
        and $AutonomicLoops[ID \ of \ s] = currentAutonomicLoop$)
15:     **if** $currentLoop > numberAutonomicLoops$ **then**
16:         $numberAutonomicLoops \leftarrow currentLoop$;
17:     **end if**
18: **end for**

Applied to our running example presented in Fig. 4:
- The *LowerBound* procedure gives the following results:

- $ParallelSets$: $\{\{Store\}, \{Catalog, ShoppingCart\}, \{Curreny\ Converter\}\}$
- lbn= 2 which is the cardinality of the second element in the ParallelSets $\{Catalog, ShoppingCart\}$

- The $ServiceRelatedParallelSets$ procedure gives the following results:

Services	Store	Catalog	ShoppingCart	Curreny Converter
ServiceRelatedParallelSets	$< 1, \emptyset >$	$< 2, \{ShoppingCart\} >$	$< 3, \{Catalog\} >$	$< 4, \emptyset >$

- The $AutonomicLoopsAssignement$ procedure gives the following results: $number\,AutonomicLoops$= 2

Services	Catalog	ShoppingCart	Store	Curreny Converter
AutonomicLoops	1	2	1	1

Applied to our running example presented in Fig. 6:
- The $ServiceRelatedParallelSets$ procedure gives the following results:

Services	S_1	S_2	S_3	S_4	S_5	S_6
ParallelSets	$< 1, \emptyset >$	$< 2, \{S_3\} >$	$< 3, \{S_2, S_5, S_6\} >$	$< 4, \{S_5\} >$	$< 5, \{S_3, S_4, S_6\} >$	$< 6, \{S_3, S_5\} >$

- The $AutonomicLoopsAssignement$ procedure gives the following results: $number\,AutonomicLoops$= 3

Services	S_3	S_5	S_6	S_2	S_4	S_1
AutonomicLoops	1	2	3	2	1	1

4 Experiments

In service research field, there are two types of compositions of services: behavior-based and architecture-based compositions. Behavior-based compositions of services are generally sparse graphs where nodes represent services and operators and links represent dependencies between services and operators. Architecture-based compositions of services can be sparse or dense graphs where nodes represent services and links represent dependencies between services.

To evaluate our algorithm for the optimization of MAPE-K loops for SBAs in the cloud, we have considered two datasets, one for architecture-based compositions and one for behavior-based compositions. At the best of our knowledge, there is no public and open source dataset for architecture-based compositions of services. Therefore, in Section 4.1, we give the results of experiments performed on a realistic dataset based on randomly generated graphs, which represented architecture-based compositions of services. But in Section 4.2 we give results related to a real dataset from IBM that contains 560 BPMN business process. All the computation times are achieved on intel® Core^{TM} i5 CPU a 2.53 GHz 2.53GHz, RAM 4Go.

As we will explain in Section 5, at the best of our knowledge none of the existing approaches tackles the problem of optimizing the number of autonomic managers whiles avoiding the bottleneck problem. Consequently, we are not able to cover any comparison with an existing approach. Therefore, for both experiments, we studied the time complexity of our algorithms and the quality of their results in the sense of the closeness of results to the lower bound numbers results of the *Lower Bound* procedure.

4.1   Experiments on Architecture-Based Compositions

To consider a realistic dataset, we have covered different graphs to represent different types of compositions of services. In fact, our generated graphs are constructed as follows. For each graph of order n we consider to represent a SBA that should be connected. Consequently, this later should contain at least $n - 1$ edges (when it is a tree). To cover different types of SBAs with the same order n, we have considered different graphs with different number of edges starting from $n - 1$ edges until $3.2 * (n - 1)$ (i. e. 320% of $(n - 1)$). In fact, we did not consider additional graphs with more edges, since we found out that beyond $2.2 * (n - 1)$, the lower bound number is n. Then the number of needed loops for a graph of order n, in this case, is n.

For our experimentation, we have varied graphs' order 10 times from 10 to 100. Real datasets, such as the IBM DataSet [7], show that 99% of service-based applications are within this order range (less than 100). In addition for each order n, we considered 12 densities (from 100% of $(n - 1)$ to 320% of $(n - 1)$) and for each density, we considered 10 randomly generated graphs. In total, we have considered 1200 generated graphs. Table 1 summarize the characteristics of our dataset.

Table 1. Characteristics of generated graphs (the values presented in this table are the number of edges of the graph and n is the number of nodes)

% of n-1 / n	100%	120%	140%	160%	180%	200%	220%	240%	260%	280%	300%	320%
10	9	11	13	14	16	18	20	22	23	25	27	29
20	19	23	27	30	34	38	42	46	49	53	57	61
30	29	35	41	46	52	58	64	70	75	81	87	93
40	39	47	55	62	70	78	86	94	101	109	117	125
50	49	59	69	78	88	98	108	118	127	137	147	157
60	59	71	83	94	106	118	130	142	153	165	177	189
70	69	83	97	110	124	138	152	166	179	193	207	221
80	79	95	111	126	142	158	174	190	205	221	237	253
90	89	107	125	142	160	178	196	214	231	249	267	285
100	99	119	139	158	178	198	218	238	257	277	297	317

As depicted in Fig. 7, that presents the evolution of percentage of the lower bound number with respect to the service number using different densities, when the number of edges for a graph of order n is beyond $2.2 * (n - 1)$, the lower bound number is n. Then the number of needed loops is n. Therefore, we limited our experimentations'analysis for quality of results, of the *AutonomicLoopsAssignement* procedure, to graphs with number of edges are starting from $n-1$ up to $2.2*(n-1)$, for graphs of order n.

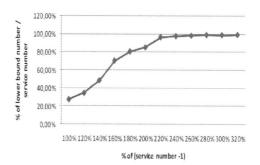

Fig. 7. Evolution of % of lower bound number/service number using different densities

Complexity. It is obvious that the time complexity of Algorithms 1, 3 and 4 is polynomial whereas the theoretical time complexity of Algorithm 2 is exponential (i.e. $o(2^n)$ where n is the order of the considered graph). In fact, the time complexity is equal to $o(|ParallelSets|)$ which is bounded by $o(2^n)$. Nevertheless, from a practical point of view, the execution time of our algorithm is reasonable. For the 1200 considered graphs the execution time does not exceed 0.24 seconds.

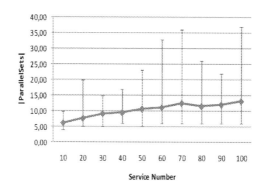

Fig. 8. Evolution of ParallelSets'cardinality using different type of graphs

As it is shown in Fig. 8, the number of sets of services that can be run in parallel ($|ParallelSets|$) is small with respect to graphs' order. For instance, the number of parallel sets for graphs of order 100 does not exceed 37. In addition, the curve of $|ParallelSets|$ is linear with a very low slope.

Quality. According to our assumptions depicted in Section 2.4,when the number of MAPE-K loops result of the *AutonomicLoopsAssignement* procedure is equal to the lower bound number result of the *LowerBound* procedure, then this former number is optimal. Applied to our dataset, our algorithm gives excellent results since it obtained optimal results, in the above sense, for 94% of the considered graphs. Beyond optimal results, let's analyze the quality of non-optimal ones (6% of the considered graphs). The quality of a given result is measured by the difference, in terms of number of assigned loops, between the lower bound obtained by the *LowerBound* procedure, on one hand, and the number of loops obtained by the *AutonomicLoopsAssignement* procedure on the other hand. The lower this difference is the better it is.

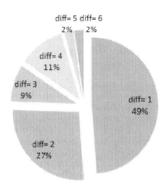

Fig. 9. Average of difference percentages

As it is shown in Fig. 9, the difference for non-optimal results (which constitute themselves 6% or the whole results) does not exceed 6 loops, where for 49% among them, the difference is equal to one. Note as it is shown in Fig. 6, the needed assigned loops for a given SBA can be greater than the lower bound obtained by the *LowerBound* procedure.

4.2 Experiments on Behavior-Based Compositions

To evaluate our Algorithms, we also used an IBM DataSet that contains 560 BPMN business processes, which represent a real dataset of behavior-based compositions of services available in the IBM WebSphere Business Modeler tool. A process node can be startEvent, endEvent, task, exclusiveGateway, parallel-Gateway, inclusiveGateway or subProcess. The number of process nodes varies between 7 and 533 while the number of task varies between 2 and 106.

Complexity. From a practical point of view, the execution time of our algorithm on the IBMs dataset is reasonable. In fact, for the 560 considered business processes, the execution time does not exceed 0.1 second.

Quality. According to our assumptions depicted in Section 2.4, when the number of MAPE-K loops result of the *AutonomicLoopsAssignement* procedure is equal to the lower bound number result of the *LowerBound* procedure, then this former number is optimal. Applied to the IBMs dataset, our algorithm gives excellent results since it obtained optimal results, with respect to the above sense, for 100% of the considered business processes.

5 Related Work

In Cloud and distributed environments, there are several research works related to autonomic computing as well as optimization of Cloud resource consumption. At the best of our knowledge, these proposals treat the two areas separately. In the following, we give an overview of some of these works.

5.1 Autonomic Computing

One of the pioneers in the Autonomic Computing field is IBM that proposed a dedicated toolkit [18]. In this work, authors gave the IBMs definition of Autonomic Computing as well as the needed steps to define autonomic resources for the management of components. The proposed toolkit is a collection of technologies and tools that allows a user to develop autonomic behavior for his/her systems. One of the basic tools is the Autonomic Management Engine that includes representations of the MAPE-K loop that provides self-management properties to managed resources.

Beside the IBMs work, Buyya et al. proposed a conceptual architecture to enhance autonomic computing for Cloud environments [5]. The proposed architecture is basically composed of a SaaS web application used to negotiate the SLA between the provider and its customers, an Autonomic Management System (AMS) located in the PaaS layer. The AMS incorporates an Application scheduler responsible of assigning Cloud resources to applications. It also incorporates an Energy efficient scheduler that aims to minimize the energy consumption of all the system. The AMS implements the logic for provisioning and managing virtual resources.

In [21], authors proposed an Autonomic Network-aware Meta-scheduling (ANM) architecture capable of adapting its behavior to the current status of the environment. This work is based on a Grid Network Broker (GNB) that represents the autonomic network-aware meta-scheduler. GNB chooses the most appropriate resource to run jobs. An autonomic loop is implemented to adjust the scheduling task to improve job completion times and resources utilization. Whenever the selected resource did not respond to the required QoS, other resources are checked until a suitable resource is found.

In [19], authors introduced a framework that tackle management and adaptation strategies for component-based applications. In their approach, the authors separate Monitoring, Analysis, Planning and Execution concerns by implementing each one of them as separate components that could be attached to a managed component.

de Oliveira et al [15] proposed a framework for self-management of systems which focuses on the coordination of autonomic managers in the Cloud. The authors proposed an architectural model for autonomic managers coordination that meets the Cloud architectural constraints from the perspective of loose coupling and information hiding. Two kinds of autonomic managers are presented in this paper. The first kind consists in managing the applications at the SaaS layer, which is called Application Autonomic Manager (AAM). The second kind consists in managing the IaaS layer, which is called Infrastructure Autonomic Manager (IAM). In this paper, authors proposed to assign one AM to each managed system that can be one application or the whole infrastructure.

All these autonomic computing approaches have been interested in modeling and implementing of autonomic environments without making any effort for optimizing autonomic managers used for the management of applications. In contrast, in our work, we propose a novel approach to optimize autonomic resources used for the management of service-based applications.

5.2   Optimization of Cloud Resources

In their work [6], Chaisiri et al. proposed an optimal Cloud resource provisioning (OCRP) algorithm for the management of virtual machines. This work can help the consumer to decide whether to purchase reserved or on-demand instances of Cloud computing resources in each time slot with the objective of reducing the total provisioning cost.

Babu et al. [3] introduced a generic algorithm to allocate virtual machines optimally in Cloud environments. Initially they proposed to assign each application to a virtual machine and compute the remaining capacity. Therefore they apply a genetic algorithm in order to have an optimal allocation to the virtual machines, with the maximum remaining capacity.

Yusoh et al. [9], presented a service deployment strategies for efficient execution of Composite SaaS applications in the Cloud. The objective was to determine which services should be assigned to which virtual machines. To achieve this objective, authors took inter-service communication and parallelism among services into consideration. They proposed an approach to minimize communication costs by assigning interrelated services in the same virtual machine and increasing the potential execution parallelism by assigning two independent services in different virtual machines when application is modeled as a Directed Acyclic Graph (DAG).

In [8], authors presented a novel approach to schedule elastic processes in the cloud. They define a system model and an optimization model which is aiming at minimizing the total leasing cost for Cloud-based computational resources. The problem addressed is to determine which services should be assigned to which virtual machines.

In [10], authors proposed an algorithm for scheduling of workflow applications in geographically distributed Clouds taking into account interdependence between workflow steps and permits to assign each tasks to Cloud resources in order to minimizing cost and execution time according to the preferences of the user.

In [17,22], authors presented a Particle Swarm Optimization (PSO) based algorithm to optimize the schedules tasks in workflow applications among Cloud services that takes computation cost and data transmission cost into account in order to minimize the execution cost when application is modeled as a DAG.

Arya et al. [2], reviewed the basis workflow scheduling algorithms that are important for cloud environments. Different methods are used in these algorithm (i.e., Particle Swarm Optimization, Heuristic based Genetic Algorithms, etc.) and several factors are considered such as the execution time, resource utilization, cost optimization, etc.

At the best of our knowledge, in the works related to optimization of Cloud resource mainly those we cite above the number of Cloud resources is assumed to be known in advance. While one can imagine adapting these proposed algorithms to optimize autonomic managers? consumption, by considering an autonomic manager as a cloud resource, these works can not address our objective. In fact, in these work, the number of Cloud resources is assumed to be known in advance, while in our work the number of autonomic managers is not known in advance. In addition, some of these works don't address applications with dependency relationships. The work we present in this paper is novel in the sense that (1) it tackles the problem of optimization at the SaaS level (particularly for SBPs) while considering applications with dependency relationship and (2) it tackles the problem of autonomic computing when the number of autonomic managers isn't known in advance.

6 Conclusion and Future Work

In this paper, we present a novel approach to optimize autonomic managers used for the management of service-based applications. Our approach consists in (1) determining all sets of services for a given SBA that can be run in parallel, which aims to determine the lower bound number of MAPE-K loops, and (2) assigning MAPE-K loops to services. The proposed algorithms are of acceptable time complexity from a practical point of view. The execution time on graphs of different types and orders does not exceed 0.24 seconds. To evaluate the quality of results, we have conducted more than 1200 of experiments on graphs of a realistic dataset. Experiments results show that our algorithm has an excellent behavior for architecture-based compositions and for those based on behavior.

The work we achieved is very promising and several perspectives are under study. Among others, we aim, in the short term, at considering estimations on execution time of service when determining and assigning MAPE-K loops to services. Another possible extension, if such information is not available, is an online approach that consists in determining and assigning, within a time window, MAPE-K loops to services during their execution. In a longer term, we aim at considering an approach to determine and assign MAPE-K components, rather than loops, to services. Since monitors, analyzers, planners, executers, and knowledge bases component may not be used in the same way in the management of services, we can envisage to assign some MAPE-K components to several services running in parallel and dedicate some others to one service at a time depending on their usage.

References

1. An architectural blueprint for autonomic computing. Tech. rep., IBM (2005)
2. Arya, L., Verma, A.: Workflow scheduling algorithms in cloud environment - a survey. In: Engineering and Computational Sciences (RAECS) (2014)
3. Babu, K.D., Kumar, D.G., Veluru, S.: Optimal allocation of virtual resources using genetic algorithm in cloud environments. In: Proceedings of the 12th ACM International Conference on Computing Frontiers (2015)
4. Booch, G., Rumbaugh, J., Jacobson, I.: Unified Modeling Language User Guide. Addison-Wesley Professional (2005)
5. Buyya, R., Calheiros, R.N., Li, X.: Autonomic cloud computing: open challenges and architectural elements. CoRR (2012)
6. Chaisiri, S., Lee, B.S., Niyato, D.: Optimization of resource provisioning cost in cloud computing. IEEE Transactions on Services Computing (2012)
7. Fahland, D., Favre, C., Koehler, J., Lohmann, N., Völzer, H., Wolf, K.: Analysis on demand: Instantaneous soundness checking of industrial business process models. Data Knowl. Eng. (2011)
8. Hoenisch, P., Schuller, D., Schulte, S., Hochreiner, C., Dustdar, S.: Optimization of complex elastic processes. IEEE Transactions on Services Computing (2015)
9. Huang, K.C., Shen, B.J.: Service deployment strategies for efficient execution of composite saas applications on cloud platform. Journal of Systems and Software (2015)
10. Juhnke, E., Dornemann, T., Bock, D., Freisleben, B.: Multi-objective scheduling of BPEL workflows in geographically distributed clouds. In: IEEE International Conference on Cloud Computing (CLOUD) (2011)
11. Juric, M.B.: Business Process Execution Language for Web Services BPEL and BPEL4WS, 2nd edn. Packt Publishing (2006)
12. Marino, J., Rowley, M.: Understanding SCA (Service Component Architecture). Addison-Wesley Professional (2009)
13. Mell, P.M., Grance, T.: The NIST definition of cloud computing. Tech. rep. (2011)
14. Mohamed, M., Amziani, M., Belaïd, D., Tata, S., Melliti, T.: An autonomic approach to manage elasticity of business processes in the Cloud. Future Generation Computer Systems (2014)
15. de Oliveira, F., Ledoux, T., Sharrock, R.: A framework for the coordination of multiple autonomic managers in cloud environments. In: IEEE 7th International Conference on Self-Adaptive and Self-Organizing Systems (SASO) (2013)
16. (OMG), O.M.G.: Business process model and notation (BPMN). Tech. rep. (2011)
17. Pandey, S., Wu, L., Guru, S., Buyya, R.: A particle swarm optimization-based heuristic for scheduling workflow applications in cloud computing environments. In: 24th IEEE International Conference on Advanced Information Networking and Applications (2010)
18. Redbooks, I., Organization, I.B.M.C.I.T.S.: A Practical Guide to the IBM Autonomic Computing Toolkit. IBM Corporation, International Technical Support Organization (2004)

19. Ruz, C., Baude, F., Sauvan, B.: Flexible adaptation loop for component-based SOA applications. In: 7th International Conference on Autonomic and Autonomous Systems ICAS (2011)
20. The Apache Software Foundation: Getting started with Tuscany. http://tuscany.apache.org/getting-started-with-tuscany.html
21. Tomás, L., Caminero, A.C., Rana, O., Carrión, C., Caminero, B.: A gridway-based autonomic network-aware metascheduler. Future Gener. Comput. Syst. (2012)
22. Wu, Z., Ni, Z., Gu, L., Liu, X.: A revised discrete particle swarm optimization for cloud workflow scheduling. In: International Conference on Computational Intelligence and Security (CIS) (2010)
23. Yangui, S., Tata, S.: The spd approach to deploy service-based applications in the cloud. Concurrency and Computation: Practice and Experience (2014)

TrustedMR: A Trusted MapReduce System Based on Tamper Resistance Hardware

Quoc-Cuong To[1,2(✉)], Benjamin Nguyen[1,2(✉)], and Philippe Pucheral[1,2(✉)]

[1] SMIS Project, INRIA Rocquencourt, 78153 Le Chesnay, France
{quoc-cuong.to,benjamin.nguyen,philippe.pucheral}@inria.fr
[2] PRiSM Laboratory, 45, Av. des Etats-Unis, 78035 Versailles, France
{quoc-cuong.to,benjamin.nguyen,philippe.pucheral}@prism.uvsq.fr

Abstract. With scalability, fault tolerance, ease of programming, and flexibility, MapReduce has gained many attractions for large-scale data processing. However, despite its merits, MapReduce does not focus on the problem of data privacy, especially when processing sensitive data, such as personal data, on untrusted infrastructure. In this paper, we investigate a scenario based on the *Trusted Cells* paradigm : a user stores his personal data in a local secure data store and wants to process this data using MapReduce on a third party infrastructure, on which secure devices are also connected. The main contribution of the paper is to present *TrustedMR*, a trusted MapReduce system with high security assurance provided by tamper-resistant hardware, to enforce the security aspect of the MapReduce. Thanks to TrustedMR, encrypted data can then be processed by untrusted computing nodes without any modification to the existing MapReduce framework and code. Our evaluation shows that the performance overhead of TrustedMR is limited to few percents, compared to an original MapReduce framework that handles cleartexts.

Keywords: Privacy-preserving · Tamper-resistant hardware · MapReduce

1   Introduction

We are witnessing an exponential creation and accumulation of personal data: data generated and stored by administrations, hospitals, insurance companies; data automatically acquired by web sites, sensors and smart meters; and even digital data owned or created by individuals (e.g., photos, agendas, invoices, quantified-self data). It represents an unprecedented potential for applications (e.g., car insurance billing, carbon tax charging, resource optimization in smart grids, healthcare surveillance). However, as seen with the PRISM affair, it has also become clear that centralizing and processing all one's data in external servers introduces a major threat on privacy. To face this situation, personal cloud systems arise in the market place (e.g., Cozy Cloud[1], SeaFile[2], to cite a few) with the aim to give the control back to individuals on their data. According to [29], a Personal Cloud could be defined as a way to aggregate

---

[1] http://cozy.io/

[2] http://seafile.com/en/home/

© Springer International Publishing Switzerland 2015
C. Debruyne et al. (Eds.): OTM 2015 Conferences, LNCS 9415, pp. 38–56, 2015.
DOI: 10.1007/978-3-319-26148-5_3

the heterogeneous personal data scattered in different areas into one (virtual) cloud, so that a person could effectively store, acquire, and share his data. This user-centric definition illustrates the gravity shift of information management from organizations to individuals [16]. But this raises a critical question: how to perform big data computations crossing information from multiple individuals?

Trusting a regular Cloud infrastructure to host personal clouds and perform global computations on them is definitely not an option. Privacy violations are legion and arise from negligence, attacks and abusive use and no current server-based approach seems capable of closing the gap[3]. Cryptographic-based solutions have been proposed (e.g., [8, 18, 22]) to guarantee that data never appear in the clear on the servers but they provide either poor performance, poor security or support a very limited set of computations. Consequently, several attempts of personal data management decentralization have appeared (e.g., [1, 3, 17]). While these solutions increase the control of each individual on his data, they complexify big data computations crossing data from several individuals. Solutions have been proposed to solve specific problems like data anonymization [2] or SQL-like queries [21] over decentralized personal data stores. However, data availability can no longer be assumed in this context because individuals can disconnect their personal data stores at their will. Hence the semantics of these computations must be revisited with an open world assumption in mind.

This paper explores a new alternative where individual's data is hosted by a Cloud provider but the individual retains control on it thanks to a personal secure hardware enclave. This alternative capitalizes on two trends. On one side, Cloud providers (e.g., OVH in Europe) now propose to rent private (i.e., unshared) physical nodes to individuals at low cost. On the other side, low cost secure hardware devices like personal smart tokens become more and more popular. Smart tokens have different form factors (e.g., SIM card, USB token, Secure MicroSD) and names but share similar characteristics (low cost, high portability, high tamper-resistance), introducing a real breakthrough in the secure management of personal data [3]. Combining both trends seems rather natural and leads to the infrastructure pictured in Figure 1. This is nothing but a regular Cloud infrastructure with personal secure devices connected to its storage and computing nodes. Hence, each individual could upload his data on the Cloud in an encrypted form and retain the control on it thanks to a Trusted Data Server hosted in his own secure device [1]. Hence the name personal enclave since the Cloud provider has no way to get access to the secrets stored in each secure device nor can tamper with their processing. This architecture differs from [5] where a shared server is hosted in a single tamper-resistant processor. This architecture can be seen as a clustered implementation of the Trusted Cells vision [3], that is to say a set of low power but highly trusted computing nodes which can communicate and exchange data among them through an untrusted Cloud infrastructure to perform a secure global computation.

In this article, we focus on the MapReduce framework [11] to perform big data computations over personal data. With MapReduce, developers can solve various cumbersome tasks of distributed programming simply by writing a map and a reduce function. The system automatically distributes the workload over a cluster of commodity machines, monitors the execution, and handles failures. Current trends show

---

[3] http://www.datalossdb.org/

that MapReduce is considered as a high-productivity alternative to traditional parallel programming paradigms for a variety of applications, ranging from enterprise computing to peta-scale scientific computing. However, the raw data can be highly sensitive: at the 1Hz granularity provided by the French Linky power meters, most electrical appliances have a distinctive energy signature. It is thus possible to infer from the power meter data inhabitants activities [15]. With the architecture presented in Fig. 1, raw data of each individual could be uploaded in an encrypted form in the Cloud while the cryptographic keys remain confined to the individual's secure device. With appropriate execution and key exchange protocol a global computation can occur with the guarantee that no adversary can get any clear text data nor infer any value at the intermediate steps of the processing.

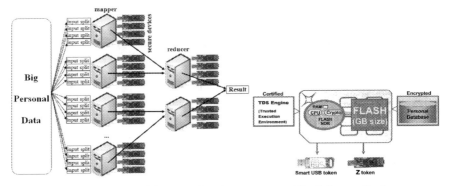

Fig. 1. Cloud infrastructure with personal enclaves   **Fig. 2.** Secure Device

MapReduce was born to meet the demand of performance in processing big data, but it is still missing the function of protecting user's sensitive data from untrusted mappers/reducers. Although some state-of-the-art works have been proposed to focus on the security aspect of MapReduce, none of them aims at data privacy (see section 2). Based on the architecture presented in Figure 1, this paper proposes a MapReduce-based system, addressing the following four important issues:

1. **Security**: How to perform a MapReduce computation over personal data without revealing sensitive information to untrusted mappers/reducers nodes?
2. **Performance**: How to keep acceptable MapReduce performance, that is to say a small overhead compared with processing cleartext data?
3. **Generality**: How to support any form of Map and Reduce functions?
4. **Seamless integration**: How to answer the preceding questions without changing the original MapReduce framework?

The rest of this paper is organized as follows. Section 2 discusses related works. Section 3 states our problem. Section 4 presents our proposed solution and Section 5 analyses its security. Section 6 measures the performance and section 7 concludes.

2   Related Works

2.1   Security in MapReduce

Mandatory Access Control (MAC) and Differential Privacy. [19] proposes the Airavat that integrates MAC with differential privacy in MapReduce framework. Since Airavat adds noise to the output in the reduce function to achieve differential privacy, it requires that reducers must be trusted. Furthermore, the types of computation supported by Airavat are limited (e.g., SUM, COUNT). The other drawback of Airavat is that the security mechanisms are implemented inside the open infrastructure. Hence, their trustworthiness should still be verified. Finally, they have to modify the original MapReduce framework to support MAC.

Integrity Verification. In other directions, [23] replicates some map/reduce tasks and assign them to different mappers/reducers to validate the integrity of map/reduce tasks. Any inconsistent intermediate results from those mappers/reducers reveal attacks. However, with only the data integrity, they cannot preserve the data privacy since the mappers/reducers directly access to sensitive data in cleartexts. So, these works are orthogonal to our works in which we aim at protecting the data privacy.

Data Anonymization. [26] claims that it is challenging to process large-scale data to satisfy k-anonymity in a tolerable elapsed time. So they anonymize data sets via generalization to satisfy k-anonymity in a highly scalable way by MapReduce.

Hybrid Cloud. Some works [24, 25] propose the hybrid cloud to split the task, keeping the computation on the private data within an organization's private cloud while moving the rest to the public commercial cloud. Sedic [24] requires that reduction operations must be associative and the original MapReduce framework must be modified. Also, the sanitization approach in Sedic may still reveal relative locations and length of sensitive data, which could lead to crucial information leakage in certain applications [25]. To overcome this weakness, [25] proposes tagged-MapReduce that augments each key-value pair with a sensitivity tag. Both solutions are not suitable for MapReduce job where all data is sensitive.

Encrypting Part of Dataset. In arguing that encrypting all data sets in cloud is not effective, [27] proposes an approach to identify which data sets with high frequency of accessing need to be encrypted while others are in cleartexts. This solution is not suitable for the case where all data have the same frequency of accessing or data owner does not want to reveal even a single tuple to untrusted cloud.

Other works **support very specific operations**. [7] searches encrypted keywords on the cloud without revealing any information about the content it hosts and search queries performed. [6] presents EPiC to count the number of occurrences of a pattern specified by user in an oblivious manner on the untrusted cloud. In contrast to these works, our work addresses more general problems, supporting any kind of operations.

2.2   Security in Other Systems

Secure Hardware at Server Side. Some works [5, 4] deploy the secure hardware at server side to ensure the confidentiality of the system. By leveraging server-hosted tamper-proof hardware, [5] designs TrustedDB, a trusted hardware based relational database with full data confidentiality and no limitations on query expressiveness. However, TrustedDB does not deploy any parallel processing, limiting its performance. [4] also bases on the trusted hardware to securely decrypt data on the server and perform computations in plaintext. They present oblivious query processing algorithms so that an adversary observing the data access pattern learns nothing.

Secure Hardware at Client Side. Even equipped with secure hardware on server, [5, 4] does not solve the two intrinsic problems of centralized approaches: (i) users get exposed to sudden changes in privacy policies; (ii) users are exposed to sophisticated attacks, whose cost-benefit is high on a centralized database [3]. So some works [21, 2, 3] are based on secure hardware at client side to solve these problems. The work in [2] proposes a generic Privacy-Preserving Data Publishing protocol, composed of low cost secure tokens and a powerful but untrusted supporting server, to publish different sanitized releases to recipients. Similarly, [21] proposes distributed querying protocols to compute general queries while maintaining strong privacy guarantees.

Centralized DaaS Without Secure Hardware. Many works [18, 22] have addressed the security of outsourced database services (DaaS) by encrypting the data at rest and pushing part of the processing to the server side but none of them can achieve all aspects of security, utility, and performance. In terms of utility and security, the best theoretical solution such as fully homomorphic encryption [12], allows server to compute arbitrary functions over encrypted data without decrypting. However, this construction is prohibitively expensive in practice with overhead of $10^9 \times$ [22]. In term of performance, CryptDB [18] provides provable confidentiality by executing SQL queries over encrypted data using a collection of efficient SQL-aware encryptions. But this system is not completely secure since it still uses some weak encryptions (e.g., deterministic & order-preserving encryptions [8]). Similarly, MONOMI system [22] securely executes arbitrarily complex queries over sensitive data on an untrusted database server with a median overhead of only 1.24× compared to an un-encrypted database. However, this system still uses some weak encryption schemes (e.g., deterministic encryption) to perform some SQL operations (e.g., Group By, equi-join).

As a conclusion, and to the best of our knowledge, no state-of-the-art MapReducre works can satisfy the three requirements of security, utility, performance, and our work is the first MapReduce-based proposal, that inherits the strong privacy guarantees from [21], achieving a secure solution to process large-scale encrypted data using a large set of tamper-resistant hardware with low performance overhead.

3   Context of the Study

3.1   Architecture

The architecture we consider is decentralized by nature. As pictured in Fig. 2, each individual is assumed to manage her data by means of a Trusted Data Server embedded in a secure device. We make no assumption about how this data is actually gathered and refer the reader to other papers addressing this issue [1, 17]. We detail next the main components of the architecture.

The Trusted Data Servers (TDSs). A TDS (as defined in [1]) is a DBMS engine embedded in an individual's secure device. It manages the individual's personal data and can participate in distributed queries while enforcing access control rules and opt-in/out choices of the individual. A TDS inherits its security from the Secure Device hosting it. Despite the diversity of existing hardware solutions, a Secure Device can be abstracted by (1) a Trusted Execution Environment and (2) a (potentially un-trusted) mass storage area. E.g., the former can be provided by a tamper-resistant microcontroller while the latter can be provided by Flash memory (see Fig. 2). Since Secure Devices exhibit high security guarantee [1], the code executed by them cannot be tampered. This given, the contents of the mass storage area can be protected using cryptographic protocols. Most Secure Devices provide modest computing resources (see section 6) due to the hardware constraints linked to their tamper-resistance. On the other hand, a dedicated cryptographic co-processor usually handles cryptographic operations very efficiently (e.g., AES and SHA). Hence, even if there exist differences among Secure Devices, all provide *much stronger security guarantees* combined with a *much weaker computing power* than any traditional server.

The MapReduce Server. Due to their limited capacity, TDSs need a powerful Supporting Server running MapReduce framework to provide communication, intermediate storage and global processing services that TDSs cannot provide on their own. Being implemented on regular server(s), e.g., in the Cloud, mappers/reducers exhibit these properties: (1) Low Security, and (2) High Computing Resources.

3.2   Threat Model

TDSs are the unique element of trust in the architecture and are considered *honest*. Part of the Map and Reduce code embedded in TDSs is also assumed to be trusted. No trust assumption needs to be made on the querier either because (1) TDSs will not accept to participate to queries sent by a querier with insufficient privileges and (2) the querier can gain access only to the final result of the query computation (not to the raw data), as in traditional database systems. Preventing inferential attacks by combining the result of a sequence of authorized queries as in statistical databases and PPDP work is orthogonal to this study.

The potential adversary is consequently the mappers/reducers. We consider *honest-but-curious* mappers/reducers (i.e., which try to infer any information they can but strictly follows the protocol). Considering *malicious* mappers/reducers (i.e., which may tamper the protocol with no limit, including denial-of-service) is of little interest to this study. Indeed, a malicious mappers/reducers is likely to be detected with an irreversible political/financial damage and even the risk of a class action.

4   Proposed Solutions

4.1   MapReduce Job Execution Phases

The MapReduce programming model, depicted in Figure 3, consists of a map(k_1; v_1) function and a reduce(k_2; list(v_2)) function. The map(k_1; v_1) function is invoked for every key-value pair $<k_1; v_1>$ in the input data to output zero or more key-value pairs of the form $<k_2; v_2>$. The reduce(k_2; list(v_2)) function is invoked for every unique key k_2 and corresponding values list(v_2) in the map output. reduce(k_2; list(v_2)) outputs zero or more key-value pairs of the form $<k_3; v_3>$. The MapReduce programming model also allows other functions such as (i) partition(k_2), for controlling how the map output key-value pairs are partitioned among the reduce tasks, and (ii) combine(k_2; list(v_2)), for performing partial aggregation.

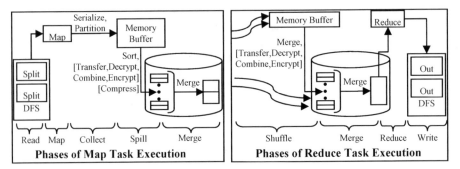

Fig. 3. Detail execution of map and reduce task

In the next section, we propose a solution so that we do not need to modify this original model. We use the encryption scheme to allow the untrusted mappers/reducers participate in the computation as much as possible and transfer the necessary computations that cannot be processed on server to TDSs. These transfer and computation on TDSs happen in parallel to speed up the running time.

4.2   Proposed Solution

Our proposed solution, called *ED_Hist*, builds on previous histogram-based techniques [20, 21] to prevent inferential attacks over encrypted data. Informally speaking, to prevent the frequency-based attack on deterministic encryption (*dEnc* for short) that encrypts the same cleartexts into the same ciphertexts, and to allow untrusted server group and sort the encrypted tuples (that have the same plaintext values) into the same partitions, *ED_Hist* transforms the original distribution of grouping attributes, called A_G, into a *nearly equi-depth histogram* (due to the data distribution, we cannot have exact equi-depth histogram). A nearly equi-depth histogram is a decomposition of the A_G domain into buckets holding *nearly* the same number of true tuples. Each bucket is identified by a hash value giving no information about the position of the bucket elements in the domain. Figure 4a shows an example of an original distribution and Figure 4b is its nearly equi-depth histogram.

There are three benefits in using nearly equi-depth histogram: i) allow mappers/reducers participate in the computation as much as possible (i.e., except the combine and reduce operations, all other operations can be processed in ciphertexts), without modifying the existing MapReduce framework; ii) better balance the load among mappers/reducers for skewed dataset; and iii) prevent frequency-based attack.

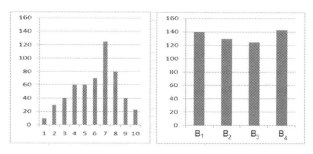

Fig. 4. Example of nearly equi-depth histogram

The protocol is divided into three tasks (see Figure 3, 5).

Collection Task. Each TDS allocates its tuple(s) to the corresponding bucket(s) and sends to mappers/reducers tuples of the form $(F(k), nEnc(u))$ where F is the mapping function that maps the keys to corresponding buckets:

$$bucketId = F(k)$$

and *nEnc* is the non-deterministic encryption that can encrypt the same cleartext into different ciphertext. Assume the cardinality of k is n, and F maps this domain to b buckets, then we have:

$$B_1 = F(k_{11}) = F(k_{12}) = ... = F(k_{1d})$$
$$B_2 = F(k_{21}) = F(k_{22}) = ... = F(k_{2e})$$
$$...$$
$$B_b = F(k_{b1}) = F(k_{b2}) = ... = F(k_{bz})$$

From that, the average number of distinct plaintext in each bucket is: $h=(d+e+...+z)/b=n/b$

When this task stops, all the encrypted data sent by TDSs are stored in DFS, and are ready to be processed by mappers/reducers.

Map Task. This task is divided into five phases:

1. Read: Read the input split from DFS and create the input key-value pairs: $(B_1, nEnc(u_1)), (B_2, nEnc(u_2)), ... (B_b, nEnc(u_m))$.

2. Map: Execute the user-defined map function to generate the map-output data: $map(B_i; nEnc(u_i)) -> (B'_i; nEnc(v_i))$. If the map function needs process complex functions that cannot be done on encrypted data (i.e., $v_i = f(u_i)$), connections to TDSs will be established to process these encrypted data.

3. Collect: Partition and collect the intermediate (map-output) data into a buffer before spilling.

4. Spill: Sort, if the combine function is specified: parallel transfer encrypted data to TDSs to decrypt, combine, encrypt, and return to mappers, perform compression if specified, and finally write to local disk to create file spills.

5. Merge: Merge the file spills into a single map output file. Merging might be performed in multiple rounds.

Reduce Task. This task includes four phases:

1. Shuffle: Transfer the intermediate data from the mapper nodes to a reducer's node and decompress if needed. Partial merging and combining may also occur during this phase.

2. Merge: Merge the sorted fragments from the different mappers to form the input to the reduce function.

3. Reduce: Execute the user-defined reduce function to produce the final output data. Since the reduce function can be arbitrary, and therefore encrypted data cannot be executed in reducers, they must be transferred to TDSs to be decrypted, executed the reduce function, encrypted, and returned to reducers. The difference between the output of the reduce function of traditional MapReduce with TrustedMR is that each input key represents different cleartext values, so the output key of the reduce function also represents different values: $(B'_1; list(nEnc(v_1)) \rightarrow (nEnc(k_{11}); nEnc(f(v_{1i}))),$ $...,(nEnc(k_{1d}); nEnc(f(v_{1m}))).$

4. Write: Compressing, if specified, and writing the final output to DFS.

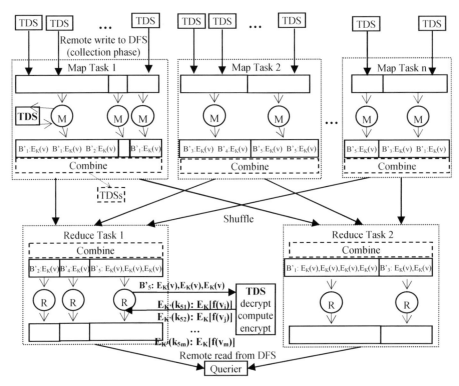

Fig. 5. Proposed solution

Among all phases in both map and reduce tasks, with the plaintext data mapped using the *ED_Hist*, the existing MapReduce framework can be used without being modified because each mappers/reducers can do all operations (i.e, map, partition, collect, sort, compress, merge, shuffle) on the mapped data, except the combine and reduce function. Since the combine and reduce functions must process on cleartexts, encrypted data are transferred back to TDSs for decrypting, computing, encrypting the result and returning to mappers/reducers. To reduce the overhead of transferring large amount of data between TDSs and mappers/reducers, each mappers/reducers split the data into smaller pieces and send it in parallel to multiple TDSs. With this way, the transferring time is reduced. Fig. 6 is the pseudocode for map/reduce function.

```
method Map (bucket B_i; encrypted value nEnc(u_i))
1. emit(bucket B'_i, nEnc(v_i))

method Combine (bucket B'_i; list [nEnc(v_1), nEnc(v_2),..])
1. form the partition: nEnc(v_1), nEnc(v_2),..nEnc(v_p)
2. create connection and send data to TDSs
3. in each TDS:
4.     unmap bucket: F^(-1)(B'_i) -> k_{i1}, k_{i2}, .., k_{in}
5.     decrypt nEnc(v_i) -> v_i
6.     compute r_{ij} = f(v_i) having the same k_{ij}
7.     encrypt result r_{ij} -> nEnc(r_{ij})
8.     map to bucket: F(k_{i1}) = F(k_{i2}) =..= F(k_{in}) = B'_i
9. emit (bucket B'_i; nEnc(r_{ij}))

method Reduce (bucket B'_i; list [nEnc(r_{ij}),..])
1-7. similar to Combine function from step 1 to 7
8.     emit (nEnc(k_{,}); nEnc(r'_{,}))
```

Fig. 6. Map, Combine, and Reduce methods

Note that it is not possible to do the whole map and reduce tasks within TDS because the modest computing resource of TDS does not allow deploying the Hadoop. Also, data transfer between mappers/reducers and TDS are mandatory to keep the Hadoop framework unchanged. So, low power TDSs cannot do more than contributing to the internal execution of the map and reduce tasks.

4.3   How Our Proposed Solution Meets the Requirements

Informally speaking, the security, utility and efficiency of the protocol are as follows (we formally prove the efficiency and security in the next sections):

Security. Since TDSs map the attributes to nearly equi-depth histogram, mappers/reducers cannot launch any frequency-based attack. What if mappers/reducers acquire a TDS with the objective to get the cryptographic material (i.e., a sort of collusion attack between mappers/reducers and a TDS)? As stated in section 3, TDS code cannot be tampered, even by its holder. Whatever the information decrypted internally, the only output that a TDS can deliver is a set of encrypted tuples, which does not represent any benefit for mappers/reducers.

Performance. The efficiency of the protocol is linked to the parallel computing of TDSs. Both the collection task and combine, reduce operations are run in parallel by all connected TDSs and no time-consuming task is performed by any of them. As the experiment section will clarify, each TDS manages incoming partitions in streaming because the internal time to decrypt the data and perform the computation is significantly less than the time needed to download the data. By combining the parallel computing, streaming data, and the crypto processor that can handles cryptographic operations efficiently in TDSs, our distributed model has acceptable and controllable performance overhead as pointed out in experiment.

Generality. Since the data is processed by trusted TDSs in cleartext, our solution can support any form of Map and Reduce functions.

Seamless Integration: Because we do not need to modify the original MapReduce framework, our solution can easily integrate with the existing framework. ED_Hist helps mappers/reducers run on encrypted data exactly as if they run on cleartext data without modifying the original MapReduce framework (i.e., as pointed out in section 4.2, the only tasks that mappers/reducers cannot run on encrypted data are combine and reduce).

Beside the four essential requirements above, we can easily show that our solution provides also a correct and exact result. Since mappers/reducers are honest-but-curious, it will strictly follow the protocol and deliver to the querier the final output. Unlike the differential privacy, mappers/reducers do not sanitize the output (to achieve the differential privacy), so the final output is exact. If a TDS goes offline in the middle of processing a partition, and therefore cannot return result as expected, mappers/reducers will resend that partition to another available TDS after waiting the response from disconnected TDS a specific interval.

5   Privacy Analysis

5.1   Security of Basic Encryption Schemes

In cryptography, indistinguishability under chosen plaintext attack (IND-CPA) [30] (which is proved to be equivalent to semantic security [14]) is a very strong notion of security for encryption schemes, and is considered as a basic requirement for most provably secure cryptosystems. While *nDet_Enc* is believed to be IND-CPA [32], *Det_Enc*, on the other hand, cannot achieve semantic security or indistinguishability due to lack of randomness in ciphertext. The maximum level of security for *Det_Enc* that can be guaranteed is PRIV [31] which is a weaker notion of security than IND-CPA. Then, it is important to understand how much (quantitatively) less secure the *Det_Enc* and *ED_Hist* are, in compare with *nDet_Enc*. To address this question, we use the *coefficient* to measure the security level of *Det_Enc* and *ED_Hist*, given the *nDet_Enc* as the highest bound of security level.

5.2   Information Exposure with Coefficient

In this section, in order to quantify the confidentiality of each encryption scheme, we measure the information exposure of the encrypted data they reveal to SSI by using the approach proposed in [10] which introduces the concept of coefficient to assess the exposure. To illustrate, let us consider the example in Fig. 7 where Fig. 7a is taken from [10] and Fig. 7b is the extension of [10] applied in our context. The plaintext table Accounts is encrypted in different ways corresponding to encryption schemes. To measure the exposure, we consider the probability that an attacker can reconstruct the plaintext table (or part of the table) by using the encrypted table and his prior knowledge about global distributions of plaintext attributes.

Although the attacker does not know which encrypted column corresponds to which plaintext attribute, he can determine the actual correspondence by comparing their cardinalities. Namely, she can determine that I_A, I_C, and I_B correspond to attributes Account, Customer, and Balance respectively. Then, the IC table (the table of the inverse of the cardinalities of the equivalence classes) is formed by calculating the probability that an encrypted value can be correctly matched to a plaintext value. For example, with *Det_Enc*, $P(\alpha = Alice) = 1$ and $P(\kappa = 200) = 1$ since the attacker knows that the plaintexts *Alice* and *200* have the most frequent occurrences in the Accounts table (or in the global distribution) and observes that the ciphertexts α and κ have highest frequencies in the encrypted table respectively. The attacker can infer with certainty that not only α and κ represent values *Alice* and *200* (*encryption infe-rence*) but also that the plaintext table contains a tuple associating values *Alice* and *200* (*association inference*). The probability of disclosing a specific association (e.g., *<Alice,200>*) is the product of the inverses of the cardinalities (e.g., $P(<\alpha,\kappa> = <Alice,200>) = P(\alpha = Alice) \times P(\kappa = 200) = 1$). The *exposure coefficient* $\mathcal{E}$ of the whole table is estimated as the average exposure of each tuple in it:

$$\varepsilon = \frac{1}{n}\sum_{i=1}^{n}\prod_{j=1}^{k} IC_{i,j}$$

Here, n is the number of tuples, k is the number of attributes, and $IC_{i,j}$ is the value in row i and column j in the IC table. Let's N_j be the number of distinct plaintext values in the global distribution of attribute in column j (i.e., $N_j \leq n$).

ACCOUNTS			DETERMINISTIC ENCRYPTION				IC TABLE OF DETERMINISTIC ENCRYPTION		
Account	Customer	Balance	Enc_tuple	I_A	I_C	I_B	ic_A	ic_C	ic_B
Acc1	Alice	500	x4Z3tfX25hOSM	π	α	μ	1/6	1	1/3
Acc2	Alice	200	mNHg1oCO10p8w	ω	α	κ	1/6	1	1
Acc3	Bob	300	WslaCvfyF1Dxw	ξ	β	η	1/6	1/4	1/3
Acc4	Chris	200	jpO8eLTVgwV1E	ψ	γ	κ	1/6	1/4	1
Acc5	Donna	400	qctG6XnFNDTQc	φ	δ	θ	1/6	1/4	1/3
Acc6	Elvis	200	4QbqC3hxZHkIU	Γ	ε	κ	1/6	1/4	1

a

NON-DETERMINISTIC ENCRYPTION			EQUI-DEPTH HISTOGRAM			IC TABLE OF NON-DETERMINISTIC ENCRYPTION		
I_A	I_C	I_B	I_A	I_C	I_B	ic_A	ic_C	ic_B
π	λ	μ	π	α	μ	1/6	1/5	1/4
ω	α	χ	π	α	κ	1/6	1/5	1/4
ξ	β	η	π	β	μ	1/6	1/5	1/4
ψ	γ	κ	ξ	β	κ	1/6	1/5	1/4
φ	δ	θ	ξ	δ	μ	1/6	1/5	1/4
Γ	ε	τ	ξ	δ	κ	1/6	1/5	1/4

b

Fig. 7. Encryption and IC tables

As pointed out above, the encrypted centralized databases [22] use *Dec_Enc* that opens the door for frequency-based attack. However, when using *nDet_Enc*, the more secure encryption scheme than *Det_Enc*, it cannot help MapReduce framework process encrypted data since mappers/reducers cannot group and sort the same en-crypted tuples into the same partition. Equi-depth histogram overcomes the weakness of these two schemes.

Using *nDet_Enc*, because the distribution of ciphertexts is obfuscated uniformly, the probability of guessing the true plaintext of α is P(α = *Alice*) = 1/5. So, $IC_{i,j} = 1/N_j$ for all i, j, and thus the exposure coefficient of *nDet_Enc* is:

$$\varepsilon_{nDec\_Enc} = \frac{1}{n}\sum_{i=1}^{n}\prod_{j=1}^{k}\frac{1}{N_j} = 1/\prod_{j=1}^{k}N_j$$

For the nearly equi-depth histogram, each hash value can correspond to multiple plaintext values. Therefore, each hash value in the equivalence class of multiplicity *m* can represent any *m* values extracted from the plaintext set, that is, there are $\binom{N_j}{m}$ different possibilities. The identification of the correspondence between hash and plaintext values requires finding all possible partitions of the plaintext values such that the sum of their occurrences is the cardinality of the hash value, equating to solving the NP-Hard *multiple subset sum problem* [9]. We consider two critical values of collision factor *h* (defined as the ratio G/M between the number of groups G and the number M of distinct hash values) that correspond to two extreme cases (i.e., the least and most exposure) of ε_{ED_Hist}: (1) *h* = *G*: all plaintext values collide on the same hash value and (2) *h* = 1: distinct plaintext values are mapped to distinct hash values (i.e., in this case, the nearly equi-depth histogram becomes *Det_Enc* since the same plaintext values will be mapped to the same hash value).

In the first case, the optimal coefficient exposure of histogram is:

$$\min(\varepsilon_{ED\_Hist}) = 1/\prod_{j=1}^{k}N_j$$

because $IC_{i,j} = 1/N_j$ for all i, j. For the second case, the experiment in [9] (where they generated a number of random databases whose number of occurrences of each plaintext value followed a Zipf distribution) varies the value of *h* to see its impact to ε_{ED_Hist}. This experiment shows that the smaller the value of *h*, the bigger the ε_{ED_Hist} and ε_{ED_Hist} reaches maximum value (i.e., max(ε_{ED_Hist}) ≈ 0.4) when *h* = 1.

The exposure coefficient gets the highest value when no encryption is used at all and therefore all plaintexts are displayed to attacker. In this case, $IC_{i,j} = 1 \;\forall\; i, j$, and thus the exposure coefficient of plaintext table is (trivially):

$$\varepsilon_{P\_Text} = \frac{1}{n}\sum_{i=1}^{n}\prod_{j=1}^{k}1 = 1$$

In short, *ED_Hist* is more secure than *Det_Enc*, and at some point the *ED_Hist* can get the same high security as *nDet_Enc*. Specifically, if all plaintext values collide on the same mapped value, *ED_Hist* has the least exposure, similar to *nDet_Enc*. On the contrary, if distinct plaintext values are mapped to distinct hash values, *ED_Hist* exposes the most amount information to server (i.e., in this case, the nearly equi-depth histogram becomes *Det_Enc* since the same plaintext values will be mapped to the same value).

The information exposures among our proposed solutions are summarized in Fig. 8. In conclusion, the information exposures of *nDet_Enc*, *Det_Enc* and *ED_Hist* have the following order: $\varepsilon_{nDec\_Enc} \leq \varepsilon_{ED\_Hist} \leq \varepsilon_{Dec\_Enc} < 1$, meaning that *ED_Hist* is the intermediate between *nDet_Enc* and *Det_Enc*.

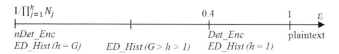

Fig. 8. Information exposure among encryption schemes

6 Performance Evaluation

This section evaluates the performance of our solution. By nature, the behavior of secure devices is difficult to observe from the outside and integrating performance probes in the embedded code significantly changes the performance. To circumvent this difficulty, we first perform tests on a development board running the same embedded code (including the operating system RTOS) and having the same hardware characteristics (same microcontroller and Flash storage) as our secure devices. This gave us the detail time breakdown on the secure hardware (i.e., transfer, I/O, crypto, and CPU cost). Then we use the Z-token described below to test on the larger scale (i.e., running multiple Z-tokens in parallel) in the real cluster. We also compare the running time on ciphertext and that on cleartext to see how much overhead incurred. We finally increase the power of the cluster by scaling depth (i.e., increase the number of Z-tokens plugged in each node) and scaling width (i.e., increase the number of nodes) to see the difference between the two ways of scaling.

6.1 Unit Test on Development Board

To see the detail time contributing to the total execution time on the secure hardware, we performed unit tests on the development board presented in Fig. 9a. This board has the following characteristics: the microcontroller is equipped with a 32 bit RISC CPU clocked at 120 MHz, a crypto-coprocessor implementing AES and SHA in hardware (encrypting or decrypting a block of 128bits costs 167 cycles), 64 KB of static RAM, 1 MB of NOR-Flash and is connected to a 1 GB external NAND-Flash and to a smartcard chip hosting the cryptographic material. The device can communicate with the external world through USB connection.

We measured on this device the performance of the main operations influencing the global cost, that is: encryption, decryption, communication and CPU time. Fig. 9b depicts this internal time consumption of this platform. The transfer cost dominates the other costs due to the connection latencies. The CPU cost is higher than cryptographic cost because (1) the cryptographic operations are done in hardware by the crypto-coprocessor and (2) TDS spends CPU time to convert the array of raw bytes (resulting from the decryption) to the number format for calculation later and some extra operations. Encryption time is much smaller than decryption time because only the result of the aggregation of each partition needs to be encrypted. TDSs handle data from mappers/reducers in stream due to the fact that encryption and CPU time is less than transfer time and I/O operations. So, TDSs can process the old data while receiving the new one at the same time.

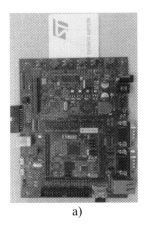
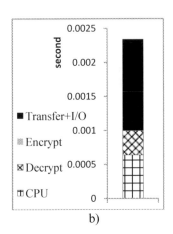

a)

b)

Fig. 9. Unit test on real hardware

6.2   Experimental Setup

Our experiment conducted with secure devices has been performed on a cluster of Paris Nord University. Each node is equipped with 4-core 3.1 GHz Intel Xeon E31220 processor, 8GB of RAM, and 128GB of hard disk. These nodes run on Debian Wheezy 7 with unmodified Hadoop 1.0.3. It is the Cloud provider who decides number of map/reduce tasks. The number of TDSs is also fixed by Cloud provider who plugs these tokens. The experiments will give hints how to choose the number of tokens and nodes. We run the Hadoop in parallel on ZED secure tokens (Fig. 10).

6.3   Scaling with Parallel Computing

Figure 12 shows the performance overhead when processing ciphertext over cleartext. There is no difference in map time but the reduce time in ciphertext is much longer than that of cleartext. This is due to the time to connect to Z-token and process the encrypted data inside the Z-token. In this test, only one Z-token is plugged to each node. That creates the bottleneck for the ciphertext processing because Z-token is much less powerful than the node that has to wait Z-token to process the encrypted data. While the cleartext data is processed directly in the powerful node, the ciphertext has to be transferred to tokens for processing. In this way, computation on ciphertext incurs three overhead in compared with the cleartext: i) time to transfer the data from node to token (including the connection time and I/O cost), ii) time to decrypt the data and encrypt the result, iii) the constraint on the CPU and memory size of token for computation inside the token.

To alleviate this overhead, we plug multiple tokens to the same node and process the ciphertext in parallel in these tokens. Figure 11 shows the 20 tokens run in parallel and plugged to the same node. In Figure 13, when the number of tokens plugged to each node increases, the reduce time decreases gradually and approaches that of cleartext. Specifically, when the number of tokens increases from 1 to 20, the average speedup is 1.75. When we plug 32 tokens to each node, the reduce time reaches 5.49

(seconds), which gives approximate 10% longer than cleartext. Hence, the overhead is controllable by increasing the number of tokens plugged per reducer.

Fig. 10. ZED token (front and back sides)

Fig. 11. Twenty tokens running in parallel

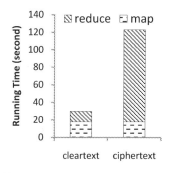

Fig. 12. Running time of cleartext & ciphertext

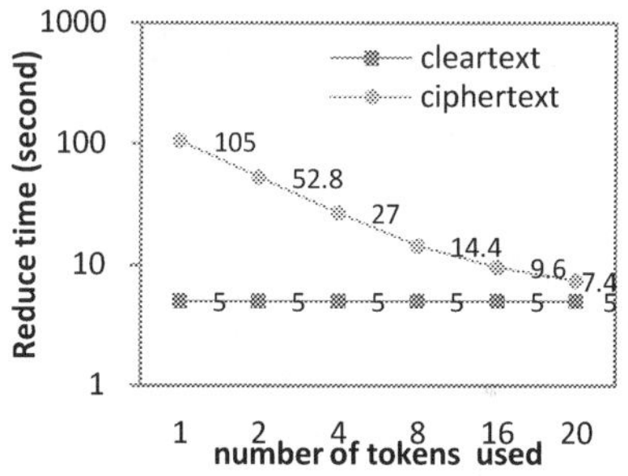

Fig. 13. Scaling depth

6.4   Scaling Depth versus Scaling Width

In traditional MapReduce, the cluster can be scaled depth by increasing number of processors per node or scaled width by increasing number of nodes. In TrustedMR, since the cluster depends on the tokens for cryptographic operations, we scale depth by increasing the number of tokens (i.e., from 1 to 4) plugged to each node. We also scale width by increasing number of nodes (i.e., from 1 to 4), and then we compare the two ways of scaling. In this test, we also increase the size of the dataset (i.e., from 2 million tuples to 4 million tuples) to see how the running time varies.

In Figure 14 & 15, when we increase the number of nodes in the cluster and keep the same number of tokens on each node, the reduce time decreases accordingly and vice versa. Also, with the same number of tokens, plugging them to the same node or to multiple nodes gives almost no difference in term of running time (e.g., the reduce time of 4 nodes with each node having only 1 token is only few percent difference from that of 1 node having 4 tokens plugged). Furthermore, the average speedup of scaling width is 1.74 which is only 2% different from that of scaling depth (i.e., 1.71). In conclusion, scaling depth yields nearly the same performance as scaling width. The only factor that affects the overall performance of the cluster is the total number of tokens plugged to this cluster, no matter how they are distributed to each node. Based on this conclusion, we measure the performance with the configuration of 5 nodes having 20 tokens plugged in each node (i.e., 100 tokens in total) and use this measurement (together with the speedups measured above) to simulate the performance with larger scale and bigger dataset (at the moment, it is difficult to perform large scale experiments with smart tokens due to the hardware cost[4]). Figure 16 shows the performance with the 1TB dataset. When the number of nodes in the cluster increases (with the number of tokens plugged in each node fixed at 20), the running time reduces correspondingly. The time to process 1 TB data is acceptable (e.g., a few minutes) when we have enough nodes in the cluster.

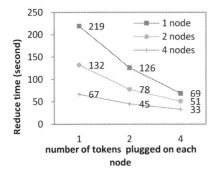

Fig. 14. Reduce time for 2 million tuples

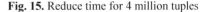

Fig. 15. Reduce time for 4 million tuples

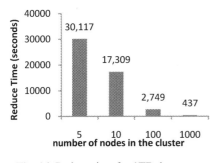

Fig. 16. Reduce time for 1TB dataset

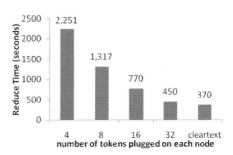

Fig. 17. Comparison of TrustedMR and [13]

To compare with state-of-the-art work in the literature, Figure 17 compares the reduce running time of TrustedMR with the Hadoop system running in cleartext in [13]. The experiment in [13] runs on a Hadoop cluster of 16 Amazon EC2 nodes of the c1.medium type with the 10GB dataset. We simulate our system with 16 nodes and vary the number of tokens to compare. It is easy to see that when the number of tokens plugged on each node increases, the overhead performance decrease thanks to the parallel computation of tokens. Although it is only a rough comparison, it gives

---

4 We have only 100 tokens, so this is the possible maximum number of tokens we can use for the experiments.

the illustration that the performance overhead of TrustedMR is not very far (i.e., 1.2× longer) from the original Map Reduce program running in cleartext.

7   Conclusion

This paper proposed a new approach to process big personal data using MapReduce while maintaining privacy guarantees. It draws its novelty from the fact that (private) user data remains under the control of its owner, itself embedded in a secure enclave within the untrusted Cloud platform. Our solution meets four main requirements, namely security, performance, generality, and seamless integration. Our future work will (1) extend threat model to consider strong adversaries capable of compromising tamper-resistant devices and (2) perform comparisons with other server-based architectures exploiting secure hardware (e.g., IBM 4765 PCIe Crypto Coprocessor).

Acknowledgement. The authors wish to thank Nicolas Greneche from University of Paris Nord for his help in setting up the cluster for the experiment. This work is partially funded by project ANR-11-INSE-0005 "Keeping your Information Safe and Secure".

References

1. Allard, T., Anciaux, N., Bouganim, L., Guo, Y., Le Folgoc, L., Nguyen, B., Pucheral, P., Ray, I., Ray, I., Yin, S.: Secure Personal Data Servers: a Vision Paper. VLDB, 25–35 (2010). Singapore
2. Allard, T., Nguyen, B., Pucheral, P.: MET$_A$P: Revisiting Privacy-Preserving Data Publishing using Secure Devices. DAPD (2013)
3. Anciaux, N., Bonnet, P., Bouganim, L., Nguyen, B., Popa, I.S., Pucheral, P.: Trusted cells: a sea change for personal data services. In: CIDR, USA (2013)
4. Arasu, A., Kaushik, R.: Oblivious query processing. In: ICDT (2014)
5. Bajaj, S., Sion, R.: TrustedDB: a trusted hardware based database with privacy and data confidentiality. In: SIGMOD Conference 2011, pp. 205–216 (2011)
6. Blass, E., Noubir, G., Huu, T.V.: EPiC: Efficient Privacy-Preserving Counting for MapReduce. IACR Cryptology ePrint Archive, 452 (2012)
7. Blass, E.-O., Di Pietro, R., Molva, R., Önen, M.: PRISM – privacy-preserving search in MapReduce. In: Fischer-Hübner, S., Wright, M. (eds.) PETS 2012. LNCS, vol. 7384, pp. 180–200. Springer, Heidelberg (2012)
8. Boldyreva, A., Chenette, N., Lee, Y., O'Neill, A.: Order-preserving symmetric encryption. In: Joux, A. (ed.) EUROCRYPT 2009. LNCS, vol. 5479, pp. 224–241. Springer, Heidelberg (2009)
9. Ceselli, A., Damiani, E., De Capitani di Vimercati, S., Jajodia, S., Paraboschi, S., Samarati, P.: Modeling and assessing inference exposure in encrypted databases. ACM TISSEC **8**(1), 119–152 (2005)
10. Damiani, E., Capitani Vimercati, S., Jajodia, S., Paraboschi, S., Samarati, P.: Balancing confidentiality and efficiency in untrusted relational DBMSs. In: CCS, pp. 93–102 (2003)

11. Dean, J., Ghemawat, S.: MapReduce: Simplified Data Processing on Large Clusters. Commun. ACM **51**(1), 107–113 (2008)
12. Gentry, C.: Fully homomorphic encryption using ideal lattices. In: STOC, pp. 169–178 (2009)
13. Herodotou, H., Babu, S.: Profiling, What-if Analysis, and Cost-based Optimization of MapReduce Programs. PVLDB **4**(11), 1111–1122 (2011)
14. Goldwasser, S., Micali, S.: Probabilistic encryption. Journal of Computer and System Sciences **28**(2), 270–299 (1984)
15. Lam, H.Y., Fung, G.S.K., Lee, W.K.: A Novel Method to Construct Taxonomy Electrical Appliances Based on Load Signatures. IEEE Transactions on Consumer Electronics **53**(2), 653–660 (2007)
16. Mun, M., Hao, S., Mishra, N., et al.: Personal data vaults: a locus of control for personal data streams. In: Proc. of the 6th Int. Conf on Emerging Networking Experiments and Technologies (Co-NEXT 2010), New York, USA, December 2010
17. de Montjoye, Y.-A., Wang, S.S., Pentland, A.: On the Trusted Use of Large-Scale Personal Data. IEEE Data Eng. Bull. **35**(4), 5–8 (2012)
18. Popa, R.A., Redfield, C.M.S., Zeldovich, N., et al.: CryptDB: protecting confidentiality with encrypted query processing. In: SOSP, pp 85–100 (2011)
19. Roy, I., Setty, S., Kilzer, A., Shmatikov, V., Witchel, E.: Airavat: security and privacy for MapReduce. In: USENIX NSDI, pp. 297–312 (2010)
20. Hacigumus, H., Iyer, B., Li, C., Mehrotra, S.: Executing SQL over encrypted data in database service provider model. In: ACM SIGMOD, Wisconsin, pp. 216–227 (2002)
21. To, Q.C., Nguyen, B., Pucheral, P.: Privacy-preserving query execution using a decentralized architecture and tamper resistant hardware. In: EDBT, pp. 487–498 (2014)
22. Tu, S., Kaashoek, M.F., Madden, S., Zeldovich, N.: Processing analytical queries over encrypted data. In: PVLDB, pp 289–300 (2013)
23. Wei, W., Du, J., Yu, T., Gu, X.: SecureMR: a service integrity assurance framework for MapReduce. In: ACSAC, pp. 73–82 (2009)
24. Zhang, K., Zhou, X., Chen, Y., Wang, X., Ruan, Y.: Sedic: privacy-aware data intensive computing on hybrid clouds. In: CCS, pp. 515–526 (2011)
25. Zhang, C., Chang, E., Yap, R.: Tagged-MapReduce: a general framework for secure computing with mixed-sensitivity data on hybrid clouds. In: CCGrid, pp 31–40 (2014)
26. Zhang, X., Yang, L.T., Liu, C., Chen, J.: A Scalable Two-Phase Top-Down Specialization Approach for Data Anonymization Using MapReduce on Cloud. IEEE Transactions on Parallel and Distributed Systems **25**(2), 363–373 (2014)
27. Zhang, X., Liu, C., Nepal, S., Pandey, S., Chen, J.: A Privacy Leakage Upper-bound Constraint based Approach for Cost-effective Privacy Preserving of Intermediate Datasets in Cloud. IEEE Transactions on Parallel and Distributed Systems **24**(6), 1192–1202 (2013)
28. Directive 95/46/EC of the European Parliament and of the Council of October 24, 1995 on the protection of individuals with regard to the processing of personal data. Official Journal of the EC, 23 (1995)
29. Wang, J., Wang, Z.: A Survey on Personal Data Cloud. The Scientific World Journal (2014)
30. Katz, J., Lindell, Y.: Introduction to Modern Cryptography: Principles and Protocols. Chapman and Hall/CRC (2007)
31. Bellare, M., Boldyreva, A., O'Neill, A.: Deterministic and efficiently searchable encryption. In: Menezes, A. (ed.) CRYPTO 2007. LNCS, vol. 4622, pp. 535–552. Springer, Heidelberg (2007)
32. Arasu, A., Eguro, K., Kaushik, R., Ramamurthy, R.: Querying encrypted data (tutorial). In: ACM SIGMOD Conference (2014)

Similarity and Trust to Form Groups in Online Social Networks

Pasquale De Meo[1], Fabrizio Messina[2]([✉]), Giuseppe Pappalardo[2],
Domenico Rosaci[3], and Giuseppe M.L. Sarnè[4]

[1] DICAM, University of Messina,
Polo Universitario Viale Annunziata, 98168 Messina, Italy
pdemeo@unime.it

[2] DMI, University of Catania, V.le Andrea Doria 6, 95125 Catania, Italy
{messina,pappalardo}@dmi.unict.it

[3] DIIES, University "Mediterranea" of Reggio Calabria,
Via Graziella, Feo di Vito, 89122 Reggio Calabria, RC, Italy
domenico.rosaci@unirc.it

[4] DICEAM, University "Mediterranea" of Reggio Calabria,
Via Graziella, Feo di Vito, 89122 Reggio Calabria, RC, Italy
sarne@unirc.it

Abstract. Social Sciences identify similarity and mutual trust as main
criteria to consider in group formation processes. On this basis, we
present a group formation technique which exploits measures of both
similarity and trust, in order to improve the compactness of groups in
Online Social Networks. Similarity and trust have been jointly exploited
to design two algorithms designed to match groups and users, in order
to capture the gain of a user who desires to join with a group and the
benefit of the group itself. Experimental results show that trust is more
valuable than similarity in forming groups and that the two proposed
algorithms are capable to deal with large networks.

1 Introduction

Social capital refers to the *collective value associated with a social network*, as
stated in the recent discussions on *Social Capital theory* [5,33]. In particular, by
the "collective approach"[33] Social Capital is viewed as a *collective resource*, or
a *collective property* and it is based on *the quality of the relationships among
actors within a collectivity*. In other words *social capital no longer resides with
an individual but exists through relationships between actors, it is based on the
density of interactions* between individuals of the collectivity [5]. Social capital
easily generalizes virtual communities: as a remarkable example we cite Online
Social Networks (OSNs) which allow members sharing common interests to form
thematic groups (hereafter groups), where related activities (e.g. events, discussions, etc) can take place. The impressive and increasing number of thematic
groups, e.g. on Facebook, is the proof that they actually catalyze the interest of
users worldwide [24]. In this context, it is easily deducible as number and quality

© Springer International Publishing Switzerland 2015
C. Debruyne et al. (Eds.): OTM 2015 Conferences, LNCS 9415, pp. 57–75, 2015.
DOI: 10.1007/978-3-319-26148-5_4

of activities (i.e. interactions) taking place in OSN groups assume high signifi-cance for the entire OSN, and activities within OSN groups strictly depend on the composition of groups itself.

Basing on the premises above, in this work we pose our attention on the density of interactions between users in OSN groups – assumed that it reflects the Social Capital of the OSN, as stated before – observing that the process of driving group formation and their evolution – widely investigated by researchers [3,17, 21] – may have a significant impact on it. In a simpler way, by acting on the group formation processes it should be possible to improve the *social capital* of the OSN. To this aim, a first, common strategy to drive the formation of groups is to exploit a *similarity metric* [7,16,35] by simply considering the matching degree between the interests and the needs of an individual and those of groups [34]. Many of existing algorithms just reflect such an approach and are mainly based on a similarity measure to suggest groups to users. Another possible strategy requires to consider *mutual trust* among individuals, by considering the recent users' concerns about privacy and security issues in social groups [33]. This approach comes from the consideration that members of *trust communities* are able to share their thoughts and experiences in a more comfortable environment, as they are mutually trusted [9].

Starting from the aforementioned approaches, in this paper we propose to combine similarity and trust measures in order to drive group formations in OSNs, with the purpose of improving the density of mutual users' interactions. For this purpose, we define the *compactness* measure as linear combination of similarity and trust, i.e. it takes into account like-minded and trusted users. Secondly, we design two algorithms exploiting compactness measure to match groups and users, in order to capture respectively the gain of a user who desires to join with a group and the benefit a group receives if a new user is accepted. The proposed approach is supported by a multi-agent scenario where each user is equipped with a personal agent monitoring his/her interests and preferences and, analogously, each group is associated with a group agent which acts in the interest of its group members by collaborating with their personal agents.

Two different scenarios are addressed. In the former, each user is allowed to access all the groups available on the OSN. A scalable algorithm, called User-To-Groups (*U2G*), allows us to solve the problem of finding the k groups by providing the largest social capital as a matching problem. In the second scenario, each user can not access all the available groups but, at query time, he can sequentially extracts information about available groups. In this case we designed an *online variant* of the *U2G* algorithm (named *U2G-O*), which is based on the well known *secretary problem* [13]. On the other side, we designed an algorithm to assist the group administrator in computing the convenience to admit the user into the group.

To prove that the U2G algorithm is convergent, i.e. that it is actually capable of improving the compactness of groups, we show a theoretical result about its convergence rate. Tests on simulated data have shown that trust and similarity can be profitably combined to yield more accurate results, especially when more relevance is given to trust, coherently with the Social Capital theory [5,33]. This later result means that in real OSNs, perhaps, it is more important to form groups of trusted users rather than groups of only like-minded people. We also discovered that the online variant (U2G-O) of the proposed algorithm is able to produce an approximate solution in a quick fashion and our approach appears to be scalable and suitable to efficiently process large amount of user- and group-related data referred to large OSN instances.

The paper is structured as follows. Section 2 describes the model along with measure definitions, while Sections 3 presents the U2G and U2G-O algorithms along with some theoretical results. Section 4 illustrates the experimental results. In Section 5 we compare our work with related literature and, finally, in Section 6 we draw our conclusions and future works.

2   Trust, Similarity and Compactness

Let $\mathcal{S} = \langle \mathcal{U}, \mathcal{G} \rangle$ be a generic OSN, where $\mathcal{U}$ is the set of *users* and $\mathcal{G}$ is the set of *groups*.

Review and Helpfulness. We suppose that any user $u \in \mathcal{U}$ can rate any item i belonging to any category of interest $c \in \mathcal{C}$ (e.g comments to commercial products, videos, ...) and also *review* rating posted by other users about i. A *review* is denoted as a triple $\mathbf{r}_{u,i} = \{rt, c, h\}$ where: rt is a *rating* ranging in [0,5] that u assigned to i; c is the *category* of i; h is the *helpfulness* to measure to what extent the rating rt associated with the review $r_{u,i}$ is valuable for taking a choice. We denote by $\bar{\mathbf{r}}_u$ the *review history* associated with u and by $\mathcal{RH}$ the collection of the review histories. Besides, *i)* the helpfulness of a review is calculated as the average of the scores assigned by the users to a u's review, and *ii)* the field category is computed by exploiting a technique derived from LDA (Latent Dirichlet Allocation) [4] to map user tags onto *topics*, which might support the assignment of categories to items. Note that both the helpfulness and the category fields are optional data.

Users and Group Profiles. We suppose that each user u is associated with a personal intelligent agent [37] a_u and each group g with an administrator agent a_g. In particular, each user agent a_u stores in its user profile p_u *i)* all the u's interests, *ii)* all the u's behaviors, *iii)* the preferred access mode for groups which u is interested to join with and *iv)* the level of trust of u with respect to his/her OSN peers, as described below:

• **Interest.** Let $c \in \mathcal{C}$ be a category, $u \in \mathcal{U}$ a user and $\bar{\mathbf{r}}_u$ his/her review history. The interest $I_u(c) : \mathcal{U} \times \mathcal{C} \to [0,1] \subset \mathbb{R}$, and the interest $I_g(c) : \mathcal{G} \times \mathcal{C} \to [0,1] \subset \mathbb{R}$ are computed as follows:

$$I_u(c) = \frac{|\{\mathbf{r}_{u,i} : i \in c\}|}{|\bar{\mathbf{r}}_u|} \qquad I_g(c) = \frac{\sum_{u \in g} I_u(c)}{|g|}$$

- **Behavior.** We suppose to classify users' interactions in order to check if their behaviors are "compatible" with those of the groups. A function $\zeta_u :$ $\mathcal{U} \times \mathcal{B} \rightarrow \{\text{True}, \text{False}\}$ is defined, where $\mathcal{B} = \{b_1, b_2, \ldots, b_p\}$ is the set of possible behaviors, and $B_u = \{\zeta_u(b)| \quad b \in \mathcal{B}\}$. Similarly, a function ζ_g is defined as follows:

$$\zeta_g(b) : \mathcal{G} \times \mathcal{B} \rightarrow \{\text{True}, \text{False}\}, \quad \zeta_g(b) = \text{True} \Leftrightarrow \frac{|\{v \in g : \zeta_v(b) = \text{True}\}|}{|G|} > \beta_g$$

where $\beta_g \in [0,1] \subset \mathbb{R}$. Finally, $B_g = \{\zeta_g(b)|b \in \mathcal{B}\}$.

- **Access mode.** It is the access mode guaranteed to the external users to the content available for a particular group. To this purpose, functions $A_u : \mathcal{U} \rightarrow L$, $A_g : \mathcal{G} \rightarrow L$ are defined, where L is the list of available access modes, where A_u indicates the preferred set of access modes of a user u, and A_g the same set for a group g. We suppose that *open, closed, secret* are the modes admitted and that the administrator of a group can decide how users can access to its group.

- **Trust.** It identifies the level of trust assigned by a user u to any peers v, denoted by $t_{u \rightarrow v}$, $v \in \mathcal{U}$, $v \neq u$. In general, the level of trust of a user u (group g) with respect to a group g (user u), is denoted by $t_{u \rightarrow g}$ $(t_{g \rightarrow u})$, and computed as an average value:

$$t_{u \rightarrow g} = \frac{\sum_{v \in g} t_{u \rightarrow v}}{|g|} \qquad t_{g \rightarrow u} = \frac{\sum_{v \in g} t_{v \rightarrow u}}{|g|}$$

Measures $t_{u \rightarrow g}$ and $t_{g \rightarrow u}$ are used to determine the trustworthiness of a group g as perceived by u and vice versa. In particular, the trust of a user u vs another user v is computed as the sum of two terms. The first is the *reliability* $(rel_{u \rightarrow v})$ and specifies how much a user trusts another user. The other is the *reputation* (rep_u) and represents how much the user communities considers trustworthy a user. More formally:

$$t_{u \rightarrow v} = \alpha_u \cdot rel_{u \rightarrow v} + (1 - \alpha_u) \cdot rep_v \qquad rep_v = \frac{1}{|\mathcal{U}|} \sum_{y \in \mathcal{U}} rel_{y \rightarrow v}$$

It is easy to observe that reliability is asymmetric (i.e. $rel_{u \rightarrow v} \neq rel_{v \rightarrow u}$) and updated by a_u each time u provides a feedback on v (i.e. evaluates a review posted by v). Since the *reputation* of a user v is defined as the average of all the reliability values, we assume that these values can be collected by a suitable software agent acting as a crawler[6].

Updating Users and Group Profiles. Users and group agents update their profiles p_u and p_g as described below.

– Each agent a_u updates the interest $I_u(c)$ in the category c as $I_u(c) = \theta \cdot I_u(c) + (1 - \theta) \cdot \delta$, with $\theta, \delta \in [0,1] \subset \mathbb{R}$, where θ is the relevance given to the values of $I_u(c)$ assumed in the past, and δ is the contribution given by a_u to $I_u(c)$ for the u's action (e.g., rating an item).

–Whenever user u performs one or mores actions, his/her agent a_u analyzes them to update the boolean variables contained in B_u. Therefore it sends such new values to the group agents a_g of its own groups that, in turn, will update the variables contained in their B_g.

– Lists A_u and A_g are updated similarly to B_u and B_g.
– Each agent a_u re-computes the trust measure $t_{u,v}$ each time u expresses an evaluation (i.e. "feedback") about a post authored by another user v.

2.1 Similarity and Compactness

Compactness, denoted as $\sigma_{u,v}$ is computed by means of three contributions c_A, c_B and c_I as:

$$c_A = \{1 \quad \text{if } A_u = A_v; \quad 0 \quad \text{otherwise}\}$$

$$c_B = 1 - \frac{1}{|B|} \sum_{b_i \in B} |\zeta_u(b) - \zeta_v(b)| \qquad c_I = 1 - \frac{1}{|C|} \sum_{c \in C} |I_u(c) - I_v(c)|$$

$$\sigma_{u,v} = \frac{w_A \cdot c_A + w_B \cdot c_B + w_I \cdot c_I}{w_A + w_B + w_I}, \qquad w_A, w_B, w_C \in [0,1] \subset \mathbb{R}.$$

Similarities $\sigma_{u,g}$ between a user u and a group g are computed in a similar way.

Compactness between two users u and v is denoted as $\gamma_{u \to v}$, and computed by combining $\sigma_{u,v}$ and $t_{u \to v}$ as:

$$\gamma_{u \to v} = w_u \cdot \sigma_{u,v} + (1 - w_u) \cdot t_{u \to v}$$

where $w_u \in [0,1] \subset \mathbb{R}$ is the relevance given by u to trust vs similarity. And, given the asymmetric nature of $\tau_{u \to v}$, it results that $\gamma_{u \to v} \neq \gamma_{v \to u}$.

At the same way, compactness between a user u and a group g ($\gamma_{u \to g}$) and that perceived by a group g vs a user u ($\gamma_{g \to u}$) are defined as follows:

$$\gamma_{u \to g} = w_u \cdot \sigma_{u,g} + (1 - w_u) \cdot t_{u \to g} \qquad \gamma_{g \to u} = w_g \cdot \sigma_{g,u} + (1 - w_g) \cdot t_{g \to u}$$

3 Associating Users and Groups

As specified in Section 1, Social Capital is strongly related to the density of interactions among the users of the groups itself. Since mutual trust and similarity of interests increase the probability of interactions among users, in this work, compactness $\gamma_{u \to g}$ ($\gamma_{g \to u}$) is adopted to measure the growth of the Social Capital in a given community, e.g. a group within OSN. In particular, it is used to design two algorithms aimed at driving group formation.

Let $\mathcal{G} = \{g_1, g_2, \ldots, g_n\}$ be the set of groups belonging to an OSN $\mathcal{S}$, and let $k_{\text{MAX}} \in \mathbb{N}^0$ be a threshold specifying the number of groups the generic user u wants to join with[1]. In particular, for a given a subset $\mathcal{K} \subseteq \mathcal{G}$, the benefit received by u in joining with all the groups belonging to $\mathcal{K}$ is denoted by $\sum_{g_i \in \mathcal{K}} \gamma_{u \to g_i}$. Therefore,

---

[1] We can assume $k_{\text{MAX}} \ll n$ [28,36]

finding the subset $\mathcal{K}^\star \subseteq \mathcal{G}$ having the largest value of $\sum_{g_i \in \mathcal{K}'} \gamma_{u \to g_i}$, under the constraint $|\mathcal{K}^\star| = k_{\text{MAX}}$, is equivalent to solve the following optimization problem:

$$\max \phi = \sum_{g_i \in \mathcal{G}} \gamma_{u \to g_i} x_{u \to g_i}$$

$$\text{s.t.} \sum_{g_i \in \mathcal{G}} x_{u \to g_i} = k_{\text{MAX}}, \quad x_{u \to g_i} \in \{0, 1\}$$

where $x_{u \to g_i} = 1$ iff $g_i \in \mathcal{K}^\star$.

In other words, an *assignment* $\mathbf{x}_u \in \mathbb{R}^n$ is defined so that the i-th component of $\mathbf{x}_u^{(i)} = 1$ iff $x_{u \to g_i} = 1$, otherwise $\mathbf{x}_u^{(i)} = 0$. This problem has a trivial solution ϕ^{OPT} associated with an *optimal assignment* $\mathbf{x}_u^{\text{OPT}}$, associated with those k_{MAX} groups in $\mathcal{G}$ provided with the largest compactness.

In order to find such a solution, a brute-force strategy is not feasible due to the high number of users and groups. Indeed, in such a context, a single users is not able to: i) process such a large amount of data; ii) compute the compactness of each group due to the highly dynamic nature of groups. In particular, with respect to the second issue, the assumption that each user agent is able to compute the compactness values $\gamma_{u \to g_i}$ of all groups needs to be relaxed. As a consequence, Section 3.1 starts with the assumption that each user agent is able to know only a subset of the OSN groups.

3.1   The Algorithms U2G and U2G-O

The algorithm *U2G*, shown as Algorithm 1, is designed to find the k_{MAX} groups to which u might join with. It is based on the assumption that each user agent knows a subset of groups $\mathcal{G}$ and their respective compactness values. That is to assume that the generic user agent a_u is able to sample at least m groups from $\mathcal{G}$. Moreover, X denotes the set of the groups u joined in the past, by assuming that a_u stores into an internal cache their profiles.

Each time, say r, Algorithm 1 is executed by agent a_u, it returns an assignment $\mathbf{x}_u^r$ (denoted as S in Algorithm 1). In the following Theorem 1 it is i) proved that the sequence $\{\phi(\mathbf{x}_u^r)\}$ of the corresponding values of the objective function always converges to the optimal solution ϕ^{OPT}. Moreover, ii) the convergence rate of the algorithm is quantified.

Theorem 1. *Let $\mathbf{x}_u^r$ be the assignment produced by Algorithm U2G at the r-th epoch and $\Pr(t)$ be the probability that the algorithm finds the optimal solution in exactly t epochs. As a consequence, it results that:*

- *the sequence $\{\phi(\mathbf{x}_u^r)\}$ is convergent to ϕ_{OPT};*
- *the ratio $\nu(t) = \frac{\Pr(t+1)}{\Pr(t)}$ is no less than $\left(1 + \frac{1}{t}\right)^{k_{\text{MAX}}}$.*

Proof. Firstly, it can be observed as the sequence $\{\phi(\mathbf{x}_u^r)\}$ is *bounded*. To this purpose, by contradiction, suppose $\{\phi(\mathbf{x}_u^r)\}$ not bounded, i.e., for any arbitrary

---

Algorithm 1. The U2G algorithm

Data: u: a user, X: the set of groups joined in the past, $m \in \mathbb{N}^0$, k_{MAX}: the number of groups u can join with

Result: A set S of groups

Let Y be a set of m random groups sampled in the OSN; Let $Z = X \bigcup Y$;

for $g \in Y$ **do**

    a_u sends a message to a_g;

    a_u receives the profile p_g from a_g;

end

Let $\mathcal{S} \subset Z$, with $|\mathcal{S}| = k_{\mathsf{MAX}}$ the set of groups of Z having the highest values of compactness;

for $g \in \mathcal{S}$ **do**

    if $g \notin X$ **then**

        a_u sends a join request to the agent a_g that also contains the profile p_u of u;

    end

end

for $g \in X$ **do**

    if $g \notin S$ **then**

        a_u deletes u from g;

    end

end

return S

---

list af available access modes $L > 0$ (see Section 2) there is an index $\bar{r}$ such that $\{\phi(\mathbf{x}_u)^{\bar{r}}\} > L$. Due to the arbitrary choice of L, it is possible to fix $L > \phi^{\mathsf{OPT}}$; consequently, it will be $\{\phi(\mathbf{x}_u)^{\bar{r}}\} > \phi^{\mathsf{OPT}}$ but it contradicts that ϕ^{OPT} is the maximum of ϕ. Then, note that the sequence $\{\phi(\mathbf{x}_u)^r\}$ is monotonically non-decreasing because only when the algorithm can increase the value of ϕ the assignment $\mathbf{x}_u^r$ is updated. Therefore, the sequence $\{\phi(\mathbf{x}_u)^r\}$ results to be bounded, monotonically non-decreasing and then convergent. It converges to $\sup \phi_{\bar{r}}(\mathbf{x}_u)$ that is equal to ϕ^{OPT}.

To proof the second part of the theorem, we assume that $\Pr(t)$ is the probability that Algorithm U2G generates the optimal solution in *exactly* t epochs. In other words, the Algorithm U2G accesses to m_t groups and the k_{MAX} groups with the highest compactness with respect to u must belong to the mt visited groups. Therefore there exist $\binom{m_t}{k_{\mathsf{MAX}}}$ possible configurations, in which the k_{MAX} groups $i)$ belongs to the first m_t visited groups and $ii)$ can freely distributed across the n available groups in $\binom{n}{k_{\mathsf{MAX}}}$ ways. By applying the definition of binomial coefficient, $\Pr(t)$ can be computed as:

$$\Pr(t) = \frac{\binom{m_t}{k_{\mathsf{MAX}}}}{\binom{n}{k_{\mathsf{MAX}}}} = \frac{m_t \, (m_t - 1) \, (mt - 2) \ldots (m_t - k_{\mathsf{MAX}})}{n \, (n - 1) \, (n - 2) \ldots (n - k_{\mathsf{MAX}})}$$

and by some simple manipulations $\Pr(t)$ assumes the following expression:

$$\Pr(t) = \left(\frac{mt}{n}\right)^{k_{\text{MAX}}} \times \frac{\left(1 - \frac{1}{mt}\right)\left(1 - \frac{2}{mt}\right)\cdots\left(1 - \frac{k_{\text{MAX}}}{mt}\right)}{\left(1 - \frac{1}{n}\right)\left(1 - \frac{2}{n}\right)\cdots\left(1 - \frac{k_{\text{MAX}}}{n}\right)}$$

Now, by assuming $\nu(t) = \frac{\Pr(t+1)}{\Pr(t)}$, its extended form can be written as:

$$\nu(t) = \left(\frac{t+1}{t}\right)^{k_{\text{MAX}}} \times \frac{\left(1 - \frac{1}{m(t+1)}\right)\left(1 - \frac{2}{m(t+1)}\right)\cdots\left(1 - \frac{k_{\text{MAX}}}{m(t+1)}\right)}{\left(1 - \frac{1}{mt}\right)\left(1 - \frac{2}{mt}\right)\cdots\left(1 - \frac{k_{\text{MAX}}}{mt}\right)}$$

from which by observing that

$$1 - \frac{j}{m(t+1)} > 1 - \frac{j}{mt}$$

then it results

$$\nu > \left(\frac{t+1}{t}\right)^{k_{\text{MAX}}} = \left(1 + \frac{1}{t}\right)^{k_{\text{MAX}}} \qquad (\text{where} \ \ j = 1\ldots k_{\text{MAX}})$$

that ends the proof.

Algorithm U2G-O. In a more realistic scenario, user agents are not able to retrieve neither $\mathcal{G}$ nor a subset of it. Instead, it is realistic to assume that a_u can only retrieve the information about a group g_i and eventually computing the compactness $\gamma_{u \to g_i}$ of u with respect to g_i.

   In order to approach this new version of the problem, we have taken inspiration from the the well-known *secretary problem* [13], which, in turn, consists in selecting the best candidate among a set of candidates applied for a position. Candidates are interviewed in a random order by assuming that the hiring manager doesn't knows in advance their curricula. After each interview, an irrevocable decision must be taken immediately.

   The best known strategy to maximize the probability to choose the best candidate is quite simple but accurate [2,12], as described below. Let n be the secretaries that have to be interviewed and suppose to fix an integer ℓ, such that $1 \leq \ell \leq n$. The first ℓ candidates constitutes a *reference set* that we denote as $\mathcal{R}$. Then the remaining $n - \ell$ candidates will be interviewed and the first of them which is better than all the candidates in $\mathcal{R}$ will be hired. The key phase of this algorithm is the choice of the set $\mathcal{R}$. For instance, if $\ell = |\mathcal{R}| = 1$ the algorithm might select the second worst candidate; conversely, if $\ell = n - 1$ the best candidate will be found because all the candidates will be examined, but it is too time-expensive. Finally, if $\ell = \lceil \frac{n}{e} \rceil$ then the probability of making the best choice will be at least $\frac{1}{e}$ [13].

   Similarly, in our problem we assume that, in a random order, the compactness of the groups are known and the optimal set k_{MAX} (out of n) of groups, such that the expected sum of their compactness values $\gamma_{u \to g}$ is maximum, has to be found. Note that in the case $k_{\text{MAX}} = 1$ our problem is the same that the mentioned secretary problem and, therefore, the following strategy can be applied [2]:

Step 1 Observe the first t groups, let t be a random integer and let $\mathcal{R}$ be the set formed by the observed groups. Consider $\mathcal{R}$ as *sample set* and t as *sample size*. For each group g in $\mathcal{R}$ we also register its compactness with respect to u.

Step 2 Let $\mathcal{T} \subseteq \mathcal{R}$ be the set formed by the k_{MAX} groups in $\mathcal{R}$ with the largest compactness values. Moreover, we suppose that groups in $\mathcal{T}$ are sorted in decreasing order of compactness with respect to u. Let g_m be the last group in $\mathcal{T}$; its compactness versus u is $\gamma_{u \to g_m}$.

Step 3 If arrives a group g_x such that $\gamma_{u \to g_x} > \gamma_{u \to g_m}$, then it will replace g_m.

The algorithm U2G-O takes a stream of values representing compactness values as input and it relies only on the visited groups to generate a solution. Similarly to [1], we acknowledge that it is advantageous to fix $t = \bar{t} = \lfloor \frac{n}{e} \rfloor$ and in this case the ratio between the solution generated by the U2G-O algorithm deviates from the optimal one will be no more than $\frac{1}{e}$. Finally, the value $\bar{t} = \lfloor \frac{n}{e} \rfloor$ will be called *reference sample size*.

Algorithm 2. The G2U Algorithm

Data: r, a user who sent a joining request to g. K, the current set of users in g
Result: The updated set K
for $u \in K$ **do**
| a_g sends a message to a_u;
end
for $u \in K \bigcup \{r\}$ **do**
| Compute $\gamma_{g \to u}$
end
Let $\pi = \dfrac{\sum_{u_i \in g} \sum_{u_j \in g} \gamma_{u_i \to u_j}}{|g|(|g|-1)/2}$ $\forall \langle u_i, u_j \rangle \in g,\ u_i \neq u_j$;
Let $\mathcal{S} = \varnothing$;
for $u \in K \bigcup \{r\}$ **do**
| **if** $\gamma_{g \to u} \geq \pi$ **then**
| | $\mathcal{S} = \mathcal{S} \bigcup \{u\}$;
| **end**
end
Let $\mathrm{Top}_{\mathcal{S}}$ be the set of top-n_{MAX} users in $\mathcal{S}$;
if $r \in \mathcal{S}$ **then**
| a_g accepts the join request of r;
end
for $u \in K \wedge u \notin \mathcal{S}$ **do**
| a_g deletes u from g;
end
return K

3.2   Algorithm G2U

Algorithm G2U is executed by every group agent a_g whenever an agent r sends a joining request for the group g. To this purpose, suppose that the size of each group $g \in \mathcal{G}$ cannot be greater than a threshold n_{MAX} fixed by the group administrator, and that a_g stores into its internal cache K the profiles of the users in g. The approach is very simple. First of all, a_g will update the profiles of its own users by sending them a message. Afterwards, all the compactness $\gamma_{g \to u}$ are updated and the threshold π is computed as the average of all the mutual compactness. Finally, the set K of the users in g is updated by selecting the top-η_{MAX} users having a compactness $\gamma_{g \to u}$ greater than threshold π.

4   Experimental Evaluation

In order to test the proposed approach some simulations were performed as detailed in the following of this Section.

Compactness of each group was measured as the *average* value of all the compactness within the same group – an extension of the average dissimilarity usually adopted in Clustering Analysis [29] – denoted as AC_g. Also the average value of all AC was computed, and is denoted as MAC:

$$AC_g = \frac{\sum_{x,y \in g, x \neq y} \gamma_{x \to y}}{|g|} \qquad MAC = \frac{\sum_{g \in G} AC_g}{|G|}$$

U2G. Experimental Setup. The behaviors of 150 OSN groups and 42,000 users have been simulated. To this aim, users and groups were provided with suitable profiles, as described in Section 2. The details of the generated profiles and other simulation parameters are listed in Table 1. Group affiliation was randomly assigned to each user (no more than 20 groups per user). In order to set a constraints on the maximum number of groups any user can join with, we based on behaviors observed in real OSN, for which each user generally join with at most 200 groups[28,36]. The maximum number of requests sent to new groups by a user in each simulation step was limited to 5. After that users and group profiles were generated, the initial value of MAC resulted equal to 0.3; we denote such an initial configuration as random, being users randomly assigned to groups.

Table 1. Simulation parameters.

Parameter	Value	Parameter	Value
$|\mathcal{G}|$	150	$I_u(c)$	random
k_{MIN}	0	A_u	{O:0.7, C:0.2, S:0.1}
k_{MAX}	200	$|B|$	6 different behaviors
n_{MIN}	0	B_u	random in $\{T, F\}^6$
n_{MAX}	200	ω_u	0.5
N_{REQ}	5	ω_g	0.5

U2G. Compactness vs Similarity. Starting with the `random` configuration, the *U2G* algorithm was applied for 20 epochs of execution per user. Two different versions of the same algorithm were executed: *U2G-comp* adopts the compactness function to perform matching, while *U2G-diff* adopts the similarity function alone. The MAC values achieved by the two algorithms for different epochs are graphically depicted in Figure 1. With respect to the `random` configuration, the results show that the *U2G-comp* algorithm increases the compactness in OSN groups of about 33% while by using the only similarity the MAC increment is of about 11.2%. Moreover, both the U2G-diff and U2G-comp algorithms converge in about 7 epochs, such a result is in accord with Theorem 1. By this first set of results it can be stated that it is convenient to consider trust and similarity together to form groups.

U2G. Trust vs Similarity. A further experiment on simulated data, was performed in order to study the weight assignment which can provide the largest increasing of MAC. In particular, the study was conducted by means of the range $\omega_u \in \{0.2, 0.3, \ldots, 0.8\}$. Results are shown in Figure 2, which makes evidence that the highest increment in MAC (with respect to the `random` configuration) is reached when ω_u is in the range $[0.2, 0.4]$ while it sharply decreases when $\omega_u > 0.5$. These results show that it is better grouping together individuals trusting each other rather than users resulting similar only for profiles.

U2G-O. Experimental Settings. To test the performance of the U2G-O algorithm we simulated an OSN having a number of groups varying from 5,000 to 25,000, and k_{MAX} spanning in the set $\{15, 20, 50, 70, 120, 200\}$. In this case a "quality index" Q was computed as:

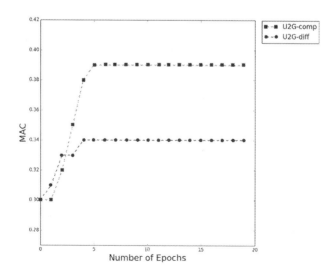

Fig. 1. MAC vs epochs obtained by the U2G-comp and U2G-diff algorithms.

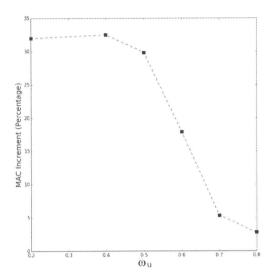

Fig. 2. MAC increment vs ω obtained by the U2G-comp algorithm.

$$Q = 1 - \frac{\phi^{\text{OPT}} - \phi(\mathbf{x}_u)}{\phi^{\text{OPT}}}$$

where $\mathbf{x}_u$ is the outcome assignment of $U2G$-O produced at each iteration, $\phi(\mathbf{x}_u)$ the associated value of the objective function, and ϕ^{OPT} is the optimal solution. Note that, since $\phi^{\text{OPT}} \geq \phi(\mathbf{x}_u)$ for any $\mathbf{x}_u$, Q always ranges in $[0, 1]$ and the higher Q, the better the approximation is.

In the first experiment the quality of the $U2G$-O algorithm was measured by setting the sample size t equal to the theoretical bound $\lfloor \frac{n}{e} \rfloor$, being n the number of groups. Figure 3 shows Q with respect to the number of groups; results put in evidence how Q is always greater than 0.82. Moreover, the lower k_{MAX}, the higher Q: in fact, if k_{MAX} is low, the probability to find the k_{MAX} groups having the highest compactness in the sample set is high and, therefore, the $U2G$-O algorithm gives a high chance to find the optimal solution even if it is restricted to view only the sample set. To reduce the number of groups viewed by the algorithm $U2G - O$ we carried out a second experiment where the number of groups was set to 10,000, and a sample size belonging to k_{MAX} to $\lfloor \frac{n}{e} \rfloor$ was used. Having to select at least k_{MAX}, we considered a sample size at least equal to k_{MAX}. In Figure 4, the obtained results show as Q quickly increases if the sample size increases: so, for example, with $k_{\text{MAX}} = 15$ it is sufficient to choose a sample size equal to 50 for achieving $Q > 0.8$. The worst case happens if the sample size is equal to k_{MAX} but it is worth noting that always it is $Q > 0.5$. In the last experiment, for each investigated value of k_{MAX}, the sample varied in size and we computed the number ns of steps executed by the algorithm U2G-O before its stop (when generated the approximate solution) by using a population of 10,000 units. Results depicted in Figure 5 show as ns linearly increases, in an

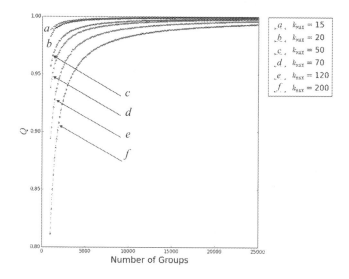

Fig. 3. Quality of the U2G-O algorithm vs. the number of available groups

independent way from the value of k_{MAX}. Such a result might appear counter-intuitive because if we enlarge the sample size, we also need to reduce the size of the space the *U2G-O* algorithm needs to explore and, consequently, we would expect that ns decreases in accordance with the sample size increasing.

However, large sample size values implies that the probability to find the top k_{MAX} groups in the reference set increases and, as a consequence, it will be harder to update the assignment generated by visiting only those groups belonging to the reference set. From this set of experiments we can deduce that the U2G-O algorithm is really competitive because it approximates the correct solution within a precision of the 90%, although it can knows only a limited part of the group population.

5 Related Work

An exhaustive discussion about the scientific literature involved on the matter presented in this paper requires too much space and, therefore, only those approaches that, to the best of our knowledge, come closest to it will be examined.

Group Formation and Evolution. Social Sciences and, more recently, Computer Science [3], extensively investigated on the mechanisms underlying groups formation and their evolution by exploiting a great variety of approaches.

In this context, a well known theory about groups formation is the *common identity and common bond* [30]. Basing on this theory, *i*) shared interests (i.e. similarity) and *ii*) strong personal ties with other group members are considered key elements to induce users to join with a group. Authors of [17] empirically

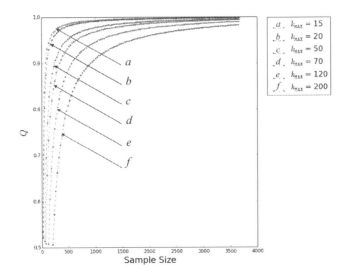

Fig. 4. Quality of the U2G-O algorithm vs. the sample size

verified the common identity and the common bond theory by means of a framework which exploits some metrics capable of capturing the main features. An interesting result is proposed in [3] which considers two communities (i.e. Live-Journal and DBLP[2] networks) on which the act to join with a group can be modeled in the same terms of spreading new ideas, although the two communities give a different meaning to the concept of group. In particular, group affiliation is modeled through the probability p that a user u will join with a group G, while that of the group growth is analyzed by considering the factors yielded an increase in the number of group members in a particular time frame.

The clustering properties of groups are studied in [21] by using diffusion processes; authors state as groups mainly growth for diffusion are usually smaller than other groups. Authors of [24] presented results which are in line with that of [21]: 500 thousands Facebook groups, created in 8 day, were observed for a period of 3 months. They made evidence that i) about 57% of groups did not create new content after the 3 months while ii) the social capital and group activity intensity resulted as the success keys. Note that the main findings of the cited contribution can be considered orthogonal to our proposal. Furthermore, in our work we consider as very relevant the role of trust in building groups and, to this purpose, we define the compactness to assess the benefit a user can get back from joining with a group.

Matching User and Group Profiles. Give suggestions to user about groups to join with is known as *affiliation recommendation* [35]. At this aim, profiles of users and groups can be matched [7,10,34,35]. An early contribution can be found in [34], on which six different measures to compute the similarity degree

---

[2] http://dblp.uni-trier.de/

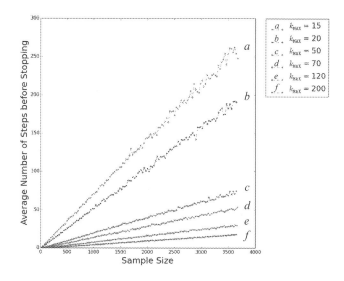

Fig. 5. Number of Steps carried out by the U2G-O algorithm before stopping.

of a user and a group are discussed and compared. Chen *et al.* [7] proposed an algorithm, called *Combinational Collaborative Filtering* where it is adopted an Expectation-Maximization-like approach, on a Gibbs sampling, to suggest users with new friend relationships and new communities (i.e. groups) which join with. Vasuki *et al.* [35] investigated on the co-evolution of the friend relationships between a user and the affiliation network (suitably modeled by a bipartite graph). As result, a good predictor for groups users will join with in the future might be realized by coupling friendship information and information referred to past groups.

An internetworking scenario is analyzed in [10] by assuming that users can desire to join with more OSNs at the same time. Users are supported by suggestions about the groups/OSNs which him/her can affiliate. Such suggestions are generated by exploiting a truncated version of the Katz coefficient [22] computed over an hypergraph representing OSN resources, groups and users.

A probabilistic framework modeling the users preferences to join with groups is proposed and experimentally validated in [16].

Our approach differs from the presented studies because, differently from them, it gives a rich framework modeling user's interests, information describing user's behaviors and social relationships (encoded as trust relationships). Besides, we consider in the policies followed in accessing groups, the past user's behaviors and combine both trust and similarity in group formation processes.

Trust in OSN membership. *Trust* is considered an important parameter when admitting/accepting a user in OSN groups, as the high level of mutual users trust motivates them to stay into a group, to work with others [31] and to access services otherwise unavailable [26]. As a consequence, trust is a key component of any relationship that is fundamental for the surviving of online communities [32]. In the OSN context, the main aspects of trust are the: informative sources [8]; aggregation rules [11]; trust inference [23]. In particular, the first issue involves direct and indirect opinions (i.e. reliability and reputation), respectively derived by personal past experiences and by opinions provided by other users [19,27] but, for the sparsity of OSNs relationships, reputation is usually predominant.

Ziegler and Golbeck [15] argue that trust must reflect user similarity and proposed a formal framework to show the relationship existing between trust and similarity by assuming that, for a given domain, trusted peers are on average considerably more similar to their sources of trust than arbitrary peers. As a consequence, on the basis of [15], we can deduce that clusters of mutual trusted OSN users should result also similar among them for some aspect of common interest and could represent the potential kernels of OSN groups.

Different authors tried to identify OSN clusters of trusted users by means of *trust chains* (i.e. direct or indirect paths linking more users by trust relationships). For instance, in [25] is proposed an extended Advogato trust metric incorporating the social relationships strength. The TidalTrust algorithm [14] executes a modified Breadth First Search to find all the shortest path linking two users (not directly connected) in an incremental way by computing the user's trust rating as a weighted average of trust ratings from the source to the target users. SWTrust [20] is a framework incorporable in different trust models to generate small trusted subgraphs of large OSNs by using a breadth-first search algorithm based on the *weak ties* theory on the spread of information in OSNs [18] and by inferring trust values.

6 Conclusions and Future Work

In this paper we exploited a parameter, named compactness, to drive group formation in social networks. Compactness measure is obtained from experimental observations about similarity and mutual trust in OSNs. Similarity and trust are combined together to drive group formation such that the probability of mutual interactions among users of the same group becomes higher. This approach eventually lead benefits in terms of Social Capital, i.e. in terms of quality and density of interactions between OSN user affiliated within the same group.

Algorithm U2G (Users-to-Groups) exploits the compactness measure to allow software agents – on behalf of OSN users and groups – to manage group evolutions in a dynamic fashion. Its variant – called U2G-O – is designed to address a more realistic scenario on which user agents are not able to access information about more than one group at a given time. Experimental results have shown as they are overlapped to those generated by the algorithm U2G, i.e. it approximates the correct solution with a higher precision.

Finally, from the obtained results, it is possible to note as the combined use of trust and similarity yields meaningful advantages in selecting and forming groups. For our ongoing researches, we are designing some experiments on large data sets collected from real OSN in order to verify the effectiveness of the proposed approach in a real context.

Acknowledgements. This work has been partially supported by the following projects:

- **PRISMA** PON04a2 A/F funded by the Italian Ministry of Education, University, and Research
- **TENACE PRIN Project** (n. 20103P34XC) funded by the Italian Ministry of Education, University and Research,
- Program "Programma Operativo Nazionale Ricerca e Competitività" 2007-2013, project **BA2Kno** (Business Analytics to Know) PON03PE_00001_1, in "Laboratorio in Rete di Service Innovation",
- Program "Programma Operativo Nazionale Ricerca e Competitività" 2007-2013, **Distretto Tecnologico CyberSecurity** funded by the Italian Ministry of Education, University and Research.

References

1. Babaioff, M., Immorlica, N., Kempe, D., Kleinberg, R.D.: A knapsack secretary problem with applications. In: Charikar, M., Jansen, K., Reingold, O., Rolim, J.D.P. (eds.) RANDOM 2007 and APPROX 2007. LNCS, vol. 4627, pp. 16–28. Springer, Heidelberg (2007)
2. Babaioff, M., et al.: Online auctions and generalized secretary problems. ACM SIGecom Exchanges **7**(2), 7 (2008)
3. Backstrom, L., et al.: Group formation in large social networks: membership, growth, and evolution. In: Proc. of the 12th ACM SIGKDD, pp. 44–54. ACM Press (2006)
4. Blei, D., et al.: Latent Dirichlet Allocation. J. of Machine Learning Research **3**, 993–1022 (2003)
5. Brunie, A.: Meaningful distinctions within a concept: Relational, collective, and generalized social capital. Social Science Research **38**(2), 251–265 (2009)
6. Chau, D.H., et al.: Parallel crawling for online social networks. In: Proc. of the 16th WWW, pp. 1283–1284. ACM (2007)
7. Chen, W., et al.: Combinational collaborative filtering for personalized community rrecommendation. In: Proc. of ACM SIGKDD, pp. 115–123. ACM (2008)
8. De Meo, P., Ferrara, E., Rosaci, D., Sarnè, G.M.L.: How to improve group homogeneity in online social networks. In: Proc. of the 14th CEUR Workshop Proc., WOA 2013, vol. 1099. CEUR-WS.org (2011)
9. De Meo, P., Nocera, A., Rosaci, D., Ursino, D.: Recommendation of reliable users, social networks and high-quality resources in a social internetworking system. AI Communications **24**(1), 31–50 (2011)
10. De Meo, P., Nocera, A., Terracina, G., Ursino, D.: Recommendation of similar users, resources and social networks in a social internetworking scenario. Information Sciences **181**(7), 1285–1305 (2011)
11. Dellarocas, C.: Designing reputation systems for the social web. SSRN Electronic Journal (2010)
12. Dynkin, E.: The optimum choice of the instant for stopping a markov process. Sov. Math. Dokl. **4**, 627–629 (1963)

13. Freeman, P.: The secretary problem and its extensions: A review. International Statistical Review, 189–206 (1983)
14. Golbeck, J.: Computing and applying trust in web-based social networks. (2005)
15. Golbeck, J., Hendler, J.: Inferring binary trust relationships in web-based social networks. ACM Transactions on Internet Technology (TOIT) **6**(4), 497–529 (2006)
16. Gorla, J., et al.: Probabilistic group recommendation via information iatching.In: Proc. of WWW 2013, pp. 495–504. ACM Press (2013)
17. Grabowicz, P., et al.: Distinguishing topical and social groups based on common identity and bond theory. In: Proc. of WSDM, pp. 627–636. ACM (2013)
18. Granovetter, M.: The strength of weak ties: A network theory revisited. Sociological Theory **1**(1), 201–233 (1983)
19. Huynh, T., Jennings, N., Shadbolt, N.: An integrated trust and reputation model for open multi-agent systems. Autonomous Agents and Multi-Agent Systems **13**(2), 119–154 (2006)
20. Jiang, W., Wang, G., Wu, J.: Generating trusted graphs for trust evaluation in online social networks. Future Generation Computer Systems **31**, 48–58 (2014)
21. Kairam, S., et al.: The life and death of online groups: predicting group growth and longevity. In: Proc. of WSDM, Seattle, USA, pp. 673–682. ACM (2012)
22. Katz, L.: A new status index derived from sociometric analysis. Psychometrika **18**(1), 39–43 (1953)
23. Kim, Y., Song, H.: Strategies for predicting local trust based on trust propagation in social networks. Knowledge-Based Systems **24**(8), 1360–1371 (2011)
24. Kraut, R., Fiore, A.: The role of founders in building online groups. In: Proc. of the 17th CSCW, Baltimore, Maryland, pp. 722–732. ACM Press (2014)
25. LePine, J.A., Methot, J.R., Crawford, E.R., Buckman, B.R.: A model of positive relationships in teams: the role of instrumental, friendship, and multiplex social network ties. personal relationships. In: The Effect on Employee Attitudes, Behavior, and Well-being, Routledge, New York, pp. 173–194 (2012)
26. Lin, N.: Social capital: a theory of social structure and action (structural analysis in the social sciences). Cambridge University Press (2002)
27. Messina, F., Pappalardo, G., Rosaci, D., Santoro, C., Sarné, G.M.L.: A trust-based approach for a competitive cloud/grid computing scenario. In: Fortino, G., Badica, C., Malgeri, M., Unland, R. (eds.) IDC 2012. SCI, vol. 446, pp. 129–138. Springer, Heidelberg (2012)
28. Mislove, A., et al.: Measurement and analysis of online social networks. In: Proc. of the ACM SIGCOMM Conf. on Internet Measurement, pp. 29–42 (2007)
29. Pearson, R.K., et al.: Quantitative evaluation of clustering results using computational negative controls. In: Proc. of the 2004 SIAM Int. Conf. on Data Mining, pp. 188–199 (2004)
30. Prentice, D., et al.: Asymmetries in attachments to groups and to their members: Distinguishing between common-identity and common-bond groups. Personality and Social Psychology Bulletin **20**(5), 484–493 (1994)
31. Putnam, R.D.: Bowling together. OECD Observer, pp. 14–15 (2004)
32. Sheldon, P.: I'll poke you. you'll poke me! self-disclosure, social attraction, predictability and trust as important predictors of facebook relationships. Cyberpsychology: Journal of Psychosocial Research on Cyberspace **3**(2), 67–75 (2009)
33. Sherchan, W., Nepal, S., Paris, C.: A survey of trust in social networks. ACM Computing Surveys (CSUR) **45**(4), 47 (2013)

34. Spertus, E., et al.: Evaluating similarity measures: a large-scale study in the orkut social network. In: Proc. of SIGKDD 2005, pp. 678–684. ACM (2005)

35. Vasuki, V., Natarajan, N., Lu, Z., Savas, B., Dhillon, I.: Scalable affiliation recommendation using auxiliary networks. ACM Transactions on Intelligent Systems and Technology **3**(1), 3 (2011)

36. Wilson, R., Gosling, S., Graham, T.: A review of Facebook research in the social sciences. Perspectives on Psychological Science **7**(3), 203–220 (2012)

37. Wooldridge, A., Jennings, N.R.: Agent theories, architectures, and languages: a survey. In: Wooldridge, M.J., Jennings, N.R. (eds.) ECAI 1994 and ATAL 1994. LNCS, vol. 890, pp. 1–39. Springer, Heidelberg (1995)

Supporting Peer Help in Collaborative Learning Environments: A Discussion Based on Two Case Studies

Luana Müller[✉], Letícia Lopes Leite, and Milene Selbach Silveira

Faculdade de Informática, PUCRS, Av. Ipiranga 6681, Porto Alegre, RS 90619-900, Brazil
{luana.muller,leticia.leite,milene.silveira}@pucrs.br

Abstract. In this paper, we present a discussion about peer help systems based on two case studies that promote their use in a collaborative learning environment. Peer help systems aim to promote and encourage the use of help systems. Through them, users interact in pairs in order to complement the assistance provided by online help systems. We highlight the importance of this alternative type of help system and the advantages of its use by promoting not only help by users interactions, but also useful information for systems designers to improve their systems and to understand the interaction problems found by users during the process of using a system.

Keywords: Collaborative learning environments · Peer help systems · Help systems

1   Introduction

According to Willis [23], the availability of an effective help system will allow users to acquire the skills and knowledge required to operate an application easily [23]. Similarly, the work of Silveira et al. [17], based on Semiotic Engineering, advocates that careful design of help systems is essential in order to explain the designers vision about their systems and better ways (and reasons) for users to interact with them. This kind of strategic information is rarely found within a help system.

The operational and tactical levels are explained by the details about what is necessary to execute each available application task, how these tasks can be played and who the user must be. The strategic level brings the reason to execute the tasks in a determined way and moment, showing the designer's view about the tasks and how important it is to execute them in such way that the designer described. Typically, we find operational and tactical information in help systems' answers from questions such as "What is this?" or "How do I do this?" [17][18].

However, regardless of their content, help systems are not often accessed by users needing assistance because help systems usually do not address the users' specific problems [21]. Besides that the strategic questions that are important to make them able to appropriate themselves to the application in order to successfully achieve their interaction goals are not provided.

Considering the difficulties of help systems to answer users' specific questions, help from other people is a common alternative [4]. In this sense, we believe that

© Springer International Publishing Switzerland 2015
C. Debruyne et al. (Eds.): OTM 2015 Conferences, LNCS 9415, pp. 76–89, 2015.
DOI: 10.1007/978-3-319-26148-5_5

fostering cooperation between users through computational tools can contribute to sharing information and experience about the knowledge they have built.

The cooperation between users is the core of the peer help approach. As stated by Kumar [10], a peer help system represents a network that integrates users and a system that knows these users, and the help requests that were sent by them. Based on this, the system tries to establish a more effective interaction between pairs of users in order to help them solve their questions. The users' exchange of information can provide mutual learning, both for the user that is requesting help and the user that is helping [12].

This paper focuses on peer help approaches and their possible applications in collaborative learning environments. According to Medeiros et al. [7], "the collaborative learning environments are not simply channels for the transmission of information, but environments where users can construct knowledge through conversation and collaboration, providing many possibilities for the user interaction synchronous and asynchronous".

We believe that users' collaboration can facilitate their understanding about these environments, contributing to a better appropriation of the tools and resources available. As stated by Wenger [22], learner communities, in which the components share information within an environment, can develop ties that reinforce the learning outcomes. In the first presented study, the focus is to support users' communication by the use of specific textual expressions. These expressions can help users to better specify their questions and thus, help the users that are providing help to understand the problem. The second study integrates peer help systems and recommender systems' algorithms to provide social matching [20] in order to improve the process of pair formation.

The following sections present the background, the two case studies, the discussion of their results, conclusions and future prospects for this work.

2   Background

In this section, we present the main subjects that underlie this research: Peer Help Systems and Collaborative Learning Environments.

2.1   Peer-Help Systems

According to Spool and Scanlon [19], users seek help for two reasons: when they are confused by the interface or when they need to find specific information. Belkin [1] complements this by saying that when people search for information they hope to solve a problem or achieve some goal, because their current knowledge is inadequate. Based on that, we assume that the system should help the user to find the answer quickly and consistently, providing an effective search for information.

Given this perspective, we observed that peer help initiatives incorporate dynamicity and agility to the solution of questions and, above all, encourage the use of help systems through collaboration among users.

According to Kumar [10], the focus of peer help is the support offered by the users of the application. Other components can be identified as well, such as the dedication of more experienced users who are available to assist in answering questions, the help system that provides information about the application, and resources and tools available to support (chat and forum, among others).

Pressley et al. [14] list some pedagogical advantages in the use of peer help systems:

- Motivating the socialization of users in the context of work and increasing their motivation by promoting social recognition of their knowledge;
- Providing a stronger learning experience for the person seeking help;
- Promoting processes of self-learning and self-reflection for the user who helps his/her peer, occurring mutual learning;
- Facilitating social interaction in the group and helping creating personal relationships among members.

We believe that adding peer help features to online help systems can assist and promote their use. In addition to clarifying questions in a more natural and simple form, because is closer to what happens every day, they also motivate people, encouraging the development of collaborative networks and knowledge dissemination.

2.2   Collaborative Learning Environments

According to Medeiros et al. [7], in an age where the Internet and web applications are fundamental for the development of human interaction, the landscape of education continues to change due to constant evolution of computer-supported collaborative learning.

Facilities for production and access to materials in collaborative learning environments are promoted by their communication mechanisms, management data tools and telecommunication resources in general and they allow us to say that the implementation of collaborative systems in education is increasing.

Given the multiplicity of applications and the diversity of users, it is very important that those environments are simple and easy to use, so that their users do not consume much time learning how to use the interface. Navigation in a virtual environment should emphasize the understanding of the content available and encourage the interactions that will contribute to learning. As social platforms [14], collaborative learning environments need to be designed not merely to distribute knowledge but also to provide conditions through which knowledge is shared and new knowledge is created or exchanged through the collaborative process.

However, using collaborative learning environments to support teaching is not always a simple task. Questions related to the use of the environment can disperse the users' attention and make them lose focus. The increasing use of collaborative learning environments and their distinct users' profiles means that they should be simple, easy to use and provide some kind of help to these users.

3   User Studies

The first case study presents a peer help architecture for collaborative learning environments (PHAVEA) that can be applied in any platform from these environments as an attempt to provide a better way to help users to use the environment [11].

The second study [13] intends to identify the criteria used by users to choose someone to help them with their questions, and to use these criteria to recommend users in a peer help system. These two case studies are presented in the next sections.

3.1   Case Study 1: Helping to Focus on the Questions

The need to provide better ways to present an online help system and its communication with the user has contributions from several areas. Semiotic Engineering [6], for instance (by the use of communicability expressions[1]), can contribute to a better specification of the users' questions. Consequently there is a better understanding of these questions by those who will assist them. The work of Silveira et al. [18] was the first step in this direction and their proposal had a direct influence on the development of this first case study. The use of communicability expressions allows the involved users to share a common vocabulary, a factor that can greatly contribute to the success of their communication and thus to a better understanding of the collaborative system in use.

In this case study, these expressions were used in order to qualify and motivate the answering of questions about collaborative learning environments.

The following subsections describe the initial set of expressions used to support communication, the software architecture developed to support this interaction, a prototype that implemented it and a user study related to it.

Initial Set of Expressions. Given the use of communicability expressions as a way of supporting dialogue between pairs of users, it was necessary to define an initial set of expressions to be used. To do so, two studies were carried out considering the main users of these environments: professors and students [11]. The studies' goal was to capture and analyze the expressions used by the users in their search for help. In both cases, the peer help system was simulated by person-to-person interaction.

The first study had the participation of four university professors. All of them used to use the collaborative learning environment in their daily activities. None of them used the help system available in the environment, choosing to ask someone else when they had questions about how to perform some task.

The studies were done individually and all interactions were video recorded for later analysis. The participants had to perform three distinct tasks and, in case of questions, they were invited to ask questions to a "helper" (an observer who played the role of a help system).

The students' study was conducted in two undergraduate classrooms, one with 31 students and the other with 25. This study was carried out the beginning of the school

---

[1] Communicability expressions [6] are associated to users' communication breakdowns, generating support for the identification and fix of failures during software development.

year and at that time, the students did not have much knowledge about the use of learning environments.

Most of the students (76.8%) have never used the environments' help system. The study was done in a computing laboratory, at two different times, separating the two classes. The study procedure was the same for both classes. All the interactions between the students and the helper were done through a forum available inside the environment.

After a deep analysis of the question-answering process of all studies, an initial set of expressions was elaborated, composed by the most commonly used expressions.

Table 1. Initial set of expressions

	Expression
Original	What is this?
	What is this for?
	How do I do this?
	Where is it?
	I give up.
	What now?
Identified	What do I type here?
	Why do I do that?
	What happens if I do this?
	Why did not anything happen?
	What does this item relate to?
	What is the purpose of this option?
	What is the difference between ... and ...?

Table 1 presents this set. It was possible to identify the expressions that already exist in Silveira, Barbosa and de Souza [18] proposal as well as new contributions.

PHAVEA Architecture. This architecture is based on the existence of two independent repositories: the repository of information about the collaborative system and the repository of information about peer help, both providing an independent technological platform, allowing the architecture to be embedded in any collaborative system. All the information needed for the peer help operation stays in its own base, and only the logon information is used from the collaborative system's database. In the collaborative system's logon page, the user data is captured and, after this, the peer help system does not consult any further information from the host system, i.e. the peer help does not use any other kind of routine or database from the collaborative system that incorporates PHAVEA.

The peer help repository supports the help requests and assistance process. The help request process begins with the demandant[2] selecting a user to provide assistance to him. The system provides a list that contains all collaborative system users that

---

[2]   In this work, the user who consults the peer help system is called a demandant; and the user who answers his questions is called an assistant.

agreed to provide assistance to other users, apart from his/her study area. In this list, the demandant must select one of the available assistants. Due to the fact that the system's goal is to provide peer help about the system, the group of assistants tends to be composed of users with diverse characteristics and knowledge.

The ordering of the list of available assistants is composed by the information about the assistance provided by each user, displaying the names of those who have provided more aid at the end of the list. This initiative aims to better distribute the requests to the assistants. After selecting an assistant, the demandant must select the communicability expression that better represents his/her difficulty and must identify the subject of the question.

Through the definition of the pair of users (demandant and assistant) the communication is established and the assistance process begins. According to the PHAVEA architecture, the communication can make use of tools such as chat, forum, remote access, among others. When assistance is completed, the demandant evaluates the received assistance, generating necessary data for system's maintenance.

Moreover, the proposed architecture stores a record of assistances and their evaluations into a database that allow other users of the collaborative system to reassess and review the solution presented by assistants. The review aims to provide an analysis of the assistance by a greater number of users and thus can influence the constitution of a FAQ database. The result of the reclassification of an assistant considers all evaluations given and this is generated   by an arithmetic average of all of those evaluations provided by users who have accessed the related answer. The equation used to calculate this average is:

$$Cat = \left(\sum x - \sum y\right) * P$$

Where:

x ← represents positive ratings;

y ← represents negative ratings;

P ← represents the user (requesting help) profile level (1 to beginning user; 2 to intermediate user; 3 to advanced user).

The use of the arithmetic average for reclassification of assistant is due to the fact that, for the system, users do not have different profiles, so the weight of the evaluation of a user is considered identical to any other user evaluation.

It is important to highlight that this architecture proposes the provision of a peer help system that would complement the help that has already been incorporated into the environment.

Prototype. The proposed architecture can be associated to any collaborative system. In this work it was implemented on Moodle (Modular Object-Oriented Dynamic Learning Environment)[3] through a prototype called Peer Help Plugin.

The prototype interface presented the number of online users and the number of available assistants, allowing users with questions to check the availability of other community members to provide assistance.

If any of the available expressions meet the demandant's needs, he/she may use the "Free Question" option, where the user can describe his/her complete question. Free

---

[3]   moodle.org

questions are also registered in the database for future reference and, based on these questions, new expressions can incorporate the expressions' database.

When the assistance process starts, the communication between users of the Peer Help Plugin occurs through a chat tool. It should be noted that the first message between the pair of users starts with the selection of a communicability expression. However, the exchange of messages occurs freely, allowing the use of new communicability expressions in the interactive discourse and generating support for their incorporation into the expressions' database.

The end of the assistance can be requested by either of the users (demandant or assistant). When it is concluded, an evaluation form of the received assistance is presented to the demandant. This information will be used to qualify the assistance, and may indicate question-answers that can be incorporated into a FAQ database, or even into the help system of the collaborative learning environment.

User Study. The analysis of the use of the prototype was done with intended users of this kind of systems (professors and students) aiming to identify new system features and analyze the use of communicability expressions to support peer help assistance.

The studies had the participation of three university professors and 25 students. The studies were conducted at different times: one with the professors and another with the students. Considering that users would be more concerned with the handling of tools they are not frequently in contact with, it was opted to use a resource that is not commonly used by these users (the collaborative text).

By accessing the collaborative learning environment to view the activities to be carried out, the users could propose to be assistants themselves. Thus, the system identified those who could provide assistance to other users. During the professors' experiment, there were two assistants who provided four assistances; and, during the students' experiment, 10 assistants provided 12 assistances.

The user study allowed the identification of the most used expressions to start an assistance service. They were as follows: "How do I do this?", "Where is it?", "What is this?", and "What do I type here?". And during the chat interactions, the most used expressions were "What now?" and "How do I do this?". The use of such expressions identified users' focus on accomplishing the task and, in most cases, asking for step-by-step instructions for performing a task.

We observed that the use of peer help was fairly simple; there were no questions about its operation. The choice of a tool that users are familiar with (chat) contributed to interactions in an organized and dynamic way. Nonetheless, the possibility of evaluating assistance was a motivating factor for high quality assistance (the assistances were only closed when the user's question was clear).

3.2   Case Study 2: Helping Focusing on the Pair Formation

When we talk about contextualized questions, a kind of question where users ask for help from another person, the research paradigm is different from the traditional one (that uses keywords in order to retrieve information). This paradigm is named a village paradigm [5]. This name is inspired by the way that information is widespread in a village. In the village context, the information is socially disseminated (person to person) and the main way to find an answer is looking for the right/best person to answer.

This paradigm is characterized by the use of natural language to ask questions and by the real time generated answers. Considering these principles, peer help systems aid users' interactions by helping them find other users to help.

The peer help system selects and suggests a person that can help a particular user, creating a pair of users that will interact supported by the system. The second case study proposes the integration of recommendation techniques and peer help systems in order to improve the process of pair combination. This proposal intends to promote a better user experience with help systems and the environment.

This study intended to identify the criteria used by users to choose someone to help them in their questions and use these criteria to generate a recommendation of a user to answer the question through a peer help system.

To understand users' preferred criteria to choose a person to ask for help and then identify which of these criteria could be used in the proposed recommendation process, it was applied an online questionnaire with potential users of collaborative learning environment.

Pair Formation Process. Based on the online questionnaire results [13] it was defined which and how users' criteria should be used in the process.

Through our online survey, from the users who reported that they frequently had questions related to the use of the environment, 67% of them were users with a professor profile. Thus, we decided to focus our process on professors because they are the responsible for configuring the environment and its subjects, adding and setting resources and tools that will be used by their students. The results of the experiments made with PHAVEA architecture show that users with a professor profile had more questions related to how to use the environment [11].

The following items represent the users' criteria and their application:

1. Configured tools: focusing on the professor's profile and based on the fact that they are responsible for configuring the environment, the items selected to find similarity indices between users and make the recommendation were configured resources and activities. The similarity will be measured through Pearson's correlation coefficient [8].
2. Technical knowledge and receptivity: these criteria can be defined by the answers given by the users. PHAVEA architecture suggests classifying users in levels using an equation that considers the users' knowledge and receptivity to increase these levels. Based on this, we decided to use PHAVEA's equation in order to define users' levels.

    In this case study it was defined that the user will be classified as a beginner when the result is less than or equal to three; intermediate when the equation's result is greater than three and less than or equal to six, and advanced when the equation's result is greater than six.
3. Time of use: it can be measured based on the amount of time each user has been using the environment. Consequently, the question will be received by the user that is using the environment for the longest time.

The pair formation process will execute up to three steps:

First: the algorithm will search for similar users (users with similar configured tools) in the user group. This user group will consist of:

— All users - if the user that registered the question did not specify the resource/activity that the question is related to.
— All users that state that they have the ability to use the resource/activity asked about in the question - if the user that registered the question specified the resource/activity the question is related to.

Second: if the first step found more than one user, the algorithm will search inside the pool of similar users for someone at the same level as the user that submitted the question.

Third: if the second step found more than one user, the algorithm will search for the user that has used the environment for the longest amount of time (this time is given by the user when she/he registers in the system).

If more than one user is still found, the algorithm will choose one randomly. If there were no users found in one of the steps, the algorithm goes on to the next one. If only one user was found in one of the steps, regardless of which step, this user will receive the question and the rest of the search process will be ignored.

Help Request and Assistance Process. The Help Request process starts with the user registering in the system, when he/she informs his/her user's profile. During this phase the user needs to classify the resources and activities that he/she used to configure on Moodle environment, and he/she also needs to inform his/her knowledge level on the use of each one. The knowledge level goes from zero (the user does not know how to configure the resource/activity) to four (the user knows how to configure the resource/activity and use it frequently).

After that, the user is able to register new questions in the system. During the register of his/her question, he/she can inform the related resource and activity. According to this information and the information about his/her profile and the profile of the other registered users, the pair selection process is executed, searching for the best user to answer that question.

After setting the user who will answer the question, the assistance process begins. The chosen user receives the question, and it remains available to him/her in the system to be answered at any moment.

After checking the question that needs to be answered, the user can answer it or inform that he/she does not know how to answer it. In the second case, the question will return to the system that will check for a new user to answer it, executing the selection process again.

In case he/she decides to answer the question, the question and the answer will return to the user who asked and he/she will be able to classify the answer as positive or negative. In case of a positive evaluation, the question is finished and the system will make it available in the system FAQ, where the question will be available to future research. In case of a negative evaluation, the question is send to a new user to try a new answer. This new user will be also selected according to the process previously described.

Prototype. Although the concept of peer help systems being usually a synchronous system with questions and answers in real time, in this study an asynchronous system was developed to allow more access flexibility to the users. The prototype was developed using Java and MySql database.

User Study. The sample (selected by convenience) of users who used the prototype was composed of 33 professors that used to use Moodle in their academic activities. From these 33 registered users, 25 inserted questions in the prototype and 22 received questions.

The average of Moodle' resources and activities used by these users were 11.

During the period of two weeks, 72 questions were registered, being 16 of these not answered. Out of the 56 remaining questions, 42 were answered and positively qualified, 13 were answered and negatively qualified, and one was answered but not qualified by the user who asked it before the end of the study period.

As mentioned before, when the question is negatively qualified the algorithm finds another user to try a new answer. In the second search for an answer, five out of these 13 questions were not answered, six were answered and positively qualified, one was answered and negatively qualified, and one was answered and not qualified. The question that was negatively qualified was submitted to a third trial. However, it was not answered.

The study verified that during those two weeks the algorithm of pair selection was executed 115 times and in only 12 cases the algorithm did not find similar users. In these cases, the system used the second and third steps to find the pair.

4   Discussion

The idea of "users helping users" to understand a system (or its interface) is the essence of peer help systems. They aim to support the process of seeking help not only through traditional help content, but also mainly through the interaction between users [14]. Horowitz and Kamvar [5] stated that the use of communication tools that promote one-on-one communication can create an intimacy that encourages collaboration. These characteristics enable and encourage the exchange of messages between the users involved in the interactive discourse, thus facilitating clarification of questions. According to Borges and Baranauskas [2], the learner's progress occurs during the interactive cycle of exchanging information.

However, only the interaction between users does not guarantee effective clarification of questions, since the exchange of messages between them in order to resolve a question could suffer from noise and could not be fully understood by those involved. We argue that (1) users need help to better specify their questions in order to establish a more effective communication, and also (2) to find the best answers it is necessary to find the best user possible to answer them [5].

Trying to help users in their search for help, the first case study presented a set of expressions to specify the users' questions. In spite of the users' agreement with the benefits of using the expressions ("certainly the use of keywords helps the identification of the question" and "questions from the beginning of the system helped me to understand my classmate's questions. After this I only talked to him to show him step by step", for instance), some expressions were confusing and needed to be reviewed ("the term 'this' present in some expressions is a problem, because it gives an indication of something that was seen on the screen" and "the question marks in the expressions confuse the inclusion of the question complement because they give the idea of a completed sentence", for instance).

The second study intended to find the best assistant, but even when found, sometimes the assistant simply did not answer the questions. This is a fundamental point, cited in both studies: the success of both approaches (and of the peer help approach in general) depends on the commitment of the users that will answer the questions. The second study brought information that allowed us to analyze specific kinds of questions, hardly found in help systems: the strategic ones.

In a deep analysis of help requests in the second study, we found that out of the 72 questions asked, 16 were classified as operational, 30 tactical, 24 strategic and two tactical-strategic (we use the classification provided by [17][18]). The strategic questions are related to information "beyond" the interaction, such as possibilities of use of the distinct resources available in learning situations and their impact in all the teaching and learning processes.

This analysis reinforces the importance of help systems and that their content presents more than operational and tactical information. Furthermore, the availability of communication channels to the users is also important: designers cannot possibly think of all possible uses of specific resources, since these questions arise through the day-to-day use of these environments.

Distinct types of assistance could be available in the environments. In addition to the designer's vision of the possibilities and impacts of the system's use in the particular field to which it is addressed, peer-help allows users to share their own experiences. Moreover, the availability of online forums and communities associated to the environment may also be important assistance tools.

More importantly, a help system should not be viewed as an alternative to good (bad) design. We hope the discussion presented here can help designers and users to understand its importance: the more a user understands a system and its possibilities of use, the better he/she can use it. The best vehicle to provide this knowledge is the help system, and, as highlighted here, collaboration through it.

5   Conclusion

The evolution of computing has promoted changes in people's behavior, work and habits. Currently, it is integrated into our everyday lives and, therefore, making use of technology has become a necessity for almost everyone. However, despite the widespread use of computer resources, many users still encounter difficulties.

The search for a solution to an interaction problem or difficulty is still done, in most cases, through search engines, by questioning other users or through trial and error. Help systems are one of the last options used in these situations [13]. One of the major reasons for the low use of help systems in general is the lack of diversified possibilities to access their content and people's frustrations when using them previously.

Alternative ways to access help can attract new users and restore the confidence of those who felt frustrated by previous experiences. Similarly, the developers of collaborative learning environments (and collaborative systems in general) should be encouraged to use cutting-edge research products and propose innovative strategies, not only to meet users' needs, but also to satisfy them and encourage them to use these systems.

It is necessary to apply the perspectives proposed by Kammersgaard [9] to collaborative systems and online help systems in order to improve their development, instigate their action and increase their use:

- Dialogue-partner: which suggests that the system should be intelligent to interact with the user;
- Tool: which defines the system as a tool that allows users to work better, increasing their cognitive ability;
- Media: which proposes that the system acts as a communication tool between people.

Focusing on the collaborative learning environments, the two case studies presented try to help users to solve their questions about these environments through peer help systems. These environments are considered by both cases to be propitious to the users' questions because of the number of configurable items they present.

Cesarini et al. [3] reinforces the idea that collaborative learning environment is propitious to questions, showing a different perspective. According to them, the learning environments are not adapted to specific needs of the participants and the materials and activities are the same for all students not considering their differences.

It was possible to observe that the use of peer help systems in these environments collaborated with users by solving their questions and helping them, and also it was possible to check through other perspectives the advantages of its use.

In order to achieve their goals, users need first to establish them, according to what they understand about what it is possible to be done in the system. However, according to De Souza [5], the users' semiosis can be wrong about how to establish their goals, plans or operations necessary. These different levels of misconception can be categorized as strategic (establishing the goals), tactical (planning to achieve the goals) and operational (planning execution). In the case of strategic information, it is hard to find it inside some applications. This specific failure is not a characteristic of the analyzed environment (Moodle), but from the habit of not making this kind of information available.

Based on the presented studies, we believe that it is fundamental to think about strategic questions, not only making this kind of information available through the help systems but also offering peer help resources, through which users can interact with each other, bringing their contributions to the system and its use.

In the future, we intend to investigate the use of gamification in order to promote users' collaboration, giving them incentives to help other users using badges, status, points etc. We also intend to get more data, especially real use data, to study all of the phenomena related to these interactions and to look for ideas to improve this relationship, the use of the system, and the satisfaction of the user about it.

References

1. Belkin, N.J.: Helping people find what they don't know. Communications of the ACM **43**(8), 58–61 (2000)
2. Borges, M.A.F., Baranauskas, M.C.C.: CollabSS: a Tool to Help the Facilitator in Promoting Collaboration among Learners. Educational Technology & Society **6**(1), 64–69 (2003)
3. Cesarini, M., Monga, M., Tedesco, R.: Carrying on the e-learning process with workflow management engine. In: Proceedings of the 2004 ACM symposium on Applied computing, pp. 940–945 (2004)
4. Constant, D., Sproull, L., Kiesler, S.: The kindness of strangers: the usefulness of electronic weak ties for technical advice. Organization Science **7**(2), 119–135 (1996)
5. Horowitz, D., Kamvar, S.D.: The anatomy of a large-scale social search engine. In: Proceedings of 19th International Conference on World Wide Web, pp. 431–440 (2010)
6. De Souza, C.S.: The Semiotic Engineering of Human-Computer Interaction. The MIT Press, Cambridge (2005)
7. Medeiros, F., Gomes, A., Amorim, R., Medeiros, G.: Redesigning collaboration tools to enhance social presence in online learning environments. In: Antunes, P., Gerosa, M.A., Sylvester, A., Vassileva, J., de Vreede, G.-J. (eds.) CRIWG 2013. LNCS, vol. 8224, pp. 175–191. Springer, Heidelberg (2013)
8. Jannach, D., Zanker, M., Felfernig, A., Friedrich, G.: Recommender systems: an introduction. Cambridge University Press, Cambridge (2011)
9. Kammersgaard, J.: Four different perspectives on human-computer interaction. International Journal of Man-Machine Studies **28**(4), 343–362 (1988)
10. Kumar, V.: An instrument for providing formative feedback to novice programmers. In: Proceeedings of Annual Meeting of American Educational Research Association, pp. 71–76 (2004)
11. Leite, L.L., Silveira, M.S.: Afinando a comunicação entre pares para melhorar a compreensão da mensagem do designer. In: Proceedings of X Simpósio de Fatores Humanos em Sistemas Computacionais (IHC 2011), pp. 139–148 (2011)
12. McCalla, G.I., Greer, J.E., Kumar, V.S., Meagher, P., Collins, J.A., Tkatch, R., Parkinson, B.: A peer help system for workplace training. In: Proceedings of 8th World Conference on Artificial Intelligence in Education, pp. 183–191 (1997)
13. Müller, L., Silveira, M.S.: Help! i need somebody… help! not just anybody: applying recommender system techniques in peer help systems. In: Proceedings of the IADIS Conference WWW/Internet, pp. 83–90 (2014)
14. Pressley, M., Wood, E., Woloshyn, V., Martin, V., King, A., Menke, D.: Encouraging mindful use of prior knowledge: Attempting to construct explanatory answers facilitate learning. Educational Psychologist **27**(1), 91–109 (1992)
15. Razmerita, L.: Collaboration using social media: the case of podio in a voluntary organization. In: Antunes, P., Gerosa, M.A., Sylvester, A., Vassileva, J., de Vreede, G.-J. (eds.) CRIWG 2013. LNCS, vol. 8224, pp. 1–9. Springer, Heidelberg (2013)
16. Ribak, A., Jacovi, M., Soroka, V.: Ask before you search: peer support and community building with reachout. In: Proceedings of ACM 2002 Conference on Computer Supported Cooperative Work, pp. 126–135 (2002)
17. Silveira, M.S., Barbosa, S.D.J., de Souza, C.S.: Augmenting the affordance of online help content. In: Proceedings of IHM-HCI 2001, pp. 279–296 (2001)

18. Silveira, M.S., Barbosa, S.D.J., de Souza, C.S.: Designing Online Help Systems for Reflective Users. Journal of the Brazilian Computer Society **9**(3), 25–38 (2004)
19. Spool, J., Scanlon, T.: Making online information usable. HyperViews **3**(4), 5–7 (1996)
20. Terveen, L., McDonald, D.W.: Social matching: a framework and research agenda. In: Proceedings of ACM Transactions on Computer-Human Interaction, pp. 401–434 (2005)
21. Vouligny, L., Robert, J.M.: Online help system design based on the situated action theory. In: Proceedings of 2nd Latin American Conference on Human-Computer Interaction, pp. 64–75 (2005)
22. Wenger, E.: Communities of Practice: The Social Nature of Learning. Healthcare Forum Journal **39**(4), 20–26 (1996)
23. Willis, M.: Building effective help systems: modelling human help seeking behavior. In: Proceedings of 18th Australia Conference on Computer-Human Interaction, pp. 433–436 (2006)

Finding Collective Decisions: Change Negotiation in Collaborative Business Processes

Walid Fdhila[1], Conrad Indiono[1(✉)], Stefanie Rinderle-Ma[1],
and Rudolf Vetschera[2]

[1] Faculty of Computer Science, University of Vienna, Vienna, Austria
{walid.fdhila,conrad.indiono,stefanie.rinderle-ma}@univie.ac.at
[2] Faculty of Business, Economics and Statistics,
University of Vienna, Vienna, Austria
rudolf.vetschera@univie.ac.at

Abstract. Change propagation has been identified as major concern for process collaborations during the last years. Although changes might become necessary for various reasons, they can often not be kept local, i.e., at one partner's side, but must be partly or entirely propagated to one or several other partners. Due to the autonomy of partners in a collaboration, change effects cannot be imposed on the partners, but must be agreed upon in a consensual way. In our model of this collective decision process, we assume that each partner that becomes involved in a negotiation has different alternatives on how a change may be realized, and evaluates these alternatives according to his or her individual costs and benefits (utilities). This paper presents models from group decision making that can be applied for handling change negotiations in process collaborations in an efficient and fair way. The theoretical models are evaluated based on a proof-of-concept prototype that integrates an existing implementation for change propagation in process collaborations with change alternatives, utility functions, and group decision models. Based on simulating a realistic setting, the validity of the approach is shown. Our prototype supports the selection of change alternatives for each partner during negotiation that depending on the group decision model used, provides solutions emphasizing efficiency and/or fairness.

1 Introduction

Collaborative business processes, in which a set of partners collaborate in order to achieve a common business goal G [2], have become an important way of coordinating economic activities. For example, in virtual factories different manufacturers collaborate in the production of goods like cars [25]. Technically, this is realized by a process choreography where the role of each partner is defined in the form of a public process. The latter describes the way a partner interacts with the other partners and the required data to be exchanged for the collaboration (inputs and outputs) [28]. Each role in the choreography; i.e., public process, is associated with a public goal G_i. In order to fulfill its role reflected by the public process, a partner develops its business logic based on a so called

© Springer International Publishing Switzerland 2015
C. Debruyne et al. (Eds.): OTM 2015 Conferences, LNCS 9415, pp. 90–108, 2015.
DOI: 10.1007/978-3-319-26148-5_6

private process that is consistent with the public process. Due to confidentiality reasons, the details of the private process are hidden from the partners, only the public process as an abstraction of the private process is visible to the outside.

It should be noted that for fulfilling a role, a partner might develop alternative consistent private processes [27], each with an associated cost and possibly different private goal g_i[1]. Indeed, according to a partner business strategy, the private and public goals can diverge, but they should always align with the common goal G (of the collaboration). Since the private process represents the business logic of a given partner, it cannot be fully transparent to the other partners. Consequently, a partner can solely view the public process of the other partners, which serves as part of the SLA (Service Level Agreement) [17]; i.e. the contract. The SLA can also include non-functional requirements such as QoS or costs [17].

It is optimistic to say that once the collaboration is set, the business processes will not change. In fact, due to many factors; e.g., optimization, evolving business needs, changing laws (compliance), a process is often subject to change [6,9]. Different alternatives of change formulations (process changes) can correspond to the same business change. For example, due to a change of the marketing strategy, different approaches can be adopted, and consequently different process configurations.

In a collaboration, a change rarely confines itself to a single partner, but might lead to knock-on effects on the associated partners; i.e., change propagation. As set out in [7], change propagation is realized by following these three steps:

- Private-to-public propagation (Pr2Pu): Changes are propagated from the private process to the corresponding public process of the same partner. This has consequences on the public goal of the partner G_i.
- Public-to-public propagation (Pu2Pu): Changes are propagated to the affected partners; i.e. the effects on their public processes. This has consequences on the common business goal G and the public goals G_i of the affected partners.
- Public-to-private propagation (Pu2Pr): Changes are propagated to the corresponding private processes of the affected partners. This has consequences on the goals g_i

Due to the autonomy and independence of partners in a collaboration, change effects cannot be imposed on the partners, but must be agreed upon in a consensual way. Hence, a propagation to a partner might result in a potentially costly and time-consuming negotiation process.

In a collaboration, two constellations are possible: (i) all partners know each other (which entails a negotiation that involves all partners) (ii) some partners are only visible to a subset of partners, for example, in supply chains. Specifically, constellation (iii) entails P2P negotiations that involve only a subset of partner, or transitive negotiations. Consequently, with respect to the constellation, a full or P2P negotiation can be envisaged.

---

[1] Compare to different goals for process variants as described in, e.g., [21].

The arising research question is: How to find a collective decision on the concrete realization of a change propagation among the affected partners in a process collaboration in a fair and efficient way? A solution should specifically support the affected partners to choose from their set of possible change alternatives associated with respective goals g_i the best one for them given a fair and efficient solution for the entire choreography and its associated common goal G. Addressing this research question requires a synthesis of research from the field of group decisions and negotiations on the one hand, and process change on the other hand, which poses new challenges for both fields. The present paper aims at this synthesis. Although the paper thus integrates known results from both fields (in particular, well known concepts in the area of group decisions), this synthesis is still important. Firstly, the concepts presented here were, to the best of our knowledge, previously not considered in the area of process management. Furthermore, concepts from group decisions usually deal with abstract decision alternatives. In the present paper, we show how models of cooperative processes, and changes made both to public and private processes, can be mapped to the level of abstraction required by group decision models.

This paper presents models from group decision making that can be applied for handling change negotiations in process choreographies in an efficient and fair way. The theoretical models are evaluated based on a proof-of-concept prototype that integrates existing implementation for change propagation in process choreographies with change alternatives, utility functions, and group decision models. Based on simulating a realistic setting, the validity of the approach is shown. Our prototype supports the selection of change alternatives for each partner during negotiation that depending on the group decision model used, provide solutions emphasizing efficiency and/or fairness.

The remainder of the paper is structured as follows: Section 2 introduces change negotiation scenarios and describes a motivating example. Section 3 formalizes the problem of change negotiations in process choreographies and Section 4 introduces three evaluation approaches of change alternatives. Section 5 evaluates and analyzes the approaches through a prototype proof of concept. Finally, Section 6 describes the related work and Section 7 concludes the paper.

2   Change Negotiation Scenarios and Motivating Example

This section explains different negotiation scenarios and introduces a motivating example to illustrate the change negotiation problem.

2.1   Change Negotiation Scenarios

As aforementioned, change alternatives are derived from a set of possible process changes across partners, which could result from different scenarios. In particular, we can distinguish three different scenarios:

1. One partner (say partner A) has to make a mandatory change to its (private) processes, for example because of a change in legal requirements, which

renders the existing process impossible (e.g., because it now violates some new legal requirements). For this scenario, we assume that there is only one possible change to A's private process.

2. One partner initiates a change, either because of a change in the environment, or because the partners wants to change the process to improve it or to exploit a new business opportunity. In contrast to scenario 1 above, we assume for this scenario that there are several possible private changes of A, which are then propagated through the network. All possible change alternatives considered result from this propagation.

3. In addition to scenario 2, we now also assume that the other partner B responds to the propagated change proposals of A by proposing alternative changes to the public processes (which result from a propagation of changes to the private processes of B, that B develops in response to the changes proposed by A).

If each change in the private process of one partner results in exactly one possible change of the public process of that parter, and each change in the public process of one partner requires exactly one change in the public process of the other partner, then scenario 1 leads to a unique outcome at the group level and does not require any further negotiation between partners. The change in partner B's public process could still be implemented via several different changes in partner B's private processes. However, since these changes do not affect partner A, they do not need to be decided at the group level. As explained above, partner B can select the change to its private processes that on the one hand implements the required change to partner B's public processes, and on the other hand optimizes partner B's private goal.

In contrast, scenario 2 provides an opportunity for a real group decision. The different changes proposed by partner A will most likely not be exactly equivalent even to that partner. Although it is unlikely that one partner will propose a change which is extremely bad from that partner's perspective, one can expect partners to include change alternatives which are slightly worse to them than other proposals, in order to broaden the set of alternatives. Since the situation is not a zero sum game, it is possible to have some alternatives, which are better for all partners, and thus to have efficient alternatives and actually create value for both partners. However, since it can be difficult for one partner to estimate the full consequences of proposed changes for the other partner, it is quite likely that the range of outcomes present in the set of alternatives under discussion will be different for partners. Alternatives will likely be quite similar from the perspective of partner A initially triggering the change, but could vary considerably from the perspective of partner B (if some of these alternatives have very negative effects on partner B, of which partner A is initially not aware).

In particular in such a setting, the third scenario will likely take place, and partner B will also make some counter-proposals for changes to the public processes. These changes must then be propagated from B's public processes to A's public processes, and A must find changes in its private processes to implement them. Since B might also be unaware of the difficulties some of these changes will cause for A, it is to be expected that this set of alternatives will span a wider range of outcomes also for A compared to scenario 2 above.

If such counter-proposals are made, the entire set of process changes considered is the union of the set of changes proposed by A and those proposed by B. One can also imagine a situation in which the intersection of the proposals of both parties is considered. However, since this is a dynamic process, that would in fact mean that B is granted a veto on proposals made by A, he can eliminate them by not nominating them himself. In such a setting, it would not make sense for B to propose any change that has not already been proposed by A, since it would also not be contained in the intersection. Thus, using the intersection would lead to a quite narrow set of alternatives, which are very similar both from A's and from B's perspective. We thus consider an approach using the union of both sets of proposals to be more suitable to find creative solutions.

2.2 Motivating Example

Consider the collaboration scenario between a *bank* and an *insurance company* as shown in Fig. 1 to provide new services; e.g., retirement funds and financial consultancy. The collaboration combines expertise and customer base of both partners in order to increase the benefits in terms of reputation and marketshare; i.e., the **global goal** of the collaboration.

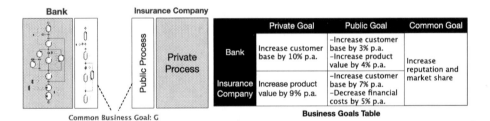

		Private Goal	Public Goal	Common Goal
Bank	Increase customer base by 10% p.a.	–Increase customer base by 3% p.a. –Increase product value by 4% p.a.	Increase reputation and market share
Insurance Company	Increase product value by 9% p.a.	–Increase customer base by 7% p.a. –Decrease financial costs by 5% p.a.	

Business Goals Table

Fig. 1. Process Collaboration: Example from Financial Domain

Each partner contributes to this global goal in a different way (through its public process), and aligns with a public goal. For example, the *bank* contributes through its financial expertise with the **public goal** of increasing its customer base by 3% p.a. and its product value by providing additional insurance offers. Similarly, the *insurance company* aims at increasing its customer base by 7% p.a. and reducing its financial costs through its partnership with the bank. Additionally, each of both partners holds a **private goal**, which is aligned with its private business process. For instance, one of the private goals for the *bank* constitutes an increase of the total customer base by 10% p.a., of which 3% is covered by this collaboration.

Now, we assume that the *bank* wants to apply a new marketing strategy through a categorization of its customers. This leads to a major change in the private process of the *bank*, by for example, creating a different procedure for each customer category; e.g., *gold category* customers receive additional insurance coverage and high saving interest rates. It should be noted that the implementation of this marketing strategy can be achieved in many ways (i.e., different alternatives). Each of these alternatives can directly affect the public model and consequently the collaboration with the *insurance company*. Similarly, each of them corresponds to a change alternative for the *insurance company*'s public process with a different impact on its public and private goals.

With respect to the multitude of choices; i.e., change alternatives, a negotiation process is required to decide on the changes to be implemented. The negotiation involves the *bank* and the *insurance*, which collectively try to find an alternative that is aligned with the common goal and the respective private and public goals. An evaluation of the alternative costs helps selecting a fair and efficient solution.

3   Problem Formulation

This section formalizes the problem of change negotiations in process choreographies.

3.1   Process Changes

We model possible process changes as discrete alternatives. Each such alternative represents a coherent change made to a public or private process model, and alternatives are exclusive in the sense that exactly one of the alternatives can be implemented. This implies that different variants of changing the process (even if they are different only on a small part of the total change) are considered as two different alternatives, and that maintaining the current process is also one of the alternatives (although it might have rather negative consequences, e.g., if due to a change in regulations the current process is no longer allowed and would lead to high fines).

We denote the j-th alternative for a change in partner i' *private* process by δ_i^j and the j-th alternative for a change in that partner's *public* process by σ_i^j. In the present paper, we only consider two actors $i \in \{A, B\}$.

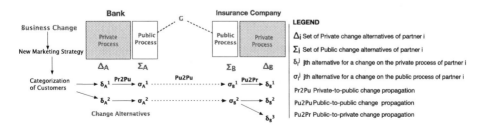

Fig. 2. Example from Financial Domain: Propagation and Negotiation Scenario

As described in the example from financial domain (cf. Figure 2), changes in the public and private processes of the same partner are not independent of each other. A change to the public process can possibly be implemented by different changes to the private process. We denote the set of possible changes to the private process, which can be used to implement change σ_i^j to the public process by $\Delta_j(\sigma_i^j)$.

3.2   Goals and Preferences

We distinguish three levels of goals in the model:

1. *Common goals G* refer to the goals of the collaboration. They depend only on the public process, and are shared by all partners.
2. *Public goals G_i* of partner i are goals which are relevant only to partner i, but of which all partners are aware, and which are also influenced only by the public processes.
3. *Private goals g_i* of partner i are also only relevant to partner i, and furthermore they are only known to that partner. Their fulfillment depends on the private and public processes of partner i, and could also be influenced by the public processes of the other partners.

For simplicity, we consider only one common goal, and one public and private goal per partner in this paper. Extension to multiple goals at each level is straightforward, but would increase the complexity of notation without providing much additional insight for the purpose of the present paper.

The dependence of these goals on changes to the public and private processes can thus be expressed as

$$G = G(\sigma_1^j, \sigma_2^j, \ldots, \sigma_N^j) \tag{1}$$

$$G_i = G_i(\sigma_i^j, \sigma_{-i}^j) \tag{2}$$

$$g_i = g_i(\delta_i^j, \sigma_i^j, \sigma_{-i}^j) \tag{3}$$

where $-i$ refers to all partners except partner i.

Only the private goal of a partner is influenced by changes to the private process of that partner. Thus we can always assume that a partner selects the change to its own private process, that best fulfills the private goal of the same partner.

$$\delta_i^j = \arg \max_{\delta_i^j} g_i(\delta_i^j, \sigma_i^j, \sigma_{-i}^j)$$

$$\text{s.t.} \tag{4}$$

$$\delta_i^j \in \Delta_j(\sigma_i^j)$$

Although this implies a sequence between changes to the public and the private processes in which the public process is changed first, this does not imply that the entire change process cannot be triggered by a change to the private process of one partner, only that final adjustments are to be made to the private process after fixing the public processes (cf. Section 2.1 above for details).

Consequently, the impact of changes on all goals (common goal, public and private goals of each partner) can be seen as being dependent on the changes to the public processes of all partners. The common decision problem of the partners thus consists in agreeing on a new set of public process models. Each design alternative, which can be considered by the partners, therefore consists of a vector of changes to each of the partner's public process model, which can be written as $(\sigma_i^j, \sigma_2^j, \ldots, \sigma_N^j)$, or more specifically in the case of two partners considered here as (σ_A^j, σ_B^j). For simplicity, we write this entire vector of changes as $\boldsymbol{\sigma} = (\sigma_i^j, \sigma_2^j, \ldots, \sigma_N^j)$

When evaluating possible process changes, each partner takes into account the common goal as well as its public and private goals. We represent this simultaneous overall evaluation of all goals via a multi-attribute utility function [14]

$$u_i = w_i^G v_i^G(G) + w_i^p v_i^p(G_i) + w_i^r v_i^r(g_i) \tag{5}$$

where w_i^G, w_i^p, and w_i^r refer to the weights which partner i assigns to the common goal, its own public goal and its own private goal, respectively, and $w_i^G + w_i^p + w_i^r = 1$. The functions v_i^G, v_i^p and v_i^r are the partial utility functions of that partner which transform these goals onto a common utility scale. For simplicity, we assume that these functions are linear and are scaled so that the worst possible outcome in each goal is assigned a partial utility value of zero and the best outcome in each goal is assigned a partial utility value of one. Thus, for the common goal, the partial utility function (which in that case is identical for all partners) is

$$v^G = \frac{G - \underline{G}}{\overline{G} - \underline{G}} \tag{6}$$

where $\overline{G}$ and $\underline{G}$ are the best and worst possible values of the common goal, respectively. Partial value functions for the other goals can be defined analogously.

Since outcomes in all goals depend on changes to the public process models, the total utility for each partner will also depend on these changes:

$$u_i(\boldsymbol{\sigma}) = w_i^G v_i^G(G(\boldsymbol{\sigma})) + w_i^p v_i^p(G_i(\boldsymbol{\sigma})) + w_i^r v_i^r(g_i(\boldsymbol{\sigma})) \tag{7}$$

Note that in (7), the first two terms refer to goals which are known to all partners, while the third term refers to partner i's private goal, which is not known to the other partner. Information provided by one partner about the utility it will achieve when a certain change to the public processes is implemented therefore is based on some information which the other partner cannot verify. This could create incentives to misrepresent the effect of changes on one's private goals (for example, to avoid a certain change, one could indicate that this change would be even more damaging to one's private goals than it really is). In this paper, we do not take into account this form of strategic behavior by the partners and assume that for the sake of maintaining a long term partnership, partners will refrain from such behavior.

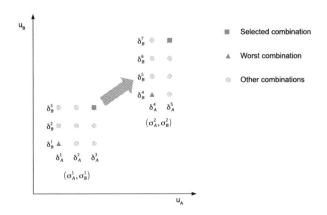

Fig. 3. Public and Private Process Changes and Utilities

Figure 3 illustrates the relationship between changes to private processes, changes to public processes, and utilities. The axes represent utilities of both partners. Consider the change to public processes indicated by (σ_A^1, σ_B^1). For this change in public processes, there are three possibilities to implement it in the private processes of A indicated as δ_A^1, δ_A^2 and δ_A^3. Since changes in A's private process only affect the utility of partner A, consequences of these changes are all located on a horizontal line. Similarly, we assume that there are also three possible changes to the private processes of B labeled δ_B^1, δ_B^2, and δ_B^3. In utility space, the consequences of these changes are located on a vertical line, so all possible combinations of changes to private processes are located in the grid shown in the lower left part of Figure 3. Assuming that each partner implements the change to its private processes which optimizes its own utility, the change to public processes indicated by (σ_A^1, σ_B^1) will lead to the upper right corner point of that grid, where the changes δ_A^3 and δ_B^3 are implemented. Similarly, another change to public processes (σ_A^2, σ_B^2) leads to another grid. Obviously, the number of changes to private processes of the partners which can implement a given change in public processes does not have to be the same neither across partners, nor across different changes to the public processes, so we show here only two private changes for partner A, but four for B. Still, assuming optimizing behavior of all partners, this set of changes to the public processes will lead to an evaluation corresponding the the upper right corner of the respective grid.

With respect to the example introduced in Section 2, Figure 4 summarizes the different change dependency graphs; i.e., propagation alternatives, as well as the corresponding cost graphs. A cost graph, uses the cost functions defined previously and a change propagation alternative in order to generate a cost alternative. The evaluation of an alternative cost depends on the adopted negotiation method; e.g., additive, Nash-bargaining, as will be defined in the next section.

	Alternative 1		Alternative 2		Alternative 3	
Propagation Graph	σ_A^1 ·········· σ_B^1 δ_A^1 δ_B^1		σ_A^2 ·········· σ_B^2 δ_A^2 δ_B^2		σ_A^2 ·········· σ_B^2 δ_A^2 δ_B^3	
Cost Graph	$G(\sigma_A^1, \sigma_B^1)$ $G_A(\sigma_A^1 \cdot \sigma_B^1)$ $G_B(\sigma_A^1 \cdot \sigma_B^1)$ $g_A(\delta_A^1, \sigma_A^1 \cdot \sigma_B^1)$ $g_B(\delta_B^1, \sigma_A^1 \cdot \sigma_B^1)$		$G(\sigma_A^2, \sigma_B^2)$ $G_A(\sigma_A^2 \cdot \sigma_B^2)$ $G_B(\sigma_A^2 \cdot \sigma_B^2)$ $g_A(\delta_A^2, \sigma_A^2, \sigma_B^2)$ $g_B(\delta_B^2, \sigma_A^2, \sigma_B^2)$		$G(\sigma_A^2, \sigma_B^2)$ $G_A(\sigma_A^2 \cdot \sigma_B^2)$ $G_B(\sigma_A^2 \cdot \sigma_B^2)$ $g_A(\delta_A^2, \sigma_A^2, \sigma_B^2)$ $g_B(\delta_B^3, \sigma_A^2, \sigma_B^2)$	

Fig. 4. Example from Financial Domain: Change Alternatives Table

4   Collective Decision

The partners have to jointly agree on a change $\sigma = (\sigma_A, \sigma_B)$ to the public processes. This is a decision situation in which the decision of each partner (the public process change of each partner) affects the outcome for all partners. Furthermore, these decisions are not independent of each other, since changes to the public processes of all partners must be compatible with each other. For example, if partner A changes its public process so that it no longer generates an output which is required from the entire process, then partner B must change its process so that it now provides that output. Such decision problems are often referred to as group decision problems, and are also studied in the field of cooperative game theory. In the following paragraphs, we will present several solution concepts from these fields for this type of problems.

In general, solutions to collective decision problems can be evaluated using the criteria of efficiency and fairness [29]. The approaches we survey below are based on systems of axioms, that describe the precise criteria of fairness and efficiency used, as well as the necessary trade-off between the two concepts.

Efficiency in the most general sense can be defined via the concept of Pareto-optimality. A solution is Pareto-optimal if no other solution exists, which would make at least one partner better off, and no partner worse off, than the solution under consideration [1]. Pareto-optimality can thus be defined if individual preferences are represented by rankings of alternatives. However, if preferences are only specified as rankings, Arrow's well known impossibility theorem [1] holds. This theorem indicates that no mapping from individual rankings to a group ranking exists, that in addition to Pareto optimality fulfills the conditions of universal domain (i.e., a group ranking is obtained for any profile of individual rankings), independence of irrelevant alternatives (i.e., the ranking of two alternatives in the group ranking does not depend on the availability of some other alternative), completeness and transitivity of the group ranking as well as the non-dictatorship condition (no group member uniquely determines the group's ranking).

In the preceding section, we have defined the evaluation of the partners for each possible package of changes to the public processes in terms of cardinal utilities to avoid this problem. In this setting, efficiency can be defined as maximizing the total output to the group, i,e. the sum of utilities. If, as defined above, utilities are all scaled between zero and one, then

$$Eff = \frac{1}{N} \sum_{i=1}^{N} u_i(\boldsymbol{\sigma}) \tag{8}$$

is an indicator of efficiency, which is scaled so that one indicates perfect efficiency.

Fairness refers to the balance of payoffs between the partners. In the case of two partners, fairness can be measured by contract imbalance, which is the difference in utilities between the partners:

$$F = 1 - |u_A(\boldsymbol{\sigma}) - u_B(\boldsymbol{\sigma})| \tag{9}$$

It can be shown that cardinal utilities can be aggregated in a way that is compatible with very similar requirements as Arrow's axioms [5,13]. A group utility function which fulfills these axioms is the additive function

$$\max U(\boldsymbol{\sigma}) = \sum_i w_i u_i(\boldsymbol{\sigma_i}) \tag{10}$$

where w_i is a weight assigned to member i's preferences in the group. The additive structure of the group utility function implies that utilities of different members are perfectly substitutable. Additive group utilities, which are sometimes also referred to as utilitarian solutions [15], therefore exclusively focus on efficiency.

In contrast, solution concepts from cooperative game theory also take fairness into account. The best known solution concept of cooperative game theory is the *Nash bargaining solution* [18], which selects the alternative that maximizes

$$\max N(\boldsymbol{\sigma}) = \prod_i (u_i(\boldsymbol{\sigma}) - d_i) \tag{11}$$

where $u_i(\boldsymbol{\sigma})$ is again the utility which partner i assigns to the proposed set of process changes, and d_i is partner i's utility for the *disagreement point*, i.e. the solution that would obtain if the partners did not agree on some alternative. For the problem at hand, the disagreement point can be interpreted as a situation in which no change takes place and thus the current processes continue to be used.

The Nash bargaining solution is based on the following set of axioms [18]:

1. Independence of linear transformation of utilities:
   The solution remains the same, when any individual utility function is changed by a linear transformation.
2. Pareto condition:
   The solution is not dominated by another feasible solution.
3. Symmetry:
   If both partners are symmetric (i.e. for each possible alternative, there exists another alternative in which payoffs to partners are exchanged), they receive the same payoff in the solution.

4. Independence of irrelevant alternatives:
   If some alternatives other than the solution are eliminated from the set of alternatives, the solution stays the same.

The axiom of symmetry introduces some notion of fairness to the Nash bargaining solution. Still, it can be shown that among comparable solutions, the Nash bargaining solution puts a comparatively high weight on efficiency [22]. Another important characteristic of the Nash solution for our problem is independence of linear transformation of utilities. Although one might argue that consequences of process changes for firms can usually be evaluated in terms of money, even monetary consequences could have a different relevance for the partners involved. The same absolute amount might be a significantly higher financial burden for a comparatively small firm than for a large corporation. In the additive model (10), such differences would have to be taken into account by assigning different weights w_i to partners.

In literature, independence of irrelevant alternatives is often seen as a problematic axiom [11,16]. One can argue that the bargaining power of a partner depends on which alternatives are available. Consider a situation in which the solution gives to each partner a payoff which is approximately in the middle of the range of possible payoffs for that partner. Then suddenly, all alternatives which would be better than that solution for one partner become unavailable. Because of independence of irrelevant alternatives, the Nash bargaining solution would still give both partners the same payoff as before, which is now the best outcome for one partner, but only an average outcome for the other one. This could be considered unfair. Since the axiom does not cover the case that new alternatives are added, it is even possible to construct examples in which alternatives are added which are better for both parties, but one partner receives less than in the solution of the original problem.

The Raiffa-Kalai-Smorodinski (RKS) solution [11,16] replaces the axiom of independence of irrelevant alternatives by the axiom of monotonicity. This axiom states that if a problem is extended by alternatives which dominate the solution of the original problem, then the new solution must also dominate the previous solution (i.e. no partner must be worse off, and at least one partner must be strictly better off in the new solution). The RKS solution maximizes the payoff to the partner whose utility is smallest. It therefore follows the principle of egalitarism by considering the partner who is worst off [15].

Considering just the minimum of utilities would introduce a dependence on the scaling of utilities. This problem can easily be avoided by scaling the utilities of all partners so that for each partner, the best feasible outcome is assigned a utility of one. The RKS solution can thus be represented as [16]

$$\max K(\boldsymbol{\sigma}) = \min_i \frac{u_i(\boldsymbol{\sigma})}{\max_{\boldsymbol{\sigma} \in \Sigma} u_i(\boldsymbol{\sigma})} \tag{12}$$

A similar transformation can also be applied to the additive model (10). Note, however, that it leads to a violation of the axiom of independence of irrelevant alternatives, since the transformed utilities of each partner now depend on the availability of the best solution for each partner.

All three solutions can be interpreted as special cases of a general α-fair social welfare function [4]

$$A(\boldsymbol{\sigma}) = \sum_i \frac{u_i(\boldsymbol{\sigma})^{1-\alpha}}{1-\alpha} \tag{13}$$

For $\alpha = 0$, (13) corresponds to (10), for $\alpha \to 1$, it approaches the Nash bargaining solution (11) and for $\alpha = \infty$, it corresponds to (12).

5   Implementation and Analysis

This work has been integrated into an existing change propagation framework [6] that is able to simulate various choreography settings for stress testing change propagations. This simulation framework served as the basis for ensuring the correctness of the change propagation algorithms [6], as well as the data source for devising a change mining algorithm for change prediction [8]. In the context of this work, we have extended the change propagation framework by designing and implementing a new package for simulating change negotiation scenarios using the mathematical models described in the previous section. Concretely, we have implemented the *additive, Nash bargaining* and the *RKS* solutions.

As a sample scenario we have implemented the example shown in figure 1 consisting of the two partners: *bank* and *insurance*. Although this example consists of only two partners, we have kept the implementation as generic as possible, being able to generate change propagation scenarios consisting of an unlimited number of partners. The restriction to two partners is kept in this paper to be able to graphically illustrate the results of the resulting negotiation outcome.

Using the change propagation framework, several change scenarios have been generated. The effects of each change on the different partners is calculated through the same framework. Each change and its effects is considered as an alternative and is associated with a cost. The basis of choice during the change negotiation is represented by a single change propagation alternative, as can be seen in the *Change Alternatives Cost Table* in Fig. 4. An alternative is defined as a unique pair of private changes, with their associated public changes. Since goals and costs, especially private ones, require intimate details of partners during a negotiation example, we have opted to estimate both private and public costs in our simulation by randomizing their values in the range [0..1]. Each partner's utility is then derived based on these private as well public random costs. As we want to compare the group ranking functions themselves, even random values should allow correct rankings, and highlight the most fair and effective change negotiation alternatives.

The following table 1 illustrates parts of the extracted log file after a complete change negotiation simulation. Each row represents the ranking of a single alternative, where the alternative is represented by the partner utilities: *Bank*

Table 1. Negotiation Log sample

Bank (U)	Insurance (U)	Scoring Function	Score Value
0.3729	0.4785	Additive	0.4257
0.3729	0.4785	Nash-Bargaining	0.1784
0.3729	0.4785	RKS	0.7793
0.3729	0.3861	Additive	0.3795
0.3729	0.3861	Nash-Bargaining	0.1439
0.3729	0.3861	RKS	0.9658

Utility and *Insurance Utility.* The associated score value shows the outcome of applying the respective ranking function. In this particular instance, the highest score is attained with the alternative where the *Bank*'s utility is measured at 0.3729 and the associated *Insurance*'s utility at 0.3861 with the final *RKS* score of 0.9658. This alternative is higher ranked compared to the next best alternative (with *Insurance*'s utility at 0.4785) due to the fairness criteria, which prefers alternatives where both partner utilities do not stray away too far from each other.

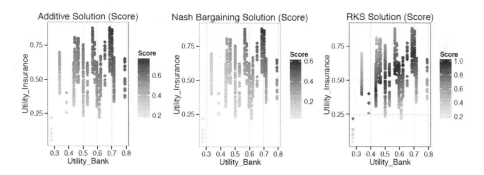

Fig. 5. Decision options for multiple propagation scenario

For evaluating the group ranking functions, we have taken the complete negotiation log as described in table 1 and visualized in Fig. 5. The charts are split into the three group ranking functions, each highlighting the final ranking score of all alternatives. A change negotiation scenario is represented as one vertical line with the corresponding alternatives. The x-axis depicts the *Bank*'s utility while the y-axis depicts the *Insurance* utility values. The final ranking score is represented in the hue of the color of a unique point representing one alternative. The darker the color, the better ranked are the alternatives. As can be seen in the charts, the *additive* solution seems to prefer *efficient* solutions, while disregarding fairness. This can be identified by the grouping of the black points

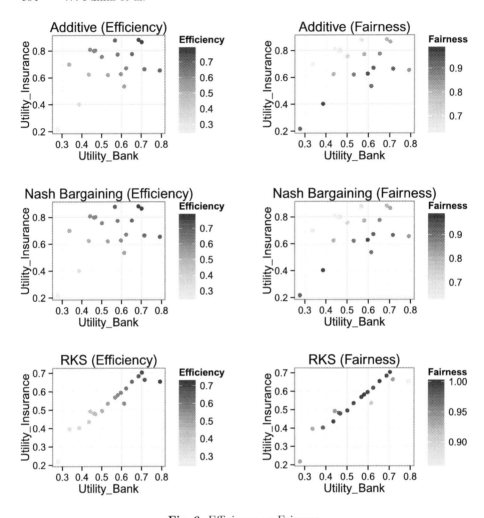

Fig. 6. Efficiency vs Fairness

as alternatives on the upper half of the chart for the *additive* ranking function chart. This is due to the behaviour of the *additive* function, which ranks alternatives with increasing partner utilities higher, without considering the difference between the utilities; i.e., fairness (cf. Equation 10). Similarly, the *Nash Bargaining* solution also prefers *efficient* solutions, and disregards those that are considered unfair. This behavior can be identified by the dark colors grouped in the upper-right hand corner of the respective chart. This can be explained by the multiplication of partner utilities (cf. Equation 11). Finally, the *RKS* solution seems to prefer more balanced alternatives to the other solutions, as the black colored points form a diagonal line from the bottom left to the upper-right corner of the chart. Indeed the *RKS* function chooses alternatives with less spread between partner utilities (cf. Equation 12).

Figure 6 shows the behavior of the best alternatives of each negotiation scenario generated by each negotiation function. In particular, it classifies these alternatives with respect to their efficiency and fairness (cf. Equations 8, 9). Both the *additive* and *Nash bargaining* functions pick up similar best alternatives per scenario for both *efficiency* and *fairness*.

In contrast, the *RKS* function selects the most fair solutions as best alternatives, which are not necessarily efficient. This is shown through the color difference between the *efficiency* and the *fairness* graphs. For example, for *utility_bank* = 0.5 and *utility_insurance* = 0.5 the fairness in the *RKS* is superior to 0.95, while the efficiency is less than 0.5. The same alternative is not picked up as best solution by both the *additive* and *Nash bargaining* functions.

6 Related Work

The research presented in this paper integrates three areas, i.e., process choreographies, change and change propagation, and collective decision making through negotiations. In each of the areas, a multitude of research questions and approaches exist. Hence, the following discussion will concentrate on the interfaces between the areas.

Change propagation in process choreographies has been addressed by different approaches as shown in a recent survey [7]. In [6,8], the process of changing a process choreography is outlined and mentions negotiations as building block of this process. However, the approaches [6,8] focus on structural correctness of changes and the prediction of change impacts, but have not addressed the negotiation of changes so far. [9,27] deals with correctness and consistency during change propagation as well, but does not focus on negotiation aspects.

In the web service area in general, negotiation is part of the service discovery phase [23]. Negotiation has also been identified as part of building process choreographies, specifically for contracting [20] and the interface design [19,26]. Moreover, negotiation protocols and strategies have been offered in the context of service level agreements between different partners, e.g., [10].

Although the solution concepts we presented in this paper, and the trade-off between fairness and efficiency which they represent, are well known concepts in the areas of collective decision making, the present problem also provides some innovative aspects for that field. Models of collective decision making usually assume that group members have a direct evaluation of the alternatives under discussion, or in some cases describe the underlying preference structure of group members by referring to risk or to separate attributes of the decision alternatives. e.g.,[12,24]. The situation we are considering here is different because of the hierarchical relationship between public and private process models. This hierarchical structure allows partners to adapt their private processes, within the boundaries of the public process, to optimally fulfill their own private goals. Although we have shown that the model can ultimately be mapped back to one in which the collective decision determines the outcome for each partner, this is still an important extension to standard models of collective decision making.

In [3], State Charts are proposed to capture different e-negotiation models as business processes. Moreover, it is described how these models can be mapped onto BPEL models for web service orchestrations. The difference to the work at hand is that neither choreographies nor changes have been considered. Moreover, [3] focuses on e-negotiation protocols such as Dutch auction.

Overall, to the best of our knowledge, an approach that addresses the interfaces between all three areas, i.e., process choreographies, change, and negotiation, has not been proposed so far.

7   Conclusion

In a collaborative environment, changes to business processes are not confined to one partner, but have to be propagated through the processes of several partners. Since such changes affect the performance of processes of all involved partners, a collective decision problem arises.

In the present paper, we have raised the question whether models and methods from various theories of collective decision making can help to find a joint solution to this problem. The methods we studied in this paper clearly show the central dilemma of collective decision making, that is to find a balance between efficiency and fairness. Depending on how this trade-off is resolved, different solution concepts can be recommended.

One important assumption made in this paper is that all partners provide correct and truthful information about the possible impact of process changes on their public goals and utilities. While this assumption seems reasonable in a cooperative environment characterized by a high level of mutual trust, there is still the possibility that not all partners behave in that way, and some might at least slightly distort information in order to reach a solution that better fits with their own interest. Analyzing the effects of such strategic behavior thus leads to additional questions, that need to be addressed in future research.

Although the models we have discussed in this paper provide normatively appealing and axiomatically founded solutions to group decision problems, they do not describe the actual negotiation process by which such solutions can be reached. Future research thus needs to address this problem from a more dynamic perspective and include the actual bargaining process between partners that might be involved in finding a solution. Addressing these issues could eventually extend the first steps taken in this paper towards a directly applicable framework for collectively evaluating and choosing changes to process choreographies in an efficient and fair way.

Acknowledgments. The work presented in this paper has been conducted within the C^3Pro project funded by the Austrian Science Fund (FWF): I743.

References

1. Arrow, K.J.: Social Choice and Individual Values, 2nd edn. Yale University Press, New Haven (1963)
2. Barros, A., Dumas, M., Oaks, P.: Standards for web service choreography and orchestration: status and perspectives. In: Bussler, C.J., Haller, A. (eds.) BPM 2005. LNCS, vol. 3812, pp. 61–74. Springer, Heidelberg (2006)
3. Benyoucef, M., Rinderle, S.: Modeling e-negotiation processes for a service oriented architecture. Group Decision and Negotiation 15(5), 449–467 (2006)
4. Bertsimas, D., Farias, V.F., Trichakis, N.: On the efficiency-fairness trade-off. Management Science 58(12), 2234–2250 (2012)
5. Dyer, J.S., Sarin, R.K.: Group preference aggregation rules based on strength of preference. Management Science 25, 822–832 (1979)
6. Fdhila, W., Indiono, C., Rinderle-Ma, S., Reichert, M.: Dealing with change in process choreographies: Design and implementation of propagation algorithms. Information Systems 49, 1–24 (2015)
7. Fdhila, W., Knuplesch, D., Rinderle-Ma, S., Reichert, M.: Change and compliance in collaborative processes. In: Services Computing. IEEE (2015)
8. Fdhila, W., Rinderle-Ma, S., Indiono, C.: Memetic algorithms for mining change logs in process choreographies. In: Franch, X., Ghose, A.K., Lewis, G.A., Bhiri, S. (eds.) ICSOC 2014. LNCS, vol. 8831, pp. 47–62. Springer, Heidelberg (2014)
9. Grossmann, G., Mafazi, S., Mayer, W., Schrefl, M., Stumptner, M.: Change propagation and conflict resolution for the co-evolution of business processes. International Journal of Cooperative Information Systems 24(01) (2015)
10. Hani, A.F.M., Paputungan, I.V., Hassan, M.F.: Renegotiation in service level agreement management for a cloud-based system. ACM Computing Surveys (CSUR) 47(3), 51 (2015)
11. Kalai, E., Smorodinsky, M.: Other solutions to Nash's bargaining problem. Econometrica 43(3), 513–518 (1975)
12. Keeney, R.L.: Foundations for group decision analysis. Decision Analysis 10(2), 103–120 (2013)
13. Keeney, R.L., Kirkwood, C.W.: Group decision making using cardinal social welfare functions. Management Science 22, 430–437 (1975)
14. Keeney, R.L., Raiffa, H.: Decisions with Multiple Objectives: Preferences and Value Tradeoffs. J. Wiley & Sons, New York (1976)
15. Konow, J.: Which is the fairest one of all? A positive analysis of justice theories. Journal of Economic Literature 41, 1188–1239 (2003)
16. Livne, Z.A.: Axiomatic charaterizations of the Raiffa and the Kalai-Smorodinsky solutions to the bargaining problem. Operations Research 37(6), 972–980 (1989)
17. Ludwig, H., Keller, A., Dan, A., King, R., Franck, R.: A service level agreement language for dynamic electronic services. Electronic Commerce Research 3(1–2), 43–59 (2003)
18. Nash, J.F.: The bargaining problem. Econometrica 18(2), 155–162 (1950)
19. Papazoglou, M.: Web services: principles and technology. Pearson Education (2008)
20. Paurobally, S., Tamma, V., Wooldridge, M.: A framework for web service negotiation. ACM Transactions on Autonomous and Adaptive Systems (TAAS) 2(4), 14 (2007)
21. Ponnalagu, K., Narendra, N.C., Ghose, A., Chiktey, N., Tamilselvam, S.: Goal oriented variability modeling in service-based business processes. In: Basu, S., Pautasso, C., Zhang, L., Fu, X. (eds.) ICSOC 2013. LNCS, vol. 8274, pp. 499–506. Springer, Heidelberg (2013)

22. Rachmilevitch, S.: The Nash solution is more utilitarian than egalitarian. Theory and Decision, pp. 1–16 (2014)
23. Roman, D., Keller, U., Lausen, H., de Bruijn, J., Lara, R., Stollberg, M., Polleres, A., Feier, C., Bussler, C., Fensel, D., et al.: Web service modeling ontology. Applied ontology **1**(1), 77–106 (2005)
24. Sarabando, P., Dias, L.C., Vetschera, R.: Mediation with incomplete information: Approaches to suggest potential agreements. Group Decision and Negotiation **22**(3), 561–597 (2013)
25. Schulte, S., Schuller, D., Steinmetz, R., Abels, S.: Plug-and-play virtual factories. IEEE Internet Computing **5**, 78–82 (2012)
26. Traverso, P., Pistore, M., Roveri, M., Marconi, A., Kazhamiakin, R., Lucchese, P., Busetta, P., Bertoli, P.: Supporting the negotiation between global and local business requirements in service oriented development. In: Proceedings of the 2nd International Conference on Service Oriented Computing, New York, USA (2004)
27. van der Aalst, W.M.P.: Inheritance of interorganizational workflows: How to agree to disagree without loosing control? Information Technology and Management **4**(4), 345–389 (2003)
28. Weske, M.: Business process management: concepts, languages, architectures. Springer Science & Business Media (2012)
29. Zukerman, M., Mammadov, M., Tan, L., Ouveysi, I., Andrew, L.L.H.: To be fair or efficient or a bit of both. Computers and Operations Research **35**, 3787–3806 (2008)

Real-Time Relevance Matching
of News and Tweets

Sei Onishi[1]($\boxtimes$), Yuto Yamaguchi[2], and Hiroyuki Kitagawa[3]

[1] Graduate School of Systems and Information Engineering,
University of Tsukuba, Tsukuba, Japan
`sei0024@kde.cs.tsukuba.ac.jp`
[2] Center for Computational Sciences, University of Tsukuba, Tsukuba, Japan
`yuto@kde.cs.tsukuba.ac.jp`
[3] Faculty of Engineering Information and Systems,
University of Tsukuba, Tsukuba, Japan
`kitagawa@cs.tsukuba.ac.jp`

Abstract. Given a news article, how many tweets are relevant to it in Twitter? Can we continuously collect only such tweets in real-time? In this paper, we propose a method for matching news articles and tweets in real-time. By collecting tweets relevant to news articles, we can get reactions to news articles such as sentiments and opinions from Twitter users. Our contributions are two-fold: (a) flexibility: our method collects the appropriate number of tweets for various kinds of news articles, each of which has the different number of tweets that mention it. (b) efficiency: our method can reduce the update time of an inverted index which is used for efficient matching of news articles and tweets. Also, we experimentally demonstrate the effectiveness of our method on streams of news articles and tweets from Yahoo!News and Twitter, respectively. We use the area under the ROC curve (AUC) to compare the accuracy of our method and that of baselines. The comparison shows that the AUC of our method is higher than that of the baselines by up to 22.7%. Furthermore, our method can update its index about 10 times faster compared to the existing technique.

1 Introduction

Given a news article, how many tweets are relevant to it in Twitter? Can we continuously collect only such tweets in real-time? In this paper, we propose a method for real-time matching of news articles and tweets. By collecting tweets relevant to news articles, we can get reactions to news articles such as sentiments and opinions from Twitter users. These reactions can be used for various analyses of the news article (e.g., sentiment analysis and opinion mining [11] [1] [8]). Therefore, it is important to collect tweets relevant to news articles.

Figure 1 shows the inputs and outputs of our method. The matching problem is informally stated as follows: **given** news articles and tweets, **find** tweets which are relevant to news articles. Relevant tweets to a news article are defined as tweets that mention this news article.

© Springer International Publishing Switzerland 2015
C. Debruyne et al. (Eds.): OTM 2015 Conferences, LNCS 9415, pp. 109–126, 2015.
DOI: 10.1007/978-3-319-26148-5_7

Challenges. There are two challenges, which we tackle in this paper: (a) *Different popularity of each news article*; in general, each news article has different popularity depending on the news content. Hence, the number of tweets relevant to a news article is different for each news article, which requires to collect the appropriate number of tweets for each news article. (b) *Flood of news articles and tweets*; a large amount of news articles and tweets are published in real-time. Hence, an efficient approach which handles such news articles and tweets arriving as a flood is needed.

Present Work. In this paper, we propose a method that matches news articles and tweets, to tackle the aforementioned challenges. Our method continuously receives streams of news articles and tweets as inputs, and then outputs the matching results between those news articles and tweets in real-time. The matching of news articles and tweets is based on the similarity between the contents of news articles and of tweets.

As we mentioned, the number of relevant tweets for each news article is greatly different. Popular news articles have a large number of relevant tweets, while unpopular news articles have a small number of relevant tweets. To address this problem, we predict the potential number of relevant tweets for each news article by using the tweets that are posted before the publication of news articles. This flexibility results in a better matching because we get a large number of relevant tweets for popular news articles while we get a small number of relevant tweets for unpopular news articles. The existing method [15] that collects top-k relevant tweets for all news articles does not have this flexibility.

In addition, our method efficiently handles news articles and tweets revising the existing method [15]. The existing method efficiently matches news articles and tweets by using an inverted index of news articles with tree structures. However, updating the index with tree structures are computationally expensive. To solve this problem, our method efficiently matches news articles and tweets by using a simple index which does not have an additional structure. Hence, our method can reduce the update time of the index compared with the existing method.

Contributions. In summary, our main contributions are as follows:

1. Flexibility: Our method collects the appropriate number of tweets for various kinds of news articles, each of which has the different number of tweets that mention it.
2. Efficiency: Our method can reduce the update time of an inverted index which is used for efficient matching of news articles and tweets.

We experimentally demonstrate the effectiveness of our method on streams of news articles and tweets from Yahoo!News and Twitter, respectively. We use the area under the ROC curve (AUC) [5] to compare the accuracy of our method and that of baselines. The comparison shows that the AUC of our method is higher than that of the baselines by up to 22.7%. Furthermore, our method can update its index about 10 times faster compared to the existing technique.

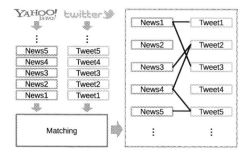

Fig. 1. Input and output: Streams of news articles and tweets are continuously received as input and the matching results between those news articles and tweets are outputted.

2   Related Work

In this section, we briefly review the related work on Twitter.

Analysis of Twitter. Kwak et al. [7] analyzed Twitter from several perspectives and reported that the majority of trending topics shared on Twitter are headline news articles or persistent news articles. Petrovic et al. [12] showed Twitter covers the most of the events that are published by newswire providers. Hu et al. [6] analyzed a news spread on Twitter, and they showed Twitter has great potential in news reporting. Osborne and Dredze [10] showed that Twitter is a more preferred medium than Facebook or Google Plus if we want to share the breaking news.

News and Twitter. Shi et al. [14] connected news articles and Twitter conversations by using hashtags. Our method differs from their approach, since our method takes into account the similarity between the contents of a news article and a tweet. As the most related study, we would mention Shraer et al. [15]. They proposed a top-k publish-subscribe approach with tweets in real-time. Their approach maintains the current top-k tweets that have largest similarity for each news article. However, each news article has different popularity depending on the news content. In our method, in order to collect the appropriate number of tweets for each news article, we determine a different threshold value of similarity for each news article.

Potential of Twitter. Tweets are often used for various kinds of analyses such as sentiment analysis and opinion mining [11] [1] [8] [2]. Meanwhile, by using tweets, the summarization of specific topics has been studied in a number of works [13] [4] [9] [3]. If we can collect tweets related to a news article, it is possible that we perform sentiment analysis, opinion mining, and the summarization about news articles using tweets.

3 Problem Formulation

This section defines some terminologies and formulates the problem of matching news articles and tweets. Let m be a tweet, s be a news article, and w be a word. Tweet m and news article s are defined as a set of words. A set of tweets and a set of news articles are denoted as M and S, respectively. The number of occurrences of word w in tweet m (news article s) is denoted as $n(m, w)$ $(n(s, w))$. These symbols are listed in Table 1.

Table 1. Symbols and Definitions

Symbols	Definitions
w	Word
m	Set of words in a tweet
M	Set of tweets
$n(m, w)$	The number of w in a tweet m
s	Set of words in a news article
S	Set of news articles
$n(s, w)$	The number of w in a news article s

Using these terminologies, the problem of matching news articles and tweets is formulated as follows:

Problem. (Matching news articles and tweets)

Given: set of news articles S and set of tweets M,
Find: subset of tweets $M' \subset M$ that is relevant to each news article s in S.

Relevant tweets to a news article are defined as the tweets that mention this news article.

4 Existing Techniques

In this section, we describe a *top-k publish-subscribe (Top-k pub-sub)* approach for news articles and tweets. The top-k pub-sub maintains the current top-k tweets for each news article. Shraer et al. [15] proposed the top-k pub-sub called *DAAT for pub-sub (DAAT)* and *DAAT for pub-sub with skipping (DAAT-skip)*. DAAT is a basic approach for the top-k pub-sub, and DAAT-skip is the efficient DAAT approach. We describe DAAT in Section 4.1 and DAAT-skip in Section 4.2.

4.1 DAAT for Pub-Sub

This section describes DAAT, which is a basic approach of top-k pub-sub. When a new tweet is published, DAAT decides whether the new tweet is inserted into the current top-k tweets of each news article. Each news article has the threshold that is the similarity of the current k-th tweet and the news article. If the similarity of the new tweet and the news article is larger than the threshold, the current k-th tweet is removed, and then the new tweet is inserted into the current top-k.

Approach. DAAT calculates the similarity of a news article and a tweet by using an inverted index called a *story index*. The story index is an inverted index composed of posting lists $L_1, L_2, ..., L_n$ where n is the number of indexed words. Posting list L_i for word w consists of pairs of a news article ID and a *partial score*. The partial score is the contribution of word w_i in a news article to the similarity. For example, Shrear et al. [15] uses the similarity that is a variant of cosine similarity as follows:

$$sim(s, m) = \sum_{w \in s \cup m} n(m, w) \cdot idf^2(w) \cdot \sqrt{\frac{n(s, w)}{|s|}} \tag{1}$$

where $idf(w) = 1 + \log\left(\frac{|S|}{1 + |\{s \in S | n(s,w) > 0\}|}\right)$ is inverse document frequency of word w in news articles. In this case, partial score $ps(s, w)$ is $idf^2(w) \cdot \sqrt{\frac{n(s,w)}{|s|}}$. By using the story index, DAAT computes the similarity of a new tweet and each news article in the ascending order of news article ID.

Algorithm. Algorithm 1 is a pseudo-code of DAAT, excerpted from [15]. When a new tweet m arrives, it checks the posting lists for words included in m. Current positions are initialized as the first entry of posting list of word w_i (lines 2–3). Among the current positions, we pick up a news article with the smallest ID (line 5). The similarity is calculated between the news article with the ID and the new tweet m (line 9), and then the corresponding current positions are advanced to next entries (line 10). If the similarity is larger than the threshold for the news article with the ID, the current k-th tweet is removed, and the new tweet is inserted into the current top-k (lines 11–15).

Algorithm 1. DAAT [15]

Input : Index of S, Tweet m
Input : $R_{s_1}, R_{s_2}, ..., R_{s_n}$ – min-heaps of size k for all news articles in S
Output: Updated min-heaps $R_{s_1}, R_{s_2}, ..., R_{s_n}$

1 Let $L_{w_1}, L_{w_2}, ..., L_{w_n}$ be the posting lists of words in m
2 **for** $i \in [1, 2, ..., |m|]$ **do**
3   Reset the current position in L_{w_i} to the first entry

4 **while** *not all lists exhausted* **do**
5    $s \leftarrow \min_{1 \le i \le |m|} L_{w_i}.cur$
6    $sim \leftarrow 0$
7   **for** $i \in [1, 2, ..., |m|]$ **do**
8   **if** $L_{w_i}.cur = s$ **then**
9        $sim \leftarrow sim + n(m, w_i) \cdot L_{w_i}.curPs$
10   Advance by 1 the current position in L_{w_i}

11    $\mu_s \leftarrow$ min. similarity of a tweet in R_s if $|R_s| = k$, 0 otherwise
12   **if** $\mu_s < sim$ **then**
13   **if** $|R_s| = k$ **then**
14   Remove the least similarity tweet from R_s
15   Add (m, sim) to R_s

16 **return** $R_{s_1}, R_{s_2}, ..., R_{s_n}$

Fig. 2. Example of DAAT: This is an example that matches a new tweet m containing five words $w_1, \ldots, w_5$ and seven news articles $s_1, \ldots, s_7$ by using DAAT. Each news article has a threshold that is the similarity of its k-th tweet.

Example. Figure 2 is an example of processing of DAAT. The example matches seven news articles $s_1, \ldots, s_7$ and a new tweet m containing five words $w_1, \ldots, w_5$. Each news article has a threshold that is the similarity of its k-th tweet.

Current positions are initialized to the first entries of posting lists (the white arrows of solid line in Figure 2). Then we pick up a news article for the similarity computation: The news article IDs at the current positions are s_1, s_2, and s_3. Thus news article s_1 is selected. By using the partial scores, the similarity can be computed as $2 + 3 = 5$ (for the sake of simplicity, the contribution of tweets is ignored here). The current positions pointing news article s_1 are advanced to the next entries (the white arrows of dotted line in Figure 2). Subsequently, the similarity is compared to the threshold of the corresponding news article. Since the similarity (5) is less than the threshold (30), the tweet is not inserted into the top-k of news article s_1. DAAT repeats the above procedure until all news articles are processed.

4.2   DAAT for Pub-Sub with Skipping

This section describes DAAT-skip, which reduces the number of similarity calculation by using the upper bound of similarity of a news article and a tweet.

Main Idea. The upper bound can be calculated by summing the maximum contributions of words that appear in both the news article and the tweet. The maximum contribution of word w_i is scored by using the posting list of word w_i as follows:

$$UB(w_i) = \alpha_{w_i} \cdot \max_{s \in L_{w_i}} ps(s, w_i) \qquad (2)$$

where α_{w_i} is the contribution of word w_i in a tweet (e.g., $\alpha_{w_i} = n(m, w_i)$ in the case of Equation 1). Thus, the upper bound of similarity between news article s and tweet m is expressed as follows:

$$UB(s, m) = \sum_{w_i \in s \cap m} UB(w_i) \geq sim(s, m)$$

Hence, we do not require to calculate the similarity between a tweet and news articles that have thresholds larger than $UB(s, m)$.

Approach. In order to reduce the calculation cost of upper bounds of similarity, DAAT-skip is processed in the following procedure. First, posting lists are sorted by news article identifiers at the current positions in ascending order. Then, we look for news articles meeting the following condition:

$$\sum_{j \leq i} UB(w_j) \leq \mu_s \tag{3}$$

where μ_s is the threshold of news article s in list L_i. We select the pivot story that is the news article with smallest identifier from those news articles, and define the list that contain pivot story as pivot list. If the news article identifier of the current position of L_1 and the news article identifier of the current position of the pivot list are same, we calculate similarity of the tweet and the news article and consider for insertion into the current top-k tweets of the news article. Otherwise, the current positions of $L_1, ..., L_{i-1}$ are advanced to positions of news articles whose identifiers are equal or greater than the pivot story identifier.

Shraer et al. [15] maintain a balanced binary tree for each posting list to efficiently find news articles that meet the aforementioned condition in formula (3). On the other hand, it may take a long time to update a story index, because it need to update both the posting list and the balanced binary tree.

5   Proposed Method

In this section, we describe our method that matches news articles and tweets. Figure 3 shows the overview of our method. When a news article is published, our method predicts an appropriate threshold of similarity for the news article by using *prior tweets*. Prior tweets of a news article are the tweets published before the publication of the news article. Then, we update the story index by adding the news article with the threshold. When a tweet is posted, we calculate the similarity of the tweet and each news article by using a story index. If the tweet has a similarity greater than the threshold of a news article, the tweet is decided to be relevant to the news article. In our method, we use a similarity measure based on Shraer's similarity [15] (Equation 1):

$$sim(s, m) = \sum_{w \in s \cup m} I(m, w) \cdot idf^2(w) \cdot \sqrt{\frac{n(s, w)}{|s|}} \tag{4}$$

$$I(m, w) = \begin{cases} 1, & \text{if } w \in m \\ 0, & \text{otherwise} \end{cases}$$

where $idf(w)$ is the same as Shraer's similarity. (we call Equation 4 *proposed similarity*). We describe the effectiveness of proposed similarity in Section 6.

The proposed method consists of the following two steps:

1. **Predicting threshold:** When a news article is published, our method predicts an appropriate threshold for the news article by using prior tweets.
2. **Matching:** When a tweet is posted, our method efficiently matches news articles and the tweet by using a story index.

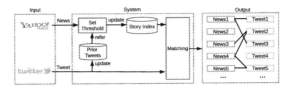

Fig. 3. Overview of our method: This figure shows the flow of the process of our method. Given a news article, our method sets the threshold of similarity for the news article. Then, we update the story index by adding the news article with the threshold. Given a tweet, using the story index, news articles having greater similarity are matched and outputted.

5.1   Predicting Threshold

In this section, we describe the method of predicting a threshold of similarity for a news article. When a news article is published, our method predicts the threshold by using prior tweets. The threshold is used to match the news article and a new tweet: If a similarity of the new tweet and the news article is larger than the threshold, we maintain the tweet for the news article.

Main Idea. We describe our method by using an example. Figure 4 shows the distributions of similarity of tweets for a news article in NEWS30 (described in Section 6). The x-axis shows the publication time of a tweet, when the publication time of the news article is zero. The y-axis shows the similarity of the news article and a tweet. A point shows the similarity of each tweet, and red points show the similarity of relevant tweets in RELEVANT (described in Section 6). Figure 4(a) illustrates the distribution of similarity of prior tweets, and Figure 4(b) depicts that of *posterior tweets*. Posterior tweets of a news article are the tweets published after the publication of the news article.

In Figure 4(b), relevant tweets are in the low-density area. On the other hand, irrelevant tweets are in the high-density area. Therefore, we set a threshold between the high-density area and the low-density area.

Approach. To calculate the threshold for a news article, we define the density of similarity y as the average number of tweets having similarity with $\frac{h}{2}$ range from y, formally:

$$d_s(y) = \frac{\left|\left\{m \in M_s | (y - \frac{h}{2}) \leq sim(s, m) < (y + \frac{h}{2})\right\}\right|}{h}$$

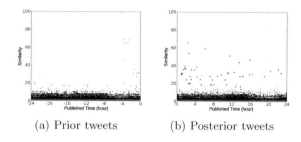

(a) Prior tweets   (b) Posterior tweets

Fig. 4. These are the distributions of similarity of tweets for a news article in NEWS30. A point shows a similarity of tweet, and red points show a similarity of relevant tweet in RELEVANT. The x-axis shows the publication time of a tweet, when the publication time of the news article is zero. The y-axis shows the similarity of the news article and a tweet. If we can determine the threshold between the high-density area and the low-density area in prior tweets, we can collect only relevant tweets in posterior tweets.

Algorithm 2. Predicting threshold

    Input : News article s, Prior tweets M, p, h, δ
    Output: θ_s – a threshold of news article s
1 $M_s = \{m \in M | sim(s, m) > 0\}$
2 Sort M_s in the ascending order of $sim(s, m)$
3 $sim_{max} \leftarrow \max_{m \in M_s} sim(s, m)$
4 $D \leftarrow \emptyset,\ y \leftarrow 0,\ i \leftarrow 0,\ j \leftarrow 0$
5 **while** $y \leq sim_{max}$ **do**
6   **while** $sim(s, m_i) < y + h/2$ **do**
7         $i \leftarrow i + 1$
8   **while** $sim(s, m_j) \leq y - h/2$ **do**
9         $j \leftarrow j + 1$
10     $d_s(y) \leftarrow (i - j)/h$
11   Add $d_s(y)$ to D
12     $y \leftarrow y + \delta$
13 Sort D in the ascending order of y
14 $d_s^{max} = \max_{0 \leq y \leq sim_{max}} d_s(y)$
15 **for** $d_s(y) \in D$ **do**
16   **if** $d_s(y) < d_s^{max} \cdot p$ **then**
17        $\theta_s \leftarrow y$
18   **return** θ_s

---

where M_s is a set of tweets such that $sim(s, m) > 0$ for news article s, and h is the similarity range which takes a value greater than 0.

Our method calculates the density values of every y by changing with δ using prior tweets, in order to predict the appropriate threshold. Then, we set the threshold to the smallest y satisfying the following condition:

$$d_s(y) < d_s^{max} \cdot p \qquad (5)$$

where d_s^{max} is the maximum of the density for news article s, and p is controllable parameter which determines acceptable density and takes a value in the range $[0, 1]$.

Algorithm. Algorithm 2 is a pseudo-code of our prediction method. Given news article s, our method selects tweets such that $sim(s, m) > 0$ from prior tweets of s (line 1). Then, we pick up the maximu similarity in M_s (line 3). Our method calculates the density of each similarity y at interval of δ until the maximum similarity in M_s (lines 5–12). If we find the smallest y which satisfies Condition 5 (line 16), y is returned as the threshold.

Example. Figure 5 shows an example of our prediction method for the same news article as in Figure 4. Figure 5(a) illustrates the schematic of applying the prediction method to the example in Figure 4(a). The calculated densities are shown in Figure 5(b). The x-axis is a similarity, and the y-axis is the density of the similarity. We find the first density that satisfies Condition 5. Thus, we determine the threshold as 10.

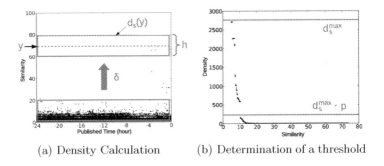

(a) Density Calculation   (b) Determination of a threshold

Fig. 5. (a) **Density Calculation:** Our method calculates the density values of every y by changing with δ using prior tweets, in order to predict the appropriate threshold. (b) **Determination of a threshold:** Our mathod sets the threshold to the smallest y which has the density lower than $d_s^{max} \cdot p$

5.2   Matching Method

In this section, we propose DAAT for variant thresholds (DAAT/VAT). DAAT/VAT can reduce not only the matching cost of news articles and tweets, but also the update time of a story index.

Main Idea. In order to reduce the number of news articles needed to calculate similarity, DAAT/VAT uses an upper bound of similarity of a tweet. The upper bound can be obtained by summing the maximum contributions of words in the tweet. The maximum contribution of word w_i is calculated by using the posting list of word w_i as in Equation 2 in Section 4.2. Thus, the upper bound of similarity of tweet m is as follows:

$$UB(m) = \sum_{w_i \in m} UB(w_i) \geq \max_{s \in S} sim(s, m)$$

Hence, we do not need to calculate similarity between the tweet and news articles that have a threshold larger than $UB(m)$.

In DAAT/VAT, we sort the entries of each posting list in the ascending order of their thresholds. DAAT/VAT calculates the similarity of a tweet and each news article in the ascending order of their thresholds by using a similar way to DAAT until reaching a news article which has a threshold larger than $UB(m)$. We can reduce the matching cost of a tweet and news articles, because we do not require to calculate the similarity of a tweet and all news article. In addition, we can save the small updating cost of an index, because it is a simple scheme unlike DAAT-skip which maintains a balanced binary tree for each posting list.

Algorithm. Algorithm 3 is a pseudo-code of DAAT/VAT. We calculate the upper bound of similarity of a tweet (lines 3–4). We pick up the news article ID with the smallest threshold in the current positions (line 6). We calculate the similarity between the new tweet and each news article (lines 9–12), and then the corresponding current positions are advanced to next entries (line 13). We compare the similarity and the threshold (lines 14–15), which is determined by the prediction method in Section 5.1. If all the current positions reach the news article that has the threshold larger than the upper bound, the algorithm terminates.

Algorithm 3. DAAT/VAT

Input : tweet m
Input : $\Theta = [\theta_{s_1}, \theta_{s_2}, ..., \theta_{s_n}]$
Input : $R_{s_1}, R_{s_2}, \cdots, R_{s_n}$
Output: Updated $R_{s_1}, R_{s_2}, \cdots, R_{s_n}$

1 Let $L_{w_1}, L_{w_2}, ..., L_{w_n}$ be posting list of terms in m
2 $UB \leftarrow 0$
3 **for** $i \in [1, 2, ..., |m|]$ **do**
4    $UB \leftarrow UB + UB(w_i)$

5 **while** *true* **do**
6    $s \leftarrow$ the news article ID with the lowest threshold in the current positions
7   **if** $UB < \theta_s$ **then**
8   **return**

9    $sim \leftarrow 0$
10   **for** $i \in [1, 2, ..., |m|]$ **do**
11   **if** $L_{w_i}.cur = s$ **then**
12       $sim \leftarrow sim + L_{w_i}.curPs$
13   Advance by 1 the current position in L_{w_i}

14   **if** $sim \geq \theta_s$ **then**
15   Add m to R_s

Example. We describe the processing of DAAT/VAT by using an example in Figure 6. The example shows the matching of a new tweet m containing five words $w_1, ..., w_5$ and seven news articles $s_1, ..., s_7$. Each news article has a threshold that is determined by the prediction method in Section 5.1.

First, we calculate the upper bound of similarity of the tweet ($UB(m) = 18$). Then, we calculate similarity between a news article and the tweet in a similar approach to DAAT. If the similarity of the new tweet is larger than the threshold, we add the tweet to the results of the news article. DAAT/VAT repeats the process until it reaches the news articles that have the thresholds larger then the upper bound of similarity of the tweet. In this example, we do not require to calculate the similarity with s_5, s_3, and s_1.

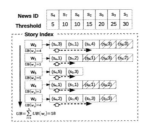

Fig. 6. Example of DAAT/VAT: This is an example that matches a new tweet m containing five words $w_1, \ldots, w_5$ and seven news articles $s_1, \ldots, s_7$ by using DAAT for variant thresholds. Each news article has a threshold that is determined by the prediction method in Section 5.1.

6   Experimental Evaluation

We performed experimental evaluations to answer the following questions:

- **Similarity comparison:** Is the proposed similarity measure better than other possible measures?
- **Accuracy:** How accurate is our proposed method compared to the baselines?
- **Update time:** How much time does our proposed method require to update the story index?
- **Matching time:** How much time does our proposed method require to match a newly arrived tweet and news articles?

Condition. We used Intel®Core™i7-2600 CPU @ 3.40GHz and 32GB Memory.

Datasets. We used news articles and tweets obtained from Yahoo!News and Twitter. The five datasets are constructed as follows:

- NEWS is a dataset containing 1,037 Japanese news articles published in 2014/6/9.
- NEWS30 is a dataset containing 30 Japanese news articles randomly selected from NEWS.

- CORPUS is a dataset containing 32,295 Japanese news articles published from 2014/5/1 to 2014/6/1. This dataset is used for calculating the IDF in the similarity score.
- TWEET is a dataset containing 2,575,198 Japanese tweets published from 2014/6/8 to 2014/6/11.
- RELEVANT is a dataset containing tweets which are relevant to news articles in NEWS30. These tweets are decided to be relevant by three human evaluators. In one-day posterior tweets of each news article, we showed top-1000 tweets with the highest proposed similarity values in TWEET to the evaluators and the evaluators classified these tweets into one of the four categories: (1) relevant, (2) a little relevant, (3) a little irrelevant, and (4) irrelevant. If the majority of evaluators select (1) or (2), then the corresponding tweets are decided to be relevant tweets for the news article.

6.1   Similarity Comparison

In this experiment, we compared our proposed similarity measure and the other similarity measures.

Setup. For each news article in NEWS30, by using similarity measure, we ranked tweets in TWEET or in RELEVANT that were published within 24h after the news article was published. We compared four similarity measures: (a) Cosine similarity, (b) Jaccard similarity, (c) Shrear's similarity (Equation 1), and (d) the proposed similarity.

To compare the four similarity measures, we employ the Mean Reciprocal Rank (MRR) which is defined as

$$MRR = \frac{1}{N} \sum_{i=1}^{N} \frac{1}{r_i} \ , \ r_i = \begin{cases} i, & \text{if } m_i \in RELEVANT \\ 0, & \text{otherwise} \end{cases}$$

where m_i is the ith tweet and N is the number of tweets. The experiment was performed as follows: (1) We calculated the similarity between news articles and tweets by using the four similarity measures. (2) We computed MRR of the top-100 tweets for each news article. (3) We computed the average MRR of all news articles.

We used MeCab [1] for morphological analysis. We only used general noun, proper noun, adjectival noun, and verbal noun when calculating the similarity scores.

Table 2. Average of MRR

Cosine	Jaccard	Shrear's	Proposed
0.0221	0.0289	0.0182	0.0324

---

[1] http://mecab.googlecode.com/svn/trunk/mecab/doc/index.html

Results and Discussion. Table 2 shows the results. We can see that the proposed similarity shows the largest MRR value. In Shrear's similarity, some tweets that contain a lot of the same words degrade the total MRR value, because this similarity takes the number of word occurrences into account. Short tweets tend to have large cosine similarity to news articles that share the same words with those tweets regardless of its topics, which leads to the low MRR value. Although Jaccard similarity shows somewhat high MRR value, it does not take IDF into account, leading to the lower MRR than that of our proposed similarity. From these results, we adopt the proposed similarity in our method.

6.2   Accuracy

In this experiment, we compared the accuracy of our proposed method and that of baseline methods.

Setup. We compared three methods as follows:

- *Top-k*: A method that collects top-k tweets with highest similarity scores for each news article. This method corresponds to the Top-k pub-sub approach [15].
- *Constant*: A method that sets the same threshold t of similarity score to all news articles. The method collects only tweets that have higher similarity score than the threshold.
- *Proposed*: Our proposed method that is explained in Section 5.

The three methods were compared by using news articles in NEWS30 and tweets in RELEVANT. To evaluate the three methods, we employed the receiver operating characteristic curve (ROC curve) [5] and the area under the ROC curve (AUC) [5]. ROC curve is a plot which is used to evaluate the accuracy of a binary classifier algorithm. The curve represents the true positive rate and the false positive rate at various threshold settings in the binary classifier algorithm. AUC is the area under the ROC curve. AUC is used to compare the accuracy of binary classifier algorithms. AUC takes values in range [0,1]. If an algorithm performs perfect binary classification, AUC is 1. While another algorithm which classifies randomly, then AUC is 0.5. In this experiment, we used 12 typical parameter values in each method to draw ROC curve. In *Top-k*, parameter k is 25, 50, 100, 200, 300, 400, 500, 600, 700, 800, 900, 1000. In *Constant*, parameter t is 5, 7.5, 10, 12.5, 15, 20, 25, 30, 35, 40, 45, 50. In *Proposed*, parameter p is 0, 0.0001, 0.0005, 0.001, 0.005, 0.01, 0.05, 0.1, 0.25, 0.5, 0.75, 1. Our method used other parameter values as $h = 10$, $\delta = 0.1$, and the one-day prior tweets of the news articles in TWEET to determine the threshold values. We treated relevant tweets of each news article to be correct when calculating the ROC curve.

Results and Discussion. Figure 7 shows ROC curve of the compared three methods. The x-axis indicates false positive rate, and the y-axis indicates true

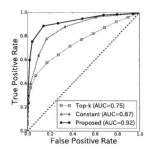

Fig. 7. ROC curve: This figure shows ROC curve of *Top-k*, *Baseline*, and *Proposed* methods. The x-axis indicates false positive rate, and the y-axis indicates true positive rate. *Top-k*, *Baseline*, and *Proposed* is represented by using line with square, triangle, and circle, respectively. A dotted line represents ROC curve of random classifiers. *Proposed* is always above the other methods, and AUC of *Proposed* (0.92) is higher than that of others (0.75, 0.87).

positive rate. *Top-k*, *Constant*, and *Proposed* are represented by using lines with squares, triangles, and circles, respectively. A dotted line represents ROC curve of random classifiers.

The ROC curve of *Proposed* is always above that of other methods. The AUC of *Proposed* (0.92) is higher than that of others (0.75, 0.87). This means that our method collects the appropriate number of tweets compared with other two methods. *Top-k* has the lowest AUC, because the number of relevant tweets is different for each news article. Hence, it is necessary to collect many irrelevant tweets, in order to collect the most of relevant tweets. *Proposed* shows high true positive rate and low false positive rate, because our method can determine an appropriate threshold for each news article. The reason that the AUC of *Proposed* is higher than that of *Constant* is that an appropriate threshold is different depending on news articles.

6.3 Update Time

In this experiment, we compared the required time to update the story index of DAAT/VAT and DAAT-skip [15]. There are two operations in updating when a new news article arrives: (1) **Insertion**: a newly arrived news article is inserted into the story index. (2) **Deletion**: the oldest news article in the story index is deleted. We compared these two operations of DAAT/VAT and DAAT-skip.

Setup. DAAT-skip is described in Section 4.2. The original DAAT-skip is designed for finding the top-k similar tweets for news articles, which means that our proposed method and DAAT-skip address slightly different problems. Hence, to make DAAT-skip to be applicable to the problem we address in this paper (with news updates), we used the same threshold values which are static for each news article (i.e., do not change over time), leading to running on the same condition. Our method used $p = 0.004$, $h = 10$, and $\delta = 0.1$ as the parameters.

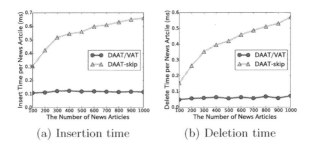

(a) Insertion time   (b) Deletion time

Fig. 8. (a) **Insertion time:** We compare the insertion time of DAAT/VAT and DAAT-skip. The x-axis indicates the number of news articles inserted into the story index, and the y-axis indicates the average insertion time to insert one news article. DAAT/VAT reduces the insertion time of news article for story index by up to 82.5% compared to DAAT-skip. (b) **Deletion time:** We compare the deletion time of DAAT/VAT and DAAT-skip. The x-axis indicates the number of news articles deleted from the story index, and the y-axis indicates the average deletion time to delete one news article. DAAT/VAT reduces the deletion time of news article for story index by up to 89.0% compared to DAAT-skip.

In this experiment, we used news articles in NEWS and one-hour prior tweets for each news article in TWEET. To compute the update time, we first insert all news articles into the story index, and then delete them from the story index.

Results and Discussion. Figure 8(a) shows the results for the insertion time. The x-axis indicates the number of news articles inserted into the story index, and the y-axis indicates the average insertion time to insert one news article. It is shown that DAAT/VAT reduces the insertion time required by DAAT-skip by up to 82.5%. Also, Figure 8(b) shows the results for the deletion time. The x-axis indicates the number of news articles deleted from the story index, and the y-axis indicates the average deletion time to delete one news article. DAAT/VAT also reduces the deletion time by up to 89.0%.

Why can DAAT/VAT reduce the required time to update (i.e., insertion and deletion) time? The reason is that DAAT-skip needs to maintain balanced binary trees for each story index. On the other hand, DAAT/VAT does not need to construct and maintain that kind of tree structures.

6.4   Matching Time

In this experiment, we evaluated the time of DAAT/VAT required to match the news articles and tweets.

Setup. We compared matching time required by DAAT/VAT and by DAAT-skip. For the same reason as in the previous section, we used the threshold values which are static for each news article. For the parameters of our method, we set

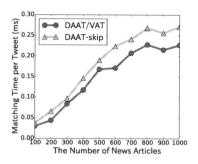

Fig. 9. Matching time: We compared matching time required by DAAT/VAT and by DAAT-skip. The x-axis indicates the number of news articles that are already inserted into the story index prior to the matching. The y-axis indicates the matching time required to match a newly arrived tweet to one news article. DAAT/VAT reduces the matching time of a news article and a tweet by up to 33.2% compared to DAAT-skip.

$p = 0.004$, $h = 10$, and $\delta = 0.1$. We used news articles in NEWS and 100,000 posterior tweets in TWEET for each news article. Also, to predict a threshold, we used one-hour prior tweets in TWEET for each news article. To compute the matching times, we first insert all the news articles into the story index, and then we match all the tweets with the inserted news articles.

Results and Discussion. Figure 9 shows the results. The x-axis indicates the number of news articles that are already inserted into the story index prior to the matching. The y-axis indicates the matching time required to match a newly arrived tweet to one news article.

DAAT/VAT reduces the matching time by up to 33.2% compared with DAAT-skip. DAAT-skip requires more time to match tweets and news articles than DAAT/VAT, because DAAT-skip needs to traverse the balanced binary trees to find the news articles to skip the similarity computations. On the other hand, DAAT/VAT skips the unnecessary computations by simply scanning the one-dimensional list of thresholds of news articles.

7   Conclusion

In this paper, we have proposed a novel method for the problem of matching news articles and tweets in the real-time condition where floods of tweets and news articles arrive. Our main contributions are summarized as follows:

1. Flexibility: Our method collects the appropriate number of tweets for various kinds of news articles by predicting the threshold of similarity for each news article (Figure 7).
2. Efficiency: Our method can reduce the update time of a story index which is used for efficient matching of news articles and tweets, leading to enable

us to handle a large amount of news articles and tweets (Figures 8(a), 8(b), and 9).

Also, we experimentally demonstrated the effectiveness of our method on streams of news articles and tweets from Yahoo!News and Twitter. Concretely, we show that the area under the ROC curve (AUC) of our method is higher than that of the baselines by up to 22.7%. It is also shown that our method reduces the insertion time and deletion time of an inverted index by up to 82.5% and 89.0% compared to the existing technique, respectively. Furthermore, matching time of news articles and tweets is also reduced by up to 33.2% compared to the existing technique.

Acknowledgement. This research was partly supported by the program "Research and Development on Real World Big Data Integration and Analysis" of MEXT and the Grant-in-Aid for Scientific Research (B) (#26280037) from JSPS.

References

1. Agarwal, A., Xie, B., Vovsha, I., Rambow, O., Passonneau, R.: Sentiment analysis of twitter data. In: LSM, pp. 30–38 (2011)
2. Amati, G., Bianchi, M., Marcone, G.: Sentiment estimation on twitter. In: IIR, pp. 39–50 (2014)
3. Canneyt, S.V., Feys, M., Schockaert, S., Demeester, T., Develder, C., Dhoedt, B.: Detecting newsworthy topics in twitter. In: SNOW-DC@WWW, pp. 25–32 (2014)
4. Chakrabarti, D., Punera, K.: Event summarization using tweets. In: ICWSM (2011)
5. Fawcett, T.: An introduction to ROC analysis. Pattern Recognition Letters **27**(8), 861–874 (2006)
6. Hu, M., Liu, S., Wei, F., Wu, Y., Stasko, J.T., Ma, K.L.: Breaking news on twitter. In: CHI, pp. 2751–2754 (2012)
7. Kwak, H., Lee, C., Park, H., Moon, S.B.: What is twitter, a social network or a news media? In: WWW, pp. 591–600 (2010)
8. Luo, Z., Osborne, M., Wang, T.: Opinion retrieval in twitter. In: ICWSM (2012)
9. Nichols, J., Mahmud, J., Drews, C.: Summarizing sporting events using twitter. In: IUI, pp. 189–198 (2012)
10. Osborne, M., Dredze, M.: Facebook, twitter and google plus for breaking news: is there a winner? In: ICWSM (2014)
11. Pak, A., Paroubek, P.: Twitter as a corpus for sentiment analysis and opinion mining. In: LREC (2010)
12. Petrovic, S., Osborne, M., McCreadie, R., Macdonald, C., Ounis, I., Shrimpton, L.: Can twitter replace newswire for breaking news? In: ICWSM (2013)
13. Sharifi, B., Hutton, M.A., Kalita, J.K.: Experiments in microblog summarization. In: SocialCom/PASSAT, pp. 49–56 (2010)
14. Shi, B., Ifrim, G., Hurley, N.: Be in the know: Connecting news articles to relevant twitter conversations. CoRR, Vol. abs/1405.3117 (2014)
15. Shraer, A., Gurevich, M., Fontoura, M., Josifovski, V.: Top-k publish-subscribe for social annotation of news. PVLDB **6**(6), 385–396 (2013)

Context-Aware Process Injection
Enhancing Process Flexibility by Late Extension of Process Instances

Nicolas Mundbrod[(⊠)], Gregor Grambow, Jens Kolb, and Manfred Reichert

Institute of Databases and Information Systems, Ulm University, Ulm, Germany
{nicolas.mundbrod,gregor.grambow,jens.kolb,manfred.reichert}@uni-ulm.de
http://www.uni-ulm.de/dbis

Abstract. Companies must cope with high process variability and a strong demand for process flexibility due to customer expectations, product variability, and an abundance of regulations. Accordingly, numerous business process variants need to be supported depending on a multiplicity of influencing factors, e.g., customer requests, resource availability, compliance rules, or process data. In particular, even running processes should be adjustable to respond to contextual changes, new regulations, or emerging customer requests. This paper introduces the approach of context-aware process injection. It enables the sophisticated modeling of a context-aware injection of process fragments into a base process at design time, as well as the dynamic execution of the specified processes at run time. Therefore, the context-aware injection even considers dynamic wiring of data flow. To demonstrate the feasibility and benefits of the approach, a case study was conducted based on a proof-of-concept prototype developed with the help of an existing adaptive process management technology. Overall, context-aware process injection facilitates the specification of varying processes and provides high process flexibility at run time as well.

Keywords: Process injection · Process flexibility · Process variability · Process adaptation · Data collection processes

1 Introduction

In today's globalized world, companies face various challenges like increased customer expectations, complex products and services, demanding regulations in different countries, or fulfillment of social responsibility. As a result, companies need to cope with high process variability as well as a strong demand for process flexibility. This means that in many of their business processes the course of action is influenced by an abundance of *process parameters* like external context factors, intermediate results, and process-related events (e.g., successful termination of process steps). Consequently, ordinary process models comprise complex decisions allowing for various alternative courses of actions as well as

© Springer International Publishing Switzerland 2015
C. Debruyne et al. (Eds.): OTM 2015 Conferences, LNCS 9415, pp. 127–145, 2015.
DOI: 10.1007/978-3-319-26148-5_8

interdependencies among these decisions that are hardly comprehensible for process modelers. In addition, an automated, controlled and sound adaptation of (long-running) processes instances is required to address contextual changes, new regulations, or emerging customer requests at run-time.

The complex development, production, or reporting processes in the automotive and electronics industry may be regarded as valuable examples [8,12,18]. Typically, these processes rely on the companies' sensitive supply chains. Hence, business partners and diverse activities have to be incorporated dynamically on demand. The following application scenario (cf. Fig. 1), we derived in the context of a case study, illustrates the complexity and dynamics of such processes.

Application Scenario: **Data Collection Processes**
Due to regulations, an automotive manufacturer needs to provide sustainability information. In particular, sustainability indicators relating to its production are requested: one indicator deals with the REACH[a] compliance of the entire company, another one addresses the greenhouse gas emissions during the production of a certain product. To gather the data, process *Data Collection 1* is deployed to request a REACH compliance statement from a supplier. Additionally, two other suppliers must be contacted to report the greenhouse gas emissions (process *Data Collection 2*). While both data collection processes have activities in common, many activities are specifically selected for each process. A request regarding REACH compliance, e.g., implies a legally binding statement and, thus, a designated representative must sign the data. However, if the CEO was not available, activity *Sign Data* can be delayed or skipped.

---
[a] Regulation (EC) No 1907/2006: Registration, Evaluation, Authorisation and Restriction of Chemicals

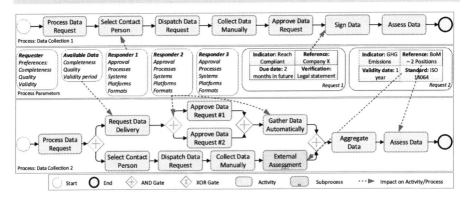

Fig. 1. Application Scenario with two Data Collection Processes

To systematically support long-running and varying processes that require (data-driven) run-time flexibility, we introduce the approach of *context-aware process injection* (CaPI). Taking the current context of a process into account,

CaPI enables the controlled, but late injection (i.e., insertion) of process fragments into a lean base process. Using so-called *extension areas*, the correctness of the process' control and data flow is ensured after injecting process fragments at run time. The feasibility of CaPI is demonstrated by implementing a proof-of-concept prototype based on existing adaptive process management technology.

Underpinning our research, we applied the *design science* research methodology [15]. In particular, our work can be categorized as a *design- and development-centered approach* accordingly. Based on an analysis of application scenarios (e.g., [8,11,17]) and process-related backgrounds (cf. Sect. 2) as well as the evaluation of existing approaches (cf. Sect. 7), we iteratively elaborated the CaPI approach (cf. Sect. 3). The latter comprises the specification of its components (cf. Sect. 4). Furthermore, we give insights into the *process of context-aware process injection* (cf. Sect. 5). To validate the approach, a poof-of-concept prototype was developed enabling the usage and evaluation in different application scenarios (cf. Sect. 6). Finally, Section 8 concludes the paper giving a summary and an outlook.

2   Backgrounds

To make CaPI applicable to existing activity-centric process modeling notations, it relies on the process model definition given in Def. 1.

Definition 1. *A **process model** PM is a tuple* (N, E, NT, ET, EC) *where:*

- N *is a set of process nodes and* $E \subseteq N \times N$ *is a precedence relation (directed edges) connecting process nodes,*
- $NT : N \rightarrow \{Start, End, Activity, ANDsplit, ANDjoin, ORsplit, ORjoin, XORsplit, XORjoin, DataObj\}$ *assign to each* $n \in N$ *a node type* $NT(n)$; *N is divided into disjoint sets of start/end nodes* C ($NT(n) \in \{Start, End\}$), *activities* A ($NT(n) = Activity$), *gateways* G ($NT(n) \in \{ANDsplit, ANDjoin, ORsplit, ORjoin, XORsplit, XORjoin\}$), *and data objects* D ($NT(n) = DataObj$),
- $ET : E \rightarrow \{ControlEdge, LoopEdge, DataEdge\}$ *assigns a type* $ET(e)$ *to each edge* $e \in E$,
- $EC : E \rightarrow Conds \cup \{True\}$ *assigns a transition condition or true to each control edge* $e \in E, ET(e) \in \{ControlEdge, LoopEdge\}$.

Note that we take sound process models for granted, i.e., a process model has one start (no incoming edges) and one end node (no outgoing edges) [17]. Further, the process model has to be *connected*, i.e., each activity can be reached from the start node, and from each activity the end node is reachable. Data consumed (delivered) as input (output) by the process model is written (read) by the start (end) node. Finally, branches may be arbitrarily nested, but must be safe (e.g., a branch following an XORsplit must not merge with an ANDjoin). Due to lack of space, we refer to literature for a detailed look on process model soundness [19]. Def. 2 introduces the notion of a *SESE (Single Entry Single Exit)* fragment:

Definition 2. *Let* $PM := (N, E, NT, ET, EC)$ *be a process model and* $N' \subseteq N$ *be a subset of activities. The subordinated process model* PM' *induced by* N' *and their corresponding edges* $E' \subseteq E$ *is denoted as* **Single Entry Single Exit (SESE)** *fragment iff* PM' *is connected and has exactly one incoming and one outgoing edge connecting it with PM. If* PM' *has no preceding (succeeding) nodes,* PM' *has only one outgoing (incoming) edge.*

Based on a process model PM, a process instance PI may be created, deployed and executed at run time. Def. 3 defines a process instance formally:

Definition 3. *A* **process instance** PI *is defined as a tuple* (PM, NS, Π) *where:*

- $PM := (N, E, NT, ET, EC)$ *denotes the process model PI is executed on,*
- $NS : N \to \{\texttt{NotActivated}, \texttt{Activated}, \texttt{Running}, \texttt{Skipped}, \texttt{Completed}\}$
  describes the execution state of each node $n \in N$ *with* $NT(n) \neq \texttt{DataObj}$,
- $\Pi := \langle e_1, \ldots, e_n \rangle$ *denotes the current execution trace of PI where each entry* e_k *is related either to the start or completion of an activity.*

3   Context-Aware Process Injection in a Nutshell

The key objective of CaPI is to ease the sophisticated modeling of process variants at design time and to enable the automated, controlled adaption of processes at run time. Therefore, the central entity of CaPI is the *context-aware process family* (CPF) (cf. Fig. 2). In detail, a CPF comprises a *base process* model with *extension areas* (cf. Sect. 4.1), *contextual situations* (cf. Sect. 4.3) based

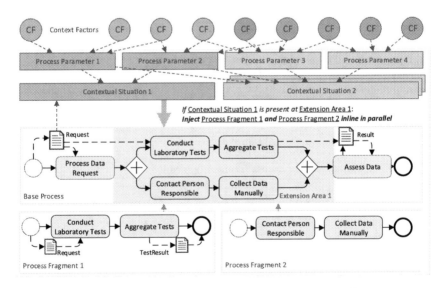

Fig. 2. Overview of a Context-Aware Process Family

on *process parameters* (cf. Sect. 4.2), a set of *process fragments* injected at the extension areas at run time, and a set of *injection specifications* (cf. Sect. 4.4).

Establishing the *separation of concerns* principle for modeling process variants, the *base process model* solely contains decisions and activities shared by all variants of the process, known at build time, and not being changed at run time. By contrast, *extension areas* represent the dynamic part of the process. Hence, a process modeler may focus on modeling predictable activities first to add the dynamic parts of the base process model subsequently. In particular, extension areas are used to automatically inject process fragments into the base process at run time based on the present *contextual situation* as well as on well-defined *injection specifications*. An extension area allows for the dynamic injection of any number of parallel process fragments. In turn, contextual situations are defined through conditions expressed in first-order logic taking *process parameters* and even data objects of the base process model into account. In this context, process parameters are connected to dynamic, external factors influencing the process injection's decision making. While injecting process fragments, CaPI takes care of correct data flow mappings as well: data objects of an injected process fragment are automatically connected to existing ones of the base process.

By this means, CaPI enables controlled, but dynamic configurations and changes of long-running and varying processes at run time. Through relying on insertions of process fragments solely, CaPI allows process modelers to increasingly focus on the particular variants instead of struggling with a highly complex process model capturing all variants.[1] Furthermore, process modelers may directly integrate contextual influences into the modeling of variants as complex external context factors are abstracted by meaningful process parameters and reusable contextual situations. In turn, CaPI is able to cope with contextual runtime changes through the late evaluation of contextual situations at given extension areas to finally inject the proper process fragments. Thereby, the automated and consistent construction of data flow between the injected process fragments and the underlying base process mitigates the efforts of involved users. Further, it empowers process activities to seamlessly read and write data.

Before presenting the key components of a CPF and CaPI, Def. 4 formally specifies the concept of a *context-aware process family* (CPF). Note that a process fragment may be the base process of another CPF and, thus, modularization can be achieved as well (recursive nesting is disallowed).

Definition 4. *A **context-aware process family** is defined as a tuple $CPF = (BP, EA, PP, CS, PF, IS)$ where:*

- *BP is the base process model,*
- *EA is a set of extension areas in the BP,*
- *PP is a set of process parameters,*
- *CS is a set of contextual situations,*

---

[1] Note that other kind of dynamic changes, like deleting or moving activities, may be also introduced by authorized users based on the features of the adaptive process management technology [6] used.

- *PF is a set of* process fragments; *each process fragment is a process model,*
- *IS is a set of* injection specifications.

4   Components of Context-Aware Process Families

4.1   Extension Areas

In order to enable the controlled extension of processes at run time, extension areas are introduced representing the dynamic part of a CPF. Based on the current contextual situation, process fragments may be dynamically injected into extension areas at run time. More precisely, an extension area is defined by two extension points—each referring to a node (i.e. start/end nodes, activities, gateways) of the base process model (cf. Fig. 3). If the nodes referenced by the extension points directly precede each other, a process fragment can be easily injected into the base process. If some nodes exist in between, a process fragment may be injected among these nodes (cf. Sect. 4.4) or, alternatively, gateways may be employed to insert the process fragment in parallel. The different possibilities of injecting process fragments are discussed in Section 5. Def. 5 formally describes extension areas and posits constraints to ensure that the injection of process fragments into a base process BP always leads to a modified, but still sound process BP'. In this context, overlaps of extension areas may result in problems regarding the concurrent injection of process fragments (cf. Sect. 5.2).

Definition 5. *Let $CPF = (BP, EA, PP, CS, PF, IS)$ be a context-aware process family and $BP = (N, E, NT, ET, EC)$ be the base process. Every **extension area** $ea \in EA$ is described by a set of two extension points $\{EP_s, EP_e\} \subseteq N \times \{Pre, Post\}$ where:*

- *Every extension point $EP_x = (n_x, scope), x \in \{s, e\}$ refers to corresponding nodes $n_x \in N$, $NT(n_x) \neq DataObj$ in BP and additionally exposes a scope; the latter determines whether ea starts (ends) just before (scope = Pre) or directly after (scope = Post) the referenced node n_x,*
- *EP_s (EP_e) may only refer to the scope Post (Pre) of the start (end) node of BP; EP_s (EP_e) must not refer to the end (start) node of BP,*
- *The referenced nodes $n_s, n_e \in N$ embrace a subordinated process model PM' induced by a subset of activities $N' \subseteq N$ and respective edges $E' \subseteq E$; PM' always corresponds a SESE fragment and must not contain any other extension areas starting (ending), but not ending (starting) in PM' (nesting of extension areas is allowed, but no overlaps).*

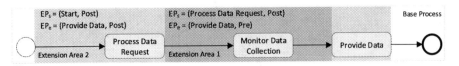

Fig. 3. Examples of Extension Areas in a Base Process

4.2   Process Parameters

Typically, long-running and varying processes are influenced by context factors, e.g., the number of involved parties or the availability of data. To include such context factors into the decision making regarding the injection of process fragments and hence the concrete course of action of the overall process, we utilize a predefined set of *process parameters* (cf. Def. 6). The set of process parameters additionally enables the exchange of entire CPFs between application scenarios as it abstracts from a concrete set of context factors (i.e., only a mapping between the context factors and process parameters need to be conducted again).

Definition 6. *Let $CPF = (BP, EA, PP, CS, PF, IS)$ be a context-aware process family. A **process parameter** $pp \in PP$ is a tuple $(ppDefault, ppValue, ppDom)$ where:*

- *$ppDefault \in PPDom$ is an optional default value of the process parameter,*
- *$ppValue \in PPDom$ is the current value of the process parameter,*
- *$ppDom \subseteq Dom$ is the domain of pp with Dom denoting the set of all atomic domains (e.g., String, Integer)*

Note that value $ppValue$ of process parameter pp is set by a context mapping (component) at run time (cf. Sect. 5.2). To focus on the controlled process adaption, we rely on simple rule-based mapping for context factors (cf. Fig. 4).

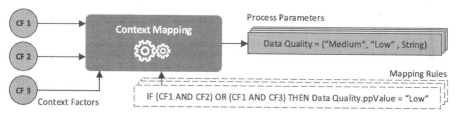

Fig. 4. Illustrative Mapping of Context Factors on Process Parameters

Consequently, process parameters may be also leveraged to provide meta information regarding the current execution trace (cf. Def. 3) or the process fragments injected at run time. Such process parameters can then be used to model interdependencies among contextual situations and process fragments, respectively. Finally, a process parameter may have compound values (e.g., sets, lists) as well—however, we omit a formal definition of complex parameters here.

4.3   Contextual Situations

A specific process variant may rely on several occurring *contextual situations*, which are based on the combination of various process parameters and, especially, their current values. For example, a company may insist on a four-eyes-principle approval process in case data is intended for a specific customer group or relates to a specific regulation. Hence, the same contextual situations may be leveraged at different extension areas to inject process fragments. Based on this observation, contextual situations (cf. Fig. 5) are defined by conditions expressed in a first-order logic relying on the set of process parameters (cf. Sect. 4.2) and data objects of the base process (cf. Def. 7). As opposed to traditional modeling of business processes, we enable the integration of external context factors as well as reutilization of contextual situations across the process model. As default process parameters may provide meta information regarding the current execution trace or the process fragments injected at run time, interdependencies can be modeled in contextual situations correspondingly.

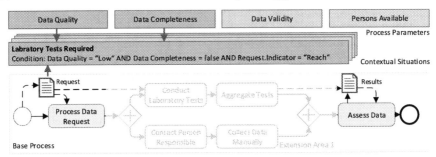

Fig. 5. Contextual Situation based on Process Parameters and Data Objects

Definition 7. *Let $CPF = (BP, EA, PP, CS, PF, IS)$ be a context-aware process family and $BP = (N, E, NT, ET, EC)$ be the corresponding base process. A **contextual situation** $cs \in CS$ is defined by a condition expressed in first-order logic. For every predicate $par_k \; \theta \; val_k, \theta \in \{ "=", " \leq ", \ldots \}, val_k \in Dom(par_k)$ of the condition, par_k either corresponds to a process parameter ($par_k \in PP$) or a data object ($par_k \in N, NT(par_k) = DataObj$).*

4.4 Injection Specifications

Finally, *injection specifications* determine the injection of a process fragment to an extension area in a given contextual situation (cf. Def. 5). To ensure data flow correctness after the injection, in addition, the mapping of data elements is considered in the injection specifications. Especially, this includes a mapping of required input and output data objects of the process fragment (or, to be more precise, of their activities) to the existing data objects of the base process. This mapping may be even extended to data objects of other process fragments, which are supposed to be injected in the base process as well (cf. Sect. 5).

Definition 8. *Let $CPF = (BP, EA, PP, CS, PF, IS)$ be a context-aware process family and $BP = (N, E, NT, ET, EC)$ be the corresponding base process. An **injection specification** is $\in IS$ corresponds to a tuple $(EA_{IS}, CS_{IS}, PF_{IS}, InjType, InjPattern, InjRate, InjTrigger, InjRank, DR, DW)$ where:*

- $EA_{IS} \in EA$ *is a specific extension area, $CS_{IS} \in CS$ a specific contextual situation, and $PF_{IS} \in PF$ a specific process fragment,*

- $InjType := \{\texttt{Inline}, \texttt{Sub-process}\}$ is the injection type denoting whether PF_{IS} is injected inline or as a sub-process,
- $InjPattern := \{\texttt{Parallel}, \texttt{Sequential}\}$ is the injection pattern denoting whether PF_{IS} is injected in parallel to the existing control flow between the extension points of EA_{IS} or sequentially into the existing control flow,
- $InjRate := \{\texttt{Single}, (\texttt{Multiple}, fre)\}$ is the injection rate denoting whether PF_{IS} is injected once or multiple times at EA_{IS}; the latter requires attribute $fre \in \mathbb{N}$ determining how often PF_{IS} shall be injected at EA_{IS} in parallel,
- $InjTrigger$ determines the point in time an injection is triggered. It is defined by a conditional predicate par θ val with $par \in N \bigcup PP$; further $par \in N \Rightarrow NT(par) = DataObj, \theta \in \{``=``, `` \leq ``, \ldots\}, val \in Dom(par)$,
- $InjRank \in \mathbb{N}$ is a number to create a ranking among injections specifications as they may match concurrently; all injection specifications for one particular extension area must expose different values,
- $DR : InputData_{PF_{IS}} \rightarrow DO$ is a set of mappings of input data objects $InputData_{PF_{IS}}$ of PF_{IS} to data objects $DO \in N_{BP} \bigcup (N_{PF} \setminus N_{PF_{IS}})$ of the base process BP or of other process fragments $PF \setminus PF_{IS}$,
- $DW : OutputData_{PF_{IS}} \rightarrow DO$ is a set of mappings of output data objects $OutputData_{PF_{IS}}$ of PF_{IR} to data objects $DO \in N_{BP} \bigcup (N_{PF} \setminus N_{PF_{IS}})$ of the base process BP or of other process fragments $PF \setminus PF_{IS}$.

The injection trigger ($InjTriger$) enables the injection of a process fragment at an extension area as soon as a given process parameter or data object exposes a certain value (see Sect. 5.2 for details). Furthermore, the number of process fragments to be injected may be dynamically set based on the current contextual situation. Both concepts increase the flexibility provided to long-running and varying processes. The ranking ($InjRank$) of injection specifications becomes necessary as several contextual situations may occur concurrently and, hence, several injections (cf. Sect. 4.4) may be concurrently triggered. Through the ranking, especially, sequential injections of process fragments can be accomplished in a well-defined order. Sect. 5 presents details on context-aware process injection based on injection specifications.

5   The Process of Context-aware Process Injection

This section discusses the *process of context-aware process injection* to reveal the interplay and benefits of the introduced components and concepts. In particular, we show how to employ CaPI entities to properly inject process fragments at extension areas in given contextual situations. Thereby, we both discuss alternatives to specify CPFs at design time as well as the process of context-aware process injection at run time.

5.1   The Modeling of Context-aware Process Families

As a prerequisite, the base process of a context-aware process family must be defined first. Therefore, either a new process model needs to be created or an existing one is modified accordingly. Note that the resulting base process model solely contains the set of activities shared by all process variants, known at build time, and usually not being changed at run time. Drawing upon, the extension areas are then defined by selecting corresponding nodes in the base process.

Subsequently, the set of process parameters must be specified as the latter provides the basis for defining contextual situations and, finally, the injection specifications. In this context, a process modeler may demand a set of pre-defined process parameters that allow modeling interdependencies among process fragments. For example, the list of process fragments injected in the base process at run time may be made available through such a pre-defined process parameter. Note that this approach also allows for the incorporation of data objects, which belong to other process fragments, into the data mapping declared in an injection specification.

Based on the given process parameters and data objects, the set of contextual situations can be defined appropriately. The latter then enables a process modeler to finally define injection specifications. Altogether, three alternative modeling perspectives can be provided to a process modeler (cf. Fig. 6):

- *Situation-based perspective*: for every contextual situation, one may determine the process fragments to be injected at given extension areas.
- *Location-based perspective*: for each extension area, one may define the process fragments to be injected in a given contextual situation.
- *Artifact-based perspective:* one may stepwise take process fragments to define in which contextual situation they shall be injected at given extension areas.

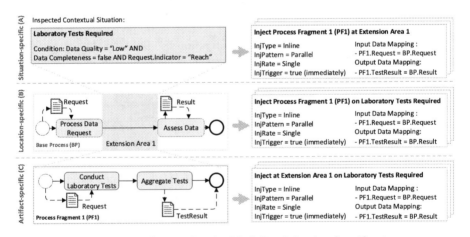

Fig. 6. Three Approaches for Modeling Injection Specification

As illustrated in Fig. 6, from each perspective the modeling still leads to the creation of injection specifications for the given CPF. However, a process modeler may use her favorite approach or even mix the approaches in relation to her personal preferences.

Since many activities and decisions in the control flow of the base process may be data-driven, the mapping of the injected data objects must be accomplished to successfully conduct CaPI. This very essential part for supporting process variants is consistently and easily achieved by selecting the data objects in both the base process model and the process fragments to create the required mapping (cf. Sect. 4.4). Note that this is a clear advantage of CaPI in comparison to many existing approaches (cf. Sec. 7) as the latter do not allow for (automatic) data mapping and, hence, process users are burdened with this issue at run time. As process fragments may be injected at different extension areas, one may want to link a data object to another data object of a process fragment injected earlier in the base process. Hence, a interdependency between such two process fragments must be created accordingly: process parameters providing meta information regarding the current execution trace (cf. Sect. 4.2) are leveraged to enhance the contextual situation for a process fragment. The latter can be easily automated as soon as one adds corresponding references to data objects of process fragments to be injected earlier. Finally, in case a process fragments is injected multiple times at an extension area, CaPI allows for referencing data objects of the injected fragments by adequate identification mechanisms.

5.2   The Execution of Context-Aware Process Families

As opposed to configuration approaches (cf. Sec. 7), CaPI enables the late configuration of processes at run time. The latter allows evaluating the contextual situations just in the moment a process adaptation is required. Therefore, a $CPF = (BP, EA, PP, CS, PF, IS)$ is deployed and executed in a process-aware information system (PaIS). After successful deployment, the base process instance $BPI = (BP, NS, \Pi)$ is continuously monitored by a dedicated CaPI application (cf. Sect. 6.1) continuously monitoring the BPI regarding reached extension areas and current contextual situations.

If an extension area $ea \in EA$ is reached and, especially, its first extension point refers to a node with scope $\texttt{Pre}$ ($EP_s = (n_x, \texttt{Pre}), n_x \in N, BP = (N, E, NT, ET, EC)$), the determination of the contextual situations will be started as soon as the previous node will have been completed ($n_{x-1} \in N$, $NS(n_{x-1}) = \texttt{Completed}$). In turn, if the first extension point refers to a node with scope $\texttt{Post}$ ($EP_s = (n_x, \texttt{Post})$), the determination will be started as soon as n_x will have been completed ($NS(n_x) = \texttt{Completed}$). In case the extension area is surrounded by a loop in the BPI, the injection specification can be evaluated in the first iteration or in every iteration of the loop structure (depends on preferences and the support by th underlying PaIS). After successfully determining the set of contextual situations CS_{ea}, it becomes possible to derive the set of utilizable injection specifications IS_{ea} for finally adapt the BPI adequately.

For every process specification $is \in IS_{ea}$ with $is = (ea, cs_{is}, pf_{is}, InjType_{is},$ $InjPattern_{is}, InjRate_{is}, InjTrigger_{is}, InjRank_{is}, DR_{is}, DW_{is})$, the point of time the process injection shall be accomplished, must be regarded based on condition $InjTrigger_{is}$. If the latter is already met when reaching ea, pf_{is}

will be immediately injected according to the below-mentioned steps. Otherwise, the injection of pf_{is} will be postponed until $InjTrigger_{is}$ is fulfilled. In case the condition is never satisfied, pf_{is} could be injected at the very end of the control embraced by an extension area or not be injected at all (depends on preferences set initially). If pf_{is} shall be lately injected, the current states of the nodes embraced by ea must be taken into account: if there is only one running node $n_x \in N(i.e.NS(n_x) = $ Running), pf_{is} will be injected directly after n_x. However, if there are several concurrently running nodes $n_k \in N, k = 1, \dots, n(i.e.NS(n_k) = $ Running), pf_{is} will be injected directly after the gateway finally merging the branches on which the nodes $n_1, \dots, n_n$ are situated on. Finally, if several injection specifications are sharing the same contextual situations and injection trigger, the injection rank $InjRank_{is}$ is considered (cf. Sect. 4.4). After the consideration of $InjTrigger_{is}$ and $InjRank_{is}$, the following procedures are applied in general (cf. Fig. 7):

1. $InjPattern_{is} = $ Parallel $\wedge InjRate_{is} = $ Single, $\Rightarrow pf_{is}$ will be injected inline (or as a sub-process depending on $InjType_{is}$) and in parallel to the existing control flow,
2. $InjPattern_{is} = $ Parallel $\wedge InjRate_{is} = $ (Multiple, fre), $\Rightarrow pf_{is}$ will be injected inline (or as a sub-process) fre times with surrounding ANDsplit / ANDjoin gateways in parallel to existing control flow,
3. $InjPattern_{is} = $ Sequential $\wedge InjRate_{is} = $ Single $\Rightarrow$, pf_{is} will be injected inline (or as a sub-process) into the existing control flow,
4. $InjPattern_{is} = $ Sequential $\wedge InjRate_{is} = $ (Multiple, fre), $\Rightarrow pf_{is}$ will be injected inline (or as a sub-process) fre times with surrounding ANDsplit / ANDjoin gateways into the existing control flow.

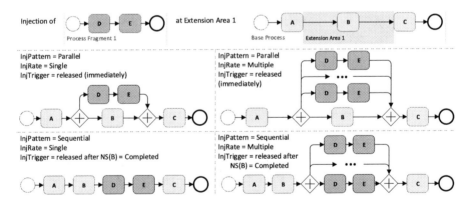

Fig. 7. Realization of Process Injection based on Injection Specifications

The detailed procedures to inject a process fragment pf_{is} are exemplarily discussed for the case $InjPattern_{is} = $ Parallel $\wedge InjType_{is} = $ Inline, assuming $InjTrigger_{is}$ has already been satisfied: first, start and end nodes $n^s_{pf_{si}}, n^e_{pf_{is}} \in N_{pf_{is}}$ of pf_{is} are removed. Then all remaining nodes $n^k_{pf_{is}} \in N_{pf_{is}}$

as well as one ANDsplit $n_{ANDsplit}$ and one ANDjoin gateway $n_{ANDjoin}$ are added to the nodes of the base process N_{BP}. Subsequently, six control edges are created: one edge connects n_p preceding the extension area with $n_{ANDsplit}$, two edges link $n_{ANDsplit}$ to $n_{pf_{is}}^{s+1}$, which succeeds the (removed) start node of pf_{is}, and n_{p+1}, which is the first node in the control flow embraced by ea. Subsequently, $n_{pf_{is}}^{e-1}$ (i.e, the last node of pf_{is}) and ea (i.e, last node of the control flow embraced by ea) are connected with $n_{ANDjoin}$. Finally, $n_{ANDjoin}$ is linked to n_s, which is the first node succeeding ea.

Finally, the correct data flow between injected nodes and existing nodes of the base process must be established. As this is automatically performed at run time, process participants are not burdened with this challenging task. We exemplarily present the data input mapping for the inline injection of a single fragment PF_{IS} (cf. Fig. 8): for every node $n_{pf_{is}}$ of pf_{is} with data edge $e_{di} = (di_{pf_{is}}, n_{PF_{IS}}) \in E, ET(e) = \texttt{DataEdge}$ from a input data object $di_{pf_{is}}, di_{pf_{is}} \in InputData_{pf_{is}}$, a new edge $e_{di\text{-}new} := (do_{BP}, n_{pf_{is}})$ is created based on mapping $dr = (di_{pf_{is}}, do_{BP}), dr \in DR$. e_{di} is deleted afterwards and if there are no further edges connecting $di_{pf_{is}}$ to nodes, $di_{pf_{is}}$ will be deleted as well.

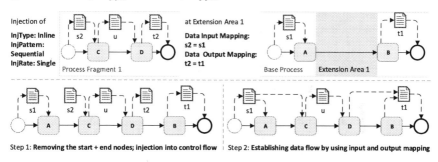

Fig. 8. Data Mapping Example for an Injected Process Fragment

6   Validation

As the CaPI approach explicitly addresses long-running processes showing high variability, which often take place in rather sensitive businesses, a mature and powerful implementation is required to conduct valuable empirical studies to successfully validate the concepts presented in this work. To prepare such studies, we developed a sophisticated proof-of-concept prototype whose details are presented in the following. Further, we conducted a first case study in the automotive and electronics industry to receive important feedback regarding both the approach in total as well as the proof-of-concept prototype in particular.

6.1   Proof-of-Concept Prototype

To establish a powerful implementation as a solid basis for future empirical studies, the CaPI proof-of-concept prototype is based on the conceptual architecture shown in Fig. 9. In particular, we realized the prototype using Aristaflow adaptive process management technology [6]. The latter allows modeling, deploying, and executing well-structured business processes. Further, it provides sophisticated and sound change operations to adapt running process instances at run time [16]. Hence, AristaFlow provides the basic execution platform required to conduct the sound injection of process fragments as well as the proper assignment of data objects for the injected activities at run time.

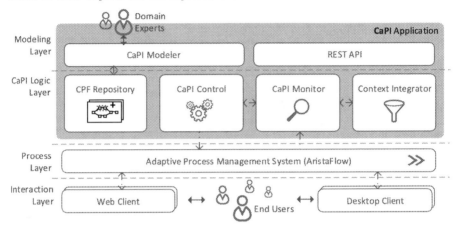

Fig. 9. Overview on the CaPI Architecture

Realized with Java Enterprise Edition 7, the CaPI application comprises a web-based sub-module enabling domain experts to conveniently model CPFs (*CaPI Modeler*) as well as sub-modules *CPF Repository*, *CaPI Monitor*, *CaPI Control*, and *Context Integrator* representing the CaPI core functions required at run time.

Through appropriate web-based user interfaces, a domain expert may first specify the mappings of the available context factors to process parameters and the one of the process parameters to contextual situations accordingly. Based on these preparations, she may create injection specifications by putting together the CaPI core components extension areas, contextual situations and process fragments via *drag and drop*. As proposed in Sect. 5.1, for this purpose, we implemented the different perspectives a domain expert may use to create an injection specification. Consequently, Fig. 10 exemplarily illustrates the situation-based perspectives showing a base process with two extension areas (see Marking (a)) for a data collection process regarding Reach Compliance of several suppliers (cf. Sect. 1). Both extension areas are needed to prepare and perform data collection activities for every involved supplier according to their capabilities (i.e. context factors). In particular, if a supplier hosts a well-reachable in-house system providing required data, the process fragment *"Perform Data Collection IHS"* is injected for every involved supplier at the second extension area.

Overall, the CPFs modeled by domain experts are managed in the CPF Repository. At run time, CaPI Control interprets the CPF specifications to detect the deployment of a CPF base process in AristaFlow and to continuously monitor the execution of the base process accordingly. Therefore, CaPI Control is registered as a dedicated service in AristaFlow to receive any status updates of activities as well as to actively acknowledge the start of every activity in the base process. Based on this approach, CaPI control detects when achieving an extension area, subsequently evaluates the valid contextual situations, and finally injects the specified process fragments on demand. For the example of Fig. 10, either *"Perform Data Collection IHS"* or *"Web-based Data Collection"* are injected at the second extension area according to the given contextual situations at run time (see Marking (b)).

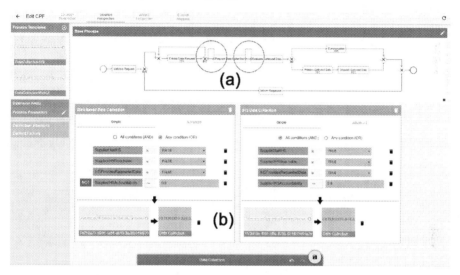

Fig. 10. Screenshots of the CaPI Situation-based Modeling Perspective

6.2   Case Study

After demonstrating the technical feasibility, we also conducted a case study based on data collection processes in the automotive and electronics industry (cf. Sect. 1) in the scope of the SustainHub[2] project. More precisely, we therefore modeled several data collection processes of an automotive manufacturer with its dynamic, data-driven injections of process fragments. Ensuing, we conducted qualitative interviews with project partners to receive their feedback. For the interviews, we presented both the approach and the existing functionality based on the modeled data collection process. Altogether, we received valuable, but of course limited feedback regarding *better modularity, increased confidentiality,* and *comprehensible monitoring.*

---

[2] SustainHub (Project No.283130) is a collaborative project within the 7th Framework Programme of the European Commission (Topic ENV.2011.3.1.9-1, Eco-innovation).

Regarding modularity, CaPI may reduce the complexity of long-running, varying process models to create more comprehensible and appropriate process models according to given contextual situations. The partners stated that the size and complexity of process models typically determine the rate of modeling errors. CaPI may provide a different way of modeling such complex and varying processes without these errors. However, the possibilities and ease-of-use regarding the modeling of contextual situations and injection specifications will mainly determine the effectiveness and efficiency of CaPI in comparison to the traditional approach of maintaining one large-sized process model. At design time, the systematic management of large process models also raises the problem of confidentiality. All possible decisions and activities including the linkage to roles, data, and other resources are accessible in total. According to the partners, modeling a process based on CaPI may provide possibilities to separate common activities and control flow from specific, confidential process fragments injected in contextual situations. Regarding confidentiality at run time, CaPI may provide only activities and control flow elements executed for monitoring purposes. Thereby, monitoring may be more comprehensible and descriptive in comparison to showing execution traces in large and complex process models.

7   Related Work

Classifying CaPI, we propose an implemented approach for the automated, context-aware extension of process instances at run time to cope with process variability and to increase process flexibility. Related work addresses the configuration of process models before deployment, the adaptation of process instances at run time, the late selection of sub-process, the late composition of services [3, 17], and, in broader sense, aspect-oriented programming. In the following we discuss the commonalities and differences of related work in comparison to CaPI.

Approaches for process configuration, e.g., [9] or [7], aim at the modification of a reference process model to configure process model variants before process run time. Therefore, these approaches employ various transformations like adding process fragments, deleting activities, or changing control flow as well as properties of activities. However, these powerful transformations can be only applied, based on current information, before the process has been deployed. Instead, CaPI enables the injection of process fragments at run time. Further, CaPI considers context- and process-specific data at run time to support both process variability and process flexibility for long-running processes. Regarding automated adaptation of process instances at run time, rule-, case, and goal-based approaches may be taken into account [17]. Based on ECA (Event-Condition-Action), the rule-based approaches automatically detect exceptional situations and determine process instance adaptations required to handle these exceptions. Especially, AgentWork [13] is based on a temporal ECA rule model and enables automated structural adaptations of a running process instance (e.g., to add process fragments or to delete them) to cope with unplanned situations. However, CaPI entities allow for the specification of process variants instead of coping with unexpected failure events. Concretizing loosely specified processes, approaches for *late selection* typically rely on placeholder activities to integrate sub-processes in a base process at run time. While [1] suggests that the selection of the process fragment is primarily done by the process participants, [14] proposes an automatic, multi-staged approach to select sub-process at run time. Further, CaPI may be compared to process-based composition methods allowing for the late selection of service implementations [2,4,5]. These approaches share the abstract definition of a business process at design time. Each activity in the business process corresponds to a service specification and provides a placeholder for services matching the specification. Either upon invocation time or at run time, service implementations matching the specification are automatically selected from a registry based on QoS attributes or selection rules. By contrast, CaPI's extension areas in combination with injection specifications enable both the inline insertion of process fragments as well as the integration of process fragments as sub-processes. While placeholder activities are limited regarding the assignment of input and output data, the declaration of data mappings in the injection specifications enables the direct access to of activities in the process fragments to data objects in the base process.

Regarding related work in a broader sense, CaPI can be also well compared to *aspect-oriented programming* (AOP) [10]. AOP represents a programming paradigm for object-oriented programming and it targets high modularity by allowing and realizing the separation of system-level cross-cutting concerns from the actual key functionality. While AOP is also relying on injections at so-called *join points*, CaPI, by contrast, targets at the increased modularity of varying processes by separating activities, which are always performed, from activities and sub-processes performed in certain, pre-defined contextual situations.

8   Conclusion

In a nutshell, this work presents an approach for supporting long-running processes being subject to high variability by the context-aware and automated injection of process fragments at run time. Especially for long-running processes, the important configuration addressing process variety can hardly be performed solely at build time. However, existing approaches either focus on build-time configurations or allow for the late selection of process fragments based on placeholder activities. Consequently, the CaPI approach addresses this gap through providing context-aware configuration support at run-time based on the injection of process fragments. Finally, we further addressed the important data mapping for injected process fragments as well as we implemented a proof-of-concept prototype demonstrating the mentioned CaPI benefits.

In future research, we will conduct comprehensive experiments using the prototype to further examine the process of context-aware process injection. We further intend to enhance the CaPI modeler and to strengthen the context mapping by employing complex event processing.

Acknowledgement. This research was partially conducted within the SustainHub research project (Project No.283130) funded by 7th Framework Programme of the European Commission (Topic ENV.2011.3.1.9-1, Eco-innovation).

References

1. Adams, M., ter Hofstede, A.H.M., Edmond, D., van der Aalst, W.M.P.: Worklets: a service-oriented implementation of dynamic flexibility in workflows. In: Meersman, R., Tari, Z. (eds.) OTM 2006. LNCS, vol. 4275, pp. 291–308. Springer, Heidelberg (2006)
2. Aggarwal, R., Verma, K., Miller, J., Milnor, W.: Constraint driven web service composition in METEOR-S. In: Proc. SCC 2004, pp. 23–30 (2004)
3. Ayora, C., Torres, V., Weber, B., Reichert, M., Pelechano, V.: VIVACE: A framework for the systematic evaluation of variability support in process-aware information systems. Information and Software Technology **57**, 248–276 (2015)
4. Canfora, G., Di Penta, M., Esposito, R., Villani, M.L.: A framework for QoS-aware binding and re-binding of composite web services. J. Systems and Software **81**(10), 1754–1769 (2008)
5. Casati, F., Shan, M.C.: Dynamic and adaptive composition of e-services. Information Systems **26**(3), 143–163 (2001)
6. Dadam, P., Reichert, M.: The ADEPT Project: A Decade of Research and Development for Robust and Flexible Process Support - Challenges and Achievements. Computer Science - Research and Development **23**(2), 81–97 (2009)
7. Gottschalk, F., van der Aalst, W.M.P., Jansen-Vullers, M.H., La Rosa, M.: Configurable workflow models. Int. J. Coop. Inf. Sys. **17**(02), 177–221 (2008)
8. Grambow, G., Mundbrod, N., Steller, V., Reichert, M.: Challenges of applying adaptive processes to enable variability in sustainability data collection. In: SIMPDA 2013, pp. 74–88. CEUR Workshop Proceedings (2013)
9. Hallerbach, A., Bauer, T., Reichert, M.: Context-based configuration of process variants. In: Proc. TCoB 2008, pp. 31–40 (2008)
10. Kiczales, G., Lamping, J., Mendhekar, A., Maeda, C., Lopes, C., Loingtier, J.-M., Irwin, J.: Aspect-oriented programming. In: Akşit, M., Matsuoka, S. (eds.) ECOOP 1997. LNCS, vol. 1241, pp. 220–242. Springer, Heidelberg (1997)
11. Lanz, A., Kreher, U., Reichert, M., Dadam, P.: Enabling process support for advanced applications with the aristaflow BPM suite. In: Proc. Business Process Management 2010 Demo Track. CEUR Workshop Proceedings (2010)
12. Müller, D., Reichert, M., Herbst, J.: A new paradigm for the enactment and dynamic adaptation of data-driven process structures. In: Bellahsène, Z., Léonard, M. (eds.) CAiSE 2008. LNCS, vol. 5074, pp. 48–63. Springer, Heidelberg (2008)
13. Müller, R., Greiner, U., Rahm, E.: AgentWork: a workflow system supporting rule-based workflow adaptation. Data & Knowledge Engineering **51**(2), 223–256 (2004)
14. Murguzur, A., De Carlos, X., Trujillo, S., Sagardui, G.: Context-aware staged configuration of process variants@runtime. In: Jarke, M., Mylopoulos, J., Quix, C., Rolland, C., Manolopoulos, Y., Mouratidis, H., Horkoff, J. (eds.) CAiSE 2014. LNCS, vol. 8484, pp. 241–255. Springer, Heidelberg (2014)

15. Peffers, K., Tuunanen, T., Rothenberger, M.A., Chatterjee, S.: A Design Science Research Methodology for Information Systems Research. J. Management Information Systems **24**(3), 45–77 (2007)
16. Reichert, M., Dadam, P.: ADEPTflex - Supporting Dynamic Changes of Workflows Without Losing Control. J. Intelligent Information Systems **10**(2), 93–129 (1998)
17. Reichert, M., Weber, B.: Enabling Flexibility in Process-Aware Information Systems: Challenges, methods, technologies. Springer, Heidelberg (2012)
18. Tiedeken, J., Reichert, M., Herbst, J.: On the Integration of Electrical/Electronic Product Data in the Automotive Domain. Datenbank Spektrum **13**(3), 189–199 (2013)
19. van der Aalst, W.M.P., ter Hofstede, A.H.M.: Verification of Workflow Task Structures: A Petri-net-based Approach. Inf. Sys. **25**(1), 43–69 (2000)

A Multi-view Learning Approach
to the Discovery of Deviant Process Instances

Alfredo Cuzzocrea[1,2]($\boxtimes$), Francesco Folino[1], Massimo Guarascio[1],
and Luigi Pontieri[1]

[1] ICAR Institute, National Research Council, Rende, Italy
{cuzzocrea,ffolino,guarascio,pontieri}@icar.cnr.it
[2] DIA Department, University of Trieste, Trieste, Italy

Abstract. Increasing attention has been paid of late to the problem of detecting and explaining "deviant" process instances, i.e. instances diverging from normal/desired outcomes (e.g., frauds, faults, SLA violations), based on log data. Current solutions allow to discriminate between deviant and normal instances, by combining the extraction of (sequence-based) behavioral patterns with standard classifier-induction methods. However, there is no general consensus on which kind of patterns are the most suitable for such a task, while mixing multiple pattern families together will produce a cumbersome redundant representation of log data that may well confuse the learner. We here propose an ensemble-learning approach to this deviance mining tasks, where multiple base learners are trained on different feature-based views of the given log (obtained each by using a distinguished family of patterns). The final model, induced through a stacking procedure, can implicitly reason on heterogeneous kinds of structural features, by leveraging the predictions of the base models. To make the discovered models more effective, the approach leverages resampling techniques and exploits non-structural process data. The approach was implemented and tested on real-life logs, where it reached compelling performances w.r.t. state-of-the-art methods.

Keywords: Business process intelligence · Classification · Deviation detection

1 Introduction

Large amounts of log data are continuously gathered in many organizations during the execution of business processes. Such data are a precious source of information, which can support ex-post process analysis and auditing tasks, with the help of automated business intelligence techniques, like those developed in the field of Process Mining.

In particular, increasing attention has been paid to the problem of detecting and explaining "deviant" process instances in a process log, i.e. instances that diverge from normal or desirable outcomes (e.g. frauds and other security breaches, faults, SLA violations, non-compliance to regulatory rules). In fact,

© Springer International Publishing Switzerland 2015
C. Debruyne et al. (Eds.): OTM 2015 Conferences, LNCS 9415, pp. 146–165, 2015.
DOI: 10.1007/978-3-319-26148-5_9

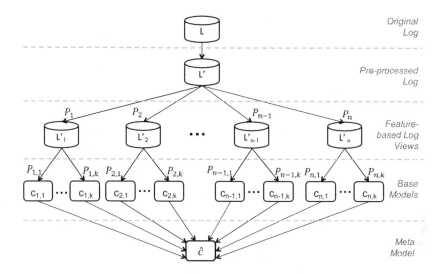

Fig. 1. Conceptual data-processing flow of the proposed approach: original data, transformed data, and discovered deviation-detection models.

the occurrence of such a deviance often impacts negatively on the performances of a business process, and it may cause severe damages to an enterprise in terms of extra-costs (e.g., due to the application of penalties) or missed earning opportunities, or even permanent loss of reputation.

Several approaches [3,19–21,24,25] have been proposed, which all combine the extraction of (sequence-based) behavioral patterns with standard propositional classifier-induction methods, in order to extract a model for discriminating between deviant and normal instances, while using the discovered patterns as summarized behavior-oriented data features. However, these approaches suffer from some major drawbacks, as discussed next.

First of all, due to their traditionally focus on balanced data, classical classifier-induction techniques may perform badly in a deviance mining setting, where deviant instances often correspond to rare behaviors. In such a case, indeed, the typical optimization strategy followed by these techniques (meant to minimize the global number of misclassification errors or, equivalently, to maximize the overall accuracy of the model) is likely to yield a model that cannot recognize deviant instances adequately.

On the other hand, it is not easy in general to decide which kinds of behavioral patterns (e.g. n-grams or sequence-based/alphabet-based tandem/maximal repeats) is the most effective choice for producing the vector-space representation of the log that will be eventually used, as a training set, for inducing a deviation detection model. This motivate previous attempts of using heterogenous representations mixing multiple families of patterns [21]. However, such an approach is likely to yield a cumbersome and redundant representation of the training data that may well confuse the learner, and eventually yield ineffective models.

Contribution. In order to overcome the above limitations, we propose a novel approach to the detection of deviant behaviors. The approach essentially consists in extracting an ensemble of classification models, induced (by applying several learning algorithms) from different propositional views, say $L'_1, \ldots, L'_n$, of the given log, say L. Each of these views represents a vector-space encoding of the traces stored in L, which combines both context information and a distinguished set of structural features capturing relevant behavioral patterns (as in [3]). Such a variegate multi-view collection of classifiers is made undergo a meta-learning scheme that eventually yields a higher-order classification model. Such a model, by combining the predictions made by the base ones, somewhat reasons on the whole heterogeneous set of structural features, at a higher level of abstraction.

In order to make the model more effective and robust to the cases where deviant instances are far less than normal ones, the approach leverages a resampling technique, and fully exploits context-oriented data associated with the process instances.

A summarized pictorial representation of the main data analysis tasks that compose our approach is shown in Figure 1. The figure presents, in particular, the relationship between the original log and different datasets derived from it through the application of pre-processing (specifically, resampling) and feature extraction techniques. Two layers of deviation-detection models are eventually discovered: a collection of base models (learnt by applying k different classifier-induction methods to one of the n feature-based views derived from the log), and a meta model, which integrates the predictions of the base models in order to implement a "high-order" deviation detection scheme.

The approach has been implemented in a prototype system, and tested on real-life logs, where it obtained compelling achievements w.r.t. state-of-the-art methods.

Organization. The rest of the paper is organized as follows. After providing a brief overview of related work in Section 2, we introduce some basic concepts and notation in Section 3. The specific learning problem addressed in this work is formally stated in Section 4, which also illustrates our technical solution to the problem, and some implementation details. An empirical analysis of the approach in a real-life scenario is discussed in Section 5, while a few concluding remarks are drawn in Section 6.

2   Related Work

Process Deviance Mining. The term "deviance mining" [21] indicates a class of process mining algorithms meant to discriminate (and possibly explain) log traces featuring a deviant behavior w.r.t. the normal or legitimate one. As discussed in [21], current deviance mining solutions adopt two alternative kinds of approaches: *(i) model delta analysis*, and *(ii) sequence classification*.

The former kind of approach consists in applying a process discovery technique to both normal and deviant traces separately. The two resulting models are then compared manually with the aim of identifying distinctive patterns for both classes of traces.

By converse, the usage of sequence classification techniques [3, 19, 20, 24] enable for discriminating deviant traces in an automated way, by learning some kind of classification model (e.g. a decision tree), after labeling all log traces as either deviant or normal. Since current approaches rely on standard classifier-induction algorithm, a critical point consists in defining a propositional encoding of the given traces, which can effectively capture relevant (and possibly distinguishing) behavioral patterns.

Three main classes of patterns have been used in the literature, in order to produce such a feature-based representation of each log trace, where each pattern is used as a distinguished attribute: *activity-based patterns*, *sequence-based patterns*, and *discriminative patterns*. Activity-based patterns [24] simply correspond to the different activities appearing in the log; for each trace and each activity, the latter is regarded as an attribute, whose value is usually set to the number of times it occurs in the trace.

More sophisticated sequence-based patterns were exploited in [3, 23], in order to capture the occurrence of typical execution schemes, prior to applying classic classification techniques (namely, *decision tree* and *association rule* classifiers). These patterns include *tandem repeats*, *maximal repeats*, *super-maximal repeats*, and *near super-maximal repeats* [4], as well as set-oriented abstractions of them, such as *alphabet tandem repeats*, and *alphabet maximal repeats* [5].

A special kind of "discriminative patterns" was introduced in [20] for recognizing failures among the traces of a software system, consisting each of a sequence of atomic event types. These patterns are (possibly non contiguous) frequent subsequences that are also correlated with the target class, based on Fisher score.

To date, there is no general consensus on which pattern family (e.g. tandem repeats, maximal repeats) must be used to derive a vector-space view of the log traces in a deviation-mining analysis. In fact, the empirical analysis of all the above-mentioned sequence classification methods presented in [21] showed that, although activity-based patterns and/or discriminative patterns sometimes perform better than others, all approaches have difficulty in discriminating and explaining certain deviances. The authors conjectured that some richer encoding of the traces (e.g. exploiting further kinds of patterns) could help better discriminate deviant cases. However, as noticed in [3], when increasing the number of patterns, the representation of the traces becomes rather cumbersome and sparse, and risks undermine the quality of the discovered models, as a consequence of the "curse of dimensionality" problem. This problem may exacerbate when mixing different kinds of patterns together (as proposed in [3]), since a redundant representation of the traces would be produced, which may well confuse the learner, even when some (greedy) feature selection/reduction mechanism is used.

Ensemble Learning Methods. These methods [13] constitute an effective flexible solution for improving classifier performances. In a nutshell, the core idea of ensemble approaches is to combine a set of models, all addressing the same mining task, in order to obtain a better composite global model. Specifically, when applied to a classification task, the prediction for any new instance is made by suitably combining the predictions made by all the models in the ensemble. When the learners are trained on different complementary views of the input dataset, the resulting meta-model will work on a space of high-level features (corresponding to the predictions made by the base models), which summarize the heterogeneous and large set of raw features that appear in those views.

Each ensemble method is defined in terms of three different elements: *(i)* the *base induction algorithms* (a.k.a. base learners), *(ii)* an *ensemble generation strategy*, specifying how different base models are to be built, by applying some base learner to a subset of the instances in the original training set, and *(iii)* a *combination strategy*, specifying how the different models in the ensemble are to be eventually integrated.

Three standard combination strategies were defined in literature: *bagging*, *boosting*, and *stacking*. Roughly speaking, in bagging schemes [7] different training datasets are used to learn the base learners, while the final prediction is performed by either uniformly averaging or voting over class labels. In the boosting strategy [17] instead, an iterative procedure modifying the distribution of the training examples is exploited to focus on those that are hard to classify correctly. The basic idea is to train, at each round, a new model compensating the errors made by former models. Unlike bagging, boosting assigns weights to each training example, and the prediction results from a weighted average scheme. Stacking [28] (a.k.a. "stacked generalization") adds a further meta-learning level on the top of the base learners in order to combine their predictions, where a new model is trained to make a final prediction, which uses all the predictions made by the base learners as additional features of the data instances.

By the way, various meta-learning methods have been proposed in the literature that do not follow an ensemble-learning approach. In particular, *co-training* techniques [2, 30] adopt a semi-supervised learning paradigm, where the scarcity of labelled data is compensated by training different predictors using different "sufficient" data views (or different learning algorithms/settings), and let the classifiers label some unlabeled instances for each other. However, these meta-learning approaches are inherently less scalable than the standard ensemble learning schemes discussed before, where different base models are trained in an independent (and possibly parallelized) way.

We pinpoint that the usage of ensemble learning techniques for the discovery of deviance detection models is novel in itself. Moreover, to the best of our knowledge, the combination of such an approach with the extraction of multiple views of the log (based on different sets of behavioral patterns) has never been explored in the literature.

3   Preliminaries and Formal Framework

Log Data. Whenever a process is enacted, a *trace* is recorded for each process instance (a.k.a "case"), which stores the sequence of *events* that happened along the execution of the instance. Let E and T denote the universes of all possible events and traces for the process under analysis, respectively.

For each trace $\tau \in T$, let $\tau[i]$ be the i-th event of τ, for $i \in \{1, \ldots, len(\tau)\}$, where $len(\tau)$ denotes the number of events in τ. Let also $prop(\tau)$ be a tuple storing a number of data properties associated with τ (e.g. case attributes or environmental variables). Moreover, let $PROP(T)$ be the relation consisting of all the data attributes associated with T's traces, so that $prop(\tau) \in PROP(T)$ for any $\tau \in T$. Focusing on the list of data values stored in these tuples, we will sometimes regard $prop(\tau)$ and $PROP(T)$ as a vector and a vector space, respectively.

Usually, any event $e \in E$ can be viewed as a tuple $\langle cID, A, R, t, x_1, \ldots, x_n \rangle$, where cID is the identifier of a process instance, t is a timestamp, A is an activity identifier, R is a resource identifier (i.e. the identifier of the agent that performed the activity), and attributes $x_1, \ldots, x_n$ encode further properties of e.

In particular, let us assume that a function α exists that maps each event e to the corresponding activity $\alpha(e)$ identifier —i.e. $\alpha(e) = A$. In general, such a function plays a key role in process mining settings, since it allows to bring the analyzed log to a suitable level of abstraction. Indeed, by abstracting each event e of a given trace into its corresponding activity label $\alpha(e)$, we can obtain an abstract representation of the whole trace. More precisely, for each trace $\tau \in T$, let $\alpha(\tau)$ be the sequence obtained by replacing each event in τ with its abstract representation: $\alpha(\tau) = \langle \alpha(\tau[1]), \ldots, \alpha(\tau[len(\tau)]) \rangle$.

A *log L* (over T) is a multiset containing a finite number of traces from T. We will denote as $events(L)$ the multiset of events that feature in (some trace of) L.

Let $\mu : T \rightarrow \{0, 1\}$ be a (unknown) function, allowing for discriminating all possible deviant cases from normal ones, that assigns a class label $\mu(\tau)$ to each $\tau \in L$, such that $\mu(\tau) = 1$ if τ is deviant, and $\mu(\tau) = 0$ otherwise.

Our ultimate aim is to obtain a *deviance detection model (DDM)*, i.e. a classification model estimating the (deviance-related) class label of any (unseen) process instance. Such a model can be represented as a function $\tilde{\mu} : T \rightarrow \{0, 1\}$ approximating μ over the entire universe of traces. Discovering a DDM is an induction problem, where the log L is the collection of training instances, and the function μ is known for each trace $\tau \in L$. In the following, we will only consider DDMs that work with a propositional representation of the traces, hence requiring a preliminary mapping of the latter onto some suitable space of features.

Feature-Based Representation of Traces. Once log traces have been turned into symbolic sequences, a wide range of sequence classification techniques could be applied in order to discover a deviance-oriented classification model. However, in general, this is not a valid solution for analyzing the logs produced by many business processes, due to the peculiar nature of these processes, where complex control-flow logics (e.g., loops, parallel execution, synchronization, exclusive choices, etc.) usually govern the execution of the activities, and impact on the possible sequences that can be stored in the log.

A consolidated approach to the analysis of process logs relies on extracting behavioral patterns that can capture the occurrence of typical execution schemes [3,23]. These patterns can be then used as high-level behavioral features for producing a vector-space representation of the original traces, where each trace is converted into a tuple registering a sort of correlation between the trace and one of the discovered patterns. At this point, whatever standard classification algorithm (such as the *decision tree* and *association rule* classifiers used in [3,23]) can be exploited to extract a deviance-detection model $\tilde{\mu}$ out of this propositional view of the log.

Various kinds patterns have been used in the literature to capture common subsequences of activities that recur in a log (within a single trace or across multiple ones). These patterns can be grouped into four main *pattern families*: *individual activities* [24], *sequence patterns* (including tandem repeats, maximal repeats, super-maximal repeats, and near super-maximal repeats) [4], *alphabet patterns* (including alphabet tandem repeats, and alphabet maximal repeats) [5], and *discriminative patterns* [20]. Individual activities are enough when the occurrence of a particular activity in a trace really helps identify deviant cases. However, reckoning deviant behaviors may require the usage of more complex patterns, providing a hint for the control-flow structure of the process. In these cases both sequence and alphabet patterns can be exploited. In particular, the latter kind of patterns is derived from sequence ones by simply relaxing the ordering of events (in order to unify different interleaving of parallel activities). Discriminative patterns represent frequent (possibly non contiguous) subsequences of activities having a discriminative power (measured via *Fisher score* in [20]) w.r.t. the target class.

Given a set P of patterns of the kinds described above, a vector-space representation of each trace τ can be built by projecting τ onto the space of the patterns in P. As a result, a propositional representation of τ is obtained that summarizes the sequence of events appearing in τ. Such a representation of the structure of a trace (i.e. of its associated sequence of events) can be extended with non-structural data, when learning a DDM via standard classifier-induction methods. More formally:

Definition 1 (*f-View*). Let $\tau \in \mathcal{T}$ be a trace, α the (event abstraction) function mapping each event to the respective process activity, and $P = [p_1, \ldots, p_q]$ be a list of (behavioral) patterns defined over the activity labels produced by α. Then, the *feature-based view* (*f-View*) of τ w.r.t. P, denoted by $f\text{-}View(\tau, P)$, is a tuple in $\mathbb{R}^q$ such that: $f\text{-}View(\tau, P) = prop(\tau) \oplus \langle val(\tau, p_1), \ldots, val(\tau, p_q) \rangle$, where $\oplus$ stands for tuple concatenation and $val(\tau, p_i)$, for $i \in \{1, \ldots, q\}$, is some function for computing the value that the feature (corresponding to the pattern) p_i takes on τ. □

Function $val(\tau, p_i)$ can be defined in different ways, depending on the application context. In general, two common criteria are used by current approaches to quantify the correlation between a trace τ and a pattern p_i: counting the number of times that p_i occurs in (the abstract representation of) τ, or simply registering the presence of p_i in (or the absence of p_i from) τ by way of a boolean flag. In the current implementation of our approach, the former option is used for individual-activity patterns, and the latter for any other kinds of patterns. As an example, let a and b be two activity labels produced by α on the given log, say L, and let a,b a tandem-repeat pattern extracted from L. Then, in our vectorial representation of any L's trace, say τ, a and b are considered as two boolean attributes (indicating whether τ contains a and b, respectively), while the pattern a,b gives rise to an integer attribute (storing how many times a and b occur one after the other within τ).

The vector-space representation of log traces defined above can be given as input to any standard classifier-induction method, in order to eventually discover a deviance-detection model (DDM). Indeed, any given labeled log L (i.e. a log where each instance is labelled as normal or deviant) can be turned into a propositional training set, denoted by $f\text{-}View(L, P)$, where each tuple encodes both the structure and the data associated with a trace of L, in addition to its class label. More precisely, $f\text{-}View(L, P)$ is a multiset that contains, for each trace $\tau \in L$, a tuple $f\text{-}View(\tau, P) \oplus \langle \mu(\tau) \rangle$ with the same multiplicity of τ. Clearly, the last value in each of the tuples appearing in $f\text{-}View(L, P)$ is the (known) class label of the corresponding trace, which represents the target of prediction; all the remaining values will play as input/descriptive features, which the learner can use to predict the class of any (possibly novel) trace.

Combining Multiple Base Classifiers Via Stacking. In our ensemble learning setting, the problem of combining multiple base DDMs into a single overall DDM is faced as an inductive (meta-) learning task, according to the strategy of stacking [28]. The meta-DDM is trained again with the help of a standard classifier-induction algorithm, provided with a propositional view of the given log, where the predictions made by the base learners for each trace of the log are used as high-level features of the trace, in addition to its intrinsic data properties. Such a representation of the traces is formally described next.

Definition 2 (*s-View*). Let $\tau \in \mathcal{T}$ be a trace, $CL = [c_1, \ldots, c_k]$ be a list of DDMs, and $PL = [P_1, \ldots, P_k]$ be a list of pattern lists, such that P_i is the specific list of patterns used to train model c_i, for $i \in \{1, \ldots, k\}$. Let us represent each DDM as a function $c_i : PROP(\mathcal{T}) \times \mathbb{R}^{|P_i|} \to \{0, 1\}$ that maps the feature-based representation $f\text{-}View(\tau)$ of any trace $\tau \in \mathcal{T}$ to a class label —where $|P_i|$ stands for the number of patterns in the list P_i. Then, the *stacking-oriented view* (*s-View*) of τ w.r.t. CL and PL, denoted by $s\text{-}View(\tau, CL, PL)$, is a tuple in $PROP(\mathcal{T}) \times \{0, 1\}^k$ such that: $s\text{-}View(\tau, CL, PL) = prop(\tau) \oplus \langle c_1(f\text{-}View(\tau, P_1)), \ldots, c_k(f\text{-}View(\tau, P_k)) \rangle$, where $\oplus$ denotes tuple concatenation and $c_i(f\text{-}View(\tau))$ is the boolean label assigned by model c_i to (the feature-based representation of) τ, for $i \in \{1, \ldots, k\}$. $\square$

Given a log L, a list CL of DDMs and a list PL of associated pattern lists, a combined DDM can be learnt by applying another classifier-induction method to a propositional view of L. This view, denoted as $s\text{-}View(L, CL, PL)$, is a multiset containing, for each trace $\tau \in L$, a tuple $sView(\tau, CL, PL) \oplus \langle \mu(\tau) \rangle$ with the same multiplicity of τ. The last value of each tuple in $s\text{-}View(L, CL, PL)$ plays as the (deviance-oriented) class label, while the remaining values are used as input/descriptive features to predict the class.

4   Problem Statement and Solution Approach

A feature-based log view like the one described in the previous section can be exploited to discover a deviance detection model. However, correctly separating deviant cases from normal ones is often a hard task, which poses several critical issues.

First of all, there is no general evidence about which pattern family should be preferred when deriving a vector-space representation of the log traces for deviance mining purposes. This motivates the attempt of exploiting heterogeneous representations mixing up different families of patterns. For example, a combination of sequence and alphabet patterns was used in [3]. The combination individual-activity patterns with both sequential, alphabet and discriminative patterns was analyzed in [21], as a way to improve the accuracy of a model leveraging the former kind of patterns only. However, the pattern generation phase may produce a very large number of patterns, and likely a sparse representation of the traces, which exposes the discovered classification models to the "curse of dimensionality" problem. In particular, when different pattern families are combined, a redundant encoding may be produced for each trace, featuring a high number of mutually correlated features, which may well confuse many learning algorithms —consider, e.g., the fact that the presence of a tandem repeat a,b implies the presence of both activities a and b (viewed as "individual-activity" patterns). In order to deal with such an issue, we propose an ensemble-learning approach, where different base learners are trained on the feature-based views produced by using distinguished family of patterns. This way, the final model, combining the predictions of all base models, can implicitly reasons on heterogeneous kinds of structural features at a higher level of abstraction, without directly working with them all.

Secondly, the discovery of deviant instances must be often carried out in scenarios where normal instances are much more than deviant ones. A dataset where a class largely overcomes the other one(s) in terms of number of examples is known in the literature as case of "class imbalance". Learning a classification model in such a situation is universally reckoned as a very challenging task for classic approaches, which tend to have bad performances in the recognition of the minority class (despite usually obtaining good global accuracy scores). In order to cope with such an issue, our discovery approach leverages a basic *oversampling* method, which attenuates the degree of class imbalance by simply replicating examples of the minority class.

The remainder of this section illustrates, in three separate subsections, the specific kind of prediction model that we want to induce from a log, our discovery approach, and some details on its current implementation, respectively.

4.1   Target Deviance-Detection Model (HO-DDM)

Our ensemble-based learning approach relies on inducing multiple classification models from different propositional views of the input log (based on different kinds of patterns). Specifically, each of these views is obtained by mapping the original traces onto a distinguished set of sequence-based behavioral patterns (according to the encoding scheme in Definition 1), extracted from the log while regarding each of its traces as a sequence of process activities.

The ultimate result of our approach is a novel multi-view (and multi-level) kind of deviance detection model, named *High-Order Deviation Detection Model* (HO-DDM), which is formally defined next.

Definition 3 (HO-DDM). Let L be a log over some proper trace universe $\mathcal{T}$ and event universe E, and $\mathcal{F}$ be a set of pattern families. Then a *High-Order Deviance Detection Model* (HO-DDM) for L w.r.t. $\mathcal{F}$ is a triple of the form $H = \langle CL, PL, \hat{c} \rangle$, where: *(i)* $PL = [P_1, P_2, \ldots, P_k]$ is a list of pattern lists, consisting each of patterns from a distinct pattern family in $\mathcal{F}$; *(ii)* $CL = [c_1, c_2, \ldots, c_k]$ is a list of base DDMs such that, for each $i \in \{1, \ldots, k\}$, the model $c_i : PROP(\mathcal{T}) \times \mathbb{R}^{|P_i|} \to \{0, 1\}$ (learnt by using $f\text{-}View(L, P_i)$ as training set) maps the propositional representation[1] $f\text{-}View(\tau, P_i)$ of any trace $\tau \in \mathcal{T}$ to a class label in $\{0, 1\}$; and *(iii)* $\hat{c} : PROP(\mathcal{T}) \times \{0, 1\}^k \to \{0, 1\}$ is a (meta) classifier that estimates the class of any trace $\tau \in \mathcal{T}$, based on its ("stacking-oriented") representation $s\text{-}View(\tau, [c_1, \ldots, c_k], [P_1, \ldots, P_k])$. □

This model encodes a sort of high-order deviance detector, where the predictions of all the discovered base classifiers are combined with the help of a second-level classifier (discovered through a stacking-based meta-learning strategy, as explained later on). Interestingly, the model can be applied to any unseen trace τ, in order to estimate whether τ is deviant or not. To this purpose, each base model c_i in the ensemble is applied to the vector-space representation $f\text{-}View(\tau, P_i)$ of τ produced according to the list P_i of patterns c_i is associated with, as specified in Definition 1. The predictions made by all the base models in CL are then combined into a single prediction by the meta-model $\hat{c}$. The latter model takes as input a propositional view of τ mixing the original data properties of τ (stored in $prop(\tau)$) with the class labels assigned to τ by the base models.

4.2   Algorithm HO-DDM-mine

Our approach to the discovery of a HO-DDM from a given log L is summarized in Figure 2 in the form of an algorithm, named HO-DDM-mine.

The algorithm follows a two-phase computation strategy. In the first phase (Steps 2-10), a number of base classifiers are discovered by applying a given set (specified via the input parameter $\mathcal{M}$) of inductive learning methods to different views of L, obtained each by projecting the traces in L onto a different space

---

[1] $PROP(\mathcal{T})$ is the space of all the data attributes associated with the traces of $\mathcal{T}$ (cf. Section 3).

Input: A log L, over event universe E and trace universe $\mathcal{T}$;
Params: A set $\mathcal{F} = \{F_1, \ldots, F_n\}$ of pattern families, $resampleMode \in \{\texttt{NONE}, \texttt{OS}\}$,
                $resampleFactor \in \mathbb{N}$, a set $\mathcal{M} = \{M_1, \ldots, M_n\}$ of classifier-induction methods,
                a (meta) classifier-induction method $\hat{M}$, max. number q of patterns per family;
Output: An HO-DDM for L w.r.t. $\mathcal{F}$;

```
 1.  CL := [ ];  PL := [ ];  // initialize both lists CL and PL as empty
 2.  for i = 1, ..., |F| do
 3.       P := minePatterns(L, Fi, q);  // extract a list P of patterns of family Fi
 4.       Compute TS = f-View(L, P);  // cf. Definition 1
 5.       if sMode = OS then reBalance(TS, resampleFactor);
 6.       for j = 1, .., |M| do
 7.            Induce a DDM c by applying method Mj to TS;
 8.            append(CL, c);  append(PL, P);
 9.       end
10.  end
11.  Compute SS = s-View(L, CL, PL);  // cf. Definition 2
12.  Induce a meta-classifier ĉ by applying method M̂ to SS;
13.  return ⟨CL, PL, ĉ⟩.
```

Fig. 2. Algorithm HO-DDM-mine

of features. In the second phase (Steps 11-12), all of these base classifiers are combined into a single DDM, based on a meta-learning (stacking) procedure.

In more detail, the different views of L are produced according to a given set $\mathcal{F}$ of pattern families (specified by the analyst as one of the input parameters of the algorithm): for each pattern family, a list P of relevant patterns of that family are extracted from the log L by using function minePatterns (Step 3). The second parameter of the function is right the reference family of patterns, while the third is the maximum number of patterns that can be generated for each family. In the current implementation of the approach, the selection of the q-top patterns is based on their frequency: the patterns with the highest q values of support in the log are kept, and returned as output.

Based on the list P of patterns extracted, a propositional view TS of L is produced, where each trace τ of L is turned into a tuple $f\text{-}View(\tau, P)$ —mixing both the data properties of τ and its representation over the space of P's patterns (Step 4), as described in Definition 1— and labelled with its associated class (i.e. either deviant or normal).

Before the classifier-induction methods specified in the input list $\mathcal{M}$ are applied to TS, in order to generate different base classifiers (Steps 6-9), the log can be further preprocessed in a way that reduces the imbalance of the two classes (namely, deviant instances vs. normal ones). Specifically, when the analyst decides to set the input parameter $sMode$ to $\texttt{OS}$, an oversampling procedure is applied to TS with the help of function reBalance, which alters the classes' distribution by simply repeating each deviant trace in the training log a number $resampleFactor$ of times (Step 5). No rebalancing is done instead when $sMode = \texttt{NONE}$.

Once all base classifiers have been induced, and stored in the list CL, they are combined into a single overall meta-classifier according to a stacking strategy. To this purpose, first an *s-View* SS of L is computed (Step 11) according to Definition 2; then a meta-classifier $\hat{c}$ is induced from SS, by applying the learning method $\hat{M}$ —still specified by the analyst, as one of the input parameters of the algorithm.

The last step of the algorithm simply combines the discovered base classifiers (with their associated pattern lists) and the meta-classifier into an overall HO-DDM.

4.3   Implementation

The discovery approach described above has been fully implemented into a Java prototype system. The system combines different functionalities, organized in four modules: *(i)* a *data transformation* module, supporting the derivation of all the kinds of log views (namely, *f-View* and *s-View*) employed by our approach; *(ii)* a *pattern extraction* module; *(iii)* a *classifier induction* module; *(iv)* a *model evaluation* module; The second module extracts and uses four different types of structural patterns defined in [4,5], by leveraging the plugin *Signature Discovery* available in the ProM framework [1]: *tandem repeats*, *alphabet tandem repeats*, *maximal repeats*, and *alphabet maximal repeats*. The extracted patterns are then used by the *data transformation* module to produce a boolean vector-space representation of the given traces, where each pattern is regarded as a distinguished attribute, taking a value of 1 iff the pattern occurs in the trace. The latter module also supports the derivation of a bag-of-activity representation of the traces.

The *classifier induction* module implements the following algorithms by taking advantage of the popular library *Weka* [16]: *A1DE*, a variant of the AODE method [26]; the decision-tree learning method *J48* [22]; the *k-NN* procedure *IBk*; the *LibSVM* Support-Vector-Machines classifier [10] with a Radial-Basis-Function kernel; the rule-base classifier *JRip* [27]; and a Neural-Network classifier [29], computing a multi-layer perceptron network via a standard back-propagation scheme (with an automated setting of the number of layers of the network).

The *model evaluation* module supports the evaluation of any discovered HO-DDM, by providing the analyst with several quality metrics, specifically tailored to our deviance detection setting, and described in details in the following section.

The system also allows the analyst to apply any discovered HO-DDM to new log traces, hence helping evaluating whether they represent deviant instances or not.

5   Experiments

In order to assess the capability our approach of effectively recognizing deviant behaviors, we conducted a series of tests on a real-life log, storing information on the clinical pathways of gynecologic cancer patients within a Dutch hospital, and made available as a benchmark dataset for the *2011 BPI Challenge* [14].

5.1   Dataset

Basically, the log registers information concerning the activities (mainly corresponding to the application of treatments) performed on patients suffering from common types of cancers to the genital tract. The raw event log contains 150291 events, referring to 624 distinct activities, and 1142 cases, corresponding each to a distinguished patient.

A number of attributes are stored for each case, which include the age of the respective patient, and two categories of attributes that concern the kinds of illness the patient was diagnosed with: "diagnosis code" and "diagnosis". Precisely, a case may be associated with up to 16 alpha-numeric diagnosis codes (e.g., M13, M12, 106), stored into different attributes of the form *Diagnosis code, Diagnosis code:1, . . . , Diagnosis code:15*, each referring to a distinguished type of cancer at a certain stage of malignancy. For example, code M13 identifies a kind of cervix cancer. Similarly, each case contains 16 attributes of category "diagnosis" —namely, *Diagnosis, Diagnosis:1, . . . , Diagnosis:15*— that can store each a short description of an illnesses (e.g. "maligniteit ovarium", "maligne neoplasma cervix uteri") diagnosed to the patient.

The main event attributes stored in the log are: *concept:name* (resp., *Activity code*), storing the name (resp., code) of the activity performed; *Specialism code*, storing the code of the medical specialism related to the activity; *org:group* and *Producer code*, which both represent the activity's executor, but at different granularity levels. Specifically, attribute *org:group* indicates the department/lab where the activity was performed, while the latter attribute stores an identifier of the person who performed the activity.

Since the traces in the log have no predefined class label, in order to make them suitable for a deviance mining task, we firstly marked each of them as either "normal" (label = 0) or "deviant" (label=1), by adopting one of the deviance criteria (namely, the one referred to as $BPIC11_{CC}$) introduced in [21]. Specifically, we labeled as deviant all the traces referring to patients diagnosed with a cervix cancer, i.e. all the traces where attribute *Diagnosis* evaluates "cervix cancer". Notably, we choose this particular definition of "deviant" clinical cases because it corresponds to the highest class imbalance ratio, among all those explored in [21]: 225 deviant cases (less than 20% of all traces) vs. 917 normal ones.

For the sake of fairness, we preprocessed the log by removing all the attributes (including those of categories "diagnosis code", "diagnosis", and "treatment code") directly linked to the class label, which would make trivial the deviance detection task.

5.2   Evaluation Metrics

Different evaluation metrics exist in the literature for testing the effectiveness of classification models in the presence of a rare class. Indeed, the usage of metrics that do not adequately accounts for the rarity of such a minority class may lead to overestimating the real capability of a classifier to correctly recognize the instances of that class. In the following we only concentrate on a binary imbalanced classification problem (as our deviance detection problem is), where the "positive" class label (namely 1) is assigned to deviant (typically rare) instances, while the "negative" class (namely 0) is assigned to the remaining (normal) ones.

Some core count-based statistics (usually shown in the form of a "confusion" matrix) for evaluating a classifier are: *(i)* *True Positives* (TP), i.e. the number of positive cases correctly classified as such; *(ii)* *False Positives* (FP), i.e. the number of negative cases incorrectly classified as positive; *(iii)* *False Negatives*, i.e. the number of positive cases incorrectly classified as negative; and *(iv)* *True Negatives*, i.e. the number of negative cases correctly classified as such.

Classification *accuracy* is the fraction of cases classified correctly: $(TP + TN)/(TP + FP + FN + TN)$. Despite this is a widespread evaluation metric, it is not appropriate when the classes are imbalanced. For instance, in a log where only 1% of traces are deviant, a simple model that predicts every trace as normal would have an accuracy of 99%, although it does not recognize any deviant instance.

A popular metrics that can be safely used over imbalanced data is the *area under the ROC curve* (AUC) [6]. Essentially, ROC curves are a visual tool for comparing the performances of different classifier induction methods, over a Cartesian plane where the vertical and horizontal axes represent the *true positive rate* ($TPR = TP/(TP+FN)$) and *false positive rate* ($FPR = FP/(TN+FP)$), respectively. A ROC curve of an induction method is drawn by plotting the score pairs (TPR, FPR) of different classification models discovered with the method. This curve essentially shows to what extent the "accuracy" (measured via the TPR score) on positive examples tends to drop when reducing the error rate (measured via the FPR score) on negative examples. AUC is a compact average measure for the performances of a classifier (the higher the AUC, the better the classifier), which let us to quantify its classification potential.

The geometric mean $\sqrt{TPR \cdot TNR}$, namely *G-mean*, was introduced in [18] as another performance metrics suitable for the case of imbalanced classes. The best classifier according to this metrics is the one that maximizes the accuracies on both classes, while keeping them balanced.

We also evaluated the standard *Precision* (P) and *Recall* (R) measures on the class of deviant instances, in order to support fine grain analyses on the misclassification errors made over those instances: $P = TP/(TP + FP)$ and $R = TP/(TP + FN)$.

5.3   Parameter Settings

Two key ingredients of our approach are: *(i)* the kind of patterns used to project the log traces onto a vector space, and *(ii)* the classifier-induction methods employed to derive, from such a feature-based representation of the traces, the base and combined models that compose the overall HO-DDM returned by the approach.

As concerns the former point, as a first family of behavioral patterns, denoted by IA (i.e. *individual activities*), we simply considered all the process activities in their own. In this case, for any trace, we regard each activity, say a, as an additional (pattern-oriented) feature of the trace, storing the number of times that a occurs in the trace. In order to produce more sophisticated representations of traces' behaviors, we considered (as also done in [3, 21]) all the sequence-based patterns described in Section 4.3, possibly capturing control-flow constructs (e.g., subprocesses, loops, and parallelism) ruling the behavior of the analyzed process: *tandem repeats* (TR), *alphabet tandem repeats* (ATR), *maximal repeats* (MR), and *alphabet maximal repeats* (AMR). As mentioned previously, all patterns but AI ones, were used as boolean attributes when computing the *f-View* of each trace, taking a value of 1 if the pattern occurs in the trace, and 0 otherwise. Similarly to [21], we considered the following heterogenous families of patterns: *(i)* {IA}, i.e. individual activities used alone (producing a bag-of-activity representation of traces' structure); *(ii)* {IA,TR}, i.e. the combination of individual activities and of tandem repeats; *(iii)* {IA,ATR}, i.e. individual activities combined with alphabet tandem repeats; *(iv)* {IA,MR}, i.e. individual activities plus maximal repeats; *(v)* {IA,AMR}, i.e. individual activities plus alphabet maximal repeats.

These pattern families were provided as input to algorithm HO-DDM-mine (via parameter $\mathcal{F}$), in order to make it build 5 different views of the given log.

A fixed setting was used in all the tests for the parameters q and *resampleFactor*. The former was always set to 250 as in [21], while parameter *resampleFactor* (really used by algorithm HO-DDM-mine only when *resampleMode* = OS) was kept fixed to 2. This way, all the deviant (i.e. positive) traces in the log were duplicated, thus raising the ratio between deviant and normal traces from 1:4 to about 1:2.

As to the induction of (both base and combined) classifiers, we resorted to all of the algorithms currently implemented in our prototype system, as described in Section 4.3. In particular, for the (second-layer) combined classifier, we always used to algorithm *A1DE* (i.e. we fixed $\hat{M} = A1DE$), pragmatically reckoned as a robust and effective solution over a wide range of tests. We pinpoint, that we obtained similar results when using other methods for the meta-classification task, but we omit details on such a kind of analysis for lack of space. Different methods were used instead in our tests to induce the base classifiers of the ensemble: the decision-tree learning method *J48* [22]; the *k-NN* procedure *IBk* (with k fixed to 10); the multi-layer perceptron method (denoted hereinafter as *ANN*) [29]; the *LibSVM* Support-Vector-Machines classifier [10] with an RDF kernel; and the rule-base classifier *JRip* [27].

Combined with the fixed settings described above, we considered three different configurations of algorithm HO-DDM-mine: *(1)* NO_RESAMPLING, where no resampling procedure (i.e. *resampleMode* =NONE) is applied to the transformed log (in order to reduce the class imbalance ratio), and the same set of (base) inductive learning methods as in [21], i.e. $\mathcal{M} = \{J48, IBk, ANN\}$ is used; *(2)* RESAMPLING, using our basic oversampling scheme (i.e. *resampleMode* = OS and *resampleFactor* = 2), along with the same battery of base classifiers as in the previous configuration (and in [21]); *(3)* RESAMPLING + MORE_CLASSIFIERS, which uses the same oversampling setting

Table 1. Prediction results on the $BPIC11_{CC}$ log by HO-DDM-mine and its competitor Nguyen et al.[21]. All the values were computed by averaging the results of 5 trials, performed according to a 5 fold cross-validation scheme. For each metrics, the best outcome is reported in bold.

Methods	AUC	G-Mean	R	P
HO-DDM-mine (RESAMPLING + MORE_CLASSIFIERS)	**0.853±0.053**	**0.736±0.022**	**0.598±0.042**	**0.742±0.049**
HO-DDM-mine (RESAMPLING)	0.819±0.044	0.722±0.047	0.584±0.080	0.715±0.047
HO-DDM-mine (NO_RESAMPLING)	0.813±0.026	0.648±0.039	0.469±0.056	0.502±0.082
Nguyen et al.[21] (BEST_OF_BEST)	0.798±0.000	0.599±0.000	0.412±0.000	0.496±0.000
Nguyen et al.[21] (BEST_AVG_RANK)	0.798±0.034	0.597±0.043	0.397±0.072	0.493±0.084

as in configuration 2 (i.e. $resampleMode = \mathtt{OS}$ and $resampleFactor = 2$) while exploiting all the classifier-induction methods provided by our prototype system (i.e. $\mathcal{M} = \{J48, IBk, ANN, LibSVM, JRip\}$).

5.4 Test Results

In order to assess the validity our approach, we conducted a series of tests on the real log described before. Table 1 summarizes the results obtained by algorithm HO-DDM-mine, compared with those of the deviance mining approach proposed in [21].

For the sake of comparison, as discussed in details in the previous subsection, we used the same families of patterns and the same (or a slightly enlarged) collection of classifier-induction methods as in [21]. However, our approach neatly differs from the one in [21] in two respects: *(i)* the possibility to exploit an oversampling mechanism, and *(ii)* the usage of an automated ensemble-based strategy, which intelligently integrates the models discovered by applying those different learning methods to different pattern-based views of the log —each of these models is used instead in [21] as an alternative "isolated" solution to the deviance detection problem.

Since the approach in [21] consists in applying each learning method to each distinct view of the log (generated according to one of the pattern families described in the previous subsection), it would produce a total of 15 independent DDM models —namely, $J48_{\{IA\}}$, ..., $J48_{\{IA+AMR\}}$, $IBk_{\{IA\}}$, ..., $IBk_{\{IA+AMR\}}$, $ANN_{\{IA\}}$, ..., $ANN_{\{IA+AMR\}}$— which should be compared with the ones discovered by our approach. For the sake of conciseness and readability, we just report, as separate rows of Table 1, a summary of the best performances achieved by the competitor approach, computed according to two different criteria: *(i)* BEST_OF_BEST, and *(ii)* BEST_AVG_RANK.

The BEST_OF_BEST row simply reports, for each evaluation method, the best value obtained by all of the different configurations of the approach in [21]. Clearly, this row provides an overestimated evaluation of the competitor approach, which may not correspond to any actual configuration of it. In a sense, this row is a sort of upper bound for the performance of all the considered configurations of the competitor.

In order to provide a more realistic (yet concise) term of comparison, we defined a second criterion, denoted by BEST_AVG_RANK, for aggregating the results obtained with the approach of [21]. Let C be the set of all DDM models discovered by the tested methods, and $V = \{AUC, G\text{-}Mean, R, P\}$ be the set of metrics considered in our evaluation setting. For any model $c \in C$ and any metrics $m \in M$, let $score(c, m)$ be the value returned by evaluating m against c. Based on these values, we ranked the models in C over each metrics. For example, $rank(c, m) = 1$ (resp., $rank(c, m) = k$) iff c is the best (k-th best) performer according to metrics m.[2] Considering all metrics equally important for assessing the quality of a DDM, we computed an overall average ranking score for each model $c \in C$ as follows: $rank(c) = .25 \times (rank(c, AUC) + rank(c, G\text{-}Mean) + rank(c, R) + rank(c, P))$. We eventually selected, among all the models discovered by (using different configurations of) the approach of [21], the one reaching the highest value of the overall ranking score $rank$.

According to this ranking criterion, the model found with method IBk on individual-activities features (i.e., by using only the family IA of patterns) was deemed as the best results of the approach in [21] (with an average rank of 1.75). The last row of Table 1 (marked as BEST_AVG_RANK) reports the quality measures received by this model, as a second term of comparison for our approach. Clearly, the performances of our competitor in its BEST_OF_BEST setting are always better than that in the BEST_AVG_RANK one. Therefore, in the following, we will focus our comparative analysis on the ("optimistic" for the competitor) BEST_OF_BEST scenario.

From the figures in Table 1, we can deduce some interesting observations. First, the proposed approach, even in the basic NO_RESAMPLING configuration, performs always better (over all the quality metrics) than the competitor, whatever configuration is used for the latter. This confirms the validity of using an ensemble-learning approach to the deviance detection problem, which seems to take the best of different data transformation and data mining schemes, and improve the performances of them all.

The gain w.r.t. the approach in [21] becomes more marked when using our (basic) oversampling procedure (i.e. configuration RESAMPLING). In more detail, even though the increment in terms of AUC is moderate (2.62%), we can observe a significant gain for the metric $G\text{-}Mean$ (20.53%), and a noticeable 44.15% (resp. 41.74%) achievement in terms of precision (resp. recall).

Further improvement is obtained by our approach when letting it use a broader range of base classifiers, i.e. when using the RESAMPLING + MORE_CLASSIFIER configuration, which exploits $LibSVM$ and $JRip$ as further base learners. Indeed, in this case, a gain of 6.89% (resp., 22.87%, 49.59%, 45.14%) is obtained in terms of AUC (resp., $G\text{-}Mean$, precision, recall) w.r.t. the overestimated BEST_OF_BEST configuration.

In summary, it seems that the combination of an oversampling method with our ensemble-learning strategy helps obtain higher improvements (w.r.t. the

---

[2] In order to deal with numeric approximation, we considered as equivalent any two scores x, y such that $|x - y| \leq .05 \times \min(x, y)$.

competitor supervised deviance-detection approach) than exploiting a wider range of base classifiers.

Before leaving this section, it is worth noticing that `HO-DDM-mine` took an average time of 25.13 seconds to compute a `HO-DDM` in the tests described so far. This corresponds to less than a 1% increase w.r.t. the time that would be spent by launching all the considered configurations of the approach of [21] (using different sets of behavioral patterns and different classifier-induction algorithms), in order to eventually select the best among the models discovered by them. Notably, a great fraction (namely, 98%) of the computation time was spent in the extraction of the behavioral patterns, which was particularly expensive for the case of tandem repeats and maximal repeats. This suggests that higher scalability could be obtained by using some more aggressive strategy for pruning the search space when computing such patterns, rather than simply using an extract-and-filter strategy (like that used in the current implementation of our approach).

6   Conclusion

We proposed an approach to the supervised detection of deviant behaviors, based on a novel multi-view ensemble learning scheme, where different learning methods are applied to different pattern-based views of a given log. Specifically, each view corresponds to a vector-space encoding of the traces, combining both context data and structural features (captured effectively by way of behavioral patterns). This collection of classifiers is eventually made undergo a meta-learning procedure, which produces an integrated high-order deviance detection model as an ultimate result. To make the approach more robust w.r.t. the classes' skewness we explored the usage of a basic resampling technique. Preliminary tests performed on a real-life log proved that the approach can achieve compelling performances w.r.t. a recent deviance mining method.

As to future work, besides testing our approach over a wider range of real logs, we plan to extend it by: *(i)* combining the pattern extraction method with an event abstraction approach, capable to automatically extract high-level activity concepts from log events (as in [15]), hence removing the assumption that an event abstraction function is already available for the events; *(ii)* integrating a cost-sensitive learning method, as a more sophisticated and flexible solution for dealing with class imbalance and with the need of minimizing a certain kind of misclassification errors over deviant traces; *(iii)* detecting deviant process instances at run time, and on the possibility to use co-training techniques [2,30] whenever the amount of labelled data is not sufficient to induce an accurate DDM. Moreover, we will investigate on extending our approach towards incorporating innovative aspects such as *privacy-preservation* (e.g., [12]), *accuracy control* (e.g., [11]), and *adaptivity* (e.g., [8]).

Acknowledgements. This work was partly funded by Italian Ministry of Education, Universities and Research within research projects `PONO3PE_00032_02` and `PONO3PE_00032_03`.

References

1. van Dongen, B.F., de Medeiros, A.K.A., Verbeek, H.M.W.E., Weijters, A.J.M.M.T., van der Aalst, W.M.P.: The ProM framework: a new era in process mining tool support. In: Ciardo, G., Darondeau, P. (eds.) ICATPN 2005. LNCS, vol. 3536, pp. 444–454. Springer, Heidelberg (2005)
2. Blum, A., Mitchell, T.: Combining labeled and unlabeled data with co-training. In: Proceedings of the Eleventh Annual Conference on Computational Learning Theory, pp. 92–100. ACM (1998)
3. Bose, R.P.J.C., van der Aalst, W.M.P.: Discovering signature patterns from event logs. In: IEEE Symp. on Computational Intelligence and Data Mining (CIDM 2013), pp. 111–118 (2013)
4. Bose, R.P.J.C., van der Aalst, W.M.P.: Abstractions in process mining: a taxonomy of patterns. In: Dayal, U., Eder, J., Koehler, J., Reijers, H.A. (eds.) BPM 2009. LNCS, vol. 5701, pp. 159–175. Springer, Heidelberg (2009)
5. Bose, R.P.J.C., van der Aalst, W.M.P.: Trace clustering based on conserved patterns: towards achieving better process models. In: Rinderle-Ma, S., Sadiq, S., Leymann, F. (eds.) BPM 2009. LNBIP, vol. 43, pp. 170–181. Springer, Heidelberg (2010)
6. Bradley, A.P.: The use of the area under the ROC curve in the evaluation of machine learning algorithms. Pattern Recognition **30**(7), 1145–1159 (1997)
7. Breiman, L.: Bagging predictors. Machine Learning **24**(2) (1996)
8. Cannataro, M., Cuzzocrea, A., Mastroianni, C., Ortale, R., Pugliese, A.: Modeling adaptive hypermedia with an object-oriented approach and XML. In: Proc. of Second International Workshop on Web Dynamics, pp. 35–44 (2002)
9. Clarke, B.: Comparing bayes model averaging and stacking when model approximation error cannot be ignored. The Journal of Machine Learning Research **4**, 683–712 (2003)
10. Cortes, C., Vapnik, V.: Support-vector networks. Machine Learning **20**(3), 273–297 (1995)
11. Cuzzocrea A.: Accuracy control in compressed multidimensional data cubes for quality of answer-based OLAP tools. In: Proc. of 18th International Conference on Scientific and Statistical Database Management, pp. 301–310 (2006)
12. Cuzzocrea, A., Russo, V., Saccà, D.: A robust sampling-based framework for privacy preserving OLAP. In: Song, I.-Y., Eder, J., Nguyen, T.M. (eds.) DaWaK 2008. LNCS, vol. 5182, pp. 97–114. Springer, Heidelberg (2008)
13. Dietterichl, T.: Ensemble Learning (2002)
14. van Dongen, B.: Real-life event logs - hospital log (2011). http://dx.doi.org/10.4121/uuid:d9769f3d-0ab0-4fb8-803b-0d1120ffcf54
15. Folino, F., Guarascio, M., Pontieri, L.: Mining predictive process models out of low-level multidimensional logs. In: Jarke, M., Mylopoulos, J., Quix, C., Rolland, C., Manolopoulos, Y., Mouratidis, H., Horkoff, J. (eds.) CAiSE 2014. LNCS, vol. 8484, pp. 533–547. Springer, Heidelberg (2014)
16. Frank, E., Hall, M.A., Holmes, G., Kirkby, R., Pfahringer, B.: Weka - a machine learning workbench for data mining. In: The Data Mining and Knowledge Discovery Handbook, pp. 1305–1314. Springer (2005)
17. Freund, Y., Schapire, R.E.: Experiments with a new boosting algorithm. In: Proc. of 13th Int. Conf. on Machine Learning (ICML 1996), pp. 148–156 (1996)
18. Kubat, M., Holte, R., Matwin, S.: Learning when negative examples abound. In: van Someren, M., Widmer, G. (eds.) ECML 1997. LNCS, vol. 1224, pp. 146–153. Springer, Heidelberg (1997)

19. Lakshmanan, G.T., Rozsnyai, S., Wang, F.: Investigating clinical care pathways correlated with outcomes. In: Daniel, F., Wang, J., Weber, B. (eds.) BPM 2013. LNCS, vol. 8094, pp. 323–338. Springer, Heidelberg (2013)

20. Lo, D., Cheng, H., Han, J., Khoo, S.C., Sun, C.: Classification of software behaviors for failure detection: a discriminative pattern mining approach. In: Proc. of 15th Int. Conf. on Knowledge Discovery and Data Mining (KDD 2009), pp. 557–566 (2009)

21. Nguyen, H., Dumas, M., La Rosa, M., Maggi, F.M., Suriadi, S.: Mining business process deviance: a quest for accuracy. In: Meersman, R., Panetto, H., Dillon, T., Missikoff, M., Liu, L., Pastor, O., Cuzzocrea, A., Sellis, T. (eds.) OTM 2014. LNCS, vol. 8841, pp. 436–445. Springer, Heidelberg (2014)

22. Quinlan, J.R.: C4.5: programs for machine learning. Morgan Kaufmann Publishers Inc., San Francisco (1993)

23. Sun, C., Du, J., Chen, N., Khoo, S.C., Yang, Y.: Mining explicit rules for software process evaluation. In: Proc. of Int. Conf. on Software and System Process (ICSSP 2013), pp. 118–125 (2013)

24. Suriadi, S., Wynn, M.T., Ouyang, C., ter Hofstede, A.H.M., van Dijk, N.J.: Understanding process behaviours in a large insurance company in australia: a case study. In: Salinesi, C., Norrie, M.C., Pastor, Ó. (eds.) CAiSE 2013. LNCS, vol. 7908, pp. 449–464. Springer, Heidelberg (2013)

25. Swinnen, J., Depaire, B., Jans, M.J., Vanhoof, K.: A process deviation analysis – a case study. In: Daniel, F., Barkaoui, K., Dustdar, S. (eds.) BPM Workshops 2011, Part I. LNBIP, vol. 99, pp. 87–98. Springer, Heidelberg (2012)

26. Webb, G.I., Boughton, J.R., Wang, Z.: Not so naïve Bayes: aggregating one-dependence estimators. Machine learning **58**(1), 5–24 (2005)

27. Witten, I.H., Frank, E.: Data Mining: Practical Machine Learning Tools and Techniques, 2nd edn. (Morgan Kaufmann Series in Data Management Systems). Morgan Kaufmann Publishers Inc. (2005)

28. Wolpert, D.H.: Original contribution: Stacked generalization. Neural Networks **5**(2), 241–259 (1992)

29. Zhang, G.P.: Neural networks for classification: a survey. IEEE Transactions on Systems, Man, and Cybernetics, Part C: Applications and Reviews **30**(4), 451–462 (2000)

30. Zhou, Z.-H., Chen, K.-J., Jiang, Y.: Exploiting unlabeled data in content-based image retrieval. In: Boulicaut, J.-F., Esposito, F., Giannotti, F., Pedreschi, D. (eds.) ECML 2004. LNCS (LNAI), vol. 3201, pp. 525–536. Springer, Heidelberg (2004)

A Genetic Algorithm for Automatic Business Process Test Case Selection

Kristof Böhmer[(⊠)] and Stefanie Rinderle-Ma

Faculty of Computer Science, University of Vienna, Vienna, Austria
{kristof.boehmer,stefanie.rinderle-ma}@univie.ac.at

Abstract. Process models tend to become more and more complex and, therefore, also more and more test cases are required to assure their correctness and stability during design and maintenance. However, executing hundreds or even thousands of process model test cases leads to excessive test suite execution times and, therefore, high costs. Hence, this paper presents a novel approach for process model test case selection which is able to address flexible user-driven test case selection requirements and which can integrate a diverse set of knowledge sources to select an appropriate minimal set of test cases which can be executed in minimal time. Additionally, techniques are proposed which enable the representation of unique coverage requirements and effects for each process node and process test case in a comprehensive way. For test case selection, a genetic algorithm is proposed. Its effectiveness is shown in comparison with other test case selection approaches.

Keywords: Process modeling and design · Process testing · Test case selection · Genetic algorithm

1 Introduction

Over the past years, processes have risen to deeply integrated solutions which are extremely important for various organizations. Hence, ensuring the stability and correctness of processes is a crucial challenge [11]. Several approaches for process verification exist [14], that focus on structural and behavorial correctness of process models. Specifically, when implementing process models, *testing* has proven a valuable complement to capture the process behavior at runtime, e.g., with respect to process data [18]. Testing concentrates on creating and executing test cases on the tested process model [13]. At minimum a test case consist of input data, which is used to initialize a new instance of the process under test, and an expected execution path that should be followed by the process model instance when executing the test case [18]. A fault can be detected, e.g., when an execution path deviates from the expected test case execution path [18].

Testing plays an important role in process model design, development, and maintenance because it allows to identify faults early during these phases [18]. As process models tend to become more and more complex, manual test case

© Springer International Publishing Switzerland 2015
C. Debruyne et al. (Eds.): OTM 2015 Conferences, LNCS 9415, pp. 166–184, 2015.
DOI: 10.1007/978-3-319-26148-5_10

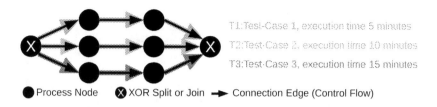

Fig. 1. Test case selection example with coverage illustration

generation becomes time-consuming and, therefore, expensive [17]. Hence, automatic test case generation tools emerged which quickly generate hundreds or even thousands of test cases to completely test a single process model [9].

Each individual test case might be executed quickly. However, executing *all* test cases may still require an excessive amount of time and, therefore, results in high costs [5]. Hence, it becomes necessary to apply test case *selection* and *minimization* techniques. Those techniques select an appropriate[1] subset of the available test cases to be executed. If the subset is small and efficient enough then significant time-savings are achieved [5,12].

Take, for example, the process model shown in Fig. 1. It's tested by three test cases, whereby the first covers the top most path, the second the middle path and so on. Assume that the user requirement is to cover 75% of the process model (i.e., 75% node coverage, so 75% of all nodes are tested by test cases)[2]. Then possible subsets would be to select T1 and T2 (combined execution time 15 minutes), T2 and T3 (25 minutes), or T1 and T3 (20 minutes). However, if the selected test cases should be executed in the minimum possible amount of time then the selection technique must select T1 and T2 as the optimal subset.

Identifying an *optimal* test case subset results in a combinatorial explosion problem [5] (the complexity is exponentially related to the amount of test cases). Hence, it cannot be solved in polynomial time [8]. So, existing approaches utilize heuristics, such as the Greedy Algorithm, which allow to find solutions where analytical algorithms are infeasible because of the huge search space [5].

We have analyzed existing process model test case selection and minimization approaches and found that those are *inflexible* regarding the supported user-defined coverage requirements, only use a *incomprehensive* representation of each node's unique coverage requirements, and also model the coverage effects of each test case in a *limited* fashion. Hence, existing work is not suitable for answering the following research questions:

RQ1. How can node coverage effects for process model test cases be modeled in a more comprehensive way?

---

[1] Appropriate means that user-defined requirements are fulfilled such as a minimal coverage objective, e.g., that a minimal amount of process nodes is tested.

[2] Multiple coverage metrics exist such as path, branch, or node coverage. However, in this paper we will, for the sake of brevity, only use *node coverage*. However, we are confident that a generalization to other coverage metrics is possible.

RQ2. How can the unique coverage requirements of each process node be determined and utilized during process model test case selection?

RQ3. Is it possible to integrate and utilize more complex process model test case selection requirements than supported by existing work (e.g., to optimize the selected test cases based on their execution time)?

RQ4. Whether and how can Genetic Algorithms be utilized to identify an appropriate set of test cases during process model test case selection?

In this paper we want to address the identified limitations and concentrate our efforts on test case selection in the process modeling domain. Therefore, we propose a comprehensive representation of test case coverage effects along with a novel approach to identify the unique coverage requirements of each process node. Here we exploit the fact that different kinds of nodes in a process model may have a different complexity, e.g., tasks versus gateways [3]. Additionally, we prove the applicability of Genetic Algorithms for process model test case selection and show, by using an evaluation and a prototypical implementation, that the presented approach supports more complex and flexible selection requirements than existing work.

This paper is organized as follows. Coverage metrics, prerequisites, and ways to improve the current situation are discussed in Section 2. Section 3 describes the proposed genetic test case selection approach. Evaluation, corresponding results and their discussion are presented in Section 4. Section 5 discusses related work. Conclusions and future work is given in Section 6.

2   Coverage Metrics

This section introduces coverage metrics for test case selection based on a given process model O. O is defined as directed graph $O := (N, CE, DE)^3$ where N denotes the set of process nodes, CE the set of control flow edges, and DE the set of data flow edges. As auxiliary functions (cf. [15]), we utilize the direct successors of a node n as $n\bullet := \{n' \in N \mid (n, n') \in CE\}$ for the control flow and $n\circ := \{n' \in N \mid (n, n') \in DE\}$ for the data flow. The direct predecessors of n can be defined accordingly by $\bullet n := \{n' \in N \mid (n', n) \in CE\}$ for the control flow and $\circ n := \{n' \in N \mid (n', n) \in DE\}$ for the data flow.

In this paper, we are mainly interested in the execution path of each test case, especially to determine which process model nodes are covered (i.e., tested) by each test case. So a test case is formally defined as:

Definition 1 (Test Case). *A test case v on a process model $O = (N, CE, DE)$ is defined as $v := (N_v, CE_v, enabled)$ with $N_v \subseteq N$, $CE_v \subseteq CE$, and enabled $\in$ $\{0, 1\}$ where N_v and CE_v form the expected test case execution path and enabled indicates if the test case should be executed (1) or not (0). The ordered set V of all test cases v on a process model O is denoted as test suite, which can be*

---

[3] The notion of directed graphs corresponds to the internal representation in order to cover different prevalent process modeling notations such as BPMN [10].

configured to create a test suite configuration V_i where all test cases are enabled or not (i.e., v.enabled is set to 1 or 0).

Test case selection starts with a test suite V (consisting of all available test cases for the process model O) and a set of requirements R which are user-defined, such as, the minimal node coverage should be 75%. The requirements contained in R must be satisfied to find a test suite configuration (i.e., deciding which test cases should be executed when executing the test suite) which provides an adequate testing of the process. Hence, the challenge is to find a minimal subset $V' \subseteq V$ that satisfies all requirements in R.

One typical requirement is that the process must be completely covered (i.e., each node must be tested by the selected test cases). For this, mostly, simple coverage metrics are used. For example, a process node is already marked as completely covered, and therefore, fully tested, when it is checked by at least one test case. However, this approach ignores that each process node has a *unique* complexity and significance [3] and therefore should be covered by an individually adjusted number of test cases to achieve an optimal coverage.

2.1   Optimal Coverage: Optimal Number of Test Cases per Node

This approach is called optimal coverage because it determines an optimal coverage value (i.e., how many test cases should be used to test it) based on various complexity metrics individually for each process node. We assume that if a process node (e.g., an activity or gateway) is more complex than another one, it must be tested more thoroughly (i.e., covered by more test cases) and, therefore, must be assigned a higher optimal coverage value. We suggest to determine the optimal coverage value $C_o(j)$ of node j as the weighted sum over selected complexity metrics $comp_i(j)$ for node j, $(i = 1, \ldots, n)$:

$$C_o(j) := 1 + \left\lceil \sum_{i=1}^{n} w_i \cdot comp_i(j) \right\rceil \qquad (1)$$

In Eq. 1, $w_i \in [0, 1]$ defines the weight for metric $comp_i(j)$. Moreover, a minimal coverage of 1 is assigned to each node, i.e., each node must be covered by at least a single test case. The complexity metrics and the weights reflect the process node coverage requirements. One example for a complexity metric is the Fan-In/Fan-Out metric (cf. [7]): for node j it sums over the number of successors $|j \bullet|$ and predecessors $|\bullet j|$ of node j and divides this sum by the maximum Fan-In/Fan-Out value over all nodes of the process model.

Two types of metrics are considered in this paper. First, *generic metrics* that are based on the process model itself which incorporate the *node complexity* (the structural *Fan-In/Fan-Out metric*), the *process structure* (a node is positioned in sequences or more complex loops, error, or concurrent paths), or the *node position* (a fault at an early executed node affects more follow up process nodes than a fault at a late node). Second, metrics that are supported by *historic data* (e.g., log files), such as *previously identified faults* (it is then more likely to find another fault), *node execution frequency* (an fault does have an higher effect if the faulty node is executed more frequently), *previous coverage* (if a node was not covered during previous tests, then it should be checked during follow up tests), *error path probability* (if a node frequently has to fall back to its error path it more likely contains a fault), *frequency of data-modifications* (we assume that a node which modifies multiple variables has likely a higher internal complexity than a node which modifies only one variable), and *known changes* (if a process node is changed then those changes should be checked with tests).

Example: Node j has three incoming edges and one outgoing edge. It is analyzed using the Fan-In/Fan-Out metric[4] with a weight of 1. Further, the node with the maximum Fan-In/Fan-Out metric of the whole process model has four incoming and two outgoing edges. Then $comp_{fan}$ would generate the following result:$(1 + 3)/(2 + 4) = 0.\overline{66}$. The total optimal coverage can then be calculated by $C_o(j)$ using $1 + \lceil (1 \cdot 0.\overline{66}) \rceil = 2$, i.e., two test cases are required to throughly test j, when considering its complexity. Existing approaches would ignore the node complexity and hence test it with a single test case. This could result in not detecting faults that will be found by the proposed approach. Why? Because, each node has a specific *internal node behavior*[5] which can, for example, contain multiple execution branches. Imagine that the internal node behavior contains a single conditional branch which provides two execution paths (e.g., for premium or normal customers), then a single test case will most likely only test one of the branches so 50% percent of the node's internal behavior and it will require at least two test-cases to throughly test the node. Note, that we are assuming that the mentioned complexity metrics also allow to assess the nodes internal complexity (e.g., a node with many incoming edges most likely has a more complex internal behavior then a node with only one incoming edge).

2.2   Test Coverage Metrics: Coverage of all Enabled Test Cases

The following coverage calculation approaches are applied individually on each process node j to determine, given a test suite configuration V_i and a process model O, which test coverage is achieved by V_i on j.

Traditional Coverage. The *traditional coverage* is based on existing coverage calculation approaches. The traditional coverage cov_{tr} is calculated for a process node j and a test suite configuration V_i by analyzing the test paths of each enabled test case $v = (N_v, CE_v, 1)$ (cf. Eq. 2).

$$cov_{tr}(j, V_i) := \sum_{v=(N_v, CE_v, 1) \, \in \, V_i} count_{tr}(v, j) \qquad (2)$$

---

[4] This example only utilizes, for the sake of brevity, the Fan-In/Fan-Out metric. The test case selection prototype (cf. Sect. 4), however, uses all the mentioned metrics (see previous paragraph).

[5] Note, each node's functionality is determined by its internal behavior (e.g., realized as a web-service or application) that is executed when execution the process node.

If j is covered by an enabled test case (i.e., it is contained in $j \in N_v$ of $v = (N_v, CE_v, 1)$), its coverage value is increased by one, cf. Eq. 3.

$$count_{tr}(v, j) := \begin{cases} 1 & \text{if } j \in N_v \\ 0 & \text{otherwise.} \end{cases} \quad (3)$$

Neighborhood Coverage. Neighborhood coverage reflects that, in a process, each node depends on its predecessors. Hence, if the predecessor of a node j is faulty then j might never be executed (e.g., the process might terminate because of a fault before reaching j) or has to deal with incorrect data/states. We propose that this should not only be reflected by increasing the optimal coverage (because of the increased complexity if multiple predecessors can affect a single node), but also by acknowledging that each test case that is executed on a predecessor of j also has a slightly positive effect on j itself. Therefore, j's coverage value should slightly be increased if one of its predecessors is tested. Hence, we are proposing to calculate the individual neighborhood coverage of each process node and combine it with its respective traditional coverage to provide a comprehensive representation of each test case's positive effects.

This a) motivates the test case selection algorithm to select test cases which together achieve a broad coverage of functionality supported by the process model under test and b) reflects the positive effects of each test case more comprehensively during test case selection. Why a)? Because with neighborhood coverage the test case selection algorithm gains less additional total coverage from covering close paths (i.e., paths that all concentrate on one function) than without. Hence, it is additionally motivated to cover paths (and therefore functions) which are more diverse and further apart from each other. Both advantages increase the probability that test cases selected by the proposed approach will more likely detect faults than test cases selected by existing approaches.

The neighborhood coverage value for a node j is calculated by analyzing each enabled test case, i.e., $\forall v = (N_v, CE_v, 1)$ over process model $O = (N, CE, DE)$ to identify the *neighborhood path start nodes* $N_{NPS,v}$ by (cf. Alg. 1):

$$N_{NPS,v} := \{k \in N_v \mid \exists p \in N \setminus N_v \text{ with } k \in \bullet p)\} \quad (4)$$

Neighborhood path start nodes are nodes that are covered by test case v, but also have direct successors that are *not* covered by v. Subsequently, all identified neighborhood path start nodes are analyzed, i.e., $\forall s \in N_{NPS,v}$, to determine all direct successors which are not covered by v using:

$$N_{FNN,s,v} := \{a \in N \mid a \in s \bullet \wedge a \notin v.N_v\} \quad (5)$$

Finally, the successors of all nodes in $N_{FNN,s,v}$ are searched for j to calculate j's neighborhood coverage (cf. Alg 2).

Example: Consider Fig. 2a with test suite configuration V_i containing a single[6] enabled test case v with $N_v = \{A, B, \ldots, F, G\}$. Obviously, B is the only neighborhood path start node, i.e., $N_{NPS,v} = \{B\}$. In turn, B results in the set $N_{FNN,B,v} = \{H, K\}$, i.e., H and K are situated in a neighboring path to the path covered by test case v, but are not covered by v themselves.

Assume that the neighborhood coverage is to be determined for node L. For this, all successors of H and K are searched until L is found or the search reaches a node which is covered by v. During the search, the nodes on the "search paths" are numbered consecutively (using counter c). The number indicates the number of edges or the distance respectively between L and the neighborhood path start node B. The greater the distance, the less the neighborhood coverage. This is expressed by a coverage reduction factor cov_{red} that indicates how quickly the positive effect of the test case v is reduced when getting further away from nodes covered by v. For $cov_{red} = 0.2$, a node numbered with 1 would be assigned 0.8 of the traditional coverage effect of the neighborhood start node. Here it is assumed that the traditional coverage of v on the neighborhood path start node is always 1. Hence, if j (so $j = L$) is the node marked with a 2 i.e., the node that is two "steps" far from the *neighborhood path start node*, so $c = 2$, then the control flow neighborhood coverage effect on L can be calculated by $max((1 - (2 \cdot 0.2)), 0) = 0.6$ when using a cov_{red} of 0.2.

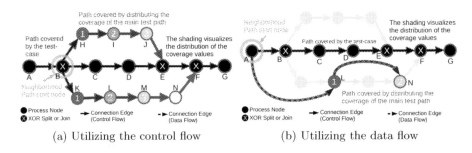

(a) Utilizing the control flow   (b) Utilizing the data flow

Fig. 2. Illustrating the concept of neighborhood coverage

Algorithms 1 and 2 focus on the process control flow. Neighborhood coverage can also refer to the process data flow denoted by the data flow edges DE of a process model $O = (N, CE, DE)$. The data flow based approach uses different sets to determine the neighborhood path starts nodes, i.e., they are based on the data flow edges DE instead of the control flow edges, i.e., $DN_{NPS,v} := \{k \in N_v \mid \exists p \in N \setminus N_v \text{ with } k \in op)\}$ and $DN_{FNN,s,v} := \{a \in N \mid a \in s \wedge a \notin v.N_v\}$. In Fig. 2b, hence, $DN_{NPS,v} = \{A\}$ and $DN_{FNN,A,v} = \{L\}$ hold. Based on

---

[6] Note, if a test suite contains multiple enabled test cases then the neighborhood coverage is calculated individually for each test case v on j. Subsequently each individual neighborhood coverage effect of each test case is added up to calculate V_i's total neighborhood coverage effect on j.

Algorithm NeibCov(V_i, j, cov_{red})
  $cov_{nbh}=0$
  Data: process node j to be analyzed, test suite configuration V_i, and coverage
    reduction factor cov_{red}
  Result: the neighborhood coverage cov_{nbh} of j
  foreach *test case* $v \in V_i$ *with* $v.enabled = 1$ **do**
    foreach *neighborhood path start node* s *in* $N_{NPS,v}$ **do**
      foreach $fs \in N_{FNN,s,v}$ **do**
        cov_{nbh}+=NeibCovRecur($j, s, fs, v, 1, cov_{red}$)   /* adds up the achieved
        neighborhood coverage of each v on j */
      end
    end
  end
  return cov_{nbh}

Algorithm 1. Neighborhood coverage calculation (pseudo code)

Recursive Subroutine NeibCovRecur(j, s, n, v, c, cov_{red})
  Data: process node to search for j, current neighborhood path start node s, current
    analyzed node n, analyzed test case v, step counter c, and a coverage reduction
    factor cov_{red}
  Result: cov_{nbh} of j for process model branch starting with s
  if $j = n$ *(i.e., the searched node j is found)* **then**
    return $max((1 - (c \cdot cov_{red})), 0)$ /* calculate the neighborhood coverage */
  else if $n \in N_v$ *(i.e., the currently analyzed node n is covered by v)* **then**
    return *0*   /* stop the search for this branch */
  else
    c=c+1   /* increase the step counter by one */
    foreach $n^* \in n\bullet$ *(i.e., $n^* \in no$ for the data flow)* **do**
      return NeibCovRecur(j,s,n^*,v,c,cov_{red})   /* recursively analyze all
      successive branches */
    end
  end
  return 0

Algorithm 2. Neighborhood coverage calculation subroutine (pseudo code)

these sets Alg. 1 and 2 can be used analogously. In the example depicted in Fig. 2b, starting from A nodes L and N are successively numbered with 1 and 2 respectively as they are connected via data edges. Assume a reduction factor of $cov_{red} = 0.2$. Then the neighborhood coverage $cov_{nbh}(L)$ of v turns out as 0.8 and for N as 0.6 respectively based on test case v.

Coverage Degeneration. If multiple test cases are applied on the same process node, partly similar *internal node behavior* (cf., Sect. 2.1) is likely executed and, therefore, tested by multiple test cases. Hence, we assume that the individual positive effect (i.e., the likelihood that a test case detects a not yet identified fault) of an additional test case is higher when, e.g., a node is currently only covered by two test cases as it would be if the same node is already covered by ten test cases. Hence, we advocate to slightly decrease the additional coverage gain of each test case if multiple test cases are covering the same process node. We denote this by the term *coverage degeneration* which is captured by a coverage degeneration factor that is determined for each coverage metric.

  For *traditional coverage* $cov_{tr}(j, V_i)$ of a node j based on test suite configuration V_i (cf. Eq. 2), the degeneration factor results (cf. Eq. 6) from weighing the number of enabled test cases with a user-defined factor $w_{deg} \in [0,1]$ and putting it into relation with the maximum possible factor $w_{degMax} \in [0,1]$, i.e., putting a limitation to the degeneration. Assume that 10 enabled test cases cover j, $w_{deg} = 0.05$, and $w_{degMax} = 0.3$, then the coverage degeneration factor for traditional coverage turns out as $1 - min(((10-1)*0.05), 0.3) = 0.7$. Hence, the achieved traditional coverage will be multiplied with 0.7 to reduce it by 30% from 10 (+1 for each test case) to 7.

$$cov_{tr}^{deg}(j, V_i) = 1 - min(((|\{v = (N_v, CE_v, 1) \in V_i \mid j \in N_v\}| - 1) \cdot w_{deg}), w_{degMax}) \tag{6}$$

The degeneration factor of the *neighborhood coverage* metrics is also based on the number of enabled test cases. More precisely, each enabled test case in V_i is analyzed to count how many test cases generate a positive neighborhood coverage (cf. Alg. 2) on j (cf. Eq. 8 and 9). Subsequently, the number of test cases is also multiplied with w_{deg}, cf. Eq. 7, to calculate the neighborhood coverage degeneration factor. Again w_{degMax} limits the maximum possible degeneration.

$$cov_n^{deg}(j, V_i, cov_{red}) = 1 - min(((cov_{nc}^{deg}(j, V_i, cov_{red}) - 1) \cdot w_{deg}), w_{degMax}) \tag{7}$$

$$cov_{nc}^{deg}(j, V_i, cov_{red}) = \sum_{v=(N_v, CE, 1) \in V_i} \sum_{s \in N_{NPS,v}} \sum_{fs \in N_{FNN,s,v}} count_n^{deg}(j, s, fs, v, cov_{red}) \tag{8}$$

$$count_n^{deg}(j, s, n, v, cov_{red}) = \begin{cases} 1 & \text{if } NeibCovRecur(j, s, fs, v, 1, cov_{red}) > 0 \\ 0 & \text{otherwise.} \end{cases} \tag{9}$$

The degeneration factors for the data flow (i.e., $Dcov_n^{deg}$) can be calculated analogously. Due to space restrictions we again abstain from a detailed definition.

By applying the described coverage degeneration technique the proposed test case selection approach gains a more comprehensive view on the coverage effects of each test case, than existing work, and therefore will more likely identify faults that are missed by existing test case selection approaches.

Final Process Node Coverage. The presented metrics, i.e., traditional coverage as well as neighborhood coverage for control and data flow, together with degeneration factors are combined to a comprehensive coverage metric for process nodes (cf. Eq. 10) which takes a node j, a test suite configuration V_i, and a coverage reduction factor cov_{red} (applied when determining the neighborhood coverage) to determine the coverage which is achieved by V_i on j. Note, $DNeibCov_n(V_i, j, cov_{red})$ calculates the neighborhood coverage based on the process model's data flow.

$$\begin{aligned} C_s(V_i, j, cov_{red}) = {} & cov_{tr}^{deg}(j, V_i) \cdot cov_{tr}(V_i, j) \\ & + cov_n^{deg}(j, V_i, cov_{red}) \cdot NeibCov(V_i, j, cov_{red}) \\ & + Dcov_n^{deg}(j, V_i, cov_{red}) \cdot DNeibCov(V_i, j, cov_{red}) \end{aligned} \tag{10}$$

The proposed concepts address the first two identified research questions by providing a more comprehensive view on coverage calculation and coverage requirements than existing process test case selection work. However, we also want to provide a solution to address flexible requirements and questions such as "Which test cases should be selected to get the maximum possible coverage within three hours test suite execution time?". We assume that Genetic Search Algorithms can play a viable role to address such challenges.

3   Genetic Selection Algorithm

A Genetic Algorithm (GA) is a search heuristic that mimics natural selection [4]. The first step is to determine the *individuals* of the problem and their encoding. For test case selection, intuitively, the test cases are *encoded* as binary genes and combined to individuals, i.e., the test suits. Multiple individuals then form the *population*. Each individual is assessed using a *fitness function* that can calculate the individual's quality. Subsequently the individuals with the highest quality (i.e., fitness) are selected and combined (i.e., by applying *crossover* and *mutation*) to form the next generation of the population. Repeatedly applying the last step typically increases the average quality of the whole population over time and allows to find an adequate solution to the search problem.

Genetic Encoding. Each potential test suite configuration V_i (cf. Def. 1) consists of multiple test cases, i.e., the $V_i :=< v_1, \dots, v_k >$ which is encoded in a binary way based on the value of the attribute *enabled* in each v:

$$V_i^{enc} :=< v_1.enabled, \dots, v_k.enabled > \tag{11}$$

Generating the First Population. The first population (i.e., the initial set of all currently evolving test suite configurations, $P :=< V_1^{enc}, \dots, V_S^{enc} >$ where S is the user chosen maximum *population_size*) is generated randomly. More precisely, *population_size* test suite configurations V_i^{enc} are generated and filled with randomly generated genes (i.e., test case *enabled* states). A random number $rand \in [0,1]$ is generated for each test case in V_i. If $rand$ is lower then 0.5 then the test case (i.e., the gene) is disabled (0), else enabled (1).

Fitness Function. A fitness function allows to assess the quality (i.e., fitness level) of each individual (i.e., of each test suite configuration). For example, here the quality is measured by taking the test suite coverage, which is achieved by a specific test suite configuration, in relation to the required test suite configuration execution time. We assume a test suite configuration with a higher fitness level as better than one with a lower fitness value.

The following fitness function (cf. Eq. 13) utilizes Eq. 12, to asses the achieved test coverage of a test suite configuration V_i^{enc7}. Therefore Eq. 12 adds up and determines (by using Eq. 10) the coverage of each process node j. We assume,

---

[7] Note, that V_i^{enc} can always be decoded into a specific V_i by using the known V and setting the respective *enabled* states.

that a node does not gain any advantage from achieving a coverage level which is above its own calculated optimal coverage level (cf. Eq. 12, Eq. 13, and Eq. 14). Hence, we take the minimum between the achieved final coverage C_s (cf. Eq. 10) of the node j and its optimal coverage C_o (cf. Eq. 1). The added up coverage is then divided by the maximum possible optimal coverage (i.e., the sum of all nodes' optimal coverage) to normalize the generated result.

$$cov_r(V_i, cov_{red}) = \frac{\sum\limits_{j \in N} min(C_o(j), C_s(V_i, j, cov_{red}))}{\sum\limits_{j \in N} C_o(j)} \tag{12}$$

The first fitness function, cf. Eq. 13, utilizes a user-chosen minimum test coverage value $cov_{obj} \in [0, 1]$ and assesses a test suite configuration V_i to check if V_i achieves at least cov_{obj} percent of the total possible optimal coverage within minimal test suite execution time.

$$fit_{minT}(V_i, cov_{obj}, cov_{red}) = \begin{cases} cov_r(V_i, cov_{red})/100 & \text{if } cov_r(V_i, cov_{red}) < cov_{obj} \\ \dfrac{\sum\limits_{j \in N} min(C_o(j), C_s(V_i, j, cov_{red}))}{x} & \text{otherwise.} \end{cases} \tag{13}$$

Specifically, fit_{minT} starts by determining if the minimum coverage objective cov_{obj} is already fulfilled by comparing the average node coverage of V_i (using $cov_r(V_i, cov_{red})$, Eq. 12) with cov_{obj}. If the cov_{obj} is not fulfilled then the achieved coverage is divided by 100 and returned. Hence, the fitness increases when additional test cases are enabled, such that the GA is motivated to enable at least enough test cases to achieve a minimum coverage of cov_{obj}.

If the cov_{obj} is fulfilled then the achieved coverage is divided by x. x is defined as the sum of the total execution times over all enabled test case in V_i. Calculating the execution time of a single test case v starts by determining the average execution time (e.g., based on timestamps stored in recorded process execution logs[8]) of each node which is part of the execution path N_v. Subsequently, the average execution times of each node in N_v are summed up to calculate v's expected total execution time. Hence, the fitness increases by preferring test cases that are executed quickly while providing a high amount of additional coverage.

The second fitness function $fit_{max}(V_i, cov_{red})$ (cf. Eq. 14) assesses a test suite configuration V_i to check if V_i achieves the maximum possible total process model coverage in at most g total test suite execution time. Therefore, it calculates the total test coverage achieved by V_i and multiplies it with a dynamic penalty factor if the total execution time x of V_i is too high compared to the user chosen maximum execution time objective g (cf. Eq. 15).

$$fit_{max}(V_i, cov_{red}) = \left[\sum\limits_{j \in N} min(C_o(j), C_s(V_i, j, cov_{red})) \right] \cdot (1 - d(g, x)) \tag{14}$$

---

[8] Note, if no execution logs are available then the expected execution times can still be specified manually, e.g., by a domain expert.

$$d(g, x) = \begin{cases} 0 & \text{if } x \leq g \\ 1 & \text{if } x \geq g \cdot 2 \\ \frac{(x-g)}{g} & \text{otherwise.} \end{cases} \qquad (15)$$

Equation 15 checks if the total test suite execution time of V_i (i.e., x) is below the user chosen execution time objective g. If x is below g (i.e., the total execution time is below the chosen maximum one) then no penalty is applied. The maximum penalty of 1 is applied if x is twice as high than g. Finally, if x is between g and and two times g then a fraction of the maximum penalty is applied to increase the flexibility of the presented approach. Hence, the algorithm is able to select a test suite configuration which is slightly above the chosen maximum execution time if it provides a dramatic coverage improvement for only a slight miss of the execution time objective.

Selection of Parents. Parents must be selected to create offspring that can form the next generation [4]. Therefore, the user chooses an *offspring_rate* that controls how many percent of the old generation will be selected as parents and replaced with their children to generate the next generation. The selection process itself is based on the Tournament Selection [4] technique. Hence, the algorithm randomly chooses individuals and compares their fitness. The individual with the highest fitness is selected until *offspring_rate* percent of the *population_size* are chosen. Tournament Selection was chosen because the selection pressure can be controlled by varying the amount of compared individuals and it also showed encouraging results when we compared it with other selection techniques during the preliminary tests.

Crossover and Mutation. The proposed GA utilizes Multi Point Crossover [4]. Hence, two parent individuals are selected and a crossover operation is applied to generate two new individuals (children). Therefore, *crossover_points* $\in [0, I]$ (i.e., the user chosen amount of crossover points, where I holds the amount of test cases stored in a single individual) points are randomly chosen and ordered. Then the algorithm iterates through all points and the section between the last point and the current one is swapped between the parents [4]. After crossover, each generated child is mutated. Hence, the mutation algorithm iterates through all genes of the child and generates a random value $rand \in [0, 1]$ during each iteration. If $rand < mutation\_rate$ then the current gene is replaced by a randomly generated one [4]. Multi Point Crossover was chosen because it provides the necessary flexibility to adapt it for each problem size using the *crossover_points* variable. Finally the generated children replace their parents to create the next generation of the population.

Termination. The GA terminates automatically when the termination condition, to repeat the algorithm for *max_generation* number of times, is satisfied. It returns the best individual, i.e., the test suite configuration with the highest fitness value, found until then.

Genetic algorithms provide flexibility (e.g., a custom fitness function can be integrated to address unique coverage selection requirements) and customizability (e.g., by providing a way to exchange algorithm components, such as the applied crossover method, or by allowing to customize the algorithm's parameters for various problem sizes). Hence, we propose genetic algorithms as an expandable foundation for process model test case selection and continue by evaluating their effectiveness in comparison with other test case selection techniques.

4   Evaluation

To assess the feasibility of the proposed process model test case selection approach it was evaluated using three different process models with increasing size and complexity. Additionally it was compared with alternative selection techniques, namely *random* and *adaptive greedy* selection.

Designing Test Problems. The test data which was used for the evaluation consists out of a) three process models (with low, medium, and high complexity) b) test cases (one test case was generated for each possible execution path for each model) and c) historic data (e.g., recorded execution logs, to determine the execution frequency of a node or its average execution time). All test data were artificially generated and each evaluated test case selection technique was executed on each of the three models and their related data (i.e., test cases and historic data). Each test case was sextupled so simulate that the internal behavior of process nodes is typically very complex and, therefore, multiple test cases with various test data are required to thoroughly test it.

The process model generation starts with an initial model with a low complexity (20 nodes, 42 test cases, 7 unique execution paths), which was then extended by adding additional paths and XOR splits to generate a model with medium complexity (80 nodes, 120 test cases, 20 paths) and high complexity (266 nodes, 390 test cases, 65 paths). Finally, artificial historic data (i.e., execution log data) were generated in a deterministic way, e.g., the node execution time was determined from the node position and a default execution timespan. Hence, the test data is "stable" and can be reproduced for future evaluations.

Metrics and Evaluation. The random, genetic, and adaptive greedy test case selection techniques were compared as follows. First the proposed genetic search algorithm based approach tried to answer one of two questions a) "Which test cases should be executed to achieve a X percent process node coverage within a minimal test suite execution time?" or b) "Which test cases should be executed to achieve the maximum possible coverage in Y minutes test suite execution time?". Subsequently, the timespan which is required to execute the test suite configuration which was identified by the proposed genetic search algorithm (for questions a or b) was calculated. Finally, the determined timespan was used by the other two evaluated selection techniques (random selection and adaptive greedy selection). Both selected one test case after another until selecting another test case would create a test suite configuration which requires more time to execute than the one identified by the proposed genetic algorithm based technique.

The *random selection* technique randomly selects each test case from a list of not yet selected test cases. *Adaptive greedy selection*, however, analyzes and orders each available not yet selected test case based on its additional coverage/ required execution time balance. Finally, the test case which provides the most additional coverage for the least additional execution time is chosen. The *genetic selecting* technique utilizes the approach described in Section 3. The test suite configurations (i.e., the configuration identified by each of the three selection algorithms) were evaluated by determining the achieved final average node coverage, cf. Eq. 12 (i.e., the optimal coverage, C_o (cf. Eq. 1), of each node $j \in N$ of a process model $O = (N, CE, DE)$ is added up and then compared with the added up achieved final node coverage, C_s (cf. Eq. 10), provided by the analyzed test suite configuration). In addition, fault coverage was determined by assigning artificial faults to each process node. We assume that a test suite configuration V_i would find more faults for the process node j if the achieved final coverage gets closer to the optimal coverage of j (cf. Eq. 16).

$$fault(V_i, j, cov_{red}) = \begin{cases} 1 & \text{if } C_s(V_i, j, cov_{red}) > 0 \wedge C_s(V_i, j, cov_{red}) \leq C_o(j) \cdot 0.25 \\ 3 & \text{if } C_s(V_i, j, cov_{red}) > C_o(j) \cdot 0.25 \wedge C_s(V_i, j, cov_{red}) \leq C_o(j) \cdot 0.50 \\ 5 & \text{if } C_s(V_i, j, cov_{red}) > C_o(j) \cdot 0.50 \wedge C_s(V_i, j, cov_{red}) \leq C_o(j) \cdot 0.75 \\ 7 & \text{if } C_s(V_i, j, cov_{red}) > C_o(j) \cdot 0.75 \\ 0 & \text{otherwise.} \end{cases}$$

$$(16)$$

$$faultCoverage(V_i, cov_{red}) = \frac{\sum_{j \in N} fault(V_i, j, cov_{red})}{|N| \cdot 7} \qquad (17)$$

Note that cov_{red} represents the user chosen *coverage reduction factor* which is utilized at $C_s(V_i, j, cov_{red})$ (i.e., the coverage calculation, cf. Eq. 10) during the incorporation of the neighborhood coverage of j. For example, if the achieved coverage (for the process node j) would be between 25% and 50% of j's optimal coverage, then it was assumed that three out of seven faults would be found by the test suite for the node j. Finally, the detected faults for each node were added up and divided through the maximum possible detectable amount of faults to normalize the result of Eq. 17.

Results. The evaluation results were generated by applying all three evaluated test case selection techniques (the proposed genetic selection algorithm, random test case selection, and adaptive greedy selection) on the described three test problems. For each test problem two questions were analyzed a) "Which test cases should be executed to achieve a X percent coverage within a minimal test suite execution time?" whereby X is 20, 40, 60, or 80 percent of the maximal possible optimal total process coverage and b) "Which test cases should be executed to achieve the maximum possible coverage in Y minutes test suite execution time?" whereby Y is 20, 40, 60, or 80 percent of twice the time which would be necessary to execute each process node once.

Primary tests were executed to identify appropriate configuration values for the designed genetic test case selection technique. *Mutation_rate* (0.5%), w_{deg} (i.e., coverage degeneration, 10%), w_{degMax} (i.e., maximal coverage degeneration, 50%), cf. Eq. 6 and 7, cov_{red} (i.e., neighborhood coverage reduction per step, 30%), cf. Alg. 1 and 2, all weights w (e.g., for coverage metrics, 1) and *offspring_rate* (50%) were fixed for all three test problem complexity levels. The value of *max_generation* (low complexity test problem:300, medium:500, high:800), *population_size* (200, 400, 800) and *crossover_points* (4, 8, 15), chosen individuals for tournament selection (3, 5, 10), however, were chosen individually to reflect the increasing test problem complexity. For example, it was found that a low number of *crossover_points* would, naturally, exchange very large chunks of test case configurations during child generation. This hardens the fine tuning of the identified results during the final stage of the search (this challenge increases from small to large test problem complexity/sizes, so the number of *crossover_points* was increased whenever the test problem complexity increases).

The results show that GA outperforms the random and adaptive greedy selection techniques (cf. Fig. 3 and 4). It is also noticeable that GA benefits from increasing the test problem complexity. The GA generated a 3.6%/3.5% higher coverage/fault detection, compared to the adaptive greedy selection technique for questions a, for the low complexity test problem, while for the test problem with high complexity the genetic selection technique provides a 9%/10.3% higher coverage/fault detection than the adaptive greedy selection (cf. Table 1 and 2).

We conclude that GA is able to make better use of the additional flexibility (i.e., it can be chosen from more test cases or more test suite execution time is permitted) provided by more complex test problems. Hence, it is better suited for complex process models and selection requirements than the compared techniques but still provides at least equally good results for all other problems. The improvement is even higher if the results are compared with random selection. The evaluation also shows comparable results for question b (cf. Fig. 4).

Note, that the results were generated by averaging the outcome of 100 runs of the random and genetic approach on each problem and question, so that the randomized behavior of those approaches does not falsify the results (e.g., because of a single "randomly" generated outstanding good or bad result).

5   Related Work

Related work can be classified into two categories: test case selection and minimization. Minimization is only partly relevant for this paper because it concentrates less on selection, but more on test suite redundancy prevention, i.e., removing test cases that are only covering process parts that are already sufficiently tested by other test cases. However, the research areas are connected and the proposed approach can be used to generate results which are comparable to existing minimization approaches, e.g., by defining a 100% coverage objective

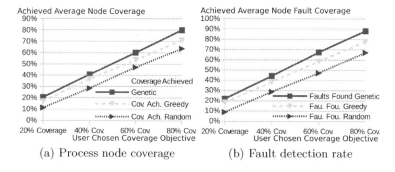

(a) Process node coverage

(b) Fault detection rate

Fig. 3. Average across all three process model complexities for question a (User chosen coverage objective)

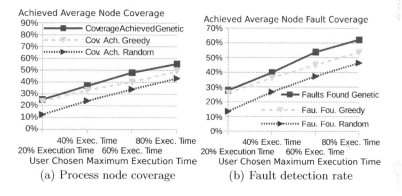

(a) Process node coverage

(b) Fault detection rate

Fig. 4. Average across all three process model complexities for question b (User chosen maximum test suite execution time)

which should be reached in minimal test suite execution time. Hence, this section also discusses minimization approaches.

Two strategies are currently applied to achieve minimization. One option is to analyze and minimize an already existing set of test cases (also called test suite). Farooq and Lam describe their minimization objective as a Traveling Sales Man [6] or an Equality Knapsack problem [5]. Subsequently, they apply Evolutionary Computation heuristics to search for a minimal set of test cases that still provides full structural coverage. However, the authors only used their approach to minimize test cases which were generated through model based software testing using UML activity diagrams. Alternatively, the test case generation algorithms can try to generate a duplicate/redundancy free test suite. [1] utilizes Orthogonal Array Testing (a statistical method that calculates which parameter values should be tested in which combination) and semantic constraints to reduce the amount of generated process model test cases. [2] instead searches for an optimal amount (e.g., minimal amount of test points which are necessary to achieve a

Table 1. Raw evaluation results for question a (User chosen coverage objective)

Process Complexity, Node Coverage Objective	Proposed Genetic Selection Approach		Adaptive Greedy Selection		Random Selection	
	Achieved Coverage	Detected Faults	Achieved Coverage	Detected Faults	Achieved Coverage	Detected Faults
Low, 20% Coverage	21.2%	23.5%	19%	21.4%	8.1%	3.2%
Medium, 20% Coverage	20.5%	21.5%	15%	16.4%	10.2%	10.8%
High, 20% Coverage	20.2%	21%	17%	17.5%	15.7%	13.2%
Low, 40% Coverage	41.6%	46.4%	38.7%	40%	25.3%	26.7%
Medium, 40% Coverage	40%	42.7%	35.1%	37.1%	31%	30.2%
High, 40% Coverage	40%	43.3%	36.1%	37.8%	29%	29.5%
Low, 60% Coverage	60.2%	70.7%	53.4%	62.2%	50.3%	48.7%
Medium, 60% Coverage	60%	65.9%	53%	56.6%	45.7%	46.6%
High, 60% Coverage	60%	65.4%	54.6%	56.4%	45.3%	45.7%
Low, 80% Coverage	80%	94.2%	69%	81.4%	65%	69.6%
Medium, 80% Coverage	80%	86.9%	73%	78.7%	66%	68.5%
High, 80% Coverage	80%	83.1%	71%	73.2%	60%	63.1%

Table 2. Raw evaluation results for question b (User chosen maximum test suite execution time)

Process Complexity, Max Execution Time Objective	Proposed Genetic Selection Approach		Adaptive Greedy Selection		Random Selection	
	Achieved Coverage	Detected Faults	Achieved Coverage	Detected Faults	Achieved Coverage	Detected Faults
Low, 20% Execution Time	32.1%	37.1%	32.1%	37.1%	11%	13%
Medium, 20% Execution Time	24.6%	24.6%	20.3%	20.3%	14.7%	14.2%
High, 20% Execution Time	18.9%	21.3%	18.1%	20.62%	11.8%	13.1%
Low, 40% Execution Time	43%	47.1%	41.6%	45.2%	29.3%	30%
Medium, 40% Execution Time	36.6%	37.6%	31.5%	33.3%	21.2%	27.8%
High, 40% Execution Time	30.5%	34.7%	26.1%	30.1%	21.7%	22.3%
Low, 60% Execution Time	53.6%	64.3%	48.1%	55.7%	38.5%	44.1%
Medium, 60% Execution Time	48.1%	50.5%	39.2%	41.2%	35%	35.8%
High, 60% Execution Time	42.1%	46.8%	33.1%	38%	28.2%	32%
Low, 80% Execution Time	61.1%	70.7%	55%	60.5%	47.9%	56.5%
Medium, 80% Execution Time	56.4%	60.7%	50.1%	52.6%	43.1%	45.6%
High, 80% Execution Time	48.8%	55.2%	42.6%	48%	38.6%	37.1%

user chosen coverage level) of test points were sensors can be added to a process model to detect faulty behavior.

Selection analyzes all test cases and selects those which provide the most value. [12] selects all test cases which cover process model areas which were changed since the last test runs. Ruth [16] instead concentrates on external partners and selects only test cases which cover a process partner that was adapted. Ruth's approach requires that each partner process definition is publicly available which is rather unlikely in real world scenarios.

Overall, existing work is frequently utilizing simple and relatively inflexible selection requirements such as "Which test cases should be selected to achieve a 100% coverage?" and therefore is, e.g., not trying to optimize test suite execution times to their full potential. Additionally, existing work is treating each process node equally and is, therefore, not respecting its unique coverage requirements (i.e., current work is counting a node as completely tested if at least a single test case tests this node once, independently from the nodes' complexity), which reduces the likelihood to identify a fault because important nodes are not tested as thoroughly as necessary. Finally, we found that existing work does not utilize a comprehensive approach (such as the presented Neighborhood Coverage) to describe test case coverage effects.

6   Conclusions

This paper provides coverage metrics and a Genetic Algorithm (GA) for test case selection specifically geared towards process model testing ($\mapsto$ **RQ1** and **RQ2**). The evaluation results support their feasibility even for complex process models. It is also shown that historic information such as log files can positively influence the generated results. They enable the incorporation of test case execution times, hence enabling the selection of those test cases that fulfill user-chosen requirements in minimal time. Especially the last point was not addressed until now by process model test case selection work. The presented GA basically enables the creation of more flexible test case selection approaches for process models (addressing **RQ3** and **RQ4**). It can also be adapted to meet unique user requirements, such as "node X must always be tested", "only the partner processes should be tested", or "only modified process parts should be tested", by configuring adequate optimal coverage calculation metrics. As shown, flexibility can be further increased based on different fitness functions. Overall, this work provides the most comprehensive and flexible process model test case selection solution so far, especially because it takes the *characteristics* of process models, e.g., by integrating neighborhood coverage metrics and execution log files, into account. Future work will incorporate process model test case prioritization and minimization by, for example, analyzing the applicability and feasibility of flexible GA for these domains. In addition we want to conduct a case study to assess the impact of the proposed coverage metrics (e.g., optimal coverage or neighborhood coverage) on the test selection quality in real world scenarios.

References

1. Askaruinisa, A., Abirami, A.: Test case reduction technique for semantic based web services. Computer Science & Engineering **3**, 566–576 (2010)
2. Borrego, D., Gómez-López, M.T., Gasca, R.M.: Minimizing test-point allocation to improve diagnosability in business process models. Systems and Software **11**, 2725–2741 (2013)
3. Cardoso, J.: Process control-flow complexity metric: an empirical validation. In: Services Computing, pp. 167–173. IEEE (2006)
4. Eiben, A., Smith, J.: Introduction to evolutionary computing. Natural Computing Series. Springer (2008)
5. Farooq, U., Lam, C.P.: Evolving the quality of a model based test suite. In: Software Testing, Verification and Validation, pp. 141–149. IEEE (2009)
6. Farooq, U., Lam, C.P.: A max-min multiobjective technique to optimize model based test suite. In: Software Engineering, Artificial Intelligences, Networking and Parallel/Distributed Computing, pp. 569–574. IEEE (2009)
7. Gruhn, V., Laue, R.: Complexity metrics for business process models. In: Business Information Systems, pp. 1–12 (2006)
8. Harman, M., Jones, B.F.: Search-based software engineering. Information and Software Technology **14**, 833–839 (2001)
9. Kaschner, K., Lohmann, N.: Automatic test case generation for interacting services. In: Feuerlicht, G., Lamersdorf, W. (eds.) ICSOC 2008. LNCS, vol. 5472, pp. 66–78. Springer, Heidelberg (2009)

10. Kriglstein, S., Wallner, G., Rinderle-Ma, S.: A visualization approach for difference analysis of process models and instance traffic. In: Daniel, F., Wang, J., Weber, B. (eds.) BPM 2013. LNCS, vol. 8094, pp. 219–226. Springer, Heidelberg (2013)

11. Leymann, F., Roller, D.: Production workflow concepts and techniques. Prentice Hall PTR (2000)

12. Li, B., Qiu, D., Ji, S., Wang, D.: Automatic test case selection and generation for regression testing of composite service based on extensible bpel flow graph. In: Software Maintenance, pp. 1–10 (2010)

13. Li, Z.J., Sun, W., Jiang, Z.B., Zhang, X.: BPEL4WS unit testing: framework and implementation. In: Web Services, pp. 103–110. IEEE (2005)

14. Mendling, J.: Metrics for process models: empirical foundations of verification, error prediction, and guidelines for correctness. LNBIP, vol. 6. Springer, Heidelberg (2008)

15. Rinderle, S., Reichert, M., Dadam, P.: Flexible support of team processes by adaptive workflow systems. Distributed and Parallel Databases **16**, 91–116 (2004)

16. Ruth, M.E.: Concurrency in a decentralized automatic regression test selection framework for web services. In: Mardi Gras Conference, pp. 7:1–7:8. ACM (2008)

17. Stoyanova, V., Petrova-Antonova, D., Ilieva, S.: Automation of test case generation and execution for testing web service orchestrations. In: Service-Oriented Systems Engineering, pp. 274–279. IEEE (2013)

18. Zakaria, Z., Atan, R., Ghani, A.A.A., Sani, N.F.M.: Unit testing approaches for BPEL: a systematic review. In: Asia-Pacific Software Engineering, pp. 316–322. IEEE (2009)

Discovering BPMN Models with Sub-Processes and Multi-instance Markers

Yuquan Wang[1], Lijie Wen[1(✉)], Zhiqiang Yan[2], Bo Sun[1], and Jianmin Wang[1]

[1] School of Software, Tsinghua University, Beijing, China
{wangyuquanliuli,zhiqiang.yan.1983}@gmail.com,
{wenlj,jimwang}@tsinghua.edu.cn, haizhibogoon@163.com
[2] School of Information, Capital University of Economics and Business, Beijing, China
wenlj@tsinghua.edu.cn

Abstract. Massive event logs are produced in information systems, which record executions of business processes in organizations. Various techniques are proposed to discover process models reflecting real-life behaviors from these logs. However, the discovered models are mostly in Petri nets rather than BPMN models, the current industrial process modeling standard. Conforti et al. and Weber et al. propose techniques that discover BPMN models with sub-processes, multi-instance, etc. However, these techniques are made for event logs with special attributes, e.g., containing attributes about primary and foreign keys, which may not commonly appear in event logs. For example, logs from the OA (office automation) systems of CMCC (China Mobile Communications Corporation) do not contain such data. To solve this issue, this paper proposes two techniques that can discover BPMN models with sub-processes and multi-instance markers with event logs containing less event attributes. One of our techniques only requires four event attributes: case id, task name, start time and end time. Experimental evaluations with both real-life logs and synthetic logs show that our techniques can indeed discover process models with sub-process and multi-instance markers from logs with less event attributes, and are more accurate and less complex than those derived with flat process model discovery techniques.

1 Introduction

Nowadays, business process management is one of the most important methods for organizations to enhance their efficiency of management. Business processes are implemented in information systems of organizations to be (semi-)automatically executed, which is an effective and efficient way to manage and control their operations. As the number of processes grows, massive amount of logs are recorded in information systems. Process discovery technology enables the extraction of knowledge from logs, which helps process analyzers better understand (the executions of) their business processes. Variant process discovery algorithms have been proposed [1-9], which balance tradeoffs between accuracy and complexity of the discovered process models.

© Springer International Publishing Switzerland 2015
C. Debruyne et al. (Eds.): OTM 2015 Conferences, LNCS 9415, pp. 185–201, 2015.
DOI: 10.1007/978-3-319-26148-5_11

However, process models discovered from these algorithms are mostly in Petri nets rather than BPMN, the industrial standard notation for process modeling [1-9]. Although BPMN models can be transformed from Petri nets, such BPMN models mainly contain activities and gateways. Few researches take sub-process and multi-instance into consideration, which are important characteristics of BPMN 2.0. Sub-process is a part of the whole process model, which is usually defined separately and called by a complex or call activity. A sub-process can be broken down into another level of details. Multi-instance means there are several instances responding to the activity, and it has two types: sequential and parallel, which implies the activity or sub-process should be executed sequentially or concurrently. In this paper, we mainly focus on parallel multi-instances for the following reason. The behavior of sequential multi-instances is the same as loops, which can be mined as loop structures as most process discovery algorithms proposed; while seldom algorithms [14,18] consider parallel multi-instances.

Table 1. Simplified traces from CMCC

cid	tn	pn	st	Et	trans	cid	tn	pn	st	et	trans
1	A	pa	0	10	{(B,pb)}	3	A	pa	0	10	{(C,pc)}
1	B	pb	10	20	{(D1,pd1),(D1,pd2)}	3	C	pc	10	20	{(D1,pd1),(D1,pd2)}
1	D1	pd1	20	30	{(E1,pe1),(F1,pf1),(F1,pf2)}	3	D1	pd1	20	30	{(E1,pe1),(F1,pf1),(F1,pf2)}
1	D1	pd2	20	35	{(E1,pe2),(F1,pf3)}	3	D1	pd2	20	35	{(E1,pe2),(F1,pf3)}
1	E1	pe1	30	40	Ø	3	E1	pe1	30	40	Ø
1	F1	pf1	30	45	Ø	3	F1	pf1	30	45	Ø
1	F1	pf2	30	47	{(G1,pg1)}	3	F1	pf2	30	47	{(G1,pg1)}
1	F1	pf3	35	40	Ø	3	F1	pf3	35	40	Ø
1	E1	pe2	35	50	{(G1,pg2)}	3	E1	pe2	35	50	{(G1,pg2)}
1	G1	pg1	47	55	Ø	3	G1	pg1	47	55	Ø
1	G1	pg2	50	60	{(H,ph)}	3	G1	pg2	50	60	{(H,ph)}
1	H	ph	60	70	Ø	3	H	ph	60	70	Ø
2	A	pa	0	10	{(C,pc)}	4	A	pa	0	10	{(B,pb)}
2	C	pc	10	20	{(D2,pd1),(D2,pd2)}	4	B	pb	10	20	{(D2,pd1),(D2,pd2)}
2	D2	pd1	20	30	{(F2,pf1),(F2,pf2)}	4	D2	pd1	20	30	{(F2,pf1),(F2,pf2)}
2	D2	pd2	20	35	{(E2,pe1)}	4	D2	pd2	20	35	{(E2,pe1)}
2	F2	pf1	30	38	Ø	4	F2	pf1	30	38	Ø
2	F2	pf2	30	40	{(G2,pg1)}	4	F2	pf2	30	40	{(G2,pg1)}
2	E2	pe1	35	45	{(G2,pg2)}	4	E2	pe1	35	45	{(G2,pg2)}
2	G2	pg1	40	50	Ø	4	G2	pg1	40	50	Ø
2	G2	pg2	50	60	{(H,ph)}	4	G2	pg2	50	60	{(H,ph)}
2	H	ph	60	70	Ø	4	H	ph	60	70	Ø

Example 1. We illustrate four simplified traces from an event log of CMCC in Table 1. It mainly consists of six attributes: case id, task name, start time, end time, executor, and transfer information (indicating which events will be executed next and by whom). The first case in Table 1 can be represented as <A,B,D1,D1,E1,F1,F1,F1, E1,G1,G1,H>. The first line of the first case tells us event A is executed by executor pa from time 0 to 10, and is followed by task B to be executed by executor pb.

The second line of the first case tells us event B is executed by pb from time 10 to 20, and is followed by two events named D1 concurrently. Current techniques, e.g., BPMN Analysis (using Heuristics Miner) in ProM, can only discover a model like that in Figure 1(b) while apparently the correct model should be like the model in Figure 1(a) if taking start time and end time into consideration.

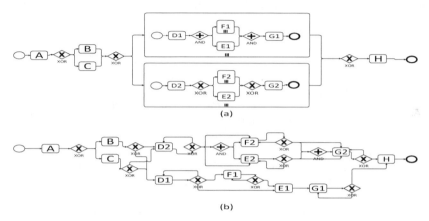

(a)

(b)

Fig. 1. BPMN model obtained with and without applying the proposed technique

Conforti et al. [14] and Weber et al. [18] proposed techniques that can discover sub-processes, multi-instance markers, etc. These techniques rely on some special event attributes in event logs to discover dependencies between events, e.g. primary and foreign key, and hierarchies are indicated by these dependencies, which are further used to discover sub-processes, multi-instance markers, etc. However, these attributes may not commonly appear in event logs, e.g., logs from CMCC. In addition, it is unpractical to add primary key and foreign key to the log manually, thus techniques in [14, 18] cannot discover sub-processes and multi-instance markers for event logs from CMCC.

Therefore, in this paper, we present two techniques that can discover BPMN models with sub-processes and multi-instance activity markers from event logs, like the one in CMCC shown in Table 1.

Challenges: With sub-process and multi-instance added to a process model, techniques like [1-10] cannot be applied directly to analyze relations between tasks. There are two main significant challenges to detect sub-process and multi-instance as follows.

1) It is hard to analyze relations between tasks with multi-instance marker. For example, if a sub-process containing several tasks is marked as multi-instance, like the model in Figure 1(a), sub-process containing tasks "E1" and "G1" is marked as multi-instance, though task G1 should always happen after task E1 in one sub-process instance, we can still see task G1 occur before tasks E1 in a log as it can happen before another task instance E1 in another sub-process executed simultaneously. Therefore, it is hard to determine the relations between tasks.

2) It is hard to discover sub-process and multi-instance with less information. Most logs do not contain either the aforesaid transfer information or attributes to find primary key and foreign key used in [14], so it's necessary to find a way to discover sub-process and multi-instance just by commonly existing attributes, e.g., case id, task name, start time and end time.

Contribution: The paper presents two different techniques to discover sub-process and multi-instance.

1) We propose an algorithm to discover sub-process and multi-instance by exploiting the aforesaid six attributes shown in Table 1. Figure 2 shows the procedure of our proposed techniques. Given an event log, an instance tree is constructed for each case, which is used to analyze hierarchy of events. Then the hierarchy tree is constructed based on the analysis, which can be used to check multi-instance in a process model. Also, the log is decomposed into sub-logs and each node in the hierarchy tree corresponds to a sub-log. Finally, sub-models are discovered from sub-logs and composed into the required process model based on the hierarchy tree.

2) We propose a heuristic algorithm to discover sub-process and multi-instance by just making use of four attributes: case id, task name, start time and end time. Although it has lower accuracy in some scenarios as a tradeoff, it is more flexible for input logs. The steps of the heuristic algorithm are the same as those in the previous algorithm.

Fig. 2. Procedure to mine BPMN models with sub-processes and multi-instance

The remainder of the paper is organized as follows. We first introduce preliminaries in Section 2. Then we present two algorithms to discover BPMN models with sub-processes and multi-instance markers in Section 3. Experiments are shown in Section 4. Section 5 introduces related work and Section 6 concludes the paper.

2   Preliminaries

Each event log consists of cases; each case consists of events that are related to the case; each event has attributes. The event we use in this paper consists of six attributes: a case id, a task name[1], an executor name, a start-time, an end-time, and transfer info.

Definition 1 (Event, Attribute). An event defined in this paper consists of six attributes, which is formally described as a tuple e = (cid, tn, pn, st, et, trans):

1. cid ∈ T is the case id of event e, where T is the set of all case ids.
2. tn ∈ Σ is the task name of event e, where Σ is the set of all task names.

---

[1] In this paper we suppose that no two tasks in a process model have identical names.

3. $pn \in \Phi$ is the name of the executor who executes event e, where Φ is the set of all executor names.
4. $st \in \Omega$ is the start time of event e, where Ω is the set of all timestamps.
5. $et \in \Omega$ is the end time of event e.
6. $trans = \{t_1, \ldots, t_i, \ldots, t_n\}$, for all $0 < i < n+1$, $t_i = (tn_i', pn_i')$, $tn_i' \in \Sigma$, $pn_i' \in \Phi$ is an element in the set of transfer info of event e, which indicates the name of the task (i.e., tn_i') executed after event e by the person pn_i'.

Definition 2 (Case, Event Log). A case consists of an ordered list of events with the same case id. An event log consists of a set of cases.

3   Instance Tree and Hierarchy Tree

The content of this section is fourfold. Firstly, the definition of (heuristic) instance tree is presented. Then, hierarchy for events is proposed. Thirdly, a hierarchy tree is defined based on instance trees and hierarchies. Finally multi-instance for event unions (nodes in a hierarchy tree) is defined.

Instance tree is of normal tree structure, which indicates the execution orders of events in a case. Formally:

Definition 3 (Instance tree). Given a case c, its corresponding instance tree itree(c) = (E, R) where:

1. E is a set of events in c.
2. $R \in E \times E = \{(e1, e2) | (e2.tn, e2.pn) \in e1.trans\}$ is a set of sequential relationships between events that indicate their execution orders, e.g., e2 is executed directly after e1.

Example 2. Take the first case of example 1 as an example, see the instance tree as shown in Figure 3 with Cid=1. As the transfer info indicates, one relationship (edge) is added from event A to event B and two edges are added from event B to two events D1. Similarly, the instance trees for other three cases are also showed in Figure 3.

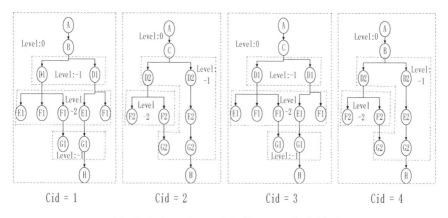

Fig. 3. Instance trees of the four cases in Table 1

The event log from CMCC contains the transfer information, which tells us the next events to be executed and the persons who execute them. Based on this information, we know exactly which node should follow which in an instance tree. However, not every log contains this information. Therefore, a heuristic instance tree is proposed in Definition 4, which can be constructed with only four attributes: case id, task name, start-time, and end-time.

Definition 4 (Heuristic instance tree). Given a case c, its corresponding heuristic instance tree hitree(c) = (E, HR) where:

1. E is a set of events in c.
2. $HR \in E \times E = \{(e1, e2) | e1.et \leq e2.st \wedge \nexists e3, e1.et < e3.et \leq e2.st\}$ is a set of heuristic sequential relationships between events that are induced by the start and end execution times of events.

For example in Table1, heuristic instance trees are the same as the instance trees for these four cases, as shown in Figure 3. In most cases, we can build heuristic instance tree correctly as the start-time of an event is usually the end-time of previous event. However, this is not always the case. When there are events ending at the same time, heuristic instance tree can be different with the corresponding instance tree. We will evaluate this in Section 4.

To deal with the situation that there is a multi-instance at the beginning or end of a case, an event "start" can be added to the beginning of the case and an event "end" can be added to the tail of the case.

The event's hierarchy is analyzed by **concurrence** in instance trees. When an event in an instance tree has more than one child (these children events are executed concurrently), the children events' hierarchy should be one level lower. The hierarchy is back to one level higher when the concurrence ceases, i.e., all children finish executing except one. Otherwise, the hierarchy remains unchanged.

Definition 5 (Hierarchy). Let L be an event log, C_L be the set of cases in L, and E_c be the set of events of a case $c \in C_L$. Hierarchy describes which level an event is in, and which events are connected with the event in the previous level. Formally the hierarchy for an event e in a case $c \in C_L$ is a tuple h(e,c)=(tn, level, leftParentSet, rightParentSet), where:

1. $tn \in \Sigma$ is the task name of event e.
2. $level \in Z$ is an integer indicating event e's hierarchy. The smaller the level is, the lower hierarchy event e is in.
3. $leftParentSet \subseteq E_c$. If it is of the highest level, leftParentSet is an empty set. Otherwise, event e is mined as (a part of) a sub-process, and leftParentSet is a set of events that are followed by the sub-process.
4. $rightParentSet \subseteq E_c$. If it is of the highest level, rightParentSet is an empty set. Otherwise, event e is mined as (a part of) a sub-process, and rightParentSet is a set of events that are following the sub-process.

The hierarchy for an event e in a log L is a tuple h(e,L)=(tn, level, leftParentSet, rightParentSet), where:

1. tn ∈ ∑ is the task name of event e.
2. level = min{h(e,c).level|c ∈ C_L ∧ e ∈ E_c ∧ e.tn = tn} is the minimum level for e in all cases.
3. leftParentSet = ∪$_{(e,c)∈EC}$h(e,c).leftParentSet is the union of leftParentSets for e, in which cases e is of its lowest level, where EC={(e,c)| c ∈ C_L ∧ e ∈ E_c ∧ e.tn = tn ∧ h(e,c).level=level}.
4. rightParentSet = ∪$_{(e,c)∈EC}$h(e,c).rightParentSet is the union of rightParent-Sets for e, in which cases e is of its lowest level.

Example 3. Take the first instance tree in Figure 3 as an example to analyze an event's hierarchy. Originally we set event A of level 0, event B is of the same level with event A. There are two nodes named D1 concurrently executed after event B, therefore D1 should have a lower hierarchy than B. Thus we set D1's level to-1. The leftParentSet of D1 is set as {B}, because this is where the hierarchy becomes lower. There is no event being executed concurrently with event H. Therefore, H should have the same hierarchy as event B and its level is set back to 0. The rightParentSet of D1 is set as {H}, because this is where event's level back to 0. Then we analyze two branches after event B recursively and set event E1, F1 to be level -2 and G1 to be level -1. Table 2 shows all events' hierarchies in first case.

Table 2. Events' hierarchies in first case

Event	Hierarchy
A	(A, 0, Ø, Ø)
B	(B, 0, Ø, Ø)
D1	(D1, -1, {B}, {H})
E1	(E1, -2, {D1}, {G1})
F1	(F1, -2, {D1}, {G1})
G1	(G1, -1, {B}, {H})
H	(H, 0, Ø, Ø)

The hierarchy of event D1 in the first case is h(D1,case1) = (D1, -1, {B}, {H}), while in the third case is h(D1,case3) = (D1, -1, {C}, {H}), which means both event B and C can be followed by sub-process containing event D1. Therefore the hierarchy of event D1 in the log should be h(D1,L) = (D1, -1, {B,C},{H}).

There are two special cases when analyzing the end-point of concurrent events, which are shown in Figure 4. The first case is shown in Figure 4(a). Event C is set as level 0 in left part as no other event is executed concurrently, but as level -1 in right part as event E is executed concurrently with event C. Maybe node C in left part is just delayed for some reasons. Therefore, we always keep the lowest hierarchy (smallest level value). The second case is shown in Figure 4(b). Though the lower event E is executed alone, we still don't think that the concurrent sub-processes end as there is another E in another branch. Thus we define event F as where level back to 0.

After analyzing the hierarchy for each event, we can construct the corresponding hierarchy tree. Event unions, consisting of events, are nodes of a hierarchy tree.

Definition 6 (Event Union). Let L be an event log, C_L be the set of cases in L, and E_L be the set of events of L. Given the hierarchies of each event in E_L, E_L can be divided into a set of event unions, denoted as EU. An event union, denoted as eu∈EU, is a subset of E_L. An eu consists of more than one event: $|eu|>1 \wedge e \in eu$ iff ($\forall e1 \in eu$, h(e,L).level=h(e1,L).level)$\wedge$($\exists e1 \in eu, \exists c \in C_L$,((e,e1)∈itree(c).R$\vee$(e1,e)∈itree(c).R$\vee$ ($\exists e2 \in E_L$-eu,{e,e1}⊆h(e2,L).rightParentSet∪h(e2,L).leftParentSet); otherwise the event union eu consists of one event.

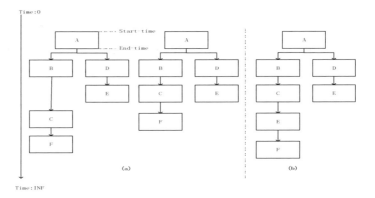

Fig. 4. Special cases when analyzing hierarchy

Proposition 1. Let L be an event log, and E_L be the set of events of L. All event unions of E_L consist of a partition of E_L.

Firstly, each event should be in some event union. From Definition 6 we know that each event is either in an event union consisting of multiple events or one event. Secondly, each event should be only in one event union. Suppose an event is in two event unions, and then, according to Definition 6, all events in these two event unions should be in one event union, i.e., these two unions should be joined into one.

Definition 7 (Hierarchy tree). Let L be an event log, C_L be the set of cases in L, and E_L be the set of events of L. The hierarchy tree for log L is htree(L) = (EU,UR) where:

1. EU is the set of event unions of E_L.
2. UR ∈ EU×EU={(eu1,eu2)|eu1,eu2 ∈ EU $\wedge$ $\exists e1 \in eu1$ $\wedge$ $\exists e2 \in eu2$, e1 ∈ h(e2,L).rightParentSet$\vee$e1∈h(e2,L).leftParentSet} is a set of sequential relationships between unions of events.

Note that the hierarchy tree in Definition 6 and 7 is based on instance trees (itree(c)), which can be easily replaced by heuristic instance trees (hitree(c)). It also applies to all definitions and algorithms in the remainder of this paper. As far as we know, this is the **first** time to propose the definition of hierarchy tree, which is based on analysis of concurrence on instance tree.

Example 4. The hierarchy tree for the event log in Table 1 is shown in Figure 5. Events A, B, C, H consist of one subset, because they are of level 0, and {B,C}, {H} are the leftParentSet and rightParentSet of eu1 and eu2 and A, B, C are connected in the instance tree shown in Figure 4. Events D1 and G1 consist of one subset, because they are of level -1, and they are the leftParentSet and rightParentSet of eu4 and eu5. An edge from eu1 to eu2 is added because eu2 should be treated as a sub-process of eu1.

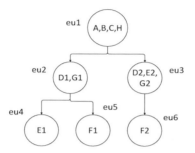

Fig. 5. Hierarchy tree for the event log in Table 1

As described in Definition 8, the event unions (nodes of a hierarchy tree) that should be marked as multi-instance if and only if there exists an event in an instance tree, such that the event has at least two relationships (edges) that connect with events (can be instances of one identical event) in the event union.

Definition 8 (Multi-instance for event union). Let L be an event log, C_L be the set of cases in L, and E_L be the set of events of L. The hierarchy tree for log L is htree(L). The set of event unions that are marked as multi-instance is denoted as Meu(L). Meu(L)= {eu∈htree(L).EU|∃c∈C_L, ∃e1,e2∈eu, ∃e∈itree(c).E, e1.tn = e2.tn ∧(e,e1) ∈itree(c).R ∧(e,e2) ∈itree(c).R }.

Example 5. See the instance tree in Figure 3 with Cid = 1, event B has relationships with two events labeled as D1. This indicates that node eu2 in the hierarchy tree in Figure 5 should be marked as multi-instance.

4   Procedure to Discover BPMN Models

Core definitions of this paper are presented in Section 2, based on which this section presents how to discover hierarchical BPMN models.

As already shown in Figure 1, six steps are required. Algorithm 1 presents the corresponding six steps of discovering a hierarchical BPMN model with multi-instance markers from a given event log: 1) construct an instance tree for each case of a given event log (Line2-3); 2) analyze instance trees and get hierarchy levels for all events in the given log (Line4-7); 3) construct a hierarchy tree based on the results of the last two steps (Line 8); 4) analyze whether a union of events (a node of hierarchy tree) has multi-instance property (Line 9); 5) project log based on unions of events (Line 10), which means generating new log for each node in hierarchy tree; 6) discover a BPMN model (can be transformed from a Petri net) from each projected log, mark multi-instance activities and sub-processes, and integrate them into a hierarchical BPMN model (Line 11-12). This section focuses on the first four steps because the last two steps are based on existing techniques [7, 13, 15].

The complexity of the first step is $O(N \cdot L)$ where N is the number of cases in the log and L is the average length of cases. The complexity of the second step is $O(N \cdot L \cdot \log(L))$. The complexity of the third step is $O(N_{tm}^2)$ where N_{tm} is the number of different task names in the log, which is much smaller than N. The complexity of the fourth step is $O(N \cdot L)$ and the complexity of the fifth step is $O(N \cdot L \cdot N_h)$ where N_h is the number of nodes in hierarchy tree. The complexity of the sixth step is depending on the complexity of existing flat discovery techniques. So the complexity of the technique is $O(N \cdot L \cdot (\log(L) + N_h))$, not counting the existing process discovery step.

Algorithm 1. BPMNMiner

	Input : Log L; **Output** : BPMN model;
	Begin
1	Let C_L be the set of cases in L; Let E_L be the set of events in L;
2	**Foreach** $c \in C_L$ **do**
3	ITree = itree(c); //Step 1, Definition 3, Definition 4
4	**Foreach** $e \in Ec$ **do**
5	h(e,c); //Step 2, Definition 5
6	**foreach** $e \in E_L$ **do**
7	h(e,L); //Step 2, Definition 5
8	hierarchyTree = htree(L);//Step 3, Definition 6
9	EU_m = Meu(L);//Step 4, Definition 7
10	Project log L based on event unions of hierarchyTree;//Step 5 [13,15]
11	Discover sub-models for all event unions;// Step 6 [7]
12	Mark these sub-models related to elements in EU as multi-instance in a higher level model; // Step 6
	return BPMNmodel

Example 6. Take the event log in Table 1 as input for Algorithm 1. The outputs are shown in Figure 6 and Figure 1(a). In Figure 6, top is the discovered model for eu1 in Figure 5 (already converted to BPMN), where X1 indicates eu2 and X2 indicates eu3 in Figure 5. X1 and X2 are marked as multi-instance and complex activities. BPMN model Y1 and Y2 in Figure 6 corresponds to eu5 and eu6 in Figure 5. Figure 1(a) provides an integrated view of models shown in Figure 6.

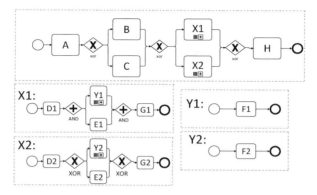

Fig. 6. Hierarchical BPMN model with multi-instance

5   Experimental Evaluation

This section presents the experiments we run to evaluate the techniques via real-life and artificial process logs. In the evaluation we compared two proposed techniques with Heuristic Miner. Heuristic Miner provides the best result among existing techniques of accuracy according to [16], and techniques [14, 18] that discover BPMN model with multi-instance markers need sub-process id extraction, which is not applicable for our data set. Therefore, we use the results of Heuristic Miner as a basis.

Fitness and simplicity are introduced to measure the performance of these mining methods. Fitness [17] measures the conformance between the mined model and the given log. The fitness value is determined by replaying the log on the model, i.e., for each trace, the "token game" is played. If fitness = 1 then the log can be parsed by the model without any error. Simplicity measures the complexity of the discovered model, i.e., the ratio between the actual number of arcs and the maximum possible number of arcs in any model with the same number of nodes. It is much easier for person to understand a discovered model with a lower simplicity.

5.1   Evaluation Based on Real-Life Logs

We first use real-life logs to test the performance of two proposed techniques. The real-life dataset comes from CMCC for the process of application for communication tools. There are 24 logs in dataset, among which 8 logs contains sub-process and multi-instance markers, so we use these 8 logs in our experiment.

We show the basic characteristics of these logs in Table 3. We have 57 different cases in first log and 20 different cases in other logs. All of them contain more than ten distinct tasks.

Table 3. Characteristics of real-life logs

Log id	1	2	3	4	5	6	7	8
Number of cases	57	20	20	20	20	20	20	20
Distinct tasks	11	12	12	10	15	11	16	18
Total events	728	194	370	215	275	397	698	522

Figure 7 shows the fitness and simplicity values for the model discovered from each technique (Heuristic miner (HM) with default configuration, our technique with instance trees (BPMN-Miner), and our technique with Heuristic instance trees (H-BPMN-Miner)). For all of these logs, our techniques perform better than Heuristic Miner, not only on the accuracy, but also on the simplicity. For example, Figure 8 shows the process model discovered by Heuristic Miner with the log in Table1. Although, the accuracy of the model in Figure 8 is 0.938, it contains too many hidden transitions and becomes complicated. Also we cannot see any multi-instance in the model. The model in Figure 1(a) shows the process model discovered using our techniques.

From the evaluation for H-BPMN-Miner, we can know that in most scenarios, it returns the same results as BPMN-Miner. However, if there are two events ending at the same time, the heuristic instance tree constructed for this case may not be the same as the corresponding instance tree, thus leading to lower accuracy. For example, as shown in Figure 7(a), for the second log, the accuracy and complexity of the discovered model using H-BPMN-Miner is not as good as BPMN-Miner, but still better than HM.

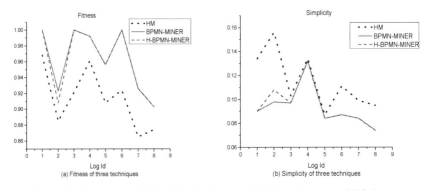

Fig. 7. Performance of HM, BPMN-Miner, H-BPMN-Miner on real-life logs

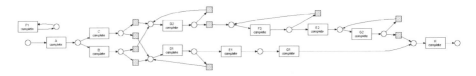

Fig. 8. Discovered model of the log in Table 1 via HM

5.2   Evaluation Based on Artificial Logs

In this section we use artificial logs to measure performance of proposed techniques because real-life logs may not cover all test cases. Five artificial logs contain different structures, e.g., choice, parallel, loop, sub-process and multi-instance. More detail is shown in Table 4.

We also implement a plug-in to do the simulation of BPMN model with sub-process and multi-instance markers. For each model, we simulate 1000 cases for mining. We present more details in Table 5.

Table 4. Structures of artificial logs

Log id	Choice	Parallel	Loop	Sub-process	Multi instance	Multi-level sub-process
1	√			√	√	
2		√		√	√	
3			√	√	√	
4				√	√	√
5	√	√	√	√	√	√

Table 5. Characteristics of artificial logs

Log id	1	2	3	4	5
Case	1000	1000	1000	1000	1000
Distinct tasks	7	6	10	8	12
Total events	22820	24758	14013	30430	57236

Figure 9 shows the fitness and simplicity values for the models discovered from each technique. Similar to results in evaluation of real-life logs, BPMN-Miner gets the best results in all scenarios. In most cases, H-BPMN-Miner can get result as good as BPMN-Miner except for the last two logs because there are too many sub-processes executed concurrently and some of them end in same time. Thus the heuristic instance tree cannot be built correctly. In addition, both BPMN-Miner and H-BPMN-Miner get simpler model than Heuristic Miner.

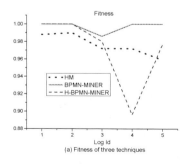
(a) Fitness of three techniques

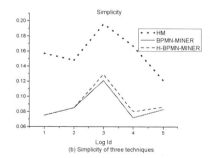
(b) Simplicity of three techniques

Fig. 9. Performance of HM, BPMN-Miner, H-BPMN-Miner on artificial logs

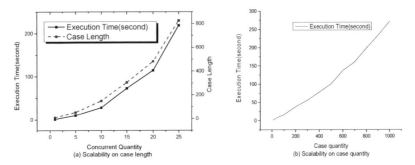

Fig. 10. Scalability of BPMN-Miner

We also do evaluation on the scalability of the proposed techniques as shown in Figure 10. We use the last artificial log that contains all common structures to generate logs. Figure 10(a) shows how the average case length and execution time change with the concurrent quantity increasing while keeping case quantity equal to 50. We can see the similar growth trend of two curves. Figure 10(b) shows time performance with case quantity getting larger while keeping the case average length equal to 50. Time increases almost linearly with increasing case quantity, which meets the expectation of complexity analysis.

From the experiments we conclude that our techniques can discover a BPMN model with sub-processes and multi-instance markers from a given event log. The discovered models not only achieve high accuracy, but also keep low complexity by using hierarchical structure, which can help people understand the process more clearly. Also the efficiency of the techniques is good, which can discover process models in terms of seconds running on a laptop in our experiments. All the experiments are run on a laptop with the Intel Core 2 Duo processor T7500 CPU (2.2GHz, 800MHz FSB, 4MB L2 cache), 4 GB DDR2 memory, the Windows 7 operating system and the SUN Java Virtual Machine version 1.6.

6   Related Work

This section provides an overview of techniques for automated discovery of process models, including both flat and hierarchical process models.

There are various techniques proposed for automated discovery of flat process models. In 2004, Wil M.P. van der Aalst proposed α algorithm [1] that leads the trend of automated discovery of process models. The α algorithm constructs a Petri net by inferring relations between pairs of events in the log (direct follows, causality, conflict and concurrency). The α algorithm works well in most cases, but it cannot deal with the situation with short loops, non-free-choice constructs, invisible tasks, duplicate tasks and OR-split/join constructs. To overcome these shortcomings, a series of α-based algorithms were proposed. The α+ algorithm [2], tsinghua-α algorithm [3], α++ algorithm [4], α# algorithm [5], α* algorithm [6] are all extensions to α algorithm to overcome its shortcomings. Weijters et al. [7] proposed the Heuristics Miner, which extracts not only dependencies between events but also the frequency of each dependency. It constructs the Petri net by heuristic rules, thus it is robust to noise. Genetic Algorithm Miner (GA) [8] is developed to benefit from global search information. It can produce process models with good fitness but it is time consuming and hard to use because of its various parameters.

Only a few techniques have the ability to discover process models other than Petri nets, such as Declarative model [10, 11] and BPMN model [12, 18, 19]. The technique proposed in [11] shows how to discover a simple and comprehensive Declarative model via the technique similar to Apriori algorithm. Paper [12] presents a technique that discovers flat BPMN models with swim lanes. Paper [19] presents techniques to discover BPMN model and conformance checking on BPMN model. However, neither of them supports sub-processes and multi-instance markers. Although most of automated discovery algorithms produce flat process models, there are still some techniques to mine hierarchical process models. One of them is the two-phase mining approach [13]. It uses pattern detection techniques to find a sub-process that works fine in most cases. However, it is unable to deal with cases with multi-instance. The technique proposed in [14] is able to discover boundary events, multi-instances and sub-processes, but it depends on the specific input. Also the technique in [18] can discover sub-process with multi-instance markers, but similar to [14], it needs sub-process ID extraction, which is domain-specific, requires expert knowledge, and can generally not be fully automated.

7   Conclusion

This paper proposes two techniques to solve the problem of discovering a BPMN model with sub-process and multi-instance markers. The first one uses these six attributes to discover BPMN models with sub-processes and multi-instance markers, while the second one only requires the first four attributes. Experiments show that these techniques can discover BPMN models, of these the accuracy and complexity are better than models discovered by existing techniques.

There are some improvements that can be done in our future work. Firstly, the BPMN elements that can be discovered using techniques in this paper are limited. Discovering more elements, such as boundary events, from event logs can be studied. Secondly, in some event logs of CMCC, we find that an activity or sub-process with the multi-instance marker can be called recursively. The techniques in this paper cannot solve this situation yet, which will be studied.

Acknowledgement. The research is supported by National Science Fund No.61402301, No.61472207 and No.61325008, the research fund of Capital University of Economics and Business, 00791462722336, 00791465730165, and the special fund for innovation of Shandong, China project No.2013CXC30001.

References

1. van der Aalst, W.M.P., Weijters, T., Maruster, L.: Workflow mining: Discovering process models from event logs. IEEE Transactions on Knowledge and Data Engineering **16**(9), 1128–1142 (2004)
2. de Medeiros, A.K.A., van Dongen, B.F., van der Aalst, W.M.P., Weijters, A.J.M.M.: Process mining for ubiquitous mobile systems: an overview and a concrete algorithm. In: Baresi, L., Dustdar, S., Gall, H.C., Matera, M. (eds.) UMICS 2004. LNCS, vol. 3272, pp. 151–165. Springer, Heidelberg (2004)
3. Wen, L., Wang, J., van der Aalst, W.M.P., et al.: A novel approach for process mining based onevent types. Journal of Intelligent Information Systems **32**(2), 163–190 (2009)
4. Wen, L., van der Aalst, W.M.P., Wang, J., et al.: Mining process models with non-free-choice constructs. Data Mining and Knowledge Discovery **15**(2), 145–180 (2007)
5. Wen, L., Wang, J., Sun, J.: Mining invisible tasks from event logs. In: Dong, G., Lin, X., Wang, W., Yang, Y., Yu, J.X. (eds.) APWeb/WAIM 2007. LNCS, vol. 4505, pp. 358–365. Springer, Heidelberg (2007)
6. Li, J., Liu, D., Yang, B.: Process mining: extending α-algorithm to mine duplicate tasks in process logs. In: Chang, K.C.-C., Wang, W., Chen, L., Ellis, C.A., Hsu, C.-H., Tsoi, A.C., Wang, H. (eds.) APWeb/WAIM 2007. LNCS, vol. 4537, pp. 396–407. Springer, Heidelberg (2007)
7. Weijters, A.J.M.M., van der Aalst, W.M.P., de Medeiros, A.K.A.: Process mining with the heuristics miner-algorithm. Technische Universiteit Eindhoven, Tech. Rep. WP **166**, 1–34 (2006)
8. Buijs, J.C.A.M., van Dongen, B.F., van der Aalst, W.M.P.: A genetic algorithm for discovering process trees. In: 2012 IEEE Evolutionary Computation, pp. 1–8 (2012)
9. Kindler, E., Rubin, V., Schäfer, W.: Process mining and petri net synthesis. In: Eder, J., Dustdar, S. (eds.) BPM Workshops 2006. LNCS, vol. 4103, pp. 105–116. Springer, Heidelberg (2006)
10. Pesic, M., Schonenberg, H., van der Aalst, W.M.P.: Declare: Full support for loosely-structured processes. In: 11th IEEE International Enterprise Distributed Object Computing Conference, EDOC 2007, pp. 287–287. IEEE (2007)
11. Pesic, M., van der Aalst, W.M.P.: A declarative approach for flexible business processes management. In: Eder, J., Dustdar, S. (eds.) BPM Workshops 2006. LNCS, vol. 4103, pp. 169–180. Springer, Heidelberg (2006)
12. De Weerdt, J., vanden Broucke, S.K.L.M., Caron, F.: Bidimensional process discovery for mining BPMN models. In: Fournier, F., Mendling, J. (eds.) BPM 2014 Workshops. LNBIP, vol. 202, pp. 529–540. Springer, Heidelberg (2015)
13. Li, J., Bose, R.P.J.C., van der Aalst, W.M.P.: Mining context-dependent and interactive business process maps using execution patterns. In: Muehlen, Mz, Su, J. (eds.) BPM 2010 Workshops. LNBIP, vol. 66, pp. 109–121. Springer, Heidelberg (2011)
14. Conforti, R., Dumas, M., García-Bañuelos, L., La Rosa, M.: Beyond tasks and gateways: discovering bpmn models with subprocesses, boundary events and activity markers. In: Sadiq, S., Soffer, P., Völzer, H. (eds.) BPM 2014. LNCS, vol. 8659, pp. 101–117. Springer, Heidelberg (2014)
15. Ekanayake, C.C., Dumas, M., García-Bañuelos, L., La Rosa, M.: Slice, mine and dice: complexity-aware automated discovery of business process models. In: Daniel, F., Wang, J., Weber, B. (eds.) BPM 2013. LNCS, vol. 8094, pp. 49–64. Springer, Heidelberg (2013)

16. De Weerdt, J., De Backer, M., Vanthienen, J., et al.: A multi-dimensional quality assessment of state-of-the-art process discovery algorithms using real-life event logs. Information Systems **37**(7), 654–676 (2012)

17. Rozinat, A., van der Aalst, W.M.P.: Conformance testing: measuring the fit and appropriateness of event logs and process models. In: Bussler, C.J., Haller, A. (eds.) BPM 2005. LNCS, vol. 3812, pp. 163–176. Springer, Heidelberg (2006)

18. Weber, I., Farshchi, M., Mendling, J., Schneider, J.G.: Mining processes with multi-instantiation. In: ACM/SIGAPP Symposium on Applied Computing (ACM SAC), Salamanca, Spain, April 2015

19. Kalenkova, A.A., van der Aalst, W.M.P., Lomazova, I.A., et al.: Process Mining Using BPMN: Relating Event Logs and Process Models. Software and Systems Modeling, 1–25 (2015)

Information Quality in Dynamic Networked Business Process Management

Mohammad R. Rasouli[✉], Rik Eshuis, Jos J.M. Trienekens,
Rob J. Kusters, and Paul W.P.J. Grefen

School of Industrial Engineering, Eindhoven University of Technology,
P.O box: 513, 5600 MB Eindhoven, The Netherlands
{M.Rasouli,H.Eshuis,J.J.M.Trienekens,p.w.p.j.grefen}@tue.nl,
Rob.Kusters@ou.nl

Abstract. The competition in globalized markets forces organizations to provide mass-customized integrated solutions for customers. Mass-customization
of integrated solutions by business network requires adaptive interactions between parties to address emerging requirements of customers. These adaptive
interactions need to be enabled by dynamic networked business processes
(DNBP) that are supported by high quality information. However, the dynamic
collaboration between parties can result in information quality (IQ) issues such
as information syntactic and semantic misalignment, information leakage, and
unclear information ownership. To counter negative consequences of poor IQ
on the performance, the orchestrator of business network needs to clearly recognize these IQ issues. In this paper, we develop and evaluate a framework to
address potential IQ issues related to DNBP. The development of the framework is based on a three step methodology that includes the characterization of
dynamism of networked business processes, the characterization of IQ dimensions, and the exploration of IQ issues. To evaluate the practical significance of
the explored IQ issues, we conduct a case study in a service ecosystem that is
shaped by a car leasing organization to provide integrated mobility solutions for
customers.

1 Introduction

The competition in the current business environment forces organizations to concentrate on core competencies and outsource other activities. This fact leads vertically
integrated organizations towards networked businesses. Within a networked business
different autonomous parties collaborate together to provide a product or service for
customers. On the other hand, based on several developments, especially in the context of marketing, manufacturing and operations management, the networked businesses need to shift from the provision of single products or services towards the
co-creation of integrated solutions for customers [1]. The co-creation of integrated
solutions necessitates shaping value networks that are characterized by adaptive interaction between parties within a networked business [2]. The complexity of this context requires paying much more attention to how parties interact, not only to what

© Springer International Publishing Switzerland 2015
C. Debruyne et al. (Eds.): OTM 2015 Conferences, LNCS 9415, pp. 202–218, 2015.
DOI: 10.1007/978-3-319-26148-5_12

they exchange. This requires seeing interaction between parties within the networked (i.e. inter-organizational) business processes point of view [3]. A networked business process is enacted by two or more autonomous organizations, of which at least one organization exposes a non-black box projection of the explicit control flow structure of an internal process to the other organization(s) [3]. In this way, the adaptive inter-actions between parties can be seen in the form of dynamic networked business proc-esses (DNBP).

On the other hand, business processes need to be supported by high quality infor-mation. Information quality (IQ) typically is defined by information "fitness for use" [4]. This definition of IQ states that the quality of information can be measured by the value which the information provides to the user of that information. The user of in-formation might be an automated application, an organization, or any other entity that uses information [5]. Since a business process consists of a set of data items (like Customer, Order, and Product), in this paper we consider a business process as a user of information. So, the quality of information is determined by its fitness to be used by a business process. However, as we discuss in Section 3, the networked and dynamic nature of DNBP results in issues like syntactic and semantic information heterogeneity, diversified security policies to access information, and inconsistent ontologies. These issues threaten the fitness of information to be used by inter-organizational business processes. Though different research studies have been con-ducted that address IQ issues in networked business processes (e.g. [6-9], research on the issues resulting from dynamism of these processes is still missing.

In this research we aim to explore IQ issues that are caused by the dynamism of networked business processes. For this purpose, we conduct a design science research approach which is elaborated in Section 2. Based on this approach, we develop and evaluate *a framework that addresses the information quality issues resulting from different levels of dynamism in networked business processes.* The development of the framework which consists of three steps is discussed in Section 3. These three steps enable the exploration of IQ issues resulting from the dynamism of networked busi-ness processes in a structured way. The practical significance of the explored IQ issues is evaluated through a case study performed in a car leasing networked organi-zation in Section 4. We discuss related work in Section 5. The paper is concluded in Section 6.

2   Research Approach

Based on the design science research approach [10] we conduct this research within two main phases, respectively, the development phase and the evaluation phase, see Figure 1. Within the development phase we build a framework that can be used to predict possible IQ issues resulting from the dynamism of networked business proc-esses. The investigation of the practical significance of the predicted IQ issues is done within the evaluation phase. These two phases are elaborated further.

Development phase (section 3)   **Evaluation phase** (section4)

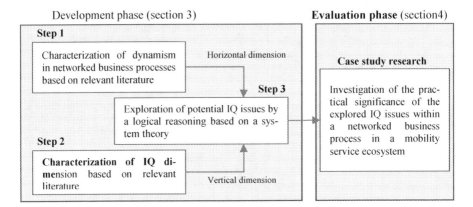

Fig. 1. The research approach

2.1   Development Phase

The dynamism of networked business processes results in the change of information requirements of these processes. Due to this change, the fitness of information to support networked business processes can be negatively affected (i.e. IQ issue). Our aim in this phase is to develop a framework for the exploration of IQ issues resulting from dynamism of networked business processes in a structured way. For this purpose, we conduct the development of the framework within three steps; see Figure 1, the development phase.

Within the first step we characterize different levels of dynamism in networked business processes. This characterization is established upon the relevant literature on the dynamism in networked business processes. Within the second step, we characterize different dimensions of IQ. This characterization is also based on the relevant literature. Finally, within the third step, we deductively explore IQ issues resulting from each level of dynamism in networked business processes. For this deductive exploration we use a logical reasoning based on system theory that distinguishes between the structure and dynamics of a phenomenon [11]. These three steps are elaborated further in section 3.

2.2   Evaluation Phase

For the evaluation of the practical significance of deductively explored IQ issues, we conduct a case study. The case study is a relevant approach for our research, because it enables to investigate the chain of the empirical evidences that support (or reject) the emergence of the explored IQ issues in a real life situation [12]. With respect to the contextual implications of the developed framework (i.e. the dynamic environment), we must select a networked business as a case that embraces dynamism between parties in different levels. For this purpose, we conduct the case study in a networked business that is shaped by a car leasing organization to provide integrated mobility solutions for customers. Within this networked business we select an inter-organizational process for invoicing customers. This case study is elaborated further in section 4.

3   Exploration of IQ Issues in DNBP

Based on the aforementioned approach, we conduct the development of the framework within three steps. These steps are elaborated further.

3.1   Characterization of Dynamism in Networked Business Processes

Previous research has investigated different aspects of dynamism in networked businesses (e.g. [13, 14]). From the strategic point of view, the dynamic capabilities perspective has been regarded as a relevant basis to explore the dynamism of networked businesses [14]. Based on this perspective, the dynamism of networked businesses is due to the need to respond to environmental changes. The environmental changes can be responded through the adaption of internal resources within a networked business. Based on [14], the adaption of internal resources is realized by operating dynamism and partnering dynamism. Both of these dynamisms can cause to the dynamism of networked business processes.

The operating dynamism reflects the need to change the business processes to respond environmental requirements. Regarding the inter-organizational nature of business processes within a networked business this change can be done at the internal or external level of a networked business process [15]. The internal level is of an intra-organizational nature and refers resources of a certain organization (especially technological resources like workflow management systems or process-aware information systems). The change in the internal level occurs within the borders of a party. Based on the BPEL standard [16] this change can be reflected in the business orchestration model of a party. But, the external level is of inter-organizational nature and specifies the interaction with external parties within a networked business. At this level, process models need to be market-specific. This means that business processes in external level have to conform to standards and/or technology used in a specific market. Based on the BPEL standard, the change in the external level of an inter-organizational process can be addressed by a network choreography diagram. The change in internal and external processes itself can be refined into different types (e.g. see [17, 18]). We plan to study these more refined change types in future work.

On the other hand, dynamism in networked business processes can also result from dynamic partnering. This dynamism can be viewed as dynamic collaboration between interdependent parties in the form of instant virtual organizations to respond for an emerging opportunity in the environment [19]. This dynamism originates from the independence of parties within a networked business to participate in collaboration or leave that.

Summarizing, based on the above discussion, in this paper we characterize the dynamism in networked business process within three levels. As we mentioned, other aspects (like different types of the change that have been addressed in process flexibility literature or the customer dynamism) can also be added. But, due to the need for managing the scope of the research we concentrate on these three levels of dynamism:

- Dynamic partnership that reflects the adding a new party, removing an existing party, or switching a party with another. This dynamism can result from the autonomy of parties, the change in the requirements of customers, and failure of an existing party.
- Dynamic external process that addresses the change of an external process by a party. This change might be because of the decision to participate in a new market or the change in standards or technologies used within a market.
- Dynamic internal process that points out the alteration of an intra-organizational process by a party. This change might result from the need to align internal processes within a party with environmental requirements or the emergence of new technologies that can be used by a party.

3.2   Characterization of Different Dimensions of IQ

The concept of quality is closely coupled with the determination of relevant metrics to assess and improve it. This has been reflected in the context of IQ research by the characterization of IQ dimensions. Different research studies, which generally rely on empirical methods, have been conducted to explore IQ dimensions (e.g. [20-22]). Though there are a number of differences between these different representations of IQ dimensions due to the contextual nature of quality, they are basically consistent [23]. In this paper, within different representation of IQ dimensions, we rely on the framework for IQ dimensions proposed by [20], which is called the PSP/IQ model, see Table 1. This model characterizes IQ dimensions within four quadrants (are elaborated further). This characterization provides a beneficial insight to explore IQ issues resulting from dynamic networked business processes. We choose this model since the logic behind the characterization of IQ dimensions enables to represent the relationship between different levels of dynamism of networked business processes and IQ dimensions.

Table 1. IQ dimensions based on PSP/IQ model

	Conforms to Specifications	**Meets or Exceeds Consumer Expectations**
Product Quality	Sound Information The characteristics of the information supplied meet IQ standards	Useful Information The information supplied meets information consumer task needs.
Service Quality	Dependable Information The process of converting data into information meets standards.	Usable Information The process of converting data into information exceeds information customer needs.

The PSP/IQ model distinguishes between information products and information services as well as the internal and external views to quality. Information product considers information as a product that needs to be produced by a manufacturing process with an end-product of information stored in a database. But, information service focuses on the activities occurring after information is stored as an end-product in a databases to enable consumers to obtain and use information. Information products need to be converted to information services to be used by information consumers. This conversion can be done by an automated application or by a manual procedure. On the other hand, internal and external views have been established upon the general quality literature that describes quality as conformance to specification and as exceeding consumer expectations. In this way, the PSP/IQ model characterizes IQ dimensions within four quadrants, see Table 1.

3.3   Exploration of IQ Issues Resulting from DNBP

For the exploration of IQ issues resulting from DNBP, we rely on a logical reasoning based on system theory [11]. The system theory distinguishes between the structure and dynamics views on a phenomenon. The structure view represents the static relationship between elements within a phenomenon. The dynamics view shows the impact of change of an element on other elements.

For the representation of structure of elements, we rely on the theoretical background about the relationship between IQ and DNBP based on information governance theory. Information governance theory sees information as a business resource that links between business and IT [24]. Information (as a business resource) needs to conform to a set of quality metrics (that are referred by IQ dimensions) to effectively support networked business processes. In this way, the quality of certain information is determined through a set of metrics that reflect the extent to which information requirements of networked business processes are met by that information. To represent this relationship we use a class diagram; see Figure 2. This diagram states that information is provided by parties and is used by internal and

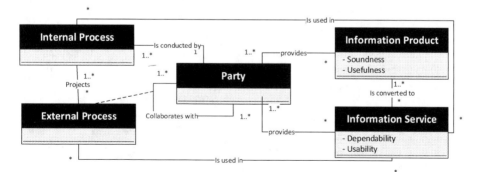

Fig. 2. The relationship between IQ and networked business processes (structure view)

external business processes. The quality of certain information is determined based on its fitness to be used by a certain networked business process.

By using the represented relationship between networked business processes and IQ in Figure 2, we explore the impact of DNBP on IQ dimensions. This exploration is based on the dynamics view of system theory. To conduct a logical reasoning for the exploration of impact of DNBP on IQ dimensions, we rely on the conceptual model of sources of IQ issues proposed by [25]. This conceptual model specifies three types of changes (as sources of issues) resulting in IQ issues. These sources of IQ issues are respectively, context change, changes to information entity, and change to underlying entity. Based on this, we explore how DNBP trigger these three sources of IQ issues and what are the resulting IQ issues; see Figure 3. In doing so, we deduce six lines originating from three levels of DNBP that trigger sources of IQ issues. Then regarding Fig.2, we infer which dimensions of IQ can be affected by each triggering line of sources of IQ issues. This deductive reasoning leads to the exploration of 13 IQ issues resulting from DNBP; see Table 2. The line of reasoning for each of predicted IQ issues is recognizable by the assigned numbers for each of IQ issues. For example, regarding Figure 3, IQ issue 1(i.e. syntactic and semantic inconsistency of information product representation) can occur because of the context change that is triggered by dynamic partnering. We elaborate each of predicted IQ issues further.

1. Syntactic *and semantic inconsistency of information products*: Dynamic partnering leads to the production of a certain information product by different parties, who might be switched with each other. Regarding the nature of networked business, each of party might have different rules (syntactic) and different language and norms (semantic) for the representation of information products. This difference in rules and language can result in syntactic and semantic inconsistency of information products within a networked business.

2. *Repetitive information product:* Dynamic partnership highlights loose linkages between parties resulting in more independence of parties within a networked business. This independent view to the reality by each party causes to repetitive information products that are distributed between parties.

3. *Incompleteness of information product to support emerging requirements:* An information product, which embraces a set of values, has been designed and produced to support a certain requirement of business processes. Dynamism in external and internal business processes can result in new information requirements. The gap between produced information values and required information values to support the emerging business processes results in incompleteness issue [26].

4. *Long-winded information product*: In line with the previous bullet, the change of business process requirements would cause to meaningless information values within information products [25, 26]. These meaningless information values conflict with the concise dimension of IQ and leads to long-winded information products.

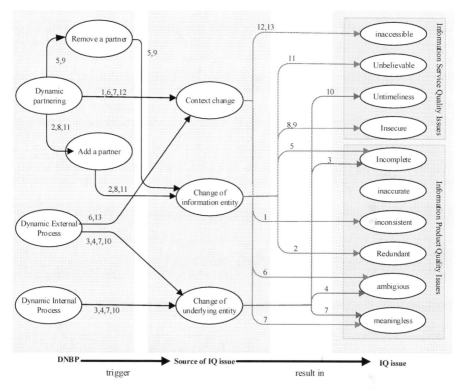

Fig. 3. IQ issues resulting from DNBP (dynamics view)

5. *Lose of relevant information product:* In networked businesses information products are distributed among all parties. Leaving of the network by one of the parties could result in the loss of valuable and relevant information that is needed to conduct networked business processes.

6. *Garbling information product*: The syntactic and semantic inconsistency of information product representation, which are caused by dynamic partnership and dynamic external processes, conflict with the understandability of information products by information consumers.

7. *Accumulation of irrelevant information product*: The change of information consumer's requirements, originating from dynamism in all three levels, can lead to meaningless information products that do not support any business process requirement in reality [26].

8. *Information leakage*: Dynamic partnering in a networked business shift the transactional governance mechanisms towards trust based mechanisms [27, 28]. However, the trust-based mechanisms can increases the threat of information leakage through opportunist parties.

9. *Information ownership*: information exchange within a networked business results in the colocation of information between parties. Because of the dynamic partnership, a party might leave the network, but its collocated information be used by other parties.

Table 2. IQ issues resulting from dynamic networked business processes

IQ dimensions				Dynamic partnership	Dynamic external process	Dynamic internal process
Information service quality	Usability			11. Unknown information service provenance 12. Semantic misalignment of information services	13. Syntactic misalignment of information services	
	Dependability			8. Information leakage 9. Information ownership	10. Decrease of information service continuity	
Information product quality	Usefulness			5. Lose of relevant information product	6. Garbling information product	7. Accumulation of irrelevant information product
	Soundness			1. Syntactic and semantic inconsistency of information product representation 2. Repetitive information product	3. Incompleteness of information product to support emerging requirements 4. Long-winded information product	

Levels of dynamic networked business processes

10. *Decrease of information service continuity*: Dynamic external processes leads to the change of standards that information services need to conform. However, some information providers might not be able (or not aim) to conform to new standards. Also the change in internal processes might result in not updating the information products supporting an information service. These issues disturb the continuity of an information service.

11. *Unknown information service provenance*: in the context of the networked business the assessment of information believability and reputation is mostly based on the information provenance [5, 29]. However, dynamic partnership makes it difficult to clearly recognize an information service provenance.

12. *Semantic misalignment of information services*: semantic inconsistency of information products distributed between parties (as discussed before) results in difficulties to exchange information within a networked business properly [30]. The semantic misalignment makes it difficult to manipulate and integrate information.

13. *Syntactic misalignment of information services*: Using different standards for inter-organizational interaction resulting from dynamic external processes, disturbs the possibility of information exchange between parties and limits the accessibility of information services [31].

These explored IQ issues reflect the possible negative consequences of dynamic collaborations on information resources. In addition to these explored IQ issues, the domain-specific characteristics of information can result in other IQ issues. For example the clinical information in the health care domain or financial information in banking industry can deal with more IQ issues. Though the proposed framework cannot be considered as a complete framework for networked business in different domains, but the structured and reliable steps proposed in this research can be used to explore domain-specific IQ issues in these specific domains as well.

4   The Evaluation of the Practical Significance of the Explored IQ Issues

In this section we evaluate the practical significance of the deductively explored IQ issues resulting from DNBP. For this purpose, as described in Section 2.2, we conduct a case study in which we explore how the dynamism of networked business processes results in the explored IQ issues. To do so, we select a networked business that is orchestrated by a car leasing organization (we refer by CLO). The CLO as the main orchestrator of this networked business has developed a strategic plan to provide an integrated mobility solution for customers rather than offering an asset-based single service. The provision of the integrated mobility solution requires a dynamic interaction between parties within the networked business for the co-creation of value-in-use for customers. For this purpose, the CLO already has developed a new business model that indicates its plan to collaborate with different autonomous parties (reflecting the dynamic partnering for the provision of integrated mobility solution). However all of planned collaborations have not been realized yet, but the CLO has already developed some networked business processes supporting a part of the planned inter-organizational collaborations. Within these networked business processes, we select a process to invoice customers. A customer within the service ecosystem of mobility solution can get services from different parties, but does not need to pay them separately and he/she only pays for a package of integrated solution for a certain period of time (e.g. six month or a year). During this period of time, a customer can request for an invoice that reflects all services that he/she has got. The CLO needs to gather information from all parties within the network about the provided services by each of parties and integrate them to invoice customers. This networked business process is dynamic, because the parties can be switched (i.e. the dynamic partnering), the standards of information exchange between parties can be changed (i.e. the dynamic external process view), and also each party can decide about the change of its internal processes (i.e. the dynamic internal process view).

To explore the IQ issues within this dynamic networked business process, we represent the "invoice customer" process by using of the business process choreography and orchestration diagrams. The choreography diagram shows the interaction between parties to invoice a customer. The orchestration diagram shows the internal processes within each party. To do so, we rely on data from "CoProFind" project that has already done in the CLO [32]. For the triangulation of data and also to evaluate the correctness of our interpretation from data about the IQ issues (i.e. the construct validity), we have conducted two in-depth interviews with domain experts in enterprise architecture department of the CLO. Also to test the internal validity of our find-ings by the analysis of the gathered data, we conduct a workshop with people from procurement, IT, and finance departments.

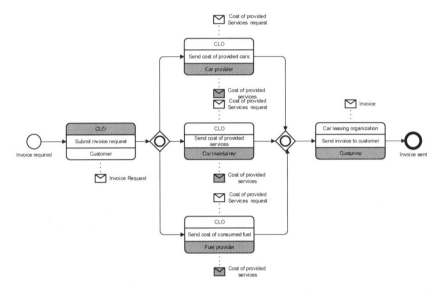

Fig. 4. The choreography diagram of "invoice customer" process in a service ecosystem for mobility solution provision

Based on the gathered data, the choreography diagram of "invoice customer" net-worked business process is shown in Figure 4. This diagram represents the interac-tions between CLO and other service providers (including car provider, car maintain-ers, and fuel service providers) to invoice a customer. The orchestration diagrams that show the internal processes within each of these parties are available on *http://is.ieis.tue.nl/research/bpm/raso15/*. Based on these diagrams, we investigate how the predicted IQ issues result from the dynamism of targeted networked business process in different levels. The results of this investigation are represented in Table 3.

The findings presented in Table 3 shows the practical significance of the explored IQ issues in a real-life situation. Most of these findings are based on the facts that already exist and can be observed directly in the CLO (findings related to the IQ issue 1, 2, 4, 5, 6, 7, 12 and 13). Since the CLO is in a transition from stable interactions with suppliers towards completely dynamic collaborations, we cannot observe some of the predicted IQ issues directly. However, people who are involved in in-depth interviews and the final workshop strongly expect the emergence of other predicted IQ issues as a consequence of dynamism in the invoice networked business. Based on the results from this case study, the CLO clearly find out the negative consequences of dynamic collaboration with its partners. By using of the results of this case study, the CLO has already decided to develop guidelines to encounter IQ issues resulting from its dynamic business model. Also the CLO has recognized the need for taking into consideration the IQ program as a part of its strategic transition plan.

Table 3. Findings that show the practical significance of predicted IQ issues resulting from DNBP

1. Syntactic and semantic inconsistency of information products	A customer can get maintenance services from different maintainers (due to the dynamism of partners). So the information related to maintenance services is distributed among different maintainers. On the other hand, these maintainers use different types of databases to store data. Also due to the lack of using a single standard, each maintainer has its own characterization from the maintenance services.
2. Repetitive information product	The customer information is replicated in different databases owned by different parties. Within orchestration diagrams we found nine different databases that store customers' information. It means that a customer needs to provide his/her information (including ID, driving license, and so on) at least nine times within this service ecosystem. The change of parties and adding new parties also require customers for the new registration when he/she wants to get a service.
3. Incompleteness of information product to support emerging requirements	CLO has already decided to reflect the customer experience about the provided solution in the invoice for customers (i.e. change in internal process). For this, they need to integrate a customer's experience from the interaction with each of parties. However some parties assess the customer's experience on the provided service, but most of them do not. So, CLO deals with the information product incompleteness to respond this requirement.
4. Long-winded information product	Regularly car providers (e.g. car rentals) produce the information related to car deficiencies in each interaction with customers. However, based on the integrated mobility solution business model, since customers do not pay for the asset (i.e. the car), but pay for the service (i.e. the mobility service), so the information related to the deficiencies are not meaningful any more.
5. Loss of relevant information product	It happens quite frequently that when a customer requests for an invoice, a partner who had provided some services for customers, has already left the networked business and so the CLO doesn't access to the required information to invoice customer.
6. Garbling information product	Because of the syntactic and semantic inconsistency of information provided by maintainers, CLO cannot interpret and integrate information correctly. Sometimes, this causes to invoices with duplicated or illusive items that are complained by customers.
7. Accumulation of irrelevant information product	As a consequence of the production of meaningless information (as discusses in 4), a large amount of irrelevant information is accumulated within parties' databases.
8. Information leakage	The provision of integrated solution is based on the prediction of desired customer experience. For this purpose, CLO gets the information of customer experience from the interaction with each of parties within a data warehouse. This data warehouse is also used by parties to tailor their services to a customer. Since the access to this data ware house is based on trust management mechanisms (due to the dynamism of network), sometimes some parties link to the network only to use these shared information and then leave it.

Table 3. (*Continued.*)

9. Information ownership	As aforementioned, the information within the data warehouse for the customer experience management is produced by all parties. This data warehouse also embraces the information produced by parties that already have left the networked business. CLO needs to encounter information ownership issues to use this data warehouse.
10. Decrease of information service continuity	The message between CLO and current fuel provider has already been exchanged by using of a pre-defined standard (based on XML). Fuel providers set their system according to their main customers. If CLO decides to change the message exchange standard (to be able to collaborate with other fuel provider), it is not guaranteed that current fuel provider be able to provide information service based on new standard.
11. Unknown information service provenance	CLO relies on information provided by parties to invoice. Because of the dynamism of networked business, it is not possible for CLO to accredit all parties within the value network. Because of this, customers sometimes complain about the services (especially maintenance services) that they have not received but are reflected in the invoice.
12. Semantic misalignment of information services	As aforementioned, parties use different language to provide information services. However standardization in each segment (i.e. parties within an industry, like car providers) helps to encounter this issue, but, because of the dynamic nature of the network, the standards are not regarded by all parties. Also the semantic integration of data between different segments is still a problem.
13. Syntactic misalignment of information services	Due to different formats of received information (particularly from maintainers), CLO cannot integrate information automatically. For example, in most of the cases, information received from car maintainers need to be re-entered by a user in CLO.

5   Related Work

IQ issues within the borders of an organization have been sufficiently addressed in previous research (e.g. [5, 21, 25, 33]). Inter-organizational interactions between parties within a networked business lead to a new set of syntactic and semantic issues. The IQ issues relating to inter-organizational interactions in stable networked businesses (like a supply chain) are also explored in previous research (e.g. [8, 34, 35]). These previous research in stable networked businesses, based on their perspective on IQ, can be classified in two main groups:

- Information integration perspective on IQ in networked (cooperative) information systems (like [34, 35]), which aims to provide solutions to deal with IQ issues in such systems;
- Business engineering perspective on IQ in business networking (like [8]), which identifies IQ related requirements in the context of business networking;

This research steps further in the context of IQ in business networking from two aspects:

- While related previous research mostly focused on IQ issues in stable business networking, this research concentrates on IQ issues resulting from the dynamism of networked business processes. In this way, the explored IQ issues in this research are different from those that have been addressed in previous studies (like [8, 34, 35]). This difference is mostly related to the origination of the explored issues (i.e. dynamism of interaction between parties). This difference in the origination of IQ issues needs to be taken into consideration for the development of effective solutions to deal with them.
- This research relies on the business engineering view on IQ issues, but regarding the classification of IQ issues within information product and information service quality, it also can be used as a comprehensive set of requirements to evaluate information integration initiatives in the context of dynamic business networking. For instance, based on Table 2, information product related issues can be resolved by information integration in database level through solutions like database-oriented middlewares. But, information service related issues can be resolved by service integration solutions like component-oriented middlewares. Indeed, the classification of the explored IQ issues helps information integration solution architects to evaluate different IT solutions in a structured way.

From the solution point of view, IQ in the context of a single organization seems to be a mature research field. Different organizational solutions (like the information governance programs), architectural solutions (like data ware-house and master data management) and technological solutions (like middleware technologies) have been developed to counter with the IQ issues within organization boundaries [5]. In the context of inter-organizational interactions, since most of IQ issues originate from syntactic and semantic heterogeneity of information services provided by different parties, proposed solutions have been focused on these issues [36]. Most of these solutions, like standardization based middlewares to deal with syntactic inconsistency or ontology matching solutions to deal with semantic inconsistency are sufficiently respond to IQ issues in stable networked businesses [37, 38]. But, due to the difficulties resulting from dynamism in networked businesses - like short term partnering of parties coming from various contexts, distributed governance power between all parties and lack of centralized control- the effectiveness of aforementioned solutions in the context of dynamic networked businesses is doubtful. Particularly, the ontological alignment that enables semantic interactions between parties cannot be easily handled in dynamic networked businesses [37]. This means that most of IQ issues in the context of dynamic networked businesses, as explored in this research, are challenging issues and more research in relevant domains is need to be conducted to respond these issues effectively. Indeed, this research highlights a comprehensive set of challenging issues as requirements of dynamic business networking.

Since explored IQ issues cannot be handled easily in the context of dynamic networked businesses (as discussed), the shift from stable inter-organizational interactions towards a dynamic business networking can result in the emergence of new risks - like the operation disruption, or irrational decision making- originating from low quality information. This means that a networked business needs to balance between market forces to provide mass customized integrated solutions for customers necessitating more dynamic interactions with partners and IQ requirements to support processes and decisions. In other words, the governor of a networked business must trade-off between market value obtained from dynamic interactions and risks originated from low quality information [39]. In addition, a strategic transition plan to move towards a dynamic networked business needs to the high consideration to emerging IQ issues. However, based on our observation, the IQ issues are usually neglected in such strategic transition plans.

In the studied case, because of the central role of the CLO as the orchestrator of networked business, IQ issues resulting from dynamic collaboration can be recognized and managed by this organization. However, within networked businesses that there is no central actor for the orchestration, the IQ issues can increase dramatically. Indeed, it can be said that the IQ issues resulting from dynamic interactions can be intensified in a networks that do not have a central orchestrator.

6   Conclusion

In this paper we explored IQ issues resulting from the dynamism of networked business processes. Indeed, the core contribution of this paper is the identification of a comprehensive set of IQ issues in the context of dynamic business networking in a structured way. The structured and reliable steps proposed for the exploration of IQ issues can be used by networked businesses in different industries to explore domain-specific IQ issues as well. The practical significance of the explored IQ issues is evaluated by conducting a case study research in a networked business that provides integrated mobility solution for customers. The proposed list of IQ issues can be used as a checklist to assess (or develop) information systems supporting inter-organizational business processes. They also can be considered as dynamic business networking requirements from the IQ point of view that need to be responded by organizational, architectural, or computational solutions.

However theoretical and practical significance of proposed IQ issues are addressed in this paper, but more exploratory research in different domains is needed to enhance the completeness of the framework. Also the combination of proposed three levels of dynamic networked business process with the aspects of process flexibility would be a good direction for future research.

References

1. Vargo, S.L., Lusch, R.F.: Evolving to a new dominant logic for marketing. Journal of Marketing **68**, 1–17 (2004)
2. Rasouli, M.R., Kusters, R.J., Trienekens, J.J., Grefen, P.W.: Service orientation in demand-supply chains: towards an integrated framework. In: Camarinha-Matos, L.M., Afsarmanesh, H. (eds.) Collaborative Systems for Smart Networked Environments. IFIP AICT, vol. 434, pp. 182–193. Springer, Heidelberg (2014)
3. Grefen, P.: Networked business process management. International Journal of IT/Business Alignment and Governance (IJITBAG) **4**, 54–82 (2013)

4. Wang, R.Y.: A product perspective on total data quality management. Communications of the ACM **41**, 58–65 (1998)
5. Sadiq, S.: Handbook of data quality. Springer (2013)
6. Hartono, E., Li, X., Na, K.-S., Simpson, J.T.: The role of the quality of shared information in interorganizational systems use. International Journal of Information Management **30**, 399–407 (2010)
7. Li, S., Lin, B.: Accessing information sharing and information quality in supply chain management. Decision Support Systems **42**, 1641–1656 (2006)
8. Otto, B., Lee, Y.W., Caballero, I.: Information and data quality in business networking: a key concept for enterprises in its early stages of development. Electronic Markets **21**, 83–97 (2011)
9. Falge, C., Otto, B., Osterle, H.: Data quality requirements of collaborative business processes. In: 2012 45th Hawaii International Conference on System Science (HICSS), pp. 4316–4325. IEEE (2012)
10. von Alan, R.H., March, S.T., Park, J., Ram, S.: Design science in information systems research. MIS Quarterly **28**, 75–105 (2004)
11. Von Bertalanffy, L.: General system theory; a new approach to unity of science. 1. Problems of general system theory. Human Biology **23**, 302 (1951)
12. Yin, R.K.: Case study research: Design and methods. Sage publications (2013)
13. Rasouli, M.R., Trienekens, J.J., Kusters, R.J., Grefen, P.W.: A Dynamic Capabilities Perspective on Service-orientation in Demand-supply Chains. Procedia CIRP **30**, 396–401 (2015)
14. Sambamurthy, V., Bharadwaj, A., Grover, V.: Shaping agility through digital options: Reconceptualizing the role of information technology in contemporary firms. MIS Quarterly, 237–263 (2003)
15. Eshuis, R., Grefen, P.: Constructing customized process views. Data & Knowledge Engineering **64**, 419–438 (2008)
16. Anders, T.A.C. F., Dholakia, H., Goland, Y., Klein, J., Leymann, F., Roller, D., Smith, D., Thatte, S., Trickovic, I., et al.: Business Process Execution Language for Web Services, Version 1.1. Standards proposal by BEA Systems. In: International Business Machines Corporation, Microsoft Corporation, SAP AG, Siebel Systems (2002)
17. Reichert, M., Weber, B.: Enabling flexibility in process-aware information systems: challenges, methods, technologies. Springer Science & Business Media (2012)
18. Schonenberg, H., Mans, R., Russell, N., Mulyar, N., van der Aalst, W.: Process flexibility: a survey of contemporary approaches. In: Dietz, J.L.G., Albani, A., Barjis, J. (eds.) Advances in Enterprise Engineering I. Lecture Notes in Business Information Processing, vol. 10, pp. 16–30. Springer, Heidelberg (2008)
19. Mehandjiev, N., Grefen, P.: Dynamic business process formation for instant virtual enterprises. Springer (2010)
20. Kahn, B.K., Strong, D.M., Wang, R.Y.: Information quality benchmarks: product and service performance. Communications of the ACM **45**, 184–192 (2002)
21. Strong, D.M., Lee, Y.W., Wang, R.Y.: Data quality in context. Communications of the ACM **40**, 103–110 (1997)
22. Wang, R.Y., Strong, D.M.: Beyond accuracy: What data quality means to data consumers. Journal of Management Information Systems, 5–33 (1996)
23. Batini, C., Cappiello, C., Francalanci, C., Maurino, A.: Methodologies for data quality assessment and improvement. ACM Computing Surveys (CSUR) **41**, 16 (2009)

24. Kooper, M.N., Maes, R., Lindgreen, E.R.: On the governance of information: Introducing a new concept of governance to support the management of information. International Journal of Information Management **31**, 195–200 (2011)

25. Stvilia, B., Gasser, L., Twidale, M.B., Smith, L.C.: A framework for information quality assessment. Journal of the American Society for Information Science and Technology **58**, 1720–1733 (2007)

26. Wand, Y., Wang, R.Y.: Anchoring data quality dimensions in ontological foundations. Communications of the ACM **39**, 86–95 (1996)

27. Provan, K.G., Kenis, P.: Modes of network governance: Structure, management, and effectiveness. Journal of Public Administration Research and Theory **18**, 229–252 (2008)

28. Zaheer, A., Venkatraman, N.: Relational governance as an interorganizational strategy: An empirical test of the role of trust in economic exchange. Strategic Management Journal **16**, 373–392 (1995)

29. Artz, D., Gil, Y.: A survey of trust in computer science and the semantic web. Web Semantics: Science, Services and Agents on the World Wide Web **5**, 58–71 (2007)

30. Li, X., Madnick, S., Zhu, H.H., Fan, Y.: Reconciling semantic heterogeneity in web services composition. Composite Information Systems Laboratory Working Paper (2009)

31. Seguel, R., Eshuis, R., Grefen, P.: Architecture Support for Flexible Business Chain Integration Using Protocol Adaptors. International Journal of Cooperative Information Systems **23** (2014)

32. Lüftenegger, E.: Service-Dominant Business Design., Ph.D. thesis, Published by Beat research school, Eindhoven University of Technology (2014)

33. Xu, H., Horn Nord, J., Brown, N., Daryl Nord, G.: Data quality issues in implementing an ERP. Industrial Management & Data Systems **102**, 47–58 (2002)

34. Batini, C.: A survey of data quality issues in cooperative information systems. Pre-conference ER tutorial (2004)

35. Mecella, M., Scannapieco, M., Virgillito, A., Baldoni, R., Catarci, T., Batini, C.: Managing data quality in cooperative information systems. In: Meersman, R., Tari, Z. (eds.) CoopIS 2002, DOA 2002, and ODBASE 2002. LNCS, vol. 2519, pp. 486–502. Springer, Heidelberg (2002)

36. Hasselbring, W.: Information system integration. Communications of the ACM **43**, 32–38 (2000)

37. Izza, S.: Integration of industrial information systems: from syntactic to semantic integration approaches. Enterprise Information Systems **3**, 1–57 (2009)

38. Otero-Cerdeira, L., Rodríguez-Martínez, F.J., Gómez-Rodríguez, A.: Ontology matching: A literature review. Expert Systems with Applications **42**, 949–971 (2015)

39. Tallon, P.P.: Corporate governance of big data: Perspectives on value, risk, and cost. Computer **46**, 32–38 (2013)

Utilizing the Hive Mind – How to Manage Knowledge in Fully Distributed Environments

Thomas Bach[✉], Muhammad Adnan Tariq, Christian Mayer,
and Kurt Rothermel

Institute for Parallel and Distributed Systems,
University of Stuttgart, Stuttgart, Germany
{thomas.bach,adnan.tariq,christian.mayer,
kurt.rothermel}@ipvs.uni-stuttgart.de
http://www.uni-stuttgart.de

Abstract. By 2020, the Internet of Things will consist of 26 Billion connected devices. All these devices will be collecting an innumerable amount of raw observations, for example, GPS positions or communication patterns. In order to benefit from this enormous amount of information, machine learning algorithms are used to derive knowledge from the gathered observations. This benefit can be increased further, if the devices are enabled to collaborate by sharing gathered knowledge. In a massively distributed environment, this is not an easy task, as the knowledge on each device can be very heterogeneous and based on a different amount of observations in diverse contexts. In this paper, we propose two strategies to route a query for specific knowledge to a device that can answer it with high confidence. To that end, we developed a confidence metric that takes the number and variance of the observations of a device into account. Our routing strategies are based on local routing tables that can either be learned from previous queries over time or actively maintained by interchanging knowledge models. We evaluated both routing strategies on real world and synthetic data. Our evaluations show that the knowledge retrieved by the presented approaches is up to 96.7% as accurate as the global optimum.

Keywords: Knowledge retrieval · Distributed knowledge · Confidence-based indexing · Query routing

1 Introduction

In many areas, such as social media or the Internet of Things (IoT) an enormous amount of data is produced. According to Cisco [7], the IoT alone will generate over 400 ZB of data annually by 2020. This data will mainly be in the form of raw observations, ranging from GPS positions to video streams, made by billions of interconnected devices, such as smart phones or myriads of ubiquitous sensors integrated in many modern devices. All these observations can be processed to generate knowledge. For example, by monitoring its GPS position over time, a

© Springer International Publishing Switzerland 2015
C. Debruyne et al. (Eds.): OTM 2015 Conferences, LNCS 9415, pp. 219–236, 2015.
DOI: 10.1007/978-3-319-26148-5_13

smart phone can learn the working place and home of its owner [1]. Starting from such basic knowledge, more complex inferences about the owners habits and daily routine are possible. Over time the phone can provide valuable knowledge to the user, for example, the best time to leave home dependent on the travel time to work. Greater benefit can arise if knowledge is not only generated and used locally, but also made accessible to others. In order to generate synergy effects, the devices of all users could form a hive mind. For example, by sharing knowledge about commuting habits, this hive mind can help to coordinate commuting, reduce traffic jams, save energy, and reduce CO_2 emissions [19].

One way of sharing knowledge is collecting at a central location, such as a cloud or a data center. This recent practice of massive data centralization has raised huge privacy concerns [16], as centralized data is regularly subject to breaches [11]. However, today there is nothing like one single central location to share all knowledge, the opposite is the case. Today every smart phone, every application and every company, every connected entity is gathering and analyzing as many observations as possible. In general, all these entities are not willing to share their, possibly private, observations directly [33]. For example users are uncomfortable sharing their exact GPS trajectories. However, in order to benefit from the knowledge and experience of other entities they might be willing to share gathered knowledge. This might be their knowledge about traffic at a specific road segment during the morning rush hour.

For instance, a public transport company could be interested in gathering knowledge about traveling patterns of its customers, while customers might be interested in more exact and up to date train timings and delay reports. In order to harness all these diverse sources of knowledge, we envision a scenario where many heterogeneous entities can share knowledge they have derived from many (possibly private) observations. Whenever an entity needs to acquire specific knowledge, such as knowledge about the traffic at a specific road, it can request this knowledge from other entities.

To enable such a fully decentralized system, all entities need to have the ability to search for (i.e., query) and retrieve specific knowledge generated by other entities. Locating knowledge in a fully decentralized system is a great challenge as we are facing three core difficulties. First, there exists no central index of all available knowledge. Second, knowledge is evolving fast, as previous observations may become outdated over time and new observations, made in different contexts, arise. Finally, knowledge is very heterogeneous, as each node learns individually, based on possibly high dimensional observations. Therefore, the learned knowledge is different, dependent on the number of observations and the context they are made in. For example, the traveling time between a users workplace and home might be dependent on weather, public holidays, time of the day, road works, etc. In consequence, the confidence with that a node can answer a specific query depends mainly on the context and amount of observations.

In order to tackle these issues, we propose two different routing strategies to retrieve specific knowledge by forwarding a query to the node that can answer it with high confidence. At the first glance, this problem looks as if it could be solved with a traditional peer-to-peer (P2P) approach. Traditional P2P-systems, however, cannot be applied as they are mainly designed for exact query searches. In knowledge retrieval, many nodes may be able to answer a query. The confidence in these answers, however, may be completely different as nodes have gathered completely different knowledge. Furthermore, traditional P2P-systems assume homogeneous attributes for searching, however, knowledge is usually learned with respect to many different contexts that even differ between the devices.

In particular, our contributions are as follows: Based on our query model, we present two different, fully distributed, strategies to route a query to a node that can answer it with high confidence. To that end, we developed a confidence metric that takes the number and variance of observations into account. We evaluate both routing strategies on a synthetic- and a real-world data-set. In order to show that our algorithms can deal with heterogeneous, high dimensional data, we evaluated them in combination with an dimension selection technique to avoid the curse of dimensionality. Our results show, that the knowledge retrieved by the presented approaches is up to 96.7% as accurate as the global optimum.

2   System Model and Problem Formulation

We assume a fully distributed system of heterogeneous computing nodes $S = \{S_1, ..., S_k\}$. These nodes can join and leave the system at any time and fail temporarily or permanently. They can range from user owned portable edge computing devices, such as laptops and desktop computers, to private cloud instances or even third party services located in the nearby fog or big data centers. All nodes communicate on a peer-to-peer basis and form an acyclic, undirected topology. Maintaining such a topology, even under dynamic conditions, is a well studied problem (e.g., [6]) and is, therefore, not discussed in this paper.

Each node $S_i \in S$ collects raw observations o_j (e.g., GPS positions) produced by arbitrary sensors or mobile devices like smart phones. Machine learning algorithms, such as Markov Models, Conditional Random Fields (CRF), Bayesian networks, etc., can then be used to derive knowledge from these raw observations. In this paper, we use N-dimensional spaces to represent the raw observations o_j. This way, observable attributes, like time or position are represented by dimensions and every observation o_j as a point in space ($o_j \in \mathbb{R}^N$). For instance, in a traffic scenario, a concrete journey would be defined by its start-time, end-time, start-coordinates, and end-coordinates and represented as a point in N-dimensional space. Based on this representation, learning approaches, such as linear regression, multivariate adaptive regression, or time series analysis, can be applied to derive knowledge, e.g., the travel time between two locations with respect to the time of the day. In the following, we use the term knowledge model KM^{S_i} to represent the observations collected by a node S_i and the corresponding knowledge derived from these observations.

As all nodes make observations individually and, thereby, gather different observations in their knowledge models KM^{S_i}, the nodes have different confidence in the knowledge they have gathered. For example, a person traveling only in one part of the city has intuitively higher confidence in estimated travel times in that part of the city than a person traveling mainly in another part.

To retrieve specific knowledge from the knowledge model, a query is issued. Such a query can be retrieving the travel time in the context of a journey at a specific time of the day. In an N-dimensional space ($\mathbb{R}^N$), we define a query $\vec{q}$ as a tuple:

$$\vec{q} = (\delta, \omega, \rho_{\vec{q}}) \tag{1}$$

This tuple consists of a context (δ), a request (ω), and required confidence ($\rho_{\vec{q}}$). We define the context as a point in a subspace $\mathbb{R}^C \subsetneq \mathbb{R}^N$, where N is the total number of dimensions and C is the number of dimensions in the subspace of the context.

$$\delta \in \mathbb{R}^C : C < N. \tag{2}$$

Similarly, the request is defined as an element in a different subspace $\mathbb{R}^R \subsetneq (\mathbb{R}^N \setminus \mathbb{R}^C)$, where R is the number of dimensions of the requested subspace.

$$\omega \in \mathbb{R}^R : R \leq N - C. \tag{3}$$

In a traffic scenario, for example, the knowledge models could consists of four dimensions (source, destination, travel time, and time of the day). A query $(\delta, \omega, \rho_{\vec{q}})$ to retrieve travel time for a specific journey can be structured as follows: context (δ) = (source, destination, time of the day) and request (ω) = (travel time) and confidence ($\rho_{\vec{q}}$) = 0.8.

Based on the above discussion, we can now define the concrete knowledge retrieval problem. Given i) a dynamic set of nodes $S = \{S_1, ..., S_k\}$, ii) continuously evolving and heterogeneous knowledge models KM^{S_i} maintained by each node $S_i \in S$ and iii) a knowledge retrieval query $\vec{q}$, our objective is to find the node $S_j \in S$ that can answer the query $\vec{q}$ with confidence $\rho > \rho_{\vec{q}}$.

In the following, we first introduce the notion of confidence and establish a metric to determine the confidence of a knowledge model KM^{S_i} to answer a specific query $\vec{q}$ (cf. Sec. 3). Afterwards, we present two algorithms that utilize the confidence metric to route a query for specific knowledge towards the node that can reply with the required confidence (cf. Sec. 4). Finally, we thoroughly evaluate and compare the performance of the proposed routing algorithms on synthetic and real-world data (cf. Sec. 5).

3   Confidence

In this section, we develop a notion of confidence and introduce a metric that reflects the confidence with that a query can be answered by a specific knowledge model KM^{s_i}. As observations in a knowledge model are usually neither concentrated in a single area of the model, nor distributed equally, it is not desirable to assign a single confidence value to a whole knowledge model. Instead, we use clustering to group similar observations and determine the confidence of these clusters individually.

3.1   Clustering

In order to cluster the observations in a knowledge model, we can use well known algorithms, such as K-means [5], spectral clustering [28], hierarchical clustering [12], etc. However, these algorithms need to know the number of clusters (denoted as K) in advance. Determining the number of clusters, however, is not easy and is usually based on preknowledge or practical experience. In our case, choosing the number of clusters K is even more difficult, as different knowledge models may witness highly heterogeneous observation patterns.

Clearly, the observations in each knowledge model are directly dependent on real world events. These real world events are usually highly chaotic as they are based on a vast amount of influence factors (Butterfly Effect). Therefore, the observations stored in the knowledge models can be treated as independent random variables. Consequently, the arithmetic mean of these observations follows a Gaussian distribution according to the central limit theorem [14]. Based on this we can conclude that the observations in each knowledge model are a combination of several Gaussian distributed clusters, located in different "areas" of the model. To determine the actual number of clusters, we use the following algorithm: We start by assuming a single cluster ($K = 1$) in a knowledge model and perform a statistical test for the hypothesis that all observations of the cluster follow a Gaussian distribution. If this test fails, we increase the assumed number of clusters by one ($K = K + 1$) and repeat the process. This process terminates, when all observations assigned to each cluster are following a Gaussian distribution. This approach is similar to the G-Means algorithm [9].

3.2   Cluster-Based Confidence

Now that the clusters are obtained, in the following we present how to determine the confidence in these clusters. Usually, machine learning algorithms are performed on a large number of observations. If not enough observations are available (for example, in the region of a query), machine learning algorithms can not derive meaningful information. Thus, we base our confidence metric on the amount and variance of observations in a cluster. The combination of both parameters is important as they can be misleading if interpreted individually. The number of observations in a cluster for example does not tell anything about the cluster's usability for learning, as the observations can be highly variant. Consider for instance, a cluster that models the waiting time at a busy intersection of a road. If the cluster consists of observations scattered over the whole day, then it might not be qualified to answer a query for the waiting time at a specific time of the day. On the other hand, low variance alone is also not adequate, as the variance can be based on a very small number of observations.

$$\rho(\overrightarrow{q}, \overrightarrow{c}_c, \Sigma_c, N_c) = N_c \cdot f_N(\overrightarrow{q}, \overrightarrow{c}_c, \Sigma_c) \tag{4}$$

This duality is reflected in our confidence metric ρ (Eq. 4) that consists of a N-dimensional Gaussian distribution function f_N, multiplied by the number of points (N_c) in a cluster c. The Gaussian distribution function f_N is characterized by the mean value $\vec{c}_c$ (also termed as centroid) and variance Σ_c of the cluster c. This way, the confidence value behaves according to the distribution of observations and is proportional to the total number of observations in a cluster. We used a Gaussian distribution function in Eq. 4 for two reasons. First, as stated in Sec. 3.1 the observations in each cluster are following this distribution. Second, it enables the confidence in a cluster to degrade exponentially, such that queries $\vec{q}$ close to the centroid $\vec{c}$ of a cluster have high confidence, while with a continuously growing distance to the centroid, the confidence gets exponentially worse. As our knowledge models are N-dimensional spaces, clusters can have different variance in each dimension. Moreover, clusters can be clinched or rotated in different dimensions. Thus we use a multivariate Gaussian distribution function (cf. Eq. 5) that uses a covariance matrix Σ_c to take the variance in the different dimensions into account. Figure 1(a) shows the confidence for a cluster in a two dimensional knowledge model. The confidence of a cluster to answer a certain query is then the confidence value ρ of a cluster c at the point of a query $\vec{q}$, i.e. $\rho_{\vec{q}} = \rho(\vec{q}, \vec{c}_c, \Sigma_c, N_c)$.

$$f_N(\vec{q}, \vec{c}_c, \Sigma_c) = \frac{1}{(2\pi)^{0.5N}|\Sigma_c|^{0.5}} \exp^{-0.5(\vec{x}-\vec{c}_c)^T \Sigma_c^{-1}(\vec{q}-\vec{c}_c)} \tag{5}$$

3.3   Discussion

The above presented confidence metric can be used to compare the confidence of two knowledge models, however, the value of confidence is unbounded. This makes it difficult to determine when a knowledge model has "good enough" knowledge or is saturated (as each cluster in a knowledge model can have arbitrarily large number of observations). To solve this problem, we propose to artificially bound the confidence ρ^B as shown in Eq. 6.

$$\rho^B(\vec{q}, \vec{c}, \Sigma, N_c) = min(1, N_c \cdot f(\vec{q}, \vec{c}, \Sigma)) \tag{6}$$

The behavior of this bounded confidence function (ρ^B) is shown in Fig. 1(b). The figure shows the confidence with that a cluster can answer a query with respect to the distance between a query and the cluster center. According to Eq. 6 we assume a saturation when the confidence value exceeds 1. On the left side of Fig. 1(b), clusters with the same variance and different number of observations are compared. On the right side, clusters with the same number of observations and different variance are compared. This shows, how the saturation of a cluster is dependent on the variance and number of observations. In essence, clusters with low variance need less observations to saturate then clusters with high variance.

Another approach would be to employ domain specific knowledge to define when a cluster is saturated or has "good enough knowledge". For instance, by introducing a threshold that specifies the minimal distance between two observations in a cluster. If all the observations of a cluster obey the threshold criteria,

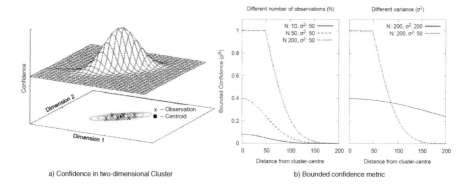

a) Confidence in two-dimensional Cluster   b) Bounded confidence metric

Fig. 1. Confidence dependent on distance to cluster-center, variance, and number of observations. Multivariate Gaussian distance function for all queries.

the cluster is assumed to have maximal confidence. Mathematically this threshold can be defined as the mean distance between observations in a cluster.

4 Routing

Now that the confidence metric is defined, we describe the routing of queries towards the nodes that can reply with the desired confidence. In particular, each node S_i maintains a routing model $RM_{S_n}^{S_i}$ for each direct neighbor $S_n \in S \setminus S_i$. A routing model $RM_{S_n}^{S_i}$ is an N-dimensional space (similar to the knowledge model) and summarizes the knowledge that is reachable (by forwarding the query) through the respective neighbor S_n.

On receiving a query $\overrightarrow{q}$ (cf. Sec. 2) a node S_i decides whether to answer $\overrightarrow{q}$ based on its local knowledge model KM_{S_i} or to forward $\overrightarrow{q}$ to one of its neighbor $S_n \in S \setminus S_i$. In more detail, a node S_i uses its knowledge model KM_{S_i} to calculate the confidence ρ at the point of the query $\overrightarrow{q}$ and reply $\overrightarrow{q}$ locally if $\rho > \rho_{\overrightarrow{q}}$. Otherwise, S_i uses the routing model $RM_{S_n}^{S_i}$ maintained for each of its neighbor S_n to calculate the estimated confidence with which $\overrightarrow{q}$ can be answered if forwarded to that respective neighbor S_n. The query $\overrightarrow{q}$ is finally routed to the neighbor with the highest estimated confidence. In the following, we present two different strategies to maintain the routing models and route queries.

4.1 Knowledge Aggregation Based Routing

With *Knowledge Aggregation Based Routing* (KAR) the routing models $RM_{S_n}^{S_i}$ that a node S_i maintains for each neighbor S_n are managed in a proactive fashion. In general, a routing model contains the summary of the knowledge reachable through a neighbor. This is done by enabling routing models to store the (subset of) N-dimensional observations that are reachable through the respective neighbors. The observations stored in a routing model are clustered similar to that of knowledge model and, thus, the calculation of confidence is alike.

To maintain routing models, each node S_n sends a compact representation of the clusters in its knowledge model KM_{S_n} to all of its neighbors. This compact representation includes the number of observations N_c, the centroid $\overrightarrow{c}_c$, and the covariance matrix Σ_c of each cluster c in the knowledge model. Moreover, the node S_n also sends to each neighbor S_i the compact representation of the observations stored in the RM of its other neighbors. This is required to ensure that the routing model not only contains the summary of the knowledge available in the knowledge model of the direct neighbor but also the knowledge reachable by routing the query through that neighbor.

On receiving the compact cluster representation from S_n, the node S_i can regenerate clusters along with all the observations in its routing model $RM_{S_n}^{S_i}$, representing the knowledge available through S_n. A complete regeneration is not very scalable for clusters containing a large number of observations, therefore, we introduce a regeneration factor $\delta \in (0, 1]$ that controls the fraction of observations that are regenerated $(N_c \cdot \delta)$.

To regenerate the clusters described by the received compact cluster representation $(N_c, \overrightarrow{c}_c, \Sigma_c)$, we use an approach described in [10]. This approach consists of three steps, shown in Fig. 2. First, we generate the desired number of observations $(N_c \cdot \delta)$ following a multivariate Gaussian distribution. Second, we skew and rotate the resulting point-cloud (the new cluster) according to the provided covariance matrix Σ_c. In the final step, we translate each point of the new cluster by the given centroid $\overrightarrow{c}_c$.

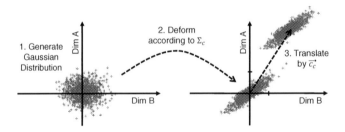

Fig. 2. Transforming a normal distributed cluster into a cluster rotated and skewed according to given compact cluster information.

Fig. 3 shows the KAR strategy for a network consisting of four nodes (S_1, S_2, S_3, S_4). To reduce complexity only relevant routing and knowledge models are shown. Initially, all routing models of node S_1 (i.e., $RM_{S_2}^{S_1}$ and $RM_{S_3}^{S_1}$) are empty, as shown in Fig. 3(a). Afterwards, S_2 and S_4 generate the compact cluster representation for their knowledge and routing models (cf. Fig. 3(b)) and send these representations to S_1 (cf. Fig. 3(c)). From the received compact representations S_1 regenerates its routing model for S_2 and S_3 (i.e., $RM_{S_2}^{S_1}$ and $RM_{S_4}^{S_1}$ respectively), as depicted in Fig. 3(d).

As the knowledge models are subject to continuous change, each node is responsible for keeping the routing models, maintained at other nodes, up to

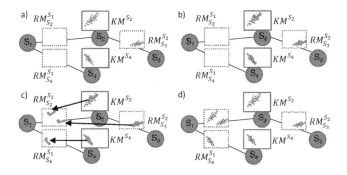

Fig. 3. Propagating the knowledge and generating the routing models.

date. If a node detects a significant change of knowledge in its own models, it generates new compact cluster representation and forwards it to its neighbors.

Routing a Query. Routing of a query works as described in the beginning of this section. To determine the confidence in both models (i.e., KM and RM), we use the confidence metric described in Sec. 3.

4.2   Query Learning Based Routing

In a large-scale system, the routing models of the previously introduced KAR strategy require frequent updates. This is due to the continuously evolving knowledge models, as well as the unpredictable churn caused by joining and leaving nodes at arbitrary times. To reduce the overhead of managing the routing models, we designed a query learning based routing strategy (QLR) that continuously learns the routing models of a node, based on previously routed queries. This means, whenever a query was answered successfully, a feedback is send backwards on the routing path to the source of the query. This feedback consists of the query $\vec{q}$ and the confidence $\rho_{\vec{q}}$ with that it was answered. Whenever a node S_i receives such a feedback from a neighbor S_n, it adds the query-confidence pair $(\vec{q}, \rho_{\vec{q}})$ to its respective routing model $RM_{S_n}^{S_i}$ (cf. Fig. 4(a)).

Routing a Query. With QLR, routing works exactly as described in the beginning of this section. However, as we are storing query-confidence pairs in the routing models, instead of observations, we have to estimate the confidence for an incoming $\vec{q}_{in}$ (i.e., the confidence with that the incoming query $\vec{q}_{in}$ can be answered or forwarded) a bit different. This is done in three steps: First, the query-confidence pairs in each routing model $RM_{S_n}^{S_i}$ are clustered with the weighted K-means clustering algorithm [5], where the queries represent points that are clustered and their respective confidence value is used as a weight (cf. Fig. 4). In consequence, the centroid of each cluster is not in the middle of the

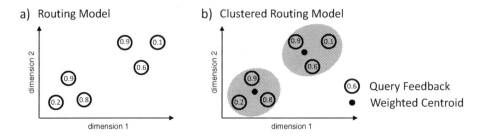

Fig. 4. a) A routing model containing query feedback with confidence values. b) Routing model after clustering.

cluster, but rather drawn towards the query-confidence pairs that have high confidence values (cf. Fig. 4(b)). We named such a centroid *weighted centroid*, $\vec{c}_w$. Second, we calculate the euclidean distance d between the incoming query $\vec{q}_{in}$ (for which the confidence has to be estimated) and the weighted centroid $\vec{c}_w$ (i.e., $d = \vec{q}_{in} - \vec{c}_w$). Third, we estimate the confidence of incoming query $\rho_{\vec{q}_{in}}$ by weighing this distance d according to the distribution of confidence values in the query-confidence pairs of the cluster, represented by the distribution function $f_c(d)$ (i.e., $\rho_{\vec{q}_{in}} = f(d)$).

To determine this distribution function $f_c(d)$, we start with the generic form of a Gaussian function (cf. Eq. 7), dependent on the parameters a_1 and a_2.

$$f_c(x) = a_1 exp(\frac{-x^2}{2a_2^2})$$ (7)

To calculate these parameters we need two additional equations that specify our requirements for the distribution function f_c. The first requirement states that if the distance between the weighted centroid $\vec{c}_w$ and the query $\vec{q}_{in}$ is zero, the confidence should be equivalent to the confidence value of the weighted centroid μ_{conf} (Eq. 8).

$$f_c(0) = \mu_{conf}$$ (8)

The second requirement states that the confidence of a cluster should decrease with increasing distance between incoming query $\vec{q}_{in}$ and $\vec{c}_w$, proportional to the standard deviation of the confidence values σ_{conf} in the query-confidence pairs, i.e., for high standard deviation in the confidence values of the query-confidence pairs in the cluster, f_c should decrease slower than for low standard deviation. This is expressed by Eq. 9, where σ_c is the standard deviation of the cluster, μ_{conf} the confidence value of the weighted centroid $\vec{c}_w$ and σ_{conf} the standard deviation of the confidence values of the query confidence pairs.

$$f_c(\sigma_c) = |\mu_{conf} - \sigma_{conf}|$$ (9)

Based on above two requirements we can now determine a_1 and a_2 and get the following distribution function.

$$f_c(d) = \mu_{conf}(\frac{\mu_{conf} - \sigma_{conf}}{\mu_{conf}})^{\frac{d^2}{\sigma_c^2}} \qquad (10)$$

Discussion. As described above, QLR uses past queries to keep routing models up-to-date. However, sometimes, it might be necessary to proactively explore the knowledge reachable through different neighboring nodes. This is, for example, necessary to bootstrap the system or when not enough queries are routed through a node. In this case, a node issues exploration queries. This can be done randomly or interest-based, i.e., a node can either try to learn about an area of interest or just a randomly selected area. An exploration query is a regular query with additional selectivity and hop count parameters, that control the magnitude of exploration. The *selectivity* parameter controls the number of neighbors to which a query is sent. The *hop count* parameter controls the depth of exploration and is decreased on reception by every node.

Furthermore, in dynamic environments, the query-confidence pairs stored in the routing models may become stale and should be removed. We use a *decay based* approach, where the confidence values of the query-confidence pairs $(\overrightarrow{q}, \rho_{\overrightarrow{q}})$ stored in the routing models decay according to a specified decay factor α over time $\rho_{new} = \rho \cdot \alpha$. When the confidence value has become lower than a certain threshold, the query-confidence pair is removed from the routing model.

5   Evaluation

In this section, we evaluated the knowledge retrieval strategies (KAR and QLR), presented in Sec. 4, w.r.t. network size, message overhead and retrieval quality. We also evaluated the influence of protocol specific parameters such as hop count and selectivity for QLR and the regeneration factor δ for KAR. Furthermore, we show that our routing strategies can work, even when a large number of dimensions in the knowledge models contain noise. To evaluate the performance in the presence of noise, we used a dimension selection algorithm in combination with QLR.

We implemented our retrieval strategies on top of the network simulator PeerSim [18] and performed our evaluations on a compute cluster, consisting of 24 Intel®Xeon®, 3.00GHz CPUs, with a total of 377.8GB of RAM. We measured the retrieval quality θ as retrieved confidence divided by global maximum confidence ($\theta = \frac{\rho_{ret}}{\rho_{max}}$).

We performed our evaluations on synthetic and real world data. To produce synthetic data we randomly generated clusters in the knowledge models of each node in a way, that neighboring nodes contained similar observations. Such a localization is realistic in many scenarios, for example, when neighboring devices collect similar observations, or can be created by an overlay network. We plan to cover the creation of such an overlay network in future work. To evaluate our approach on real world data, we used the GeoLife data set [32,30,31]. This data set represents mobility data and contains 17,621 GPS trajectories gathered by 178 people, mainly around Bejing.

5.1   Knowledge Aggregation Routing (KAR)

In the following, we evaluated the Knowledge Aggregation Routing (KAR) strategy presented in Sec. 4.1. In Fig. 5, we measured the retrieval quality (θ) for different network sizes, real world, and synthetic data. We compared our results to a random routing strategy, also using the real world data set, because this strategy can be seen as a lower bound for routing performance. During this experiment we used a regeneration factor of 1 ($\delta = 1$) (cf. Sec. 4.1). The reason for the reduced retrieval quality of the real world data is due to massively overlapping and highly similar knowledge in the knowledge models. This leads to suboptimal routing decisions, because a node cannot clearly distinguish the best neighbor to forward the query. However, as we can see, the retrieved quality is still significantly better than the random approach.

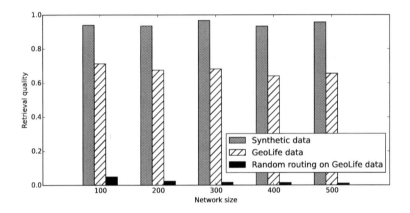

Fig. 5. Retrieval quality of KAR for different network sizes.

In Fig. 6 (left) we evaluated the retrieval quality for different regeneration factors δ (cf. Sec. 4.1). Overall, the routing quality decreases only slightly with the regeneration factor, as long as all clusters have a certain minimal size which is the case for the synthetic data and the synthetic data with GeoLife sized clusters, where we used the average cluster size of the GeoLife data set. However, the GeoLife data set also contains many clusters with very few observations. If the number of observations in these small clusters is further reduced the retrieval quality becomes worse.

To get an indicator, if the real world data provided by the GeoLife data set can be modeled as a multivariate Gaussian distribution, we performed the Kolmogorov Smirnov goodness-of-fit test. The subject of this test is the hypothesis, that we can represent a real world cluster by its respective multivariate Gaussian distribution. In statistical testing, the so called p-value is calculated to indicate if the hypothesis under test needs to be rejected. A large p-value provides evidence that the hypothesis is true. We tested 14000 real world clusters, obtained

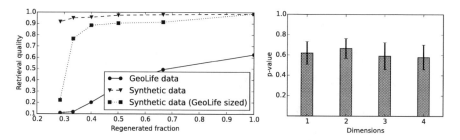

Fig. 6. Left: Routing quality for different regeneration factors (δ). Right: The p-values for clusters of different dimensionality.

from the GeoLife data set and plotted the mean of the p-value for up to four dimensional clusters in Fig. 6 (right). With a p-value significantly above the usual threshold of 0.05, we can conclude that it is reasonable to use multivariate Gaussian distributions to represent real world clusters.

5.2   Query Learning Based Routing (QLR)

Similar to the evaluations for KAR, we determined the retrieval quality of QLR for different network sizes, real and synthetic data. As we can see in Fig. 7, the retrieval quality of QLR on synthetic data is not as high as with KLR. The reason is that in KAR every node regenerates clusters similar to the "original" clusters of its neighbors in its routing models. This leads to a precise representation of the clusters in the routing models. However, the advantage of QLR lies in its higher retrieval quality for real world data. Because QLR is building its routing models based on the success of previous queries, it can better reflect the real world distribution of observations in the knowledge models of its neighbors.

In QLR, each node has to gather a number of queries in its routing model, before reasonable routing performance can be reached. This *learning phase* is clearly visible in Fig. 8, where we compared the bootstrapping of QLR with KAR. We can see, that the retrieval quality for QLR is gradually increasing with an increasing amount of queries, while the retrieval quality of KAR immediately jumps from low to high after all routing models have been successfully generated.

We use exploration queries in QLR to probe the knowledge available in the network and keep routing models up-to-date. In our system, two parameters (selectivity and hop count) controls the spread of these exploration queries. In Fig. 9, we evaluated the influence of these parameters on the retrieval quality and message overhead. We measure the exploration query overhead as the number of exploration queries per "retrieval" query. Comparing message overhead and retrieval quality, we can see that it is not necessary to choose high values for selectivity and hop count. Instead, it seems adequate if each node explores its closer neighborhood. For instance, setting selectivity and hop count to two results in high retrieval quality and low message overhead.

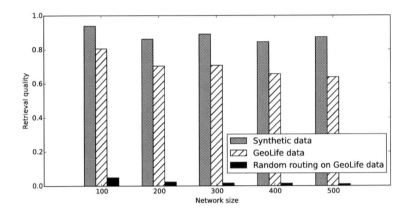

Fig. 7. Retrieval quality for different network sizes.

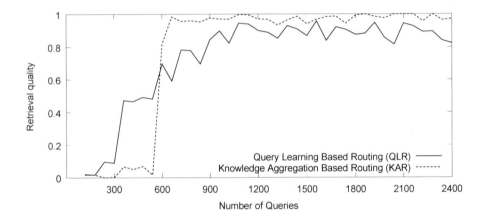

Fig. 8. The retrieval quality w.r.t. the number of queries for KAR and QLR.

As already mentioned in Sec. 1, the knowledge of the different nodes can be heterogeneous and high dimensional, which may result in sub optimal routing. In order to deal with this challenge, literature proposes various dimension selection approaches [29,15]. We extended QLR to select the most important dimensions for query routing using a simple variance based dimension selection approach. In a nutshell, our approach determines the important dimensions of a routing model based on the variance of the observations in each dimension. If the observations in one dimension exceed a certain variance threshold, the dimension is marked as not important. To evaluate this, we started with four dimensional observations and added up to 20 highly variant (noisy) dimensions. Fig. 10 compares the retrieval quality of QLR with dimension selection to QLR without dimension selection. The figure clearly shows, that QLR with dimen-

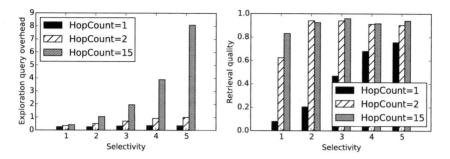

Fig. 9. Impact of hop-count and selectivity on message overhead and retrieval quality.

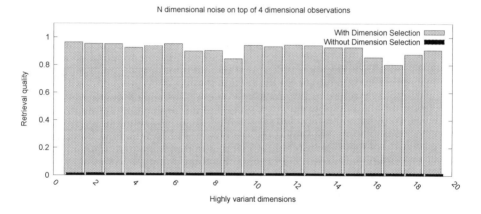

Fig. 10. Querying high dimensional knowledge with and without dimensionality reduction.

sion selection can perform almost without loss of retrieval quality, even in the presence of 20 highly variant dimensions.

6   Related Work

Retrieving information from a distributed system is a well-studied research problem [20,25,21,13,22,24,28,27]. In this section, we review the related work in a chronological order.

An early bulk of work is centered around the question of how to find and retrieve specific data items or files in a distributed P2P system, given by exact keys, such as hash values. Examples of such systems are Chord [25], CAN [20] and Pastry [21]. While Chord allows only one dimensional keys for the distributed search, routing in CAN is performed based on a multidimensional, euclidean key space. These systems are, however, only suitable for the retrieval of items that can be identified by an unique index.

The second wave of data retrieval systems identified the need for more complex queries, such as multidimensional range queries (e.g. *retrieve all people with age ≥ 18 and income $\geq 50k$*). Examples include Mercury [3], Squid [23] and Znet [24]. These systems enable clients to retrieve data within a specified range of values of certain attributes. The attribute space has to be partitioned and mapped to the participating peers. Data locality in the multidimensional space can be achieved with dimensionality reduction techniques such as space-filling curves (e.g. [8]). However, range-queries are often too restricted, for instance, if there is sparse or no data in the specified range. For example, a person with $income = 49,99k$ might be interesting for the query issuer, too.

To fill this gap, another branch of research enabled semantic and similarity search in a P2P-environment [22]. Two examples are pSearch [26] and Semantic Small World [13]. Both provide routing mechanisms to find similar data items to a certain multidimensional query. In Semantic Small World, a node maintains links to nodes with similar data items and some long range contacts to distant nodes. This enables efficient routing of arbitrary multidimensional queries to retrieve semantically related data items.

Other approaches [17] [4] [2] provide nearest neighbor search, i.e., finding the k closest data items in a large collection of high dimensional data, where a predefined similarity measure, such as euclidean distance defines *closeness* of data items. These systems aim to find peers with data that is similar to the query, while ignoring the quality and confidence of retrieved information. To the best of our knowledge, there is no approach in the literature enabling scalable, quality-oriented knowledge retrieval in a distributed environment.

7   Conclusion

Today, many devices, such as smart phones, gather an enormous amount of observations. Machine learning algorithms can be used to derive knowledge from these observations. In order to benefit from this enormous amount of distributed knowledge, we need methods to search and retrieve specific knowledge. To accomplish this, we first developed a metric to determine the confidence in the local knowledge of each device. This confidence metric takes the number and variance of observations made by each device into account. Based on this confidence metric, we proposed two methods to route a query for specific knowledge to a device that can answer it with high confidence. To that end, each device maintains routing models that can either be learned from previous queries or maintained actively by exchanging knowledge models. Our evaluations show, that the knowledge retrieved by our approaches is up to 96.7% as accurate as the global optimum.

Acknowledgment. The authors would like to thank the European Union's Seventh Framework Programme for partially funding this research through the ALLOW Ensembles project (project 600792).

References

1. Ashbrook, D., Starner, T.: Using GPS to learn significant locations and predict movement across multiple users. Personal and Ubiquitous Computing **7**(5) (2003)
2. Batko, M., Gennaro, C., Zezula, P.: A scalable nearest neighbor search in P2P systems. In: Ng, W.S., Ooi, B.-C., Ouksel, A.M., Sartori, C. (eds.) DBISP2P 2004. LNCS, vol. 3367, pp. 79–92. Springer, Heidelberg (2005)
3. Bharambe, A.R., Agrawal, M., Seshan, S.: Mercury: supporting scalable multi-attribute range queries. In: ACM SIGCOMM Computer Communication Review, vol. 34, pp. 353–366. ACM (2004)
4. Chen, D., Zhou, J., Le, J.: Reverse nearest neighbor search in peer-to-peer systems. In: Larsen, H.L., Pasi, G., Ortiz-Arroyo, D., Andreasen, T., Christiansen, H. (eds.) FQAS 2006. LNCS (LNAI), vol. 4027, pp. 87–96. Springer, Heidelberg (2006)
5. Chen, X., Yin, W., Tu, P., Zhang, H.: Weighted k-means algorithm based text clustering. In: Proceedings of the 2009 International Symposium on Information Engineering and Electronic Commerce, IEEC 2009, pp. 51–55. IEEE Computer Society, Washington, DC (2009). http://dx.doi.org/10.1109/IEEC.2009.17
6. Cheng, C., Cimet, I., Kumar, S.: A protocol to maintain a minimum spanning tree in a dynamic topology. In: Symposium Proceedings on Communications Architectures and Protocols, SIGCOMM 1988. ACM (1988)
7. Cisco: Cisco global cloud index: Forecast and methodology, 2013–2018 (2014). http://www.cisco.com/c/en/us/solutions/collateral/service-provider/global-cloud-index-gci/Cloud_Index_White_Paper.html
8. Ganesan, P., Yang, B., Garcia-Molina, H.: One torus to rule them all: multi-dimensional queries in p2p systems. In: Proc. of the 7th Int. Workshop on the Web and Databases: Colocated with ACM SIGMOD/PODS 2004. ACM (2004)
9. Hamerly, G., Elkan, C.: Learning the k in k-means. In: Thrun, S., Saul, L., Schölkopf, B. (eds.) Advances in Neural Information Processing Systems, vol. 16, pp. 281–288. MIT Press (2004)
10. Hernádvölgyi, I.: Generating random vectors from the multivariate normal istribution. Tech. rep., University of Ottawa, Canada, Ottawa, ON (1998)
11. informationisbeautiful.net: World's biggest data breaches (2015). http://www.informationisbeautiful.net/visualizations/worlds-biggest-data-breaches-hacks/
12. Johnson, S.: Hierarchical clustering schemes. Psychometrika **32**(3), 241–254 (1967)
13. Li, M., Lee, W.C., Sivasubramaniam, A.: Semantic small world: an overlay network for peer-to-peer search. In: Proceedings of the 12th IEEE International Conference on Network Protocols, ICNP 2004, pp. 228–238. IEEE (2004)
14. Lindley, D.V.: Introduction to probability and statistics from bayesian viewpoint, part 1 probability, vol. 1. CUP Archive (1965)
15. Lu, Y., Cohen, I., Zhou, X.S., Tian, Q.: Feature selection using principal feature analysis. In: Proc. of the 15th Int. Conf. on Multimedia, pp. 301–304. ACM (2007)
16. Madden, M.: Privacy and cybersecurity: Key findings from pew research (2015). http://www.pewresearch.org/key-data-points/privacy/
17. Malkov, Y., Ponomarenko, A., Logvinov, A., Krylov, V.: Approximate nearest neighbor algorithm based on navigable small world graphs. Information Systems **45**, 61–68 (2014)
18. Montresor, A., Jelasity, M.: Peersim: a scalable p2p simulator. In: IEEE Ninth Int. Conf. on Peer-to-Peer Computing, P2P 2009, pp. 99–100. IEEE (2009)

19. Ogallo, H.G., Jha, M.K., Marroquin, O.: Studying the impacts of vehicular congestion and offering sustainable solutions to city living. In: Proceedings of the 2nd International Conference on Sustainable Cities, Urban Sustainability and Transportation (SCUST 2013) (2013)

20. Ratnasamy, S., Francis, P., Handley, M., Karp, R., Shenker, S.: A scalable content-addressable network. ACM SIGCOMM Computer Communication Review **31**, 161–172 (2001)

21. Rowstron, A., Druschel, P.: Pastry: scalable, decentralized object location, and routing for large-scale peer-to-peer systems. In: Guerraoui, R. (ed.) Middleware 2001. LNCS, vol. 2218, p. 329. Springer, Heidelberg (2001)

22. Sahin, O.D., Emekci, F., Agrawal, D.P., El Abbadi, A.: Content-based similarity search over peer-to-peer systems. In: Ng, W.S., Ooi, B.-C., Ouksel, A.M., Sartori, C. (eds.) DBISP2P 2004. LNCS, vol. 3367, pp. 61–78. Springer, Heidelberg (2005)

23. Schmidt, C., Parashar, M.: Squid: Enabling search in dht-based systems. Journal of Parallel and Distributed Computing **68**(7), 962–975 (2008)

24. Shu, Y., Ooi, B.C., Tan, K.L., Zhou, A.: Supporting multi-dimensional range queries in peer-to-peer systems. In: Fifth IEEE International Conference on Peer-to-Peer Computing, P2P 2005, pp. 173–180. IEEE (2005)

25. Stoica, I., Morris, R., Karger, D., Kaashoek, M.F., Balakrishnan, H.: Chord: A scalable peer-to-peer lookup service for internet applications. ACM SIGCOMM Computer Communication Review **31**(4), 149–160 (2001)

26. Tang, C., Xu, Z., Mahalingam, M.: pSearch: Information retrieval in structured overlays. ACM SIGCOMM Computer Communication Review **33**(1), 89–94 (2003)

27. Tariq, M.A., Koldehofe, B., Bhowmik, S., Rothermel, K.: Pleroma: a SDN-based high performance publish/subscribe middleware. In: Proceedings of the 15th International Middleware Conference, Middleware 2014, pp. 217–228. ACM, New York (2014). http://doi.acm.org/10.1145/2663165.2663338

28. Tariq, M.A., Koldehofe, B., Koch, G.G., Rothermel, K.: Distributed spectral cluster management: a method for building dynamic publish/subscribe systems. In: Proceedings of the 6th ACM int. Conf. on Distributed Event-Based Systems, pp. 213–224. ACM (2012)

29. Yu, L., Liu, H.: Feature selection for high-dimensional data: a fast correlation-based filter solution. ICML **3**, 856–863 (2003)

30. Zheng, Y., Li, Q., Chen, Y., Xie, X., Ma, W.Y.: Understanding mobility based on GPS data. In: Proceedings of the 10th International Conference on Ubiquitous Computing, pp. 312–321. ACM (2008)

31. Zheng, Y., Xie, X., Ma, W.Y.: Geolife: A collaborative social networking service among user, location and trajectory. IEEE Data Eng. Bull. **33**(2), 32–39 (2010)

32. Zheng, Y., Zhang, L., Xie, X., Ma, W.Y.: Mining interesting locations and travel sequences from GPS trajectories. In: Proceedings of the 18th International Conference on World Wide Web, pp. 791–800. ACM (2009)

33. Ziegeldorf, J.H., Morchon, O.G., Wehrle, K.: Privacy in the internet of things: threats and challenges. Security and Communication Networks **7**(12), 2728–2742 (2014)

∂u∂u Multi-Tenanted Framework: Distributed Near Duplicate Detection for Big Data

Pradeeban Kathiravelu[✉], Helena Galhardas, and Luís Veiga

INESC-ID Lisboa, Instituto Superior Técnico,
Universidade de Lisboa, Lisbon, Portugal
pradeeban.kathiravelu@tecnico.ulisboa.pt

Abstract. Near duplicate detection algorithms have been proposed and implemented in order to detect and eliminate duplicate entries from massive datasets. Due to the differences in data representation (such as measurement units) across different data sources, potential duplicates may not be textually identical, even though they refer to the same real-world entity. As data warehouses typically contain data coming from several heterogeneous data sources, detecting near duplicates in a data warehouse requires a considerable memory and processing power.

Traditionally, near duplicate detection algorithms are sequential and operate on a single computer. While parallel and distributed frameworks have recently been exploited in scaling the existing algorithms to operate over larger datasets, they are often focused on distributing a few chosen algorithms using frameworks such as MapReduce. A common distribution strategy and framework to parallelize the execution of the existing similarity join algorithms is still lacking.

In-Memory Data Grids (IMDG) offer a distributed storage and execution, giving the illusion of a single large computer over multiple computing nodes in a cluster. This paper presents the research, design, and implementation of ∂u∂u, a distributed near duplicate detection framework, with preliminary evaluations measuring its performance and achieved speed up. ∂u∂u leverages the distributed shared memory and execution model provided by IMDG to execute existing near duplicate detection algorithms in a parallel and multi-tenanted environment. As a unified near duplicate detection framework for big data, ∂u∂u efficiently distributes the algorithms over utility computers in research labs and private clouds and grids.

Keywords: Near Duplicate Detection (NDD) · In-Memory Data Grid (IMDG) · MapReduce

1 Introduction

Data quality must be ensured for a proper functioning of data-driven information systems. As data warehouses are constructed from multiple data sources, near duplicate entries are common, often with multiple entries referring to the same

© Springer International Publishing Switzerland 2015
C. Debruyne et al. (Eds.): OTM 2015 Conferences, LNCS 9415, pp. 237–256, 2015.
DOI: 10.1007/978-3-319-26148-5_14

entity. Data sources may contain inconsistencies in the data representation that will coexist when migrated to the data warehouse. Therefore, data cleaning [1] is essential for a cost-effective maintenance of enterprise data warehouses.

Due to the different multiple non-standard APIs and representations used in collecting the data and different storage media used in storing the data collected by different organizations, integrating and federating data from several data sources to create a data warehouse also introduces quality issues into the data, such as duplicate entries that are represented with minor differences [2]. Near duplicate detection algorithms were developed to find these "almost identical" entries, and clean the data warehouses in a cost and power efficient manner.

Data cleaning frameworks were designed to ensure the quality of data. They consist of many different use cases such as finding and eliminating exact or near duplicate entries, and manually or automatically correcting corrupted data entries or entries that have representation errors or inconsistencies [1]. Finding near duplicates over big data requires large memory and processing power. As data entries consist of multiple entries with multiple attributes, two or more entries may still point to a single real-world entity, while a few attributes of them may be slightly different due to the differences in data representation in the original sources [3]. Moreover, finding near duplicates often requires text processing across massive datasets with efficient matchmaking that involves searching over a collection of large text.

Parallel and distributed programming can be leveraged to provide a perception of a large memory and processing power, executing across multiple computers in a cluster. Most near duplicate detection algorithms are sequential, though recently MapReduce based approaches have been exploited [4].

In-memory data grids [5] are distributed computing frameworks that offer a view of a large computer by unifying the resources available from the computing nodes of a distributed computer cluster. Many in-memory data grid frameworks exist, including open source (Hazelcast [6], Infinispan [7], Gridgain [8]) and proprietary (Terracotta BigMemory[1], Oracle Coherence [9], IBM WebSphere eXtreme Scale [10]). They are used in industry and research for distributing long running and resource consuming applications across multiple computing nodes. We claim that a framework leveraging an in-memory data grid should be able to extend the existing near duplicate detection algorithms to execute across a cluster in a parallel and distributed manner.

This paper presents $\partial u \partial u$, a distributed architecture for near duplicate detection. It proposes an efficient distribution strategy for the blocks identified by the block detection algorithms, over the IMDGs, by adapting the existing block detection algorithms to execute on a computer cluster or a public/private cloud. $\partial u \partial u$ leverages MapReduce frameworks offered by the IMDG in finding the blocks that should be compared for identifying the potential duplicates. $\partial u \partial u$ ensures that the strategy and algorithms are loosely coupled to the base algorithms, hence having the potential to distribute multiple algorithms, along with the potential to configure them based on user preferences.

---

[1] http://terracotta.org/products/bigmemory

In the upcoming sections, we will further analyze the proposed $\partial u \partial u$ distributed parallel near duplicate detection framework. In Section 2, we discuss the preliminary background and related work on near duplicate detection algorithms and efforts on distributing them. Section 3 discusses the design and architecture of the proposed multi-tenanted framework for near duplicate detection. Section 4 elaborates on the implementation details of the $\partial u \partial u$ framework. Section 5 depicts the ongoing experimental evaluations of the prototype implementation, and discusses the results obtained. Finally, Section 6 drives us to the conclusion of this research discussing its current state and the possible future enhancements.

2   Background and Related Work

2.1   Near Duplicate Detection

Efficient and declarative data cleaning frameworks were built to get higher precision and recall in cleaning the data (e.g., [11]). Expressive models and declarative languages have been researched and developed for an efficient near duplicate detection. Near duplicate detection algorithms have been extended to exploit machine learning to automate the duplicate detection and elimination [12], offering an adaptive execution of the algorithm [13]. Nevertheless, user involvement and manual data recovery is often necessary at execution time to ensure that the merged data is free from errors and inconsistencies [14].

The Merge/Purge problem is defined as the task of efficiently unioning two or more data sources into a single data source, finding the matches across the data sources, and finally merging them [15]. Since comparing each entry of a data source against each of the entries in the other data source is a quadratic time process, adaptive and intelligent algorithms are essential to execute this process for large data bases. The sorted neighborhood method partitions the data source and sorts the entries in the neighborhood before the merge phase, utilizing parallel processing [15]. PPJoin [16] is an efficient similarity join algorithm developed by research, that outputs pairs of near duplicates from the input data.

Blocking Keys in Similarity Join: Blocking keys are the attributes of the data sources that are used as the pivot for sorting and deciding the neighbors and clusters in the data set [17]. Choosing the right blocking key is essential for an accurate detection of near duplicates, as choosing the wrong attribute as the blocking key will bring unrelated entries closer, hence increasing the number of true negatives found, while reducing the efficiency.

Primary keys of relational tables are also good candidates for the blocking key as they are unique, and we do not expect them to have duplicates. If carefully chosen, blocking keys bring the right values closer in a typical blocking algorithm, because they are used to sort the entries, thus increasing the accuracy, precision, recall, and performance significantly. For instance, if the objective is to find near duplicates in a table storing data about people, then we could choose, first name, last name, and address as the blocking keys as these attributes can often be considered as being free of errors. Furthermore, multi-pass approach over multiple blocking keys [15] offers a higher accuracy for the trade-off of execution time, by repeating the execution with the data sorted using different blocking keys. It offers a more accurate duplicate detection, though it consumes more time if the multiple passes are executed sequentially.

There has been extensive research in efficient similarity join and many exact similarity join algorithms have been developed. A positional filtering principle has been exploited for finding the similarity scores for near-duplicate detection [16]. Near duplicate detection algorithms are generalized to exploit the parallel and distributed execution frameworks. MapDupReducer extends the PPJoin near duplicate detection algorithm to execute over MapReduce frameworks [18]. A three step approach constitutes by: (i) computing data statistics to generate good signatures; (ii) extract record IDs (RID); and (iii) perform the actual join, has been implemented in a parallel manner leveraging the MapReduce framework [4].

MapDupReducer and Dedoop [19] generalize the existing near duplicate detection algorithms to execute in a MapReduce framework. However, they do not consider all aspects of the near duplicate detection, and are coupled to the MapReduce framework and to the chosen near duplicate detection algorithms. Currently, there is no distributed data cleaning framework that can be adopted to execute existing near duplicate detection algorithms with minimal code change when migrating from the implementation for a sequential execution to a distributed execution.

2.2 In-Memory Data Grids

Java in-memory data grids provide a distributed execution and storage model for data executions in the grid-scale. They offer scalability and seamless integration with persistent storage. Hazelcast, Infinispan, Terracotta BigMemory, Oracle Coherence, IBM WebSphere eXtreme Scale, VMWare vFabric GemFire[2], Gigaspaces XAP [20], and Gridgain are some of the currently most used platforms for distributed execution and storage [21–23].

Table 1 presents a comparison of the in-memory data grid platforms, Hazelcast 3.4, Infinispan 7.2.3, Terracotta BigMemory 4.3, and Oracle Coherence 12.1.3. Terracotta is a server-client architecture, while the other data grids have a grid architectural topology. Distributed atomicity and concurrency are ensured through distributed data structures such as distributed lock, distributed atomic long, distributed atomic reference, and distributed atomic semaphores, in Hazelcast, Terracotta, and Coherence. DistributedAtomicLong is a distributed implementation of AtomicLong, the concurrent atomic Long data structure offered by Java. Similarly, the other distributed data structures are distributed implementations of the relevant concurrent data structures as well. Infinispan does not offer these distributed atomic data structures.

Hazelcast also offers a multimap structure, where each key can contain multiple values, which is a feature that is not supported by the other data grids. Replicated maps with active and passive replication are supported by all data grids except

---

[2] http://www.vmware.com/products/vfabric-gemfire/

Table 1. Comparison of in-memory data platforms

	Hazelcast	Infinispan	Terracotta BigMemory	Oracle Coherence
License	Apache License v.2.0.	Apache License v.2.0.	Proprietary License	Proprietary License
Architectural topology	Grid	Grid	Client-Server	Grid
Distributed Atomicity				
Lock & Atomic Long	✓	X	✓	✓
Atomic Ref & Semaphore	✓	X	✓	X
Maps				
Distributed Maps	✓	✓	✓	✓
Replicated Maps	✓	✓	X	✓
Multimaps	✓	X	X	X
Distributed Execution				
Executor Service	✓	✓	X	X
MapReduce	✓	✓	X	✓
Elasticity	✓	✓	X	✓

Terracotta. Hazelcast and Infinispan provide distributed execution through their implementation of a distributed executor service, MapReduce, and elasticity across a cluster as well as a private, public, or hybrid cloud deployment. Terracotta and Coherence offer a relatively limited support for distributed execution.

Hazelcast supports consistent hashing for partitioning the data of the instances of Hazelcast distributed data structures. Locality of the related objects can be ensured using the PartitionAware interface of Hazelcast. Data partition table is achieved for each distributed object by calculating *hash(key) % partitionCount. partitionCount* is by default chosen to be 271, a prime number, reasonably big enough for the real world enterprise cluster configurations.

In-memory data grids are used in research to distribute the storage and execution across multiple computing nodes. $Cloud^2 Sim$ leverages Hazelcast and Infinispan to execute cloud simulations on top of a computer cluster [24]. A cloud based document classification has been implemented using Gridgain, in research [25].

However, in-memory data grids are not leveraged in existing near duplicate detection approaches to distribute the execution efficiently to utilize the data grid resources. Advances in distributed computing and big data should be leveraged for an enterprise level near-duplicate detection and data cleaning. Further research is necessary to adopt the existing algorithms to the distributed computing platforms, while developing more efficient near duplicate detection algorithms.

3   Solution Architecture

We propose ∂u∂u, a distributed and parallel near duplicate detection framework for heterogeneous data sources. Near duplicate detection algorithms are invoked when integrating multiple data sources, or constructing a data warehouse from multiple data sources. PPJoin is used as the default core algorithm behind the $\partial u \partial u$ near duplicate detection framework.

Figure 1 depicts a high level architecture of $\partial u \partial u$. An instance of Hazelcast executes in each node of a cluster of computers. The Hazelcast instances form one or more Hazelcast clusters. $\partial u \partial u$ executes on top of each Hazelcast instance, hence distributing the work load across the multiple instances. Each of the $\partial u \partial u$ instances stores part of the data sets to be compared for near duplicate detection as local objects in the memory partitions allocated for the Hazelcast instance running in the node. Each instance executes the near duplicate detection algorithm on the data partition stored in the instance.

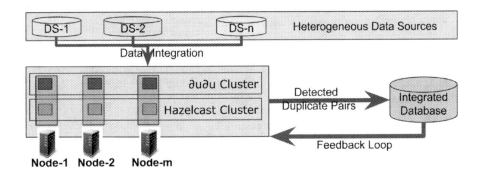

Fig. 1. Deployment Architecture of $\partial u \partial u$

Multiple heterogeneous data sources are connected to $\partial u \partial u$, and the data is integrated across the cluster. $\partial u \partial u$ executes the near duplicate detection in a distributed manner. Finally, the detected near duplicate pairs are written to the integrated data source.

3.1 $\partial u \partial u$ Multi-tenanted Parallel Executions

The distributed execution framework is initialized before the near duplicate detection process is started. Algorithm 1 depicts the initialization process of the deployment. A policy file consisting of crucial information such as the *blockingKeySet* is input to the algorithm, along with the list of *nodes*. *blockingKeySet* is a set consisting of one or more attributes from the data sources that are chosen as the attributes or blocking keys to consider as the basis for the near duplicate detection. When $\partial u \partial u$ initializes, the blockingKeySet is retrieved from the policy file, using the *getBlockingKeySet()* (invoked in line 2).

Initially, a Hazelcast instance is initialized in each of the nodes, and join the coordinator cluster by the *joinCluster()* method (invoked in line 4). For each of the blocking key in the blockingKeySet, the *joinCluster()* method initializes an execution cluster by starting an instance to form a cluster. The Hazelcast instances in the coordinator cluster are called coordinator instances, while the other instances are called executor instances as they execute the near duplicate detection algorithm. Each coordinator instance is responsible for coordinating the executor instances in the same node, as it is aware of the instances in its own computer node.

Algorithm 1. ∂u∂u Initialization

1: **procedure** *initialize(nodes, policy)*
2:      *blockingKeySet* ← *policy.getBlockingKeySet()*
3:      **for all** (*node* **in** *nodes*) **do**
                                                    ▷ Let all the nodes join the coordinator cluster.
4:          *joinCluster(node, coordinator)*
5:      **end for**
6:      *adaptiveScale(blockingKeySet, policy)*
                                    ▷ Monitors the health and scale the clusters accordingly.
7:      **for all** (*blockingKey* **in** *blockingKeySet*) **do**
8:          *index* ← *generateIndex(nodes.count())*
                                                    ▷ At least one node joins a cluster.
9:          *joinCluster(nodes.get(index), blockingKey)*
10:     **end for**
11:     *initDataSourcesIntegrator()*
12:     *initIntegratedDatabase()*
13: **end procedure**

Each cluster is considered a tenant, since it is unaware of the instances in other clusters. Instances in the coordinator cluster initialize the health monitor thread, by invoking the adaptiveScale() with the blockingKeySet and the scaling and monitoring policies as the input. The health monitor thread monitors the load in the instances, and overall health of the nodes, including the consumption of memory and processing power and execution speed or throughput. The health information is used for scaling the system adaptively.

The coordinator instance spawns executor instances in the computer node it is executing. It exploits local distributed atomic shared flags ensuring that only one instance is spawned. *generateIndex()* (invoked in line 8) generates an index to choose one node among all the available nodes, in which an executor instance will be spawned to initialize the execution cluster.

The clusters are initialized during the start up of the first iteration of near duplicate detection with a given blocking key. Blocking key is used as the cluster ID. The first instance spawned with a given ID creates and initializes the relevant cluster. The *adaptiveScale()* (invoked in line 6) spawns additional instances at a latter time based on the load of the existing instances in the computation. The latter instances join the relevant existing cluster identified by the cluster ID, to scale the cluster.

Multi-pass approaches of near duplicate detection algorithms are generally slower than a single-pass executes with a single blocking key, as regular multi-pass approaches execute the algorithm multiple times sequentially. To overcome this situation, $\partial u \partial u$ initializes and executes separate execution clusters for each blocking key, and hence the execution can be as fast as a sequential execution of single pass. Which node to spawn the instance to create the execution cluster for a given blocking key is decided by $generateIndex()$ function. The index can be a random number inferior to the number of nodes, such that a random node can create a cluster. Furthermore, $generateIndex()$ can be more intelligent, since it can choose the node that is less loaded, or that has the least number of instances executing. Multi-tenanted executions are executed in parallel. Final results over the multiple pass are computed by the coordinator instances.

Once all the execution clusters are joined and initialized, data sources and the integrated database are connected and initialized through the relevant drivers, by invoking $initDataSourcesIntegrator()$ (invoked in line 11) and $initIntegratedDatabase()$ (invoked in line 12). Once initialized, the data flow is initiated from the data sources into the in-memory data grid. Once the near duplicate detection workflow is completed, the duplicate data pairs are written to the integrated database.

The initialization process creates and initializes multiple execution clusters and a single coordinator cluster, which are separated from each other. Hence, multi-tenancy is ensured in $\partial u \partial u$ by the design. By offering a multi-tenanted parallel processing architecture, coordinated for multi-pass over multiple keys, $\partial u \partial u$ offers a more accurate and precise duplicate detection than the single-pass near duplicate detection.

Figure 2 shows how the multi-tenanted environment of $\partial u \partial u$ is constructed by multiple Hazelcast clusters for an efficient near duplicate detection in a sample deployment. The active instances in the clusters are highlighted (and indicated by thick border) in Figure 2, and the instances that are currently not being executed are also indicated (in dotted lines as the border in Figure 2) for the nodes and clusters as the potential instances. It is possible to initiate multiple instances in a single node to join the same cluster (such as i_{2b}, i_{2b1}, and i_{2b2} instances executing from node 2 as part of the cluster b).

In the sample deployment represented in Figure 2, coordinating cluster functions as a cluster to manage the near duplicate detection workflows from the other clusters, which consists of multiple executions with different blocking keys in each cluster. Each cluster is isolated and protected from other clusters, while being completely aware of the other instances of the same cluster. Hence, $\partial u \partial u$ deployment offers a tenant-aware parallel execution for multiple composite blocking keys.

The $\partial u \partial u$ deployment is represented using a matrix notation of (Node X Tenant), representing each node's contribution to each tenant/cluster. Three separate matrices represent (i) currently executing instances, (ii) maximum number of executing instances allowed by the policy, as defined by the user, and (iii) minimum executing instances required by the policy. A tenant represents a cluster. A node may consists of zero, one, or more executing instances in each cluster. One of the

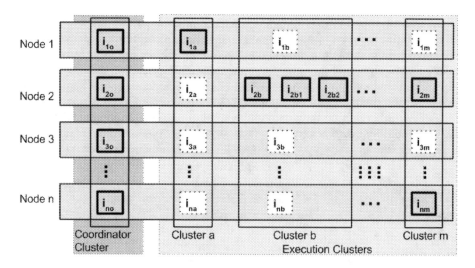

Fig. 2. Deployment of Hazelcast Clusters

instances from the coordinator cluster is often designated as the Master Coordinator instance, which handles centralized logic such as logging the execution, handling interrupts, and receiving user inputs run time. The matrix for the multi-tenanted deployment depicted by Figure 2 is given by Equation 1 showing only the executing instances, while differentiating the slave and master instances.

$$
\partial u \partial u = \begin{array}{c} \\ \mathbf{Node}_1 \\ \mathbf{Node}_2 \\ \mathbf{Node}_3 \\ \vdots \\ \mathbf{Node}_n \end{array} \begin{array}{c} \mathbf{C} \\ \left(\begin{array}{ccccc} C_{N1} & M_a & 0 & \dots & 0 \\ C_{N2} & 0 & M_b + 2S_b & \dots & M_m \\ C_{N3} & 0 & 0 & \dots & 0 \\ \vdots & \vdots & \vdots & \vdots & \vdots \\ C_{Nn} & 0 & 0 & \dots & S_m \end{array} \right) \end{array} \quad (1)
$$

Here,

$\forall \, n \in \mathbb{Z}^+$: C_{Nn} represents the coordinator instance for the node $Node_n$.

$\forall \, \alpha \in \{a, b, \dots, m\}$: M_α represents the master instance for the cluster $Cluster_\alpha$; S_α represents a slave instance for the cluster $Cluster_\alpha$.

In a near duplicate detection execution with a single blocking key, functionality of the coordinator will be limited to just monitoring and scaling the execution. Hence, it can be omitted, in a simple static deployment with an attribute pre-defined as the blocking key. Moreover, as more instances are added to each cluster adaptively by the coordinator, the execution inside a cluster is distributed uniformly. The instance that created the cluster remains the master instance of the cluster, which will execute the tasks that cannot be distributed, such as combining the final results and cross-checking the redundancy before returning the results to the coordinator or before writing to the integrated database if coordinator does not exist in the deployment.

In a multi-pass with multiple blocking keys, each pass with a given key is offered a separate cluster for its isolated parallel execution. In a near duplicate detection execution defined with m blocking keys, $\partial u \partial u$ will consist of $(m + 1)$ Hazelcast clusters, where m clusters are execution clusters, and one cluster is the coordination cluster. Each node hosts an instance in the coordinator cluster, that is responsible for monitoring the instances of the same node in the execution clusters. Based on the load of the execution for any given execution, an instance is involved in the execution by the coordinator.

Instances in the coordinator cluster of each node function as the local coordinator instance of the node. Hence the coordinator instances monitor the load of each executions and adaptively involve more instances to each execution based on the load. One or more designated nodes, which are usually from the coordinator cluster, are responsible for fetching the data from the data sources and writing back the detected duplicate pairs to the integrated database. When a master instance of a cluster is gracefully shutdown, one of the other instances known as the slave instances will become the new master instance of the cluster.

3.2   Distributed Execution Framework

Algorithm 2 describes the execution of the coordinator instances. Clusters are identified by the respective blocking key that they are executing for, as their cluster name. Hence, blockingKeySet represents all the clusters in the deployment. $fetchDataFromDatasources()$ (invoked in line 2) fetches the data partitions from the data sources in a distributed manner, and stores the data partition objects in the distributed shared memory offered by Hazelcast.

The coordinator instance initializes the instances of each of the execution clusters that reside in the same node as the coordinator instance, identified by their respective blocking key, by invoking the $initInstance()$ (in line 5). Once initialized, $executeInstance()$ (invoked in line 6) starts the execution of each execution instance, on the relevant data partitions. Each cluster receives the entire data during the course of execution either all at once or in batches, as this would be a multipass over the entire data set with near duplicate detection algorithms with different blocking keys applied as the base. However, each instance will have just a partition of the entire data, and the near duplicate detection algorithm execution for a blocking key is done in a distributed manner.

Once the instances return the duplicate pairs, they will be added to the $duplicatePairs$ distributed map (invoked in line 7). $updateStatus()$ (invoked in line 8) updates the status flag for the cluster periodically during the execution, representing the status of the $\partial u \partial u$Join action. If just a single blocking key is used, coordinator will write the duplicate pairs to the integrated database, as soon as the data is received.

The multi-pass with multiple keys can be executed independently in each cluster, or streamlined across the clusters to start executing based on the cleaned data returned from a previous cluster. Streamlining the clusters is expected to offer a higher accuracy, where independent parallel executions are expected to offer a higher throughput, as they do not rely on the completion of the other clusters on

Algorithm 2. *Coordinator Execution*

1: **procedure** $\partial u \partial u Join(blockingKeySet, policy)$
2:     $dataPartition \leftarrow fetchDataFromDatasources()$
3:     **repeat**
4:         **for all** $(blockingKey$ **in** $blockingKeySet$) **do**
5:             $initInstance(blockingKey)$
6:             $executeInstance(blockingKey, policy, dataPartition)$
7:             $duplicatePairs.add(receive(blockingKey.instances))$
8:             $updateStatus(blockingKey)$
9:         **end for**
10:        $Join(duplicatePairs)$
11:    **until** $(allReceived(blockingKeySet, dataPartition, cleanData))$
12:    $write(integratedDatabase, duplicatePairs)$
13: **end procedure**

---

the data partitions. If the data was streamlined across the clusters for the multiple blocking keys, the coordinator will ensure that all the passes have completed on the clean data. If the multi-pass was independent across the clusters with pointers to data duplicated across the clusters, coordinator will also executes *join*() (invoked in line 10) on the entries to merge all the detected duplicate pairs. This final join of the duplicatePairs is delegated to the coordinator instances in each of the nodes, which is done in a distributed manner. *write*() (invoked in line 12) finally writes the duplicate pairs to the integrated database.

Adaptive Scaling. Algorithm 3 describes the health monitoring and adaptive scaling thread of the coordinator instances. The coordinator monitors each instance in its nodes for its health, and the load in the execution instances are retrieved by the node.getInstance(..).getLoad() method (invoked in line 4). When the load is found to be greater than or equal to the maximum threshold for the particular cluster (as retrieved from policy.maxThreshold, in line 5) and the number of instances in that cluster is lower than the maximum permissible instance, a new instance is spawned in the node to join the cluster.

Similarly, when the load is found to be lower than the minimum threshold and the number of instances in the cluster is higher than the minimum required instances, an instance is shut down based on the policies (by invoking terminateInstance() in line 9). *wait*() ensures a time interval between the scaling decisions (as in lines 7 and 10) as well as the monitoring executions (as in line 12) to avoid jitter, cascaded scaling, and potential performance overhead. coordinator.status.update() (invoked in line 15) ensures that the coordinator instances are informed of the final status after the execution of the health monitoring and adaptive scaling thread.

The monitoring and scaling thread executes throughout the execution of the main thread. For each monitoring iteration, the coordinator status is updated with the outcome. The data objects stored inside the terminated instance will be reassigned to the current executing instances. Synchronous backups can be enabled by changing the Hazelcast configuration file, such that a copy of each of the data object is stored in another instance. This avoids the data loss during an abrupt termination of an instance, hence providing fault-tolerance. Synchronous backup copies the data real time to another instance. To avoid the performance overhead, asynchronous backups may be used. However, in case of a hardware failure and crashing the nodes, a few of the distributed objects would be left outdated with the asynchronous backups, depending on the time the data partition was last updated.

Algorithm 3. *∂u∂u Adaptive Scaling*

1: **procedure** ADAPTIVESCALE(*blockingKeySet, policy*)
2:   **repeat**
3:     **for all** *blockingKey* **in** *blockingKeySet* **do**
4:       *load ← node.getInstance(blockingKey).getLoad()*
5:       **if** *load ≥ policy.maxThreshold()* **AND**
          spawnedInstances < policy.maxInstancesToBeSpawned **then**
6:         *joinCluster(node, blockingKey)*
7:         *wait(policy.timeBetweenScaling)*
8:       **else if** *(load ≤ policy.minThreshold)* **AND**
          spawnedInstances > policy.minInstancesToBeSpawned **then**
9:         *terminateInstance(node, blockingKey)*
10:        *wait(policy.timeBetweenScaling)*
11:      **else**
12:        *wait(policy.timeBetweenHealthChecks)*
13:      **end if**
14:    **end for**
15:    *coordinator.status.update()*
16:   **until** *(data.allReceived(blockingKeySet)*
17: **end procedure**

3.3   Near Duplicate Detection for Big Data

Algorithm 4 describes the execution of the executor instances, including the master and slave instances. *BaseJoin()* (invoked in line 8) can be any existing sequential or parallel near duplicate detection algorithm. PPJoin is extended to store the data objects and execute in a distributed in-memory data grid, as the default near duplicate detection algorithm.

All the instances, the master instance and the slave instances, consist of the same code and the data is distributed uniformly. The first instance to join the cluster is designated as the master. *initCluster()* (invoked in line 3) of the master instance initializes the cluster. In the initial iteration, the data is partitioned

---

Algorithm 4. Executor Instance Execution

1: **procedure** ∂u∂uJoin(*blockingKey*, *policy*, *dataPartition*)
2:     **if** (isMaster) **then**
3:         initCluster(*blockingKey*)
4:     **end if**
5:     **repeat**
6:         **while** (*initialIteration*) **do**
7:             **Send** Executor Service Executions To Other Instances
8:             **BaseJoin(dataPartition)**
9:         **end while**
10:        **if** (isMaster) **then**
11:            **Process** Received Partitions from Other Instances
12:            **Execute** Core Execution That cannot be Distributed.
13:        **end if**
14:     **until** (*dataPartition.delta ≥ policy.delta*)
15:     **if** (isMaster) **then**
16:         **for all** (*instance* in *getInstances(blockingKey)*) **do**
17:             dataPartition.add(dataPartitionFrom(instance))
18:             **Randomize(BaseJoin(dataPartition))**
19:         **end for**
20:         **send(coordinator, dataPartition)**
21:     **end if**
22:     *clearDistributedObjects()*
23: **end procedure**

---

across the distributed instances of the same cluster. As the data is fetched from multiple nodes, data transfer across the nodes over the network can be avoided by sending the logic to the data using the Hazelcast distributed execution framework invocations instead of pulling the data to the logic.

Base join algorithm is executed in a regular way in each of the instances over the data partitions. The partitions are transferred to the master once the first iteration is completed. If throughput is favored over accuracy, the execution can terminate after the first iteration. Otherwise, another round of base join will be executed on a randomized set of data by shuffling the data to avoid true negatives due to the duplicates ending in different Hazelcast instances. *Delta* is defined as the measure of how clean the data is, from the duplicate entries, by measuring the distance between the closest data entries eligible to suspect duplicates. The implementation of *delta* is delegated to the application layer, to be able to customize the definition of duplicates by the user. The first iteration completes when the overall *delta* of the data partition in the instance is greater than or equal to the delta defined in the policy.

The master instance executes the tasks that cannot be distributed such as computing or estimating the current delta of all the data accumulated. Once the near duplicate detection iteration is completed, the master instance receives the duplicate data pairs from the other instances, and add them up. Optionally, the data may be randomized by Randomize() (invoked in line 18) and the base join may be applied by the master. This measure is to further minimize the potential misses during the data partitioning and distribution, as only the data partitions inside each instance is compared otherwise. However, multiple iterations will cost more execution time, as expected.

Finally the data partition is sent to the coordinator instance by the master instance, using send() (invoked in line 20). In a smaller deployments without multipass, the master and coordinator instance can refer to the same instance, as there will be only a single master instance. In that case, the algorithm of the coordinator instance is executed by the master instance itself. Once the data is transferred, clearDistributedObjects() (invoked in line 22) flushes the distributed in-memory objects out of the in-memory data grid.

Mathematical Representation of $\partial u \partial u$ Execution. Data quality in $\partial u \partial u$ can be represented using mathematical models for an easy understanding. A data entry in the in-memory data grid of $\partial u \partial u$ is visualized as a function of its attributes. Hence, a data unit u consisting of multiple blocking keys x, y, and z, can be represented as, u = f(x).f(y).f(z).

Having one of the attributes as the blocking key, the data set is sorted in parallel once for each key in the cluster responsible for the key. Each attempt sorts the entries only based on the chosen key, while ignoring others. Hence, this can be realized by a partial derivative, where the blocking key is considered the partially differentiating variable. This brings data units closer inside a single partition based on the blocking key. Hence a proper selection of blocking key will bring all potential duplicates inside a single Hazelcast partition.

Multi-pass execution of the near duplicate detection algorithms can detect near duplicates more efficiently than using single-pass with just one of the attributes as the blocking key. Multi-pass over multiple blocking keys can be parallelized with all the chosen attributes as blocking keys. For representation purposes, the multi-pass approach is depicted as a set of partial derivatives as shown by Equation 2.

$$delta = \{\frac{\partial u}{\partial x}, \frac{\partial u}{\partial y}, \frac{\partial u}{\partial z}\} \tag{2}$$

where,

$$\frac{\partial u}{\partial x} = \frac{\partial f(x)}{\partial x}.f(y).f(z); \frac{\partial u}{\partial y} = f(x).\frac{\partial f(y)}{\partial y}.f(z); \frac{\partial u}{\partial z} = f(x).f(y).\frac{\partial f(z)}{\partial z} \tag{3}$$

Software Architecture. Figure 3 provides the software architecture of $\partial u \partial u$. Hazelcast is leveraged as the in-memory data grid, in the *data storage layer*. $\partial u \partial u$ can also be implemented by extending and exploiting the other in-memory data grids appropriately, instead of Hazelcast. The *distribution layer* consists of distributor and scaler. The *distributor* ensures the distribution of the objects across the instances uniformly, such that the execution load is balanced across the nodes. The scaler manages the adaptive scaling of the ∂u∂u platform.

In the *base algorithms layer*, the platform supports blocking and near duplicate detection (NDD) algorithms that are generalizations of the algorithms described in Section 2, for a distributed execution over in-memory data grids.

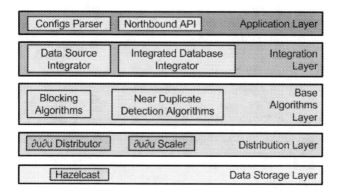

Fig. 3. Software Architecture

The *integration layer* offers two APIs: *DataSourceIntegrator* and *Integrated DatabaseIntegrator*, which can be implemented for multiple heterogeneous data sources and integrated databases. ∂u∂u also offers implementations of *DataSourceIntegrator* for common relational databases such as MySQL, and NoSQL data sources such as MongoDB, to connect them to ∂u∂u. Integration layer also consists of the implementations of Integrated DatabaseIntegrator, such as an integrator to Hadoop HDFS as the destination database to store the duplicate pairs.

Application layer offers a *configs parser*, and a *northbound API* which is the user-facing API of ∂u∂u. The applications can extend and exploit ∂u∂u for their enterprise requirements, using its northbound API. ∂u∂u configuration files consists of information such as pointers to the data sources and integrated database or data warehouse. *ConfigsParser* is responsible for parsing the configuration files, and sending the configuration information downstream to the execution algorithms.

4   ∂u∂u Prototype

∂u∂u has been implemented using Java 1.8.0 as the programming language and Hazelcast 3.4 as the in-memory data grid. MongoDB 2.4.9 and MySQL 5.5.41-0ubuntu0.14.04.1 were connected to ∂u∂u through the respective Java driver APIs, to demonstrate the potential to integrate with multiple data sources and interoperability with multiple data sources. Multiple different databases were deployed as the data sources.

Apache Hadoop 2.7.0 was used as the integrated database to store the near duplicates found from the multiple data sources. This enables collecting and storing duplicates among a large number of massive data sets. However, relational databases such as MySQL can also be used as the integrated database. The data from Mongo is copied to the $\partial u \partial u$ cluster using Mongo Java client and REST API as well as Jongo[3]. Data is transferred in a distributed manner in batches. Near duplicate detection workflows are executed in $\partial u \partial u$ and the duplicate pairs are written to the Hadoop data warehouse through the Hadoop Java client.

Instances of distributed HashMap implementation offered by Hazelcast is used as the in-memory storage for the dirty and cleaned data after fetching from the data source and before writing the clean data back to the data warehouse. Since the scaling decisions are taken by the coordinator instances in a distributed manner, scaling should be done atomically in the distributed environment to prevent cascaded scaling. Hazelcast distributed atomic long values were used as the flags to scale the system.

$\partial u \partial u$ implementation of multi-pass approaches of the PPJoin near duplicate detection algorithm use the same data sorted with different keys, potentially changing the entries that come in a single block during each iteration. Since the datasets are broken into smaller blocks of data, the execution is done in parallel. The $\partial u \partial u$ multi-tenanted execution is done using one of the two approaches: (i) The data from the data sources is duplicated and sorted accordingly using the assigned blocking key in multiple clusters; (ii) The data is sorted each time using the relevant blocking key in blocks for each cluster, and streamed across clusters. The second approach is more feasible where data duplication is costlier than streaming data across the clusters in blocks and sorting them each time with a different blocking key. In a single-pass approach, there will be no parallel execution or duplicate data entries, as there will be only one executing cluster using the single blocking key.

Data is copied from the data sources to Hazelcast in-memory data grid at once or in batches. Data can also be streamed consistently from the data sources to the data grid. Data cached in the data grid can quickly and efficiently be accessed for the execution of algorithms, than fetching the data real-time from the data sources. Figure 4 indicates how the data is partitioned and tracked across the instances inside a single cluster storing the data sets in Hazelcast.

The distributed storage, memory, and processing power are provided by the physical nodes that host the Hazelcast instances. Data sets are partitioned to store in the instances. Hence, data sets larger than the memory of any given instance can be stored in the data grid. More instances can be added to seamlessly scale the available storage in the grid for the data sets, that are stored as distributed Java objects in the Hazelcast cluster.

The partitioning is tracked by the objectIDs with pointers to initial and final IDs of each data partition. These initial IDs function as the pointers to access the physical location where a given data is stored. Each instance executes the near duplicate detection algorithm on the data partition that is stored in itself, by invoking the *execute()*.

---

[3] http://jongo.org/

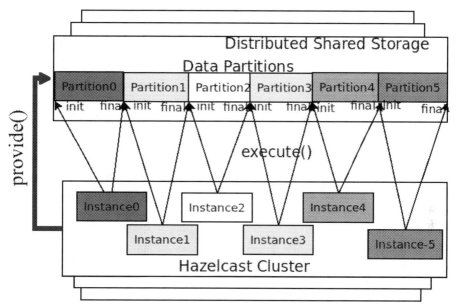

Fig. 4. Partition of storage and execution across the instances

The concurrent execution constructs (i.e. the implementation of Callable and Runnable Java interfaces) of $\partial u \partial u$ are submitted using Hazelcast ExecutorService for a distributed execution. These constructs implement the *HazelcastInstanceAware* interface, which makes them aware of the Hazelcast instance that they are executing on. This ensures that the instances execute the logic on the data that is stored in themselves, avoiding the remote executions on the distributed objects in other instances. By increasing data locality, this minimizes communication overload over the network, bandwidth consumption, and delay caused by the remote invocation.

Similarly, host awareness is ensured by leveraging the relevant Hazelcast constructs such that the objects are stored with the knowledge of which instances are stored in the same host. Blocking keys were made *PartitionAware*. *PartitionAware* interface implementation ensures that the near duplicates end in the same data partition in the Hazelcast distributed cluster, for a speedy comparison of data pairs. Hazelcast MapReduce implementation can be configured to find the initial blocks to store inside the same partition and to do the text matching inside the partitions to find the near duplicates.

5 Evaluation

We used a computer cluster with Intel   Core   i7-4700MQ CPU @ 2.40GHz × 8 processor, 8 GB memory, and Ubuntu 14.04 LTS 64 bit operating system for the evaluation of the prototypical implementation of $\partial u \partial u$. Two Mongo databases were connected as the data sources having the potential duplicate pairs, with Hadoop

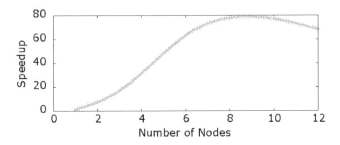

Fig. 5. Variations of Speedup with the Number of nodes

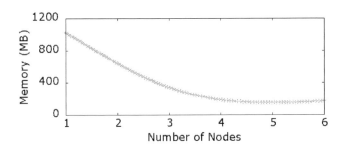

Fig. 6. Variations of Memory Consumption with the Number of Nodes

HDFS used as the integrated data base to store the detected duplicate pairs. We performed preliminary experiments to evaluate the $\partial u \partial u$ efficiency in distributing the storage and execution. We also measured its performance and speed up with multiple instances in the execution cluster, compared to the sequential execution of PPJoin in a single computer.

We used around 100 datasets of varying sizes above 1 GB with multiple number of nodes configured to execute in a cluster. Each cluster was configured to have an executor instance. We exploited the PPJoin algorithm as the distributed near duplicate detection algorithm with multi-pass in 4 different execution clusters. The number of iterations and the blocking keys were maintained to be same across all the experiments for fairness in the evaluation.

While the execution time depended on the base near duplicate detection algorithm, speed up still remained the same for the same workload during the experiments. Figure 5 shows the speedup in a distributed cluster, compared to an execution in a single instance. Each node consists of 4 clusters, with an instance per node per cluster. Due to the memory contention caused by the heavy data objects that represent the partitions of massive data in-memory for computations, $\partial u \partial u$ executes slower in a single node. For multiple nodes, it exhibits a super-linear speedup. However, a negative scalability was observed after 8 - 10 nodes as the communication and coordination overheads supersede the speedup due to the distributed execution. For an even larger dataset, further nodes can be added without introducing a negative scalability.

Figure 6 shows the variations of memory consumed by each node executing ∂u∂u, with number of nodes, when populating and integrating data repositories. Using the Hazelcast monitoring center, we observed that the data was distributed uniformly across the instances and nodes.

6 Conclusion and Future Work

∂u∂u leverages in-memory data grids as a scalable platform for near duplicate detection, adopting the existing near duplicate detection algorithms to work in a distributed environment. The multi-tenanted environment offered by ∂u∂u can provide accurate near duplicate detection for big data, by applying multi-pass approach using multiple blocking keys in a parallel execution.

By offering an efficient partitioning of data across multiple IMDG instances, ∂u∂u offers high speedup and lower communication and coordination overheads. It also provides faster near duplicate detection over big data compared to the respective sequential execution of the algorithms, while enabling executions on massive datasets which would not have been possible to execute on utility computers. While ∂u∂u has been developed for near duplicate detection for big data, it can be generalized for any data-intensive big data scenario as an adaptive distributed execution framework.

Acknowledgements. This work was supported by national funds through Fundação para a Ciência e a Tecnologia with reference UID/CEC/50021/2013, and a PhD grant offered by the Erasmus Mundus Joint Doctorate in Distributed Computing (EMJD-DC).

References

1. Rahm, E., Do, H.H.: Data cleaning: Problems and current approaches. IEEE Data Eng. Bull. **23**(4), 3–13 (2000)
2. Oliveira, P., Rodrigues, F., Henriques, P., Galhardas, H.: A taxonomy of data quality problems. In: 2nd Int. Workshop on Data and Information Quality, pp. 219–233 (2005)
3. Barateiro, J., Galhardas, H.: A survey of data quality tools. Datenbank-Spektrum **14**(15–21), 48 (2005)
4. Vernica, R., Carey, M.J., Li, C.: Efficient parallel set-similarity joins using mapreduce. In: Proceedings of the 2010 ACM SIGMOD International Conference on Management of Data, pp. 495–506. ACM (2010)
5. Di Sanzo, P., Rughetti, D., Ciciani, B., Quaglia, F.: Auto-tuning of cloud-based in-memory transactional data grids via machine learning. In: 2012 Second Symposium on Network Cloud Computing and Applications (NCCA), pp. 9–16. IEEE (2012)
6. Johns, M.: Getting Started with Hazelcast. Packt Publishing Ltd. (2013)
7. Marchioni, F.: Infinispan data grid platform. Packt Publishing Ltd. (2012)
8. Samovsky, M., Kacur, T.: Cloud-based classification of text documents using the gridgain platform. In: 2012 7th IEEE International Symposium on Applied Computational Intelligence and Informatics (SACI), pp. 241–245. IEEE (2012)
9. Seovic, A., Falco, M., Peralta, P.: Oracle Coherence 3.5. Packt Publishing Ltd. (2010)

10. Arora, P., Khandelwal, D., Marshall, J., Usha, A., Sadtler, C., et al.: Scalable, Integrated Solutions for Elastic Caching Using IBM WebSphere eXtreme Scale. IBM Redbooks (2011)
11. Galhardas, H., Florescu, D., Shasha, D., Simon, E., Saita, C.: Declarative data cleaning: Language, model, and algorithms (2001)
12. Zhang, D.Q., Chang, S.F.: Detecting image near-duplicate by stochastic attributed relational graph matching with learning. In: Proceedings of the 12th Annual ACM International Conference on Multimedia, pp. 877–884. ACM (2004)
13. Bilenko, M., Mooney, R.J.: Adaptive duplicate detection using learnable string similarity measures. In: Proceedings of the Ninth ACM SIGKDD International Conference on Knowledge Discovery and Data Mining, pp. 39–48. ACM (2003)
14. Galhardas, H., Lopes, A., Santos, E.: Support for user involvement in data cleaning. In: Cuzzocrea, A., Dayal, U. (eds.) DaWaK 2011. LNCS, vol. 6862, pp. 136–151. Springer, Heidelberg (2011)
15. Hernández, M.A., Stolfo, S.J.: The merge/purge problem for large databases. In: ACM SIGMOD Record, vol. 24, pp. 127–138. ACM (1995)
16. Xiao, C., Wang, W., Lin, X., Yu, J.X.: Efficient similarity joins for near duplicate detection. In: Proceedings of the 17th International Conference on World Wide Web, pp. 131–140. ACM (2008)
17. Christen, P.: A survey of indexing techniques for scalable record linkage and deduplication. IEEE Transactions on Knowledge and Data Engineering 24(9), 1537–1555 (2012)
18. Wang, C., Wang, J., Lin, X., Wang, W., Wang, H., Li, H., Tian, W., Xu, J., Li, R.: Mapdupreducer: detecting near duplicates over massive datasets. In: Proceedings of the 2010 ACM SIGMOD International Conference on Management of data, pp. 1119–1122. ACM (2010)
19. Kolb, L., Thor, A., Rahm, E.: Dedoop: efficient deduplication with hadoop. Proceedings of the VLDB Endowment 5(12), 1878–1881 (2012)
20. Lwenstein, B.: Benchmarking of Middleware Systems: Evaluating and Comparing the Performance and Scalability of XVSM (MozartSpaces), JavaSpaces (GigaSpaces XAP) and J2EE (JBoss AS). VDM Verlag (2010)
21. Ferrante, M.: Java frameworks for high-level distributed scientific programming (2010)
22. El-Refaey, M., Rimal, B.P.: Grid, soa and cloud computing: On-demand computing models. Computational and Data Grids: Principles, Applications, and Design, 45 (2012)
23. Mohanty, S., Jagadeesh, M., Srivatsa, H.: Extracting value from big data: in-memory solutions, real time analytics, and recommendation systems. In: Big Data Imperatives, pp. 221–250. Springer (2013)
24. Kathiravelu, P., Veiga, L.: An adaptive distributed simulator for cloud and mapreduce algorithms and architectures. In: 2014 IEEE/ACM 7th International Conference on Utility and Cloud Computing (UCC), pp. 79–88. IEEE (2014)
25. Sarnovsky, M., Ulbrik, Z.: Cloud-based clustering of text documents using the ghsom algorithm on the gridgain platform. In: 2013 IEEE 8th International Symposium on Applied Computational Intelligence and Informatics (SACI), pp. 309–313. IEEE (2013)

Multilevel Mapping of Ecosystem Descriptions
Short Paper

Matt Selway, Markus Stumptner$^{(\boxtimes)}$, Wolfgang Mayer, Andreas Jordan, Georg Grossmann, and Michael Schrefl

University of South Australia, Adelaide, Australia
{matt.selway,andreas.jordan}@mymail.unisa.edu.au,
{mst,wolfgang.mayer,georg.grossmann}@cs.unisa.edu.au,
schrefl@dke.uni-linz.ac.at

Abstract. One of the most significant challenges in information system design is the constant and increasing need to establish interoperability between heterogeneous software systems at increasing scale. Beyond individual applications, today's enterprise applications require automated information exchange across the system lifecycle of information ecosystems—large scale families of software built around official or de facto standards. The automated translation of data between the data models and languages used in these ecosystems is best addressed using model-driven engineering techniques, but requires the handling of both data and multiple levels of metadata within a single model. Standard modelling approaches are generally inconsistent with these requirements, leading to compromised modelling outcomes. In this paper we discuss the use of the SLICER framework built on multilevel modelling principles for transformation purposes. The framework provides natural propagation of constraints over multiple design and instantiation levels that cover different engineering lifecycle phases. We discuss the concept of metamodelling spaces and give an example of a concrete transformation application.

Keywords: Metamodelling · Lifecycle models · Interoperability

1 Ecosystem Interoperability

The lack of interoperability between computer systems remains one of the largest challenges of computer science and costs industry tens of billions of dollars each year [1]. Standards usually are not universal nor universally applied even within a given industry. The engineering industry refers to the set of software systems that interact to provide services across the entire system lifecycle of their domain as a *heterogeneous ecosystem*. We are engaged in the "Oil and Gas Interoperability Pilot" (or simply OGI Pilot) that aims for the automated, model-driven transformation of data during the asset lifecycle between two of the major data standards in the Oil & Gas industry ecosystem: ISO15926 [2] generally used for

C. Debruyne et al. (Eds.): OTM 2015 Conferences, LNCS 9415, pp. 257–266, 2015.
DOI: 10.1007/978-3-319-26148-5_15

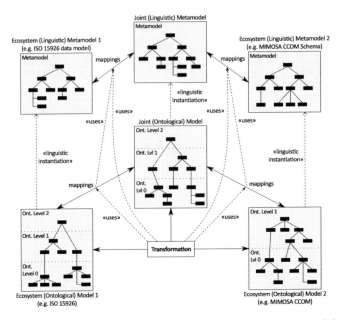

Fig. 1. Ecosystem interoperability through a joint metamodel

EPC (Engineering, Procurement, and Construction), and the MIMOSA OSA-EAI for Operations & Maintenance.[1]

During design, the specification for a (type of) pump is considered an object that must be manipulated with its own lifecycle (e.g. creation, revision, obsolescence), while during operations the same object is considered a type with respect to the physical pumps that conform to it and have their own lifecycle (e.g. manufacturing, operation, end-of-life). Furthermore, at the business/organisational level, other concepts represent categories that perform cross-classifications of objects at other levels. This leads to multiple levels of (application) data: business, specification, and physical entity level. Enabling ecosystem transformation requires a flexible conceptual framework for representing these levels of information. As transformations in the engineering domain must guarantee correctness (e.g., an incorrectly identified part or part type can result in plant failures), heuristic matching does not replace the need for a succinct and expressive conceptual model that facilitates design of the mappings by a human designer. We use a framework for ecosystem transformations based on a joint metamodel that serves as the baseline for the transferred information [3].

When trying to model ecosystem mappings in UML, aggregation is normally used in an attempt to capture the multi-level nature of the domain, and specialisation is used to distinguish the different categories (i.e. business classifications), models (i.e. designs), and physical entities of pumps. Finally, instantiation of

---

[1] Current industrial participants in the OGI Pilot include: Intergraph, Bentley, AVEVA, Worley-Parsons, IBM, Rockwell Automation, Assetricity.

singleton classes is used to model the actual catalogue, categories, models, and physical entities. This creates redundancy [4], physical entities that are not intuitively instances of their product models, and difficulty in modelling the lifecycles of both design and physical entities as well as the dynamic introduction of new business categories. This makes the definition of mappings more difficult as the real semantics of the model are hidden in implementation.

Multilevel Modelling (MLM) approaches [4–6] have been developed to address such situations, but in general use the concept of *potency*: a numeric value that requires pre-layering of levels as the main designer input, thus setting down a fixed number of levels from the start. In contrast, prior work on relationships such as specialization [7], and metaclasses [8] assumed that there can be arbitrary many levels of each. Therefore, interoperability solutions must accommodate mappings to models that may cover domains at different levels of granularity, are not designed according to the strictness criterion (i.e. only instantiation relationships may cross level boundaries), and cannot be changed to fit the needs of the interoperability designer. Transformation solutions such as [3] will therefore profit from a more flexible level definition framework.

In the context of enterprise integration frameworks, our work is situated in the space of Model-Driven Interoperability as described in [9]. Much of this work focused on Universal Enterprise Modeling Languages (UEML) [10]. Our approach assumes that in a setting of heterogeneous ecosystems, it is via effective transformation languages and meta-models where flexibility can be achieved.

2   The SLICER Relationship Framework

When examining different description levels in the engineering lifecycle, a higher level generally expresses the relationship between an entity and its definition (or description) in two possible ways: abstraction and specification. In *abstraction*, entities are grouped together based on similar properties, giving rise to a concept that describes the group. These entities may themselves be groups of concepts, thus permitting a multi-level hierarchy. With *specification*, an explicit description is given, and entities (artefacts) are produced that conform to this specification.

A *level of description* can be established either by instantiation, or by enriching the vocabulary used to formulate the descriptions. This corresponds to the concept of *extension* in specialisation hierarchies [7]: if a subclass receives additional properties (attributes, associations etc.) then these attributes can be used to impose constraints on its specification and behaviour.

Identifying levels based on the basic semantic relationships between entities enables a flexible framework for describing joint metamodels in interoperability scenarios. To support this we have developed SLICER (Specification with Levels based on Instantiation, Categorisation, Extension and Refinement) framework based on a flexible notion of levels as a result of applying the semantic relationships below. A detailed presentation of the conceptual framework and comparison to other multi-level modelling approaches was given in [11]. Figure 2 shows the application of the framework to a product catalogue example.

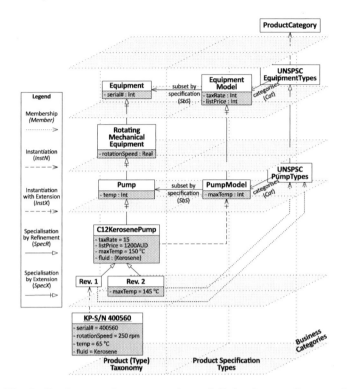

Fig. 2. Product catalogue example modelled using our framework

Instantiation and Specialisation. In contrast to previous MLM techniques, levels are not strictly specified, but dynamically derived based on finer distinctions of relations between more or less specific types. Specialisation relationships *extend* the original class (by adding attributes, associations, or behaviour, i.e., constraints or state change differentiation, *SpecX*) or *refines* it (by adding granularity to the description, *SpecR*). Of the two, only *SpecX* introduces a new model level.

Similarly, instantiation is characterised as *Instantiation with Extension* (*InstX*, allowing additional attributes) or *Standard Instantiation* (*InstN*). Instantiation always introduces additional model levels. A key difference between the two is that an object created through *InstN* cannot be instantiated further.

Categories are concepts that provide external ("secondary") grouping of entities based on some common property and/or explicit enumeration of its members. In the SLICER framework, we explicitly represent categories through two relationships: *Categorisation* (*Cat*) and *Membership* (*Member*, which we do not discuss further). *Categorisation* relates two concepts, one representing a category and the other a type, where the *members* of the category are *instances* of the type. Categories exist on the same level as the type they categorise.

Specifications are expressed via the *Subset by Specification* (*SbS*) relation, which identifies specification types and the parent type of the specification

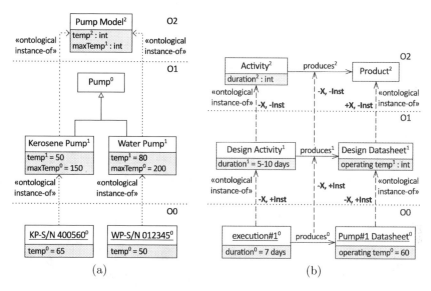

Fig. 3. (a) Potency-based based model of the product catalogue example. (b) Meta-relationship properties being used to identify whether a relationship should be specialisation or instantiation.

concepts. The specification class (for example EquipmentModel) exists at the same level as the type it refers to as it can define constraints with respect to that type.

Descriptions. A description, e.g. a set of constraints, can refer only to the attributes specific to its object (or, if the description is for a category or specification, the attributes of the type associated with the category or specification) and are inherited through specialisation, while instances of a type (and members of a category) must satisfy its description (or membership criterion).

3   Lifecycle Management

A Level Alignment Example. Using the semantic distinctions described in the previous section, other models in an ecosystem can be analysed to better identify mappings between them. We use potency-based models for the example (cf. Figures 2 & 3a), identifying the following alignment indicators:

1. An attribute with potency ≥ 2 suggests $InstX$ as the potency indicates that the attribute should be introduced to the concept at the level where its potency $= 1$ (so that it can be given a value at the next instantiation).
2. A subclass that introduces new attributes over its parent class suggests $SpecX$, while a subclass that only refines the domain of an attribute suggests $SpecR$; this is a direct corollary of the same distinction made in SLICER .
3. An object with potency $= 0$ and attributes with only potencies $= 0$ is $InstN$.
4. If all of the instances of an object are specialisations of the same class it suggests an SbS relation between the instantiated class and the specialised class.

In particular, if the class has attributes with potency > 0 or the instantiated class has attributes with potency $= 2$ it is most likely the case.

5. Specialised classes that have no attributes with a potency ≥ 1 and that are not identified as related to a specification class (see previous rule) suggests possible use of specialisation for categorisation. The introduction of attributes indicates the boundary between categorisation and categorised object(s).

Applying these rules to the example we can identify $InstN$ by rule (3) between the object at $O0$ on the left and KerosenePump, hence it can be aligned with the bottom level of the joint metamodel. At the $O1$ level, KerosenePump instantiates PumpModel from the level above which includes an attribute with potency 2; thereby identifying $InstX$ by rule (1). Moreover, by rule (2) a $SpecX$ relation is identified as KerosenePump adds attributes over the class it specialises (Pump) Finally, all of the instances of PumpModel are subclasses of Pump, matching rule (4) and indicating the relation $SbS(\text{PumpModel}, \text{Pump})$. As a result, this pattern can be matched in the joint metamodel. Note that the result would be the same if the attribute $temp^2$ were defined on Pump as $temp^1$. Finally, if the concept Pump were not modelled at all (i.e. it was completely incorporated into PumpModel) then the specialisation to some concept could still be inferred due to the combination of specialisation and instantiation embodied by potency.

Meta-relationship Properties. At first glance, the incorporation of the above described relationship patterns would appear to increase the complexity of the modeler's task, by increasing the number of basic relationships considered in a model. However, in practice it can be seen that the new relationships are really created by identifying special cases that would already have been reflected in domain models, but have usually been left implicit and hidden within generic domain associations or naming conventions (or even both, as in ISO 15926), resulting in highly complex and even inconsistent models [12]. In particular, these special cases result from the use of extension and explicit specifications. These can be considered as *meta-properties* (X+/-, S+/-) of the existing relationships, in the sense of the U, I, and R meta-properties used in OntoClean [13]. In the case of the X (extension) meta-property these can be partly automatically identified by examining property specifications. In the S (specification) case, it would be used to identify and distinguish what would before have been a generic domain association, or at best an instance of the generic D (Dependency) meta-property.

Figure 3b displays the application of the meta-properties to identify specialisation vs. instantiation. As can be seen, the bottom-most "instantiation" relationships have all been marked as *not* including extension, but incorporate instantiation as all attributes have been assigned values. Therefore, instantiation ($InstN$) is the correct relationship. In the top row, however, we can see that no instantiation occurs—the assignment of 5-10 days in Design Activity can be considered refinement as the "value" is a range and the potency remains > 0—and there is a mix of extension and not extension. Therefore, the correct relationships would be $SpecR$ between Design Activity and Activity, and $SpecX$ between Design Datasheet and Product. In practice, using these properties to automatically identify the correct relationships helps to reveal similarities between different (meta-)models when engineering transformations between them.

Metamodelling Spaces were an attempt to resolve the issue of strict metamodelling by separating modelling domains such that they have their own set of metamodel levels within their own space, irrespective of the levels of other metamodelling spaces [14]. A hierarchy of metamodelling spaces can then be formed by one way dependencies between spaces such that the source metamodelling space is on a metalevel with respect to the target space, thereby allowing the source space to reference elements on any level of the target space without violating the strictness criterion. This ensures *global strictness* of the model by eliminating cycles between meta-levels. A key aspect of using metamodelling spaces is to make appropriate use of instantiation and inheritance. This helps maintain *local strictness* within metamodelling spaces.

While this approach provided good separation of concerns, both within and between modelling spaces, it failed to account for situations where two metamodelling spaces are mutually dependent on one another, as the dependency between spaces can be only one way. For example, a process that produces a diagram that represents the process that was performed to create it (where the process metamodelling space and the product/diagram metamodelling space are separate). Moreover, it does not resolve the issue if there is a local cycle between meta-levels of a metamodelling space. For example, a class diagram that refers-to (or represents) the classes used to define the class diagram. This type of cycle between a more concrete object that represents a more abstract object from its own hierarchy occurs frequently in larger models that support ecosystem and lifecycle management. Part of the limitations of the original approach is that it attempts to stay with a four-layer architecture, such as that used by MOF/UML. When not constrained to four layers, concepts and objects can more easily be situated in the level most appropriate to their definitions.

The important point of the metamodelling spaces solution is that there is an encompassing meta-level involved that provides the definitions of relationships that pass between metamodelling spaces (and would otherwise violate the strictness criterion). The SLICER (linguistic) meta-model provides such an encompassing meta-level, which defines appropriate relationships for the crossing of metamodelling spaces and levels.

Mapping Identification and Execution. We have implemented a mapping tool, the *UniSA Transform Engine* (or, UTE), enabling data integration with transformation operators based on model-driven principles and a modular, extensible architecture. Mappings are defined in terms of fully declarative *mapping templates*—small reusable fragments—which considerably facilitate the integration process. The transformation engine uses mapping templates to find occurrences of data patterns in specific source models and composes the target model(s). OGI Pilot demonstrations of transformations from ISO 15926 to MIMOSA CCOM or vice versa have been given at industry events, e.g. ISA Automation Week.

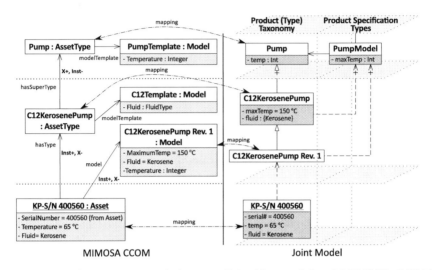

Fig. 4. Transformation example between Joint Metamodel and MIMOSA CCOM

The example in Figure 4 shows on the right a subset of a *joint model* based on our multi-level modelling framework and on the left a subset of the MIMOSA CCOM specification[2]. The MIMOSA specification is based on a UML class model (the linguistic metamodel) and a reference data library (the ontological model). CCOM provides general concepts such as Asset, AssetType, and Model in the UML model, while the reference data includes specific types, such as Kerosene Pump. Organisational instance data, such as the specific pump *KP-S/N 400560*, extends the ontological model.

There are two aspects to this: the identification of mappings between the linguistic metamodels, and those between the ontological metamodels. In the former, we can identify correlations between the *hasType* association and as an *Instantiation* in SLICER , and between *hasSuperType* and *Specialisation*. Moreover, the *model* relationship between Asset and Model can be seen as an *Instantiation* type relationship, with an implied *Specialisation* between the Model and the AssetType for the Asset. This is because the Model should incorporate all of the attributes of the *modelTemplates* associated with the hierarchy of AssetTypes.

Using this information, we can induce levels in the CCOM model, which would otherwise be flat, and align them with the Joint model to aid in identifying mappings between them. Starting with the lowest level, which is in this case the kerosene pump *KP-S/N 400560*, we can query the joint model and, using standard matching technique, identify the mapping between the two kerosene pumps. This serves as the basis for extending the mappings. By using the information in the models to determine which meta-properties hold for the CCOM relationships and by performing additional querying and reasoning on the joint model (e.g. querying the attributes of the types), further mappings can be identified.

---

[2] For simplicity, attributes are shown within the objects rather than as separate Attribute objects

Having identified these mappings in a concrete example model, we can define more abstract mapping templates for UTE. For example, one template may transform an Asset its Model (through the *model* association) and its AssetType (through the *hasType* association) into an object at the lowest level of the joint model and two types, one specialising the other, with the more specialised type being instantiated by the object. In addition, such a transformation could infer the existence of a specification somewhere in the type hierarchy such that the more specialised type is in an $InstX$ relationship with it.

4   Conclusion

The SLICER framework [11] provides a multi-level base model that allows making explicit the types of relationships that will exist between different stages in the engineering lifecycle, e.g., industrial artefacts relative to their specifications. Identifying the underlying semantics required for the relationships in such a model permits creating mappings across ecosystem boundaries, the establishment of a set of guidelines for consistent use of these relationships, so that they can be used as an aid for identifying consistent levels across mappings.

References

1. Young, N., Jones, S.: SmartMarket Report: Interoperability in Construction Industry, Technical report. McGraw Hill (2007)
2. ISO. ISO 15926 - Part 2: Data Model (2003)
3. Berger, S., Grossmann, G., Stumptner, M., Schrefl, M.: Metamodel-based information integration at industrial scale. In: Petriu, D.C., Rouquette, N., Haugen, Ø. (eds.) MODELS 2010, Part II. LNCS, vol. 6395, pp. 153–167. Springer, Heidelberg (2010)
4. Atkinson, C., Kühne, T.: The essence of multilevel metamodeling. In: Gogolla, M., Kobryn, C. (eds.) UML 2001. LNCS, vol. 2185, pp. 19–33. Springer, Heidelberg (2001)
5. Gonzalez-Perez, C., Henderson-Sellers, B.: A powertype-based metamodelling framework. Software & Systems Modeling **5**(1), 72–90 (2006)
6. de Lara, J., Guerra, E., Cobos, R., Moreno-Llorena, J.: Extending deep metamodelling for practical model-driven engineering. Computer **57**(1), 36–58 (2014)
7. Schrefl, M., Stumptner, M.: Behavior consistent specialization of object life cycles. ACM TOSEM **11**(1), 92–148 (2002)
8. Klas, W., Schrefl, M.: Metaclasses and Their Application. LNCS, vol. 943. Springer, Heidelberg (1995)
9. Chen, D., Doumeingts, G., Vernadat, F.B.: Architectures for enterprise integration and interoperability. Computers in Industry **59**(7), 647–659 (2008)
10. Ducq, Y., Chen, D., Vallespir, B.: Interoperability in enterprise modelling: requirements and roadmap. Adv. Eng. Informatics **18**(4), 193–203 (2004)
11. Selway, M., Stumptner, M., Mayer, W., Jordan, A., Grossmann, G., Schrefl, M.: A conceptual framework for large-scale ecosystem interoperability. In: Proc. ER 2015, Stockholm (to appear 2015)

12. Smith, B.: Against idiosyncrasy in ontology development. In: Proc. Formal Ontology in Information Systems (FOIS 2006), pp. 15–26 (2006)
13. Welty, C.A., Guarino, N.: Supporting ontological analysis of taxonomic relationships. Data Knowl. Eng. **39**(1), 51–74 (2001)
14. Atkinson, C., Kühne, T.: Processes and products in a multi-level metamodeling architecture. IJSEKE **11**, 761–783 (2001)

Determining the Quality
of Product Data Integration

Julian Tiedeken[1]([✉]), Thomas Bauer[2], Joachim Herbst[3],
and Manfred Reichert[1]

[1] Institute of Databases and Information Systems, Ulm University, Ulm, Germany
{julian.tiedeken,manfred.reichert}@uni-ulm.de
[2] Department Information Management,
University of Applied Sciences, Neu-Ulm, Germany
thomas.bauer@hs-neu-ulm.de
[3] ITM Group Research & Product Development MBC,
Daimler AG, Böblingen, Germany
joachim.j.herbst@daimler.com

Abstract. To meet customer demands, companies must manage numerous variants and versions of their products. Since product-related data (e.g., requirements' specifications, geometric models, and source code, or test cases) are usually scattered over a large number of heterogeneous, autonomous information systems, their integration becomes crucial when developing complex products on one hand and aiming at reduced development costs on the other. In general, product data are created in different stages of the product development process. Furthermore, they should be integrated in a complete and consistent way at certain milestones during process development (e.g., prototype construction). Usually, this data integration process is accomplished manually, which is both costly and error prone. Instead semi-automated product data integration is required meeting the data quality requirements of the various stages during product development. In turn, this necessitates a close monitoring of the progress of the data integration process based on proper metrics. Contemporary approaches solely focus on metrics assessing schema integration, while not measuring the quality and progress of data integration. This paper elicits fundamental requirements relevant in this context. Based on them, we develop appropriate metrics for measuring product data quality and apply them in a case study we conducted at an automotive original equipment manufacturer.

Keywords: Product data integration · Integration quality · Integration Process

1 Introduction

During the last 15 years, the amount of product data has more than doubled, while at the same time the duration of product development lifecycles has decreased by 25 percent [13]. In addition to product data management systems

© Springer International Publishing Switzerland 2015
C. Debruyne et al. (Eds.): OTM 2015 Conferences, LNCS 9415, pp. 267–284, 2015.
DOI: 10.1007/978-3-319-26148-5_16

[26], which track and manage changes related to product data, proprietary information systems are used by the various business divisions involved in product development to manage specific product data (e.g., test cases). In particular, many information systems were introduced to quickly adopt to new business challenges such as emerging technologies, standards, or legal regulations. Consequently, product data are scattered over a multitude of information systems managing data of different quality. Usually, distributed product data cover different perspectives on the product (e.g., requirements' specifications, geometric models, source code, and test cases), which are recorded for different purposes at different points in time. Finally, different techniques for handling variants and versions of product data are prevalent [8].

At certain points during product development, product data shall be integrated in a complete and consistent way. Note that even minor errors like, for example, a wiring harness of an automotive prototype, might lead to high costs, as construction costs of prototypes are very high. Due to heterogeneous product structures (e.g., list, hierarchy, or array representation of product parts) [4] as well as varying data quality, however, the integration of product data constitutes a challenging task. Especially, the identification of different artifacts related to the same real-world object is a cumbersome task that cannot be fully automated. As manual interaction is required, which is costly as well as time consuming, targeting at a full integration of all available product data from each application for all points in time is unfeasible.

In practice, an on-demand integration of subsets of product data is required, i.e., only those artifacts necessary to realize a particular business use case shall be integrated. As example consider the creation of a consistency check between requirements specifications on one hand and geometric models of product parts on the other.

To ensure for a high quality of incrementally integrated product data at a certain point in time, the progress of the integration process should be monitored based on proper quality metrics. Examples include metrics measuring the completeness of the correspondences between records stemming from different information systems. Note that data related to the same semantic concept may be documented in multiple information systems. Existing approaches provide integration quality metrics at the schema level, e.g., to assess the completeness of mappings between semantic concepts from different information systems. However, appropriate integration quality metrics at the data (i.e., instance) level are missing. Several challenges need to be tackled when aiming to measure the quality of product data integration. For example, companies may have numerous information systems maintaining thousands of product data artifacts. Furthermore, product data and corresponding attributes are recorded at different points in time. Finally, various stakeholders with different requirements may be involved in the integration process.

This paper addresses the following research questions: (1) How can the quality of product data integration be measured? (2) What are appropriate quality metrics for this purpose? Accordingly, the contribution of the paper are as follows: First, we present results from an in-depth requirements analysis for measuring the quality of integrated product data. Second, different quality metrics for measuring the integration of product data are elaborated. Third, we apply the metrics to a real-world case.

Section 2 presents our framework for product data integration required for understanding this work. In Section 3, we elicit requirements for measuring the quality of product data integration. To meet these requirements, Section 4 presents different metrics for assessing the progress and quality of incrementally integrated product data. A proof-of-concept prototype is presented in Section 5. In turn, in Section 6 we apply the metrics to a real-world case. Related work is discussed in Section 7. Section 8 summarizes the paper and gives an outlook.

2   A Framework for Product Data Integration

In order to integrate product data from heterogeneous, autonomous information systems several challenges need to be tackled [8]. Among others, one must cope with varying data quality, missing global identifiers, and differences regarding the management of product data variability and versions. To better understand these challenges, we analyzed a variety of information systems used in the context of product engineering by a German automotive original equipment manufacturer (OEM). Based on these practical insights as well as an in-depth literature study, we derived a framework for integrating heterogeneous product data. In detail, this framework relies on four *data integration layers*, i.e., product data collection layer, object layer, variant layer, and version layer [8].

2.1   Local and Global Product Ontology

In practice, different perspectives on product data are captured in application-specific data models. In turn, the various applications rely on different data management technologies, including relational databases, XML documents, and files. To cope with this heterogeneity, product data should be abstracted in a platform-independent way. For this purpose, in our framework product data is represented as reusable, interoperable, and platform-independent ontologies. Hence we apply the terms *schema concept* and *individual* from ontology engineering to express data model concepts as well as their extents.

A common architecture for integrating heterogeneous systems is to define a global schema into which schema concepts and corresponding data of information systems (denoted as local systems in the following) are integrated [2]. In the same manner, product data from a local information system may be abstracted into a *local product ontology* (*LPO*). The latter is then integrated into the *global product ontology* (*GPO*), which constitutes a holistic view on different product data aspects. Remember that a local information system solely maintains those parts (i.e., aspects) of the product data being relevant for specific stakeholders to accomplish their tasks (e.g., requirements engineer, CAD engineer, or test

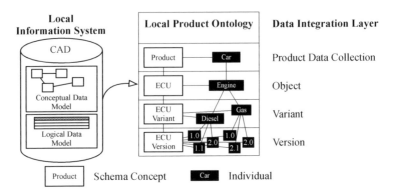

Fig. 1. Example local product ontology

manager). In realistic scenarios, a multitude of local product ontologies needs to be integrated into the global product ontology.

Fig. 1 depicts an example of a local product ontology from the automotive domain.[1] In particular, a local information system maintains geometric models of electronic control units (ECUs). Furthermore, it uses specific techniques to store ECU variants and versions. These techniques are captured in the information systems' conceptual data models. Furthermore, semantic concepts of the latter are mapped onto hierarchically structured schema concepts of a local product ontology: A *product* consists of different *ECUs*. For each ECU, different *variants* (ECU Variant) and *versions* (ECU Version) are maintained. For example, a *car* requires an ECU controlling its *engine*. Different engine types, in turn, require appropriate variants of this ECU (*Diesel, Gas*). Finally, different versions of these ECU variants must be maintained (*1.0, 1.1, 2.0, 2.1*) as well.

Like local product ontologies, schema concepts and individuals of the global product ontology are organized in four data integration layers as well. Hence, it becomes possible to integrate product data for each layer separately. As a major challenge to be tackled when integrating individuals (i.e., data entities) from a local product ontology into the global product ontology, individuals related to the same real-world object need to be identified.

2.2   Schema Concept Rules and Actions

As there are usually only few schema concepts in a local product ontology that need to be integrated into the global product ontology, this part of the integration process can be performed manually by integration experts. In turn, there may exist thousands of individuals for each schema concept, especially regarding the version layer. Consequently, the integration of individuals should be automated as far as possible in order to reduce human efforts.

---

[1] To improve readability, attributes of the schema concepts as well as corresponding attribute values of the individuals are hidden.

As discussed, product data is maintained in heterogeneous and autonomous information systems, which were designed with a specific use case in mind (e.g., requirements engineering, computer-aided design). Typically, corresponding information systems obey specific conventions for labeling individuals. Existing approaches for mapping local with global concepts are usually based on string metrics (e.g., Levenshtein distance, Hamming distance) or phonetic algorithms (e.g, Metaphone [3]). If two information systems do not rely on the same naming convention, however, respective algorithms fail in finding correspondences between individuals. Hence, other techniques are required to integrate these individuals as well.

Record linkage techniques aim to find records stemming from different data sets that refer to the same entity [10]. Some of these techniques are based on rules related to attributes of records to define whether or not two records refer to the same entity. Similarly, for each schema concept of a local product ontology, *schema concept attribute rules* (*SCARs*) are defined to determine related individuals between local and global product ontology. In particular, these rules define relationships between *attributes* of local product ontology schema concepts and the ones of global product ontology schema concepts. Furthermore, for each SCAR, a *matching function* is defined that is applied during the integration process to identify correspondences between attribute values of individuals from a local and the global product ontology.

If the naming conventions for schema concepts from a local and the global product ontology are similar or equal, matching functions based on string metrics may be defined between attributes of these schema concepts. Typically, product data stemming from different information systems share common attributes (e.g., cross-references), which may be exploited as well. Furthermore, naming conventions may share patterns. Hence, SCARs that evaluate regular expressions for attribute values of individuals from both ontologies may be defined. Finally, if no matching functions can be defined based on string metrics or regular expressions, mapping tables must be maintained. In particular, the latter are lists of corresponding source and target attribute values.

In general, the integration of local product ontologies into the global product ontology is performed biliterally; i.e., there is a one-to-one mapping between schema concepts of local and global product ontologies on each integration layer. As example consider Figure 2. For each local product ontology, Fig. 2 depicts a schema concept and a corresponding individual. For the sake of simplicity, we restrict ourselves to schema concepts and individuals at the object layer.[2] The local product ontology on the left maintains geometric models of ECUs, whereas the local product ontology on the right captures corresponding requirement documentations of these ECUs. Both schema concepts consist of four attributes (*Label, Geom, Name, Doc*). In particular, for each local product ontology schema concept, a SCAR describes the relationship to a corresponding schema concept in the global product ontology.

---

[2] SCARs for the other data integration layers are defined accordingly.

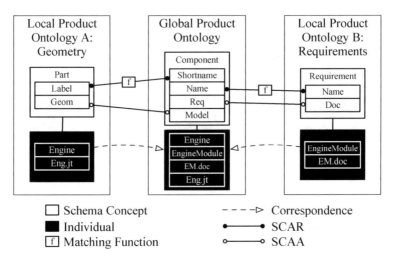

Fig. 2. SCARs and SCAAs between local and global product ontology

Since the global product ontology provides a holistic view on all product data perspectives (e.g., requirements, geometric models, or source code), mappings between attributes of local product ontology schema concepts to corresponding ones in the global product ontology must be defined. While a SCAR corresponds to a rule that relates individuals based on their schema concepts, a *schema concept attribute action (SCAA)* defines those attributes that should be integrated into the global product ontology after identifying correspondences between individuals.

For each local product ontology schema concept in Fig. 2, an SCAA is defined. In particular, attribute values (*Geom*) from individuals of *Part* (LPO A) will be copied into corresponding values (*Model*) from individuals of *Component* (GPO). In the same way, attribute values (*Doc*) from individuals of *Requirements* (LPO B) will be copied into corresponding ones (*Req*) of *Component*.

2.3   Integration Set

As a prerequisite for defining metrics measuring the quality of product data integration, several terms need to be defined. The quality metrics are based on the notion of *integration set*, which consists of a local product ontology that shall be integrated into a global product ontology. Correspondences between individuals from both ontologies are identified through the aforementioned schema concept attribute rules. In the following, the integration set as well as additional functions necessary for measuring the quality of product data integration are defined.

Definition 1 (Integration Set). An integration set $IS := (LPO, GPO, M, COR)$ is a quadruple with the following properties:

- $LPO := (SC_{LPO}, IND_{LPO}, Attr_{LPO}, AttrVal_{LPO}, HierarchySC_{LPO},$
  $HierarchyIND_{LPO}, LayerSC_{LPO}, SCAttr_{LPO}, INDAttrVal_{LPO},$
  $Member)$ defines a local product ontology, where
  - SC_{LPO} is a set of schema concepts,
  - IND_{LPO} is a set of individuals,
  - $Attr_{LPO}$ is a set of attributes,
  - $AttrVal_{LPO}$ is a set of attribute values,
  - $HierarchySC_{LPO} \subset SC_{LPO} \times SC_{LPO}$ is a set of directed edges representing the hierarchy of the schema concepts in SC_{LPO},
  - $HierarchyIND_{LPO} \subset IND_{LPO} \times IND_{LPO}$ is a set of directed edges representing the hierarchy of the individuals in IND_{GPO},
  - $LayerSC_{LPO}: SC_{LPO} \rightarrow \{PDC, OBJ, VAR, VER\}$ assigning a layer to each schema concept,
  - $SCAttr_{LPO} \subset SC_{LPO} \times Attr_{LPO}$ is a set of directed edges between schema concepts and attributes,
  - $INDAttrVal_{LPO} \subset IND_{LPO} \times Attr_{LPO} \times \mathcal{D}$ is a set of directed edges between attributes of individuals to attribute values,
  - $Member_{LPO} \subset SC_{LPO} \times IND_{LPO}$ is a set of directed edges between schema concepts and individuals
- $GPO := (SC_{GPO}, IND_{GPO}, HierarchySC_{GPO}, HierarchyIND_{GPO},$
  $LayerSC_{GPO}, Attr_{GPO}, AttrVal_{GPO}, Member)$ defines a global product ontology[3]
- $M := (SCAR, SCAA)$ defines the mapping between local and global product ontology where
  - $SCAR \subset SC_{LPO} \times SC_{GPO}$ is the a of schema concept attribute rules,
  - $SCAA \subset SC_{LPO} \times SC_{GPO}$ is the a of schema concept attribute actions
- $COR \subset IND_{LPO} \times IND_{GPO}$ is a set of correspondences between individuals from a local and the global product ontology
- $GetSC_{LPO}(l) := \{sc \in SC_{LPO} \mid LayerSC_{LPO}(sc) = l \wedge l \in \{PDC, OBJ,$
  $VAR, VER\}\}$ returns the schema concepts corresponding to a particular layer,
- $GetIND_{LPO}(sc) := \{ind \in IND_{LPO} \mid \exists \, m = (sc, ind) \in Member_{LPO}\}$
  corresponds to the set of individuals associated with a given schema concept,
- $L2GSC(sc_{LPO}) := \{sc_{GPO} \in SC_{GPO} \mid \exists \, scar = (sc_{LPO}, sc_{GPO}) \in SCAR\}$
  corresponds to the schema concept of a global product ontology onto which a schema concept of a local product ontology is mapped, and
- $GetSCAR(sc_{LPO}, sc_{GPO}) := \{scar \in SCAR \mid scar = (sc_{LPO}, sc_{GPO})\}$
  corresponds to the set of schema concept attribute rules between a schema concept from local and global product ontologies.

2.4   Initial Integration

The integration of individuals from local product ontology schema concepts with those of the global product ontology should be automated where possible. As

---

[3] Definitions of the components are similar to the ones of the LPO and are omitted for the sake of space.

local and global product ontology are structured in the same way, SCARs can be evaluated on each data integration layer. In general, the execution of the integration process is performed top-down, i.e., SCARs between the schema concepts of a local and the global product ontology located at the product data collection layer are evaluated first. Then, SCARs related to the object layer are evaluated, and so forth.

Algorithm 1 depicts this initial integration process. As input, an integration set IS is chosen (cf. Definition 1). It consists of a local and global product ontology for which a complete schema concept mapping exists, i.e., for each schema concept of the local ontology there exists at least one schema concept attribute rule as well as an action. Algorithm 1 returns a set of correspondences between individuals of schema concepts from the two ontologies.

Input: Integration set IS
Result: Set of correspondences COR
1 **foreach** $layer \in \{PDC, OBJ, VAR, VER\}$ **do**
2 $\quad$ **foreach** $sc_{LPO} \in GetSC_{LPO}(layer)$ **do**
3 $\quad\quad$ $L^{IND} = GetIND_{LPO}(sc_{LPO})$;
4 $\quad\quad$ $sc_{GPO} = L2GSC(sc_{LPO})$;
5 $\quad\quad$ $G^{IND} = GetIND_{GPO}(sc_{GPO})$;
6 $\quad\quad$ $SCAR^{L,G} = GetSCAR(sc_{LPO}, sc_{GPO})$;
7 $\quad\quad$ **foreach** $l \in L^{IND}$ **do**
8 $\quad\quad\quad$ **foreach** $g \in G^{IND}$ **do**
9 $\quad\quad\quad\quad$ $COR_{l,g} = evaluateSCAR(l, g, SCAR^{L,G})$;
10 $\quad\quad\quad\quad$ **if** $COR_{l,g} \neq \emptyset$ **then**
11 $\quad\quad\quad\quad\quad$ $executeSCAA(COR_{l,g})$;
12 $\quad\quad\quad\quad\quad$ $COR = COR \bigcup COR_{l,g}$;
13 $\quad\quad\quad\quad$ **end**
14 $\quad\quad\quad$ **end**
15 $\quad\quad$ **end**
16 $\quad$ **end**
17 **end**

Algorithm 1. Algorithm for the initial integration of an integration set

In particular, the integration of the local product ontology with the global one is performed for each data integration layer separately (Line 1), starting with the product data collection layer. For each schema concept of the local product ontology of the given layer (Line 2), its associated individuals are identified (Line 3). Then, the corresponding schema concept of the global product ontology as well as its individuals are obtained (Lines 4 and 5). Next, the schema concept attribute rules between both schema concepts are determined (Line 6). The cartesian product of all individuals of a schema concept from the local product ontology and all individuals of the corresponding one from the global product ontology is created (Lines 7 and 8). For each member of this product, the previously defined SCARs are then evaluated (Line 9).

If a correspondence between individuals l and g has been identified (Line 10), the corresponding schema attribute actions are executed (Line 11) and the correspondence is added to the result set (Line 12).

The previous steps will be repeated for each product data integration layer. After completing the integration process, individuals of a local product ontology are linked to individuals from the global product ontology. Typically, a local product ontology comprises only a subset of the product data. Therefore, multiple local product ontologies need to be integrated to obtain a holistic view.

Various stakeholders and users, who perform different tasks, are involved in this integration process. For instance, *domain experts* are responsible for defining mappings between the information systems' conceptual data models and the corresponding local product ontologies. Furthermore, they specify SCARs and SCAAs between schema concepts of local and global product ontology. This task is supported by *integration experts* that have an in-depth knowledge of interdependencies between schema concepts of the different information systems. Due to the complex nature of product data, the integration cannot be fully automated; partially, manual interaction is required, which causes high efforts.

In general, the integration algorithm may not find all corresponding individuals between local and global product ontology. Hence, *data quality experts* maintain correspondences to assure a complete and consistent integration. Finally, *end users* utilize the integrated product data from the global product ontology to realize different business use cases (e.g., management report).

3   Requirements

To support the needs of the different stakeholders involved in the integration process, metrics that allow assessing data integration quality become necessary. This section elicits the requirements for respective metrics. For this purpose, we analysed development processes for electrical and electronic components (e.g., electronic control units, sensor, and actuators) at a german automotive OEM. This includes expert interviews as well as an in-depth survey of numerous information systems maintaining product data.

Requirement 1 (Aspects). Several stakeholders are involved in the integration process (e.g., domain experts, integration experts, data quality experts, and end users) raising different requirements for measuring the quality of integrated product data. For example, domain and integration experts focus on integrating schema concepts from a local and the global product ontology and, hence, need quality metrics taking SCARs and SCAAs between schema concepts into account. In turn, end users are solely interested in individuals of the global product ontology. Thus, it should be possible to measure the quality of product data integration for different aspects of an integration set (i.e., schema concepts, individuals, or attribute values).

Requirement 2 (Perspective). Furthermore, stakeholders have different perspectives on the integration process. Domain experts and data quality experts are responsible for maintaining local product ontology aspects (i.e., schema concepts, individuals, and attributes) in relation to the global product ontology. In turn, end users consider global product ontology individuals related to a set of local product ontology. Consequently, it should be possible to measure the integration quality of integrated product data from different perspectives (local to global and vice versa).

Requirement 3 (Scope). Product data evolve over time and, hence, have different lifecycle states (e.g., *specified, designed, implemented, integrated, and released*). Since product data is managed by heterogeneous, autonomous information systems that use different techniques for dealing with product data variants and versions, entirely integrating product data at all points in time is too costly. Therefore, it should be possible to define the scope of integration quality metrics.

Requirement 4 (Monitoring). Quality gates are milstones in product development processes at which predefined requirements must be fulfilled. In the same way, it should be possible to specify reference values along the lifecycle of product data for which predefined values for different integration quality metrics must be reached. If the actual values of the quality metrics deviate from a pre-defined reference value, countermeasures may be performed to still achieve a complete and consistency integration set at a specific point in time.

4   Measuring the Quality of Product Data Integration

Quality metrics enable the different stakeholders of the product data integration process to monitor their tasks. Considering the requirements elicited in Section 3, we present metrics measuring the quality of product data integration grouped along different viewpoints (local-to-global vs. global-to-local) (cf. Req. 2) to support the various stakeholders in performing their integration tasks.

Section 4.1 presents metrics measuring the integration quality of a single local product ontology. Section 4.2 then deals with metrics that measure the integration quality of the global product ontology with respect to a given set of local product ontologies. For both viewpoints, quality metrics for different integration aspects are presented (cf. Req. 1).

4.1   Local-to-Global Mapping

Local Schema Concept Completeness. Domain and integration experts are responsible for maintaining mappings between local and global product ontology schema concepts (cf. Sect. 2). As the initial integration process may only be executed if for each schema concept there exists at least one schema concept attribute rule and action, their completeness must be determined. Hence, for a given integration set IS (cf. Definition 1), *local schema concept completeness* ($LocSCComp$) relates the set of schema concepts with at least one schema concept attribute rule and action (MPD^{SC}) to all schema concepts of a local product ontology (SC_{LPO}). If both sets are the same, the integration set is denoted as *local schema complete* (i.e., $LocSCComp = 1$):

$$LocSCComp(IS) = \frac{|MPD_{LPO}^{SC}|}{|SC_{LPO}|} \in [0, 1], \text{ where}$$

$$MPD_{LPO}^{SC} = \{sc_{LPO} \in SC_{LPO} \mid \exists\, sc_{GPO} \in SC_{GPO} \wedge$$
$$\exists\, scar = (sc_{LPO}, sc_{GPO}) \in SCAR \wedge \exists\, scaa = (sc_{LPO}, sc_{GPO}) \in SCAA\}$$

Local Individual Completeness. As the integration of product data cannot be fully automated, data quality experts must maintain correspondences between local and global product ontology individuals identified during the initial integration process. To measure the progress of the integration process, a specific data quality metric becomes necessary taking the correspondences between individuals from the local and global product ontologies into account.

Thus, for a given integration set (IS), *local individual completeness* (*LocIndComp*) is defined as the ratio of individuals of a local product ontology with at least one correspondence to an individual of the global product ontology (COR_{LPO}^{IND}) related to all individuals of the local product ontology (IND_{LPO}). If both sets are equal, the integration set is denoted *local individual complete* (i.e., $LocIndComp = 1$):

$$LocIndComp(IS) = \frac{|COR_{LPO}^{IND}|}{|IND_{LPO}|} \in [0, 1], \text{ where}$$

$$COR_{LPO}^{IND} = \{a_{LPO} \in IND_{LPO} \mid \exists\, c = (a_{LPO}, b_{GPO}) \in COR\}$$

4.2   Global-to-Local Mapping

The metrics presented so far focus on the integration quality of a local product ontology with respect to the given global product ontology. End users, in turn, are solely interested in individuals of the global product ontology being completely and consistently integrated, i.e., all necessary attribute values from global product ontology individuals are recorded to enable particular use cases.

Global Individual Completeness. The main goal of product data integration is to enable sophisticated business use cases. The latter include, for example, the creation of physical mock-ups. Since production costs of such mock-ups are very high, errors (e.g., missing attributes, inconsistent attributes) during product data integration should be avoided. Hence, each individual of the global product ontology needs to be linked to at least one individual of a local product ontology.

Formally, *global individual completeness* (*GlobalIndComp*) of multiple integration sets $IS_1, \ldots, IS_n$ corresponds to global product ontology individuals linked to at least one local product ontology individual (MPD_{GPO}^{IND}) related to all global product ontology individuals (IND_{GPO}). If both sets are equal, the integration sets is denoted *global individual complete*:

$$GlobalIndComp(IS_1, \ldots, IS_n) = \frac{|MPD_{GPO}^{IND}|}{|IND_{GPO}|} \in [0,1], \text{ where}$$

$$MPD_{GPO}^{IND} = \{ind_{GPO} \in IND_{GPO} \mid$$
$$\exists\, c = (ind_{LPO}, ind_{GPO}) \in COR_1 \cup \ldots \cup COR_n\}$$

Global Individual Attribute Completeness. Product data evolves over time and, therefore, their attributes are captured at different points in time. Though, there may be correspondences between individuals from the local product ontology and the global one. Since attribute values of individuals from local product ontologies may have not been set yet, corresponding attribute values of individuals from the global product ontology cannot be set as well. As these attribute values might be necessary to realize a particular business use case, the completeness of individual attribute values from the global product ontology must be determined. In particular, the attribute value of an individual from the global product ontology is complete, if it is not empty.

Therefore, *global individual attribute completeness* (*GlobalIndAttrComp*) of multiple integration sets $IS_1, \ldots, IS_n$ corresponds to the ratio of those individuals of a global product ontology, where each attribute value is not empty ($COMPLATTR_{GPO}^{IND}$) related to all individuals of a global product ontology (IND_{GPO}). If both sets are equal, the integration set is denoted *global attribute complete*:

$$GlobalIndAttrComp(IS_1, \ldots, IS_n) = \frac{|COMPLATTR_{GPO}^{IND}|}{|IND_{GPO}|} \in [0,1], \text{ where}$$

$$COMPLATTR_{GPO}^{IND} = \{i \in IND_{GPO} \mid \exists\, sc \in SC_{GPO} \wedge \exists\, m \in Member(sc,i)$$
$$\wedge\, \forall a = (sc, attr) \in SCAttr_{GPO}\, \exists\, v = (i, attr, val) \in INDAttrVal_{GPO}\}$$

Global Individual Attribute Consistency. After applying the initial integration process (cf. Section 2.4) there may be correspondences between multiple individuals from local product ontologies to a single individual from the global product ontology. This will be the case if attributes describing the same real-world object are documented in multiple information systems. As changes of corresponding attribute values performed in one these information systems are not always propagated to the other ones maintaining the same attribute, integration conflicts might occur during the integration process. Hence, we need an appropriate quality metric to detect such conflicts.

In particular, *global individual attribute consistency* (*GlobalIndAttrCons*) of multiple integration sets $IS_1, \ldots, IS_n$ corresponds to the difference between all individuals of a global product ontology (IND_{GPO}) and the set of inconsistent individuals ($INCON_{GPO}^{IND}$). The latter consists of all individuals, for which there are at least two corresponding individuals ind_k and ind_l from two local product ontologies LPO_k and LPO_L having SCAAs on the same attribute $attr_{GPO}$ defined, while the attribute values for ind_k and ind_l are different for this attribute. If $INCON_{GPO}^{IND}$ is an empty set, the integration set is denoted as *global attribute consistent*:

$$GlobalIndAttrCons(IS_1, \ldots, IS_n) = \frac{|IND_{GPO} \setminus INCON_{GPO}^{IND}|}{|IND_{GPO}|} \in [0,1], \text{ where}$$

$$INCON_{GPO}^{IND} = \{i \in IND_{GPO} \mid \exists\, scaa_k = (attr_{LPO}^k, attr_{GPO}) \in SCAA_k$$

$$\wedge \exists\, scaa_l = (attr_{LPO}^l, attr_{GPO}) \in SCAA_l$$

$$\wedge \exists\, a = (ind_k, i) \in COR_k \wedge \exists\, b = (ind_l, i) \in COR_l$$

$$\wedge \exists\, v_1 = (ind_k, attr_{LPO}^k, av_1) \in INDAttrVal_{LPO}$$

$$\wedge \exists\, v_2 = (ind_l, attr_{LPO}^l, av_2) \in INDAttrVal_{LPO} \wedge av_1 \neq av_2 \wedge 1 \leq k, l \leq n\}$$

As discussed, integrating all available product data would be too costly. In practice, therefore, only subsets of product data are integrated, i.e., only those local product ontology individuals are integrated into the global product ontology necessary to enable relevant business use cases. As our metrics are based on set theory and any subset of an ontology is again an ontology, the metrics may be applied to arbitrary integration sets (cf. Requirement 3).

4.3   Reference Values

The quality metrics defined in Section 4.1 and 4.2 considered the current state of the local product ontologies and the global one. To also enable use cases that consider the quality of integrated product data at a specific point in time (denoted as t_{end}), the integration set should be *global individual complete*, *global attribute complete*, and *global attribute consistent*. As the integration process requires manual interaction (e.g., to maintain correspondences between local product ontologies and the global one), its progress needs to be monitored in order to guarantee these quality properties at t_{end} (cf. Req. 4). Hence, *reference values* are defined representing benchmark values for the different integration quality metrics to be met at certain points in time $t_1, \ldots, t_n$; $t_i < t_{end}$, $i = 1, \ldots, n$.

As example consider Figure 3, which depicts the evolution of the three different integration quality metrics over time. In particular, the solid line illustrates the *global individual completeness* values for integration sets IS_1 and IS_2, while the dashed line represents the *global individual attribute completeness* values for the same sets. Finally, the dotted line illustrates *global individual attribute consistency* values. Furthermore, reference values are defined at two points in time t_1 and t_2. In particular, squares represent reference values for the first, diamonds the ones for the second, and circles the ones for the third quality metric. Note that all curves have positive and negative gradients (e.g., deletion of correspondences). Except the *global individual attribute completeness* value at t_1, the other values fall below the predefined reference values. Hence, countermeasures need to be performed to be still able to achieve the required quality properties (global individual complete, global attribute complete, and global attribute consistent) for the integration sets at t_{end}.

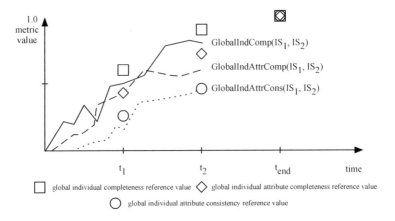

Fig. 3. Integration quality metrics over time in relation to reference values

5   Proof-of-Concept Prototype

The presented integration process as well as integration quality metrics have been implemented as a plugin for the Protégé ontology editor [15]. In particular, local and global product ontologies are represented as OWL2 ontologies [16]. To separate integration knowledge from schema concepts and individuals, SCARs, SCAAs, and resulting correspondences are maintained in a separate OWL ontology, denoted as *mapping ontology*. In particular, schema concepts are modelled as OWL2 classes, whereas SCARs and SCAAs are modelled as object types between OWL2 classes. We implemented the integration quality metrics based on semantic web rule language (SWRL) rules [17] to gather the different sets (e.g., COR_{LPO}^{IND}, $INCON_{GPO}^{IND}$). Applying these rules in a real world case study (cf. Sect. 6) revealed their limitation to ontologies with only of limited set of individuals. Consequently, we implemented the integration quality metrics with imperative functions based on the OWL API [18].

6   Case Study

The previously presented metrics have been applied in a real-world case study at a large German automotive OEM. During the development of a car, usually, mock-ups are produced to identify problems (e.g., packaging, functions) in an early development phase.

Modern cars consist of numerous electrical and electronic (E/E) components (ECUs, sensors, actuators) that enable safety systems (e.g., electronic stability control, collision avoidance system) as well as comfort systems (e.g., navigation devices, infotainment). While mechanical parts are described with geometric models, in turn, E/E components are described by multiple aspects. This includes, for instance, geometric models, funcional models, and software. Consequently, the integration of complex product data is crucial for creating prototypes. Note that a single error in one component might cause high financial losses since construction costs of prototypes are high.

The case study focuses on the practical use of the presented quality metrics on product data integration. More precisely we consider the integration of E/E components from three heterogeneous information systems: The first system maintains geometric models, while the second one stores hardware and software information; the third system captures the signals exchanged between E/E components. For each of the three information systems, local product ontologies were created (i.e., *LPO1, LPO2, LPO3*). The resulting schema concepts are depicted in Figure 4.

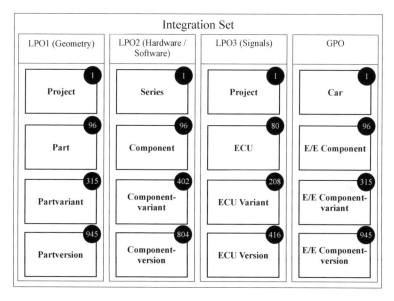

Fig. 4. E/E product data integration schema concepts and # of individuals [4]

Each local product ontology comprises of one schema concept at each data integration layer. Furthermore, each schema concept is populated with corresponding individuals. Since product data of one specific car have to be integrated, there is one individual for each schema concept at the product data collection layer. There are 96 different *parts* with 315 *partvariants*, and 945 *partversion* in the local product ontology for geometric models (*LPO1*). 96 *components* with 402 *component variants*, and 804 *component versions* (*LPO2*) as well as 80 *ECU*, 208 *ECU variants*, and 416 *ECU versions* (*LPO3*). Finally, schema concepts of the global product ontology *GPO* are defined (i.e., *CAR, E/E Component, E/E Componentvariant*, and *E/E Componentversion*). Furthermore, schema concept attribute rules and actions are defined between LPOs and the GPO. The global product ontology is populated with individuals from *LPO1*, which provides

---

[4] The circles at each schema concept show the number of corresponding individuals.

product data with the best accuracy. In detail, individuals at the object layer are labeled to comply with the pre-specified labeling schema.

Table 1 shows the values of the quality metrics after an initial integration (t_{init}). While 86 percent of the individuals of *LPO1* could be automatically mapped to corresponding ones of *GPO*, only 41 percent of the individuals of *LPO3* could be linked. The source information system of *LPO3* uses abbreviations to label individuals. Hence, no schema concept attribute rules evaluating the labels of individuals based on string metrics could be defined between *LPO3* and *GPO*. In turn, a mapping table (cf. Sect. 2.2) relating individual labels from *LPO3* to ones from *GPO* were established.

Table 1. Integration quality after initial integration

Quality Metric	t_{init}
GlobalIndComp	0.68
GlobalIndAttrComp	0.53
GlobalIndAttrCons	0.84
LocIndComp(LPO1)	0.86
LocIndComp(LPO2)	0.55
LocIndComp(LPO3)	0.41

Altogether, the following lessons learned resulted from the case study. The presented integration quality metrics could be successfully applied in practice. In particular, the latter allowed assessing the initial integration process and could be used to monitor the progress of product data integration over time. However, defining reference values for different integration quality metrics required experience in product data integration. Furthermore, the quality of the initial integration is related to the one of the product data sources to be integrated. In general, the quality of product data attributes in early stages of the product development lifecycle is rather low (e.g., missing attribute values, deprecated values). Consequently, the manual interaction efforts (e.g., maintaining correspondences between local and global product ontologies) will be higher compared to the integration of mature product data.

7   Related Work

We argued that a full integration of all product data available in any information system at any point in time is unfeasible. Similarly, [1] argues that data inconsistencies are common and hence should be tolerated. As opposed to our integration framework, the approach presented in [1] neither builds upon a global integration system nor a common data structure. Further, no quality metrics are provided.

In [9], different information quality metrics are introduced. First, *schema completeness* is defined as the ratio of its distinctive schema concepts to all schema concepts of a data integration system. Second, *schema data type consistency* is introduced as the total number of consistent attributes in relation to all attributes. Finally, the authors define *schema minimality* based on redundancy values of the entities and relations of a schema. These metrics are similar to our definitions, but neither take data completeness and consistency nor the definition of reference values into account.

In [12], the approach presented in [9] is extended with *schema structurality* and *schema proximity*. The definitions compare schema integration results. On one hand, the latter are automatically integrated by a tool, on the other they are integrated manually by experts. In detail, schema completeness is the proportion of the intersection of entities from the automatically generated schema related to all entities of the manually created schema. In our framework, the schema integration is performed manually by integration experts. Consequently, these measures cannot be applied. Furthermore, measuring the integration of data and reference values are not considered as well.

[11] proposes five quality criteria for data integration: *schema completeness*, *schema consistency*, *mapping consistency accuracy*, *minimality*, and *performance*. The approach introduces metrics measuring the integration between local schemas and a global schema. Therefore, it is related to our approach. Nevertheless, quality metrics concerning data integration are missing as well.

Altogether, we elaborated metrics measuring the quality of product data integration for different aspects (schema concepts, individuals, and attributes). While contemporary approaches solely focus on schema concepts, we provided further metrics taking the quality of data integration into account as well.

8   Summary and Outlook

In this paper, various quality metrics for measuring the integration of product data were elaborated. Based on an in-depth analysis of information systems maintaining product data at a German automotive OEM, we elicited the fundamental requirements for measuring product data integration. Furthermore, different metrics measuring the quality of product data integration were elaborated. To meet the requirements of the users involved in the integration process (e.g., domain experts, integration experts, data quality experts, and end users), appropriate quality metrics were introduced. In particular, we introduced metrics measuring product data integration of local product ontologies in relation to the global product ontology and vice versa. The presented metrics are generic in the sense that they can be applied to arbitrary subsets of local and global product ontologies. Finally, we suggested defining reference values and applied the metrics in a real-world case study. In future work, we will apply the presented metrics in further case studies from diverse domains and integrate them with product data management tools.

References

1. Easterbrook, S., Finkelstein, A., Kramer, J., Nuseibeh, B.: Coordinating Distributed ViewPoints: the anatomy of a consistency check. CERA **2**(3), 209–222 (1994)
2. Wache, H., et al.: Ontology-based integration of information - A survey of existing approaches. In: Proc. IJCAI 2001 Workshop, pp. 108–117 (2001)
3. Philips, L.: Hanging on the Metaphone. Computer Language **7**(12), 39–44 (1990)
4. Stark, J.: Product Lifecycle Management. Springer (2011)
5. Wiederhold, G., Qian, X.: Consistency control of replicated data in federated databases. In: Workshop on the Management of Replicated Data, pp. 130–132 (1990)
6. Sheth, A.P., Rusinkiewicz, M.: Management of interdependent data: specifying dependency and consistency requirements. In: Workshop on the Management of Replicated Data, pp. 133–136 (1990)
7. Wiederhold, G., Qian, X.: Modeling asynchrony in distributed databases. In: Proc. ICDE 1987, pp. 246–250 (1987)
8. Tiedeken, J., Reichert, M., Herbst, J.: On the Integration of Electrical/Electronic Product Data in the Automotive Domain. Datenbank Spektrum **13**(3), 189–199 (2013)
9. Batista, M.D.C.M., Salgado, A.C.: Information quality measurement in data integration schemas. In: Proc. QDB 2007, pp. 61–72 (2007)
10. Herzog, T.N., Scheuren, F.J., Winkler, W.E.: Data Quality and Record Linkage Techniques. Springer (2007)
11. Wang, J.: A quality framework for data integration. In: MacKinnon, L.M. (ed.) BNCOD 2010. LNCS, vol. 6121, pp. 131–134. Springer, Heidelberg (2012)
12. Duchateau, F., Bellahsene, Z.: Measuring the quality of an integrated schema. In: Proc. ER 2010, pp. 261–273 (2010)
13. Roland Berger Strategy Consultants. Mastering Product Complexity, Düsseldorf, November 2012
14. Wang, R.Y., Strong, D.M.: Beyond Accuracy: What Data Quality Means to Data Consumers. J. of Management Information Systems **12**(4), 5–33 (1996)
15. Gennari, J.H., et al.: The evolution of Protégé: an environment for knowledge-based systems development. Int. J. Hum.-Comput. Stud. **58**(1), 89–123 (2003)
16. Motik, B., et al.: OWL 2 Web Ontology Language: Structural Specification and Functional-Style Syntax. W3C recommendation 27.65 (2009)
17. Horrocks, I., et al.: SWRL: A Semantic Web Rule Language Combining OWL and RuleML. W3C Member Submission, May 21, 2004
18. Horridge, M., Bechhofer, S.: The OWL API: A Java API for OWL Ontologies. Semantic Web **2**(1), 11–21 (2011)

Inference Control in Data Integration Systems

Mokhtar Sellami[1]($\boxtimes$), Mohand-Said Hacid[2],
and Mohamed Mohsen Gammoudi[3]

[1] Higher Institute of Technological Studies of Kef/Riadi Laboratory-ENSI Tunisia,
Manouba, Tunisia
sellamimokhtar@yahoo.com
[2] Université de Lyon/LIRIS UCBL, Lyon, France
mohand-said.hacid@univ-lyon1.fr
[3] Higher Institute of Multimedia Arts of Manouba/Riadi Laboratory-ENSI Tunisia,
Manouba, Tunisia
gammoudimomo@gmail.com

Abstract. Specifying a global policy in a data integration system in a traditional way would not necessarily offer a sound and efficient solution to deal with the inference problem [8]. This is mainly due to the fact that data dependencies (between distributed data sets) are not taken into account when local policies (attached to local sources) are defined. In this paper, by using formal concept analysis, we propose a methodology, together with a set of algorithms that can help to detect security breaches by reasoning about semantic constraints. Given a set of local policies, an initial global policy and data dependencies, we propose an approach that allows the security administrator to derive a set of queries so that when their results are combined they could lead to security breaches. We detect the set of additional rules which will be used to extend the policy of the mediator in order to block security breaches. We also discuss a set of experiments we conducted.

Keywords: Access control · Data integration · Inference problem · Security and privacy – databases security · Privacy · Access controls

1 Introduction

Data integration aims at providing a unique entry point to a set of data sources. In this paper, we focus on the security challenge that mainly arises in data integration systems. In such systems, a mediator is defined. This mediator aims at providing a unique entry point to several heterogeneous sources. In this kind of architecture security aspects and access control in particular represent a major challenge. Indeed, every source, designed independently of the others, defines its own access control policy and it is important to comply with the local policies in the context of data integration. Complying with the sources' policies means that a prohibited access at the source level should also be prohibited at the mediator level. Also, the policy of the mediator needs to protect data against

C. Debruyne et al. (Eds.): OTM 2015 Conferences, LNCS 9415, pp. 285–302, 2015.
DOI: 10.1007/978-3-319-26148-5_17

indirect accesses. An indirect access occurs when one could synthesize sensitive information from the combination of non-sensitive information (and semantic constraints) collected from different sources and subject to different access control policies. Detecting all indirect accesses in a given system is referred to as the inference problem [4]. We propose a formal concept analysis based approach to derive the global policy of the mediator. The proposed approach allows preserving the local (source) policies and provides us with information about the inference problem. From the schemas and the security policies of the local sources, we derive a set of security policies (called global policy) that must be attached to the mediator. We then exploit interactions between elements of the global schema in presence of the global policy for inferring implicit combinations of queries that could lead to the violation of local security policies. Another issue is the dynamic change of the local policies and schemas. By resorting to incremental algorithms [5] in lattice construction, it is possible to avoid the regeneration of the global schema and policies from scratch. The reminder of the paper is organized as follows: Section 2 gives an overview of research effort related to our work. Section 3 introduces an example. In section 4, we describe our approach. In Section 5 describes the experiments. We conclude in section 6. Please note that because of lack of space, a research report containing more details regarding the state of the art, formal definitions of concepts used in our approach, complete examples and the theoretical complexity of the algorithms can be downloaded from http://bit.ly/1Iok4Fd.

2   Related Work

We will discuss the different approaches which are connected in any way to our problem. In addition, we will discuss different types of inferences that have been investigated so far.

2.1   Formal Concept Analysis and Access Control

The authors of [21] proposed a lattice-based solution for controlling inferences caused by unprotected aggregations. Instead of detecting inferences, they first prevent the adversary from combining multiple aggregations for inferences by restricting queries. Then, they remove remaining inferences caused by individual aggregations. In [10], the authors proposed to use attribute exploration from formal concept analysis on the dyadic formal context derived from the triadic security context to design the role based access control. In [19], a method, based on formal concept analysis, which facilitates discovering the roles from the existing permission to the user assignments, is proposed. From a technical point of view, our work extends the traditional approaches by resorting to formal concept analysis as a tool for reasoning about security policies in a distributed setting. From an application point of view, we consider a data integration scenario where it is mandatory to accommodate data dependencies, security policies and inference problems.

2.2   Views, Access Control and Inferences

Rosenthal and Sciore [15,16] have considered the problem of how to automatically coordinate the access rights of a warehouse with those of sources. The authors proposed a theory that allows automated inference of many permissions for the warehouse by a natural extension of the standard SQL grant/revoke model,[1] to systems with redundant and derived data. The authors have also defined the witness notion by including the use of views. The framework proposed by the authors determines only if a user has right to access a derived table (based on explicit permission) but our proposal goes further by determining which part of the table the user has right to access in the derived table. In [1], the authors have built on [12] to provide a way to select access control rules to be attached to materialized view definitions based on access control rules over base relations. They resort to the basic form of the bucket algorithm which does not allow to derive all relevant access control rules. In our work, we synthesize new rules from existing rules where the body of the new rules makes reference to materialized views. In [3], the authors proposed, unlike the use of authorization views, a graph-based model to define the access control rules and query profilers. These latter consist in capturing the information content of the query through the use of graphs. The major drawback of this approach is the impossibility to define permissions on a subset of tuples (selection).

2.3   Inference Problem

A number of methods have been proposed to deal with statistical attacks. These methods could be classified into three categories: query restriction [2], data perturbation [17] and output perturbation [9]. Query restriction could be performed by constraining the number of tuples that are used to construct query results. Data perturbation modifies data in such a way that it limits data inferences. Output perturbation modifies query results in order to prevent from sensitive information disclosure. Approaches dealing with semantic attacks tackle some issues that arise in traditional access control mechanisms. Semantic attacks have been identified as a serious threat to data security at a time where multilevel security policies were much popular [6,20]. In [7,8], the authors proposed a methodology that allows controlling the access to a data integration system. The methodology allows dealing with direct access and indirect access. The methodology includes two main phases: (1) *Propagation and combination of source policies* and (2) *Detection of threats*. They also proposed solutions to remedy flaws identified in the previous phases. Our approach is inspired from [8]. However, we take another look at the problem of data integration in presence of security policies. First, we generate a global schema and a global policy simultaneously. We capture the relevant elements of the data integration system in a single framework. The underlying lattice construction algorithms implicitly accommodate schema and policy changes.

---

[1] http://www.techonthenet.com/oracle/grant_revoke.php

3   Example

First, we need to introduce two definitions.

Definition 1. *(Functional Dependency)[13]. A functional dependency (FD) over a schema R is a statement of the form: R : X→Y where X, Y ⊆ schema(R). We refer to X as the left hand side (LHS) and Y as the right hand side (RHS) of the functional dependency X→Y.*

Definition 2. *(Authorization View)[14]. A set of authorization views specifies what information a user is allowed to access. The user writes the query in terms of the database relations, and the system tests (by considering the authorization views) the query for validity by determining whether it can be evaluated over the database.*

We consider a University Record System (URS) scenario where multiple systems need to share data records for cooperation purposes. Each University has a full control (*e.g.*, creation, management, etc.) over its own data records with respect to its own access control policies. To share data between the systems, a secure mediator is needed in order to facilitate access to the shared data via a global schema, while ensuring data confidentiality. This allows different users, including administrators, professors, students and researchers, to access multiple faculty or student data. In this paper, we assume (1) the mediator is built from three local sources, (2) an access control model based on constraints in an role based access control model which is associated with a resource and (3) a user is described by a set of features defining her/his Role. The enforcement of this model is done as follows: a user is allowed to access a resource if her/his profile satisfies the access constraints of that resource, otherwise, the access is denied. We use authorization views to provide a fine-grained access control.

Local Source 1
Relation : Supervisors(IDFaculty, Name, ResearchTeam, Affiliation)
Functional dependencies: IDFaculty, ResearchTeam →Name
and IDFaculty, Affiliation →ResearchTeam
Authorization views:

- V1_1_Authorization(IDFaculty)←
  Supervisors(IDFaculty,Name,ResearchTeam,Affiliation),
  $Role=DC ∨$Role=AD∨$Role=FO∨$Role=PR.
- V1_2_Authorization(Name)←
  Supervisors(IDFaculty,Name,ResearchTeam,Affiliation),
  $Role=AD ∨$Role=DC∨$Role=FO∨$Role=PR.
- V1_3_Authorization(ResearchTeam)←
  Supervisors(IDFaculty,Name,ResearchTeam,Affiliation),
  $Role=DC ∨$Role=AD∨$Role=PR.

Local Source 2
Relation: PHDStudents(StudentID, IDFaculty, ThesisTitle, ResearchTeam)
Functional dependencies: StudentID→ThesisTitle; StudentID→IDFaculty;
IDFaculty→ResearchTeam

Authorization views:

- V2_1_Authorization(StudentID)←
  PHDStudents(StudentID,IDFaculty,ThesisTitle,ResearchTeam),
  $Role=PR∨$Role=DC∨$Role=AD.
- V2_2_Authorization(IDFaculty)←
  PHDStudents(StudentID,IDFaculty,ThesisTitle,ResearchTeam),
  $Role=DC∨$Role=PR∨$Role=AD∨$Role=FO.
- V2_3_Authorization(ThesisTitle)←
  PHDStudents(StudentID,IDFaculty,ThesisTitle,ResearchTeam),
  $Role=PR∨$Role=DC.

Local Source 3
Relation: Faculty(IDFaculty, SSN, Salary, Insurance)
Functional dependencies: IDFaculty→ SSN and SSN, Insurance→ Salary
Authorization views:

- V3_1_Authorization(SSN)←
  Faculty(SSN,Salary,Insurance,IDFaculty),$Role=FO∨$Role=AD.
- V3_2_Authorization(IDFaculty)←
  Faculty(SSN,Salary,Insurance,IDFaculty),$Role=AD∨$Role=DC.
- V3_3_Authorization(Salary)←
  Faculty(SSN,Salary,Insurance,IDFaculty),$Role=FO∨$Role=AD.

4   Inference Detection: A Formal Concept Analysis Based Approach

We propose an approach for determining all the possible disclosure transactions[2] which could appear at the mediator level by exploiting the semantic constraints[3] and healing the global policy in order to deactivate the completion of such disclosure transactions. Our approach inspired from [8] is centered around three phases: (1) the generation of a global schema, global functional dependencies and a global policy from local sources and underlying policies, (2) disclosure transaction discovery and (3) policy healing.

- Phase 1: It consists in synthesizing the global policy, the global schema and the global functional dependencies. These elements are then exploited in the next phases.
- Phase 2: This phase is devoted to the detection of all sequences of queries, called disclosure transactions, which can be used to defeat the access control mechanism by exploiting the semantics of data dependencies.
- Phase 3: In this phase, we proceed to policy reconfiguration to avoid security breaches. This can be accomplished either at design time (by adding new authorization views) or at run-time (by controlling the execution of user queries).

---

[2] A disclosure transaction (DT) is a sequence of queries such that if they are evaluated and their results are combined, they will lead to security breaches and thus violating an access control policy.

[3] Which include the hidden associations between the attributes of data sources.

4.1 Synthesizing the Global Schema, the Global Policy and the Global Functional Dependencies

To synthesize the global policy and the global schema from the sources, we resort to the preliminary approach we described in [18]. Here, we briefly recall the principle of the approach. It takes as input a set of source schemas together with their access control policies and performs the following steps: First, it starts by translating the schemas and policies into formal contexts. Second, for each attribute, it identifies the set of rules which are preserved at the level of sources. This is done by computing the *supremum*.[4] Finally, it builds the global schema by combining relevant attributes. When this step is applied to our example, it derives the following[5] global schema which is composed of three virtual relations:

1. VR1(IDFaculty,Salary,SSN,Insurance,Name)←
   Supervisors(IDFaculty,Name,ResearchTeam,Affiliation),
   Faculty(IDFaculty, SSN, Salary, Insurance).
2. VR2(IDFaculty,ResearchTeam,Affiliation)←
   Supervisors(IDFaculty,Name,ResearchTeam,Affiliation),
   PHDStudents(StudentID,IDFaculty,ThesisTitle,ResearchTeam).
3. VR3(StudentID,IDFaculty,ThesisTitle)←
   PHDStudents(StudentID,IDFaculty,ThesisTitle,ResearchTeam),
   Faculty(IDFaculty, SSN, Salary, Insurance),
   Supervisors(IDFaculty, Name, ResearchTeam, Affiliation).

It also produces the following global policy which will be associated with the global schema:

- GV1_Authorization(SSN)←VR1(IDFaculty,Salary,SSN,Insurance,Name),
  $Role=AD∨$Role=FO.
- GV2_Authorization(Salary)←VR1(IDFaculty,Salary,SSN,Insurance,Name),
  $Role=AD∨$Role=FO.
- GV3_Authorization(IDFaculty)←VR1(IDFaculty,Salary,SSN,Insurance,Name),
  VR2(IDFaculty,ResearchTeam,Affiliation),
  VR3(StudentID,IDFaculty,ThesisTitle),$Role=AD∨$Role=DC.

Similarly to the generation of the global policy and the global schema, highlighting the functional dependencies at the mediator level is a way to anticipate and deal with the inference problem.

To do this, we propose to generate a global lattice using the functional dependencies associated with each local source. By exploiting the properties of the lattice, one noticed that by construction the lattice leads to the identification of overall functional dependencies. That is, the construction[6] of the lattice highlights the global functional dependencies. The construction process relies on an algorithm (Algorithm 1) that transforms all the local functional dependencies

---

[4] aka least common superconcept or least upper bound.

[5] Here, we give an extract of the results. For a complete result, please refer to http://bit.ly/1Iok4Fd.

[6] For our experiments, we use Galicia Tools to build the lattices: http://www.iro.umontreal.ca/~galicia/

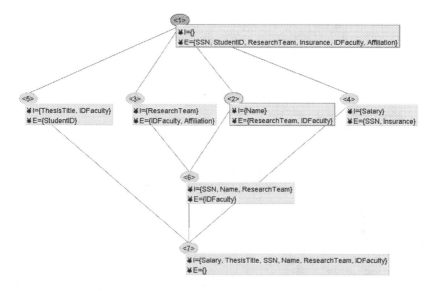

Fig. 1. Global functional dependencies organized in lattice

into formal contexts according to definition 3 and, by looping on the lattice, it derives a global functional dependency for each concept of the lattice.

Definition 3. *(A Functional Dependency as a Formal Context (O, A, R)). Given a Functional Dependency $X \to Y$, a formal context is obtained from $X \to Y$ (where γ_{FD} is a transformation function) as follows:*

$$\gamma_{FD}(X \to Y) \begin{cases} O = X \\ A = Y \\ R = 1 \end{cases}$$

By considering our running example, Algorithm 1 produces the following functional dependencies which are organized in lattice[7] (see figure 1):
$StudentID \to ThesisTitle$; $StudentID \to IDFaculty$;$SSN, Insurance \to Salary$
$IDFaculty, Affiliation \to ResearchTeam$; $IDFaculty, ResearchTeam \to Name$
$IDFaculty \to SSN$; $IDFaculty \to ResearchTeam$ AND $IDFaculty \to Name$

Please note that each source defines its policy separately and does not take into account the possible associations that can appear while combining its data with those of other sources. In addition, new semantic constraints could appear at the mediator level. These additional constraints could be used by a given user to infer sensitive information from non sensitive ones.

---

[7] Please note that, throughout the paper, we refer in the Lattice (*i.e.*, figure 1), the Intent of the formal Concept is denoted by I whereas the Extent is denoted by E.

Algorithm 1. Generation of global functional dependencies

Input: Functional dependencies FDs of a local source S_i
Output: Global Functional Dependencies FD^G
Begin:
1: $FD^G \leftarrow \oslash$;
2:   $K^{FD} \leftarrow \gamma_{FD}(FDs)$;▷
transform the FDs to a formal context (see definition 3)
3:   $L_{G_i}^{FD} \leftarrow ComputeLattice(K^{FD})$▷ compute the Lattice of the FD's Context;
4:   **for each** C_j in L_G^{FD} **do**
//Decomposition: if X → Y Z then X → Y and X→Z
5:       **for each** Y in $C_j.Extent$ **do**
6:           $FD_k \leftarrow C_j.Intent \rightarrow Y$ ▷ translate the concept into a FD
7:           **if** $FD_k \notin FD^G$ **then** add FD_k to FD^G
8:       **endfor**
9: **endfor**
10: **Return**

4.2 Discovery Phase

This phase includes two main steps: first, by resorting to formal concept analysis as a tool to characterize the global policy, we identify the profiles which should be prohibited to access some sensitive data at the mediator level. Second, one identifies threatening transactions by considering the impact of semantic constraints (*e.g.*, functional dependency) at the mediator level. First, we introduce two relevant definitions:

Definition 4. *(Authorization View Policy as a Formal Context)[18]. Let P be a set of Authorization Views V_k that govern access to the source (relation/schema) S and σ_{VBAC} be a transformation function. A formal context K (O, A, R) is obtained from P as follows*

$$\sigma_{VBAC}(P) \begin{cases} \forall\, a_i \in S, \forall\, c_j \in P,\ A = a_i \cup c_j \\ \forall\, V_k \in P \mid O = Rule_k \\ \forall\, a_i \in V_k,\ \forall\, c_j \in V_k,\ R = 1\ otherwise\ R = 0 \end{cases}$$

where A is the set of formal attributes (composed by the union of all source attributes a_i and all constraints (roles) c_j, O is the set of formal objects(authorization views) and R indicate the authorization view V_k having the query part a_i and the constraint/role c_j).

Definition 5. *(Prohibition Rules).*
Given an Access Control Constraint Context $K^{P^G}(Rule_k, c_i, R)$ obtained from the global policy using the transformation function σ_{VBAC}, The complementary relation, $\bar{R}$, corresponds to the prohibition rules: $Rule_k \bar{R} c_i$ holds iff $K^P(Rule_k, c_i) = 0$.

Computing Prohibition Rules. Prohibition rules are rules which can be used to deny the access to some data at the mediator level in order to comply with local policies. In order to detect such rules, we propose to extract the whole set of rules based on the characterization of the authorization views with a formal concept analysis. Basically, the authorization views are transformed into formal contexts and then we identify the prohibition rules by using the notion of prohibition rule introduced in definition 5. In order to represent the global policy as a formal context, we use the function σ_{VBAC} to generate the corresponding Global Policy Context.

After the extraction of the formal Contexts, we split them into two formal contexts: a formal context for access constraints and a formal context for attributes. A relationship (Rule, A∪C) ∈ R means that each profile (role) r ∈ C can access the attribute a_i. The context (Rule, A∪C, R) grants access to attributes by roles, and we can read from the context whose attributes are granted to a role.

Based on definition 5 , we obtain, from the above context, four prohibitions rules which are used in the disclosure discovery process:

- Rule 1: PR , DC → *SSN, Salary, Insurance*
- Rule 2: PR , DC → *SSN, Name, Salary*
- Rule 3: PR , DC → *Salary, Name*
- Rule 4: PR , DC → *IDFaculty, ResearchTeam, Salary*

Identification of Disclosure Transactions. By exploiting the semantics of functional dependencies, we present a naive method for automatically retrieving the set of queries which display the following property: when all the queries of a given set are executed, then the combination of their results could lead to the disclosure of sensitive information.

The principle of our approach is the following: first, we extract the functional dependencies. Then, we improve this process by taking into account the presence of prohibition rules. Finally, we show that it is sufficient to compute only the disclosure transactions by generating the lattice of functional dependencies involved in each prohibition rule.

Fo example, the following functional dependencies (1) and (2) can be used for overcoming the prohibition rule PR , DC → *Salary, Name* in order to access Salary and Name.

SSN, Insurance → *Salary* **(1)**

IDFaculty, ResearchTeam → *Name* **(2)**

To detect the sequences of violating queries, as a first step, the Formal Context (see table 1) is generated from the above functional dependencies using definition 3.

Then, by using the FD Context (see Table 1), we generate a Lattice of Formal Concepts (see figure 2) which can be used by the Algorithm 2 in order to detect the sequences of violating queries. The Lattice shows how we can exhaustively compute the disclosure transaction which can be exploited by a malicious user to infer Salary and Name by issuing the sequences of queries Q1, Q2 and Q3.

Table 1. $K^{FD}(X_i, Y_i, R)$: Functional dependencies Formal Context

X(LHS)	Y(RHS)	
	Name	Salary
IDFaculty	1	0
ResearchTeam	1	0
SSN	0	1
Insurance	0	1

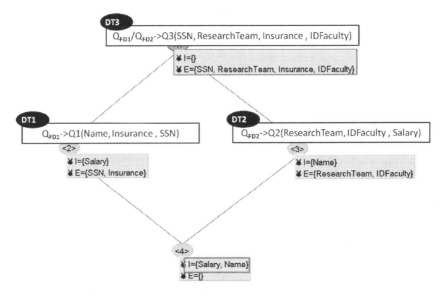

Prohibition rule 3: PR , DC →Salary, Name

Fig. 2. Disclosure Transaction Lattice of Salary, Name

The example of Figure 2 shows the lattice with four formal concepts: the topConcept C1, the FD concepts C2 and C3, and the bottom concept C4. Our algorithm exploits this lattice and for each parent concept C_i of a given concept having the attributes of the prohibition rule as Intent (*e.g.*, the bottom concept C4), it derives a Disclosure Transaction DT containing a sequence of queries. Considering our example, Algorithm 2 generates the disclosure transaction set $Set^{DT} = \{\mathcal{DT}_1(Q_{FD1}, Q_1), \mathcal{DT}_2(Q_{FD2}, Q_2), \mathcal{DT}_3(Q_{FD1}, Q_{FD2}, Q_3)\}$. So, if all the queries of any transaction $\mathcal{DT}_i$ are issued and evaluated, then the prohibition rule $Rule3$ (Salary, Name) is violated. Hence, to deal with this issue and to avoid the disclosure transaction completion, the next step consists in reconfiguring the global policy with additional rules in such a way that no transaction could be completed.

Algorithm 2. Disclosure Transaction Discovery

Input: Functional dependencies FDSet , P_ Prohibition rule policy **Output**: Disclosure Transaction Set DTSet **Begin**:

1: **for each** Rule $R_i \in$ P_ **do**
2:     $FD_{R_i} \leftarrow$ ExtractFDs(**FDSet**,R_i);
3:     $K_{R_i}^{FD} \leftarrow \gamma_{FD}(FD_{R_i})$;
4:     $L_{R_i}^{FD} \leftarrow ComputeLattice(K_{R_i}^{FD})$.
5:     **for each** C_j in $L_{R_i}^{FD}$ **do**
6:         **if** ($R_i.Att \subseteq C_j.Intent$) **then**
7:             **for each** Parent P_k of C_j in $L_{R_i}^{FD}$ **do**
8:                 $Q_{FD_s} \leftarrow Q(\{P_k.Intent \cup P_k.Extent\}$)
9:                 $Q_k \leftarrow Q(\{C_j.Intent \cup P_k.Extent\} \setminus \{P_k.Intent\})$
10:                    add $DT_i\{Q_{FD_s}, Q_k\}$ to Set^{DT} ;
11:                    $DT_n \leftarrow DT_n \cup \{Q_{FD_s}\}$
12:             **endfor**
13:         **endif**
14:     $Q_{k+1} \leftarrow Q(L_{R_i}^{FD}.TopConcept.Extent\})$
15:     add $DT_n \leftarrow \{Q_{FD_s}, Q_{k+1}\}$ to Set^{DT} ;
16:     **endfor**
17: **endfor**
18: **Return**

4.3   Policy Healing

The policy healing can be applied at two levels: First, at design time with policy completion by adding a new set of authorization rules. Such rules are applied to make sure that no transaction could be completed. Second, at runtime. This could be accomplished by means of a monitoring process which requires to store the previous queries.

Global Policy Completion. The policy completion is the step which can be used by an administrator to repair the global policy by adding new ones which can prevent the completion of transactions. The main issue is then how to identify the (minimal) set $\mathcal{Q}$ of queries from which to build the new authorization rules. The new authorization rules should display the following property: for any DT_i (disclosure transaction) at least one $Q_i \in \mathcal{Q}$ is denied. The (minimal) set of queries which would be used to generate the new authorization rules must also ensure that there are no redundant access control rules and should cover all the disclosure transactions.

The principle of the underlying algorithm (see Algorithm 3) is the following: it starts by initializing the set of revoked queries then it runs through the Galois Sub Hierarchy Lattice of Disclosure Transactions (see Figure 3). For each pair of Concepts (C_i,C_j), it checks if the hierarchy order ($C_i \leq C_j$) holds between the two concepts. If the subconcept C_i is not marked then it will be used in the

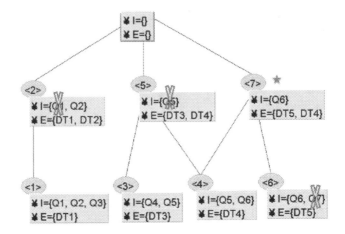

Fig. 3. Galois Sub-Hierarchy Lattice of Disclosure Transactions

queries revocation process, otherwise the superconcept C_j must be used. Finally, it generates the additional authorization views based on each revoked query we obtained.

Algorithm 3. Minimal Queries Revocation

Input: Disclosure Transaction Galois Sub Hierarchy Lattice GSH^{DT}, PG : Global Policy

Output: PG' the new Global policy with additional rules

Begin:

1: **for each** pair of Concept (C_i, C_j) in GSH^{DT} i≠j **do**
2: **if** $(C_i \leq C_j)$ **then**
3:     **if** $(C_i\,not\,marked)$ **then** $C_r \leftarrow C_j; mark\ C_j$*
4:     **else** $C_r \leftarrow C_i; mark\ C_j;$**endif**
5:     **if**$(|C_r.Intent| = 1$ **then** $Q_r \leftarrow Q_1$**else**
6:         $Q_r \leftarrow Q_1, Q_1 \in C_r.Intent$ **endif**
7:         **for each** $query\ Q_{k+1}$, **in** $C_r.Intent$ **do**
8:             **if**$(Q_{k+1} \subset Q_r)\ then Q_r \leftarrow Q_{k+1}$**endif**
9:         **endfor**
10:     **endif**
11:     add new Authorization View $GV(Q_r)$ to Global Policy PG'
12: **endfor**
13: **Return**
*:Note that all concepts of the Lattice having a label that indicates which concept has been marked by itself or by its super-concepts

---

Stop that Query. In order to ensure maximal availability of data at the mediator level while ensuring the non disclosure of sensitive information, one can choose a run-time approach which consists in monitoring the execution of queries and revokes those queries that could lead to the violation of policies. The main problem with the run-time query revocation is that it requires the storage of the past queries and the computing of the correlation between the current query and the past queries. By resorting to formal concept analysis, one can enhance the monitoring process.

5   Experiments

We provide an experimental evaluation of our proposed methodology and analysis of the proposed algorithms. We designed a synthetic scenario by using three generators. The scenario includes data sources, authorizations views and functional dependencies. The synthetic scenario (including the generators) was implemented in Java and we used the Galicia API. Experiments were carried out on a Linux PC with Ubuntu TLS 14.04, Intel Core 2 Duo CPU with 2.00GHz and 4GB RAM.

(a) **Data Sources Generator**: Given a number (N) of relations, an average number (A) of sub-elements of each relation and an average number (J) of join attributes, the source generator randomly produces a set $\sum^{R}$ of relation R(A) defined in such a way that J corresponds to the number of joins that could be built from shared attributes by the generated relations. Here, each join attribute is randomly chosen from the set of attributes of each relation. In the experiments, we considered N ranging from 5 to 20, A ranging from 10 to 20, and J ranging from 5 to 10.

(b) **Authorization Views Generator**: Given a source schema R, we consider three numbers: P (the number of authorization views), Q (the number of attributes used in the project clause of queries), and C (the number of profiles). In our experiments we considered P = 80 rules, Q= 3, and C = 10.

(c) **Functional Dependencies Generator**: Given a relational R and a natural number m, the functional dependencies generator randomly produces a set $\sum^{FD}$ consisting of functional dependencies on R, such that the average number of functional dependencies for each relation in R is m. The generator also takes two other parameters as inputs, namely LHS and RHS. LHS is the maximum number of attributes in each left hand side of the generated functional dependencies, and RHS is the maximum number of attributes in each RHS of the functional dependencies. The experiments were conducted on various $\sum^{FD}$ ranging from 10 to 80 functional dependencies per source, with the LHS containing from 3 to 10 attributes and the RHS containing from 2 to 5 attributes.

We conducted our experimental evaluation as follows. We performed a large number of trials so that, for each run, we generated a random number of sources ranging from 5 to 20, the number of attributes ranging from 10 to 20, the number of common attributes or joins ranging from 5 to 10, the number of functional

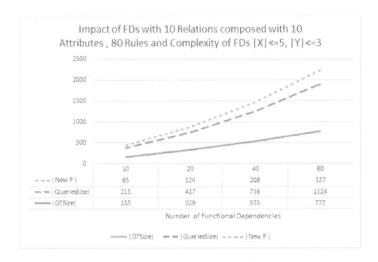

Fig. 4. Computational time for different steps of our approach

dependencies (of the form X→Y) ranging from 10 to 80 for each local source with X and Y involving 5 to 10 attributes, and 80 access control rules with 10 roles and 3 attributes.

For each set of generated tests, we measured the size and the time required to build the lattices by our algorithms for each step of our methodology including:

• $|GFDTime|$ is the necessary time to infer the global functional dependencies and $|GFDLattice|$ is the size of the obtained lattice (number of concepts).

• $|DTDTime|$ is the time required to detect all the suspicious transactions and $|DTSize|$is the number of such transactions.

•$|QueriesSize|$ is the number of queries and $|MQRTime|$ is the time required to extract a minimal query set.

• $|NewP|$: the number of added access control rules to the policy to prevent completion of prohibited transactions.

• $|LQQTime|$ and $|LQQ|$correspond to the time required to generate the lattice Query Labeling Lattice and its size respectively.

The required Time to compute the global functional dependencies and the suspicious transactions: Figure 4 shows the time required to compute the disclosure transactions. It significantly exceeds both the time required to build the lattice and the time to compute the minimal query revocation. We can also deduce that the time to compute the suspicious transactions (DTD) with 80 functional dependencies is higher than the time required to compute disclosure transaction with 20 functional dependencies. The results depict that the global time to compute the lattice of functional dependencies is between 32 and 81 seconds for data sets containing 10 to 80 functional dependencies per source.

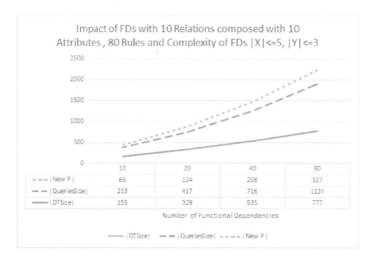

Fig. 5. Impact of functional dependencies on the global policy

Impact of functional dependencies on the global Policy: Figure 5 shows the relationship between the number of disclosure transactions and the number of additional rules. At each run, we particularly pick, as decision metric, the new rule that appears more often in DTD. The number of queries also increases with the same rate as that of functional dependencies. We also noticed that the number of access control rules, to be added, increases with the number of inferred dependencies as well as with the number of identified transactions. This means that the functional dependencies have a significant impact on defeating access control mechanisms in order to infer sensitive information from non-sensitive one.

Query Labeling Lattice: To analyze the impact of large databases with a large number of functional dependencies on the Query Labeling Lattice, we generated a dataset composed of 20 sources with 10 attributes, 80 rules and 160 functional dependencies per source.

Figure 6 shows the time required to construct such an QLL and its size. We note that the more functional dependencies we infer the more queries are identified. The results show that the size and the time required to compute the QLL increases with the number of new queries that are discovered.

Figure 7 shows the impact of functional dependencies on the time required to lock a query. We note that the time required to run through a QLL Lattice and to evaluate the policy decision for a given query increases with the number of illicit transactions as well as with the number of identified queries. They clearly indicate that the Number of queries and transactions have a significant impact on time required to lock query at run time. So the main problem of the query tracking is the enormous amount of queries that needs to be managed. Further tests will be necessary to fully understand the behavior of the Stop That Query

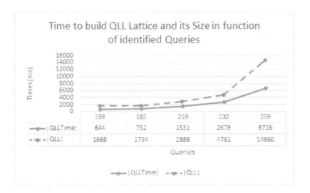

Fig. 6. Impact of identified queries on size of query labeling lattice and its time computing

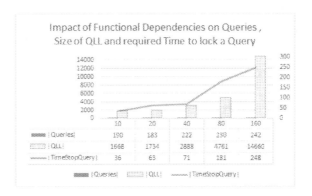

Fig. 7. Time required to lock a query of a transaction

method. However, the current track seems promising, especially if combined with the efficient and fastest algorithms [11] of lattices Construction and Navigation. Improvement to the flexibility of Stop That Queries can be achieved through approaches that adapt to Incremental algorithms of lattice construction and lattice reduction. In our approach, we mainly focused on the analysis of the performance and the scalability of our proposal for many reasons. The use of the Lattice as a common representation framework to model the global schema, policies and functional dependencies requires comparison of each of our steps to each related approaches separately. Due to this issues, it is difficult to compare our approach to the related work because there is no available implementation or experimental data sets(policies, functional dependencies and local schemas).

6   Conclusion

In this work we have investigated the problem of illicit inferences that result from combining semantic constraints with authorized information in a data integration context. We proposed an approach which exploits formal concept analysis to capture security policies and data dependencies. By resorting to formal concept analysis, we were able to build both a global schema and the underlying global policy. The global policy is refined in such a way that violating queries are blocked in advance (design time or run-time). There are many research directions to pursue: when a new source joins the system or an existing source leaves the system, it is necessary to revise the global schema and the global policy. In this case, an incremental approach should be designed. Another interesting issue is concerned with data dependencies. Indeed, there are other semantic constraints that could play an important role in inference problems. Examples are inclusion dependencies, multivalued dependencies and the partial functional dependencies. We are investigating these issues. In Future work, we intent to integrate our approach as plug-in on Talend Data Integration Studio.[8]

Acknowledgments. This work is supported by Thomson Reuters in the framework of the Partner University Fund project : Cybersecurity Collaboratory: Cyberspace Threat Identification, Analysis and Proactive Response". The Partner University Fund is a program of the French Embassy in the United States and the FACE Foundation and is supported by American donors and the French government.

References

1. Cuzzocrea, A., Hacid, M.-S., Grillo, N.: Effectively and efficiently selecting access control rules on materialized views over relational databases. In: International Database Engineering and Applications Symposium (IDEAS), pp. 225–235 (2010)
2. Denning, D.E., Schlorer, J.: Inference controls for statistical databases. Computer **16**(7), 69–82 (1983)
3. De Capitani di Vimercati, S., Foresti, S., Jajodia, S., Paraboschi, S., Samarati, P.: Assessing query privileges via safe and efficient permission composition. In: ACM Conference on Computer and Communications Security, pp. 311–322 (2008)
4. Farkas, C., Jajodia, S.: The inference problem: A survey. SIGKDD Explor. Newsl. **4**(2), 6–11 (2002)
5. Ganter, B., Wille, R.: Formal Concept Analysis: Mathematical Foundations, 1st edn. Springer-Verlag New York Inc., Secaucus (1997)
6. Goguen, J.A., Meseguer, J.: Unwinding and inference control. In: Proceedings of the 1984 IEEE Symposium on Security and Privacy, pp. 75–86. IEEE Computer Society (1984)
7. Haddad, M., Hacid, M.-S., Laurini, R.: Data integration in presence of authorization policies. In: 1th IEEE International Conference on Trust, Security and Privacy in Computing and Communications, TrustCom 2012, Liverpool, United Kingdom, June 25–27, pp. 92–99 (2012)
8. Haddad, M., Stevovic, J., Chiasera, A., Velegrakis, Y., Hacid, M.-S.: Access control for data integration in presence of data dependencies. In: Bhowmick, S.S., Dyreson, C.E., Jensen, C.S., Lee, M.L., Muliantara, A., Thalheim, B. (eds.) DASFAA 2014, Part II. LNCS, vol. 8422, pp. 203–217. Springer, Heidelberg (2014)
9. Fellegi, I.P., Phillips, J.L.: Statistical confidentiality: Some theory and application to data dissemination. In: Annals of Economic and Social Measurement, vol. 3(2), pp. 101–112. National Bureau of Economic Research, Inc. (1974)

---

[8] http://fr.talend.com/index.php

10. Kumar, C., et al.: Designing role-based access control using formal concept analysis. Security and Communication Networks **6**(3), 373–383 (2013)
11. Mouliswaran, S.C., Kumar, Ch., Chandrasekar, C., et al.: Modeling chinese wall access control using formal concept analysis. In: 2014 International Conference on Contemporary Computing and Informatics (IC3I), pp. 811–816. IEEE (2014)
12. Nait-Bahloul, S.: Inference of security policies on materialized views. rapport de master 2 recherche (2009). http://liris.cnrs.fr/~snaitbah/wiki
13. Özsu, M.T., Valduriez, P.: Principles of Distributed Database Systems, 3rd edn. Springer (2011)
14. Rizvi, S., Mendelzon, A.O., Sudarshan, S., Roy, P.: Extending query rewriting techniques for fine-grained access control. In: Weikum, G., König, A.C., Deßloch, S., (eds.) Proceedings of the ACM SIGMOD International Conference on Management of Data, Paris, France, June 13–18, pp. 551–562. ACM (2004)
15. Rosenthal, A., Sciore, E.: View security as the basis for data warehouse security. In: CAiSE Workshop on Design and Management of Data Warehouses, pp. 5–6 (2000)
16. Rosenthal, A., Sciore, E.: Administering permissions for distributed data: Factoring and automated inference. In: Proc. of IFIP WG11.3 Conf. (2001)
17. Schlörer, J.: Security of statistical databases: Multidimensional transformation. ACM Trans. Database Syst. **6**(1), 95–112 (1981)
18. Sellami, M., Gammoudi, M.M., Hacid, M.S.: Secure data integration: a formal concept analysis based approach. In: Decker, H., Lhotská, L., Link, S., Spies, M., Wagner, R.R. (eds.) DEXA 2014, Part II. LNCS, vol. 8645, pp. 326–333. Springer, Heidelberg (2014)
19. Sobieski, Ś., Zieliński, B.: Modelling role hierarchy structure using the formal concept analysis. Annales UMCS Sectio AI Informatica **10**, 143–159 (2015)
20. Su, T.-A., Özsoyoglu, G.: Data dependencies and inference control in multilevel relational database systems. In: Proceedings of the 1987 IEEE Symposium on Security and Privacy, Oakland, California, USA, April 27–29, pp. 202–211 (1987)
21. Wang, L., Jajodia, S., Wijesekera, D.: Lattice-based inference control in data cubes. In: Preserving Privacy in On-Line Analytical Processing (OLAP). AIS, pp. 119–145. Springer US (2007)

Integrated Process Oriented Requirements Management

Nikolaus Wintrich[✉], Patrick Gering, and Malte Meissner

Corporate Management, Fraunhofer IPK, Berlin, Germany
{nikolaus.wintrich,patrick.gering,
malte.meissner}@ipk.fraunhofer.de

Abstract. Within current software development projects requirements are usually derived from a technical point of view. Since these systems are part of an already existing enterprise environment and their goal is to support business processes, the focus should be shifted towards these overlaying business processes. Therefore we propose a holistic method that focuses on business processes and using them as a vantage point from which requirements are elicitated and linked to them. Based on these interconnected dependencies, functional requirements without a business relation can be identified. Furthermore, this also allows identifying aspects that are not yet covered by any requirements as well as process-oriented monitoring throughout all project phases. Existing business process management tools were extended to incorporate this method which was successfully applied within a software development project in a large, international company.

Keywords: Process management · Requirements management · Enterprise modeling · IEM · MO^{2}GO · Process assistant

1   Introduction

Software systems are the backbone of most enterprises in developed economies. They support the value-adding process across all fields and are integral to many work steps. Several factors determine whether a software system is efficient, functional or profitable. The field of Requirements Engineering (RE) is widely studied due to its frequent usage as well as the important role it plays in terms of costs, effectivity and functionality. Many advances have been made and there have been several developments, particularly in the requirement elicitation methods as well as stakeholder involvement [1, 2, 3, 4, 5, 6]. We can reduce costs, save time and provide better quality, and thus improve the quality of the elicitation process by extending two existing aspects of RE research. One has been researched in great detail, namely stakeholder involvement, whereas the other one has been somewhat neglected. The latter one are processes which we use as the main angle for the entire project, especially the requirements elicitation and monitoring.

The goal is to develop a more streamlined and holistic system. This can be accomplished by avoiding an isolated view of requirements. We seek to remedy this flaw by using both stakeholders and processes in the requirement elicitation and facilitating

C. Debruyne et al. (Eds.): OTM 2015 Conferences, LNCS 9415, pp. 303–310, 2015.
DOI: 10.1007/978-3-319-26148-5_18

said elicitation with two process management tools. This approach has already been applied in a large sized company.

The paper is organized as followed: section 2 will give a brief overview about the related work and our research goals. Our approach is presented in section 3 and the application is described in section 4. Section 5 will summarize the paper and give an outlook for future research.

2   Literature Review and Goals

Stakeholder involvement has been the most dominant trend in recent requirements elicitation and management research. In [5], part of the core definition of RE is stakeholder involvement, specifically "finding consensus with all involved stakeholders about the elicitated requirements". Stakeholder involvement has improved requirement elicitation to a certain degree, but the usual sources for these requirements are system users, management or existing systems. This usually results in requirements/systems having a large stakeholder bias which oftentimes neglects the overlaying business processes (example: stakeholder demands a function that cannot be traced back to a business process).

There are numerous techniques in the field of requirements elicitation now and they range from methods such as brain-storming, workshops or roleplaying, to the Walt Disney Method, apprenticing, artifact based observations or mind mapping [7]. These methods, if applied correctly, can be reasonably expected to fulfill stakeholder demands adequately. Only few techniques (for example: observation and system archeology) mention processes though and none of them make processes their main focus [5].

There are several existing methodologies which can be applied in order to create high quality systems that are able to fulfill their requirements, such as V XT Model, Prince2, the waterfall model, RUP or Scrum [7, 8, 9, 10, 11]. The similarities between these models are mainly their participatory system analysis, their project and phases oriented approaches, as well as an isolated view on the requirements.

Most contemporary research focuses on fulfilling a certain set of requirements, falling short of creating a holistic system. Within the current research we find the same isolated, oftentimes mirroring the shortcomings we have pointed out above, namely one sided approaches that succeed in fulfilling a certain set of requirements, but fail to conceive a holistic approach. A good example would be [12], which looks at the context between certain requirements, objects and users. Numerous issues, such as the scope of the elicitation or the appropriateness of their applicability, remain unsolved. They require a reevaluation of the original approach rather than just specialized, isolated efforts.

This is not to say that there are no approaches that deal with business processes and eliciting requirements from them. Goal trees are extracted from business processes modelled in BPMN in [13]. A similar approach is presented in [14] describing a two-step approach, the derivation of business services and the derivation of software services, where the process activities are classified as automatically, semi-automatically or manually executed.

3   Method

The integrated process oriented requirements management method combines business process management aspects, especially the business process (re-)engineering, and the requirements management into a holistic method. Like existing RE methods, our approach focusses on business processes which the new system is going to support. The final result is an integrated enterprise model where all processes and requirements are linked to each other and are properly described. By integrating process and requirements management, the definition of the to-be process and the elicitation of requirements, as well as their validation and verification can be performed alongside each other. The overall procedure of our methodology can be divided into five main steps (Fig. 1).

Fig. 1. Methodological procedure for the integrated process and requirements management

The first step is the definition of the project framework. This includes the definition of the process scope, the modeling concept (object types, granularity, correlation and spatial layout). It also includes the definition of the requirement specification template (e.g. Volere [6], IEEE [15], other), a delimitation of the software system to be developed and existing IT systems (e.g. ERP), as well as identification of interfaces. Additionally, the project structure and project team is set up as well as other organizational aspects.

It is crucial to involve as many stakeholders as possible to create a result which covers the most common requirements. Depending on the size of the company, this means that a lot of people need to be involved. From our perspective it is not efficient to directly start the requirement elicitation on such a broad spectrum. Our approach is, to create an initial to-be process and collect first requirements within a small team (core team). Therefore it is important that the members of such a team are covering all relevant parts of the company and have expertise in their work areas.

The used modeling methodology is the Integrated Enterprise Modeling (IEM) which is fully object oriented [16]. The methodology is extended in order to integrate requirements as a self-contained object. In addition, the IEM is also conform to the international standard ISO 19440 (constructs for enterprise modeling) [17] which ensures compatibility with other methodologies and tools. Since IEM models support hierarchies, a synchronized process and requirement hierarchy is defined (Fig. 2).

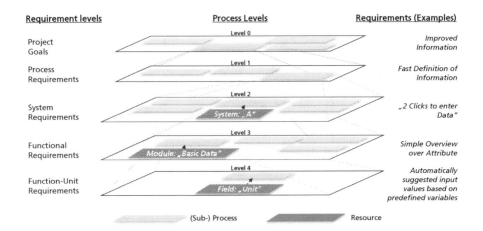

Fig. 2. Example of the process and requirements hierarchy

According to that hierarchy, each subsequent level is more detailed and the granularity of the descriptions is increased for both the processes and requirements. On the highest level (Level 0), the overall business processes are described in a highly abstract fashion. The major project goals (e.g. "improved information") were connected to these process steps. On the next level of description (Level 1), actual process requirements are described and connected (e.g. "fast definition of information"). The third level (Level 2) deals with system requirements (e.g. "2 clicks to enter data"). These system requirements were directly linked to one or more process steps, so that requirements which cannot be linked to any of these process steps are not taken into account, because they obviously have no relevance for the business processes. On the next two levels (Level 3 and 4) explicit functional and function-unit requirements were described and linked to corresponding elements.

Besides the IEM, the process modelling tool MO²GO needs to be extended as well. MO²GO, which fully supports the IEM, is a tool to display, analyze and engineer enterprise structures and processes. The client/server-based architecture of MO²GO allows the simultaneous modelling by different users.

To support requirement modelling, MO²GO needs to be extended to define requirements and link them to business processes. The requirement can be defined in two ways, either in the form of free text or by using a predefined template (which can easily be adapted to the project and/or customer needs). The same applies to the specific requirement elicitation methods. As the process step is a good starting point to define system requirements, the application of specific requirements elicitation methods ensures the envisaged completeness and helps to reveal interesting requirements, because they force the participants to think "out of the box". Our methodology integrates methods/templates like *Snow Cards [6], the Osborn-Checklist [18], Brainstorming-Paradox [19]* and *Context-Description-Templates*.

Besides these requirements which can directly be linked to any process step, some process independent requirements exist, which cannot be linked to a single process step. Such requirements (e.g. availability, scalability) are also elicited from the system perspective in order to create a holistic requirements specification. Naturally, these requirements can be linked to existing processes (like the maintenance of the system), as well. Since these processes are not within the focus of the applied business processes, such requirements are defined as process independent.

The third step of the procedure is the validation and extension of such initial integrated process and requirements system. Therefore, all relevant stakeholders need to be involved. Our approach involves a procedure with two stages, based on workshops and decentralized participation. At first, a group of representatives consisting of all relevant stakeholder groups will take part in the first of two workshops where the current results were extended and presented as well as validated. Afterwards, the participants were obliged to disseminate this information within their organizational units to acquire further feedback. Parallel to this, the current results (processes and requirements) are published online via the Process Assistant (PA) [20]. It has been developed to publish IEM based enterprise models online for a larger audience than the modeling experts in order to support employees in their daily business. It is used for centrally providing detailed process descriptions as well as all process relevant information, especially requirements including their connections, hierarchy and attributes. Additionally, a comment function was introduced to gather feedback from the stakeholders. This feedback is then finally discussed within a second workshop.

The result of step three is an integrated process and requirements system that is extended and validated by all relevant stakeholders. In the fourth step, this system is used to create the final requirements specification automatically. Therefore the information within the integrated enterprise model will be automatically transformed into a document (MS Word and PDF). In addition, via the Process Assistant, an interactive version of that requirements specification is made available via the intranet.

The final step is the trace, monitor and adaption phase. This phase runs parallel to the actual development (coding) of the IT system. The main tasks within this step are the monitoring and tracing of the requirements according to their system implementation/specification. Also included is the adaption of the business processes according to any changes resulting from the system development. Since the system specification is often realized based on different development approaches (e.g. SCRUM vs. "classical") and with specific tools (e.g. JIRA [21]) we established a synchronization between both worlds (Fig. 3). This prevents the development of software artefacts which are not related to any requirements and facilitates the identification of requirements which were not yet covered by any system specification / implementation.

The developers can keep track of the implementation phase with their tools (e.g. JIRA). The requirements are transferred from MO²GO into such tools (XML-based) wherein they are interlinked with development artifacts (e.g. user stories). A developed synchronization client ensures consistent data between MO²GO (and therefore the Process Assistant and the requirement app) and the used development tool, to assure the consistency of the connection between requirements and business processes. Changes to a requirement status are fetched by the MO²GO server automatically and the requirement cockpit always shows an up-to-date overview of the implementation status. This facilitates both process oriented reporting of the current development status as well as a development artifact related monitoring.

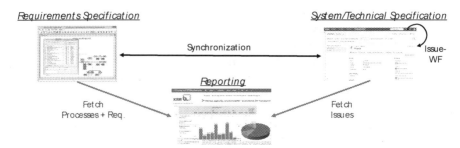

Fig. 3. Tracking and monitoring of the requirement implementation

4   Industrial Application

The integrated process and requirements management methodology described in the previous section has already been successfully applied in a software development project in a large sized company. The main goal was to create a software tool that would replace the existing one which was supporting the offer creation and order handling process. Since there were no hindrances such as old habits, we were able to reengineer the entire, overall business process according to specific process requirements such as front-loading (shift as much as possible task and process defining decisions into the early stages) and fast offer creation (time for a standard offer should not exceed 24 hours). After setting up the project framework, the work of developing the initial integrated process and requirement system could be started. In order to efficiently and timely include as many requirements and locations as possible, an expert team was created. This team consisted of ten members who were selected based on the region they hailed from and their expertise. An initial blueprint for a new offering process was created within six weeks, including the first requirements.

Two large review workshops with 80 participants were held for the extension and validation of the integrated requirements system. 800 new requirements were elicited in the first workshop, by using several methods (for example: Brainstorming Paradox, Osborn-Checklist, user stories). When it came to defining processes, the biggest challenge was to abolish old and familiar systems and to accept new methods when it came to defining processes. One clear advantage of the used modeling methodology (IEM) is, that it only consists of four model elements (order, product, resource and action), so that all workshop participants can adopt the methodology very easily and quickly.

In the time between the two workshops, participants had the assignment to validate their processes and requirements within their organizational unit. By utilizing the Process Assistant, the participants were able to observe the entire offer processes and requirements, as well as comment on them. The results were discussed, summarized and finalized in the second workshop.

The process information as well as the requirements from the integrated model were (automatically) transferred into a document. The Process Assistant was used as an interactive version of the requirements specification (Fig. 4).

With our method, the requirements specification, consisting of 2220 requirements and more than 1000 process steps was created within 5 months. In total 105 participants were directly involved. Furthermore over 600 employees of the company were partly involved (commenting, reviewing).

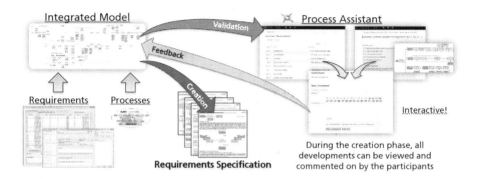

Fig. 4. Collaborative creation and validation of the processes and requirements, as well as requirements specification creation

5   Conclusion and Research Perspective

Our method is an addition to the well-established field of RE research to cover an area that has been neglected so far. We developed a holistic, integrated methodology by combining process management aspects and requirements management. This was achieved by using processes as the main angle for the elicitation and implementation period. Therefore we extended the Integrated Enterprise Modeling (IEM) Methodology and the related applications MO²GO and Process Assistant in order to include the necessary requirements perspective.

We applied our method successfully in an industrial environment. By using a high level approach, our methodology is flexible enough to adapt to individual enterprises and their demands, as well as specific requirements management methodologies. Nonetheless, it is not sufficient to simply incorporate processes into the elicitation process, because stakeholder and user involvement remains essential. Additionally, the focus on processes is insufficient by itself if it is not complimented by an in-depth elicitation, implementation and monitoring process.

Future research should focus on the longevity of these endeavors. Successful business process and requirements management is a long term endeavor [22]. The long-term perspective is oftentimes lacking in RE research and future research of this approach can fill this gap. Applying the approach to other enterprises and domains, such as product development, could also reveal potential for further development.

References

1. Panian, Z.: User Requirements Engineering and Management in Software Development. In: Mastorakis, N., Mladenov, V., Kontargyri, V.T. (eds.) Proceedings of the European Computing Conference. LNEE, vol. 28, pp. 609–620. Springer US, Boston (2009)
2. Nguyen, L., Swatman, P.A.: Managing the requirements engineering process. Requirements Engineering **8**, 55–68 (2003)
3. Jarke, M., Kethers, S., Lakemeyer, G., Gans, G.: Continuous requirements management for organisation networks: a (dis)trust-based approach. Requirements Engineering **8**, 4–22 (2003)
4. Cardoso, E., Almeida, J.P.A., Guizzardi, G.: Requirements engineering based on business process models: a case study. In: Tosic, V. (ed.) 13th Enterprise Distributed Object Computing Conference Workshops, EDOCW 2009, pp. 320–327. IEEE, New York (2009)
5. Pohl, K., Rupp, C.: Basiswissen Requirements Engineering. dpunkt-Verl, Heidelberg (2011)
6. Robertson, S., Robertson, J.: Mastering the requirements process. Addison-Wesley, Upper Saddle River (2011)
7. Rupp, C.: Requirements-Engineering und -Management. Professionelle, iterative Anforderungsanalyse für die Praxis. Hanser, München (2009)
8. Friedrich, J., Hammerschall, U., Kuhrmann, M., Sihling, M.: Das V-Modell XT. Für Projektleiter und QS-Verantwortliche kompakt und übersichtlich. Springer, Berlin (2009)
9. Barker, S.: Brilliant PRINCE2. What you really need to know about PRINCE2. Pearson Education, Harlow, UK (2013)
10. Benington, H.D.: Production of Large Computer Programs. IEEE Annals Hist. Comput. **5**, 350–361 (1983)
11. Schwaber, K.: Scrum im Unternehmen. Microsoft Press, Unterschleißheim (2008)
12. Ali, R., Dalpiaz, F., Giorgini, P.: A goal-based framework for contextual requirements modeling and analysis. Requirements Eng. **15**, 439–458 (2010)
13. De la Vara González, J.L., Sánchez Díaz, J.: Business process-driven requirements engineering: a goal-based approach (2007)
14. Neiger, D., Churilov, L.: Goal-oriented business process modeling with EPCs and value-focused thinking. In: Desel, J., Pernici, B., Weske, M. (eds.) BPM 2004. LNCS, vol. 3080, pp. 98–115. Springer, Heidelberg (2004)
15. American National Standards Institute: IEEE Guide to Software Requirements Specification, 1–24 (1984). http://ieeexplore.ieee.org/xpl/articleDetails.jsp?arnumber=278253
16. Spur, G., Mertins, K., Jochem, R.: Integrierte Unternehmensmodellierung. Beuth, Berlin (1993)
17. ISO: Enterprise integration - constructs for enterprise modelling. ISO 19440, Genève (2007)
18. Osborn, A.F.: Applied imagination. Principles and procedures of creative problem-solving. Creative Education Foundation, Buffalo, NY (1993)
19. De Bono, E.: Serious creativity. Die Entwicklung neuer Ideen durch die Kraft lateralen Denkens. Schäffer-Poeschel, Stuttgart (1996)
20. Wintrich, N.: Prozessassistent. http://www.prozessassistent.de
21. JIRA Software | Atlassian. https://www.atlassian.com/software/jira
22. Harmon, P. and Wolf, C.: The State of Business Process Management 2014 (2014). http://www.bptrends.com/bpt/wp-content/uploads/ BPTrends-State-of-BPM-Survey-Report.pdf

Supporting Structural Consistency Checking in Adaptive Case Management

Christoph Czepa[1], Huy Tran[1(✉)], Uwe Zdun[1], Stefanie Rinderle-Ma[1],
Thanh Tran Thi Kim[2], Erhard Weiss[2], and Christoph Ruhsam[2]

[1] Faculty of Computer Science, University of Vienna, Vienna, Austria
{christoph.czepa,huy.tran,uwe.zdun,stefanie.rinderle-ma}@univie.ac.at
[2] Isis Papyrus Europe AG, Maria Enzersdorf, Austria
{thanh.tran,erhard.weiss,christoph.ruhsam}@isis-papyrus.com

Abstract. Adaptive Case Management (ACM) enables knowledge workers to collaboratively handle unforeseen circumstances by making ad hoc changes of case instances at runtime. Therefore, it is crucial to ensure that various structural elements of an ACM case, such as goals, subprocesses and so on, remain consistent over time. To the best of our knowledge, no studies in the literature provide adequate support for structural consistency checking of ACM. In this paper, we introduce a formal categorization of ACM's structural features and potential inconsistencies. Based on this categorization, we develop a novel approach for structural consistency checking of ACM cases. Our approach, based on model checking and graph algorithms, can detect a wide range of inconsistencies of ACM's structural elements. The evaluation of our approach shows reasonable performance and scalability.

1 Introduction

Adaptive Case Management (ACM) is part of an emerging trend in the field of business process management that is aiming at supporting highly flexible, knowledge-intensive software systems [13]. A high degree of flexibility often comes at the cost of potential errors or inconsistencies, subsequently hampering the executability of the processes. In the context of ACM, new sources of inconsistencies occur when compared to flexible process management technology (cf. e.g., [11]). For example, a new goal could be in conflict with an existing goal or a new dependency among two tasks could make no sense because of contradicting pre- and postconditions of the tasks. Structural consistency checking focuses on revealing such internal inconsistencies and contradictions inside the structure of a case.

In this paper, we propose a novel approach for supporting structural consistency checking of ACM systems. First, we study existing ACM systems and relevant industrial standards and introduce a formal categorization of ACM's structural features and potential inconsistencies. Based on this categorization, we developed checking techniques that can discover a wide range of inconsistencies of ACM cases. Our prototype shows reasonable performance and scalability, so the proposed approach is appropriate for both runtime and design time checking.

© Springer International Publishing Switzerland 2015
C. Debruyne et al. (Eds.): OTM 2015 Conferences, LNCS 9415, pp. 311–319, 2015.
DOI: 10.1007/978-3-319-26148-5_19

2   ACM Structural Concepts and Possible Inconsistencies

In this section, we identify ACM's structural concepts and which inconsistencies can possibly occur in these structures.

2.1   Formal Definition of ACM Case Models

Our identification of ACM's structural concepts is based on a generalization of the commercial ACM solution ISIS Papyrus[1], the CMMN standard[2], and the existing ACM literature [6,9,14]. Based on this study we have derived a formal definition of a case model.

Definition 1. *A case model $\mathcal{M}$ is a tuple $(\mathcal{T}, \mathcal{G}, \mathcal{S}, \mathcal{E}, \mathcal{X}, \mathcal{C}, \mathcal{D}, \zeta_{\mathcal{E}}, \zeta_{\mathcal{X}}, \eta, \mathcal{T}_{\mathcal{F}}, \mathcal{F}, \phi, \mathcal{J}, \delta, s_m)$ where*

- *$\mathcal{T}$ is a set of tasks, $\mathcal{G}$ is a set of goals, $\mathcal{S}$ is a set of stages, $\mathcal{E}$ is a set of entry criteria, $\mathcal{X}$ is a set of exit criteria, $\mathcal{C} = \mathcal{E} \cup \mathcal{X}$ is a set of criteria,*
- *$\mathcal{D} = \mathcal{D}_{\mathcal{X}\mathcal{E}} \cup \mathcal{D}_{\mathcal{X}} \cup \mathcal{D}_{\mathcal{E}} \cup \mathcal{D}_{\mathcal{S}_{\mathcal{X}}} \cup \mathcal{D}_{\mathcal{S}_{\mathcal{E}}} \cup \mathcal{D}_{\mathcal{N}}$ is a set of dependencies, where*
  - *$\mathcal{D}_{\mathcal{X}\mathcal{E}} \subsetneq \mathcal{X} \times \mathcal{E}$ is a set of dependencies from exit to entry criteria,*
  - *$\mathcal{D}_{\mathcal{X}} \subsetneq \mathcal{X} \times (\mathcal{T} \cup \mathcal{S})$ is a set of dependencies from exit criteria to tasks, and stages,*
  - *$\mathcal{D}_{\mathcal{E}} \subsetneq (\mathcal{T} \cup \mathcal{G} \cup \mathcal{S}) \times \mathcal{E}$ is a set of dependencies from tasks, goals, and stages to entry criteria,*
  - *$\mathcal{D}_{\mathcal{S}_{\mathcal{X}}} \subsetneq (\mathcal{T} \cup \mathcal{G} \cup \mathcal{S} \cup \mathcal{X}) \times \mathcal{X}$ is a set of dependencies from stage internal tasks, stages, goals, and exit criteria to exit criteria of the stage.*
  - *$\mathcal{D}_{\mathcal{S}_{\mathcal{E}}} \subsetneq \mathcal{E} \times (\mathcal{T} \cup \mathcal{S} \cup \mathcal{E})$ is a set of dependencies from entry criteria of a stage to stage internal tasks, stages, and entry criteria.*
  - *$\mathcal{D}_{\mathcal{N}} \subsetneq (\mathcal{T} \cup \mathcal{G} \cup \mathcal{S}) \times (\mathcal{T} \cup \mathcal{S})$ is a set of dependencies from tasks, goals and stages to tasks and stages.*
- *$\zeta_{\mathcal{E}} : \mathcal{E} \mapsto \mathcal{T} \cup \mathcal{G} \cup \mathcal{S}$ is a total non-injective function which maps an entry criterion to a task, goal, or stage,*
- *$\zeta_{\mathcal{X}} : \mathcal{X} \mapsto \mathcal{T} \cup \mathcal{S}$ is a total non-injective function which maps an exit criterion to a task or stage,*
- *$\eta : \mathcal{G} \mapsto \mathcal{G}$ is a partial non-injective function which maps a goal to a parent goal*
- *$\mathcal{T}_{\mathcal{F}} \subsetneq \mathcal{T}$ is a set of process tasks, $\mathcal{F}$ is a set of subprocesses,*
- *$\phi : \mathcal{T}_{\mathcal{F}} \mapsto \mathcal{F}$ is a total function which maps a process task to a subprocess,*
- *$\mathcal{J} = \mathcal{C} \cup \bigcup_{p \in \mathcal{F}} p.\mathcal{B}$ is the joint set of criteria and conditions of all subprocesses,*
- *$\delta : \mathcal{T} \cup \mathcal{G} \cup \mathcal{S} \mapsto \mathcal{S}$ is a partial non-injective function which maps a task, goal, or stage to a parent stage, and*
- *$s_m \in \mathcal{S}$ is the main stage of the case (equivalent to a Case element in CMMN).*

2.2   Possible Inconsistencies in ACM's Structural Concepts

Dependencies among elements in ACM can be arranged to form loops. Table 1 shows two kinds of loop-related inconsistencies in ACM. If the elements in a

---

[1] http://www.isis-papyrus.com
[2] http://www.omg.org/spec/CMMN/1.0/PDF

Table 1. Loop-Related Inconsistencies in ACM

Naming	CMMN Example	ISIS Papyrus Example
Inaccessible Dependency Loop		
Potential Endless Loop		Not possible (due to hierarchical organization of goals)

loop formed by dependencies are generally inaccessible, then we call this kind of inconsistency *Inaccessible Dependency Loop*. In the given example in Table 1, *Task 1* is dependent on *Task 2* and *Task 2* is dependent on *Task 1*. Neither one is accessible due to this arrangement. Another inconsistency related to loops is called *Potential Endless Loop*, and it is found in parts of the model where loops do not include user interaction. In the example in Table 1 there is a dependency from *Goal 1* to *Goal 2* and another dependency from *Goal 2* to *Goal 1*. Because of the lack of user interactions in between these goals, there is a possibility that the case execution engine continuously reenters *Goal 1* and *Goal 2* until an action independent from this loop changes data states in a way to eventually break the loop.

Pre- and postconditions of tasks, completion criteria of goals, and dependencies among case elements are important and recurring mechanisms in ACM that guard the access to certain elements of a case, dependent on the case's data state. Table 2 summarizes inconsistencies in ACM definitions that are related to guarding constraints. If we observe just a single constraint, this isolated constraint must be inherently consistent. A simple example for a *Self-Contradictory Constraint* is `data.value == true && data.value != true` because the logical and-connected parts of this constraint can never be satisfied at the same time. We reuse this straightforward example of an unsatisfiable combination of constraints for the other possible inconsistencies that are shown in Table 2. *Directly Dependent Contradictory Constraints* occur if a dependency is defined between two constraints that contradict each other. *And-Dependent Contradictory Constraints* are contradictory constraints that are not explicitly connected by a single dependency but by an arrangement that links them together. Table 2 illustrates such an arrangement where the postconditions of both *Task 1.1* and *Task 1.2* must be met in order to allow a start of *Task 2*. Constraints in subprocesses or substructures can be contradictory to constraints of their surrounding structures. Table 2 illustrates an example of *Substructure- or Subprocess-induced Contradictions* in which the guard condition that is defined on the sequence flow in front of the end event contradicts the completion criterion of the goal. Regularly, there exist larger structures of interdependent constraints that can be composed of the aforementioned structures. An example for an *Unsatisfiable Composition of Interdependent Constraints* is given in Table 2 in which the *Main Goal* has a constraint structure that contains contradictory constraints. In particular, the

Table 2. Constraint-Related Inconsistencies in ACM

Naming	CMMN Example	ISIS Papyrus Example
Self-Contradictory Constraint	Task — Exit Criterion: data.value == true && data.value != true	Task — Postconstraint: data.value is true and data.value is false
Directly Dependent Contradictory Constraints	Task 1 ⟷ Task 2 — Exit Criterion: data.value != true Entry Criterion: data.value == true	Task 1 → Task 2 — Postconstraint: data.value is false Preconstraint: data.value is true
And-Dependent Contradictory Constraints	Exit Criterion: data.value == true — Task 1.1 / Task 1.2 → Task 2 — Exit Criterion: data.value != true	Postconstraint: data.value is true — Task 1.1 / Task 1.2 → Task 2 — Postconstraint: data.value is false
Substructure- or Subprocess-induced Contradictions	Subprocess — Task → Guard Condition: data.value == true — Entry Criterion: data.value != true / Goal	Guard Condition: data.value is true — Completion Criterion: data.value is false
Unsatisfiable Composition of Interdependent Constraints	Exit Criterion: data.value == true — Main Goal / Task 1 — Goal 2 / Goal 1 — Entry Criterion: data.value != true	Postcondition: data.value is true — Case Goal / Goal 2 / Goal 1 / Task — Completion Criterion: data.value is false
Conflicting Goals in Goal Hierarchies	Main Goal — Subgoal 1 / Subgoal 2 — data.value == true data.value != true	Case Goal — data.value is true data.value is false — Goal 2 / Goal 1

postcondition of *Task 1* contradicts the completion criterion of *Goal 2*. Such compositions can comprise several aforementioned structures. In the example, directly dependent constraints are combined with and-dependent constraints in a bigger, composite structure. Goals can be structured hierarchically [6,14]. On top of the hierarchy stands the main goal of a case which is subdivided into subgoals. In Table 2, an example of a goal hierarchy is given. Naturally, pursuing contradictory goals simultaneously would not make any sense. Knowledge workers can work towards *Subgoal 1* and *Subgoal 2* concurrently, so their completion criteria must not be contradictory.

3   Structural Consistency Checking Approach for ACM

This section introduces our proposed approach for enabling structural consistency checking in ACM. Our approach leverages model checking and graph algorithms.

Model checking performs an exhaustive check whether a model meets a given specification. A model is often defined as a state transition system, whereas specifications are usually defined in a formal language such as Computation Tree Logic (CTL). The CTL expression $EF\ p$ is satisfied if the expression p holds on at least one subsequent path. Since model checking works faster when the state space is smaller, it is a good strategy to look at isolated parts of the model first (Definitions 2, 3 and 4).

Definition 2. (Self-Contradictory Constraint) *A constraint $c \in \mathcal{J}$ is self-contradictory iff $\neg\,(EF\,(c))$.*

Definition 3. (Directly Dependent Contradictory Constraints) *Two constraints $c \in \mathcal{C}$ and $c' \in \mathcal{C}$ which are directly linked by a dependency $(c, c') \in \mathcal{D}_{\mathcal{X}\mathcal{E}} \cup \mathcal{D}_{\mathcal{S}_{\mathcal{X}}} \cup \mathcal{D}_{\mathcal{S}_{\mathcal{E}}}$ are contradictory iff $\neg\,(EF\,(e \wedge e'))$.*

Definition 4. (And-Dependent Contradictory Constraints) *Two constraints $c \in \mathcal{C}$ and $c' \in \mathcal{C}$ which are and-dependent because $\exists((c, t) \wedge (c', t')) \mid (c, t) \in \mathcal{D} \wedge (c', t') \in \mathcal{D} \wedge t = t' \wedge c \in \mathcal{C} \wedge c' \in \mathcal{C} \wedge t \in \mathcal{C} \wedge t' \in \mathcal{C}$ are contradictory iff $\neg\,(EF\,(e \wedge e'))$.*

The remainder of this section is concerned with finding contradictions in larger structures. We focus exemplary on *Dependency Loops* and *Goal Hierarchies*.

3.1   Dependency Loops

Definition 5. (Case Graph) *$G_{\mathcal{M}} = (V, E)$ is a directed graph representation of $\mathcal{M}$, where $V = \mathcal{T} \cup \mathcal{G} \cup \mathcal{S} \cup \mathcal{C} \cup \mathcal{D}$ is a set of vertices. E is a set of edges which is created as follows:*

- *An edge $(e, \zeta_{\mathcal{E}}\,(e))$ is added for every $e \mid e \in \mathcal{E}$.*
- *An edge $(\zeta_{\mathcal{X}}\,(x)\,, x)$ is added for every $x \mid x \in \mathcal{X}$.*

– An edge (f, d) is added for every $d = (f, t) \in \mathcal{D}$.
– An edge (d, t) is added for every $d = (f, t) \in \mathcal{D}$.

Definition 6. *A dependency loop $\circlearrowleft$ is given as a strongly connected component (SCC) of $G_\mathcal{M}$.*

The set of strongly connected components can be computed by Tarjan's algorithm [15].

Definition 7. (Inaccessible Dependency Loop) *A dependency loop $\circlearrowleft$ is inaccessible iff $(\nexists e \mid e \in \mathcal{E} \land \zeta_\mathcal{E}(e) \in \circlearrowleft \land e \notin \circlearrowleft) \land (\nexists d = (f, t) \mid d \in \mathcal{D} \land d \notin \circlearrowleft \land t \in \circlearrowleft \land t \in T \cup S)$*

According to this definition, a dependency loop is accessible if there exists at least either

– one entry criterion which is attached to an element of the dependency loop but is not part of the loop, or
– a dependency which points to a task or stage of the loop without being in the loop.

3.2   Goal Hierarchies

For the verification of hierarchically structured goals, we first find pairs of goals which are possibly in contradiction to each other.

Definition 8. *A goal $g \in \{x \mid x \in \mathcal{G} \land \exists \eta(x)\}\}$ is possibly in contradiction with a goal g' iff $g' \in \mathcal{G} \setminus \mathcal{G}_\eta$ where $\mathcal{G}_\eta$ is the set of parent goals of g which can be found by recursive use of η (i.e., $\eta(g), \eta(\eta(g)), \eta(\eta(\eta(g))), ...$) until η returns no further parent goal.*

Then, we can check each found possibly contradictory goal pair (g, g'). Let $g.\mathcal{E}$ denote the set of entry criteria of g and $g'.\mathcal{E}$ be the set of entry criteria of g'.

Definition 9. *(Conflicting Goals in Goal Hierarchies) Two goals g and g' are contradictory iff they are possibly in contradiction to each other (cf. Definition 8) and the formula $EF(e \land e')$ does not hold for at least one $\{e, e'\} \mid e \in g.\mathcal{E} \land e' \in g'.\mathcal{E}$.*

4   Experimental Results

Model checking is known for its high demands on computational resources. Therefore, we conducted an experiment on the performance and scalability of our approach. In this experiment, we measure the response times that are to be expected while checking a combination of string constraints with the NuSMV model checker version 2.5.4 [2]. In particular, an *and-connected* constraint term that contains between 1 and 50 string variables is created. Furthermore, the number of possible string values of each variable is between 1 and 50. This scenario is representative for checking large structures of interdependent

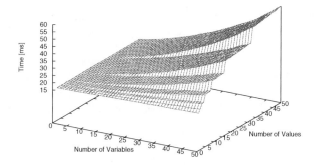

Fig. 1. Results of performance and scalability evaluation

constraints in ACM systems because a high count of interdependent constraints is to be expected. The experiment was carried out on a computer with 8 GB RAM, Intel i5-4200U CPU and SATA II SSD, as we wanted to test our approach in the usual setting of a software developer or knowledge worker. The experiment was repeated 1000 times which resulted in sufficient data. The reported values shown in Figure 1 represent the median of our measurements which is stable against statistical outliers (e.g., caused by OS activities that we cannot control). Studying the averages yields similar results and the standard deviation is not significant. Even with a large number of variables and values, the response time of the model checker stays far below 100 ms, which is still reasonable for checking large problems.

5   Related Work

Formal verification encompasses techniques such as model checking or Petri net based approaches to assert whether a model definition satisfies certain properties. Kherbouche et al. use the SPIN model checker[3] to find structural errors in BPMN 2 models [7]. Eshuis proposes a model checking approach using the NuSMV model checker for the verification of UML activity diagrams [5]. Van der Aalst defines a mapping of EPCs to Petri nets for checking structural errors [1]. Sbai et al. use SPIN for the verification of workflow nets [12]. Raedts et al. propose the transformation of models such as UML activity diagrams and BPMN 2 models to Petri nets for verification with Petri net analyzers [10]. Köhler et al. describe a process by means of an automaton and check this automaton by NuSMV [8]. El-Saber et al. [4] provide a formalization of BPMN and translate BPMN constructs to the Maude model checker [3]. None of the existing approaches proposes structural consistency checking for ACM.

---

[3] http://spinroot.com

6   Conclusion and Future Work

This paper discusses structural consistency checking of ACM. We discuss structural concepts of ACM and what inconsistencies can possibly occur in such structures. As our main contribution, we propose structural consistency checking of ACM definitions that leverages model checking and graph algorithms. Our approach is able to discover various structural inconsistencies in ACM cases. The experimental results show that our consistency checking scales well. Our approach strives for computational efficiency despite the use of model checking. This is achieved by dividing the problem of checking structural consistency of entire case models into smaller problems. As a result, if already a single isolated constraint is self-contradictory, it is not necessary to check it as part of a bigger structure that demands greater computational effort. The approach has been developed in a prototype for an industrial system and tested with real cases.

Acknowledgment. The research leading to these results has received funding from the FFG project CACAO, no. 843461 and the WWTF project CONTAINER, Grant No. ICT12-001.

References

1. Van der Aalst, W.M.P.: Formalization and verification of event-driven process chains. Information and Software Technology **41**(10), 639–650 (1999)
2. Cimatti, A., Clarke, E., Giunchiglia, F., Roveri, M.: NUSMV: A new symbolic model verifier. In: Halbwachs, N., Peled, D.A. (eds.) CAV 1999. LNCS, vol. 1633, pp. 495–499. Springer, Heidelberg (1999)
3. Eker, S., Meseguer, J., Sridharanarayanan, A.: The maude LTL model checker and its implementation. In: Ball, T., Rajamani, S.K. (eds.) SPIN 2003. LNCS, vol. 2648, pp. 230–234. Springer, Heidelberg (2003)
4. El-Saber, N., Boronat, A.: BPMN formalization and verification using maude. In: 2014 Workshop on Behaviour Modelling-Foundations and Applications (BM-FA), pp. 1:1–1:12. ACM (2014)
5. Eshuis, R.: Symbolic model checking of UML activity diagrams. ACM Trans. Softw. Eng. Methodol. **15**(1), 1–38 (2006)
6. Greenwood, D.P.A.: Goal-oriented autonomic business process modeling and execution: engineering change management demonstration. In: Dumas, M., Reichert, M., Shan, M.-C. (eds.) BPM 2008. LNCS, vol. 5240, pp. 390–393. Springer, Heidelberg (2008)
7. Kherbouche, O., Ahmad, A., Basson, H.: Using model checking to control the structural errors in BPMN models. In: 7th Intl. Conf. on RCIS, pp. 1–12 (2013)
8. Koehler, J., Tirenni, G., Kumaran, S.: From business process model to consistent implementation: a case for formal verification methods. In: 6th Intl. Conf. on EDOC, pp. 96–106 (2002)
9. Pucher, M.J.: Considerations for implementing adaptive case management. In: Fischer, L. (ed.) Taming the Unpredictable Real World Adaptive Case Management: Case Studies and Practical Guidance. Future Strategies Inc. (2011)

10. Raedts, I., Petković, M., Usenko, Y.S., van der Werf, J.M., Groote, J.F., Somers, L.: Transformation of BPMN models for behaviour analysis. In: MSVVEIS, pp. 126–137. INSTICC (2007)
11. Rinderle-Ma, S., Reichert, M., Dadam, P.: Correctness criteria for dynamic changes in workflow systems: A survey. Data & Knowledge Engineering **50**(1), 9 (2004)
12. Sbai, Z., Missaoui, A., Barkaoui, K., Ben Ayed, R.: On the verification of business processes by model checking techniques. In: 2nd Intl. Conf. on ICSTE, vol. 1, pp. 97–103, October 2010
13. Schonenberg, H., Mans, R., Russell, N., Mulyar, N., van der Aalst, W.: Process flexibility: A survey of contemporary approaches. In: Dietz, J.L.G., Albani, A., Barjis, J. (eds.) CIAO! 2008 and EOMAS 2008. LNBIP, vol. 10, pp. 16–30. Springer, Heidelberg (2008)
14. Stavenko, Y., Kazantsev, N., Gromoff, A.: Business process model reasoning: From workflow to case management. Procedia Technology **9**, 806–811 (2013)
15. Tarjan, R.: Depth first search and linear graph algorithms. SIAM Journal on Computing (1972)

A Probabilistic Unified Framework
for Event Abstraction and Process Detection
from Log Data

Bettina Fazzinga[2]([✉]), Sergio Flesca[1], Filippo Furfaro[1], Elio Masciari[2],
and Luigi Pontieri[2]

[1] DIMES, University of Calabria, Rende, Italy
{flesca,furfaro}@dimes.unical.it
[2] ICAR-CNR, Rende, Italy
{fazzinga,masciari,pontieri}@icar.cnr.it

Abstract. We consider the scenario where the executions of different business processes are traced into a log, where each trace describes a process instance as a sequence of low-level events (representing basic kinds of operations). In this context, we address a novel problem: given a description of the processes' behaviors in terms of high-level activities (instead of low-level events), and in the presence of uncertainty in the mapping between events and activities, find all the interpretations of each trace Φ. Specifically, an interpretation is a pair $\langle \sigma, W \rangle$ that provides a two-level "explanation" for Φ: σ is a sequence of activities that may have triggered the events in Φ, and W is a process whose model admits σ. To solve this problem, we propose a probabilistic framework representing "consistent" Φ's interpretations, where each interpretation is associated with a probability score.

1 Introduction

Thanks to the diffusion of various automated process management and tracing platforms, many process logs (i.e., collections of execution traces) have become available. Log data can be exploited to analyze and improve the processes, by possibly using process mining techniques [2], such as those for inducing a process model [1], for checking whether log traces comply to a model [3], and for quantifying "how much" a log and a model conform one to the other [7].

All of these techniques, however, require log events to be univocally mapped to activity concepts corresponding to some high-level view of the process, suitable for the analysis. For example, in order to evaluate the compliance (or the conformance) of a log w.r.t. a given process model, it is necessary that each event in the log refers to one of the activities that appear in the model. Unfortunately, this assumption does not hold often in practice. As a matter of fact, in logs of many real systems, the recorded events just represent low-level operations, with no clear reference to the business activities that were carried out through these operations, as shown in the following example.

© Springer International Publishing Switzerland 2015
C. Debruyne et al. (Eds.): OTM 2015 Conferences, LNCS 9415, pp. 320–328, 2015.
DOI: 10.1007/978-3-319-26148-5_20

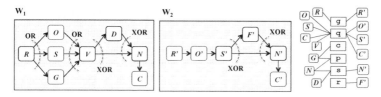

Fig. 1. Two process models (left and middle), and all the possible mappings between their activities and the low-level event types, shown inside dashed squares, that occur in the log (right).

Example 1. Consider the case of a phone company, where two business processes are carried out: 1) service activation, and 2) issue management. Assume that an abstract description of the behaviors of the two processes above is available, encoded by two models, named W_1 and W_2 and sketched in Fig. 1 in the form of *precedence graphs*. Therein, nodes and edges (some of which are labeled with typical split/join constraints) represent activities and precedence links, respectively. Basically, these models describe the corresponding processes in terms of high-level activities. In particular, W_1 (service activation) features the set of activities $\mathcal{A}_{W_1} = \{$ R *(Receive a service request)*, O *(Open a new case)*, S *(Select a service package)*, G *(Gather more information on the customer)*, V *(Validate the package)*, D *(Dispatch a contract proposal)*, N *(Notify the request's outcome)*, C *(Close the case)*$\}$. Analogously, W_2 (issue notification) features $\mathcal{A}_{W_2} = \{$ R' *(Receive a request of help)*, O' *(Open a ticket)*, S' *(Search the issue in a knowledge base)*, F' *(Fix the issue)*, N' *(Notify the solution)*, C' *(Close the ticket)*$\}$[1].

All these activities are performed via low-level operations (provided by different collaborative-work tools, including databases and communication services) that correspond to instances of the following event types: g (resp., s, c, p): *getting an email from* (resp., *sending an email to, opening a chat session with, making a phone call to*) *a customer*; r: *delivering a report*; q: *posing a query against a database*. Thus, performing any activity results in the execution of one of the above events, and the correspondence between event and activity types is *many to many*, as depicted on the right-hand side of Fig. 1. For instance, activity G *(Gather more information on the customer)* can be accomplished by either *opening a chat session with the customer* (event c) or *making a phone call to the customer* (event p). Analogously, an instance of event p can be generated by the execution of either activity G or N.

The enactments of the processes is monitored by a tracing system that stores the executions of the low-level operations triggered during the process execution. Hence, an instance of process W_1 consisting in the execution of the sequence $R\,S\,G\,V\,N\,C$ can be stored in the log as the (low-level event) *trace* g q p q s q, or as the trace g q c q p q, depending on the low-level operations triggered by each activity instance.   □

---

[1] Two disjoint sets of activities are here shown for the two models only for the sake of readability. In fact, our approach can deal with activities shared by an arbitrary number of process models.

In such a setting, we address a novel challenging analysis problem: given a log L (possibly containing traces generated by different processes), and a set $\mathcal{W}$ of candidate process models (encoded each as a set of behavioral constraints), we want to assess whether each trace in L can be regarded as an instance of each model in $\mathcal{W}$, and to what degree of confidence. In order to support such analysis, we need to *interpret* each step of the trace (i.e. each low-level event registered in the trace) as the execution of an activity from one of the process models, so that the whole trace can be eventually viewed as a instance of that model.

Example 2 (contd.). Consider the trace $\Phi=$ gqqssq. In order to interpret Φ as the result of an execution of the models in Fig. 1, we should first translate Φ into a sequence of activities σ (by interpreting each of its events as the execution of a single activity), and then interpreting σ as an instance of W_1 or W_2. Actually, as each event can have different causes (in terms of activities that have generated it), Φ may admit multiple sequences of activities "explaining" it. In turn, the same sequence of activities may be compatible with different process models. Hence, there can be multiple reasonable interpretations of Φ as a pair $\langle \sigma, W \rangle$ (where σ is a sequence of activities and W a process): those where the mappings event/activity used for obtaining σ agree with the right-hand side of Fig. 1, and σ complies with the model of W.

It is easy to see that, based on this reasoning, the only valid interpretations for Φ consist in viewing it as generated by either the sequence $ROV\,DNC$ or $RSV\,DNC$, and viewing both these sequences as generated by an instance of process W_1. In fact, any other translation of Φ into a sequence of activities consistent with the event-activity mappings in Fig. 1 does not conform to any process model.   □

Contribution. We propose a probabilistic framework for facing the interpretation problem above in a uniform synergistic way, at both mapping levels (i.e. events vs. activities, and traces vs. process models). As a matter of fact, current log abstraction techniques [4–6] do not approach this problem adequately, as they do not address the specific "interpretation" problem faced in this paper.

The ultimate result of our approach is a "conditioned interpretation set" (named *ci-set*) for each input trace Φ, which stores, for each candidate model W, the probability that Φ is an instance of W, along with probabilistically-scored mappings between the steps of Φ and instances of the activities in W. Technically, we first introduce a model for formally describing the structure of each process (via precedence constraints), and for probabilistically ranking the event-activity and trace-process mappings (via a-priori probabilities). Next, based on this model, we describe the conditioning approach for encoding all and only the interpretations of the input trace Φ, which are consistent with the structure of the processes, and the probabilities assigned to the mappings from each step of Φ to an activity, and from the whole Φ to a process. Preliminary experiments on a real-life scenario, prove that the approach is effective yet not efficient enough.

2 Preliminaries

Logs, Traces, Processes, Activities and Events. A log is a set of *traces*.
Each trace Φ describes a process instance at the abstraction level of basic *events*,
each generated by the execution of an activity. That is, an instance w of a *process*
W is the execution of a sequence $A_1, \ldots, A_m$ of *activities*; in turn, the execution
of each activity A_i generates an instance e_i of an event E_i; hence, the trace
describing w consists in the sequence $e_1, \ldots, e_m$ of event instances. For any event
e_i occurring in a trace, we assume that the starting time point of its execution
is represented in the log, and denote it as $e_i.t_s$.

In the following, we assume given the sets $\mathcal{W}$, $\mathcal{A}$, $\mathcal{E}$ of (types of) processes,
activities, and events, respectively, and denote their elements with upper-case
alphabetical symbols (such as W, A, E). Process-, activity-, and event- instances
will be denoted with lower-case symbols (such as w, a, e).

Given an event instance e, we denote the event of which it is an instance as
$E\text{-}type(e)$.

Composition Rules for the Processes (Process Models). We assume that
every process $W \in \mathcal{W}$ is "regulated" by a *"composition rule"*, that restricts
the sequences of activities that are allowed to be executed when W is enacted.
Basically, the composition rule associated with W is a pair $\langle ActSet, \mathcal{IC} \rangle$ (whose
members will be also denoted as $W.ActSet$ and $W.\mathcal{IC}$, respectively), where *Act-
Set* is the set of activities that are allowed to be executed within any instance of
W, and $\mathcal{IC}$ is a set of constraints of the form $A \Rightarrow_T B$ (called *must-constraint*)
or $A \Rightarrow_T \neg B$ (called *not-constraint*), where $A, B \in \mathcal{A}$ and T is of the form '$\leq c$',
where c is a constant. Basically, $A \Rightarrow_T B$ (resp., $A \Rightarrow_T \neg B$) imposes that, within
every instance of W, the beginning of an instance a of A always (resp., never)
precedes the beginning of an instance b of B such that the width of the interval
between the starting times of a and b satisfies T. Omitting T is equivalent to
specifying $T =$'$\leq \infty$'. The set of composition rules associated with the processes
in $\mathcal{W}$ will be denoted as $\mathcal{CR}$.

Correspondence Between Events and Activities. Under the above-
discussed assumption that the execution of an activity generates one event
instance, we consider the general case that the correspondence between activities and event types is *many to many*: different instances of the same event can
be generated by executions of different activities, and vice versa. For instance,
with reference to Example 1 (see Fig.1), activity G (*Gather more information
on the customer*) can generate an instance of either event c (*opening a chat
session...*) or of event p (*making a phone call...*), while an instance of event p
can be generated by both the activities G and N (*Notify the request's outcome*).

Given an event $E \in \mathcal{E}$, we denote as $cand\text{-}act(E)$ the set of activities whose
execution is known to possibly generate an instance of E. In turn, given an
instance e of E, we use $cand\text{-}act(e)$ as a shorthand for $cand\text{-}act(E\text{-}type(e))$:
basically, $cand\text{-}act(e)$ contains every "candidate" activity A such that e can be
viewed as the result of executing A.

3   The Interpretation Problem and Our Approach for Solving It

Problem Statement. The problem addressed in this paper is that of "interpreting" an input trace $\Phi = e_1 \ldots e_m$ from an event log. This means deciding, for each e_i of Φ, the activity $A_i \in cand\text{-}act(e_i)$ whose execution generated e_i, and, in turn, the process W whose execution caused the sequence of activities $A_1 \ldots A_m$ to be performed. When deciding this, the models of the processes encoded by the composition rules in $\mathcal{CR}$ must be taken into account.

More formally, the solution of an instance $\Phi = e_1 \ldots e_m$ of this problem is called *interpretation for Φ consistent with $\mathcal{CR}$* (or, simply, *consistent interpretation*, when Φ and $\mathcal{CR}$ are understood), and is a pair $\langle \sigma, W \rangle$, where:

- σ is called *sequence-interpretation* and is a sequence $A_1 \ldots A_m$ of activities, where each A_j is in $cand\text{-}act(e_i)$, meaning that each e_j is interpreted as the result of executing an instance of the activity A_j;
- W is called *process-interpretation*, meaning that Φ is interpreted as the result of an execution of the process W;
- σ conforms to the composition rule of W.

Example 3. Given $\mathcal{W} = \{W_1, W_2\}$, $\mathcal{A} = \{A, B, C\}$, $\mathcal{E} = \{E_1, E_2, E_3\}$, let $\langle \mathcal{A}, \{A \Rightarrow B; A \Rightarrow C\} \rangle$ be the composition rule of W_1, and $\langle \mathcal{A}, \{B \Rightarrow A; B \Rightarrow \neg C\} \rangle$ the composition rule of W_2. Moreover, assume that $cand\text{-}act(E_1) = \{A\}$, $cand\text{-}act(E_2) = \{B\}$, $cand\text{-}act(E_3) = \{A, B, C\}$. Consider the trace $\Phi = e_1 e_2 e_3$, where $E\text{-}type(e_1) = E_1$, $E\text{-}type(e_2) = E_2$, $E\text{-}type(e_3) = E_3$. If we consider only the correspondence between events and activities encoded by $cand\text{-}act(\cdot)$, Φ can be interpreted as the result of executing one of the following sequences of activities: $\sigma_1 = A\,B\,A$, or $\sigma_2 = A\,B\,B$, or $\sigma_3 = A\,B\,C$. It is easy to see that $\sigma_1 = A\,B\,A$ is inconsistent with the composition rule of W_1, but consistent with that of W_2; $\sigma_2 = A\,B\,B$ is inconsistent with both the composition rules of W_1 and W_2; finally, $\sigma_1 = A\,B\,C$ is consistent with the composition rule of W_1, but inconsistent with that of W_2. Hence, there are two consistent interpretations for Φ: $\langle A\,B\,C, W_1 \rangle$ and $\langle A\,B\,A, W_2 \rangle$.   □

Dealing with the Interpretation Problem in Probabilistic Terms. The above example describes an instance of the interpretation problem admitting multiple solutions. This situation is likely to happen frequently, for the following reasons: 1) the correspondence between events and activities is many to many, thus an event instance can be interpreted as the result of different activity executions; 2) the description of the process models provided by composition rules can be rather "loose", thus there can be process instances consistent with the composition rules of different processes: that is, the execution of a sequence of activities can be interpreted as the execution of different processes.

The presence of this uncertainty suggests to address the interpretation problem in probabilistic terms. Under the probabilistic perspective, the problem becomes that of finding all the consistent interpretations, and associating each of them with the probability of being the actual one. A starting point for probabilistically addressing the interpretation problem could be that of modeling the correspondence between events and activities probabilistically. In this direction, we assume that the many-to-many correspondence between events and activities is modeled by a probability distribution function (pdf) $p^a(A|E)$ returning the *a-priori* probability that an instance of event E is generated by an execution of A. For instance, $p^a(A_1|E_1) = 0.75$ and $p^a(A_2|E_1) = 0.25$ means that any instance of event E_1 is generated by the execution of either A_1 or A_2, and that the former case is three times more probable than the latter. This pdf is said to be *a-priori* since it assigns probabilities to the different ways of interpreting an event in terms of an activity execution, without looking at the context where the event instance happened. That is, it provides an interpretation for the events that occur in a trace without looking at the other events occurring in the trace.

Analogously, we assume given a pdf $p^a(W)$ over $\mathcal{W}$, assigning to each $W \in \mathcal{W}$ the *a-priori* probability that a trace in a log encodes an instance of W. For instance, given $\mathcal{W} = \{W_1, W_2\}$, $p^a(W_1) = p^a(W_2) = 0.5$ means that, in the absence of further knowledge, W_1 and W_2 are equi-probable interpretations of any trace.

It is worth noting that assuming that $p^a(A|E)$ and $p^a(W)$ are known is realistic: as done in our experiments, these pdfs can be obtained by computing statistics taken from historical data, or by encoding domain-expert knowledge.

We now show how the pdfs $p^a(A|E)$ and $p^a(W)$ can be exploited as a basis for probabilistically addressing the interpretation problem. We start by introducing a naive approach (that will be used in the experiments as term of comparison) and discuss its limits; then, we briefly introduce the rationale of our framework, explaining how it overcomes these limits.

Once the a-priori pdfs $p^a(A|E)$ and $p^a(W)$ are given, a naive way to solve the interpretation problem is the following: First, assume that the event instances in Φ are independent from one another; then, use the a-priori pdf $p^a(A|E)$ to probabilistically interpret each e_i in $\Phi = e_1 \ldots e_m$ as an instance of an activity A_i, and the pdf $p^a(W)$ to probabilistically interpret the whole Φ as an instance of one of the processes, say W_j. As implied by the independence assumption, every sequence-interpretation $\sigma = A_1 \ldots A_m$ obtained this way will be associated with the probability $\Pi_{i=1}^m p^a(A_i|E\text{-}type(e_i))$ (that is the product of the a-priori probabilities of the event-to-activity mappings at each step), while the process-interpretation W_j will have probability $p^a(W_j)$. Unfortunately, this naive approach is unlikely to provide reasonable results, as explained in the following example.

Example 4. Consider the scenario where the sets of processes, activities, and events are $\mathcal{W} = \{W_1, W_2\}$, $\mathcal{A} = \{A, B, C, D\}$, and $\mathcal{E} = \{E_1, E_2\}$, such that $cand\text{-}act(E_1) = \{A, B\}$ and $cand\text{-}act(E_2) = \{C, D\}$. Moreover, assume that the a-priori probabilities of the processes are $p^a(W_1) = 0.7$ and $p^a(W_2) = 0.3$, while those of the activities are $p^a(A|E_1) = p^a(B|E_1) = 0.5$; $p^a(C|E_2) = 0.8$; $p^a(D|E_2) = 0.2$.

Let $\Phi = e_1 e_2$ be the trace to be interpreted, where e_1 and e_2 are instances of E_1 and E_2, respectively. According to the a-priori pdf, if we consider the events in Φ separately, all the sequence-interpretations are: $\sigma_1 = AC$; $\sigma_2 = AD$; $\sigma_3 = BC$; $\sigma_4 = BD$.

Each sequence-interpretation is also associated with a probability, implied by p^a and the independence assumption. Thus, the probability of each sequence-interpretation σ, denoted as $p^a(\sigma)$, is the product of the a-priori probabilities of its steps. Hence:

$$p^a(\sigma_1) = p^a(A|E_1) \cdot p^a(C|E_2) = 0.4; \quad p^a(\sigma_2) = p^a(\sigma_4) = 0.1; \quad p^a(\sigma_3) = 0.4.$$

Moreover, owing to $p^a(W_1)$ and $p^a(W_2)$, we can say that Φ encodes an execution of W_1 with probability 0.7, and of W_2 with probability 0.3.

Now, assume given the context-specific knowledge that the composition rules are: $\langle \mathcal{A}, \{A \Rightarrow C; B \Rightarrow A\} \rangle$ for W_1, and $\langle \mathcal{A}, \{A \Rightarrow B; B \Rightarrow \neg C; B \Rightarrow \neg D\} \rangle$ for W_2. Given this, we have that σ_2, σ_3 and σ_4 are inconsistent with the composition rules of W_1 and W_2, and thus they turn out to be invalid sequence-interpretations. Therefore, given that σ_1 conforms to the composition of W_1 but not of W_2, σ_1 remains the only valid sequence-interpretation, and W_1 turns out to be the only valid process-interpretation. Hence, the a-priori probabilities $p^a(\sigma_1) = 0.4$ and $p^a(W_1) = 0.7$ are not reasonable, and should be revised as the sum of the probabilities of the consistent sequence-interpretations should be 1, and the same should hold for the consistent process-interpretations.   □

Our approach consists in using this naive approach to obtain some initial interpretations, and then revising them by *a-posteriori* enforcing the composition rules. In order to do this, we resort to probabilistic conditioning, that is a well-known paradigm used in the general context of forcing integrity constraints over probabilistic databases where the assumption of independence between tuples is originally used. Generally speaking, applying probabilistic conditioning for a random variable X in the presence of a set C of constraints means revising $f(X)$ into $f(X|C)$, where f is the pdf of X: that is, re-evaluating $f(X)$ conditioned to the fact that the constraints in C are satisfied. In our case, this means that we will revise the a-priori pdfs $p^a(\sigma)$ and $p^a(W)$ over the sequence- and the process-interpretations into $p^a(\sigma|\mathcal{CR})$ and $p^a(W|\mathcal{CR})$, respectively.

For instance, consider the case of Example 4. If we disregard the composition rules, the probabilities of the sequence-interpretations are the a-priori ones: $p^a(\sigma_1) = p^a(\sigma_3) = 0.4$; $p^a(\sigma_2) = p^a(\sigma_4) = 0.1$. Now, we have seen that if we take into account the set $\mathcal{CR}$ of composition rules, σ_2, σ_3 and σ_4 turn out to be inadmissible. Thus, the conditioned probabilities are:

$$p^a(\sigma_1|\mathcal{CR}) = \frac{p^a(\sigma_1)}{p^a(\sigma_1)} = 1; \quad p^a(\sigma_2|\mathcal{CR}) = p^a(\sigma_3|\mathcal{CR}) = p^a(\sigma_4|\mathcal{CR}) = 0.$$

Thus generally, the conditioned probability of a sequence-interpretation is either 0, if it is invalid, or the ratio between its a-priori probability and the sum of the a-priori probabilities of all the valid sequence-interpretations, otherwise.

In turn, the conditioned probabilities of the process interpretations are: $p^a(W_1|\mathcal{CR}) = \frac{p^a(W_1)}{p^a(W_1)} = 1$ and $p^a(W_2|\mathcal{CR}) = 0$. This corresponds to the fact that the only valid process-interpretation of Φ is W_1.

Our approach for interpreting an input trace Φ consists in revising $p^a(\sigma)$ and $p^a(W)$ into $p^a(\sigma|\mathcal{CR})$ and $p^a(W|\mathcal{CR})$ by first enumerating all the interpretations of Φ, then discarding those not satisfying the composition rules, and finally revising the a-priori probabilities of the remaining ones. More in detail, given a trace Φ a probabilistic interpretation of Φ is the set of triples $CIS_\Phi = \{\langle \sigma, W, p^a(\sigma \wedge W|\mathcal{CR}) \rangle | \langle \sigma, W \rangle$ is an interpretation for $\Phi\}$, which is named $ci\text{-}set$ for Φ in the following. It is worth pointing out that CIS_Φ implicitly represent $p^a(\sigma|\mathcal{CR})$ (resp. $p^a(W|\mathcal{CR})$) as $p^a(\sigma|\mathcal{CR}) = \sum_{\langle \sigma, W', p \rangle \in CIS_\Phi} p$ (resp. $p^a(W|\mathcal{CR}) = \sum_{\langle \sigma', W, p \rangle \in CIS_\Phi} p$).

4 Experiments

Scenario, Data, and a-priori pdfs. We tested our framework over real-like data of the administrative units of a phone company (PC). In these scenario, a process instance is a collection of activities performed by the staff of the units in response to customers' requests. We were given the scheme of the processes in terms of precedence relationships (between activities), that were easily encoded into composition rules of the form used in our framework. Moreover, we were given the sets $\mathcal{W}$, $\mathcal{A}$ and $\mathcal{E}$, and, for each $E \in \mathcal{E}$, the set $cand\text{-}act(E)$ of the activities whose execution is known to possibly generate an instance of E. Besides the composition rules the phone company gave us a set of real traces along with suitable values for the a-priori pdfs, based on their knowledge of the domain. Specifically, we were given by the phone company and the service agency 100 real traces describing different process instances. Moreover, for each original trace Φ, we were given also its correct interpretation $\langle \sigma_\Phi, W_\Phi \rangle$.

Efficiency and Effectiveness of the Conditioning Approach. In Table 1 we report the average running times of the generation of the $ci\text{-}set$ (row $Times$) vs. trace length (we did not run the generation of the $ci\text{-}set$ on traces longer than 30 as it would require too much time). It is easy to see that the generation of the $ci\text{-}set$ is feasible only on short traces (i.e., traces of length 10); more efficient approaches should be investigated for dealing with longer traces (i.e., traces of length greater than or equal to 20).

Table 1. Running time of the generation of the $ci\text{-}set$ and accuracy of activity queries.

Trace length	10	20	30
Running Times	$\approx 21\ msec$	$\approx 24\ min$	halted after 30 min
Accuracy	73%	72%	75%

We now analyze the accuracy of the interpretations. We measured the accuracy with which a *activity* queries can be answered over it. In the following, we denote as Φ the trace over which the queries are posed, and as $\langle \sigma_\Phi, W_\Phi \rangle)$ the corresponding correct interpretation. Given this, an *activity* query (over a step i) asks for the activity that has been performed at the i-th step of Φ, thus its answer is $\sigma_\Phi[i]$. The probabilistic answers to activity queries over ci-sets are the natural probabilistic extensions of their deterministic semantics. Specifically, given a ci-set CIS_Φ over Φ, the answer $q(CIS_\Phi)$ of an activity query q over step i is a set of activities, where each activity A is associated with the probability encoded in CIS_Φ that the event e_i of Φ was generated by the execution of an instance of A. Correspondingly, given an activity query q and a ci-set CIS_Φ over Φ, the accuracy of $q(CIS_\Phi)$ is measured as the probability associated with A^* in $q(CIS_\Phi)$, where A^* is the answer of q evaluated on σ_Φ. The average accuracies of the answers of activity queries, issued over all the steps of the input traces, are reported in the row *Accuracy* of Table 1. The results show that, in terms of accuracy, our approach is rather good and insensitive to the trace length.

5   Discussion, Conclusion, and Future Work

We have presented a novel probabilistic approach to the problem of interpreting a low-level log trace as an instance of one or more given process models, which relies on computing, for each model, different probability-aware event-activity mappings, which all comply with the behavioral constraints encoded in the model. The proposed model is shown to be effective, but it is not efficient enough to be used in practice. Efficiency issues will be addressed in future work.

References

1. Van der Aalst, W., Weijters, T., Maruster, L.: Workflow mining: Discovering process models from event logs. IEEE TKDE **16**(9), 1128–1142 (2004)
2. van der Aalst, W.M.P.: Process Mining: Discovery, Conformance and Enhancement of Business Processes, 1st edn. Springer Publishing Company, Incorporated (2011)
3. van der Aalst, W.M.P., de Beer, H.T., van Dongen, B.F.: Process mining and verification of properties: an approach based on temporal logic. In: Meersman, R., Tari, Z. (eds.) OTM 2005. LNCS, vol. 3760, pp. 130–147. Springer, Heidelberg (2005)
4. Baier, T., Di Ciccio, C., Mendling, J., Weske, M.: Matching of events and activities - an approach using declarative modeling constraints. In: Gaaloul, K., Schmidt, R., Nurcan, S., Guerreiro, S., Ma, Q. (eds.) BPMDS 2015 and EMMSAD 2015. LNBIP, vol. 214, pp. 119–134. Springer, Heidelberg (2015)
5. Baier, T., Mendling, J., Weske, M.: Bridging abstraction layers in process mining. Information Systems **46**, 123–139 (2014)
6. Baier, T., Rogge-Solti, A., Weske, M., Mendling, J.: Matching of events and activities - an approach based on constraint satisfaction. In: Frank, U., Loucopoulos, P., Pastor, Ó., Petrounias, I. (eds.) PoEM 2014. LNBIP, vol. 197, pp. 58–72. Springer, Heidelberg (2014)
7. Rozinat, A., van der Aalst, W.M.: Conformance checking of processes based on monitoring real behavior. Information Systems **33**(1), 64–95 (2008)

Property Hypergraphs as an Attributed Predicate RDF

Dewi W. Wardani[1,2(✉)] and Josef Küng[2]

[1] Institute for Application Oriented Knowledge Processing, Johannes Kepler University,
Altenberger Straße 69, 4040 Linz, Austria
[2] Sebelas Maret University, Jl. Ir Sutami 36 a, Surakarta, Central Java, Indonesia
{dwardani,jkueng}@faw.jku.at

Abstract. Graph databases have been getting more attention for recent applications. It's based on the idea that knowledge is better to be modeled through graph models. Graph models intuitively capture the complexity of knowledge of the real world. The property graph is a famous graph model in graph databases. Basically, a graph model is also the data model of the semantic web technology. In semantic web point of view, the simple graph-like RDF must represent any knowledge which can be sometimes quite complex. In this work we propose a new model in representing property graphs in RDF format. We name it an attributed predicate RDF. The experiments show that the attributed predicate RDF surpasses the performance of other models in the sense of query time than the other models. Additionally, the other approach only considers normal property graphs, our approach also can deal property hypergraphs as the generalization of property graphs.

Keywords: Graph model · Graph database · Property graphs · Hypergraphs · RDF · Attributed predicate

1 Introduction

The data in Web 3.0 is connected or graph model data. Graph models have some advantages and are more expressive in representing data [1] [2]. Graph models have inspired an emerging database technology, named graph databases [3], as an alternative database to the dominating relational databases. One famous graph model is the property graph, it has been used as native model by existing graph databases [4] [5]. A property hypergraph/graph intuitively and expressively captures knowledge of the real world. As an example in Figure 1.a, two nodes are involved (digraph) and more than two nodes are involved (hypergraph) in Figure 1.b. Figure 1.b is a property hypergraph, the generalization of a property graph [6].

The advantage of graph databases is the efficiency in managing data which contains many edges [7]. Regarding its advantages [8], graph databases or NoSQL databases are gaining popularity as well. In managing the property graphs/hypergraphs, it seems that graph databases are more advanced than the existing RDF store. One work [9] mentioned that native RDF stores have some limitations in representing a graph

© Springer International Publishing Switzerland 2015
C. Debruyne et al. (Eds.): OTM 2015 Conferences, LNCS 9415, pp. 329–336, 2015.
DOI: 10.1007/978-3-319-26148-5_21

oriented of the data. This problem inspired us to study that a graph-like RDF also can represent graph oriented model data even the more complex one, a property hypergraph model. The advantage of RDF over graph databases is that the graph-like RDF, even though simple, but the standard data model in Semantic Web [11].

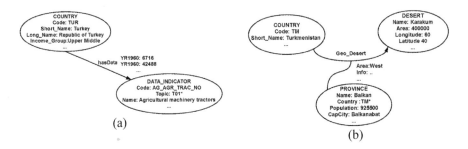

Fig. 1. The examples of (a) a property graph and (b) a property hypergraph.

Our approach is based on the extension of the predicate element of RDF. Intuitively, we can see that the edge of graphs/hypergraphs can be associated with the predicate element of RDF. We will explain it in detail in section three. This is the novelty of this work. Briefly, the objectives of our work are as below:

1. Proposing a new model in representing a property hypergraph (digraph is included) in RDF format. We name it, an attributed predicate RDF.
2. Comparing the performance of query time of our model with the existing approaches.

The remaining sections are organized as follows. Section two explains some related works. Section three is the main explanation of our approach. We conduct and discuss the result of experiments in section four. Finally, the conclusion and discussion related to the near future works in section five.

2   Related Work

The previous research proposed three possibilities to store property graphs in RDF [11]. The three approaches respectively, based on an extension of reification (RF), subProperty based (SP) and named graph based (NG). The performance results of the SP and NG were similar each other's. The NG has the lowest storage cost, but the complexity of using the element name of graph arises the complexity of NG dataset and the SPARQL will be more complicated too. Reification [10] and named graph [12] have been extended in this work to support the solution of the objectives of this work. The other scenario of this work, subProperty based (SP) uses **rdf:subProperty** to handle reify-like process, a sort of substitute of name of graph in NG approach. This work focused on a property digraph as RDF and it does not show the case of a property hypergraph which is closer to the abstraction of the real world. There are less scientific publications which study this work. This issue inspired us to do this research.

The native RDF cannot directly represent non-binary data included property graphs/hypergraphs. W3C released some standard recommendations to solve this situation. The reification [13] is the prominent work to represent non-binary data. It uses surrogate subject nodes that usually are formed as blank nodes to create statements for each element t Subject, Predicate and Object, then the surrogate nodes are used to reify additional statements of non-binary data. N-Quads [14] use the fourth element in the reification process for creating additional statements. The same idea was proposed by Named Graph [12], it uses the name of graph to wrap the statement of triple RDF then uses the name of graph to reify additional statements.

3   An Attributed Predicate RDF (AP-RDF)

3.1   The Concept of AP-RDF

Our approach is based on the extension of the predicate element of RDF. Intuitively, we can see that the edge of graph/ hypergraph can be associated with the predicate element of RDF. The nodes can be formed as the subject or the object in RDF. The property nodes can be represented through the concept of DataProperty and ObjectProperty. The sign (*) in Figure 1 is the possibility of creating ObjectProperty in RDF. Hence, we see that the predicate element can be extended to represent the properties of the edge.

Our approach, uses the example from Figure 1.a, (i) it uses the instance **:hasDataX** of predicate class/type **:hasData**, then (ii) uses the instance of predicate to create the statement of properties. This is why we name it an attributed predicate RDF because the instance of predicate connects all information which extends the binary data as an attribute of predicate, either as DataProperty or ObjectProperty.

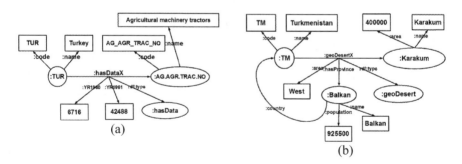

Fig. 2. The description of the graph-like of an attributed predicate RDF from Figure 1

The description of our approach for Figure 1 is described in Figure 2. By using AP-RDF approach, we obtain the RDF in Figure 1.a as below (.ttl),

:TUR   :country_code   :TUR   ;   :short_name   "Turkey"^^xsd:string   .   :AG_AGR_TRAC_NO :data_indicator_code   "AG_AGR_TRAC_NO"^^xsd:literal   ;   :data_indicator_name   "Agriculture machinery tractors"^^xsd:string .   :TUR :hasDataX :AG_AGR_TRAC_NO   .   :hasDataX rdf:type :hasData ; :YR1960 "6716"^^xsd:float .

Although simple, we will show it can manage complex property hypergraphs and this model returns good performances as well. The detail is described in the next section of this part.

3.2   Converting Property Hypergraphs to AP-RDF

There are 2 main problems in representing property hypergraphs as RDF: (i) the choosing of the node subject and the node object. The nature of RDF is that only two nodes can be involved meanwhile in hypergraphs more than two nodes are involved. (ii) Managing the rest nodes and their properties. We define some definitions to explain how to represent property hypergraph as AP-RDF.

Definition 1. (A property hypergraph)
Let H be a hypergraph, $H = \{X, E\}$ which consists of X and E. X is a set of nodes $X = \{v_1, v_2, v_3 ...v_n\}$ and E is a set non-empty hyperedges or edges $E = \{e_1, e_2, e_3 ... e_m\}$. Each node v_n and each edge e_m has key-value pair properties. $<p_iv_n, Ap_iv_n>$ are key-value properties of nodes and $<p_je_m, Ap_jv_m>$ are key-value pair properties of edge.

Regarding in choosing the node as subject and object, we define formula 1 and 2 to measure the weight of each node in the hypergraph. The weight is inspired by HITS [15] and Pagerank [16]. Considering that either sophisticated measure such as HITS or simple measure return similar result [17], we proposed the simple formulas to measure the weight of Authority (Av_n) and the weight of Hub as well of each node (Hv_n). The weight is the difference of Authority and Hub ($Wv_n = Av_n - Hv_n$). The weight will be used to determine the role of each node.

$$Av_p = \sum_{q \to p} outlinkv_q \qquad (1) \qquad Hv_p = \sum_{p \to q} inlinkv_q \qquad (2)$$

Definition 2. (The Subject, The Object, The Attributed Predicate)
Let Hx be a one hypergraph. Each hyperedge em connects to n nodes v_n, where $n \geq 2$ and each node have weight Wv_n. Each em is the class/type of predicate. The node subject v^S is where $MaxW_v = (Wv_1 ... Wv_n)$ belongs to the node, and the node object v^O is where $MinW_v = (Wv_1 ... Wv_n)$ belongs to the node. The predicate is an instance of predicate class/type ie_m. The attributes of predicate are (i) all original properties (DataProperty) of hyperedge e_m and (ii) the rest nodes of hyperedge e_m (ObjectProperty).

In case there is the same weight of nodes in a hypergraph, then we can choose any node as the subject or the object. Based on our above given definitions, we obtain the RDF of a property hypergraph in Figure 1.b as below (.ttl),

:TM :code "TM"^^xsd:string ; :name "Turkmenistan"^^xsd:string . :Karakum :name "Karakum"^^xsd:string ; :area "400000"^^xsd:float . :TM :geoDesertX :Karakum . :geoDesertX rdf:type :geoDesert ; :area "West"^^xsd:string ; :hasProvince :Balkan ; :country :TM . :Balkan :name "Balkan"^^xsd:string ; :population "925500"^^xsd:float .

We also proposed the extension of SP-RDF [11] for representing property hypergraph. We extend SP-RDF for property hypergraphs based on our proposed approach. Therefore, later on we can compare in the experiment between AP-RDF and SP-RDF for the property hypergraphs case since SP-RDF uses the native triple RDF (three elements). We use the surrogate predicate in a duplicate statement of SP-RDF as like as the instance of the class/type predicate in AP-RDF, then the rest process is the same as like as in AP-RDF. The SP-RDF for Figure 1.b as below (.ttl),

:v1 :code "TM"^^xsd:string ; :name "Turkmenistan"^^xsd:string . :v2 :name "Karakum"^^xsd:string ; :area "400000"^^xsd:float . :v1 :geoDesert :v2 . :v1 :edge :v2 . :edge rdfs:subPropertyOf :geoDesert :edge :area "West"^^xsd:string ; :hasProvince :Balkan ; :country :TM . :v3 :name "Balkan"^^xsd:string ; :population "925500"^^xsd:float .

4   The Experiment

4.1   The Dataset, the Experimental Setup and the Queries

We conducted experiments for two real datasets, WorldBank[1] and Mondial[2] datasets. We constructed property hypergraph based on the previous approach [18]. The WorldBank dataset is for a property graph case and the Mondial dataset is for a property hypergraph case. We implemented in Jena-Apache[3]. The Hardware environment for the experiments is CPU Intel i7-3540M (3.00GHz), memory 8GB (Kingston DDR3 1600 MHZ). Figure 3 shows, in general the storage and the number of statements of AP-RDFs are pretty competitive with the other models.

We prepared two types of query in each experiment: (i) the simple query (Q1 and Q2). This type of query focuses on retrieving property data in the node or joins between the same type of nodes or less number join process. (ii) The rather complex query (Q3 - Q5). This type of query focuses on retrieving data property on the edge or join between different types of nodes and or more number join process. An example: List all countries and their names (a simple query). The SPARQL (for AP-RDF):

SELECT ?code ?name

WHERE { ?ct rdf:type :Country . ?ct :hasCountry_Code ?code . ?ct :hasLong_Name ?name . }

An example: Show all indicators in the topic (T20) in JAPAN which have been increased or decreased for 4 years till 2012 (a rather complex query). The SPARQL (for AP-RDF):

SELECT ?ic ?in

WHERE   {   ?ic   rdf:type   :Indicators   .   ?ic   :hasINDICATOR_TOPIC   :T20   .   ?ic :hasINDICATOR_CODE ?ic . ?ic :hasINDICATOR_NAME ?in . :JPN ?hasDataic ?ic . :JPN ?hasDataic2 ?ic . :JPN rdf:type :Country . ?hasDataic rdf:type :hasData . ?hasDataic2 rdf:type :hasData . {{?hasDataic :hasYR2012 ?a . ?hasDataic :hasYR2011 ?b . FILTER (?a > ?b) } UNION { ?hasDataic :hasYR2011 ?b . ?hasDataic :hasYR2010 ?c .FILTER (?b > ?c) } UNION {?hasDataic :hasYR2010 ?c . ?hasDataic :hasYR2009 ?d . FILTER (?c > ?d) }} UNION {{{ ?hasDataic2 :hasYR2012 ?a2 . ?hasDataic2 :hasYR2011 ?b2 . FILTER (?a2 < ?b2) } UNION { ?hasDataic2 :hasYR2011 ?b2 . ?hasDataic2 :hasYR2010 ?c2 . FILTER (?b2 < ?c2) } UNION { ?hasDataic2 :hasYR2010 ?c2 . ?hasDataic2 :hasYR2009 ?d2 . FILTER (?c2 < ?d2) }}} }

---

[1] http://data.worldbank.org/
[2] http://www.dbis.informatik.uni-goettingen.de/Mondial/
[3] https://jena.apache.org/

The list of queries for WorldBank dataset (the first experiment): *Q1. Show all countries and indicator in topic (T20) which have been increased for 4 years till 2012; Q2. Show all countries and indicators in topic (T20), which have been increased for 4 years till 2012 but in the same time those indicators have been decreased in JAPAN ;Q3. Show all indicators in topic (T01) and topic (T02) which have been increased for 4 years till 2012 in and the same time have been decreased in JAPAN ; Q4. Show all indicators which have been increased for 4 years till 2012 in topic (T19) and topic (T20) in JAPAN and TURKEY ; Q5. Show all indicators in topic (T01) and topic (T02) which have been increased for 4 years till 2012 in and the same time have been decreased in JAPAN.*

The list of queries for Mondial dataset (the second experiment): *Q1. List the province which has lake, river, and the river as the source and the river as the estuary; Q2. List the province in the countries which the area located in continent Asia and Europe which has lake, river, the river as the source and the river as the estuary;Q3. List of countries which located in continent Africa, has relation with organization, has inflation more than 60 (Mondial point) in number and infant mortality less than 100 (Mondial point); Q4. List country name which its area located in continent Asia and Europe, has inflation more than 9% and has membership in organization; Q5. List countries which have the same membership in Organization.*

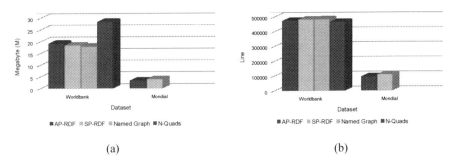

(a)   (b)

Fig. 3. The description of the dataset, (a) the storage need and (b) the number of statement of each model per dataset

4.2   The Experimental Results

In brief, to represent a property graph/hypergraph of each model: SP-RDF → S P O . S edge O . edge P O ; NG-RDF → G1 { S P O .} G2 {G1 P O .} ; NQ-RDF → S P O C1 . C1 P O C2 . ; AP-RDF → S P* O . P* P O . SP-RDF has duplicate statements of real statements which use surrogate term "edge" as the predicate in the duplicate statement, then use it to reify the other statements. The retrieval process needs to match twice for the real statement and the duplicate statement. It makes the query time to become double. The NG-RDF and NQ-RDF both have fourth element, the name of graph in Named Graph and the context element in N-Quads. The retrieval process seeks the fourth element first, then the triple statement of the graph. It obviously makes the query process longer. Meanwhile, AP-RDF only uses the instance of predicates to be matched, no need twice steps, therefore it reduces the query time.

We conducted a cold-experiment style. The first experiment for property graphs in 4 models (AP-RDF, SP-RDF, Named Graph and N-Quads) and the second experiment for property hypergraphs in 2 models (AP-RDF and SP-RDF). Figure 4 shows the comparison of the execution-time of each model. We can see here, in general, for all experiments, for simple queries there is not much difference of performances between all models because they scan less the node and its properties or have less join processes, but obviously the performance time will be different in case of rather complex queries which scan more nodes, properties have more join processes.

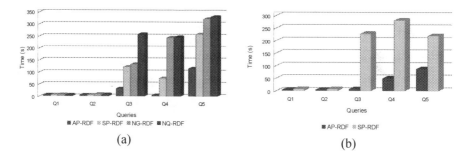

Fig. 4. The execution time (in second) per query of each model in (a) first experiment and (b) second experiment

The experimental results show that AP-RDF is a promising way in representing property hypergraphs and significantly reducing query time.

5   Conclusions and Future Works

We proposed an attributed predicate RDF (AP-RDF) to represent property hypergraphs in native triple RDF including normal digraph, whereas the previous approach was only for digraph. The main idea is making the predicate as a class/type and use the instance of a predicate to reify and to handle the statement property of an edge or the rest nodes (not Subject and Object nodes). The experimental result with two real datasets show, that AP-RDF returns better performance than the previous models, particularly for rather complex queries. In the near future works, we are going to prove that this model fits with the W3C standard semantic interpretation and study its impact in the inference process.

References

1. Chein, M., Mugnier, M.-L.: Graph-based knowledge representation: computational foundations of conceptual graphs. Springer Science & Business Media (2008)
2. Aggarwal, C.C., Wang, H.: Managing and mining graph data, vol. 40. Springer (2010)
3. Hecht, R., Jablonski, S.: NoSQL evaluation: A use case oriented survey (2011)

4. Webber, J.: A programmatic introduction to neo4j. In: Proceedings of the 3rd Annual Conference on Systems, Programming, and Applications: Software for Humanity, pp. 217–218 (2012)
5. Martinez-Bazan, N., Gómez-Villamor, S., Escalé-Claveras, F.: Dex: A high-performance graph database management system. In: 2011 IEEE 27th International Conference on Data Engineering Workshops (ICDEW), pp. 124–127 (2011)
6. Iordanov, B.: HyperGraphDB: a generalized graph database. In: Shen, H.T., et al. (eds.) WAIM 2010. LNCS, vol. 6185, pp. 25–36. Springer, Heidelberg (2010)
7. Vicknair, C., Macias, M., Zhao, Z., Nan, X., Chen, Y., Wilkins, D.: A comparison of a graph database and a relational database: A data provenance perspective. In: Proceedings of the 48th Annual Southeast Regional Conference, New York, NY, USA, pp. 42:1–42:6 (2010)
8. Angles, R.: A comparison of current graph database models. In: 2012 IEEE 28th International Conference on Data Engineering Workshops (ICDEW), pp. 171–177 (2012)
9. De Abreu, D., Flores, A., Palma, G., Pestana, V., Pinero, J., Queipo, J., Sánchez, J., Vidal, M.-E.: Choosing between graph databases and RDF engines for consuming and mining linked Data. In: COLD (2013)
10. World Wide Web Consortium and others, RDF 1.1 Primer (2014)
11. Das, S., Srinivasan, J., Perry, M., Chong, E.I., Banerjee, J.: A tale of two graphs: property graphs as RDF in oracle. In: EDBT, pp. 762–773 (2014)
12. Carroll, J.J., Bizer, C., Hayes, P., Stickler, P.: Named graphs, provenance and trust. In: Proceedings of the 14th International Conference on World Wide Web, New York, NY, USA, pp. 613–622 (2005)
13. Manola, F., Miller, E., McBride, B.: RDF primer. W3C Recomm., vol. 10 (2004)
14. Carothers, G.: RDF 1.1 N-Quads: A line-based syntax for RDF datasets. W3C Recomm. (2014)
15. Kleinberg, J.M.: Hubs, authorities, and communities. ACM Comput. Surv. CSUR **31**(4es), 5 (1999)
16. Page, L., Brin, S., Motwani, R., Winograd, T.: The PageRank citation ranking: bringing order to the web. In: Proceedings of the 7th International World Wide Web Conference, Brisbane, Australia, pp. 161–172 (1998)
17. Amento, B., Terveen, L., Hill, W.: Does 'Authority' mean quality? predicting expert quality ratings of web documents. In: Proceedings of the 23rd Annual International ACM SIGIR Conference on Research and Development in Information Retrieval, Athens, Greece, pp. 296–303 (2000)
18. Wardani, D.W., Küng, J.: Semantic mapping relational to graph model. In: 2014 International Conference on Computer, Control, Informatics and its Applications (IC3INA), pp. 160–165 (2014)

Rewinding and Repeating Scientific Choreographies

Andreas Weiß$^{(\boxtimes)}$, Vasilios Andrikopoulos, Michael Hahn,
and Dimka Karastoyanova

Institute of Architecture of Application Systems (IAAS),
University of Stuttgart, Stuttgart, Germany
{andreas.weiss,vasilios.andrikopoulos,michael.hahn,
dimka.karastoyanova}@iaas.uni-stuttgart.de

Abstract. Scientists that use the workflow paradigm for the enactment of scientific experiments need support for trial-and-error modeling, as well as flexibility mechanisms that enable the ad hoc repetition of workflow logic for the convergence of results or error handling. Towards this goal, in this paper we introduce the facilities to repeat partially or completely running choreographies on demand. Choreographies are interesting for the scientific workflow community because so-called multi-scale/field (multi-*) experiments can be modeled and enacted as choreographies of scientific workflows. A prerequisite for choreography repetition is the rewinding of the involved participant instances to a previous state. For this purpose, we define a formal model representing choreography models and their instances as well as a concept to repeat choreography logic. Furthermore, we provide an algorithm for determining the rewinding points in each involved participant instance.

Keywords: Ad Hoc changes · Choreography · Workflow · Flexibility

1 Introduction

The goal of eScience is to provide generic approaches and tools for scientific exploration and discovery [6]. The workflow technology, in this context known as *scientific workflows*, is one approach for supporting data processing and analysis. However, scientists have different requirements on workflow modeling and enactment than users in the business domain. eScience experiments often demand a trial-and-error based modeling [2] that allows the extension of incomplete models after they have already been instantiated, or their partial repetition with different sets of parameters for the convergence of results. In this context, scientists are both the designers and users of a workflow model. To support these requirements the *Model-as-you-go* approach has been introduced in [13]. The approach uses workflow technology from the business domain and adapts it for the requirements of scientists while keeping the technology's benefits such as standardization and automated error handling. One aspect of the approach is

© Springer International Publishing Switzerland 2015
C. Debruyne et al. (Eds.): OTM 2015 Conferences, LNCS 9415, pp. 337–347, 2015.
DOI: 10.1007/978-3-319-26148-5_22

the definition of two operations allowing scientists to influence the execution of a workflow in an ad hoc manner without relying on pre-specified facilities in the workflow model [14]. The *iterate* operation allows repeating workflow logic without undoing previously completed work. This is helpful for scientists to enforce the convergence of results by repeating some steps such as building a Finite Element Method grid with a different set of parameters. The *re-execute* operation also allows repeating parts of already executed workflow logic, however, completed work is compensated (undone) beforehand. This allows scientists to reset the execution environment e.g. in case of detected errors.

A limitation of the Model-as-you-go approach is the lack of support for multi-scale (e.g. space or time scales) and multi-field (e.g. physics and biology or chemistry), so-called *multi-**, experiments in cases where the experiment's mathematical models have not been merged. Such merging typically approximates descriptions of one or more scales/fields onto another scale/field, while sacrificing accuracy of the simulation results. In order to support the modeling and execution of multi-* experiments, in previous work [17] we proposed the use of choreographies and introduced the notion of *Model-as-you-go for Choreographies*. Choreographies are a concept known from the business domain. They provide a global view on the interconnection of collaborating parties such as business organizations. Unlike service orchestrations, choreographies do not have a centralized coordinator but represent the peer-to-peer-like interconnection between services or orchestrations of services [3]. However, flexibility features as provided for single scientific workflows are still missing. Scientists should be able to select a point in the choreography up to which the execution of the simulations has to be rewound before applying any desired changes and repeating the execution of the experiment. Repeating the execution instead of discarding all intermediate results saves a lot of time especially in case of long running scientific experiments.

Towards this goal, this work supports the notion of Model-as-you-go for Choreographies by providing the following contributions: based on the work of [7] and [14], we provide a *formal description of choreography models and instances* (Sec. 2). Subsequently in Sec. 3, we discuss the concept of repeating the execution of choreography instances and the *rewinding of choreography instances* to a previous state as preparatory step, and introduce an *algorithm to determine the rewinding points*. Sec. 4 compares our approach to related ones and Sec. 5 concludes the paper with an outlook on future work.

2   Formal Model

In this section, we define the underlying formal model for our approach corresponding to the life cycle phases *modeling* and *execution* of scientific choreographies [16].

2.1   Modeling Phase

A choreography model consists of at least two participants, which are represented by service orchestrations/process models. A process model is a directed, acyclic graph whose nodes represent activities. Control flow is explicitly modeled by control flow connectors linking activities. Data flow is implicitly described through the manipulation of variable values as input and output of activities. The participants communicate with each other via message links. For the purposes of this work we do not consider loops inside the process models. Formally speaking, a *process model* is a DAG $G = (m, V, i, o, A, L)$, where $m \in M$ is the name of the process model (M is the set of all names), V is the set of variables, i is the map of input variables, o is the map of output variables, A is the set of activities, and L is the set of control flow connectors (control flow links). A control flow connector $l \in L$ is a triple $l = (a_{source}, a_{target}, t \mid a_{source}, a_{target} \in A, t \in C \wedge a_{source} \neq a_{target})$ connecting a source and a target activity, while its *transition condition* (where C is the set of all conditions) is evaluated during run time [7,14]. Based on that, we define:

Definition 1 (Choreography Model $\mathfrak{C}$). *A choreography model is a directed, acyclic graph denoted by the triple $\mathfrak{C} = (m, P, ML)$, where $m \in M$ is the name of the choreography model, P is the set of choreography participants, ML is the set of message links between the choreography participants.*

A *choreography participant* $p \in P$ is a triple $p = (m, type, G)$, where $m \in M$ is the name of the participant, $type \in T$ is the type of the participant (T is the set of types), and $G \in G_{all}$ (G_{all} is the set of all process models) is a process model graph. A message link is a tuple $ml \in ML = (p_s, p_r, a_s, a_r, t)$, where $p_s, p_r \in P$ are the sending and receiving participants. For the sending and receiving participants the following holds: $p_s \neq p_r$, i.e., the sender and the receiver must not be identical; $a_s \in \pi_5(p_s.G)$ and $a_r \in \pi_5(p_r.G)$, where π_i is the projection operation on the i-th element of a tuple, are the sending and receiving activities for which holds: $a_s \neq a_r$. The transition condition $t \in C$ is evaluated during run time.

2.2 Execution Phase

Choreography models are typically not directly instantiable [3]. Instead, the process/workflow models implementing the choreography participants are instantiated. Together they form an overall virtual choreography instance. The virtual choreography instance at a given point in time can be created by reading monitoring information. We use the definitions of activity and process instances from [14] and extend them for choreography instances. Note that we describe states with the following abbreviations: (S=scheduled, E=executing, C=completed, F=faulted, T=terminated, Cmp=compensated, D=dead, Sus=suspended). Formally, a *process instance* is a tuple $p_g = (V^I, A^A, A^F, L^E, s_g)$, where V^I is the set of variable instances, $A^A \subseteq A^I$ is the set of active activity instances, $A^F \subseteq A^I$ is the set of finished activity instances, L^E is the set of evaluated links, and s_g is the state of the process instance. In general, the set of activity instances is defined as $A^I = \{(id, a, s, t) \mid id \in ID, a \in A, s \in \mathcal{S}, t \in \mathbb{N}\}$. During execution, an activity instance is identified by its id. The set $\mathcal{S} = \{S, E, C, F, T, Cmp, D\}$ contains the execution states an activity instance can take at any point in time t. The state of an activity instance $a^i \in A^I$ can be determined by the function $state(a^i)$, whereas its model element is retrieved by the function $model(a^i)$. For the set of evaluated control flow links the following holds: $L^E = \{(l, c, t) \mid l \in L, c \in \{true, false\}, t \in \mathbb{N}\}$. Evaluated links are the links that already have a truth value c assigned at an execution time t. The truth value determines if the link is followed during execution. The process instance as a whole may be in one of the following states: $s_g \in \{E, C, Sus, T, F\}$. It then follows:

Definition 2 (Choreography Instance c^i). *A choreography instance is the triple* $c^i = (P^I, ML^E, s_c)$, *where* P^I *is the set of participant instances,* ML^E *the set of evaluated message links, and* s_c *the state of the choreography instance.*

The set of participant instances P^I contains pairs of the form $p^i = (m, p_g)$, where m is the name of the participant instance and $p_g \in P_g^{all}$ (P_g^{all} is the set of all process instances) is a process instance. For ML^E the following holds: $ML^E = \{(ml, c, t) \mid ml \in ML, c \in \{true, false\}, t \in \mathbb{N}\}$, i.e., ML^E contains the instantiated message links having a truth value c indicating the outcome of the transition condition evaluation and an execution time t. The choreography instance may be in one of the following states: $s_c \in \{E, C, Sus, T, F\}$.

3   Repetition of Choreographies

In this section we discuss our approach for rewinding a choreography instance to a previous state and we introduce an algorithm for identifying rewinding points.

3.1   Concept

A basic assumption for the *Model-as-you-go for Choreographies* approach is the existence of a monitoring infrastructure as introduced in [18] capturing the execution events, providing information about instance states of the process models distributed across different execution engines, and correlating these states with the corresponding choreography model (in the graphical modeling environment a scientist uses). For our purposes, it is sufficient that only the events related to elements already described in the choreography model are monitored. Figure 1 shows an example of a choreography instance in which a part of its logic is to be repeated, and summarizes the relevant terms that are used in the following. Repeating parts of the logic of choreography instances is triggered by manually choosing a *start activity instance* in a *start participant instance* (activity instance c_1 of Participant 1 in the example) during run time via a graphical modeling tool. The *choreography wavefront* contains all currently active or scheduled activity instances, control flow connector instances, and message link instances. The execution must be suspended before starting the rewinding and the repetition of logic in order to avoid race conditions [14].

   An important concept is the notion of the *iteration body*. In [14], the iteration body is defined as the activity and evaluated link instances reachable from a

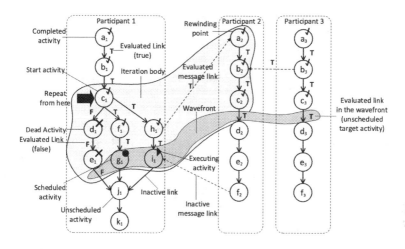

Fig. 1. Example of a choreography instance

user-selected start activity of an individual process instance. Activities that are
not yet scheduled, i.e., that are located in the future of the process instance, are
not contained in the iteration body. In Fig. 1, the iteration body of Participant 1
are the activities c_1, d_1, e_1,f_1, g_1, h_1, i_1, and the control flow connectors between
them. Note that the path $c_1 \rightarrow d_1$ has not been chosen during execution and
is marked as *dead*. However, it may be chosen after starting a repetition from
activity c_1. We extend the notion of iteration body for choreography instances.
Here, the iteration body spans across process instances and includes message
links between them. In Fig. 1, additionally to the already enumerated ones, the
activities a_2, b_2, c_2, the control flow links between them, the control flow link
$c_2 \rightarrow d_2$, and the message link $h_1 \rightarrow a_2$ are part of the *choreography iteration body*. The repetition of logic starting in one particular participant instance
affects at least all participant instances that are part of the choreography iteration body. Already finished activities in the choreography iteration body must be
rewound, i.e., either be *reset* (for iteration purposes), or *compensated* (to enable
re-execution). *Iteration* in a choreography instance is the repetition of logic in the
enacting workflow instances without undoing already completed work. The workflow instances participating in the choreography instance are collectively reset
as described for individual workflow instances in [14]. *Re-execution* in choreography instances is the repeat of choreography logic after compensating already
completed work.

In general, two cases can be distinguished. In the first case, the start participant instance is connected to other participant instances, which are reachable
from the manually selected start activity instance (c_1 in Fig. 1). The start participant instance at this point contains completed sending activities that have
sent messages to other participant instances. While the activity instance identified by the user is the *rewinding point* in the start participant instance, the

rewinding points in the connected instances have to be identified separately (cf. Sec. 3.2). In the example, activity a_2 is the rewinding point of the Participant 2 instance. Rewinding points can also be found in participants that are transitively connected and reachable from the start activity instance. Each rewinding point indicates where the resetting or compensation of activities has to stop, i.e., how the choreography wavefront has to be moved to the past of the choreography instance. In the second case, participants that are not reachable from the start activity instance may still be affected by the repetition of logic in other participant instances. Messages that are not the reply of previous requests and transmitted over incoming message links to the affected participant instances must be available again in the case of repetition. This can either be done by also determining rewinding points in the sending participant instances and rewinding and repeating logic, or by storing and replaying previously sent messages by the workflow engine responsible for the respective participant instance. The determined rewinding points are sent to the involved workflow engines to trigger the iteration or re-execution of choreography logic using a transactional protocol. This is not presented here due to space constraints.

3.2   Determining the Rewinding Points

In the following an algorithm is presented to determine the rewinding points in a choreography iteration body. Therefore, a set of auxiliary functions is defined.

Definition 3 (Function $succ$). *The* successor function $succ$ *is defined as* $succ:$ $A^I \times A^I \to \mathbb{B}$, *where* A^I *is the set of activity instances and* $\mathbb{B}$ *is the set of boolean values* $\mathbb{B} = \{true, false\}$.

The function determines if the second activity instance is reachable from the first activity instance, i.e., a successor in the process instance graph. Definition 4 describes the function for finding the set of rewinding points.

Definition 4 (Function ρ). *The* Determine Rewinding Points function ρ *is defined as* $\rho : \mathfrak{C}^I \times A^I \times P^I \times RP_{\mathfrak{C}}^{all} \to RP_{\mathfrak{C}}^{all}$, *where* $\mathfrak{C}^I$ *is the set of choreography instances,* A^I *is the set of activity instances,* P^I *is the set of participant instances, and* $RP_{\mathfrak{C}}^{all}$ *is the set that contains all* $RP_{\mathfrak{C}}$ *sets.*

$RP_{\mathfrak{C}} \subseteq P^I \times \mathcal{P}(A^I)$ is a set of pairs $\{(p^i, A_{rp}^I) \mid p^i \in P^I, a_1^i, ..., a_k^i \in A_{rp}^I \subseteq A^I\}$ consisting of a participant instance and a set of rewinding point activity instances. The reason that a participant instance can have more than one rewinding point is the existence of parallel paths in the process model graph. A participant may receive messages in parallel that result in independent rewinding points.

Definition 5 (Function χ). *The* Handle Sending Activities function χ *is defined as* $\chi : \mathfrak{C}^I \times A^I \times RP_{\mathfrak{C}}^{all} \to RP_{\mathfrak{C}}^{all}$, *where* $\mathfrak{C}^I$ *is the set of choreography instances,* A^I *is the set of activity instances, and* $RP_{\mathfrak{C}}^{all}$ *is the set of pairs containing the assignment of participant instances to their rewinding points.*

Algorithm 1. determineRewindingPoints, ρ

---

1 **input** : Choreography instance $\mathfrak{c}^i$, activity instance a^i_{start}, participant instance
        p^i, set of pairs $RP_{\mathfrak{C}} = (p^i, A^I_{rp})$
2 **output**: $RP_{\mathfrak{C}}$
3 **begin**
4 | **if** $RP_{\mathfrak{C}} = \emptyset$ **then**
5 | | $RP_{\mathfrak{C}} \leftarrow RP_{\mathfrak{C}} \cup (p^i, \{a^i_{start}\})$
6 | **end**
7 | Stack $S \leftarrow \emptyset$
8 | $S.push(a^i_{start})$
9 | **while** $S \neq \emptyset$ **do**
10 | | Activity Instance $a^i \leftarrow$ S.pop()
11 | | **if** a^i *is not marked as visited* $\wedge$ *state*$(a^i) = completed$ **then**
12 | | | mark a^i as visited
13 | | | **if** *model*(a^i) *is sending activity* **then**
14 | | | | $RP_{\mathfrak{C}} \leftarrow$ handleSendingActivities $(\mathfrak{c}^i, a^i, RP_{\mathfrak{C}})$
15 | | | **end**
16 | | | **foreach**
        $l^i = (l^x, c^x, t^x) \in \pi_4(p^i.p_g) \mid l^x.a^x_{source} = a^i \wedge state(c^x) = true$ **do**
17 | | | | $S.push(l^x.a^x_{target})$
18 | | | **end**
19 | | **end**
20 | **end**
21 | **return** $RP_{\mathfrak{C}}$
22 **end**

Algorithm 1 and the sub-routine described in Algorithm 2 show the realization of functions ρ (Definition 4) and χ (Definition 5), respectively. The main idea of the algorithm is the following: Beginning from the user-selected start activity instance, the start participant instance graph is traversed in a depth-first manner. Every activity instance with the state *completed* is marked as visited and its outgoing links, provided they have been evaluated to true, are followed. For each completed activity instance it is checked if it is a sending activity. If so, the sub-routine *handleSendingActivities* (χ) as defined in Definition 5 is invoked. The attached message link instance $ml^i_{traversed}$ of the sending activity instance a^i is retrieved by evaluating the following conditions: (i) it has been evaluated to true and (ii) there exists a receiving activity instance a^i_r in the *completed* state, i.e., a message has been sent and consumed. If $ml^i_{traversed}$ exists, the algorithm retrieves its receiving participant instance. For the receiving participant instance it is checked if it has already been (partly) traversed by the algorithm and a (preliminary) rewinding point has been found. If this is not the case, ρ is invoked recursively with the current receiving participant. If there exists already a rewinding point, it is checked if (i) the old rewinding point would be a successor of the new one or if (ii) both are in parallel branches. In case (i) the old rewinding point activity instance is removed before the new rewinding point

---

Algorithm 2. handleSendingActivities, χ

---

1 **input** : Chor. instance $\mathfrak{c}^i$, activity instance a^i, set of pairs $RP_{\mathfrak{C}} = (p^i, A^I_{rp})$
2 **output**: $RP_{\mathfrak{C}}$
3 **begin**
4 $\quad$ Message Link Instance $ml^i_{traversed} \leftarrow (ml^x, c^x, t^x) \mid (ml^x, c^x, t^x) \in ML^E \wedge$
$\quad\quad ml^x = (p^i_s, p^i_r, a^i_s, a^i_r, c) \wedge a^i = a^i_s \wedge state(c^x) = true \wedge state(a^i_r) = completed$
5 $\quad$ **if** $ml^i_{traversed} \neq \bot$ **then**
6 $\quad\quad$ Participant Instance $p^i_r \leftarrow ml^i_{traversed}.p^i_r$
7 $\quad\quad$ **if** $\nexists(p^x, A^x_{rp}) \in RP_{\mathfrak{C}} \mid p^x = p^i_r$ **then**
8 $\quad\quad\quad RP_{\mathfrak{C}} \leftarrow RP_{\mathfrak{C}} \cup (p^i_r, \{a^i_r\})$
9 $\quad\quad\quad RP_{\mathfrak{C}} \leftarrow \rho\,(\mathfrak{c}^i, a^i_r, p^i_r, RP_{\mathfrak{C}})$
10 $\quad\quad$ **end**
11 $\quad\quad$ **else if** $\exists(p^x, A^x_{rp}) \in RP_{\mathfrak{C}} \mid p^x = p^i_r$ **then**
12 $\quad\quad\quad$ Boolean $recursion \leftarrow false$
13 $\quad\quad\quad$ **foreach** $a^x \in A^x_{rp}$ **do**
14 $\quad\quad\quad\quad$ **if** $succ(a^i_r, a^x)$ **then**
15 $\quad\quad\quad\quad\quad A^x_{rp} \leftarrow A^x_{rp} \setminus a^x$
16 $\quad\quad\quad\quad\quad recursion \leftarrow true$
17 $\quad\quad\quad\quad$ **end**
18 $\quad\quad\quad\quad$ **else if** $\neg succ(a^x, a^i_r) \wedge \neg succ(a^i_r, a^x)$ **then**
19 $\quad\quad\quad\quad\quad recursion \leftarrow true$
20 $\quad\quad\quad\quad$ **end**
21 $\quad\quad\quad$ **end**
22 $\quad\quad\quad$ **if** $recursion$ **then**
23 $\quad\quad\quad\quad A^x_{rp} \leftarrow A^x_{rp} \cup a^i_r$
24 $\quad\quad\quad\quad RP_{\mathfrak{C}} \leftarrow \rho\,(\mathfrak{c}^i, a^i_r, p^i_r, RP_{\mathfrak{C}})$
25 $\quad\quad\quad$ **end**
26 $\quad\quad$ **end**
27 $\quad$ **end**
28 $\quad$ **return** $RP_{\mathfrak{C}}$
29 **end**

---

is added and in case (ii) both are kept. In both cases, ρ is invoked recursively afterwards. The recursion in one participant instance stops when all reachable completed activity instances have been marked as visited.

4   Related Work

There are several areas related to our work, such as ad hoc repetition in process instances and adaptation of choreographies during modeling and run time. In literature, the concept of ad-hoc repetition in process instances is well studied. For example, in [10] concepts and algorithms for pre-modeled or ad hoc backward jumps, which enable the repeat of logic in process instances enacted by the ADEPT Workflow Management System are presented. The Kepler system supports the concept of smart reruns [1] enabling scientists to repeat parts of a scientific workflow with a different set of parameters. Previously stored provenance information is used to avoid the repetition of parts of the workflow that do not change the overall outcome of the scientific experiment. Similarly, in [8] a system is proposed that supports scientific workflows as well as the concept of reruns of workflow logic for the validation of scientific results but not for enabling an explorative modeling approach as in our work. In [12], process flexibility types are classified. Our concept for rewinding and repeating choreography instances could be classified as *Flexibility by Deviation* – deviating from the specified control flow in the model. Similarly, our repetition is one form of the *Support for Instance-Specific Changes* as described in [15] for individual process instances. However, none of these works consider choreography instances.

Several works exist on the adaptation of choreography models. For example, in [11] the propagation of changes appearing in the private process of one choreography participant to the affected business partners is enabled without considering already running choreographed workflow instances. Formal methods are used to calculate the necessary changes and if the new message interchange is deadlock free. In [4], a generic approach for propagation of local changes to directly as well as transitively dependent business partners is shown. Reichert and Bauer [9] introduce a variant of the ADEPT system that combines the distributed execution of a partitioned workflow model with ad hoc modifications of the workflow instances. Changes on the model are efficiently transmitted to the involved execution engines. In [5], a concept for the evolution of distributed process fragments during run time is proposed identifying change regions and applying changes to the process fragment instances. The major difference of these works to our approach is that we do not start with changes on the level of the model but change running instances in an ad hoc manner.

5   Conclusions and Future Work

In this paper, we motivated the need for the capability to repeat partially or completely the logic in a choreography with a clear focus on the eScience community. Toward this goal, we presented a formal model for describing choreography models and instances. Based on the formal model, we introduced the concept of repeating logic in choreography instances, which involves the rewinding of process instances as a preparatory step. We distinguished between iteration, which executes logic again without undoing already completed work, and re-execution, which aims at the compensation of already completed work before executing it again. We proposed an algorithm that is able to identify the rewinding points for each involved participant instance.

In future, we plan to extend our formal model and proposed algorithm to also consider loop constructs and variable values. The integration of our proposal into the scientific Workflow Management System (sWfMS) [17] is ongoing work. While we currently do support the identification of rewinding points in the graphical environment of our sWfMS in an automated manner, the capability to rewind enacted choreographies through the environment is work in progress. As part of this effort, we also plan to evaluate our proposed algorithm in combination with monitoring data collected from executing simulation workflows in the context of the SimTech project.

Acknowledgments. This work is funded by the project FP7 EU-FET 600792 ALLOW Ensembles and the German DFG within the Cluster of Excellence (EXC310/2) SimTech.

References

1. Altintas, I., Barney, O., Jaeger-Frank, E.: Provenance collection support in the kepler scientific workflow system. In: Moreau, L., Foster, I. (eds.) IPAW 2006. LNCS, vol. 4145, pp. 118–132. Springer, Heidelberg (2006)
2. Barga, R., Gannon, D.: Scientific versus business workflows. In: Workflows for e-Science, pp. 9–16. Springer (2007)
3. Decker, G., Kopp, O., Barros, A.: An Introduction to Service Choreographies. Information Technology **50**(2), 122–127 (2008)
4. Fdhila, W., Rinderle-Ma, S., Reichert, M.: Change propagation in collaborative processes scenarios. In: Proceedings of CollaborateCom 2012. IEEE (2012)
5. Hens, P., Snoeck, M., Poels, G., De Backer, M.: Process Evolution in a Distributed Process Execution Environment. Int. J. Inf. Syst. Model. Des. **4**(2), 65–90 (2013)
6. Hey, T., Tansley, S., Tolle, K. (eds.): The fourth paradigm: data-intensive scientific discovery. Microsoft Research (2009)
7. Leymann, F., Roller, D.: Production Workflow - Concepts and Techniques. PTR Prentice Hall (2000)
8. Lu, S., Zhang, J.: Collaborative scientific workflows. In: Proceedings of ICWS 2009, pp. 527–534. IEEE (2009)
9. Reichert, M., Bauer, T.: Supporting Ad-Hoc changes in distributed workflow management systems. In: Meersman, R., Tari, Z. (eds.) OTM 2007, Part I. LNCS, vol. 4803, pp. 150–168. Springer, Heidelberg (2007)
10. Reichert, M., Dadam, P., Bauer, T.: Dealing with forward and backward jumps in workflow management systems. Software and Systems Modeling **2**(1), 37–58 (2003)
11. Rinderle, S., Wombacher, A., Reichert, M.: Evolution of process choreographies in DYCHOR. In: Meersman, R., Tari, Z. (eds.) OTM 2006. LNCS, vol. 4275, pp. 273–290. Springer, Heidelberg (2006)
12. Schonenberg, H., Mans, R., Russell, N., Mulyar, N., van der Aalst, W.: Process flexibility: A survey of contemporary approaches. In: Dietz, J.L.G., Albani, A., Barjis, J. (eds.) IAO! 2008 and EOMAS 2008. LNBIP, vol. 10, pp. 16–30. Springer, Heidelberg (2008)
13. Sonntag, M., Karastoyanova, D.: Model-as-you-go: An Approach for an Advanced Infrastructure for Scientific Workflows. Grid Computing **11**(3), 553–583 (2013)
14. Sonntag, M., Karastoyanova, D.: Ad hoc Iteration and Re-execution of Activities in Workflows. Int. J. on Advances in Software **5**(1 & 2), 91–109 (2012)
15. Weber, B., Reichert, M., Rinderle-Ma, S.: Change patterns and change support features - enhancing flexibility in process-aware information systems. Data Knowl. Eng. **66**(3), 438–466 (2008)

16. Weiß, A., Karastoyanova, D.: A life cycle for coupled multi-scale, multi-field experiments realized through choreographies. In: Proceedings of EDOC 2014, pp. 234–241. IEEE (2014)
17. Weiß, A., Karastoyanova, D.: Enabling coupled multi-scale, multi-field experiments through choreographies of data-driven scientific simulations. Computing, 1–29 (2014)
18. Wetzstein, B., Karastoyanova, D., Kopp, O., Leymann, F., Zwink, D.: Cross-organizational process monitoring based on service choreographies. In: Proceedings of SAC 2010, pp. 2485–2490. ACM (2010)

Enabling DevOps Collaboration and Continuous Delivery Using Diverse Application Environments

Johannes Wettinger[✉], Vasilios Andrikopoulos, and Frank Leymann

Institute of Architecture of Application Systems, University of Stuttgart,
Universitätsstr. 38, Stuttgart, Germany
{wettinger,andrikopoulos,leymann}@iaas.uni-stuttgart.de

Abstract. Aiming to provide the means for efficient collaboration between development and operations personnel, the DevOps paradigm is backed by an increasingly growing collection of tools and reusable artifacts for application management. Continuous delivery pipelines are established based on these building blocks by implementing fully automated, end-to-end application delivery processes, which significantly shorten release cycles to reduce risks and costs as well as gaining a critical competitive advantage. Diverse application environments need to be managed along the pipeline such as development, build, test, and production environments. In this work we address the need for systematically specifying and maintaining diverse application environment topologies enriched with environment-specific requirements in order to implement continuous delivery pipelines. Beside the representation of such requirements, we focus on their systematic and collaborative resolution with respect to the individual needs of the involved application environments.

Keywords: Continuous delivery · Pipeline · Requirements · Topology · DevOps

1 Introduction

Continuous delivery [3] as an emerging paradigm aims to significantly shorten software release cycles by bridging existing gaps between developers, operations personnel (system administrators), and other parties involved in the delivery process. DevOps [4] is often considered in this context as an approach to improve the collaboration between development ('dev') and operations ('ops'). As a result of improved collaboration, new software releases can be made available much faster. Especially users, customers, and other stakeholders in the fields of Cloud services, Web & mobile applications, and the Internet of Things expect quick responses to changing demands and occurring issues. Consequently, shortening the time to make new releases available becomes a critical competitive advantage. In addition, tight feedback loops involving users and customers based on continuous delivery ensure building the 'right' software, which eventually improves

© Springer International Publishing Switzerland 2015
C. Debruyne et al. (Eds.): OTM 2015 Conferences, LNCS 9415, pp. 348–358, 2015.
DOI: 10.1007/978-3-319-26148-5_23

customer satisfaction, shortens time to market, and reduces costs. Typically, cultural and organizational gaps between developers, operations personnel, and further groups appear, so these separated groups follow different goals such as 'push changes to production quickly' on the development side versus 'keep production stable' on the operations side. This often results in incompatible or even opposing processes and mindsets. By implementing continuous delivery, these goals and processes are aligned. Independent of the chosen approach to establish continuous delivery by tackling cultural and organizational issues, a high degree of technical automation is required. This is typically achieved by implementing an automated *continuous delivery pipeline* (also known as deployment pipeline) [3], covering all required steps such as retrieving code from a repository, building packaged binaries, running tests, and deployment to production. Such an automated and integrated delivery pipeline improves software quality, e.g., by avoiding the deployment of changes that did not pass all tests. Moreover, the high degree of automation typically leads to significant cost reduction because the automated delivery process replaces most of the manual, time-consuming, and error-prone steps. Establishing a continuous delivery pipeline means implementing an individually tailored automation system, which considers the entire delivery process. Furthermore, a separate pipeline has to be established for each independently deployable unit, e.g., an application or microservice [8]. As a result, a potentially large and growing number of individual pipelines has to be maintained. Along each pipeline suitable application environments (development, test, production, etc.) must be established as their key building blocks. Toward this goal, our research focuses on *dynamically and systematically establishing corresponding application environments as the building blocks of continuous delivery pipelines to improve DevOps collaboration.*

The constantly growing DevOps community supports this notion by providing a huge variety of individual approaches such as tools and reusable artifacts to implement holistic delivery automation. Prominent examples are the Chef configuration management framework[1], the Jenkins[2] continuous integration server, and Docker[3] as an efficient container virtualization approach. The open-source communities affiliated with these tools publicly share reusable artifacts to package, deploy, and operate middleware and application components. For instance, Chef's Ruby-based domain-specific language [2] can be used to create and maintain cookbooks — basically scripts to automate the deployment and wiring of different components of an application stack. These approaches are typically combined with Cloud computing [7] to enable on-demand provisioning of resources such as virtual servers and storage in a self-service manner. This is not limited to the infrastructure level, but may also include database-as-a-service and other middleware-centric offerings.

The goal of our work is to systematically handle and resolve such requirements to establish suitable application environments (development, test, production,

---

[1] Chef: http://www.chef.io

[2] Jenkins: http://jenkins-ci.org

[3] Docker: http://www.docker.com

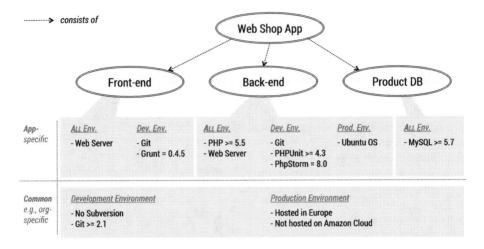

Fig. 1. Web shop application with its environment-specific requirements

etc.) as the key building blocks of continuous delivery pipelines. For this purpose, we provide the means to collaboratively maintain such application environments, allowing developers and operations personnel to share and utilize a common meta-model. As part of this effort we reuse concepts from the fields of requirements engineering and software configuration management. The major contributions of this paper can therefore be summarized by the *representation* of (i) *environment requirements* imposed by applications across different dimensions and of (ii) *application environment topologies* to interlink corresponding requirements, and (iii) the systematic *resolution* of these requirements.

The remainder of this paper is structured as follows: Section 2 presents a motivating scenario that is used throughout the rest of this work. Section 3 introduces the fundamental concepts of our proposal, together with their for-malization as environment-specific requirements. Section 4 discusses how these requirements can be resolved into concrete application environments. Finally, Section 5 concludes the paper and outlines future work.

2   Motivating Scenario

In this section we introduce a Web shop application, which is used as motivating scenario and running example for this work. Figure 1 outlines the three-tier archi-tecture of the Web application, consisting of a front-end, back-end, and product database. The front-end is implemented in HTML and JavaScript to provide the Web shop's user interface. It communicates with the PHP-based back-end using HTTP messages containing JSON data. The back-end itself provides a RESTful API to enable the HTTP-based communication with arbitrary clients such as the Web shop front-end or a mobile shopping application. Product information (inventory, etc.) are stored in the product database, which is based on a MySQL database server.

As shown in Fig. 1, diverse requirements regarding middleware, infrastructure, and tooling are attached to the application stack with respect to the different application environments. Some of them are required for all kinds of environments such as a Web server and a PHP runtime. Build tools and version control mechanisms such as Git[4] and Grunt[5] are only required for development & build environments. On the other hand, some requirements may only be relevant for operating the application in production such as using a specific operating system. Beside the distinction between environments, these requirements can be classified as *application-specific* or *common* requirements: the former ones are essential to develop and operate instances of a specific application, whereas the latter ones are application-agnostic and may be derived from organization- or domain-specific policies. As an example, such a policy could say that all data must be stored in Europe, so the whole application stack must be hosted in Europe when instantiated. In the following sections we discuss how such requirements can be represented, systematically handled, and resolved to collaboratively establish continuous delivery pipelines.

3   Fundamentals

In this section we focus on introducing a set of fundamental concepts that allow us to address the challenges identified in the previous sections. More specifically, we propose for this purpose the concept of *application environment requirements (AERs)* and discuss their relation to other existing kinds of requirements (Section 3.1). We then show how *application environment topologies (AETs)* can be used to describe application environments by interlinking AERs (Section 3.2). Finally, we outline how to collaboratively establish continuous delivery pipelines based on AERs and AETs (Section 3.3).

3.1   Application Environment Requirements

The Web shop application we introduced in Section 2 outlines several requirements attached to different parts of the application stack. These are all non-functional requirements — such as infrastructure and middleware requirements — that need to be satisfied to establish different kinds of environments for a particular application. For this purpose, we propose *application environment requirements (AERs)* as the *subset of non-functional requirements imposed by an application on its underlying environment for different stages of the application lifecycle.* We do not consider functional requirements of the application related to the application's user interface and other application features. However, we do consider the relation of AERs to other non-functional requirements. Referring to the Web shop application, for example, the requirement that the application is hosted in Europe may have been derived from a specific compliance requirement, saying that all data must stay in Europe to conform to the

---

[4] Git: http://git-scm.com
[5] Grunt: http://gruntjs.com

EU Data Protection Directive [6]. As already outlined by the Web shop example (Section 2) environment-specific AERs need to be considered and satisfied when building a corresponding environment such as a development environment or production environment. Some AERs are relevant for multiple environments such as the PHP runtime required by the back-end of the Web application: this does not only affect production and test environments, but also development environments, e.g., to allow developers to analyze the impact of their code changes immediately and locally on their developer environment.

Definition 1 (AER Predicate). *An* AER *predicate is a representation of an* AER *in predicate logic. Assuming that* $\mathcal{M} = \{im, ev\}$ *is the set of modes (im = 'immediately required', ev = 'eventually required') for AERs,* $\mathcal{E}$ *is the domain of all entities that can be potentially required (middleware, infrastructure, etc.),* $\mathcal{P}$ *is the domain of all possible properties the entities may own, and* $\mathcal{V}$ *is the domain of all potential property values, there are two valid forms of AER predicates:* $P_{<label>}^{m,<name>} : \mathcal{E} \rightarrow \{true, false\}$ *and* $P_{<label>}^{m,<name>} : \mathcal{E} \times \mathcal{P} \times \mathcal{V} \rightarrow \{true, false\}$, $m \in \mathcal{M}$.

The following AER predicates can be identified based on this definition to properly express AERs for applications such as the Web shop application described previously:

- $P_{<label>}^{im,include} : \mathcal{E} \rightarrow \{true, false\}$ implies that a solution for a particular entity $e \in \mathcal{E}$ must *immediately* exist in the application stack (e.g., the runtime in which a component is executed); otherwise the predicate evaluates to *false*.

- $P_{<label>}^{ev,include} : \mathcal{E} \rightarrow \{true, false\}$ implies that a solution for a particular entity $e \in \mathcal{E}$ must *eventually* exist in the application stack (e.g., the underlying operating system); otherwise the predicate evaluates to *false*.

Further AER predicates can be defined in this fashion such as $P_{<label>}^{im|ev,exclude} : \mathcal{E} \rightarrow \{true, false\}$ as the inversion of $P_{<label>}^{im|ev,include}$. The '|' symbol is used to indicate variants of the defined predicates, e.g., $im|ev$ to immediately or eventually exclude solutions. Moreover, $P_{<label>}^{im|ev,equals|eqGr} : \mathcal{E} \times \mathcal{P} \times \mathcal{V} \rightarrow \{true, false\}$ implies that $P_{<label>}^{im|ev,include}(e) = true$ for a particular entity $e \in \mathcal{E}$ and the given solution owns a property $p \in \mathcal{P}$ and its value equals to (or is greater than) $v \in \mathcal{V}$; otherwise the predicate evaluates to *false*. As an example referring to the Web shop application, we may define the following AER predicate to express the requirement that the back-end must be *immediately* hosted on a PHP runtime, version 5.5 or better: $P_{PHP}^{im,eqGr}$('PHP', 'version', '5.5'). Such predicates can be bundled as logical expressions using logical operators such as:

$$P_{PHP}^{im,eqGr}(\text{'PHP', 'version', '5.5'}) \wedge P_{Ubuntu}^{ev,include}(\text{'Ubuntu OS'}) \wedge ...$$

3.2   Application Environment Topologies

For the purpose of representing both the application and the environment for which AERs are defined we use the concept of an *application environment topology (AET)*. AETs can be expressed as *typed graphs* following [1], where all nodes and edges are of the form $< name : type >$ and $< type >$, respectively. Nodes represent components of the application stack, including *aaS solutions such as infrastructure-as-a-service (IaaS) and database-as-a-service (DBaaS), while edges represent the different types of relations between them, e.g., *HostedOn, DependsOn,* etc. Examples for nodes are *ApacheHTTPServer:WebServer* (named node) and *WebServer* (unnamed node). As discussed in [1], many existing works such as the TOSCA specification[6], the Cloud Blueprinting approach [9], and the CloudML language[7], as well as solutions like Amazon CloudFormation[8], the OpenNebula initiative[9], or OpenStack Heat[10], essentially build on this typed topology graph model in various forms.

In order to connect an AER with the actual application that they express requirements for, AERs are allowed to be attached to different parts of an AET. AERs for example can be attached to nodes, denoting the requirements expressed by the component on the environment, or to subgraphs in the AET, denoting requirements that need to be satisfied for all nodes in the subgraph, e.g., for the front-end of the application. An attachment map is used for this purpose:

Definition 2 (AER Attachment Map). *An* AER attachment map *is a mapping function f_{map} associated with a particular AET to assign AER predicates to specific parts of the topology. Assuming that N is the set of nodes in the topology T, $\mathcal{X}$ is the domain of logical expressions consisting of AER predicates, and $\mathcal{E} = \{development, test, production, ...\}$ representing the environments to which AERs are bound, then the mapping function is formally defined as $f_{map} : N \cup \{T\} \times \mathcal{E} \rightarrow \mathcal{X}$.*

The mapping function f_{map} is used to attach application-specific AERs to nodes in the AET and to the topology as a whole, without the need of modifying the topology definition. In case not all AERs are reflected by solutions in a topology, we refer to such a topology with an associated AER attachment map as an *unresolved topology:*

Definition 3 (Unresolved AET). *An* unresolved AET (unresolved topology) *is an application environment topology containing at least one AER that is not satisfied by an attached solution.*

Unresolved requirements can be satisfied in different ways, depending on which kind of application environment (development, production, etc.) should be described by a resulting *resolved topology:*

---

[6] TOSCA: http://www.oasis-open.org/committees/tosca
[7] CloudML: http://cloudml.org
[8] Amazon CloudFormation: http://aws.amazon.com/cloudformation
[9] OpenNebula: http://opennebula.org
[10] OpenStack Heat: https://wiki.openstack.org/wiki/Heat

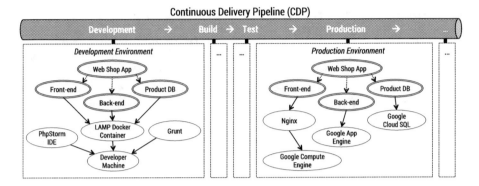

Fig. 2. Example for continuous delivery pipeline (CDP) for the Web shop application

Definition 4 (Resolved AET). *A* resolved AET (resolved topology) *is an application environment topology containing at least one solution for each AER attached to the topology.*

As an example, a PHP runtime environment may be satisfied by a corresponding Docker container[11] with minimum overhead for a development environment. However, for a production environment, an elastic platform-as-a-service solution such as Google App Engine[12] could be more appropriate. In the following, we outline how AERs and AETs are utilized to establish continuous delivery pipelines.

3.3 Continuous Delivery Pipelines (CDPs)

The eventual purpose of AERs and AETs is to systematically and collaboratively establish continuous delivery. Technically, continuous delivery pipelines have to be built and maintained for this reason. In this context, we refer to a *continuous delivery pipeline (CDP) as a delivery automation system, individually tailored and maintained per independently deployable unit such as an application or a microservice.* Thus, a CDP implements an application-specific delivery plan. Consequently, a potentially large and growing number of individual CDPs have to be established and maintained, especially when following the emerging microservice architecture style [8]. In addition, this has to be done in a collaborative manner to enable aligned and automated delivery processes, considering diverse parties that are involved such as developers and operations personnel. By resolving AERs appropriately, diverse application environments (development environment, production environment, etc.) are established as key building blocks of a CDP. Figure 2 shows an example for a CDP, considering the requirements of the Web shop application described in Section 2. Each phase of the CDP has a dedicated resolved AET attached: a development environment

---

[11] PHP Docker container: https://registry.hub.docker.com/_/php

[12] Google App Engine: https://cloud.google.com/appengine

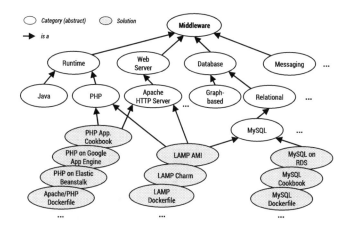

Fig. 3. Middleware solutions stored in the knowledge base and organized in a taxonomy

typically aims to be lightweight, e.g., by running the entire application stack in a single container. Moreover, development tools are required to run on the developer machine. These are not necessary in a production environment. On the other hand, a production environment would be preferably based on scalable and elastic Cloud offerings to keep the application responsive even in case a lot of load appears. In the following, we present the usage of a knowledge base and a supporting process to find suitable solutions in order to resolve AERs. In this manner, resolved topologies are created in order to instantiate specific application environments, which can then be tied together to establish a continuous delivery pipeline.

4   Requirements Resolution

In order to create an instance of a particular application environment (e.g., a development environment for the Web shop application outlined in Section 2), all AERs attached to an unresolved AET need to be satisfied. In Section 4.1 we outline the usage of a *knowledge base (KB)* for the purpose of resolving AERs. Based on the existence of such a KB, Section 4.2 discusses how diverse application environments (development, production, etc.) can be built by deriving resolved topologies.

4.1   Application Environment Knowledge Base (KB)

In order to enable the resolution of *unresolved topologies* with attached AERs we propose the use of a *knowledge base (KB)* that enables informed decision making when satisfying AERs to create resolved topologies that can be used to instantiate application environments. The KB [10] contains linked solutions such as reusable artifacts, tools, and services to manage development, infrastructure, and middleware aspects of an application environment. Technically, the KB is distributed and composed, so it is not a monolithic system. This enables the KB to be collaboratively maintained, e.g., considering experts from different domains such as developers and system administrators.

Figure 3 outlines a small selection of middleware solutions stored in the KB. These are captured in a taxonomy that consists of abstract entities (for categorization purposes) and the actual solutions. Similarly, infrastructure solutions (e.g., virtual server images), development solutions (e.g., version control and build tools), and other supplementary solutions (e.g., monitoring tools) are captured in further taxonomies stored in the KB. Links that potentially cross taxonomy boundaries are established between solutions to express dependencies such as a middleware component that relies on a particular operating system to run[13].

4.2   Building Diverse Application Environments

The ultimate goal of our work is to allow the automated building of diverse application environments as key building blocks of a continuous delivery pipeline for a particular application such as the Web shop introduced in Section 2. Therefore, we need to provide the means to derive a suitable, resolved topology that satisfies all associated AERs. The following process can be used for this purpose:

1. Define constraints to express *environment preferences* for the target environment, e.g., *minimum resource usage* for development environments vs. *resilient & elastic* for production environments.
2. Use the unresolved topology with its AER attachment map in conjunction with application-agnostic, common AERs to reason about the given AERs and constraints by querying the KB for appropriate solutions.
3. Evaluate environment preferences to filter (and potentially rank) the resulting resolved topologies.
4. Pick a suitable or, if a ranking is available, the most suitable resolved topology.

The concept of expressing additional preference requirements (environment-specific constraints in our case) is well-known, e.g., from goal-oriented approaches established in the field of requirements engineering [5]; beside the mandatory requirements (AERs in our case) that must be fulfilled by any proposed solution, (potentially prioritized) preference requirements ('nice-to-have') such as solution details and complex temporal properties are expressed and considered. This is enabled by not only searching the optimal solution based on the mandatory requirements, but also considering alternative solutions when satisfying AERs in unresolved topologies.

Building on previous work [1], the original, unresolved AET is represented as an application-specific α-*topology*; using the α-topology, a reusable γ-*topology* is

---

[13] More information on the KB is available at: http://github.com/jojow/aer-paper

derived from the knowledge base, considering all potential topology alternatives. Both α- and γ-topologies are typed graphs with inheritance (essentially, class diagrams using only association and inheritance relations, expressed as graphs), from the combination of which a set of *viable* topologies can be derived. Viable topologies in the context of [1] refer only to the fact that the topology graph is typed over the elements of the graph resulting from the union of the α- and γ-topologies, also called the μ-topology. A potentially large set of viable topologies can be created by the morphism from the type graph of the μ-topology to the typed graphs of application topologies. For this purpose, a *filter function* σ is used to prune down the number of potentially viable topologies $\mathcal{T}$. In principle, a set of constraints $\mathcal{C}$ is defined based on environment preferences for each viable topology T:

$$\sigma(T,c) = \begin{cases} T & \text{if } condition(c)\text{=}true, \\ \emptyset & \text{otherwise.} \end{cases} \text{ , where } T \in \mathcal{T}, c \in \mathcal{C}.$$

Filter functions can be chained to allow for multiple such constraints to be applied. Following [1], we also use *utility functions* to rank the filtered, viable topologies (e.g., minimum number of nodes) in order to find the most suitable topology that satisfies all AERs and the corresponding environment preferences. Any kind of function can be used as a utility function, as long as it allows for the mapping from the space of viable topologies to that of real numbers. For example, a utility function could return the number of nodes in the topology graph, aiming for minimizing the number of components required for the deployment of the application. Multiple dimensions can be combined, e.g., number of nodes with costs of operating the application under a given load, as discussed in [1]. We finally performed an evaluation using a case study based on the Web shop application[14].

5   Conclusions

Continuous delivery and DevOps have emerged with the goal to bring together developers and operations personnel by enabling their efficient collaboration. This is technically supported by establishing automated continuous delivery pipelines to significantly shorten release cycles without quality degradation. Diverse application environments (development, test, production, etc.) form the key building blocks of a continuous delivery pipeline. In the previous sections we proposed the concept of application environment requirements as a particular kind of non-functional requirements and formalized their representation using predicate logic, which allowed us to define mappings between application topologies and application environment requirements. For the resolution of these requirements into concrete environments we proposed the usage of a knowledge base in combination with a resolution process with distinct tasks. With respect

---

[14] More information on the evaluation is available at: http://github.com/jojow/aer-paper

to the latter, in this work we focused on deriving suitable application environments driven by diverse environment preferences. We plan however to extend the resolution and selection process in future work by considering costs and QoS aspects, using [1] as the basis. Moreover, we aim to use AERs and the knowledge base to support the migration of existing applications, e.g., to consider the available options for partially or fully migrating an application to the Cloud.

Acknowledgments. This work is partially funded by the FP7 EU-FET project 600792 ALLOW Ensembles.

References

1. Andrikopoulos, V., Gómez Sáez, S., Leymann, F., Wettinger, J.: Optimal distribution of applications in the cloud. In: Jarke, M., Mylopoulos, J., Quix, C., Rolland, C., Manolopoulos, Y., Mouratidis, H., Horkoff, J. (eds.) CAiSE 2014. LNCS, vol. 8484, pp. 75–90. Springer, Heidelberg (2014)
2. Günther, S., Haupt, M., Splieth, M.: Utilizing Internal Domain-Specific Languages for Deployment and Maintenance of IT Infrastructures. Tech. rep., Very Large Business Applications Lab Magdeburg, Fakultät für Informatik, Otto-von-Guericke-Universität Magdeburg (2010)
3. Humble, J., Farley, D.: Continuous Delivery: Reliable Software Releases through Build, Test, and Deployment Automation. Addison-Wesley Professional (2010)
4. Hüttermann, M.: DevOps for Developers. Apress (2012)
5. Liaskos, S., McIlraith, S.A., Sohrabi, S., Mylopoulos, J.: Representing and Reasoning About Preferences in Requirements Engineering. Requirements Engineering **16**(3), 227–249 (2011)
6. Louridas, P.: Up in the Air: Moving Your Applications to the Cloud. IEEE Software **27**(4), 6–11 (2010)
7. Mell, P., Grance, T.: The NIST Definition of Cloud Computing. National Institute of Standards and Technology (2011)
8. Newman, S.: Building Microservices. O'Reilly Media (2015)
9. Papazoglou, M., van den Heuvel, W.: Blueprinting the Cloud. IEEE Internet Computing **15**(6), 74–79 (2011)
10. Wettinger, J., Andrikopoulos, V., Leymann, F.: Automated capturing and systematic usage of devops knowledge for cloud applications. In: Proceedings of the International Conference on Cloud Engineering (IC2E). IEEE Computer Society (2015)

Ontologies, DataBases, and Applications of Semantics (ODBASE) 2015

ODBASE 2015 PC Co-Chairs' Message

The International Conference on Ontologies, DataBases, and Applications of Semantics (ODBASE) provides a forum for exchanging ideas and research results on the use of ontologies and data semantics in novel applications. The 14th ODBASE conference is held in Rhodes, Greece, on 26-30 October 2015. As in previous years, ODBASE 2015 continues to draw a highly diverse body of researchers and practitioners. ODBASE is part of the OnTheMove (OTM 2015) federated event composed of three interrelated yet complementary scientific conferences. The other two co-located conferences are CoopIS'15 (Cooperative Information Systems) and C&TC'15 (Cloud and Trusted Computing'15). These three conferences together attempt to span a relevant range of the advanced research on, and cutting-edge development and application of, information handling and systems in the wider current context of ubiquitous distributed computing.

Of particular relevance to ODBASE 2015 are papers that bridge traditional boundaries between disciplines such as databases, conceptual modeling, ontology, social networks, artificial intelligence, information extraction, and knowledge management.

This year, we received 38 abstract submissions and invited a Program Committee (PC) of 66 dedicated colleagues. Each submitted full paper was reviewed by 4-5 PC members of different research areas. As a result, the final program consists of 8 regular papers (up to 18 pages), 6 short papers (up to 8 pages), and 1 poster (up to 4 pages). Their themes span a spectrum of studies on a number of modern challenges including querying and management of linked data and OWL documents, ontology engineering, semantic matching and mapping, social network analysis, web services discovery, and mobile data. We are also grateful for John Mylopoulos for giving us an insightful keynote speech on Data Semantics in the Days of Big Data.

We would like to thank all the members of the Program Committee for their hard work in reviewing the papers. We would also like to thank all the researchers who submitted their work to the conference.

We hope that you enjoy ODBASE 2015 and have a wonderful time in Rhodes, Greece!

September 2015

Yuan An
Min Song
Markus Strohmaier

COBieOWL, an OWL Ontology
Based on COBie Standard

Tarcisio M. Farias[1(✉)], Ana Roxin[2], and Christophe Nicolle[2]

[1] Active3D, Dijon, France
t.mendesdefarias@active3D.net
[2] Checksem, Laboratory LE2I (UMR CNRS 6306),
University Bourgogne Franche-Comté, Dijon, France
{ana-maria.roxin,cnicolle}@u-bourgogne.fr

Abstract. Building Information Modelling (BIM) standards have been recognized by construction and political actors as a highly promising tool for resolving issues of data dematerialization, notably in the field of Architecture, Engineering, Construction and Facility Management. Among worldwide-adopted BIM standards, there is COBie. COBie's goals are to dematerialize building data and to enhance building information interoperability. Nevertheless, COBie data is available in static formats such as STEP or spreadsheet templates. Such formats lack logical formalisms and semantic features provided by languages such as OWL. Because of this, in this paper, we propose a method for semi-automatically conceiving an OWL ontology for the COBie standard starting from a COBie spreadsheet template. We call this ontology COBieOWL and we populate it directly from COBie spreadsheet data files as used by building actors. We also discuss various benefits of adopting our approach, for example: it reduces semantic heterogeneity of the COBie model. Besides, we discuss how COBieOWL can be linked to other LOD datasets such as FOAF.

Keywords: Building ontology · Linked data · Building Information Modelling · COBie · COBieOWL · Spreadsheet-to-OWL

1   Introduction

Building life-cycles produce important amounts of data. These data are generally hard-printed data stored in boxes and concern aspects related to building design, construction, operations and maintenance. Building Information Modelling (BIM) standards have been recognized by construction and political actors as a highly promising tool for resolving issues of data dematerialization, notably in the field of Architecture, Engineering, Construction and Facility Management (AEC/FM) [1]. In late 2006, among BIM standards, the Construction-Operations Building information exchange (COBie) [2] was created under the National Institute of Building Sciences (NIBS) Facility Maintenance and Operations Committee [3]. COBie standard addresses contractors, builders, designers and facility managers. This standard aims at delivering a novel method for sharing data during building life-cycle.

COBie's goals are to dematerialize building data and to enhance building information interoperability. Nevertheless, COBie data is available in static formats such as

© Springer International Publishing Switzerland 2015
C. Debruyne et al. (Eds.): OTM 2015 Conferences, LNCS 9415, pp. 361–377, 2015.
DOI: 10.1007/978-3-319-26148-5_24

STEP [4] or a spreadsheet template (see subsection 2.3). Such formats lack logical formalisms and semantic features provided by languages such as W3C Ontology Web Language (OWL) [5]. The lack of such formalisms raises issues related to semantic heterogeneity. Still, adopting one standard for data exchange, such as using XML [6], does not eliminate the data heterogeneity problem: it raises heterogeneity problems at a higher level. As noted by Alon Y. Halevy in [7], semantic heterogeneity appears whenever there is more than one way to structure a body of data.

OWL-based ontologies are an interesting and promising approach regarding data interoperability and exchange, mainly because they handle formal representations of data (description logic-based) over which one may perform reasoning in a decidable manner. Our choice of the OWL language for representing the COBie standard is dictated by the fact that we want to connect the COBie dataset to other Linked Open Data (LOD) datasets. Based on such assumption, in this paper, we propose a method for semi-automatically conceiving an OWL ontology for the COBie standard starting from a COBie spreadsheet template (e.g. COBie 2.4 [2]). We call this ontology CO-BieOWL and we populate it directly from COBie spreadsheet data files as used by building actors. This way, the latter do not have to learn how to use (or buy) a new software for working with COBieOWL. These advantages are very important for the adoption of BIM by building stakeholders. In [25], Eadie et al. states that the lack of flexibility, the lack of technical expertise and the cost of software are in the top four barriers for BIM adoption by non-users of BIM.

Furthermore, with regard to the Linked Open Data (LOD) context, we also propose to link COBieOWL to existing published datasets in order to enrich the existing building information on Web. Pauwels et al. in [8] proposed possible links for a building ontology based on the Industry Foundation Classes (IFC) [19] standard to other datasets in LOD. However, if we look at the LOD diagram published in August 2014 [9], no ontologies for building information have been yet proposed as part of it. Still, several initiatives such as IfcWoD [10] keep emerging for representing building data using OWL language. This also justifies our decision to use OWL because CO-BieOWL datasets can be linked to these datasets (e.g. IfcWoD datasets).

The article at hand is structured as follows: section 2 gives the scientific background for our work and presents most important related work in the considered domain; section 3 details our approach, notably the semi-automatic procedure implemented for conceiving the COBieOWL ontology; benefits of using COBieOWL for data exchange in the building context are described in section 4. Finally, we conclude this article by identifying additional works that could be undertaken.

2   Background and Related Works

2.1   Semantic Web Technologies

The Semantic Web vision allows describing meaning in a machine-readable form. For doing this, languages developed for the Semantic Web are based on standards (e.g. RDF/RDF Schema [11]) and logic-based knowledge representation formats (e.g. OWL, Web Ontology Language [5]) that allow automated reasoning. OWL is based on Description Logics (DL) formalisms. Table 1 illustrates DL syntax terms (summarized from [12]) which are used in this paper with their respective semantics. An interpretation I comprises a set Δ^I that is the domain of I and an interpretation function $\cdot^I$.

Table 1. Syntax and semantics of description logic (DL) [12].

Description	DL Syntax	Semantics
Individual name	a	a^I
Atomic role	R	R^I
Inverse role	R^-	$\{(x,y) \mid (y,x) \in R^I\}$
Atomic concept	C	C^I
Union	$C \sqcup D$	$C^I \cup D^I$
Top concept	$\top$	Δ^I
Existential restriction	$\exists R.C$	$\{x \mid some\ R^I - successor\ of\ x\ is\ in\ C^I\}$
Universal restriction	$\forall R.C$	$\{x \mid all\ R^I - successor\ of\ x\ are\ in\ C^I\}$
Nominal	$\{a\}$	$\{a^I\}$
Concept inclusion	$C \sqsubseteq D$	$C^I \subseteq D^I$
Concept equivalence	$C \equiv D$	$C^I = D^I$
Role equivalence	$R \equiv S$	$R^I = S^I$
Concept assertion	$C(a)$	$a^I \in C^I$
Role assertion	$R(a,b)$	$(a^I, b^I) \in R^I$

where a and b are individual names, A is a concept name, C and D are concepts, R and S are roles.

Open standards such as SPARQL [13] allow querying a RDF-based knowledge base, along with several additional constructs for processing results (e.g. limit, order, offset).

Rule languages can be a complement to DL-based languages (such as OWL) as they allow representing different axioms. The Semantic Web Rule Language (SWRL) [14] combines OWL and RuleML [15]. SWRL makes it possible to specify conjunctive rules over the concepts and relationships present in an OWL ontology [16].

2.2 Building Information Modelling

A building lifecycle mainly comprises three phases: design, construction and facility management. Such building lifecycle produces considerable amounts of data that have to be handled and updated by several stakeholders (e.g. architects, civil engineers, facility managers, etc.). BIM [18] is one of the latest approaches proposed in the AEC/FM domain for bridging the existing interoperability gap among current systems in this field [1].

One of the first steps in BIM standardization was conducted in 1999 by buildingSMART[1]. It resulted in the development of a model for representing the majority of components of a physical building, namely the IFC model (Industry Foundation Classes) [19].

---

[1] http://www.buildingsmart-tech.org/

2.3   COBie, Construction-Operations Building Information Exchange Standard

In 2007, COBie [2] was proposed as a simple way for sharing building information that does not include geometric modelling [20]. It is, indeed, a spreadsheet-based data format (open-standard) that contains digital information about a building. This allows the participation of several stakeholders without needing long training and new software acquisition. The purpose of COBie is to improve how information is captured during design and construction, and then provided for operations, maintenance, and asset management purposes.

COBie is a worldwide recognized standard implemented in design, construction, and maintenance commercial software for managing building information worldwide [2]. The COBie project has been led by a laboratory of the U.S. Army, Corps of Engineers. COBie provides an important flexibility because building life-cycle information can be viewed in simple spreadsheets and it allows to be used on all building projects regardless of size and technological complexity.

For each building project, one COBie file is provided. All phases of the building project (e.g. design, construction and facility management) contemplate COBie deliverables that follow the same processes used in design and construction. COBie basically represents the main information provided in paper documents into information that can be re-used through the project. Fig. 1 summarizes the COBie deliverable process.

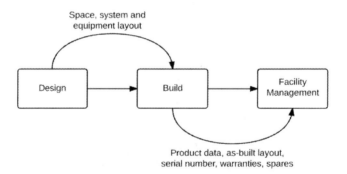

Fig. 1. Illustration of the COBie process.

In early design phases, architects propose spaces and collection of spaces for supporting the activities required by clients. This information is delivered through the schematic diagrams (i.e. schematic design drawings) that give a general view of the project considering client requirements. COBie delivers the portion of the schematic design information related to spaces, zones, and room data sheets. This COBie information is used to verify that the facility being designed satisfies the owner's (i.e. client) expectations. COBie data files consider information about spaces and architectural products and schedules as found on the schematic design documents.

Once the early design phase accomplished, engineers are responsible for the detail design phase. They develop the systems in order to supply the required services such as water, electricity, fire protection, security, etc. This information is given at the construction documents design stage. Therefore, COBie delivers as well information concerning product and equipment assets that will afterwards be managed by the facility manager or the building owner. This asset information is originated from the equipment and product specifications.

In construction phases, COBie construction deliverables are obtained from the construction documents. A COBie submission before the final completion of a building project (i.e. beneficial occupancy) allows the facility manager to start well operating the building from its occupation. A COBie as-built submission is also provided to structure all information concerning final changes and as-built conditions. Other sources such as documents containing approved submissions, warranty certificates, installation and testing of equipment documentation are also considered during construction phase. The resulting COBie deliverable is a set of operations and maintenance manuals that can be used by facility managers.

After the delivery of a building, information about maintenance and operations can be loaded by the owner or facility manager directly into a spreadsheet software or a COBie-based maintenance management system. They can begin the efficient operation of the building as well update COBie data (e.g. produced data from the building renovation).

In order to provide an easier access and vulgarization, COBie was conceived for being a spreadsheet-based exchange format. Because of this, a COBie spreadsheet template[2] is available for building actors. This template contains an "Instruction" sheet that describes general information about the COBie version and data that has to be provided. Moreover, this sheet contains information about the meanings of the various colours used for specifying if a sheet and/or a column is required to be filled with respect to precise project phases. Colour legend in COBie 2.4 template is described as follows:

- Yellow: required
- Orange: reference to other sheet or pick list
- Purple: external reference
- Green: if specified as required
- Grey: secondary information when preparing product data.

Fig. 2 displays, in yellow, the required sheets for the design phase. COBie 2.4 is composed of 20 sheets that include one instruction sheet and one Picklist sheet. The Picklist sheet contains several columns of values referenced by other column sheets. Table 2 shows all sheets (except Instruction and Picklist sheets) from the COBie 2.4 template and their contents that can be filled in accord to the building project phases. These sheets are similar to relational database tables.

---

[2]   The COBie 2.4 template and examples are available online:
       http://www.nibs.org/?page=bsa_commonbimfiles

Instruction / Contact / Facility / Floor / Space / Zone / Type / Component / System ,

Fig. 2. Some sheets from COBie 2.4 template.

Table 2. COBie 2.4 sheets and their contents.

Project phase	Sheet	Contents
Early Design	Facility	Project, site and facility
	Floor	Vertical levels and exterior areas
	Space	Spaces
	Zone	Sets of spaces sharing a specific attribute
	Type	Types of equipment, products, and materials
Detailed Design	Component	Individually named or schedule items
	System	Sets of components providing a service
	Assembly	Constituents for types, components and others
	Connection	Logical connections between components
	Impact	Economic, environmental and social impacts at various stages in the life cycle
Construction	Document	Inclusion of submission and approval documents
	Type	Insertion of manufacturer and model information
	Component	Inclusion of serial and tag data
Facility Management	Spare	Onsite and replacement parts
	Resource	Required materials, tools, and training
	Job	PM, safety, and other job plans
All Phases	Document	All applicable document references
	Attribute	Properties of referenced item
	Coordinate	Spatial locations in box, line, or point format
	Issue	Other issues remaining at handover.
	Contact	People and companies

COBie columns reference other column values by using data validation rules. For example, Fig. 3 shows the column "CreatedBy" in the Facility sheet that makes reference to values present in the "email" column from the Contact sheet.

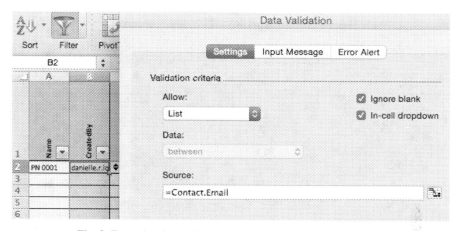

Fig. 3. Example of a Facility sheet and a data validation rule.

2.4 Related Works

As noted in the Introduction of this article, several initiatives have been undertaken regarding the use of Semantic Web technologies in the AEC/FM domain. Among those, Farias et al. in [10] propose an adaptation of the Industry Foundation Classes (IFC) model [19] into OWL which allows leveraging all modelling constraints required by the object-oriented structure of the IFC schema. This ontology is called IfcWoD and it allows sharing building information in the linked data context [17][21].

Regarding the conversion of spreadsheet files into OWL, several approaches have been proposed over the last few years. Among those we may cite approaches described in [22], [23] and [24]. Nevertheless, none of them are fully adapted for extracting all model semantics as structured in the 2.4 COBie template (e.g. COBie code colours). Various spreadsheet-to-OWL conversion approaches are based on the definition of correspondences by using a mapping language. This is not well adapted in the COBie context because each new version of COBie standard implies an update of the mapping ensemble. Consequently, this entails that users not used to these languages have to learn them. However, as we have mentioned before, COBie is a standard that aims at avoiding such additional training. Because of this, our approach relies on the spreadsheet data validation functionality for stating restriction axioms and object properties in the ontology. Moreover, column colour codes are also considered. These characteristics present in COBie spreadsheet template are not considered in the previous identified spreadsheet-to-OWL conversion approaches.

Despite extensive studies, to the best of our knowledge, there is no work proposing a semi-automatic approach for conceiving an OWL-based ontology for the COBie standard.

3   The COBieOWL Ontology

In this section, we present our approach for semi-automatically conceiving an OWL ontology based on 2.4 COBie standard (i.e. COBieOWL). We also present our method for populating this ontology with data extracted from existing COBie spreadsheets. We have used Java for coding our COBieOWL generator, along with external Application Programming Interfaces (APIs) for handling spreadsheet files (Apache POI API) [3] and OWL ontologies (OWL API)[4]. For the sake of simplicity, we do not mention concept and roles namespaces when using description logic for describing COBieOWL ontology.

3.1   A Semi-automatic Approach for the Conception of the COBie Ontology

In our approach, general rules retained for conceiving an OWL ontology for COBie standard (COBieOWL) are listed as follows:

- Each sheet from the COBie 2.4 template is mapped as an OWL class;
- Columns from sheets are mapped as OWL properties;
- Cells from the second row to the end of every sheet are mapped as property values.

Fig. 4 shows a portion of the COBie ontology as proposed. For each OWL class C corresponding to one COBie template sheet, our approach asserts the following concept inclusion: $C \sqsubseteq CobieSheet$ (i.e. C is a subclass of CobieSheet). CobieSheet is an additional concept (i.e. $CobieSheet \sqsubseteq \top$) for gathering all concrete (i.e. instantiable) concepts from COBie standard (e.g.: Facility, Floor, System, etc.).

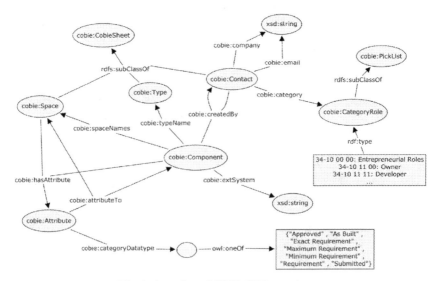

Fig. 4. A portion of COBieOWL ontology.

---

[3]   https://poi.apache.org/
[4]   http://owlapi.sourceforge.net/

Moreover, if a COBie column contains a string value that points to another column in a different sheet, then this column is mapped as an OWL object property. For referencing other sheets/columns, the COBie template implements data validation rules. We take advantage of these spreadsheet rules for asserting OWL object properties and their ranges. Indeed, the OWL range of these properties is the OWL class representing the sheet that contains the referenced column. For illustrating this, let us consider the *CreatedBy* column present in all concrete concepts from COBie. This column makes reference to "Email" column from the Contact sheet. Then, our approach defines the following axioms in COBieOWL: $Contact \sqsubseteq \top$, $\top \sqsubseteq \forall createdBy.Contact$ and $\exists createdBy.\top \sqsubseteq Cobiesheet$. Thus, this means in OWL that *cobie:createdBy* property is an OWL object property with *cobie:Contact* class as its range.

Furthermore, the most part of COBieOWL properties are functional, because we have only one value for each column cell. The *cobie:resourceNames* property is an exception. This property maps the *ResourceNames* column from the Job sheet. Cells from *ResourceNames* column have a list of resource names as values which are previously defined in the *Name* column from the *Resource* sheet. These values can be interpreted as foreign keys in a relational database context. These keys make reference to the *Resource* sheet and they are separated using commas. Therefore, *ResourceNames* column is mapped as a non-functional OWL object property and their values are *cobie:Resource* individuals. For doing so, our approach states the following axioms in COBieOWL: $Job \sqsubseteq \top$, $Resource \sqsubseteq \top$, $\top \sqsubseteq \forall resourceNames.Resource$ and $\exists resourceNames.\top \sqsubseteq Job$.

Some columns with values from a predefined list (e.g.: the *Category* column) are mapped as OWL datatype properties and the respective values are mapped as OWL enumerations (by using *owl:oneof*). Such enumeration is stated as a restriction for the respective OWL property in a specific class context. For exemplifying this, let us suppose the enumeration *ZoneType* and the *cobie:category* property. *cobie:category* is an OWL datatype property in COBieOWL representing the "Category" column from the Zone sheet. *ZoneType* (illustrated in Fig. 5) is a set of values from the correspondent Picklist of the Zone *Category* column (i.e.: $ZONETYPE \equiv \{Circulation\ Zone\} \sqcup \{Fire\ Alarm\ Zone\} \sqcup \ldots \sqcup \{Ventilation\ Zone\}$). Therefore, our approach states the following axiom in COBieOWL: $Zone \sqsubseteq \forall category.ZONETYPE$.

	AS	AT	AU	AV	AW	AX	AY
1	ZoneType	LinearUnit	VolumeUnit	CostUnit	AssemblyType	ImpactType	ImpactStage
2	Circulation Zone	inches	cubicfeet	Dollars	Fixed	Cost	Production
3	Lighting Zone	feet	cubicmeters	Euros	Optional	ClimateChange	Installation
4	Fire Alarm Zone	miles			Included	PrimaryEnergyConsumption	Maintenance
5	Historical Preservation Zone	millimeters			Excluded		Replacement
6	Occupancy Zone	meters			Layer		Use
7	Ventilation Zone	kilometers			Patch		Reuse
8					Mix		
9							
10							
11							

Spare / Resource / Job / Impact / Document / Attribute / Coordinate / Issue / PickL

Fig. 5. A portion of the PickList sheet.

When including roles in the knowledge base (KB), if a column (from a given sheet) makes reference to lists from the PickList sheet with a cardinality greater than a threshold *t,* our approach maps this column as an OWL object property. The range of these properties is a subclass of *cobie:PickList*. In this case, a column in the PickList sheet is mapped as an OWL class that is a subclass of *cobie:PickList*. We do not determine the set of strings as an enumeration by using *owl:oneOf* for lists which have the cardinality greater than *t*. Hence, the solution adopted is to define the enumeration of elements from PickList columns as asserted instances of a new class. This new class has the PickList column name and it is a subclass of the *cobie:PickList* class. However, only PickList columns which have more elements than *t* are mapped as subclasses of the *cobie:PickList* class. For our COBieOWL version, the threshold values 16 (i.e. *t* = 16). After defining the necessary concepts, one individual is created for each element. Otherwise, if there are fewer elements than *t* then an enumeration is defined by using *owl:oneof* term.

For illustrating how our approach performs the mapping of PickList into OWL, let us consider the *Category* column from Type sheet and a threshold *t* = *16*. This column has values from *CategoryProduct* column that contains about 6900 elements. These elements are mapped as instances of the *cobie:CategoryProduct* class. So, the restriction $\forall category.CategoryProduct$ is defined as superclass of *cobie:Type*. However, the *Category* column from Floor sheet is translated on an OWL datatype property that is called *cobie:categoryDatatype* since it references a column from PickList sheet with less than 16 elements. Thus, the COBieOWL generator states the following axioms: $\top \sqsubseteq \forall categoryDatatype.(xsd:string)$ and $Floor \sqsubseteq \forall categoryDatatype.(\{Floor\} \sqcup \{Roof\} \sqcup \{Site\})$. The suffix "Datatype" is added to the property name that already exists as an OWL object property and it is created as an OWL datatype property (*owl:DatatypeProperty*).

Columns in the COBie template that do not have a "Data Validation" rule for authorising that only cell values from a predefined list (e.g. one list described in the PickList sheet) are mapped as OWL datatype properties. Ranges of those datatype properties are *xsd:string* (e.g: *cobie:color*), *xsd:double* (e.g.: *cobie:coordinateXAxis*) or *xsd:integer* (e.g.: *cobie:createdOn*) types. Such property range information is not present in the COBie template. Because of this, our approach states a *xsd:string* range for all datatype properties that are missing range information in the original template. Nevertheless, we can also consider the datatype information defined in the COBie Responsibility Matrix file[5]. This file is an input of our COBieOWL generator.

All columns that are required to be filled in the COBie template have a yellow colour. These required columns are mapped as existential restrictions for the considered class (e.g.: $Document \sqsubseteq \exists name.xsd:string$). The range of some of those properties depends on their domain class. For asserting this type of restriction, we use the universal quantifier $\forall$ (for all) for specifying a class range or a set of data values allowed for a property, in the context of a specific class. This is done through a conception inclusion (i.e. subsumption). For illustrating this, let us consider the *cobie:category* property that has an union of classes as its domain (i.e. $\exists category.\top \sqsubseteq$

---

[5]   http://projects.buildingsmartalliance.org/files/?artifact_id=4093

Contact ⊔ *Document* ⊔ *Type* ⊔ ... ⊔ *Facility*). For each one of these classes, there is a range restriction for *cobie:category* property. For example, the following restrictions are asserted in COBieOWL:

- *Contact* ⊑ ∀*category*. *CategoryRole*;
- *Document* ⊑ ∀*category*. *DocumentType* ;
- *Facility* ⊑ ∀*category*. *CategoryFacility*.

Still, COBie template restrictions are not sufficient for conceiving an ontology where each class that represents a COBie sheet is equivalent to a set of both defined classes (e.g. *cobie:CobieSheet*) and anonymous classes (e.g.: ∀*category*. *CategoryFacility*). Because of this, in our ontology, anonymous classes are defined as super-classes of COBie classes.

3.2   Extending and Populating the COBieOWL Ontology

The COBie Excel template comprises a lot of information for semi-automatically conceiving the TBox of the COBieOWL ontology. Nevertheless, some minor issues have to be solved for improving this TBox before populating it (i.e. defining the AB-ox). For doing so, we import the COBieOWL ontology serialized in a Turtle[6] (TTL) format into an OWL editor such as Protégé 5.0[7] in order to improve the ontology (see Fig. 6). For example, let us consider that several datatype properties (e.g.: *cobie:coordinateXAxis*) have their ranges automatically defined as a *xsd:string* instead of a more adequate datatype such as *xsd:double*. This type of range definition is not automatically generated, mainly because such information is not explicitly declared in the template. In this case, we use an ontology editor for manually specifying such property datatypes.

Some sheets contain columns that point to rows in other sheets, notably by using two columns. This is the case for *SheetName* and *RowName* columns in the Document sheet. In the context of COBieOWL, we interpret this as a reference to another individual from another class. SheetName and RowName columns are mapped as datatype properties (*cobie:sheetName* and respectively *cobie:rowName*). Moreover, we define additional properties for linking these individuals and for increasing the expressiveness of the resulting COBieOWL ontology. For defining these extra properties, our approach identifies all sheets that contain two columns that contain references to rows in other sheets. For each one of these identified sheets, a new OWL object property is defined with *cobie:CobieSheet* as its range as follows: [sheet name] ⊑ ⊤, ⊤ ⊑ ∀[sheet name]*To*. *CobieSheet* and ∃[sheet name]*To*. ⊤ ⊑ [sheet name]. This is because *cobie:sheetName* range is a *cobie:Picklist* that contains all names of subclasses of *cobie:CobieSheet*. Furthermore, the domain asserted to *[sheet name]To* property is the OWL class representing the identified sheet.

---

[6]   http://www.w3.org/TR/turtle/
[7]   http://protege.stanford.edu/products.php

For illustrating this, let us suppose the Document sheet that contains *SheetName* and *RowName* columns. Thus, our approach states the following axioms in the COBieOWL: $Document \sqsubseteq \top$, $\top \sqsubseteq \forall documentTo.CobieSheet$ and $\exists documentTo.\top \sqsubseteq Document$. The *cobie:documentTo* property links an individual of sub-type of *cobie:CobieSheet* to an another individual of type *cobie:Document*.

Moreover, we define inverse properties of *cobie:[sheet name]To* (i.e.: *cobie:has[sheet name]*) in order to enrich the COBieOWL semantics. Considering our previous example, the property *cobie:hasDocument* is asserted as being the inverse property of *cobie:documentTo* as follows: $hasDocument \equiv documentTo^{-}$. As *cobie:hasDocument* is the inverse property of *cobie:documentTo*, the reasoner will infer that *cobie:hasDocument* is an OWL object property, its range being *cobie:Document*   (i.e.: $\top \sqsubseteq \forall hasDocument.Document$) and   its   domain *cobie:CobieSheet* (i.e. $\exists hasDocument.\top \sqsubseteq CobieSheet$).

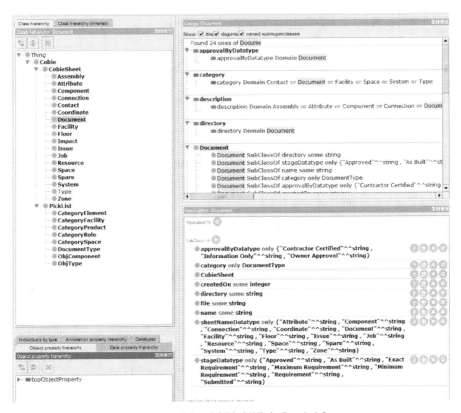

Fig. 6. Editing COBieOWL in Protégé 5.

The DL expressiveness of the resulting COBieOWL ontology is $ALCHIF^{(D)}$. This is a subset of OWL-Lite ($SHIF^{(D)}$) because there aren't transitive properties. Therefore, COBieOWL can be considered a decidable ontology. Main metrics of the COBieOWL ontology are showed in Table 3.

Table 3. COBieOWL ontology metrics.

OWL Entity	Number
Classes	30
Object properties	32
Datatype properties	125
Individuals (PickList)	9418
Inverse properties	7
DL expressiveness	$ALCHIF^{(D)}$

Once we have conceived the TBox of the CobieOWL ontology, we can populate it with data extracted from filled COBie Excel templates. For doing so, each row (except the first row) from a COBie sheet (except Instruction and PickList sheets) is mapped as an instance of one COBie OWL class representing the considered sheet. Besides, for each building project described using COBie spreadsheet files, one new knowledge base (KB) is created in the triple store (e.g. Stardog[8]). This KB contains the COBieOWL schema and it is populated with a COBie spreadsheet file for a given project.

4   Benefits of Using COBieOWL for COBie Data Exchange

In this section, we illustrate several benefits of using an OWL-based representation of building models in the BIM context. Among those we may cite the following facts: it allows addressing generic queries; it allows inferring new knowledge from existing data and it allows extending the underlying model without decreasing data interoperability by applying logical rules.

4.1   Querying with COBie Terms

Storing COBie data in the form of an OWL-based ontology allows querying building information by using a formal query language such as SPARQL. This is not possible when considering only spreadsheet software (e.g. Excel) for manipulating building data. Furthermore, we can extract building views (i.e. sub-graphs of COBieOWL) from the populated COBieOWL ontology by using SPARQL features such as CONSTRUCT. For exemplifying this benefit, let us consider that we want to retrieve a RDF subgraph containing all building information created by a specific user for a given project. Thus, for doing so, we execute the following query over a KB containing a populated COBieOWL:

```
CONSTRUCT{
    ?x ?p ?o  }   WHERE {
    ?y a cobie:Contact.
    ?y cobie:email <mailto:user1@email.com>.
    ?x cobie:createdBy ?y.
    ?x ?p ?o }.
```

---

[8] http://docs.stardog.com/

Still, spreadsheet softwares do not have an expressive query language such as SPARQL for retrieving data. Actually, these softwares are limited to keyword searches for retrieving COBie information.

4.2   Inferring New Information

As OWL is based on description logics, one of its advantages is to allow the inference of new information by applying a DL reasoner over a KB. In our case, we are using the backward-chaining reasoner implemented in the Stardog triple store. For exemplifying this advantage, we consider the object property *cobie:hasDocument* that is stated as an inverse property of *cobie:documentTo*. Therefore, the reasoner is capable of inferring new assertions regarding the *cobie:hasDocument* property based on explicitly asserted *cobie:documentTo* properties, and vice-versa. For further explanation, let us suppose the following assertions: *cobie:documentTo(doc1,type1)* and *cobie:hasDocument(type2, doc2)*. Based on these elements, the reasoner infers the following assertions: *cobie:documentTo(type2,doc2)* and *cobie:hasDocument(type1, doc1)*, where *type1* and *type2* are instances of *cobie:Type* class and *doc1* and *doc2* are instances of the *cobie:Document* class.

4.3   Flexibility for Enriching COBie Model by Applying Logical Rules

Our approach allows defining novel concepts as used by AEC/FM stakeholders notably by means of SWRL rules [14]   and its *swrlb* built-ins [14]. An ensemble of rules allows specifying additional information concerning classes and properties defined in the TBox. Notably, rules specify means for identifying and creating new information from exiting one. Hence, implicit information becomes explicit.

For illustrating this benefit, let us consider the *cobie:Component* class. This class models various building components such as windows, doors, toilets, etc. However, these components (e.g. windows) are not explicitly and formally defined in the COBie standard. They represent semi-structured data, which, again, arise semantic heterogeneity. Consequently, they increase interoperability problems. This is actually important when considering the interoperation of COBieOWL data with data from other building ontologies such as IfcWoD[10] that may contain a concept for defining windows (e.g *IfcWindow*). For tackling this problem, we propose to extend the CO-BieOWL schema with concepts that aren't present in the COBie standard (e.g. *cobie:Window*). We could thus add the concept *cobie:Window* as a subclass of *cobie:Component*. Such concept can be populated by applying rules previously defined on the top of our KB.   For example, the following SWRL rule populates the *cobie:Window* class with data described using solely original COBie concepts:

$$cobie:Component(?x) \ \wedge \ cobie:name(?x,?y)$$
$$\wedge \ swrlb:containsIgnoreCase(?y, \text{"window"})$$
$$\rightarrow \ cobie:Window(?x)$$

5   COBieOWL in the Web of Data Context

A considerable amount of structured data is published on the Web using decentralised Semantic Web technologies (e.g. RDF and HTTP URIs). In order to benefit from such data, we propose to link COBieOWL to these sources of information. For doing so, we can define mappings between COBieOWL and existing vocabularies published under the Linking Open Data project[9] such as FOAF[10] (Friend of a Friend).

FOAF is a machine-readable vocabulary for describing organizations and people. It includes properties for stating activities and relations among people and organisations. For integrating FOAF and COBieOWL, we remove existential restrictions in the *cobie:Contact* class for avoiding incoherencies and we assert the axioms below:

- $cobie:Contact \equiv foaf:Agent$
- $\exists cobie:givenName.\top \sqsubseteq foaf:Person$
- $\exists cobie:familyName.\top \sqsubseteq foaf:Person$
- $cobie:givenName \equiv foaf:givenName$
- $cobie:familyName \equiv foaf:familyName$
- $cobie:email \equiv foaf:mbox$

Linking FOAF and COBieOWL allows to automatically map AEC/FM actors' FOAF descriptions to the respective COBie building models.

Another well-known dataset is DBpedia[11]. This dataset contains structured data automatically extracted from Wikipedia. For linking COBieOWL to DBpedia, we create the property *cobie:hasDBpedia* with *cobie:CobieSheet* as its domain. For illustrating this, let us suppose a COBie project for the Capital Tower building[12]. We then assert that *:Capital_Tower* is an instance of the *cobie:Facility* class. In the DBpedia dataset, it is asserted that *dbpedia:Capital_Tower_(Singapore)* [13] is an instance of *dbpedia-owl:Building*[14]. Thus, for connecting the COBie Facility concept to the DBpedia Building concept, we state that:

$$cobie:hasDBpedia(:Capital\_Tower,\ dbpedia:Capital\_Tower\_(Singapore)\ ).$$

By doing so, we enrich our BIM model with external data published on the Web. Regarding our previous example, we can also have access to additional information not modeled in the COBie project for the "Capital Tower" building such as its former name (i.e. "PosBank Headquarters Building") and its location (i.e. *dbpedia:Robinson_Road,_Singapore*).

---

[9]   http://www.w3.org/wiki/SweoIG/TaskForces/CommunityProjects/LinkingOpenData
[10] http://xmlns.com/foaf/spec/
[11] http://wiki.dbpedia.org/
[12] http://www.skyscrapercenter.com/building/capital-tower/824
[13] http://dbpedia.org/resource/
[14] http://dbpedia.org/ontology/

6   Conclusion and Future Works

Structuring data produced by the AEC/FM industry has been addressed by building actors over the past 15 years. Main approaches focus on the standardization of BIM through formats such as IFC and COBie. These standards rely on file-based approaches for exchanging building data. However, as we have previously discussed, the sole adoption of a standard for data exchange does not eliminate the data heterogeneity problem. Additionally, a file-based data exchange approach cannot help in enriching building models without compromising data interoperability. Because of this, we propose the use of OWL for defining a COBie-based ontology, and consequently, enhancing data interoperability. In this paper, we presented an approach for semi-automatically converting the COBie spreadsheet format into an ontology for taking advantage of various benefits, for example: the possibility of querying COBie data, reducing semantic heterogeneity and enriching the COBie model. Besides, we discussed how the COBieOWL ontology can be linked to other LOD datasets such as FOAF and DBpedia.

Regarding future works, we want to take into account the alignment between CO-BieOWL and others existing ontologies such as the OWL version of CityGML [26] (based on CityGML[15] standard) and IfcWoD [10]. Moreover, we will study the feasibility of addressing queries in natural language with terms from the AEC/FM domain over the COBieOWL ontology.

Acknowledgements. This work has been financed by the French company ACTIVe3D (see http://www.active3d.net) and supported by the Burgundy Regional Council (see http://www.region-bourgogne.fr).

References

1. De Farias, T.M., Roxin, A., Nicolle, C.: A rule based system for semantical enrichment of building information exchange. In: CEUR Proceedings of RuleML (4th Doctoral Consortium), Prague, Czech Republic, vol. 1211, p. 2 (2014)
2. East, B.: Construction-Operations Building Information Exchange (COBie) (2014). http://www.wbdg.org/resources/cobie.php
3. National Institute of Building Sciences: Current Projects of the Facility Maintenance & Operations Committee. http://www.nibs.org/?page=fmoc_projects
4. Product data representation and exchange - Part 21 (ISO 10303-21:2002). http://www.iso.org/iso/home/store/catalogue_tc/catalogue_detail.htm?csnumber=33713
5. Dean, M., Schreiber, G. (eds.): OWL Web Ontology Language Reference, W3C Recommendation (2004). www.w3.org/TR/2004/REC-owl-ref-20040210
6. The World Wide Web Consortium (W3C): XML Technology. http://www.w3.org/standards/xml/
7. Halevy, A.: Why Your Data Won't Mix. Queue **3**(8), 50–58 (2005)

---

[15] http://www.citygml.org/

8. Pauwels, P., Van Deursen, D., De Roo, J., Van Ackere, T., De Meyer, R., Van de Walle, R., Van Campenhout, J.: Three-dimensional information exchange over the semantic web for the domain of architecture, engineering, and construction. Artificial Intelligence for Engineering Design, Analysis and Manufacturing 25(4), 317–332 (2011)

9. The Linking Open Data cloud diagram: State of the LOD Cloud (2014). http://linkeddatacatalog.dws.informatik.uni-mannheim.de/state/

10. De Farias, T.M., Roxin, A., Nicolle, C.: IfcWoD, semantically adapting IFC model relations into OWL properties. In: Proceedings of the 32nd CIB W78 Conference on Information Technology in Construction, October 2015, Eindhoven, Netherlands (2015) (to appear)

11. Beckett, D. (ed.): RDF/XML syntax specification (Revised), W3C Recommendation (2004). http://www.w3.org/TR/REC-rdf-syntax/

12. Krötzsch, M., Simancík, F., Horrocks, I.: A description logic primer. CoRR abs/1201.4089 (2012)

13. Clark, K.G., Feigenbaum L., Torres E. (ed.): SPARQL protocol for RDF, W3C Recommendation (2008). http://www.w3.org/TR/rdf-sparql-protocol/

14. The World Wide Web Consortium (W3C): SWRL: A Semantic Web Rule Language Combining OWL and RuleML (2004). http://www.w3.org/Submission/SWRL/

15. RuleML. http://www.ruleml.org

16. Farias, T.M., Roxin, A., Nicolle, C.: FOWLA, a federated architecture for ontologies. In: Bassiliades, N., Gottlob, G., Sadri, F., Paschke, A., Roman, D. (eds.) RuleML 2015. LNCS, vol. 9202, pp. 97–111. Springer, Heidelberg (2015)

17. Bizer, C., Heath, T., Berners-Lee, T.: Linked data - the story so far. Int. J. Semantic Web Inf. Syst. 5(3), 1–22 (2009)

18. Volk, R., Stengel, J., Schultmann, F.: Building Information Modeling (BIM) for existing buildings - Literature review and future needs. Automation in Construction 38, 109–127 (2014)

19. International Alliance for Interoperability: IFC2x Versions (2013). http://www.buildingsmart-tech.org/specifications/ifc-overview

20. East, B.: COBie Frequently Asked Questions (2011). http://www.wbdg.org/resources/cobiefaq.php

21. Heath, T., Bizer, C.: Linked Data: Evolving the Web into a Global Data Space. Synthesis Lectures on the Semantic Web: Theory and Technology, 1st edn. s.l.:Morgan & Claypool (2011)

22. O'Connor, M.J., Halaschek-Wiener, C., Musen, M.A.: Mapping master: a flexible approach for mapping spreadsheets to OWL. In: Patel-Schneider, P.F., Pan, Y., Hitzler, P., Mika, P., Zhang, L., Pan, J.Z., Horrocks, I., Glimm, B. (eds.) ISWC 2010, Part II. LNCS, vol. 6497, pp. 194–208. Springer, Heidelberg (2010)

23. Bowers, S., Madin, J.S., Schildhauer, M.P.: Owlifier: Creating OWL-DL ontologies from simple spreadsheet-based knowledge descriptions. Ecological Informatics 5(1), 19–25 (2010)

24. Jupp, S., Horridge, M., Iannone, L., Klein, J., Owen, S., Schanstra, J., Stevens, R., Wolstencroft, K.: Populous: a tool for populating templates for OWL ontologies. In: SWAT4LS (2010)

25. Eadie, R., Odeyinka, H., Browne, M., McKeown, C., Yohanis, M.: Building Information Modelling Adoption: An Analysis of the Barriers to Implementation. Journal of Engineering and Architecture 2(1), 77–101 (2014)

26. Métral, C., Falquet, G., Cutting-Decelle, A.F.: Towards semantically enriched 3D city models: an ontology-based approach. Academic Track of GeoWeb (2009)

A Semantic Graph Model

Liu Chen$^{(\boxtimes)}$, Ting Yu, and Mengchi Liu

State Key Lab of Software Engineering, School of Computer,
Wuhan University, Wuhan, China
{dollychan,yuting}@whu.edu.cn, mengchi@scs.carleton.ca

Abstract. Graph models do excel where data have an element of uncertainty or unpredictability and the relationships are data's main features. However, existing graph models neglect the semantics of node and relationship type.

To capture as much semantics as possible, we extend the nodes in graph model with some object-oriented features and edges with multiple semantic information, and propose a Semantic Graph Model (SGM). SGM is a schema-less model and supports dynamic data structures as well as extra semantics. Although the class definition is unknown at the beginning, the schema can be extracted from the semi-structured and semantic data. The excavated domain model can help further data analysis and data fusion, and it is also important for graph query optimization.

We have proposed graph create statements to represent data in SGM and have implemented a conversion layer to store, manage and query the graph upon the graph database system, Neo4j.

1 Introduction

Due to the increasing requirement of query and analysis on linked data, such as social networking, master data management, geospatial, recommendations, web RDF data, etc., graph databases have attracted a lot of interests for their ability to represent connections [1,2]. A graph consists of a set of nodes and a set of edges (or relationships) that connect them. Real world entities are represented as nodes in a graph and the ways in which those entities are related in the world as relationships. This general-purpose, expressive structure allows graph model to represent all kind of scenarios.

A consensus schema is hard to define when integrating data from the Web for data expressions as structures are uncertain and unpredictable [3,4]. For example, from the Wikipedia the structures of countries are quite different, China makes up of provinces, USA comprises states and UK includes four countries. This is an example that data from one source may have different structures, as well as data from different sources and describing different aspects of information.

This work is supported by National Natural Science Funds of China under grand numbers 61202100 and 61272110.

C. Debruyne et al. (Eds.): OTM 2015 Conferences, LNCS 9415, pp. 378–396, 2015.
DOI: 10.1007/978-3-319-26148-5_25

Schema-less graph models are suitable here to represent data from different sources with various structures.

Semantics are important for analysis and schema-less applications, and people try to capture as much semantics as possible. To our knowledge, there are two kinds of semantic data, one is the well-defined schema or pre-defined conceptual knowledge base established before instance data are created; the other is semantics lies in instance data. For example, "consists_of" is a containment relationship, which is the former kind; China includes Province Hubei and this connection has containment meaning, which is the latter kind.

The former semantic data need lots of work to conclude and integrate. Existing semantic graph models, such as RDF, SKOS and OWL, belong to this kind[5–7]. RDF can represent conceptual and reasoning rules in a triple form, while it doesn't consider the relationships between relationships. Simple Knowledge Organization System (SKOS) is an RDF vocabulary and supports semantic relationships.

For the second kind of semantic data, the extra semantics can be captured, represented and used with extracted data. Some semantics of heterogeneous data are left over and are not captured and leveraged via existing graph models, which is the task we aim at. These semantics are mainly types of nodes and relationships, and there is no way to identify and classify important entities and relationships in a graph. In the country example given above, China, USA and UK are countries, and the relationships between provinces and China, states and USA, and countries and UK are containment connections.

The more semantics we capture, the more knowledge we can use [8–11]. Additionally, the semantics of nodes and relationships are necessary for graph query optimization [12–14]. Hence, we extend the nodes in graph model with some object-oriented features and edges with multiple semantic information, and we call this extension the Semantic Graph Model (SGM).

In SGM, every node is treated as an object and objects are classified into classes. Objects have various relationships with each other. Based on the data we extract and integrate from the Web, we attach three kinds of semantics to relationships: relationship type (including containment, role and user-defined type), relationship hierarchy and inverse relationship. Some relationships are unidirectional, some are bidirectional, and some directed relationships are pairwise. Pairwise relationships have a strong dependency on each other and they are fundamentally one relationships between two objects with two different labels for two directions.

In this way, SGM can represent as much semantics as possible in a schema-less manner. What's more, due to the semantics captured and semi-structure of data, the structures of classes can be extracted from data and the domain model is obtained, and from the model more knowledge can be excavated and applies to further integrate and fuse heterogeneous data. Also, the semantics and structures of the graph are applied to query optimization.

This paper is organized as follows: Section 2 gives an overview of SGM, Section 3 and Section 4 respectively elaborate the extension of nodes and relationships, Section 5 introduces the implementation of SGM upon Neo4j [15] and finally Section 6 concludes the paper.

2   Overview

2.1   Our Model

SGM is extended based on property graph model, in which every node and relationship can have properties. Nodes are objects and relationships are connections between objects.

Every node (object) is an instance of one or multiple classes. If the class information of an object is unknown, it can be omitted. In order to represent the complex properties of real-world entities, properties of objects in SGM can have multiple value (array) and aggregation of properties. Relationships are named and directed, and always have a start and end node. In SGM, we introduce three features to relationships: relationship type (containment, role, user-defined type), relationship hierarchy and inverse relationship. Hence, an extended node EN is the expansion of a graph node N and a semantic edge SE is the extension of graph edge E in graph model $G = (N, E)$.

1. Every relationship has a label indicates its natural meaning that is the relationship name, such as friend, parent and etc. Relationship type refers to the extra semantics of the connection, like the two pre-defined types in SGM, containment and role.

   Relationships with composition semantics can be represented as containment relationships, such as relationship "consist_of", "has_a" and etc. Relationships of a type share common inference rules. General connections omit the interdependent relationship that objects to some degree depend on the object containing them. Furthermore, containment relationship is transitive such that if A contains B, B contains C then A contains C.

   Real world entities have various natural and complex properties and relationships with each other and via these relationships, objects play various roles that form their context, and then have the corresponding context-dependent properties. Even though relationships are first-class citizens in graph models, existing ones oversimplify and ignore the complex relationships and context-dependent properties. To model the dynamic aspect of an object, we introduce role relationships in SGM. An object can play the same role in different organizations or circumstances, as well as different roles in the same context. In specified context and as particular role, entity can have context-dependent properties and relationships.

   Users can classify relationships into ad hoc relationship types for different applications.

2. In some cases, the relationships between objects are exhibited in a hierarchical way from a general relationship to a more specific one. Hence, in SGM, the hierarchies of a relationships are kept.

3. In addition, there are uniliteral and mutual relationships, and as in graph relationships are directed, to represent mutual relationships, relationships in two directions are defined respectively in existing models, while in this way, the correspondence information between this two relationships is lost.

SGM supports the definition of mutual relationships in pairs to maintain their correspondence.

SGM is a schema-less and semi-structured model just like graph model; that is, there is no need to predefine schema for nodes and relationships in advance. However, with data represented in SGM, we can excavate the class definition from the object data, and generate the model graph. The extracted model summarizes and displays the structure and semantics of the object data and meaningful knowledge can be mined from it.

Also, with the knowledge of the data, graph query optimization can proceed.

2.2   Introduction of Neo4j

To manage and store data represented by SGM in a database system, we select Neo4j as the database system, transform the SGM data into structures that Neo4j can process, and at the same time keep the extra semantic information we capture in SGM. We manage and analyze data mainly extracted from the Web by taking advantage of Neo4j.

As in [16], the latest version of Neo4j released in May 2015, Neo4j is a labeled property graph making up of nodes, relationships, properties and labels. In Neo4j, Nodes contain properties. Nodes store properties in the form of arbitrary key-value pairs. In Neo4j, the keys are strings and the values are the Java string and primitive data types, plus arrays of these types. Nodes can be tagged with one or more labels. Labels group nodes together, and indicate the roles they play within the dataset. Relationships connect nodes and structure the graph. A relationship always has a direction, a single name, and a start node and an end node - there are no dangling relationships. Together, a relationship's direction and name add semantic clarity to the structuring of nodes. Like nodes, relationships can also have properties. The ability to add properties to relationships is particularly useful for providing additional metadata for graph algorithms, adding additional semantics to relationships (including quality and weight), and for constraining queries at runtime.

Cypher, the language Neo4j uses to create and query graphs, is concise and easy to use. Neo4j is a full-fledged native graph database system and achieves a good data access efficiency. We take use of features of Neo4j to keep and store data as well as their semantics. The semantics SGM capture is information of nodes and relationships, and a easy way to maintain the information is taking advantage of properties of nodes and relationships.

3   Extension of Nodes

As SGM is a schema-less model, and the properties and relationships in an object are not predefined and vary from objects to objects of a class. Hence, except the object-oriented features related to definitions of classes, like encapsulation and polymorphism, SGM extends graph model with objects and classes, and composition and inheritance.

Although the structure of a class is not known in SGM, illustrating the class an object belongs to needs not defining upfront. Additionally, the schema-less model can be used to represent the relationships between classes, like the class hierarchies.

The data collected from various sources are instances and structures extracted from the instances are schemas. Hence, there are two kinds of extended nodes (EN) in SGM: object nodes (ON) and class nodes (CN).

Definition 1. ON = (L, P), where

$L = \{l_1, ..., l_n\}$ is an optional set of class names (or labels) that the object belongs to, where $l_i \in \mathcal{L}$ with $1 \leq i \leq n$ is a class name. As an example from Fig. 1, the label of node China is Country. In SGM, the labels of an object can be omitted if the classification information is unknown.

$P = \{p_1, ..., p_n\}$ is a set of properties, where each p_i is an attribute-value and the value can be a array or a aggregated one. The value of a property can also be a node in SGM. If the value of a node property is a node, it should be represented as a relationship. Hence, the value of a node property is better not a node. A relationship property whose value is a node indicates relationship-based relationships, which will be illustrated in Section 4.1.

Definition 2. CN = (R, EP), where

$R = \{r_1, ..., r_n\}$ is a set of class hierarchical relationships as it shown in Example 1.

$EP = \{ep_1, ..., ep_n\}$ is a set of property definitions extracted from object data.

In this section, we explain the object-oriented features SGM extends and how the class information and complex property are represented in SGM.

3.1   Objects and Classes

The label of every object node makes it possible to extract the definition of every type, otherwise what we can get are the property and relationship names without classifications. Hence, a node in SGM is an object which is an instance of a particular class or multiple classes. As SGM is schema-less and there are no definitions of attributes and relationships for a given type or class of an object, and objects are not required to match a schema. The classes an object belongs to do no impact on the object and just indicates the type of the object. In some cases, the knowledge of an object's classification maybe remain unknown, and the class of an object can be a default one *Object* that is the superclass of any classes.

Although the definition of a class is not required at the beginning, the classes and structures can be extracted from the object data. The structure and content of a class may be huge because different sources depicts different aspects of data in the same domain and language expressions vary. Hence, the extracted structure is a complete representation of objects in a class and a collection of language statement of all properties of a class, in which we can find the synonym sets under the context of a class.

As the latest release of Neo4j supports nodes with labels, which can be treated as classifications of objects, we directly follow the usage of label to denote objects and classes.

3.2 Composition and Inheritance

Objects can contain other objects; this is known as object composition. As this feature is related to relationships between objects, it will be elaborated with containment relationship in Section 4.1.

With introducing classes into SGM, it's natural to support subclass relationships between classes. This is predefined conceptual knowledge and can be used for data analysis after the classes are extracted from object data. In SGM, the inheritance mainly displays a hierarchy that represents "is-a-type-of" relationships among classes. What is different from usual inheritance is that subclasses will not inherit the properties of the superclass as the definition of a superclass is unknown.

Schema information classifies objects and the class hierarchies will make sense when querying and analyzing.

In SGM, we can define classes and their inheritance relationships via class definition statements, which is new from existing graph models. Neo4j supports definition of domain model, that is the schema of the graph. However, there is no metadata of the class hierarchies. Hence, we bring a keyword *class* to create statement to indicate the class node definition.

Example 1. The following are two statements representing that Country, Province and City are subclasses of Region.

```
create class (Region), class (Country), class (Province),
    class (City), (Region) - [:subsume] -> (Country),
    (Region) - [:subsume] -> (Province), (City) - [:isa] -> (Region);
```

3.3 Complex Properties

SGM is a property graph model and every node and relationship can have properties. To directly represent multiple value and nested attributes, we support the array and aggregation of properties in SGM.

Example 2. The following is the node creation statement for Person Alice who is female, has two phone numbers (+1(613)520-2525 and +1(613)520-4049), and the address is an aggregation of four values, which are addressline "1125 Colonel By Drive", city Ottawa, country Canada and address type "Company address".

```
create (Alice:Person { gender:female,
    phone_no.:[+1(613)520-2525,+1(613)520-4049]
    address:{AddressLine1:"1125 Colonel By Drive",
        City:Ottawa, Country:Canada, Type:"Company address"}});
```

4   Extension of Relationships

In this section, we introduce semantics attached to relationships (SE): relationship type (including containment relationship, role relationship and user-defined-type relationship), relationship hierarchies and inverse relationship.

Definition 3. SE = (t, P, h, i), where
  t is the type of a relationship, and the default relationship is a general one without special semantics. t can be any value such as containment, role or other user-defined ones.
  $P = \{p_1, ..., p_n\}$ is a set of properties as it is defined in Definiton 1. The value of a relationship property can be not only text and can be other nodes, which indicates the interdependency between relationships.
  h indicates the hierarchical structure of a relationship.
  i is the inverse relationship which establishes the connection between mutual relationships.

4.1   Relationship Type

Containment Relationships. As it is mentioned in Section 3.2, Object composition is used to represent "has-a" relationships: every employee has an address, so every Employee object has a place to store an Address object. This is a feature of object-oriented model.

The address of a person is a detailed geographic location that can be represented as aggregated properties as shown in Section 3.3 and can be also represented as an entity node with a connection to the person. The description of a geographic location always contains information of country, state/province, city and street that is from a larger scale to smaller ones. That a country is comprised of states/provinces and that a state/province consists of cities are special relationships with containment semantics.

There are two reasoning rules of containment relationship. Firstly, included entities depends on larger-scale entities. Once an entity is deleted, the entities it contains will also be deleted. Secondly, the containment relationship is transitive; that is, if A contains B, and B contains C, then A contains C.

Example 3. In Figure 1, it displays the containment relationships between Country China with Province Hubei and Guangzhou, and with Municipality Beijing, as well as the containment relationships between Province Hubei and City Wuhan and Yichang. As it shows, included nodes are inside larger-scale nodes.

```
create (China:Country {name:"China"}), (Beijing:City {name:"Beijing"}),
    (Wuhan:City {name:"Wuhan"}), (Guangzhou:Province {name:"Guangzhou"}),
    (Hubei:Province {name:"Hubei"}), (Yichang:City {name:"Yichang"}),
    (China) -[containment:municipality] -> (Beijing),
```

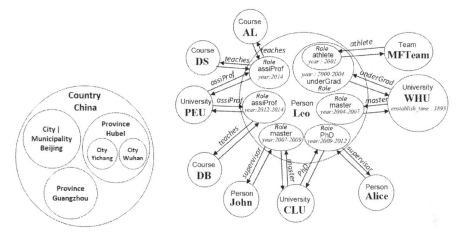

Fig. 1. A graph of containing objects.

Fig. 2. A graph of Leo's resume.

```
(China) -[containment:provinces] -> (Hubei),
(China) -[containment:provinces] -> (Guangzhou),
(Hubei) -[containment:city] -> (Wuhan),
(Hubei) -[containment:city] -> (Yichang);
```

Note that keyword *containment* is introduced to indicate the containment
semantic of the connection.

Role Relationships. An object has static aspects as well as dynamic aspects.
Real world entities have various natural and complex relationships with each
other and via these relationships, objects play various roles that form their contexts, and then have the corresponding context-dependent properties. Object
properties are often based on their contexts, and contexts can be nested to form
complex context dependent information.

For example, a student may have studied at one or more universities as an
undergraduate, master, or Ph.D student, and thus may have several distinct
properties with the same name (e.g. year). Each university involved is the context. Undergraduate, master, and Ph.D are also nested contexts for the properties. Similarly, a faculty member may have worked at one or more universities as
an assistant professor, associate professor, or full professor and thus may have
some context-dependent properties with the same name as well.

Existing graph models treat roles of an entity as individual nodes and connects role nodes with entity nodes and context organization nodes respectively,
while role nodes are not independent entities and have containing relationships
with original entity.

Example 4. A person's resume (education and career network) is a typical example that displays connections between he/she and some schools or companies, and different roles he/she plays in different organizations. In Figure 2, it illustrates the education and work experience of Person Leo. He was an undergraduate student in university WHU from year 2000 to year 2004, and as an undergraduate student, he participated the Man's Football Team in year 2001. From year 2004 to year 2007, he obtained master's degree in WHU and under this context, he was supervised by Ben and took course OS. Then he turned to university CLU and obtained master's degree for year 2007 to year 2009 and was supervised by John, and he obtained doctor's degree for year 2009 to year 2012 and switched to supervisor Alice. After getting his doctor's degree, Leo worked in university PEU as assistant professor from year 2012 to year 2014 and taught course DB. Since 2014, he is a associate professor and teaches course DS and AL.

The following statement shows how to represent above situation in SGM. It represents node Perosn Leo, and connections that Leo relates to university WHU, CLU and PEU, roles that Leo respectively plays under those contexts and context-dependent properties and relationships.

```
create (Leo:Person {name:"Leo"}), (WHU:Univ {name:"WHU"}),
    (CLU:Univ {name:"CLU"}), (OS:Course {name:"Operating System"}),
    (Ben:Person {name:"Ben"}), (DS:Course {name:"Distributed System"}),
    (Alice:Person {name:"Alice"}), (PEU:Univ {name:"PKU"}),
    (DB:Course {name:"Database"}), (John:Person {name:"John"}),
    (AL:Course {name:"Algorithm"}),
    (ManFbTeam:Team {name:"Man'sFootballTeam"}),
    (WHU) <- [:studies_in {(Leo:UnderGrad {year:2000-2004}) -
        [:participate {(Leo:Athlete {year:2001})}] -> (ManFbTeam),
      (OS) <- [:take] - (Leo:Master {year:2004-2007})
      - [:supervisor] -> (Ben)} ] - (Leo) -
    [:studies_in {(Leo:Master {year:2007-2009}) - [:supervisor] -> (John),
        (Leo:PhD {year:2009-2012}) - [:supervisor] -> (Alice)}] -> (CLU),
    (Leo) - [:works_in {(Leo:AssiProf {year:2012-2014}) - [:teaches] ->
(DB)},
        (AL) <- [:teaches] - (Leo:AssoProf {year:2014})
        - [:teaches] -> (DS)] -> (PEU);
```

On the one hand, to represent the roles Leo play under different contexts and on the other hand, to represent the relationships and properties based on the role, in the relationship that the context-dependent properties occur, there is not only text value but also node value for a relationship property, and properties with node values are also treated as relationship based relationships or context-dependent relationships. For example, in the relationship Leo studies in WHU, there are two properties in this relationship and each of the properties is an relationship between a role object derived from the role relationship and other objects. A context dependent relationship can also have context-dependent relationships, like the the relationship Leo participate Man's Football Team, which depends on the relationship that Leo is an under graduate student in WHU. Hence, the relationship behaves in nested way.

A role node, such as the node Leo:UnderGrad, is a special object node in order to represent an object combined with a certain context and context-dependent relationships by using role nodes as their start/end nodes. The role an object plays is also a class, as shown in role node Leo:UnderGrad, UnderGrad is a role class and a role class is the subclass of the class of the original object, for example UnderGrad will be a subclass of class Person. This role class and class relationship will be used when model extracting.

The following is the modeling example of Leo's resume in a different way, that is starting from organizations, WHU, CLU and PEU, Leo is connected by *role* relationships. Corresponding to every role relationship, a role node will be generated in according entity. For example, induced from role relationship underGrad between WHU and Leo, role node WHU.underGrad is generated in entity Leo. It is important to note that the role relationship *athlete* between Man's Football Team and role node WHU.underGrad Leo.

```
create (WHU) - [role:UnderGrad {year:2000-2004,
      (Leo:UnderGrad) - [:participate {year:2001}] -> (ManFbTeam)}] ->
(Leo),
   (WHU) - [role:Master {year:2004-2007}] -> (Leo),
   (CLU) - [role:Master {year:2007-2009,
      (Leo:Master) - [:supervisor] -> (John)}] -> (Leo),
   (CLU) - [role:PhD {year:2009-2012,
      (Leo:PhD) - [:supervisor] -> (Alice)}] -> (Leo),
   (PEU) - [role:AssiProf {year:2012-2014,
      (Leo:AssiProf) - [:teaches] -> (DB)}] -> (Leo),
   (PEU) - [role:AssoProf {year:2014-,
      (AL) <- [:teaches] (Leo:AssoProf) - [:teaches] -> (DS)}] -> (Leo);
```

User Defined Relationship Type. Besides the two pre-defined relationship type which has the certain inference rules, user can classify a relationship to any type according to the application requirement, and by query statements, this type property can be used to infer certain results.

4.2   Hierarchical Relationships

The relationships between objects are sometimes hierarchical from a general one to more specific ones. Usually, the most direct relationship is maintained in graph model, and the semantics indicates the meaning and structure of object connections is lost. SGM keeps the relationship with its hierarchies.

Example 5. Figure 3 shows the committee structure of CIKM 2015. The committee of CIKM 2015 is specified into relationships "General Chairs" and "Program Chairs", and "Program Chairs" is further specified for tracks, such as "Database Track" and "Tutorial Chairs".

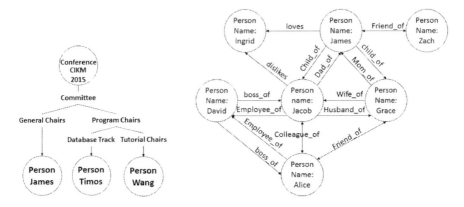

Fig. 3. The Committee of CIKM 2015.

Fig. 4. Jacob's social network (relationships and inverse relationships).

```
create (CIKM2015:Conference {name:"CIKM 2015"}),
    (James:Person {name:"James Bailey", affiliation:"The University
of Melbourne"}),
    (Timos:Perosn {name:"Timos Sellis", affiliation:"RMIT
University"}),
    (Wang:Person {name:"Wei Wang", affiliation:"University of New
South Wales"}),
    (CIKM2015) - [:Committee] - [:General_Chairs] -> (James),
    (CIKM2015) - [:Committee] - [:Program_Chairs] -
[:Database_Track] -> (Timos),
    (CIKM2015) - [:Committee] - [:Program_Chairs] -
[:Tutorial_Chairs] -> (Wang);
```

Based on the relationship of Cypher, between nodes, more notations (-[]) are used to represent the relationship hierarchy. For example, between nodes CIKM2015 and James, the relationship is comprised of two parts, from Committee to General Chairs.

4.3   Relationships and Inverse Relationships

The relationships between entities are either unilateral or mutual. Affection connections can be unilateral, for instance one man loves the other while the love may not be requited. Compared with unilateral ones, mutual relationships are more prevalent. In such a case, once a one-way connection occurs from an entity to another, the reflexive connection also needs to be established.

For mutual relationships, people always define two relationships in two directions to make the mutual semantics complete. The two relationships for a mutual connection have two features. Firstly, the label of a mutual relationship in two directions can be either the same or different. Secondly, this two relationships likewise dependent on each other, and once connection in one direction changes, the other one should change correspondingly. From the perspective of semantic capturing, the interdependency relationship between two mutually inverse relationships are important for data analysis. Existing graph models do not support this feature of mutual connections. Hence, in SGM, users can directly define mutual relationships using relationship pairs, so that the system can know and maintain the consistency of relationship pairs.

Example 6. Figure 4 illustrates a network of a person's family, friends and colleagues. Jacob and Grace are a couple and James is their child. Jacob and Alice are both employees of David. James loves Ingrid (the love is not requited), while Jacob dislikes her. Grace and Alice are friends, so are James and Zach. As the figure shows, parallel and pair directed lines indicate mutual connections, in which one is another's inverse and they have different labels. The two way lines, like friend_of can be treat as a combined pair relationships for they have the same label in two directions. Single directed lines are uniliteral relationships.

```
create (Jacob:Person {name:"Jacob"}), (Grace:Person {name:"Grace"}),
    (Ingrid:Person {name:"Ingrid"}), (James:Person {name:"James"}),
    (Zach:Person {name:"Zach"}), (David:Person {name:"David"}),
    (Alice:Person {name:"Alice"}),
    (Jacob) - [:husband_of(<- wife_of)] -> (Grace),
    (Jacob) - [:dad_of(<- child_of)] -> (James),
    (Jacob) - [:dislikes] -> (Ingrid),
    (Jacob) - [:employee_of(<- boss_of)] -> (David),
    (Jacob) - [:colleague_of] - (Alice),
    (Grace) - [:mom_of(<- child_of)] -> (James),
    (Grace) - [:friend_of] - (Alice),
    (James) - [:friend_of] - (Zach),
    (James) - [:loves] -> (Ingrid),
    (Alice) - [:employee_of(<- boss_of)] -> (David);
```

As shown above, -> indicates outgoing relationships, <- indicates the inverse ones. - represents mutual relationships with the same labels in two direction. Within a outgoing relationship, we use a clause (<-) to indicate the inverse relationship of the current one. On the one hand, it defines the inverse relationship and needs not another clause for the inverse relationship. On the other hand, it represents that that like "husband_of" and "wife_of" are conceptually inverse to each other.

5   Implementation Upon Neo4j

5.1   Data Conversion to Cypher

To represent the extra semantics introduced by SGM, we take advantage of properties and labels of Neo4j. For nodes and relationships, we assign some properties with particular functions to keep the semantics. In this section, we introduce the particular properties and structures we use for SGM in Neo4j system.

Type. *Type* is a most important property we use to represent the type of a class or a relationship. Firstly, there are three kinds of nodes in SGM: class, object and role. The type of an object node is *object* and a class node *class*. Role node is a special one that represents roles an object plays, and by the role node the context-dependent properties can be represented and kept in Neo4j. Secondly, *type* keeps the relationship type for a relationship.

Path. For a hierarchical relationship, the each layer of it may have its own properties and hierarchies are not only relationship labels. Also, two objects connected by a hierarchical relationship can be regarded as that they have connections of each layer of the hierarchies, and a general relationship contains a more specific one. Thus, for hierarchical relationship, we split the every layer out and connect the objects by them, and for the more specific relationship, its super relationships are kept in the property *path*.

Inverse. For relationships which have according interdependent inverse relationship, SGM will automatically generate their inverse ones if given the inverse clauses. To convert relationship to Cypher, two independent relationships are created from two directions, and for every relationship there is a property *inverse* indicating its inverse relationship.

New Nodes. There are situations new intermediate nodes are needed. One is for aggregated properties as Neo4j does not support aggregation of properties and new nodes are generated to capture the aggregation information of properties. The second situation is for a property when its value is a node that is the context-dependent relationship, and in this case role nodes are generated.

5.2   Query Examples

Figure 5 illustrates the results of data from above examples converted and stored in Neo4j. Note that the properties of nodes and relationships are omitted in the graph.

There give some query examples which leverage the semantics of SGM. For every query, the result is presented. As every relationship has a property type, query pattern can match the relationship by type. In this way, we can get meaningful relationships in a schema-less manner without knowing the relationship names. Moreover, we can get results with certain semantics by taking advantage of relationship semantics, like containment and role.

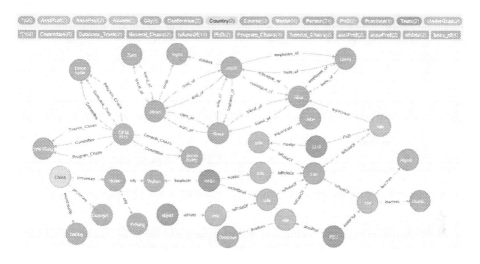

Fig. 5. Results of SGM Data Managed in Neo4j.

1. The following query finds the relationships which have containment relationship with China.

```
Match (n {name:"China"})-[r {type:"containment"}] -() return n, r;
```

The following one finds the containment topology graph of node China. Note that *1..4 means traverse the relationships in 1 to 4 hops and the condition {type:"containment"} indicates that only continue traversing if the relationship type is containment.

```
Match (c {name:"China"})-[r *1..4 {type:"containment"}] -> (p)
return c, p;
```

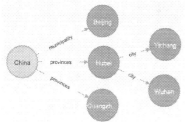

2. If we want to find China's university, the universities locating in cities and provinces China contains should be returned. Taking use of the containment relationship, directly find the universities locates where China contains regardless of the relationship labels.

```
Match (u)-[:locatesIn]->()<-[r1 *1..4
{type:"containment"}]-(c {name:"China"}) return u, r1, c;
```

3. The following query returns the object Leo and all roles he plays.
```
Match (n {name:"Leo"}) <- [:IsRoleOf] -(r) -[]- (o) return n, r, o;
```

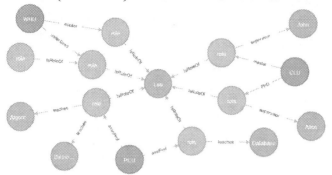

4. Find the context-dependent relationship that Leo has as a Master student.
```
Match (n {name:"Leo"}) <- [:IsRoleOf] -({name:"role:Master"})
-[r]- (o) where r.type="general" return r;
```

5. As the split of hierarchical relationship, the super relationship will contain sub relationships. Hence, for the following two queries, the result of the first one (["James Bailey","Timos Sellis", "Wei Wang"]) contains that of the second one (["Timos Sellis", "Wei Wang"]).
```
Match (c {name:"CIKM 2015"}) - [:Committee] -> (p) return p;
Match (c {name:"CIKM 2015"}) - [:Program_Chairs] -> (p) return p;
```
6. Find the relationships that have corresponding inverse relationships of Jacob.
```
Match (n {name:"Jacob"}) - [r] -> (t) - [ir] ->(n) where ir.name =
r.inverse return r,ir;
```

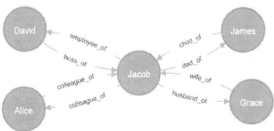

5.3   Extracted Domain Model

Model information is an outline of the nontrivial integrated heterogeneous data and provides conceptual knowledge like semantic correlation of words from a domain and etc. Additionally, the model information can be used to analyze data structure and assist query optimization, like cost estimation and optimal plan selection and etc. Although the property and relationship definitions of a class are not given at the beginning, we can extract model information from the labeled nodes and relationships.

Following statement is a part of the extracted class definition of above example data in Cypher. To distinguish the metadata from instances, the type of class nodes is specified as "class". The model information are generated.

```
create (Country:Country {name:"Country", type:"class"}),
   (City:City {name:"City", type:"class"}),
   (Province:Province {name:"Province", type:"class"}),
   (Country) - [:municipality type:"containment"}] -> (City),
   (Country) - [:city {type:"containment"}] -> (Province),
   (Province) - [:city {type:"containment"}] -> (City)
   (Univ:Univ {name:"Univ", type:"class" }),
   (Person:Person {name:"Person", type:"class"),
   (Team:Team {type:"Team", type:"class"}),
   (UdGrad:UnderGrad {name:"UnderGrad", type:"class"}),
   (Athlete:Athlete {name:"Athlete", type:"class"}),
   (Master:Master {name:"Master", type:"class"}),
   (UnderGrad) - [:IsRoleOf] -> (Person),
   (Athlete) - [:IsRoleOf] -> (UdGrad),
   (Master) - [:IsRoleOf] -> (Person),
   (Univ) - [:undergraduate {type:"role"}] -> (UnderGrad),
   (Team) - [:athlete {type:"role"}] -> (Athlete),
   (Master) <- [:master {type:"role"}] - (Univ),
   (Conf:Conference {name:"Conference", type:"class"}),
   (Conf) - [:Committee] -> (Person),
   (Conf) - [:General_Chairs {path:["Committee"]}] -> (Person),
   (Conf) - [:Program_Chairs {path:["Committee"]}] -> (Person),
   (Conf) - [:Database_Track {path:["Committee",
      "Program_Chairs"]}] -> (Person),
   (Person)- [:husband_of {inverse:"wife_of"}] -> (Person),
   (Person)- [:dad_of {inverse: "child_of"}] -> (Person),
   (Person)<- [:wife_of {inverse:"husband_of"}] - (Person),
   (Person)<- [:child_of {inverse:"dad_of"}] - (Person);
```

Figure 6 demonstrates the model information we extracted and presented in Neo4j. There are 14 classes in which 6 classes are induced from role relationships. Roughly, we can extracted some knowledge from the semantic object data. Firstly, Country consists of provinces and provinces consists of cities which are induced from containment relationships. Secondly, from role relationships, Person can play roles: undergraduate, master, athlete and etc. Thirdly, relationship "committee" can be specified as relationship "program_chairs", and if two objects only have relationship "program_chairs", we can induct that they are possibly have a relationship "committee". The quality of heterogenous data

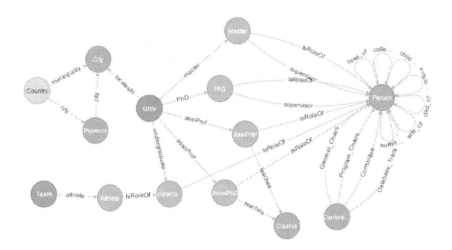

Fig. 6. Neo4j Results of Extracted Model.

varies, extracted model from data with high quality and more information can be used to complement imperfect data and benefit schema-less query.

6   Conclusion

Graph models do excel where data have an element of uncertainty or unpredictability and the relationships are the features of the data. To represent and integrate heterogeneous data and at the same time to capture as much semantics as possible, we have proposed a novel graph model called Semantic Graph Model (SGM), that extends the nodes of graph model with object-oriented features and attachs some semantics to relationships.

Objects and classes are introduced to nodes of SGM; that is, every node is an object which is an instance of one or more classes. Additionally, we have introduced two kinds of relationship: containment relationship and role relationship, a new relationship structure, hierarchical relationship, and a new relationship between relationships; that is, the relationship and its inverse relationship are coexisting. Containment relationship is introduced to represent relationships with composition semantics. Role relationship models the dynamic aspect of an object. Some relationships are directed, some are bidirectional, and some directed relationships are pairwise. Pairwise relationships have a strong dependency on each other and they are fundamentally one relationship between two objects with two different expression from two directions. Hence, aiming at these pairwise relationships, relationship and its inverse can be represented and maintained in SGM.

The features of SGM are as follows. Firstly, it is a schema-less model. Data with various structures and semantics can easily be represented with it. Secondly, besides the label of nodes and relationships, their type can be specified as well. Semantics of the data are represented and captured as what they demonstrate in sources. Thirdly, the structures and definitions of classes can be extracted from the instance data, and other knowledge can be mined from the extracted model and used on further integrate and fuse data. Finally, the extra semantics captured by SGM are important to graph query optimization.

We have also implemented a conversion layer to leverage the data management provided in Neo4j. We firstly convert the data represented in SGM to data that the graph database Neo4j can process, secondly make use of the semantics SGM captured to do some queries, and thirdly extract domain model from the object data.

In the future, we will investigate how to integrate, fuse and analyze data using SGM and how to apply SGM to applications by leveraging extracted model information, and we will study the query optimization methods taking advantage of structural semantics.

References

1. Bondy, J.A., Murty, U.S.R.: Graph theory with applications. Macmillan, London (1976)
2. Bizer, C., Heath, T., Berners-Lee, T.: Linked data - the story so far. Int. J. Semantic Web Inf. Syst., 1–22 (2009)
3. Madhavan, J., Halevy, A.Y., Cohen, S., Dong, X.L., Jeffery, S.R., Ko, D., Yu, C.: Structured data meets the web: A few observations. IEEE Data Eng. Bull. **29**(4), 19–26 (2006)
4. Talukdar, P.P., Ives, Z.G., Pereira, F.: Automatically incorporating new sources in keyword search-based data integration. In: Proceedings of the 2010 ACM SIGMOD International Conference on Management of data, pp. 387–398. ACM (2010)
5. Klyne, G., Carroll, J.J., McBride, B.: RDF 1.1 Concepts and Abstract Syntax (2014). http://www.w3.org/TR/rdf11-concepts/
6. Isaac, A., Summers, E.: SKOS Simple Knowledge Organization System Primer (2009). http://www.w3.org/TR/2009/NOTE-skos-primer-20090818/
7. Hitzler, P., Krotzsch, M., Parsia, B., Patel-Schneider, P.F., Rudolph, S.: OWL 2 Web Ontology Language Primer, 2nd edn. (2012). http://www.w3.org/TR/2012/REC-owl2-primer-20121211/
8. Suchanek, F., Weikum, G.: Knowledge harvesting in the big-data era. In: Proceedings of the 2013 ACM SIGMOD International Conference on Management of Data, pp. 933–938. ACM (2013)
9. Bizer, C., Boncz, P., Brodie, M.L., Erling, O.: The meaningful use of big data: four perspectives-four challenges. ACM SIGMOD Record **40**(4), 56–60 (2012)
10. Dong, X.L., Srivastava, D.: Big data integration. In: 2013 IEEE 29th International Conference on Data Engineering (ICDE), pp. 1245–1248. IEEE (2013)
11. Hull, R., King, R.: Semantic database modeling: Survey, applications, and research issues. ACM Computing Surveys (CSUR) **19**(3), 201–260 (1987)

12. Flesca, S., Greco, S.: Querying graph databases. In: Zaniolo, C., Grust, T., Scholl, M.H., Lockemann, P.C. (eds.) EDBT 2000. LNCS, vol. 1777, pp. 510–524. Springer, Heidelberg (2000)
13. Rodriguez, M.A., Neubauer, P.: The graph traversal pattern. In: Graph Data Management, pp. 29–46 (2011)
14. Wood, P.T.: Query languages for graph databases. SIGMOD Record, 50–60 (2012)
15. Miller, J.J.: Graph database applications and concepts with neo4j. In: Proceedings of the Southern Association for Information Systems Conference, Atlanta, GA, USA, March 23–24, 2013
16. Robinson, I., Webber, J., Eifrem, E.: Graph Databases, 2nd edn. O'Reilly Media Inc., USA (2015)

An Approach for Ontology Population Based on Information Extraction Techniques
Application to Cultural Heritage
(Short Paper)

Riyadh Benammar[1,2]($\boxtimes$), Alain Trémeau[1], and Pierre Maret[1]

[1] Université de Lyon, CNRS, UMR 5516, Laboratoire Hubert Curien, Lyon, France
[2] Université de Lyon, Institut des Sciences de l'Homme, Lyon, France
benammar.riyadh@gmail.com,
{alain.tremeau,pierre.maret}@univ-st-etienne.fr

Abstract. The Colour and Space in Cultural Heritage European (COSCH) COST action has the objective of providing true, precise and complete documentation related to cultural heritage (CH) artifacts. In order to represent and organize knowledge, COSCH developed its own ontology called $COSCH^{KR}$. This paper proposes an approach for automatically populating this ontology from CH scientific papers. We evaluate our approach in comparing manually annotated and automatically computed triples. Our results show a significant increase of the numbers of generated triples and generated properties.

Keywords: Ontology population · Information extraction · Natural language processing · Semantic web · RDF

1 Introduction

Cultural Heritage (CH) is a multidisciplinary domain that focuses on the old civilization lifestyles by studying customs, practices, places, objects, artistic expressions and values. Projects related to this domain require knowledge from different domain experts, such as experts in humanities, art historians, archaeologists, as well as experts in computer science and data acquisition technologies. COSCH (*Colour and Space in Cultural Heritage*) is a European project (COST action TD 1201). It has the objective of providing true, precise and complete documentation related to cultural heritage artefacts.[1] In order to represent and organize the knowledge relating to the different domains covered by CH, COSCH members have developed their own ontology. This ontology is called $COSCH^{KR}$. Populating this ontology requires lot of human resources and time. Fortunately there are numerous scientific papers published in the domain of CH. Therefore, we explore a way to populate the ontology by automatically extracting the knowledge specifically related to CH from scientific papers.

---

[1] http://cosch.info/

© Springer International Publishing Switzerland 2015
C. Debruyne et al. (Eds.): OTM 2015 Conferences, LNCS 9415, pp. 397–404, 2015.
DOI: 10.1007/978-3-319-26148-5_26

Our approach is based first on a text pre-processing step of all sentences, next on an extraction step of semantic relations. The aim of the pre-processing step is to cut sentences into a set of independent set of words. The second step starts by building a gazetteer for the terms (synonyms) associated to $COSCH^{KR}$ concepts names. Then, regular expressions are used to extract relations, next entities are matched with the gazetteer to identify relationships with concepts names. We evaluated our approach by comparing the triples extracted by our system with the ones manually extracted by an expert. For this, we used seven papers from different indexed journals.

The paper is organized as following: section 2 presents related works in the field of ontology population related to texts analysis. Section 3 describes the specific needs identified in the domain of Cultural Heritage. Section 4 describes the approach we proposed for the population of the $COSCH^{KR}$. Section 5 and 6 describe respectively our evaluation and conclusion of this study. To the best of our knowledge, our paper is the first attempt for providing to end-users a simple integrated tool supporting them, based on knowledge extraction features and ontology population.

2   Ontology Population

An ontology is a way to store knowledge at conceptual level (T-Box) and instance level (A-Box). Defining an ontology relies on domain experts who have to find a consensus about concepts names, their relationships and instances. This process is expensive in terms of human resources and time. For this reason researchers tried to use information extraction techniques to find automatically knowledge from text. We distinguish three scenarios for automated information extraction: (a) build an ontology from scratch, (b) populate an ontology (T-Box must already exist) and (c) enrich an existing ontology (T-Box and A-Box must already exist).

In [1], the authors have defined a process to generate ontologies from texts. It begins with a pre-processing step which consists of tokenization, morphological, and lexical processing, and chunk parsing to produce syntactic and semantic information. The construction of the ontology is done by a cyclic process that relies on the human evaluation of the generated knowledge. Another approach called *Open Information Extraction* (OIE)[2] consists of a single pass to produce semantic relations (triples) from domain-independent corpus [2]. The authors proposed to use *TEXTRUNNER*, the first scalable domain-independent OIE system. Self-Service Semantic Suite[3] proposes a cloud-based platform which gives access to multiple services for text mining, on-demand access to popular linked open data, etc. In [3] the authors defined a comprehensive process to populate ontologies. They base their approach on linguistic analysis and domain verbs extraction thanks to a scoring method (such as $tf \times Idf$ in Information retrieval). It was tested on E-Voting application. Unfortunately the authors did not get

---

[2] http://openie.allenai.org/
[3] http://ontotext.com/products/ontotext-s4/

sufficient precision and recall. Lastly, [4] is a method to remove or update a knowledge set from an ontology while preserving its validity. It has been used on dbpedia, which depends on wikipedia. It uses a framework called *"DBpedia-Live extraction"* to ensure synchronization with the knowledge source [5].

3   Ontologies versus Cultural Heritage Texts

We are focusing on mechanisms to populate the $COSCH^{KR}$ ontology from Cultural Heritage scientific papers. In a first step we focused on how CH objects are digitalized.

First, let us remark that the stop words and stemming shall be used carefully because they tend to reduce the semantic of a text. As example, in the sentence *"Images were collected by a Nikon D2x"*. *"were collected by"* shall not be replace by *"were collected"*. Contrarily, the standard use of synonyms and hypernyms [6] using for instance WordNet should be used to build a gazetteer.

In the field of Cultural Heritage, Di Buono et al. [7,8] used a NLP tool and a lexicon grammar approach to extract the knowledge associated to taxonomy. For each concept, they defined a vocabulary set using Thesauri and Guidelines of the Italian Central Institute for the Catalogue and Documentation[4]. Their grammar combines POS tags and concepts tags. It detects knowledge patterns from text. This approach is useful to populate a small ontology without extracting other potential taxonomic knowledge. Notice however that it depends of the domain experts for the definition of the local grammar.

Knowledge elicited and validated by groups of experts is precise and generally trustworthy. However, the field of Cultural Heritage involves a large number of independent fields, such as art historians, archaeologists, experts in digitization systems. Consequently, knowledge elicitation requires many experts and is very slow and not affordable.

4   Semantic Based Process for Ontology Population

In the following sub-sections we present our strategy to insert semantic relations (new instances of concepts and relations) in the $COSCH^{KR}$ ontology, extracted from a set of Cultural Heritage scientific papers.

4.1   Pre-Processing

In order to find relations between entities (also when abbreviations and pronouns are used), first we applied few pre-processing steps:

---

[4] http://www.theeuropeanlibrary.org/tel4/contributor/P02002

Co-reference Resolution. Writing texts use pronouns and abbreviations to avoid repetition and long names. This introduces ambiguity, as for example in the sentence *"Steve bought a watch for his son, because he likes it."*. The personal pronoun *"he"* may refer here to *"Steve"* or to *"his son"*.

Co-reference resolution is, as defined in [9], the process of determining whether two expressions in natural language refer to the same entity in the world. It can be based on machine learning methods, such as decision trees [9] [10] or Markov logic [11]. We need co-reference resolution to replace pronouns by their references. We decided to use the Reconcile Java Api[5] for its short running time and flexibility[12].

Sentence Splitting. Sentence splitting is an automatic process which consists to cut paragraphs into sentences. The most known tools for sentence splitting are Stanford Core NLP, OpenNLP, NLTK and Gate. Their performance varies depending on the learning corpus and the method used. In [13], the best scores were obtained with the Stanford Core NLP. We tested both Stanford Core NLP and OpenNLP in our experiments. Considering both the quality of results and the running time criteria, we stated that for a similar quality of results, OpenNLP needed a few minutes against nearly one hour for Stanford Core NLP (tested with 4 GB RAM, Intel Core i3 CPU, 2.53 GHz). These results are coherent with [14]. So we used OpenNLP for sentence splitting. Moreover, we propose to correct wrong sentences splits by merging consecutive sentences when one sentence ends with "e.g." or "i.e.".

Tokenization and POS Tagging. The tokenization consists to cuts a sentence into tokens (elementary text pieces). This task is easy for languages where words are separated by simple delimiters, as for instance in English. This task requires additional steps for some languages when words are not easily identified. Since our process is currently dedicated to English text, we decided to simply use the Stanford Parser without applying additional steps. This parser realizes text tokenization and tagging, and it generates implicit dependencies between tokens [15].

4.2   Processing

The processing step starts from independent sentences with annotated tokens (words). The aim of this processing consists of generating triples to add new individuals into the $COSCH^{KR}$ ontology. We developed a process which consists of a gazetteer construction and triples extraction based on concepts matching, as illustrated in Figure 1. The first step (pre-processing) has been already presented. The others are described in the following sub-sections.

Gazetteer Construction. A gazetteer is a map that contains keywords and the associated reference words [16]. In our case, the keywords are the concept

---
[5] https://www.cs.utah.edu/nlp/reconcile/

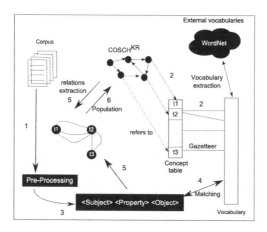

Fig. 1. Ontology population process

names from $COSCH^{KR}$ and the reference words are their "synonyms set". We build our gazetteer based on the on-line platform WordNet 3.1. For each concept name we searched for synonyms in WordNet and for those with compound names we searched for synonyms of separated words and built the union of all synonyms to get the "synonyms set".

Triples Extraction. The sentence splitting pre-processing step produces two types of sentences: simple sentences that describe one information, and compound sentences that describe more than one information. In order to generate simple triples from both types of sentences, we implemented a continuous extraction process such that the *object* of the last triple became the *subject* of the next one.

Relations Extraction. From the previous steps, a text is represented by words and the corresponding POS tags. From our experiments we observed that, generally, there are more than 50 POS tags combination of patterns in a sentence. In order to build a process that covers a maximum number of patterns, we decided to use a rule-based approach with regular expressions. We implemented an approach inspired by [17]. In [17] it is showed that the pattern with the regular expression presented above covers 85% of well-formed binary verbal relation phrases.

```
V | V P | V W*P
V = verb particle? adv?
W = (noun|adj|adv|pron|det)
P = (prep|particle|inf. marker)
s.t. ?: 0 or 1, *: 0 or many
```

Entity Extraction. For the extraction and recognition of entities we used the gazetteer previously presented. For each noun of a sentence that matches with the expression on tags (from Pann Tree Bank POS)[6] we applied the following process:

```
N*(CD|JJ)* where
N* refers to NN,NNP,NNS,NNPS (Pann Tree Bank POS)
CD to Cardinal number
JJ to Adjective
```

For instance, entities as *digital Canon EOS D60* can be extracted using this expression. If there is no verb between two entities, a *triple* can be generated with an empty *property*. We implemented a strategy which consists of deducing the *property* name from the *object*. For each word of the *object*, if it does not start with an upper case and it is neither alphanumeric nor a unit of measurement (mm, pixel, etc.), then we use this word for the *property* name, preceded by "has". This strategy follows the $COSCH^{KR}$ properties definition. It allows us to reduce the number of empty properties and to extract datatype properties instances.

The next step consists of matching each *triple* with the ontology or a subgraph of it. First, we match the *Subject* and the *Object* with the gazetteer synonyms to deduce their classes (i.e. corresponding concepts names). This step can provide zero or many results. In this case we choose the concept name with the highest frequency. For example, if the entity *"digital Canon EOS D60"* matches with *"Panorama_Scanner, Panorama_Scanner,Phase_Scanner"* then we select the class with more occurrences which is *"Panorama_Scanner"*.

Property Matching. After extracting triples, we build a SPARQL query to retrieve matching objects and data type properties with the extracted property. This SPARQL query has the form:

```
SELECT ?p
WHERE <Subject> ?p  <Object>.
```

The chosen property is the one that has the maximum of common shared words with the extracted property divided by total number of words. Finally the generated triples are added to $COSCH^{KR}$ using Jena Java Api. Such assertion does not cause any coherence problem due to the fact that our ontology version is encoded in OWL Lite. Otherwise, we should check the validity of the ontology after each insertion using a reasoner such as $HermiT$[7].

5   Evaluation and Discussion

The main objective of this work was to develop and implement a ontology population method based on information extraction from texts. As study case we considered the $COSCH^{KR}$ ontology. The method proposed consists of extracting

---

[6] https://www.ling.upenn.edu/courses/Fall_2003/ling001/penn_treebank_pos.html
[7] http://hermit-reasoner.com/

Table 1. Automatic and manual triples generation results

Article Number	1	2	3	4	5	6	7
Textual part size (KBytes)	15.5	14.5	21.8	27.3	22.4	17.9	28.2
Auto-generated triples	124	178	207	273	403	199	276
Manually annotated triples	32	42	64	54	103	63	53
New properties auto-generated	121	154	182	237	246	182	259
New properties manually added	16	22	28	36	41	26	27

semantic relations from Cultural Heritage scientific papers. The general approach used consists of a processing chain based on sub-tasks using NLP and information extraction techniques. From the first experiments done, we obtained accurate results with these techniques but sometimes they suffer from some limits and make wrong decisions. For example, when there is no space between the end of a sentence and the following one, the sentence splitter consider it as the same sentence.

Table 1 shows the results that we obtained from automatic and manual triples generation from texts. During our preliminary work we chose seven scientific papers judged by the expert rich in knowledge. The manual annotation process took him around 3 hours per paper. Notice that the number of generated triples is in both cases in direct proportion with paper size, except for papers 1 & 2. This is due to the fact that paper 2 does not contains the same amount of knowledge as paper 1. Notice also that the automatic generation provides always more triples than the manual annotation. Lastly, let us note that for both cases we get new properties that currently do not exist in the first version of the $COSCH^{KR}$.

Let us now discuss the qualitative aspect of the triples, meanwhile the expert (manual extraction) tends to extract long and compound (macro-knowledge) triples, our method tends to extract only simple triples which form is closer to the way knowledge is modeled in ontologies (micro-knowledge).

6   Conclusion

In this work we treated a problem related to semantic web and information extraction. We presented different notions about knowledge encoding and information extraction techniques used for entities extraction and semantic relations decoding from texts.

In our preliminary work, we used as study case the $COSCH^{KR}$ ontology developed by $COSCH$ team. Our objective was to populate this ontology from cultural heritage texts. We studied different methods of the state-of-the-art based on information extraction for ontology population. Then, using and combining several techniques from the state of the art, we defined a general processing chain based on WordNet that takes in input an ontology and produces in output semantic relations.

References

1. Maedche, A., Staab, S.: The text-to-onto ontology learning environment. In: Software Demonstration at ICCS-2000-Eight International Conference on Conceptual Structures (2000)
2. Etzioni, O., Banko, M., Soderland, S., Weld, D.S.: Open information extraction from the web. Communications of the ACM **51**(12), 68–74 (2008)
3. Punuru, J., Chen, J.: Learning non-taxonomical semantic relations from domain texts. Journal of Intelligent Information Systems **38**(1), 191–207 (2012)
4. Flahive, A., Taniar, D., Rahayu, W., Apduhan, B.O.: A methodology for ontology update in the semantic grid environment. Concurrency and Computation: Practice and Experience **27**(4), 782–808 (2015)
5. Morsey, M., Lehmann, J., Auer, S., Stadler, C., Hellmann, S.: Dbpedia and the live extraction of structured data from wikipedia. Program **46**(2), 157–181 (2012)
6. Shekarpour, S., Auer, S.: Rquery: Rewriting text queries to alleviate the vocabulary mismatch problem on rdf knowledge bases
7. di Buono, M.P., Monteleone, M., Elia, A.: How to populate ontologies. In: Métais, E., Roche, M., Teisseire, M. (eds.) NLDB 2014. LNCS, vol. 8455, pp. 55–58. Springer, Heidelberg (2014)
8. Pia, M.: Information Extraction for Ontology Population Tasks. An Application to the Italian Archaeological Domain **3**(2), 40–50 (2015)
9. Soon, W.M., Ng, H.T., Lim, D.C.Y.: A machine learning approach to coreference resolution of noun phrases. Computational Linguistics **27**(4), 521–544 (2001)
10. Ng, V., Cardie, C.: Improving machine learning approaches to coreference resolution. In: Proceedings of the 40th Annual Meeting on Association for Computational Linguistics, pp. 104–111. Association for Computational Linguistics (2002)
11. Poon, H., Domingos, P.: Joint unsupervised coreference resolution with markov logic. In: Proceedings of the conference on empirical methods in natural language processing, pp. 650–659. Association for Computational Linguistics (2008)
12. Stoyanov, V., Cardie, C., Gilbert, N., Riloff, E., Buttler, D., Hysom, D.: Coreference resolution with reconcile. In: Proceedings of the ACL 2010 Conference Short Papers, pp. 156–161. Association for Computational Linguistics (2010)
13. http://tech.grammarly.com/blog/posts/How-to-Split-Sentences.htm
14. Rusu, D., Dali, L., Fortuna, B., Grobelnik, M., Mladenic, D.: Triplet extraction from sentences. In: Proceedings of the 10th International Multiconference, pp. 8–12. Information Society-IS (2007)
15. De Marneffe, M.-C, Manning, C.D.: Stanford typed dependencies manual. 20090110 Httpnlp Stanford 40, 1–22, September 2010
16. Cunningham, H., Maynard, D., Bontcheva, K., Tablan, V.: Gate: a framework and graphical development environment for robust nlp tools and applications. In: Proc. 40th Anniversary Meeting of the Association for Computational Linguistics (ACL) (2002)
17. Fader, A., Soderland, S., Etzioni, O.: Identifying relations for open information extraction. In: Proceedings of the Conference on Empirical Methods in Natural Language Processing, pp. 1535–1545. Association for Computational Linguistics (2011)

Matchmaking Public Procurement Linked Open Data

Jindřich Mynarz[1]([⊠]), Vojtěch Svátek[1], and Tommaso Di Noia[2]

[1] Department of Information and Knowledge Engineering, University of Economics,
W. Churchill Sq. 4, 130 67 Prague 3, Czech Republic
{jindrich.mynarz,svatek}@vse.cz
[2] Polytechnic University of Bari, Bari, Italy
tommaso.dinoia@poliba.it

Abstract. An increasing amount of public procurement data is nowadays being ported to linked data format, in view of its exploitation by government, commercial as well as non-profit subjects. One of the crucial tasks in public procurement is matchmaking demand with supply. We conceived this task as that of finding a supplier with previous successful history of contracts similar to a current call for tenders. In this paper we show how to implement a portable matchmaking service that relies solely on the capability of SPARQL 1.1. In order to show its effectiveness, the proposed service has been tested and evaluated on the RDFized versions of 2 procurement databases: the European Union's Tenders Electronic Daily and the Czech public procurement register. We evaluate several factors influencing matchmaking accuracy, including score aggregation and weighting, query expansion, contribution of additional features obtained from linked data, data quality and volume.

Keywords: Public procurement · Matchmaking · Linked open data · SPARQL

1 Introduction

Public procurement constitutes a large share of countries' economy. For example, the financial volume of the public procurement market in the Czech Republic in 2013 accounted for 12.3 % of the country's gross domestic product.[1] The large volume of transactions in this domain gives rise to economies of scale, so that even minuscule improvements of public procurement processes can have a substantial impact. While releasing open data is frequently framed as a means to improve transparency of the public sector, it can also have a positive effect on its efficiency [8, p.69], since the public sector itself is often the primary user of open data. Using open data can help streamline public sector processes [18, p.90] and curb unnecessary expenditures [19, p.4]. The publication of public procurement data is claimed to improve *"the quality of government investment decision-making"* [12, p.2], as supervision enabled by access to data puts a pressure on

---

[1] http://www.portal-vz.cz/getmedia/8965ea38-8a96-490b-ad0f-ce4e1c0a32c9/
Vyrocni-zprava-o-stavu-verejnych-zakazek-za-rok-2013.pdf

© Springer International Publishing Switzerland 2015
C. Debruyne et al. (Eds.): OTM 2015 Conferences, LNCS 9415, pp. 405–422, 2015.
DOI: 10.1007/978-3-319-26148-5_27

contracting authorities to follow fair and budget-wise contracting procedures. This affects not only the active waste with public resources that is often caused by corruption or clientelism. In a study of Italian public sector Bandiera et al. [3, p.1282] observed that 83 % of inefficient spending in public procurement is due to passive waste that does not entail any benefit for the public decision-maker, and which is caused rather by a lack of skills or incentives. Releasing public procurement data also makes it possible to build applications on the data that assist contracting authorities to avoid passive waste and improve the quality of their decisions. Matchmaking public contracts to relevant suppliers is an example of such application that can contribute to better informed decisions that lead to more economically advantageous contracts.

In this paper we present an application of matchmaking in public procurement, in which calls for tenders (CFT) represent potential queries and potential suppliers are the resources to retrieve. The task is to support a contracting authority in preparing a CFT in terms of screening relevant suppliers for a future contract. Other matchmaking tasks are feasible as well, such as alerting businesses on relevant open CFTs, or helping contracting authorities fill in CFT's details based on past contracts, both being described in our earlier work in [16, p.6]. In our case, matchmaking covers only the information phase of market transaction [21, p.194] that corresponds to the preparation and tendering stages in public procurement life-cycle [17, p.865], during which public bodies learn about relevant suppliers and companies learn about relevant open calls.

The presented research is a part of a larger effort originally carried out within the 'procurement linked data' use case of the EU LOD2 project.[2] The first phase of this effort involved extensive data extraction, transformation, and publication according to the *Public Contracts Ontology*.[3] The second phase exploited the linked procurement datasets for matchmaking and analytic tasks. An early version of procurement matchmaker had been embedded into a prototype tool, *Public Contract Filing Application* [24, p.5–10], whose aim was to assist contracting authorities in preparation of new calls for tenders. Two contracting authorities helped to evaluate the tool including the matchmaking functionality [24, p.33–36]. They found the functionality of recommending potential suppliers beneficial, in particular for contracts with the so-called restricted procurement method that allows suppliers to be directly invited by an authority. The research presented in this paper partly extends the work carried out in the LOD2 project and reflects the findings from the end-user evaluation, as regards the requirement of larger training data with better quality. We evaluate our SPARQL-based matchmaker for public procurement linked data using several factors influencing matchmaking accuracy, including score aggregation and weighing, query expansion, contribution of additional features obtained from linked data, data quality and volume. The evaluation has been performed on 2 public procurement datasets: the EU-wide register Tenders Electronic Daily and the Czech public procurement journal.

---

[2] http://lod2.eu/WorkPackage/wp9a.html

[3] http://lov.okfn.org/dataset/lov/vocabs/pc

2   Motivating Example

In order to illustrate the described matchmaking task we present a motivating example. The following examples describe 2 contracts using the Public Contracts Ontology. Their purpose is both to give an idea of a contract's representation in RDF as such and to demonstrate the added value of using identifiers and structured data rather than plain literals.

The query contract (QC) is actually a CFT, for which its contracting authority seeks a supplier; the matched contract (MC) is a similar contract awarded in the past. The degree of similarity between them indicates whether the supplier of MC is suitable for QC as well. Listing 1 in the RDF Turtle syntax describes the contracts using mere keywords. We can see that the descriptions share the keyword "Onions", which constitutes an exact match:

```
@prefix  :  <http://purl.org/procurement/public-contracts#>  .

<query-contract> a :Contract ;
  :mainObject "Carrots"@en ;
  :additionalObject "Onions"@en .

<matched-contract> a :Contract ;
  :mainObject "Vegetables"@en ;
  :additionalObject "Onions"@en,
    "Root and tuber vegetables"@en ;
  :awardedTender [ :bidder <matched-bidder> ] .
```

Listing 1. Keyword-based descriptions

Now, in Listing 2, we switch from keyword-based to concept-based descriptions of contracts, using the SKOS version of the Common Procurement Vocabulary (CPV, see Section 3). In the CPV taxonomy the concept of "Carrots" is narrower for a concept that is narrower for "Root and tuber vegetables", which is, in turn, narrower for "Vegetables" (see the bottom of the listing).

```
@prefix  :  <http://purl.org/procurement/public-contracts#>  .
@prefix cpv: <http://linked.opendata.cz/resource/cpv-2008/
    concept/>  .
@prefix skos: <http://www.w3.org/2004/02/skos/core#>  .

<query-contract> a :Contract ;
  :mainObject cpv:03221112 ;
  :additionalObject cpv:03221113 .

<matched-contract> a :Contract ;
  :mainObject cpv:03221000 ;
  :additionalObject cpv:03221113, cpv:03221100 ;
  :awardedTender [ :bidder <matched-bidder> ] .

cpv:03221000 skos:prefLabel "Vegetables"@en .
cpv:03221100 skos:prefLabel "Root and tuber vegetables"@en .
cpv:03221112 skos:prefLabel "Carrots"@en .
cpv:03221113 skos:prefLabel "Onions"@en .

cpv:03221112 skos:broaderTransitive [
    skos:broaderTransitive cpv:03221100 ] .
```

Listing 2. Concept-based descriptions

QC and MC now become connected in 3 different ways:

– Additional object of QC ("Onions") is additional object of MC (as in the keyword approach)
– Main object of QC ("Carrots") is narrower (by 2 hops) of additional object of MC ("Root and tuber vegetables")
– Main object of QC ("Carrots") is narrower (by 3 hops) of main object of MC ("Vegetables")

Even in this simplified example, the similarity between the contracts, and, indirectly, the relevance of MC's supplier to QC, can take into account multiple inputs: taxonomic distances, relative importance of main vs. additional object, as well as the number of different connections. We will explain more details on the actual matchmaking method in Section 4.

3   Experimental Datasets

In this section we briefly describe 3 kinds of RDF resources we used, in turn. The first is the datasets describing public contracts proper. The second is the CPV dataset, which supplies the taxonomic structure for contract objects. The third, the zIndex dataset, contains a 'fairness score' of contracting authorities.

Public Procurement Linked Data. The presented matchmaker has been evaluated on 2 procurement datasets, including Czech (CZ) public procurement journal and the EU-wide register Tenders Electronic Daily (TED). These datasets expose public procurement notices informing about contracts above the financial thresholds for mandatory disclosure. The extraction and transformation of the selected datasets to linked data is described in [23, pp.18–20] and [17, pp.869–871]. Both are described using the Public Contracts Ontology, which contributes to the matchmaker's portability. We chose the dataset obtained from the Czech Public Procurement Journal as primary for the matchmaking experimentation because of its features (e.g., CPV codes or distinctions of contract lots) and an appropriate size. In Table 1 we provide a basic summary of these datasets.

Common Procurement Vocabulary. The most important linked dataset for the matchmaker is the Common Procurement Vocabulary (CPV):[4] a controlled vocabulary standardized by the EU for harmonizing the description of procured objects across the member states. The vocabulary has a mono-hierarchical structure in which the individual taxonomic links typically have the flavour of either subsumption[5] or part-whole[6] relations between CPV concepts. While the original CPV source expresses hierachical relations using the structure of numerical notations of the vocabulary's concepts, we transformed the CPV to

---

[4] http://simap.europa.eu/codes-and-nomenclatures/codes-cpv/codes-cpv_en.htm
[5] E.g., "Broccoli" has broader concept "Vegetables".
[6] E.g., "Vegetables" has broader concept "Vegetables, fruits and nuts".

Table 1. Basic statistics of the datasets used in evaluation

	CZ	TED
Number of triples	11.7 M	46.6 M
Number of awarded contracts	73.9 k	173.3 k
Number of bidders	29 k	517 k
Temporal coverage	July 2006–August 2014	2012–June 2014
Average number of contracts won by bidder	3.82	1.27

RDF[7] that makes these relations explicit using the SKOS vocabulary. *Public Contracts Ontology* [14, p.21] declares CPV concepts as range of the properties `pc:mainObject`[8] and `pc:additionalObject`, both of which are defined as sub-properties of `dcterms:subject`. The property `pc:mainObject`, defined as functional, indicates the most important object procured in the contract, whereas `pc:additionalObject` describes supplementary objects related to the contract. Using the terminology of case-based reasoning, CPV provides a "bridge attribute" that allows to derive the similarity of contracts from the shared concepts in their descriptions. CPV is available in both of the used datasets.

Fairness Index. For the Czech dataset only we were able to use annotations with zIndex.[9] It is a rating of fairness of Czech contracting authorities computed from several indicators describing various issues in public procurement, such as the use of open tendering procedures. It is represented as a number z ($0 < z \leq 1$), where 1 is assigned to contracting authorities that best adhere to the fair practices in public procurement, while the index of 0 is given to authorities that deviate from these practices the most. The zIndex is available for 63.1 % of contracting authorities present in the CZ dataset; for others we use 0.5 as a default value. There is no fairness index for the TED dataset.

4   Matchmaking Problem and Method

Matchmaking can be defined as an information retrieval task of searching the space of queries (demands) and resources (supplies), both of which are described using semi-structured data with comparable schemas, and the task results are ordered by the degree to which they fulfill the query [7, p.278]. The presented matchmaker can be described as a case-based reasoning recommender system that provides a *"form of content-based recommendation that emphasizes the use*

---

[7] https://github.com/opendatacz/cpv2rdf
[8] All vocabulary prefixes used in this paper can be resolved to their corresponding namespace URIs via http://prefix.cc.
[9] http://wiki.zindex.cz/doku.php?id=en:start

of structured representations and similarity-based retrieval during recommenda-tion" [22, p.369]. It recasts public contracts awarded in the past as cases to learn from. In this sense, the awarded contracts represent experiences of solved problems [20, p.17]. The downside of this approach is that it favors larger and longer-established bidders that were awarded with more contracts than newcom-ers to the procurement market. The matchmaker produces a ranked list of top-k most relevant matched resources for a given query resource. Fig. 1 depicts a matchmaking scenario, with the resources to be matched in bold:

- The query resource is a *call for tenders* (CFT), marked as QC (for 'query CFT'), i.e. an incomplete contract object with no awarded tender.
- The matched resources are potential bidders, as business entities that may supply what the contract demands. The diagram represents them by MB_1 and MB_2 (for 'matched business entities').
- We only consider the business entities awarded with at least 1 contract. These contracts, through which the matchmaking is carried out (MC_1 – MC_3), are analyzed with respect to the similarity to the current CFT.
- The contract-CFT similarity calculation relies primarily on the similarity of their *objects*, in terms of CPV concepts linked by the pc:mainObject (MO) and pc:additionalObject (AO) property.
- The current contracting authority (CA) preparing the CFT (QCA, for 'query CA') is only implicit in the process. However, we consider the CAs respon-sible for the relevant past contracts (such as MCA_1, for 'matched CA', in the diagram), in particular in terms of their *fairness scores* (as FS_1). The better the fairness score of a CA, the higher the contribution of the contract awarded by it to the recommendation of the awarded supplier.

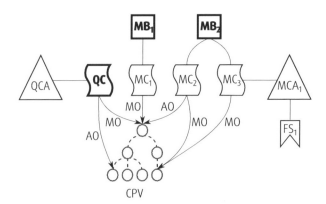

Fig. 1. Overall diagram of similarity-based contract matchmaking

4.1   Generic Method

We present a generic descriptive formalism of matching contracts (precisely, contract notices) to potential bidders, and gradually refine it to cover the notions specific to our approach. We start with the notions of contract and call for tenders. A public *contract* is a quadruple

$$c = (ca, su, obj, ctx)$$

where ca is a contracting authority (buyer), su is the supplier, obj is the object of the contract (what is provided by the supplier to the buyer) and ctx is the context of the contract, including, for simplicity, all of its aspects other than buyer, supplier and object: the conditions under which the contract is fulfilled (time, place, legal framework, etc.), but also the tendering procedure and the inherent characteristics of the contract, e.g., whether it is a standalone contract or just a part of contract, called 'lot'. Analogously, a *call for tenders* is a triple

$$cft = (ca, obj, ctx)$$

where ca is a contracting authority (potential buyer), obj is the demanded object of the anticipated contract (for which the tenders are to be submitted) and ctx is the context of the contract envisaged in the call (with similar but possibly reduced scope as for an awarded contract).

Let C be the *contract base*, i.e. the pool of all known contracts (with all possible contracting authorities) considered in the task, S is the (known) *supplier base*, i.e. the set of all past suppliers of all contracts from C, and CFT is the set of calls for tenders under consideration. From the practical point of view, it should consist of the calls of the given contracting authority for which the matchmaking task is to be carried out, namely, the *published calls* (not yet awarded to a bidder) and the *calls under preparation*. The task of matchmaking a call for tenders to potential suppliers is then cast as computation of match score from some ordinal range of values V, allowing subsequent ranking. It can be expressed by means of the following match-score abstract function:

$$mscore : CFT \times S \to V$$

Let $cft_q = (ca_q, obj_q)$ be the 'query' call for tenders for which we want to retrieve potential suppliers. In our particular model, formed by the actual data sources available, we primarily exploit the similarity at the level of contracts (call for tenders being just a reduced form of implemented contract). Therefore we introduce the notion of *contract-similarity match-score* function

$$mscore_{CS}(cft_q, su) = \underset{i}{agg^c}(adj(sim^c(cft_q, c_i), imp^c, qual(ca_i)))$$

where

- imp^c is a function returning the importance of a contract, typically based on its type (e.g., a lot is less important than a complete contract)

- **qual** is a function returning the contracting authority quality, such as a 'fairness/transparency index' of the authority; it is uniformly computed for each contract of the same authority ca_i
- **sim**^{c} is a contract similarity metric, presumably a symmetric one
- **adj** is a contract-level score adjustment operator over the values of **sim**^{c}, by **imp**^{c} and **qual**
- **agg**^{c} is a score (adjusted by **adj**) aggregation operator over all contracts $c_i = (ca_i, su, obj_i)$, i.e. those of supplier su.

Of the boldfaced template operators or metrics, **sim**^{c} is elaborated on below. For all, specific instantiations are provided in Section 4.2.

The contract similarity metric **sim**^{c} can be based on both components we distinguish for a contract: object and context. In our approach we currently only exploit the contract object, since the availability of machine-readable data is limited in the sources we address. We thus specialize the similarity metric to

$$sim^c(cft_q, c_i) = sim^{obj}(exp(obj_q), obj_i)$$

where **sim**^{obj} is a contract *object* similarity metric, and **exp** is a query expansion operator for contract objects.

Let us now define more precisely the notion of *object* of a contract. Rather than as 'physical' products or services, the objects of public procurement are mostly observed at the level of concepts, declared in controlled vocabularies such as CPV, some of which may play dominant and some other only marginal role in the same contract. Therefore we decompose obj_i (as object in contract c_i), in our model, to a multiset of *concept associations*

$$obj_i = \{(con_{i,j}, str_{i,k}))\}$$

where all concepts $con_{i,j}$ belong to a common set of concepts Con and all $str_{i,k}$ are numerical values from a certain range, presumably $0 \leq str_{i,k} \leq 1$. Each $(con_{i,j}, str_{i,k})$ pair represents an association between contract c_i and a concept, equipped with specified numerical strength. Since c_i can be associated to the same concept in multiple ways with different or equal strengths, the same $con_{i,j}$ as well as $str_{i,k}$ may repeat in obj_i, giving the possibility of multiset rather than set.

We assume that the set Con is internally (especially, hierarchically) structured such that relevance of one concept may entail relevance of some other concepts in its neighborhood. The expansion operator **exp** takes as input a contract object obj and returns a contract object **exp**(obj). At the general level, we will only require **exp** to be monotonous with respect to the concept association multiset, i.e. for every concept $con \in Con$ holds

$$(con, str) \in obj \;\; \Rightarrow \;\; (con, str) \in exp(obj)$$

As regards the similarity of two contract objects, we assume that it is to be computed at the level of concepts shared by their concept sets, taking into account the respective *strengths* of the concepts in the objects and also the prior *importance* of the concepts, obtained via the function $\boldsymbol{imp}^{con}$. The importance can be based on the concept's statistical discrimination power (which is what we exploit in our method described later), on its position in the graph structure of Con, on its assessment by a human oracle, etc. Formally,

$$\boldsymbol{sim}^{obj}(obj_q, obj_i) = \boldsymbol{agg}^{con}_j(\boldsymbol{comb}(str_{q,j}, str_{i,j}, \boldsymbol{imp}^{con}(con_j)))$$

for all j such that

$$(con_j, str_{q,j}) \in obj_q \ \wedge \ (con_j, str_{i,j}) \in obj_i$$

Here, $\boldsymbol{comb}$ is a function for combining the 3 weights into a partial similarity measure (in terms of one shared concept). Note that the 3 weights correspond to the 'strengths' of the 3 parts of the *path* connecting the query call for tenders cft_q and the matched contract c_i: edge from cft_q to con_j, edge from c_i to con_j, and concept con_j in the middle. Furthermore, $\boldsymbol{agg}^{con}$ is another aggregation operator, this time (in contrast to $\boldsymbol{agg}^c$) over the multiple shared concepts of contracts rather than over contracts themselves.

4.2   Function Instantiation

The boldfaced abstract functions from the previous subsection can be instantiated in many ways. The summary of our particular instantiation (aside $\boldsymbol{sim}^c$, already instantiated above) and of the choice/range of parameter values in the experiments, is in Table 2. Note that 'modifiers' (such as quality-based adjustment) have only been used in some of the experimental settings. The nature of these inferential procedures can be understood as reasoning under uncertainty [10]. Since $\boldsymbol{adj}$ and $\boldsymbol{comb}$ aggregate multiple 'sequential' weights over an inferential path, they are 'fuzzy-conjunctive' and can be modeled as *t-norms*. Analogously, $\boldsymbol{agg}^c$ and $\boldsymbol{agg}^{con}$ aggregate multiple 'parallel' weights affecting an inferential node, they are thus 'fuzzy-disjunctive' and can be viewed as *t-conorms*. Product $(a * b)$ and probabilistic sum $(a + b - a * b)$ are the most commonly used types of t-norm and t-conorm, respectively. However, probabilistic sum requires aggregation by multiplication, which cannot be implemented directly in SPARQL since it lacks an operator to multiply grouped bindings. Therefore, we implemented the aggregation via post-processing of SPARQL results. Eventually, since the difference on the evaluated metrics between the probabilistic sum and summation $(a + b)$ turned out to be statistically insignificant, we opted for summation, which can be computed in SPARQL and is marginally faster. We also experimented with alternative t-norms and t-conorms: Gödel's and Łukasiewicz's methods [4, p.27]. Their impact on the target metrics was however negative, as seen in the evaluation results in Section 7; we thus omit them from Table 2, for simplicity.

One more instantiation feature is the setting of association strength (str). While we always set it to 1 for the main object of the contract, it was lowered, in some configurations, for the additional object ('AO weight' in result tables).

Table 2. Instantiations of abstract functions used in experiments

Function	Instantiation	Value/range
imp^c	Two-valued function	1 for complete contract, 0.5 for lot
$qual$	For Czech contracts only: Z-index of the authority	$(0, 1]$
adj	Multiplication	
agg^c	Summation	
exp	Addition of broader/narrower concepts n hops away from the current concept	n varying from 1 to 3; strength same as for current
imp^{con}	IDF measure wrt. use in contracts	$(0, 1]$
$comb$	Multiplication	
agg^{con}	Summation	

5 Implementation

Matchmaking public contract to suitable bidders starts with retrieving similar contracts awarded in the past. For each awarded contract a similarity score is computed and the contracts are grouped by bidders that won them. Scores of each group are aggregated and sorted in descending order. In this way, matchmaking uses both semantic and statistical properties of data on which it operates. While the semantics of contracts' descriptions is employed in similarity measurement, the aggregation of scores reflects the statistics about past participation of bidders in public procurement [2, p.122].

The matchmaker is implemented using SPARQL [1] as a native way of RDF data processing. Indeed, as it operates directly on the RDF data model, there is no need for data re-formatting. In this way, the matchmaker avoids the initialization time needed for pre-processing data or training a model. Given that it needs only RDF store's indices for operation, it is well suited for streaming data that requires real-time processing. Such requirement is to a certain degree also present in the public procurement domain because its data becomes quickly obsolete due to its currency bound on fixed deadlines for tender submission. Moreover, since the matchmaker is limited to the standard SPARQL without proprietary addons or extension functions, it is portable across RDF stores compliant with the SPARQL specification. The implementation of our matchmaker bases exclusively on querying a SPARQL endpoint without any previous data preprocessing. Our tool can thus be easily deployed by any public administration exposing its data via a SPARQL endpoint with no further tool or service needed.

While RDF stores in general suffer from performance penalty compared to relational databases, recent advancements in the application of column store

```
?queryCFT (pc:mainObject|pc:additionalObject)/
  (skos:broaderTransitive|skos:narrowerTransitive)*/
  ^(pc:mainObject|pc:additionalObject)/
  pc:awardedTender/pc:bidder ?matchedBidder  .
```

Listing 3. Matchmaker's SPARQL property path

technology for RDF data improved things a lot [5, p.23]. Yet, in order to get the best performance of SPARQL, the matchmaker is limited to exact joins. Fuzzy joins over literal ranges or overlapping substrings significantly decrease the matchmaker's performance and are therefore avoided.

The basic graph pattern considered in most configurations of the matchmaker is illustrated in Listing 3 using the SPARQL 1.1 Property Path syntax.

The actual implementation of the matchmaker in SPARQL is based on nested sub-queries and **VALUES** clauses used to associate the considered properties with weights. Score aggregation is done using SPARQL 1.1 aggregates. More detailed description of the matchmaker's implementation and the API it exposes is available in [16, p.5]. Matchmaker source code is available in a public repository[10] licensed as open source under the terms of Eclipse Public License. Example SPARQL queries used by the matchmaker can be found at https://github. com/opendatacz/matchmaker/wiki/SPARQL-query-examples. A demo instance of the matchmaker's JSON-LD API configured for the data from TED is available at http://lod2-dev.vse.cz:8080/matchmaker/.

6   Evaluation Protocol

We evaluated the matchmaker's configurations on the task of predicting the contracts' winning bidders. In our setting the matchmaker predicts from the space of all bidders and not only from those that bid for a given contract, since only the identity of the awarder bidder is available in the datasets used for evaluation. In this context, winning bidders are used as ground truth and the matchmaker attempts to mimick the selection of contracting authorities. However, it is clear that the awarded bidder may not be the best match in all cases. The choice of the winner may not only reflect its suitability for a particular contract, but it can also be influenced by adverse factors including corruption, lack of information or cartel agreements. Attempting to address these factors we included zIndex as a weight in one of the matchmaker's configurations in order to take into account how well contracting authorities adhere to fair contract award procedures. The evaluation was done using offline experimental setup.

The datasets on which we evaluated the matchmaker are described in Section 3. Our evaluation setup was restricted to public contracts that announced 1 winner. However, some contracts in the considered datasets reported more that

---

[10] https://github.com/opendatacz/matchmaker

a single winner, typically because their descriptions did not distinguish between lots the contracts were composed of, so it was not possible to assign winners to the lots they were awarded. While in the Czech dataset this was the case for only a handful of contracts, in TED it accounted for 9.8 % of awarded contracts. Due to our evaluation setup we removed these contracts from the datasets used for experimentation. The datasets' statistics in Table 1 reflect this change.

We used 5-fold cross validation on the complete datasets without respecting the temporal order of contracts (i.e.we also use future contracts for matching the query contract). The folds were not overlapping, so each contract was evaluated exactly once. The results obtained for the adopted metrics were averaged over individual folds. Evaluation of statistical significance was done using the Student's t-test.

6.1   Metrics

The chosen evaluation metrics reflect the matchmaker's accuracy and variance in results. We adopted Hit-Rate at 10 (HR@10) [6, p.159] as our principal metric. This metric is defined as $\frac{number\ of\ hits}{n}$, where hits account for contracts for which the awarded bidder is found in the first 10 results of the matchmaker and n is the total number of the evaluated contracts. We prioritized this metric because the first 10 results are typically the only ones users consider.[11]

A complementary metric employed in the evaluation was mean Average Rank at 100 (AR@100). This metric is defined as $\frac{1}{n} \sum_{i=1}^{n} r_i$, where r_i ($1 \leq r_i \leq 100$) is the rank of the awarded bidder in the first 100 results of the matchmaker and n is the number of cases when the awarded contract was found in the first 100 results of the matchmaker. Note that AR cannot be used alone, since it does not penalize complete non-matches and matches below the threshold rank. AR is thus meant as a fine-grained adjustment for distinguishing between cases that all have rather high HR, which, in turn, does not account for the actual rank at all. The threshold for AR@100 was set as more relaxed as that for HR@10 such that 'less visible but not yet hopeless' matches (considering a more patient user) would only lose their weight gradually.

Apart from metrics of accuracy we consider catalog coverage [9, p.258], which measures variance of the matchmaker's results. Catalog coverage is ratio of distinct items that are effectively presented in matchmaking results I_r over all items I. If we denote the number of queries as N and the items presented for a query j as I_r^j, then catalog coverage can be computed as:

$$\frac{\left| \bigcup_{j=1...N} I_r^j \right|}{|I|}$$

Using the described evaluation protocol we conducted several experiments with different configurations of the matchmaker. We discuss the results of these experiments in the following section.

---

[11] A study claims that this is the only part considered by 91 % of search engine users (http://www.seo-takeover.com/case-study-click-through-rate-google/).

7 Comparison of the Evaluated Approaches

From the large pool of possible configurations of the matchmaker we only selected a few for evaluation of the metrics. These configurations either differ in the matchmaking method or produce the best result improvement. The following tables summarize the results obtained.

7.1 Evaluation Results

The results are presented for different matchmaker settings and varying additional object weight (AO weight). Tables 3 and 4 refer to the CZ and TED dataset, respectively. The number of configurations is higher for CZ due to its smaller size, allowing to effectively explore the space of configurations, and also due to availability of fairness index (zIndex) annotations for it; for TED we also did not perform additional deduplication. The best results for each metric are in bold font. All differences in evaluation results that we report further on as statistically significant were tested for p-values ¡ 0.01. Large size of the evaluation datasets allows us to recognize even minor but statistically significant differences.

7.2 Discussion

We applied the matchmaker using exact matches of CPV concepts with *association strenghts* set to 1 as our baseline. When varying the additional object

Table 3. Comparison of selected matchmaker's configurations on the CZ dataset

Matchmaker	AO weight	HR@10	AR@100	CC@10
Exact CPV	1	0.234	19.046	0.304
Exact CPV	0.1	0.237	18.564	0.333
Exact, Gödel comb.	0.5	0.084	32.15	0.324
Exact, Lukasiewicz comb.	0.5	0.076	32.805	0.326
Exact, product comb.	0.5	0.235	19.104	0.305
Exact, distinguishing lots	1	0.23	19.399	0.3
Exact, with zIndex	1	0.233	18.867	0.307
Exact, better deduplication	1	0.27	18.354	0.309
Exact, better deduplication	0.1	**0.273**	**18.052**	**0.337**
Expand 1 hop to broader	1	0.227	20.32	0.268
Expand 1 hop to broader, with IDF	1	0.235	19.877	0.286
Expand 1 hop to narrower	1	0.234	19.044	0.304
Expand 1 hop to narrower, with IDF	1	0.236	19.278	0.298

Table 4. Comparison of selected matchmaker's configurations on TED

Matchmaker	AO weight	HR@10	AR@100	CC@10
Exact CPV	1	0.06	**19.159**	0.065
Exact CPV	0.1	**0.06**	19.423	**0.081**
Exact, Gödel comb.	0.5	0.014	36.347	0.06
Exact, Lukasiewicz comb.	0.5	0.014	36.516	0.06
Exact, product comb.	0.5	0.059	19.744	0.069
Expand 1 hop to broader	1	0.053	21.833	0.049
Expand 1 hop to broader, with IDF	1	0.058	20.193	0.057
Expand 1 hop to narrower	1	**0.06**	19.16	0.065

inhibition (AO weight), we found that the best results for the CZ dataset can be obtained by adjusting it to 0.1. With this setting the HR@10 is increased by 0.27 %, while AR@100 improves by 2.53 %. This configuration also has a positive impact on catalog coverage, which for CC@10 increases by 2.89 %. Using this setting also improved the evaluation results for the TED dataset, as can be seen in Table 4. Having a small influence of additional objects on the similarity scores surpasses ignoring the additional objects and is also better than assigning higher weights to additional objects. We experimented with using combinations of different AO weight for query CFTs and matched contracts, but the results were worse than when the weight was set to 0.1 in both cases.

When testing different *t-norms* and *t-conorms* we set the weights to 0.5 instead of 1 because so as to allow the differences in some combination methods to manifest. The product combination clearly outperformed the others, because it reflects statistical properties of data better. If we distinguish lots from complete contracts by a decreased weight, the evaluation results get worse. When we applied zIndex fairness score as a weight for contracting authorities, we did not observe any statistically significant difference in the evaluation results.

The largest improvement of the matchmaker's evaluation results was achieved by better *deduplication* of bidders in the CZ dataset. Deduplication and fusion of bidders reduces the search space of possible matches and thereby increases the probability of finding the correct match. Deduplication led to 14.97 % decrease in the number of bidders, which in turn accounted for 3.56 % improvement in HR@10, 3.63 % improvement in AR@10, and 0.46 % improvement in CC@10. These results indicate that influence of data quality is greater than the impact of the parameters varied in the evaluation.

Query expansion did not improve the matchmaker's performance. We experimented with 1-3 hops for expansion to broader and narrower concepts. Whether we applied IDF as a weight for the expanded concepts or not, the results did not improve significantly and often even got worse. Since we did not obtain any gain by query expansion, its computational overhead clearly does not pay off.

Apart from varying single parameters, we evaluated a couple of *combinations* of the best-performing parameter settings. When we combined better dedupli-cated dataset with using 0.1 as AO weight, we got the best HR@10, which surpassed the baseline by 3.93 %, AR@10 improved by 5.22 %, and CC@10 out-performed the baseline by 3.3 %. In case this configuration was combined with 1-hop expansion to broader concepts the evaluation results got worse.

Overall, the results for the TED dataset were worse than for the CZ dataset, which is likely due to greater heterogeneity and duplicity. In effect, these results are barely usable in practice.

In order to assess the impact of data volume on the matchmaker's results we performed evaluation with reduced sample dataset. Before each experiment we temporarily removed a part of the dataset containing the links between public contracts and awarded bidders and run the 5-fold cross validation on the reduced dataset. The results show that if we reduce the Czech dataset by half, HR@10 drops by 2.73 % for the baseline configuration. If we reduce the dataset to 10 % of the original size, HR@10 decreases by 10.16 % compared to the baseline. It is worth noticing that sometimes while HR@10 decreases, AR@100 improves, highlighting that these metrics must be evaluated together. The impact of data reduction is shown in Figure 2. This demonstrates how the matchmaker leverages the volume of data using aggregations along with data semantics.

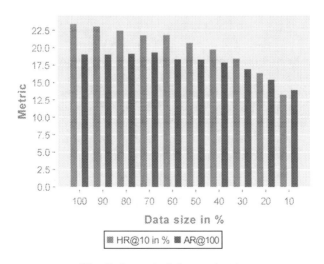

Fig. 2. Impact of data reduction

8   Related Work

In order to illustrate the progress beyond the state of the art made by the presented matchmaker, we compare it to the features provided by the publishers of public procurement data, reusers of this data, and the related research in matchmaking in general.

The search interfaces provided by the publishers of datasets employed in this paper can be used to approximate the matchmaker's functionality, although doing so requires additional manual work for the tasks that cannot be automated via these interfaces. Besides simple search, TED allows to search its archives using the Common Command Language [11]. For instance, following the example matched contract from Section 2, we can express a query for awarded contracts described by the CPV concept "Root and tuber vegetables", its narrower concepts obtained by query expansing using a wildcard, or the concept "Onions" as `TD=["Contract award"] AND PC=[032211* OR 03221113]`. This query retrieves a list of contract award notices, which a user needs to go through individually to find the awarded bidders. Aggregation of search results is possible via a statistic mode, however, awarded bidder is not among the fields users are allowed to group the results by. Approximating the matchmaker's results with this interface thus requires additional manual work. Similar matchmaking functionality may be achieved by searching XML dumps of TED data,[12] but combining it with additional data and writing expressive queries can be difficult.

The Czech public procurement journal provides a search interface that allows to query multiple fields and provides full-text search features including Boolean operators and wildcards. The expressivity of this interface allows to perform queries analogous to those for TED. The journal also exposes an XML API,[13] providing machine-readable data. However, as is the case for TED, data aggregation and combination with other sources may require a lot of effort.

Given the availability of these datasets as open data, their commercial reusers can build services similar to our matchmaker. An example reuser of TED data is Euroalert.net [15], which provides alert services matching search profiles of companies to relevant contracts. However, as the description of this service[14] suggests, the matchmaking is keyword-based without using the semantics of contracts' descriptions. For the Czech public contracts, the maintainer of the official procurement journal provides the portal Zakázky+,[15] which offers an analogous alert service using cleaner and better deduplicated data.

If we survey the related research in matchmaking, the closest work to ours is likely from Alvarez-Rodríguez et al. [2], who used SPARQL for matchmaking organizations and public procurement notices along with several methods of query expansion [2, p.118]. Unfortunately, it is difficult to determine the differences between their and our approach, because neither implementation details nor evaluation is revealed in the paper describing this work. SPARQL also served as a basis for extensions focused on similarity retrieval in iSPARQL by Kiefer el al. [13]. Unlike iSPARQL, our approach works without extending SPARQL and therefore maintains better compatibility.

---

[12] http://ted.europa.eu/TED/misc/xmlPackagesDownload.do

[13] http://vestnikverejnychzakazek.cz/en/PublishAForm/XMLInterfaceForISVZUS

[14] http://euroalert.net/en/10ders_alerts_government_contracts.aspx

[15] http://www.zakazky-plus.cz/

9   Conclusions

Public procurement is an area where the benefits of linked data technology are potentially manifold and affect numerous parties: contracting authorities, suppliers, citizens as well as supervisory bodies. In the paper we focused on the contracting authority side, namely, on the exploitation of past contracts data when creating new CFTs and assessing which business entities could potentially become suppliers; the whole task is recast as CFT-to-supplier matchmaking mainly leveraging CFT-to-contract similarity. Based on prior feedback from contracting authorities, we carried out a number of experiments on 2 procurement datasets. In summary, the influence of data volume and quality in terms of better deduplication appears greater than the impact of the parameters varied in the evaluation. Future work will also address systematic exploitation of textual description associated with the contracts, as well as geo-spatial information, such as location of the suppliers, and recency of the past contracts.

Acknowledgements. The presented research has been partially supported by the EU ICT FP7 project no. 257943, LOD2 project, by the H2020 project no. 645833 (Open-Budgets.eu), by the Italian projects PON01_03113 ERMES, PON02_00563_3470993 Vincente and PON02_00563_3446857 KHIRA, and by the long-term institutional support of research activities by Faculty of Informatics and Statistics, University of Economics, Prague.

References

1. SPARQL 1.1 Query Language. W3C recommendation. W3C, March 2013. http://www.w3.org/TR/sparql11-query/
2. Alvarez-Rodríguez, J.M., Labra Gayo, J.E., Ordoñez de Pablos, P.: Enabling the matchmaking of organizations and public procurement notices by means of linked open data. In: Cases on Open-Linked Data and Semantic Web Applications, pp. 105–131. IGI Global (2013)
3. Bandiera, O., Prat, A., Valletti, T.: Active and passive waste in government spending: evidence from a policy experiment. American Economic Review **99**(4), 1278–1308 (2009). http://www.aeaweb.org/articles.php?doi=10.1257/aer.99.4.1278
4. Beliakov, G., Pradera, A., Calvo, T.: Aggregation Functions: A Guide for Practitioners. STUDFUZZ, vol. 221. Springer, Heidelberg (2007)
5. Boncz, P., Erling, O., Pham, M.D.: Advances in large-scale RDF data management. In: Auer, S., Bryl, V., Tramp, S. (eds.) Linked open data: creating knowledge out of interlinked data. LNCS, vol. 8661, pp. 21–44. Springer, Heidelberg (2014)
6. Deshpande, M., Karypis, G.: Item-based top-n recommendation algorithms. ACM Transactions on Information Systems **22**(1), 143–177 (2004)
7. Di Noia, T., Di Sciascio, E., Donini, F.M.: Semantic matchmaking as non-monotonic reasoning: a description logic approach. Journal of Artificial Intelligence Research **29**(1), 269–307 (2007)

8. Access Info Europe and Open Knowledge Foundation. Beyond access: open government data & the right to (re)use public information. Tech. rep. (2011). http://www.access-info.org/documents/Access_Docs/Advancing/ Beyond_Access_7_January_2011_web.pdf
9. Ge, M., Delgado-Battenfeld, C., Jannach, D.: Beyond accuracy: evaluating recommender systems by coverage and serendipity. In: Proceedings of the Fourth ACM Conference on Recommender Systems, pp. 257–260. ACM, New York (2010)
10. Hajek, P.: The Metamathematics of Fuzzy Logic. Kluwer (1998)
11. ISO: Information and documentation: commands for interactive text searching. ISO 8777:1993, International Organization for Standardization (1993)
12. Kenny, C.: Publish what you buy: the case for routine publication of government contracts. Tech. Rep. 011, Center for Global Development, Washington DC, August 2012. http://www.cgdev.org/content/publications/detail/1426431
13. Kiefer, C., Bernstein, A., Stocker, M.: The fundamentals of iSPARQL: a virtual triple approach for similarity-based semantic web tasks. In: Aberer, K., et al. (eds.) ASWC 2007 and ISWC 2007. LNCS, vol. 4825, pp. 295–309. Springer, Heidelberg (2007)
14. Klímek, J., Knap, T., Mynarz, J., Nečaský, M., Svátek, V.: LOD2 deliverable 9a.1.1: Framework for creating linked data in the domain of public sector contracts. Tech. rep., LOD2 EU Project, Prague (2012). http://static.lod2.eu/Deliverables/ deliverable-9a.1.1.pdf
15. Marín, J.L., et al.: Euroalert.net: aggregating public procurement data to deliver commercial services to SMEs, pp. 114–130. IGI (2013). http://www.igi-global.com/ chapter/euroalert-net-aggregating-public-procurement/69590
16. Mynarz, J., Zeman, V., Dudáš, M.: LOD2 deliverable 9a.2.2: Stable implementation of matching functionality into web application for filing public contracts. Deliverable D9a.2.2, LOD2 EU Project (2014). http://svn.aksw.org/lod2/D9a.2. 2/public.pdf
17. Nečaský, M., Klímek, J., Mynarz, J., Knap, T., Svátek, V., Stárka, J.: Linked data support for filing public contracts. Computers in Industry 65(5), 862–877 (2014). special Issue: New trends on E-Procurement applying Semantic Technologies
18. Parycek, P., Höchtl, J., Ginner, M.: Open government data implementation evaluation. Journal of Theoretical and Applied Electronic Commerce Research 9(2), 80–99 (2014). http://www.scielo.cl/pdf/jtaer/v9n2/art07.pdf
19. Prešern, M., Žejn, G.: Supervizor: an indispensable open government application. In: Share-PSI 2.0 workshop on uses of open data within government for innovation and efficiency (2014). https://www.w3.org/2013/share-psi/wiki/images/6/ 6b/Supervizor_Slovenia_description_pdf.pdf
20. Richter, M.M., Weber, R.O.: Case-based reasoning: a textbook. Springer (2013)
21. Schmid, B.F., Lindemann, M.A.: Elements of a reference model for electronic markets. In: Proceedings of the Thirty-First Hawaii International Conference on System Sciences, vol. 4, pp. 193–201, January 1998
22. Smyth, B.: Case-based recommendation. In: Brusilovsky, P., Kobsa, A., Nejdl, W. (eds.) Adaptive Web 2007. LNCS, vol. 4321, pp. 342–376. Springer, Heidelberg (2007)
23. Svátek, V., et al.: LOD2 deliverable 9a.3.1: application of data analytics methods of linked data in the domain of PSC. Deliverable D9a.3.1, LOD2 EU Project (2014). http://svn.aksw.org/lod2/D9a.3.1/public.pdf
24. Svátek, V., et al.: LOD2 deliverable 9a.3.2: Implementation of data analytics in the public contract filing application. Deliverable D9a.3.2, LOD2 EU Project (2014). http://svn.aksw.org/lod2/D9a.3.2/public.pdf

Preference Queries with Ceteris Paribus Semantics for Linked Data

Jessica Rosati[1,2,3](✉), Tommaso Di Noia[1], Thomas Lukasiewicz[4],
Renato De Leone[2], and Andrea Maurino[3]

[1] Polytechnic University of Bari, Via Orabona, 4, 70125 Bari, Italy
{jessica.rosati,tommaso.dinoia}@poliba.it
[2] School of Science and Technology, University of Camerino,
Piazza Cavour 19/f, 62032 Camerino (MC), Italy
renato.deleone@unicam.it
[3] University of Milano-Bicocca, Piazza Dell'Ateneo Nuovo, 1,
20126 Milano, Italy
maurino@disco.unimib.it
[4] University of Oxford, Parks Road, Oxford OX1 3QD, UK
thomas.lukasiewicz@cs.ox.ac.uk

Abstract. User preferences play a central role in supporting complex and multifactorial decision processes. Every personalized information filtering system should exploit a preferences model of the user in order to match her interests as much as possible. In a Linked Open Data (LOD) setting, the problem is twofold. On the one hand, there is the need of a standard way to represent complex preferences. On the other hand, we need tools able to query LOD datasets by taking into account user's preferences. In this paper, we propose a vocabulary to represent statements formulated in terms of ceteris paribus semantics. We then show (i) how to represent a CP-net by means of this vocabulary and (ii) how to embed such compact preference model in a SPARQL 1.1 query in order to access semantic data in a personalized way.

Keywords: User preferences · Ceteris paribus · CP-nets · Linked data · Preference queries · SPARQL

1 Introduction

Dealing with user preferences is an important aspect of every application designed to provide personalized information to the end-user. The original interest in preferences can be found in decision theory, as a way to support complex, multifactorial decision processes [10], and nowadays every personalized system needs a preference model to capture what the user likes or dislikes. Once the user model has been represented, it is then exploited to filter information coming from a data source, e.g., a database, to provide a ranked list of results matching the order encoded in the preferences of the user.

© Springer International Publishing Switzerland 2015
C. Debruyne et al. (Eds.): OTM 2015 Conferences, LNCS 9415, pp. 423–442, 2015.
DOI: 10.1007/978-3-319-26148-5_28

Query languages usually let us specify the information that we want to be returned (hard constraints). However, if a user's requirements are not fulfilled, the result of the query can be the empty set. At the same time, returning huge and unordered sets of answers could be useless and even counter-productive. A possible way to bypass these issues is to allow the language to represent both hard constraints (used to return only relevant results) and soft ones, i.e., preferences (to rank the results by fulfilling user's tastes). Approaches to preference representation can be distinguished between quantitative and qualitative. The former are based on total ordering of outcomes given by a scoring function, while the latter make possible the representation of partial orders, since preferences are treated as independent dimensions. From a user perspective, a qualitative approach is more natural than the quantitative one [8]. Indeed, in the first case, the user has just to provide pairwise qualitative comparisons, while in the second case, she has to assign a value to many alternatives, which very often are represented in a multi-attribute setting. Within the database community, both Chomicki [5,6] and independently Kießling and colleagues [15,16], formalized extensions of SQL that support the specification of quantitative and qualitative queries. Regarding the Linked (Open) Data world, the notion of qualitative preferences into SPARQL queries was introduced in [19] by Siberski et al., whose *preference-based querying* language extends SPARQL through the introduction of solution modifiers (the PREFERRING clause). Their query formulation retrieves only items which are the most preferred ones, or equivalently *undominated*. The work in [13] builds upon the earlier approach of [19], but adds preferences at the level of filters rather than as a solution modifier. The *PrefSPARQL* syntax of [13] does not need any additional solution modifier to express qualitative preferences, and it bases on the expressive power of SPARQL 1.1. However, both the approaches proposed in [19] and [13] have an important limitation: they only return the undominated query results and are not able to provide an order of all the available outcomes which reflects user preferences. The size of the resulting answers set could be too small to be of practical use, especially considering the fact that user's preference model is just an approximation of what a user really wants.

In this paper, we address the problem of preference representation and reasoning with Linked Data from different perspectives. We first introduce an RDF ontological vocabulary to represent qualitative preferences over Linked Data, and then we show how our vocabulary can be used to model a CP-net [3], a powerful graphical language to represent and reason with conditional *ceteris paribus* (all else being equal) preference statements. Finally, inspired by [13], we show how to encode the CP-net in a SPARQL query able to return a **ranked list** of resources whose order reflects that of the user preferences. The main contributions of this paper are:

- presentation of an RDF vocabulary to represent qualitative preference statements over Linked Data;
- a codification into RDF triples of the qualitative preferential information encoded in a CP-net and the exploitation of *ordering queries* reasoning [3] to compute a partial order over items;

– a procedure to translate conditional preference statements into a SPARQL query, which retrieves a list of resources whose order reflects the user preferences.

The rest of this paper is structured as follows. Firstly, the semantics of CP-nets and a recap on some relevant Semantic Web technologies are provided in Section 2. In Section 3, we start by introducing an ontology to represent conditional preferences and CP-nets, and we then present an algorithm to generate a SPARQL 1.1 query able to order a set of items consistently with the CP-net. Alongside these sections we provide, by means of an example, details on RDF-based CP-nets and ordering queries. The most relevant approaches for preference-enabled SPARQL query language are analysed in Section 4. A summary and an outlook on future research close the paper.

2   Background Technologies

2.1   Ceteris Paribus Networks: CP-Nets

Utility functions can be considered as the ideal tool for representing and reasoning with preferences, but the total order they are allowed to represent does not always reflect the actual user model. Partial orders among preferences are a more natural way to represent user's tastes. Qualitative statements, e.g., "*I prefer x_i over x'_i*", permit a system to encode partial orders among user preferences thus granting the representation of a more realistic user model. A relevant framework to represent and reason with qualitative preferences is given by CP-nets (conditional preference networks) [3]. The CP-nets approach offers a formal language for expressing preferences on the values of single object variables, and provides a suitable formalism to model conditional dependence and independence of preferences under the *ceteris paribus* (all else being equal) interpretation [11]. More formally, a CP-net $\mathcal{N}$ is a graph with a vertex set $V = \{X_1,...,X_n\}$ corresponding to the variables over which preferences are expressed. Each variable X_i has a domain $dom(X_i) = \{x_{i1}, x_{i2}, ...\}$ containing the values the variable ranges over. For simplicity of presentation, in the rest of the paper, we will focus only on binary variables, i.e., $|dom(X_i)| = 2$, but the proposed approach can be easily extended to general n-ary variables. For each X_i, we identify a set of variables that we call *parents* of X_i, denoted $Pa(X_i)$, and a set of preferences, named conditional preferences, of the form $\bigwedge_j x_j | x_i \succ x'_i$ stating that "*given $\bigwedge_j x_j$ I prefer x_i over x'_i*" [1]. The set of conditional preferences associated to X_i forms the *conditional preference table* CPT(X_i). For each preference in CPT(X_i), we have $x_j \in dom(X_j)$ with $X_j \in Pa(X_i)$ and $x_i, x'_i \in dom(X_i)$. The *ceteris paribus* semantics implies that, given a particular value assignment to $Pa(X_i)$, the user determines a preference order for the values of X_i, all other things being equal. Being the CP-net a directed graph over $X_1,...,X_n$, for each variable in V, it is also possible to identify a set of *ancestors*, $Anc(X_i)$, which obviously includes the set of parents $Pa(X_i)$.

---

[1] For presentation purposes, as in [3], we ignore indifference between outcomes.

Example 1 (Books). "Paolo is planning his summer holidays, and he is going to choose the book to take to the beach. Paolo can read both English and German but during summer he would like to improve his German, so he prefers to read German books. At the same time, Paolo thinks that fantasy literature is more attractive and captivating than historical one. Finally, given a fantasy English book he prefers those being part of a saga. After all, Paolo wants to stay with his fictitious friends also during autumn and winter evenings".

Given the above description we may identify a set of Paolo's ceteris paribus preferences on books: (i) *German books are preferred to the ones from the United Kingdom*; (ii) *the same is for fantasy literature over historical one*; (iii) *given a fantasy English book, a saga is preferred over a single issue novel*. We may model the overall Paolo's profile by means of the CP-net $\mathcal{N}_{(C-LG)-SW}$ depicted in Figure 1(a). There, we have a set of binary variables $V = \{Country, LiteraryGenre, SubsequentWork\}$, whose domain is respectively given by $dom(Country) = \{C_G, C_{UK}\}$ (for *Germany* and *United Kingdom*), $dom(LiteraryGenre) = \{LG_F, LG_H\}$ (for *Fantasy* and *History*), $dom(SubsequentWork) = \{SW_{Yes}, SW_{No}\}$ (indicating that a book has a subsequent work or not). Directed arrows indicate direct influence of a variable over another one under the ceteris paribus interpretation and each variable is annotated with the corresponding CPT. In $\mathcal{N}_{(C-LG)-SW}$, the variable *Country* has no parents (and consequently no ancestor) and the same is for the variable *LiteraryGenre*. Variable *SubsequentWork* instead is conditionally dependent on both *Country* and *Literary- Genre*, that is $Pa(\text{SubsequentWork}) = \{Country, LiteraryGenre\}$ and, for this example, this set coincides with the ancestor set $Anc(\text{SubsequentWork})$. ∎

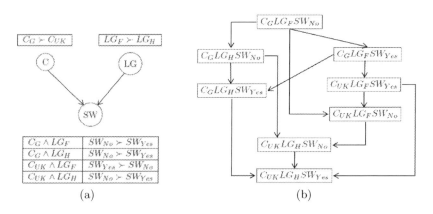

(a)   (b)

Fig. 1. The CP-net $\mathcal{N}_{(C-LG)-SW}$ (a) and the induced preference graph (b)

An outcome is a complete assignment to all the variables in V. The set of all outcomes will be denoted in what follows as $\mathcal{O}$. Hereafter we will use $o(X_i) = x_i$ to denote that to the variable X_i is assigned the value x_i in o and analogously $o(\{X_j, \ldots, X_{j+k}\}) = \{x_j, \ldots, x_{j+k}\}$ to state that $X_j = x_j, \ldots, X_{j+k} = x_{j+k}$

in o. A *preference ranking* is a partial order over $\mathcal{O}$, where $o \succ o'$ means that o is strictly preferred over o'. A CP-net induces a preference ranking under the *worsening flip* semantics. Given two outcomes o and o' of $\mathcal{O}$ there is a worsening flip from o to o' if there exists a variable $X_i \in V$, $x_i, x'_i \in dom(X_i)$ and $\{x_j, \ldots, x_{j+k}\}$ with $\{X_j, \ldots, X_{j+k}\} = Pa(X_i)$ such that: (i) $o(X_i) = x_i$ and $o'(X_i) = x'_i$, (ii) $o(\{X_j, \ldots, X_{j+k}\}) = o'(\{X_j, \ldots, X_{j+k}\}) = \{x_j, \ldots, x_{j+k}\}$, (iii) $o(V - \{X_i\}) = o'(V - \{X_i\})$ and (iv) $x_j \wedge \ldots \wedge x_{j+k}|x_i \succ x'_i$. The preference relation $\succ$ over $\mathcal{O}$ is then defined as the transitive closure of worsening flips. In Figure 1(b) we show the graph representing the partial order over outcomes for the corresponding CP-net.

We state that a CP-net $\mathcal{N}$ is *satisfiable* if there exists at least a preference ranking $\succ$ that satisfies it ($\succ$ satisfies $\mathcal{N}$ iff satisfies each of the conditions given in the CPTs of $\mathcal{N}$, under the *ceteris paribus* interpretation [3]). We also say that such a preference ranking is *consistent* with $\mathcal{N}$. By definition, given two outcomes o and o', $\mathcal{N}$ *entails* $o \succ o'$ ($\mathcal{N} \models o \succ o'$) if and only if $o \succ o'$ holds in every preference ranking $\succ$ that satisfies $\mathcal{N}$. It can be shown that preferential entailment is transitive [3]. Given a CP-net $\mathcal{N}$, there are two possible ways of comparing outcome pairs:

Dominance Query: we can ask whether $\mathcal{N} \models o \succ o'$, i.e., determine whether o is strictly preferred over o' under all consistent preference rankings. If this holds, we say that o *dominates* o' relative to $\mathcal{N}$. This is the most complex reasoning task and is NP-complete with the exception of simple cases such as binary tree-structured CP-nets [3].

Ordering Query: we can ask whether $\mathcal{N} \not\models o' \succ o$. If this holds, there exists at least one preference ordering $\succ$ consistent with $\mathcal{N}$ in which $o \succ o'$. We say that o is *consistently orderable* over o' relative to $\mathcal{N}$ (or alternatively o *weakly dominates* o').

The ordering condition is weaker than the dominance one, but in [3] one can find results which make ordering queries more attractive than dominance ones, at least for the complexity point of view.

A subclass of CP-nets has received special attention in the literature, namely, acyclic CP-nets, which are always satisfiable and have an additional useful property when comparing outcomes. First, for acyclic (not necessarily binary-valued) CP-nets, Theorem 1 provides a sound, even if incomplete, algorithm to answer *ordering queries* [3].

Theorem 1. *Let $\mathcal{N}$ be an acyclic CP-net over the variable set V, and o, o' be a pair of outcomes. We have $\mathcal{N} \not\models o' \succ o$, if there exists a variable X in $\mathcal{N}$, such that: (1) o and o' assign the same values to all ancestors of X in N and (2) given the assignment provided by o (and o') to $Pa(X)$, o assigns a more preferred value to X than that assigned by o'.*

An additional result concerns the possibility to return a positive answer for at least one of the query $\mathcal{N} \not\models o' \succ o$ or $\mathcal{N} \not\models o \succ o'$ in $O(n)$ time, where o and o' are any two possible outcomes and n is the number of variables in

CP-net $\mathcal{N}$. In Section 3 we will show how to exploit the possibility to order m different outcomes consistently with an acyclic CP-net $\mathcal{N}$ using only *ordering queries*. This further result is proved in [3] and, considering a polynomial time for ordering queries, sets up a time complexity of $O(nm^2)$ to provide a consistent order for m arbitrary outcomes.

Example 2 (Books cont'd). With regard to $\mathcal{N}_{(C-LG)-SW}$, the use of *ordering queries* between pairs of outcomes would produce the following sound ranking solution:

$$< C_G LG_F SW_{No}, C_G LG_F SW_{Yes}, (C_G LG_H SW_{No}, C_{UK} LG_F SW_{Yes}), ...$$
$$..., (C_G LG_H SW_{Yes}, C_{UK} LG_F SW_{No}), C_{UK} LG_H SW_{No}, C_{UK} LG_H SW_{Yes} >$$

where outcomes within round parentheses are not comparable. We can pick up any of them in any order and keep the ranking solution sound. Moreover, as we know that Theorem 1 is not complete we may have more sound solutions which are equivalent with each other from the user point of view. Even if completeness is a desirable property for many algorithms, in case we are interested in solving a top-k query answering problem, we will ask the query language to return just a list of available items ordered consistently with the CP-net.   ■

2.2   RDF and SPARQL

In this section we provide a brief overview of two Semantic Web technologies used in our approach: RDF [18] and SPARQL [14] which are at the basis of the Linked Open Data initiative. The Linking Open Data community project started in 2007 with the goal of extending the current Web with data published according to Semantic Web standards. The idea is to use RDF to broadcast various open datasets on the Web, as a vast decentralized knowledge graph. Among the datasets available in the LOD cloud, DBpedia is one of the main projects. It is an effort to extract structured information from Wikipedia and make it freely accessible as RDF triples. This knowledge base currently (release DBpedia 2014) describes 4.58 million resources. In addition, it is highly connected to other RDF datasets of the Linked Open Data cloud thus making DBpedia a cornerstone for the entire LOD project.

Resource Description Framework. The Resource Description Framework (RDF) is a standard model for describing information about resources on the Web. It is the building block for the Semantic Web, developed by the World Wide Web Consortium (W3C) in 1998. It allows to represent Web entities and their relations as well as to attach to them a machine understandable and processable meaning (semantics) that can be further exploited to perform automatic reasoning tasks able to infer new knowledge from the explicitly stated one. Each statement about resources is modeled in the form of a triple: *subject-predicate-object*. *Subjects* and *predicates* are represented by URIs (*Uniform Resource Identifiers*), while *objects* can be identified either by URIs or by literals (data values). As an example, the following triple is a valid RDF statement about the book *War and Peace*:

```
<http://dbpedia.org/resource/War_and_Peace>
<http://dbpedia.org/ontology/author>
<http://dbpedia.org/resource/Leo_Tolstoy>
```

where we state that the book writer is *Leo Tolstoy*. RDF information representation can be formally modeled through a labeled directed graph. In fact, the
RDF statements (triples), as a whole, form a graph where nodes are resources
connected to each other or to literal values through predicates (the graph edges).
RDF can be serialized by means of different syntaxes. The most compact is the
so called `turtle` syntax where prefixes can be used to shorten URIs. The triple
above can be rewritten according to `turtle` as:

```
@prefix db: <http://dbpedia.org/resource/>
@prefix dbo: <http://dbpedia.org/ontology/>

db:War_and_Peace  dbo:author  db:Leo_Tolstoy.
```

From an ontological point of view, an interesting built-in RDF predicate is http://
www.w3.org/1999/02/22-rdf-syntax-ns#type, which can be further abbreviated
just with a, with no prefix. It states that a resource is an instance of a class.

```
db:War_and_Peace  a    dbo:Book.
```

The previous triple asserts that *War and Peace* is an instance of the class *Book*.

Simple Protocol and RDF Query Language. SPARQL 1.1, hereafter indicated as SPARQL is the de facto query language for data stored in RDF format,
able to reflect the graph-based nature of underlying data. The query mechanism
is graph-matching. A basic SPARQL query has the form:

```
PREFIX db: <http://dbpedia.org/resource/>
PREFIX dbo: <http://dbpedia.org/ontology/>

SELECT ?genre ?page
WHERE {
   db:War_and_Peace dbo:literaryGenre  ?genre;
                    dbo:numberOfPages ?page.}
```

where we ask for all possible values that can be assigned to the variables `?genre`
and `?page` to match the graph pattern expressed in the `WHERE` clause. SPARQL
provides several solution modifiers such as `DISTINCT` to ensure unique solutions,
`GROUP BY` to calculate aggregate values for a solution, `ORDER BY` which applies
ordering conditions to a solution sequence and `LIMIT` that puts an upper bound
on the number of solutions retrieved. Additionally, the `FILTER` keyword restricts
solutions to those for which an expression evaluates to "true". The testing for
the presence or the absence of a graph pattern can be done using respectively
`FILTER EXISTS` and `FILTER NOT EXISTS`. The `IF` function form evaluates the
first argument, interprets it as a boolean value, then returns the value of a
second expression if such value is "true", otherwise it returns the value of a

third expression. Useful functions on strings are CONCAT (and its aggregated version GROUP_CONCAT) for concatenation, CONTAINS to verify if a first argument is a substring of a second one and STR returning the string representation of its argument. Finally, BIND AS can be used for binding a variable.

3   CP-Nets and Linked Open Data

In this section, we start by proposing an ontology to represent conditional preferences and CP-nets. Then we show how to use a user profile represented as an instantiation of this ontology to encode the corresponding preferences in a standard SPARQL query able to retrieve and rank resources in a personalized way.

Example 3 (Books cont'd). With respect to Paolo's preference *"given a British book whose literary genre is Fantasy, I prefer those belonging to a saga"*, if we look in DBpedia we follow, for instance, the book *GoodKnyght!*. Indeed, we have:

```
@prefix db: <http://dbpedia.org/resource/>
@prefix dbo: <http://dbpedia.org/ontology/>

db:GoodKnyght! dbo:country db:United_Kingdom ;
               dbo:literayGenre db:Fantasy_literature ;
               dbo:subsequentWork db:Whizzard! .
```

As we want to be fully compliant with the Linked Data technological stack, we need a vocabulary/ontology thus allowing the user to represent her preferences on different aspects of resources she might be interested in.   ■

Figure 2 shows an ontology to model user profiles in terms of a CP-net[2]. The main idea behind the modelling of the ontology is that we may model the preferences of a user considering the attributes of the items she is looking for, such as dbo:country, dbo:literaryGenre or dbo:subsequentWork. The ontology is composed of four main classes and ten properties. The class Value represents possible values of a variable. If we look at the book *GoodKnyght!* in Example 3, we see that the "actual values" for which the user expresses a preference are composed by both a *property*, e.g. dbo:country and its related *object*, e.g. db:United_Kingdom. This is the reason why the class Value is domain of the two properties: attribute and value. The former mapping the property, the latter mapping the object. Condition is used to express the conditional part of a preference. It is domain of the property contains whose range is Value. The class Preference represents the whole conditional statement. The properties it is domain of reflect the structure of the preferential statement "given a Condition, I prefer a Value over another Value". The last class Variable is used to model the variables of a CP-net. Indeed, it is domain of variableDomain whose range is Value as well as of the two properties parentCondition and

---

[2] The corresponding OWL file is available at
   http://sisinflab.poliba.it/semanticweb/lod/ontologies/cp-nets.owl

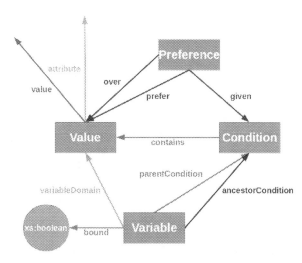

Fig. 2. A graphical representation of the ontology proposed to represent conditional statements.

`ancestorCondition` with the former being a sub-property of the latter which is in turn defined as transitive. Here we adopted the modelling choice of representing directly the conditions generated by the combination of the values in the parent variables instead of relating the variables themselves. We will see how this modelling choice will be useful when embedding the CP-net into a `SPARQL` query. Finally we have the **bound** property needed to explicitly state if the `value` associated to an `attribute` is an actual value (as for `dbo:country` and `dbo:literaryGenre`) or it represents the situation that we have (not) a triple involving the `attribute`, as for `dbo:subsequentWork`.

Example 4 (Books cont'd). The encoding which corresponds to the CP-net modeling Paolo's preferences is represented in Figure 3. For the sake of conciseness, we will always assume prefix cp: ¡http://sisinflab.poliba.it/semanticweb/lod/ontologies/cp-nets.owl#¿ in the rest of the paper. Note that the represented encoding can be used to query directly the `DBpedia` dataset.   ■

3.1 Ordering SPARQL Results via CP-Nets

Once we have a model of the user profile represented as an `RDF`-based CP-net, we may use the corresponding preferences to order a query solution set. We assume the user is looking for the best k items satisfying some (hard) constraints and that the choice for the best ones is led by her preferences, formulated according to ceteris paribus semantics, on a set of variables $V = \{X_1,...,X_n\}$. In other words, we use a CP-net $\mathcal{N}$ defined with reference to V to solve a top-k query answering problem where the ordering criterion is encoded in $\mathcal{N}$. Note that we use *item* to denote a generic `RDF` resource, while *outcome* is used for a complete assignment

```
 1 @prefix cp: <http://sisinflab.poliba.it/semanticweb/lod/ontologies/cp-nets.owl#>
 2 @prefix db: <http://dbpedia.org/resource/>
 3 @prefix dbo: <http://dbpedia.org/ontology/>
 4
 5 cp:country1 a cp:Value;
 6              cp:attribute dbo:country; cp:value db:United_Kingdom.
 7 cp:country2 a cp:Value;
 8              cp:attribute dbo:country; cp:value db:Germany.
 9 cp:genre1 a cp:Value;
10           cp:attribute dbo:literaryGenre; cp:value db:Fantasy_literature.
11 cp:genre2 a cp:Value;
12           cp:attribute dbo:literaryGenre;  cp:value db:History.
13 cp:sub1 a cp:Value;
14         cp:attribute dbo:subsequentWork; cp:value cp:subsequentWorkYes.
15 cp:sub2 a cp:Value;
16         cp:attribute dbo:subsequentWork; cp:value cp:subsequentWorkNo.
17
18 cp:conditionCG1 a cp:Condition;
19                 cp:contains  cp:country1; cp:contains  cp:genre1.
20 cp:conditionCG2 a cp:Condition;
21                 cp:contains  cp:country1; cp:contains  cp:genre2.
22 cp:conditionCG3 a cp:Condition;
23                 cp:contains  cp:country2; cp:contains  cp:genre1.
24 cp:conditionCG4 a cp:Condition;
25                 cp:contains  cp:country2; cp:contains  cp:genre2.
26
27 cp:country a cp:Variable;
28            cp:bound "true";
29            cp:variableDomain cp:country1,cp:country2.
30 cp:literaryGenre a cp:Variable;
31                  cp:bound "true";
32                  cp:variableDomain cp:genre1,cp:genre2.
33 cp:subsequentWork a cp:Variable;
34                   cp:bound "false";
35                   cp:variableDomain cp:sub1, cp:sub2;
36                   cp:parentCondition cp:conditionCG1, cp:conditionCG2,
37                             cp:conditionCG3, cp:conditionCG4;
38                   cp:AncestorCondition cp:conditionCG1, cp:conditionCG2,
39                             cp:conditionCG3, cp:conditionCG4.
40
41 cp:preference1 a cp:Preference;
42               cp:prefer cp:country2; cp:over cp:country1.
43 cp:preference2 a cp:Preference;
44               cp:prefer cp:genre1; cp:over cp:genre2.
45 cp:preference3 a cp:Preference;
46               cp:given cp:conditionCG1;
47               cp:prefer cp:sub1; cp:over cp:sub2.
48 cp:preference4 a cp:Preference;
49               cp:given cp:conditionCG2;
50               cp:prefer cp:sub2; cp:over cp:sub1.
51 cp:preference5 a cp:Preference;
52               cp:given cp:conditionCG3;
53               cp:prefer cp:sub2; cp:over cp:sub1.
54 cp:preference6 a cp:Preference;
55               cp:given cp:conditionCG4;
56               cp:prefer cp:sub2; cp:over cp:sub1.
```

Fig. 3. The RDF version of the CP-net represented in Figure 1(a).

to all the variables in V, as defined in Section 2.1. Indeed, an outcome can be seen as a partial description of the item. This implies, on the one hand, that an outcome may refer to many items and, on the other hand, that ordering items can be pursued ordering corresponding outcomes and vice versa.

In the presented approach, we concentrate on acyclic CP-nets. We adopt acyclicity to preserve the nice computational properties introduced in Section 2.1.

By using a meta-language built on top of SPARQL we may write the query representing the task we want to solve as:

```
SELECT ?item  WHERE {?item satisfies hard constraints}.
ORDER BY N
LIMIT  k
```

where *hard constraints* are represented by a SPARQL graph pattern where at least one triple has ?item as subject. We will use the notation $\mathcal{HC}(?\text{item})$ to denote the hard constraints associated to the variable ?item.

Example 5 (Books cont'd). "*Paolo really wants to relax and so he is looking only for books with more than 300 pages.*" In this case his hard constraints $\mathcal{HC}(?\text{item})$ are represented by:

```
?item a dbo:Book.
?item dbo:numberOfPages ?page.
FILTER(?page>300).                                              ■
```

From Theorem 1 in Section 2.1, we know how to build a non-increasing order of a set of outcomes $o_1, ..., o_m$ that is consistent with $\mathcal{N}$ by using only *ordering queries*. Via the same meta-language we used before, the ordering of outcomes could be done via Query 1, with which we select only the outcomes satisfying some hard constraints and order them according to a counter representing the number of outcomes they are able to weakly dominate. The query output is an ordering solution which is sound for $\mathcal{N}$.[3]

Query 1
```
SELECT ?outcome-Dominating
       (COUNT(?outcome-dominated) AS ?counter)
WHERE
{ ?outcome-Dominating   satisfies hard constraints.
  ?outcome-dominated    satisfies hard constraints.
   FILTER  { N ⊭ ?outcome-dominated ≻ ?outcome-Dominating }}
ORDER BY DESC(?counter)
```

We now show how to build an actual SPARQL query that mimics the behavior of Query 1 given a CP-net $\mathcal{N}$ represented via the ontology in Figure 2. First of all we introduce some notation needed for a better understanding of the overall approach. Given the variable $X_i \in V$ with $dom(X_i) = \{x_{i1}, x_{i2}\}$, we will use the following notation relative to the two corresponding instances $\text{cp} : \text{x}_{\text{i}1}$ and $\text{cp} : \text{x}_{\text{i}2}$ of the class cp:Value:

- $value(x_{ij})$ is the object of the triple cp:x$_{\text{ij}}$ cp:value object;
- $attribute(x_{ij})$ is the object of the triple cp:x$_{\text{ij}}$ cp:attribute object;
- we call *representative string* of x_{ij} the concatenation of the two strings represented by $attribute(x_{ij})$ and $value(x_{ij})$ respectively. We use the combination of $attribute(x_{ij})$ and $value(x_{ij})$ to represent x_{ij} as they uniquely identify a value in the domain of a variable. Indeed, in case we used only $value(x_{ij})$ ambiguous situations could arise when it is used in combination with different attributes.
- *Preferences*$(\mathcal{N})$ is the set of all the conditional preferences in the CPTs of $\mathcal{N}$;

---

[3] The query finds all the outcomes consistently orderable over at least another outcome, but the remaining ones can be easily found by looking for all the outcomes satisfying hard constraints and subtracting with MINUS the results of the query.

Finally, given an instance cp:c of the class cp:Condition we call *conditional values* of cp:c all the objects of the triples cp:c cp:contains object. For instance, with reference to Figure 3 we have that cp:country1 and cp:genre1 are the *conditional values* of cp:conditionCG1.

The SPARQL query we are going to build acts on a pair of outcomes per time by checking an *ordering query*. It starts from *Preferences*($\mathcal{N}$) and it uses the UNION of the following Query 2 and Query 3 to build all possible conditions that let to consistently order an outcome over another one. The answer to the *ordering query* grounds on the matching with one of these conditions. Eventually, all the outcomes in $\mathcal{O}$ are ordered according to the number of outcomes they weakly dominate.

Query 2

```
 1 SELECT ("VoidSet" as ?ConcatenatedAncestor) ("VoidSet" as ?ConcatenatedParent)
 2        (concat(str(?attrPrefer),str(?valuePrefer)) AS ?Prefer)
 3        (concat(str(?attrPrefer),str(?valueOver)) AS ?Over)
 4 WHERE
 5 { FILTER NOT EXISTS {?preference cp:given ?condition.}
 6   ?preference cp:prefer ?p;
 7               cp:over ?o.
 8   ?p cp:attribute ?attrPrefer;
 9      cp:value ?valuePrefer.
10   ?o cp:value ?valueOver.}
```

Query 2 processes elements of *Preferences*($\mathcal{N}$) belonging to CPTs of variables without parents. Within the query, they are represented by the variable ?preference. The selection is made possible by the FILTER NOT EXISTS on the pattern {?prefe- rence cp:given ?condition.} in line 5. The query sets the value of both ?ConcatenatedAncestor and ?ConcatenatedParent to "VoidSet" (line 1), then it computes the *representative strings*, ?Prefer and ?Over (lines 2–3), for the objects ?p and ?o of the two triples involving cp:prefer and cp:over (lines 6–10). Notice that the objects of triples involving predicate cp:attribute and having subjects ?p and ?o coincide.

Query 3

```
 1 SELECT ?ConcatenatedAncestor ?ConcatenatedParent
 2        ?Prefer ?Over
 3 WHERE
 4 { { SELECT ?V ?Acondition
 5          (GROUP_CONCAT(CONCAT(str(?attr),str(?valu e)); separator="")
 6            as ?ConcatenatedAncestor)
 7     WHERE
 8     { ?V cp:ancestorCondition ?Acondition.
 9       ?Acondition cp:contains ?a.
10       ?a  cp:attribute ?attr;
11           cp:value ?value.}
12     GROUP BY ?V ?Acondition}
13   { SELECT  ?V2 ?Pcondition
14          (concat(str(?attrPrefer),str(?valuePrefer)) as ?Prefer)
15          (concat(str(?attrPrefer),str(?valueOver)) as ?Over)
16          (GROUP_CONCAT(CONCAT(str(?attr),str(?value)); separator ="")
17            as ?ConcatenatedParent)
18     WHERE
19     { FILTER EXISTS{?preference cp:given ?Pcondition.}
20       ?preference cp:given ?Pcondition.
21       ?preference cp:prefer ?p;
```

```
22                    cp:over ?o.
23          ?V2 cp:variableDomain ?p.
24          ?p cp:attribute ?attrPrefer;
25             cp:value ?valuePrefer.
26          ?o cp:value ?valueOver.
27          ?Pcondition cp:contains ?c.
28          ?c cp:attribute ?attr;
29             cp:value ?value.}
30      GROUP BY ?V2 ?Pcondition ?attrPrefer ?valuePrefer ?valueOver}
31      FILTER(contains(?ConcatenatedAncestor, ?ConcatenatedParent) && ?V=?V2).}
```

Differently from the previous query, Query 3 is used to process preferences belonging to CPTs of variables having at least one parent. The selection is made via the FILTER EXISTS on the pattern {?preference cp:given ?Pcondition.} (line 19). For each preference, Query 3 firstly considers their parent conditions ?Pcondition (line 20) and then it extracts their corresponding *conditional values* (lines 27–29). For these latter, their *representative strings* are then computed and concatenated at lines 16–17 in ?ConcatenatedParent. The variables ?Prefer and ?Over are defined similarly to Query 2. In lines 4–12, Query 3 processes the ancestor conditions for each variable and, also in this case, it concatenates the *representative strings* of the corresponding *conditional values* in ?ConcatenatedAncestor. Query 3 acts to compute all possible combination of ?ConcatenatedAncestor and triples <?ConcatenatedParent, ?Prefer, ?Over>, i.e., to build the set of quadruples <?ConcatenatedAncestor, ?ConcatenatedParent, ?Prefer, ?Over>. As we know that for each variable, its parent set is contained in its ancestor set, we use at line 31 a FILTER condition to verify if, for each quadruple, the value of ?Concate- natedParent is contained in ?ConcatenatedAncestor, being both defined as strings. Finally, we verify in the same FILTER that the parent and the ancestor conditions, used to define a quadruple, refer to the same CP-net variable (taking into account lines 8 and 23). The UNION of Query 2 and Query 3 thus returns a set of quadruples, <?ConcatenatedAncestor, ?ConcatenatedParent, ?Prefer, ?Over>, able to consistently order an outcome over another one.

Example 6 (Books cont'd). Given Paolo's preferences in Figure 3, the execution of Query 2 and Query 3 returns the set of quadruples in Table 1. The first quadruple is returned by Query 2 and refers to preference cp:preference1 about country. According to cp:preference1 we have, for example, that $C_G LG_F SW_{Yes}$ weakly dominates $C_{UK} LG_F SW_{Yes}$. We reproduce the *ordering query* reasoning by building the two outcomes represented by the two strings c_Germany lg_Fantasy cp:sub- sequentWorkYes and c_UK lg_Fantasy cp:subsequentWorkYes respectively, and verifying that the former includes the substring ?Prefer, i.e., c_Germany, and the latter the substring ?Over, i.e. c_UK.

The third quadruple of Table 1 is a solution of Query 3 when dealing with preference cp:preference3 about variable cp:subsequentWork, which has both country and genre in the parent condition. Outcome $C_{UK} LG_F SW_{Yes}$ is consistently orderable over $C_{UK} LG_F SW_{No}$ thanks to this preference. In fact, variable cp:subsequent- Work has coincident ancestors in both the outcomes and a better value in the first one. Analogously to what we did with the first quadruple, in our *ordering query* reasoning we will use the third quadruple to compare a pair of outcomes, building their corresponding strings and verifying if they both contain ?ConcatenatedAncestor, i.e. c_UK lg_Fantasy in addiction to cp:subsequentWorkYes (?Prefer) for the former and cp:subsequentWorkNo (?Over) for the latter. ∎

Table 1. Matching Conditions for ordering queries. We use c_UK, c_Germany, lg_Fantasy and lg_History to abbreviate the *representative strings* of cp:country1, cp:country2, cp:genre1 and cp:genre2, respectively.

?ConcatenatedAncestor	?ConcatenatedParent	?Prefer	?Over
VoidSet	VoidSet	c_Germany	c_UK
VoidSet	VoidSet	lg_Fantasy	lg_History
c_UK lg_Fantasy	c_UK lg_Fantasy	cp:subsequentWorkYes	cp:subsequentWorkNo
c_UK lg_History	c_UK lg_History	cp:subsequentWorkNo	cp:subsequentWorkYes
c_Germany lg_Fantasy	c_Germany lg_Fantasy	cp:subsequentWorkNo	cp:subsequentWorkYes
c_Germany lg_History	c_Germany lg_History	cp:subsequentWorkNo	cp:subsequentWorkYes

Algorithm 1 takes as inputs user's *hard constraints* and the RDF-based CP-net and it returns *OrderingQuery*. This latter has as result all the items satisfying the hard constraints imposed in the input query which are ordered consistently with $\mathcal{N}$. The third input k represents the number of resources we are interested in.

Line 1 in Algorithm 1 computes, for each outcome o, the number of outcomes o' it dominates. The counting is made possible by the combination of the COUNT in line 1 and the GROUP BY in line 20. The corresponding ?counter variable is then used by the ORDER BY in line 21 to rank the result set, while the LIMIT of line 22 is used to select its first k elements. The loop in lines 2–16 lets to consider a pair of items per time, ?item_D and ?item_d, where D and d stand respectively for **D**ominating and **d**ominated. They both must satisfy the hard constraints, as imposed in line 3, and for each item the nested loop of lines 4–10 introduces the values corresponding to the variables in V. For each variable $X_i \in V$, Algorithm 1 distinguishes between instances of cp:Variable whose corresponding value for cp:bound is set to "false" or "true". In the first case (line 6) it checks (with the EXISTS statement) if the current item has *attribute(X_i)* among predicates. In the other case (line 8), it looks for values ?X$_i$_y of the object of *attribute(X_i)* and uses the VALUES assignment to filter only elements of the set {*value(x_{i1})*, *value(x_{i2})*}. At lines 11-15, the outcome corresponding to an item is built by concatenating the values extracted for various ?X$_i$_y together with *attribute(X_i)*. We also verify with line 17 that the pair of outcomes we are going to compare is made of distinct elements. The UNION of Query 2 and Query 3 is added at line 18. We know it returns a set of quadruples <?ConcatenatedAncestor, ?ConcatenatedParent, ?Prefer, ?Over>, able to consistently order an outcome over another one. Finally, the FILTER condition of lines 19 checks if the pair of outcomes (?outcome_D, ?outcome_d) matches one of

---

Data: *hard constraints*, RDF-based CP-net $\mathcal{N}$, number of results k

Result: OrderingQuery

```
1   OrderingQuery = SELECT ?item_D (COUNT(DISTINCT ?outcome_d) AS ?counter) WHERE { ;
2   for y ∈ {D, d} do
3       OrderingQuery += HC(?item_y) ;
4       foreach Xᵢ ∈ V do
5           if there exists cp:Xᵢ cp:bound "false"^^xs:boolean then
6               OrderingQuery += BIND(IF(EXISTS{?item_y
                attribute(Xᵢ) ?object}, cp:XᵢYes, cp:XᵢNo) AS ?Xᵢ_y).
7           else
8               OrderingQuery += item_y attribute(Xᵢ) ?Xᵢ_y. VALUES(?Xᵢ_y {(value(xᵢ₁))
                (value(xᵢ₂))})
9           end
10      end
11      OrderingQuery += BIND(CONCAT(STR( ;
12      for i = 1,…,|V| − 1 do
13          OrderingQuery += attribute(Xᵢ)), STR(?Xᵢ_y), ;
14      end
15      OrderingQuery += STR(attribute(X_|V|)), STR(?X_|V|_y)) AS ?outcome_y). ;
16  end
17  OrderingQuery += FILTER(?outcome_D!=?outcome_d) ;
18  OrderingQuery += {Query 2} UNION {Query 3} ;
19  OrderingQuery += FILTER( ((?ConcatenatedParent="VoidSet") &&
    CONTAINS(?outcome_D,?Prefer) && CONTAINS(?outcome_d,?Over) ) ||
    (!(?ConcatenatedParent="VoidSet")) && CONTAINS(?outcome_D,?ConcatenatedAncestor) &&
    CONTAINS(?outcome_d,?ConcatenatedAncestor) && CONTAINS(?outcome_D,?Prefer) &&
    CONTAINS(?outcome_d,?Over) ).;
20  OrderingQuery += GROUP BY ?item_D ;
21  OrderingQuery += ORDER BY DESC(?counter) ;
22  OrderingQuery += LIMIT k ;
23  return OrderingQuery.
```

Algorithm 1. Query Formulation

the conditions returned by Query 2 or Query 3. In particular, for quadruples with
"VoidSet" as ?ConcatenatedAncestor it is sufficient to verify if ?outcome_D
contains the better value of a preference ?Prefer and ?outcome_d contains the
relative worse value ?Over. Instead when we are dealing with preferences with
a parent, according to Theorem 1, ?outcome_D is consistently orderable over
?outcome_d if the ancestors of the discriminating variable are equal. We therefore
verify if both outcomes contains the value of ?ConcatenatedAncestor, as well
as ?Prefer just for ?outcome_D and ?Over for ?outcome_d. In conclusion, if the
outcome corresponding to ?item_D is consistently orderable over ?outcome_d we
increment of a unit its ?counter value. Through the DISTINCT solution modifier
in line 1, we count only different weakly dominated outcomes.

Example 7 (Books cont'd). The query built from the CP-net in Figure 3 together
with the hard constraints expressed by Paolo is represented in Appendix A.
Table 2 reports the results of the query posed over DBpedia with $k = 5$. The
maximum value for ?counter is 5 since there are no German historical books in
the dataset. By looking in DBpedia one can observe an exact matching with the
expected order shown in Example 2, according to the following triples.

Table 2. top-5 list of items retrieved by the ordering query in Appendix A from DBpedia.

?item_D	?Counter
db:Inkdeath	5
db:The_Neverending_Story	5
db:Inkheart	4
db:Magic_Moon	4
db:Abarat	3

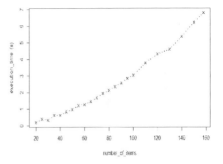

Fig. 4. Execution Time on DBpedia for the query in Appendix A.

```
@prefix db: <http://dbpedia.org/resource/>
@prefix dbo: <http://dbpedia.org/ontology/>

db:Inkdeath    dbo:country db:Germany ;
               dbo:literayGenre db:Fantasy_literature .
db:The_Neverending_Story dbo:country db:Germany ;
                         dbo:literayGenre db:Fantasy_literature .
db:Inkheart    dbo:country db:Germany ;
               dbo:literayGenre db:Fantasy_literature ;
               dbo:subsequentWork db: Inkspell .
db:Magic_Moon  dbo:country db:Germany ;
               dbo:literayGenre db:Fantasy_literature ;
               dbo:subsequentWork db:Children_of_Magic_Moon .
db:Abarat      dbo:country db:United_Kingdom ;
               dbo:literayGenre db:Fantasy_literature ;
               dbo:subsequentWork db:Days_of_Magic,_Nights_of_War .
```

We also evaluated the performance of our ordering query on progressively shrinking sets of items. The original size consists of 158 books. Results are depicted in Figure 4, which presents the query execution time as a function of the number of items to order. It shows a non-linear growing in the number of items and reveals the influence of time necessary to order m outcomes consistently with a CP-net built over n variables, $O(nm^2)$. The timing results were collected computing the mean value of 5 measurements ran on a ARCH LINUX PC with a 2.53 Ghz Intel i5 m460 Processor with 4.00 GB of RAM. We used Apache Jena Fuseki[4] as a SPARQL server for our experiments. Results refers to DBpedia 2014 release. ∎

4   Related Work

The ability to infer, model and reason with users' preferences has been recognized as a prominent research direction for many fields, especially for artificial intelligence [9]. Quantitative approaches use a scoring function to assess an order over the available outcomes, resulting in a total order. In a relational database management system, for example, the *top-k* queries return the k best matches according to a numerical score. In [17], one can find a formalism supporting ranking queries for a relational database. The qualitative approach is more general: it allows preferences to be treated independently, resulting in incomparable

---

[4] http://jena.apache.org/documentation/fuseki2/

outcomes and a partial preference order. In particular, *skyline* queries [2] extend the notion of best matching to contexts where multiple independent scores have to be taken into account. The result of a *skyline* query is a set of outcomes that are no worse than any other one across all dimensions of a set of independent boolean or numerical preferences [2]. Within the database community, the first examples of *preference-based querying* languages with a qualitative approach have been introduced by [6] and [7].

The notion of preference is of primary importance also in the Linked Open Data context. The provision of a means to enable users to look for data sources (e.g. SPARQL endpoints) and data content which is tailored to their individual preferences is one of the target of the original project by Tim Berners-Lee et al. Even the motivating example proposed in the seminal Semantic Web article [1], can be interpreted as a preference-based search, as extensively discussed in [19]. Therefore in [19] authors add preference-based querying capabilities to the most known Semantic Web query language, SPARQL. However when the paper was published it was not possible to specify multiple (independent) preference dimensions in SPARQL, and consequently the authors added the PREFERRING solution modifier. For example, Query 4 provides a preference-enabled SPARQL query for a user who is searching for an appointment, preferring excellent therapist, appointments out of the rush hour and later appointments over earlier ones if both are equal with respect to the rush hour constraint.

Query 4

```
1 SELECT ?appointment WHERE {
2   ?terapist :rated ?rating; :offers ?appointment.
3   ?appointment :starts ?start; :ends ?end.
4   PREFERRING (?rating = excellent AND
5   ?end < 1600 || ?start > 1800
6   CASCADE HIGHEST(?start))}
```

The PREFERRING clause behaves as a solution modifier, the AND keyword separates independent preference dimensions and the CASCADE keyword lets to give higher priority to the left-hand preference over the right-hand one. The *PrefSPARQL* syntax of [13] introduces preferences at the level of filters. It still uses the AND to separate independent dimensions and build what the authors called *MultidimensionalPref*. Each dimension is either a *conditional* preference (IF-THEN-ELSE) or an *atomic* preference, which in turn can be a simple expression or can involve constructs, e.g. BETWEEN (more details on the grammar of atomic preferences are in [13]). Besides the introduction of these constructs, the support for conditional preferences and the substitution of CASCADE with PRIOR TO –probably the main innovative point of [13] with respect to [19]– is that the preference-enabled query they propose can be completely rewritten using SPARQL 1.1 features. In particular [13] uses the FILTER NOT EXISTS. The translation of Query 4 according to *PrefSPARQL* query rewriting is given in Query 5.

Query 5

```
1 SELECT ?appointmentA WHERE {
2   ?terapistA :rated ?ratingA; :offers ?appointmentA.
```

```
3   ?appointmentA :starts ?startA; :ends ?endA.
4   BIND ((?ratingA = :excellent) AS ?Pref1A)
5   BIND ((?endA < 16 || ?startA > 18:00) AS ?Pref2A)
6   BIND ((?startA) AS ?Pref3A)
7   FILTER NOT EXISTS {
8      ?terapistB :rated ?ratingB; :offers ?appointmentB.
9      ?appointmentB :starts ?startB; :ends ?endB.
10     BIND ((?ratingB = :excellent) AS ?Pref1B)
11     BIND ((?endB < 1600 || ?startB > 1800) AS ?Pref2B)
12     BIND ((?startB) AS ?Pref3B)
13     FILTER (
14     ((?Pref1B > ?Pref1A)  &&
15     !((?Pref2B < ?Pref2A) || (?Pref3B < ?Pref3A && ?Pref2B = ?Pref2A)))
16     ||
17     (!(?Pref1B < ?Pref1A)  &&
18     ((?Pref2B > ?Pref2A) || (?Pref3B > ?Pref3A && ?Pref2B = ?Pref2A))))}}
```

The query looks for appointments ?appointmentA satisfying the pattern expressed in lines 2-3. The research is done verifying that there is no ?appointmentB that verifies the same pattern (lines 8-9) and dominates ?appointmentA in any preference dimension. Recall that ?appointmentB would dominate ?appointmentA if it was better in at least one dimension and no worse in the others. The independent dimensions are expressed in the two branches of the logical disjunction of line 16, that is in lines 14-15 and 17-18. The PRIOR TO preference relation is encoded in lines 15 and 18 through ||. It is worth noticing that the *MultidimensionalPref* which lets to filter the solution set in [13] is actually based on constructs implicit in the ceteris paribus semantics. The AND to link independent preference dimensions is the relation between any two variables X_1 and X_2 in $\mathcal{N}$ such that $X_1 \notin Pa(X_2)$ and vice versa. The PRIOR TO is reproduced in the relationship between a variable and its parents, since the ceteris paribus semantics implicitly ensures that parent preferences have higher priority over child preferences [3]. Finally, the IF-THEN-ELSE construct allowed in [13] is the essence of conditional preferences in CPTs.

5   Summary and Outlook

In this paper, we have shown how to query Linked Open Data datasets considering also user preferences. In particular, we have focused on qualitative preferences represented via CP-nets. We have proposed an ontological vocabulary to model CP-nets via RDF statements under the ceteris paribus semantics. Then, we have presented an algorithm to build a standard SPARQL 1.1 query encoding the CP-net and to retrieve a ranked set of resources satisfying the corresponding preferential constraints. To our knowledge, this is the first attempt to translate the semantics of a CP-net into a SPARQL query.

We are currently investigating how to extend our work to other ceteris paribus preference languages such as TCP-nets [4] or the more general CP-theories [20]. As another direction, we are working on approaches to automated CP-net elicitation [7,12].

Acknowledgements. We acknowledge partial support of PON01_00861 "SMART—Services and Meta-services for smART eGovernment".

References

1. Berners-Lee, T., Hendler, J., Lassila, O.: The Semantic Web. Sci. Am. **284**(5), 34–43 (2001)
2. Börzsönyi, S., Kossmann, D., Stocker, K.: The skyline operator. In: Proc. of ICDE, pp. 421–430 (2001)
3. Boutilier, C., Brafman, R.I., Domshlak, C., Hoos, H.H., Poole, D.: CP-nets: A tool for representing and reasoning with conditional ceteris paribus preference statements. J. Artif. Intell. Res. **21**, 135–191 (2004)
4. Brafman, R.I., Domshlak, C.: Introducing variable importance tradeoffs into CP-nets. In: Proc. of UAI, pp. 69–76 (2002)
5. Chomicki, J.: Preference formulas in relational queries. ACM Trans. Database Syst. **28**(4), 427–466 (2003)
6. Chomicki, J.: Logical foundations of preference queries. IEEE Data Eng. Bull. **34**(2), 3–10 (2011)
7. Dimopoulos, Y., Michael, L., Athienitou, F.: Ceteris paribus preference elicitation with predictive guarantees. In: Proc. of IJCAI, pp. 1890–1895 (2009)
8. Domshlak, C., Hüllermeier, E., Kaci, S., Prade, H.: Preferences in AI: An overview. Artif. Intell. **175**(7/8), 1037–1052 (2011)
9. Doyle, J.: Prospects for preferences. Comput. Intell. **20**(2), 111–136 (2004)
10. Fishburn, P.C.: Utility theory for decision making. Publications in operations research, J. Wiley (1970)
11. Fürnkranz, J., Hüllermeier, E.: Preference Learning. Springer (2010)
12. Guerin, J.T., Allen, T.E., Goldsmith, J.: Learning CP-net preferences online from user queries. In: Perny, P., Pirlot, M., Tsoukiàs, A. (eds.) ADT 2013. LNCS, vol. 8176, pp. 208–220. Springer, Heidelberg (2013)
13. Gueroussova, M., Polleres, A., McIlraith, S.A.: SPARQL with qualitative and quantitative preferences. In: Proc. of OrdRing, pp. 2–8 (2013)
14. Harris, S., Seaborne, A.: SPARQL 1.1 query language (2013). http://www.w3.org/TR/2013/REC-sparql11-query-20130321/
15. Kießling, W.: Foundations of preferences in database systems. In: Proc. of VLDB, pp. 311–322 (2002)
16. Kießling, W., Endres, M., Wenzel, F.: The preference SQL system – an overview. IEEE Data Eng. Bull. **34**(2), 11–18 (2011)
17. Li, C., Soliman, M.A., Chang, K.C.C., Ilyas, I.F.: RankSQL: Supporting ranking queries in relational database management systems. In: Proc. of VLDB, pp. 1342–1345 (2005)
18. Schreiber, G., Raimond, Y.: RDF 1.1 Primer (2014). http://www.w3.org/TR/rdf11-primer/
19. Siberski, W., Pan, J.Z., Thaden, U.: Querying the semantic web with preferences. In: Cruz, I., Decker, S., Allemang, D., Preist, C., Schwabe, D., Mika, P., Uschold, M., Aroyo, L.M. (eds.) ISWC 2006. LNCS, vol. 4273, pp. 612–624. Springer, Heidelberg (2006)
20. Wilson, N.: Extending CP-nets with stronger conditional preference statements. In: Proc. of AAAI, pp. 735–741 (2004)

Appendix A Ordering Query Example

```
prefix cp:<http://sisinflab.poliba.it/semanticweb/lod/ontologies/cp-nets.owl\#>
prefix db:<http://dbpedia.org/resource/>
prefix dbo:<http://dbpedia.org/ontology/>
```

```
SELECT ?item_D  (COUNT(DISTINCT ?outcome_d) AS ?counter)
WHERE
{ ?item_D      a dbo:Book; dbo:numberOfPages ?page_D.
  FILTER(?page_D>300). #hard constraints
  ?item_D      dbo:country ?country_D; dbo:literaryGenre ?genre_D.
  VALUES (?country_D) { (db:Germany) (db:United_Kingdom) }
  VALUES (?genre_D) { (db:Fantasy_literature) (db:History) }
  BIND (IF(EXISTS{?item_D dbo:subsequentWork ?object},
    cp:subsequentWorkYes, cp:subsequentWorkNo) AS ?subsequentWork_D).
  BIND (CONCAT(STR(dbo:country),STR(?country_D),STR(dbo:literaryGenre),
    STR(?genre_D), STR(dbo:subsequentWork), STR(?subsequentWork_D)) AS ?outcome_D).
  ?item_d      a dbo:Book; dbo:numberOfPages ?page_d.
  FILTER(?page_d>300). #hard constraints
  ?item_d      dbo:country ?country_d; dbo:literaryGenre ?genre_d.
  VALUES (?country_d) { (db:Germany) (db:United_Kingdom) }
  VALUES (?genre_d) { (db:Fantasy_literature) (db:History) }
  BIND (IF(EXISTS{?item_d dbo:subsequentWork ?object},
    cp:subsequentWorkYes, cp:subsequentWorkNo) AS ?subsequentWork_d).
  BIND (CONCAT(STR(dbo:country),STR(?country_d),STR(dbo:literaryGenre),
    STR(?genre_d), STR(dbo:subsequentWork),STR(?subsequentWork_d)) AS ?outcome_d).
  FILTER(?outcome_D!=?outcome_d).
    { # Query 2
    SELECT ("VoidSet" AS ?ConcatenatedAncestor)("VoidSet" AS ?ConcatenatedParent)
           (CONCAT(STR(?attrPrefer),STR(?valuePrefer)) AS ?Prefer)
           (CONCAT(STR(?attrPrefer),STR(?valueOver)) AS ?Over)
    WHERE
    {FILTER NOT EXISTS{?preference cp:given ?condition.}
     ?preference cp:prefer ?p; cp:over ?o.
     ?p cp:attribute ?attrPrefer; cp:value ?valuePrefer.
     ?o cp:value ?valueOver.}}
    UNION
    { # Query 3
    SELECT ?ConcatenatedAncestor ?ConcatenatedParent ?Prefer ?Over
    WHERE
    { {SELECT ?V ?Acondition
              (GROUP_CONCAT(CONCAT(STR(?attr),STR(?value)); separator="")
                 AS ?ConcatenatedAncestor)
       WHERE
       {?V cp:ancestorCondition ?Acondition.
        ?Acondition cp:contains ?a.
        ?a cp:attribute ?attr; cp:value ?value.}
       GROUP BY ?V ?Acondition}
      {SELECT ?V2 ?Pcondition
              (CONCAT(STR(?attrPrefer),STR(?valuePrefer)) AS ?Prefer)
              (CONCAT(STR(?attrPrefer),STR(?valueOver)) AS ?Over)
              (GROUP_CONCAT(CONCAT(STR(?attr),STR(?value)); separator ="")
                 AS ?ConcatenatedParent)
       WHERE
       {?preference cp:given ?Pcondition.
        FILTER EXISTS{?preference cp:given ?Pcondition.}
        ?preference cp:prefer ?p; cp:over ?o.
        ?V2 cp:variableDomain ?p.
        ?p cp:attribute ?attrPrefer; cp:value ?valuePrefer.
        ?o cp:value ?valueOver.
        ?Pcondition cp:contains ?c.
        ?c cp:attribute ?attr; cp:value ?value.}
       GROUP BY ?V2 ?Pcondition ?attrPrefer ?valuePrefer ?valueOver}
      FILTER(CONTAINS(?ConcatenatedAncestor,?ConcatenatedParent)&&?V=?V2).}}
  FILTER(((?ConcatenatedParent="VoidSet") &&
  CONTAINS(?outcome_D,?Prefer) && CONTAINS(?outcome_d,?Over)) ||
  (!(?ConcatenatedParent="VoidSet")) &&
  CONTAINS(?outcome_D,?ConcatenatedAncestor) && CONTAINS(?outcome_d,?Prefer) &&
  CONTAINS(?outcome_D,?ConcatenatedAncestor) && CONTAINS(?outcome_d,?Over)).}
GROUP BY ?item_D
ORDER BY DESC(?counter)
LIMIT 5
```

Modeling and Retrieving Linked RESTful APIs: A Graph Database Approach

Sahar Aljalbout, Omar Boucelma[✉], and Sana Sellami

Aix Marseille Université, CNRS, ENSAM, Université Toulon, LSIS UMR 7296,
13397 Marseille, France
saharjalbout@gmail.com, {omar.boucelma,sana.sellami}@univ-amu.fr

Abstract. This paper describes an approach that combines Linked Data and Graph Database concepts for modeling and retrieving RESTFul Linked APIs (Web APIs). We propose a multi-levels graph structure where the Web APIs (vertices) are connected by means of different types of links: The graph is stored in a graph database to allow graph exploration, e.g., to achieve an API discovery task for instance. The exploration/retrieval process is performed by means of graph queries: on the user (client) side, a keyword search interface is provided while, on the server side (graph database), a graph query is issued. The approach has been implemented on top of Neo4j and its cypher query language, and an experimentation has been conducted with real datasets.

Keywords: RESTful web API · Mashup · API discovery · Linked data · Graph databases · Neo4j

1 Introduction

As the amount of data is increasing on the web, Web APIs are becoming a popular way (i) for many companies to expose their data on the web and (ii) for a large amount of developers that compose existing APIs to develop new APIs, mashups and innovative applications. Despite the fact that many approaches and systems have been proposed in order to streamline the services retrieval process, web API discovery is still a difficult task.

Our research proposal relies on both Linked Data principles (LD) and Graph Databases. While we recently witnessed some studies on the relationship between APIs and Linked Data, leading to the concept of Linked APIs [1], there is no popular work that combine both LD and Graph Databases to enhance automatic discovery of Web APIs. Links between APIs will be identified, categorized and stored in a graph database, together with the APIs. Finally, the API discovery process is performed by means of graph queries: a user can submit a keyword-based query that is translated into cypher, the Neo4j query language.

The remainder of this paper is organized as follows. In section 2, present our approach for building and querying the graph of Linked Web APIs. Section 3 details the implementation and illustrates the preliminary results. Related work is discussed in Section 4, while Section 5 concludes the paper and presents some future work directions.

© Springer International Publishing Switzerland 2015
C. Debruyne et al. (Eds.): OTM 2015 Conferences, LNCS 9415, pp. 443–450, 2015.
DOI: 10.1007/978-3-319-26148-5_29

2   Linked APIs Approach

2.1   Motivation

Linked data (LD) and RESTful Web APIs share a number of similarities and differences [4]. In fact, an LD resource can be referenced with one URI, so is a RESTful Web API. Those similarities have recently led to a new RESTful Web API modeling approach as illustrated in [1,5,8] for exploiting links between APIs. Along the lines of these works, we adopted a graph database modeling approach[1]. This choice is motivated from both the formal perspective and a technology one: (i) a graph (database) model is close to the original graph abstraction, (ii) a graph database model comes often with a powerful and expressive query language, and (iii) a graph database system can be used for prototyping, hence allowing us to focus more on building a well-founded graph model of linked services.

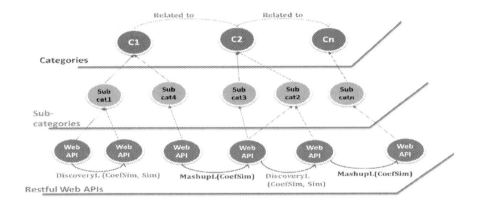

Fig. 1. Linked APIs Vision

2.2   Modeling the Graph of APIs

To build the APIs graph Fig. 1, we identified different type of links (with their semantics) between APIs. First, knowing that each API may belong to a category, e.g., twitter API belongs to the *Blogging* sub-category in a *Social* category[2], we identified two links: Subcat_Of and Belongs_To.

Belongs_To Link. The Belongs_To link is established between an API (s) and a Sub-Category (scat) if s is a member of scat.

Subcat_Of. The Subcat_Of link is established between a category (cat) and a sub-category (scat) if scat is a member of cat.

---

[1] For lack of space we skip the discussion between our graph database approach and a RDF based one, although RDF triples can be represented as a graph

[2] We are using programmableweb.com categories

Next, APIs need to be related to each other. We propose the following links: *discovery link, mashup link, tag link, artifact link*, etc. These links were created after examination of the API properties. Therefore each link is based on one or more API property. For sake of brevity, only discovery and mashup links that are described below will be illustrated in the paper:

Discovery Link. A discovery link between two APIs A and B is established if the APIs are similar according to a global similarity (coefSim) ratio based on the computation of the similarities between the name of the APIs, its operations (Op), inputs (In) and outputs (Ou).

coefSim(A,B)= w1*NameSim (APIName(A), APIName(B)) + w2*FSim(A,B) $\in [0,1]$
    where

- NameSim is a name based similarity
- w1, w2 weights introduced to asses the relevance of each kind of similarity (w1 $\in [0,1]$ and w2 = 1 - w1)
- FSim (A, B) = $2 * \dfrac{\sum OpSim(Op(A), Op(B))}{|Op(A)| + |Op(B)|} \in [0,1]$ where:
  - $OpSim(A,B) = NameSim(Op(A), Op(B)) + InSim(A,B) + OuSim(A,B)$,
  - $InSim(A,B) = NameSim(In(A), In(B)) + 2 * \dfrac{|In(A) \cap In(B)|}{|In(A)| + |In(B)|}$ is the input similarity, (respectively for $OuSim(A,B)$)

A discovery link is established between two APIs if and only if the coefSim is greater than a threshold.

Mashup Link. In most cases, API consumers are not limited to use a single API, but they are interested in multiple APIs that can work together e.g.; Trip API, Hotel API, Transportation API.Therefore, we propose a mashup link to help answer the following question: given an API A, what are the APIs that are usually composed with A and how frequently?
    Given two APIs A and B, the weight of the edge (A, B) is calculated as follows:

$$coefSim = 2 * \frac{|Mashup(A) \cap Mashup(B)|}{|Mashup(A)| + |Mashup(B)|} \tag{1}$$

where

- *Mashup(A)* is the set of mashups containing API A and *Mashup(B)* is the set of mashups containing API B.

– $|Mashup(A) \cap Mashup(B)|$ is the number of mashups containing both A and B
– $|Mashup(A)| + |Mashup(B)|$ is the number of mashups containing A, and the number of mashups containing B.

If $coefSim > threshold$, a mashup link is created between A and B.

Related To Link. Two categories C1 and C2 are connected if there exists at least one edge connecting APIs belonging to C1 to APIs belonging to C2. That is, there exists at least two APIs (A and B) such as $A \in C1$ and $B \in C2$ which are connected with a mashup link.

2.3   Modeling the Linked APIs Network

The APIs network can be considered as a multi-levels (multi-partite) graph, while at the bottom level (the APIs' one), links among APIs may also be materialized. For sake of simplicity, in the sequel of the paper, we consider this network as a graph that we define as follows:

Definition 1. The RESTful APIs graph is a directed graph $G = <V, L>$ where:

– $V = V_S \cup V_C \cup V_{SC}$ represents a set of nodes (vertices) and,
  - V_S denotes the set of APIs,
  - V_C denotes the set of categories,
  - V_{SC} is the set of sub-categories.
  Stated otherwise: $\forall v \in V, \exists t\,(type(v)) \mid t \in \{API, sub\_category, category\}$.
– A node has also a set of properties. An API node properties are name, label, URI, tag, protocol, provider, price, etc.
– L represents a set of edges (links), and each link has a set of properties. More formally:
  $\forall l \in L, \exists p\,(p = property(l)) \mid p \in \{type, coefSim, Sim\}$, where:
  - $type \in \{Belongs\_To, Subcat\_Of, Related\_To, Discovery, Mashup\}$,
  - $CoefSim$ is the similarity value between two nodes linked with l,
  - Sim is the set of common nodes properties e.g.; operations,outputs etc. Let's say that we have two APIs A and B elligible to form linked APIs on a discovery link. The sim property of that link will be calculated as follow: sim = (Op(A) $\cap$ Op(B)) $\cup$ (Ou(A) $\cap$ Ou(B)) where Op refers to API operations and Ou refers to API output.

2.4   Graph Query

In order to exploit the API graph, we currently propose two queries patterns. The first one "keyword search" exploits the discovery link and especially the "sim" property. After selecting a category and a sub category, the user submits a keyword query. We search the graph for nodes linked with a discovery link and compare the sim property of that discovery link with the keyword submitted by the user. In case of a match, a subgraph (result) is returned: only popular nodes are returned to avoid a huge graph as a result. This method accelerates the API retrieval because it targets one property of the graph links instead of several nodes properties. The second pattern, "Popular complementary api", allows retrieval of APIs that are candidate for a mashup. The user have to choose categories or sub categories to search among. Therefore, we select among these categories, APIs linked with a mashup link. Resulting APIs are sorted according to their popularity and the top k APIs are returned.

3   Implementation and Experimentation

3.1   System Architecture

Fig. 2 illustrates the functional architecture of the system which is composed mainly of three components:

1. The Extractor is in charge of extracting API properties: the Description Extractor returns the whole description of an API and submits it to the Properties Extractor which is in charge of extracting names, URLs, operations, inputs, outputs, etc. Those properties will be later passed to the linker who is in charge of creating the different types of links;
2. The Meta Data Extractor is in charge of retrieving specific information for the linkers. It relies on a Tag extractor, a correspondence mashups/API module, and Semantic Information Extractor for ontologies;
3. The Linker creates links between APIs and is composed of a set of specific modules: Artifact, Tag, Discovery and Mashup Linker(s).

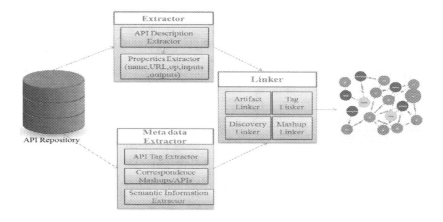

Fig. 2. System Architecture

3.2   Experimentation

Dataset: We built a Neo4J[3] graph consisting of 103 nodes and 281 relationships taken. Neo4j is a Java-based open source graph database hat comes with cypher, a powerful query language as illustrated in [12]. The nodes are divided into 8 categories and each category contains sub-categories.We consider two scenarios: Web API discovery and Popular complementary APIs search.

Web API discovery Scenario: Let us consider the set of APIs described in Table 1. This table represents the similarity value (sim) of the discovery link between a sample of Science Fiction APIs. In addition we suppose we have the following (API, popularity) value pairs: {(s33, 5), (s32, 4), (s34, 4), (s49, 3)}. The popularity of an API designates the number of mashup this API is involved in. An API that is part of many mashups will have a high popularity and will be considered as a popular one (s33 in our example).

Table 1. Relationships between the Science Fiction APIs

Source Node	Destination Node	Sim
s33	s32	$Get Author Price - Author Price$
s34	s32	$Get Author - Author$
s34	s33	$Get Author - Author$
s49	s32	$Get Author Price - Author Price$
s49	s33	$Get Author Price - Author Price$

In order to perform a Web API discovery, a user has to do the following: (1) Choose an API category,(2) Choose a sub category, (3) Submit a keyword search query.

In our case, the user is searching for APIs that return science fiction (SF) authors. This request is translated into a cypher query as illustrated in Fig. 3. As we can see, the search is filtered by "Science Fiction" (Subcategory) (lines 1-2). APIs linked with a discovery link (line 4) are explored and the user query (author) is compared to the sim property of the discovery link (line 5). Only top k ranked APIs that match are returned together with this discovery link: ranking is based on APIs popularity (lines 6-7).

```
1 MATCH (n:scat)-[l]-(m:ser)
2 WHERE(n.name='ScienceFiction')
3 WITH m
4 MATCH (m)-[r:DISCOVERY]-(b)
5 WHERE (r.Sim=~''.*Author.*") and HAS (m.pop)
6 RETURN m,m.pop
7 ORDER BY m.pop desc limit 13
```

Fig. 3. Cypher Keyword Search Query

---

[3] http://neo4j.com/

4   Related Work

Linked APIs Languages. Several languages have been proposed in the literature for modeling data services that mimics LD principles. These languages follow the Linked data principles and are translated into RDF[4]. SEREDASj [2] is a language that allows a semantic description of data services; it has been superseded by JSON-LD [5] that features a simple method to express linked data in JSON and also to add semantics to existing JSON documents. RESTdesc [4] aims to apply the vision of Linked Data to Hypermedia API.

Linked Services Networks. Recently, the linked services network has drawn attention among the web services research community. For example, in [8], authors propose a framework for defining a linked view over multiple repositories and for searching their content. Another work [9] suggested a triple view graph for modeling the web services ecosystem: (1) An API graph that connects services when they are used in the same mashup; (2) A domain graph that provides information about services that are more likely to be connected to produce innovative applications; and (3) A tag graph which connects two tags if there exist two APIs which are labeled with those tags and appear in the same mashup. In [11] an approach for providing new services based on service composition is proposed. Finally, Bennara et al. [10] exploit REST and linked data principles to facilitate discovery and composition of RESTful linked services (resources): each resource must have a descriptor that contains its meta-data.

5   Conclusion and Future Work

Whether published as part of a set of registries such as UDDI, with a more or less user-friendly interface such as programmableweb.com, the plethora of published Web APIs is still perceived as a set of sparse isolated islands of APIs, making it difficult for a user to automatically discover a Web API or to build a mashup that satisfies her needs.

In this paper, we presented an approach where a database graph-based model to structure the space of APIs. Part of the approach, we developed a discovery method where both indexing (via popular APIs, categories) and link properties querying enhance the discovery of APIs. The approach has been tested and implemented on top of Neo4j in using a realistic dataset and the results were satisfying. For future work, we plan to identify other type of links, manage large distributed graphs of APIs, conduct benchmarking experiments and, ultimately, make the graph available to the community.

---

[4] http://www.w3.org/RDF/

References

1. Domingue, J., Pedrinaci, C., Maleshkova, M., Norton, B., Krummenacher, R.: Fostering a Relationship between Linked Data and the Internet of Services. In: Domingue, J., et al. (eds.) Future Internet Assembly. LNCS, vol. 6656, pp. 351–366. Springer, Heidelberg (2011)
2. Lanthaler, M., Gült, C.: A semantic description language for RESTful data services to combat semaphobia. In: IEEE International Conference on Digital Ecosystems and Technologies (DEST), pp. 47–53 (2011)
3. Trinh, T.-D., Do, B.-L., Wetz, P., Anjomshoaa, A., Kiesling, E. Tjoa, A.M.: A drag-and-block approach for linked open data exploration. In: Proceedings of the 5th International Workshop on Consuming Linked Data (COLD 2014) Co-Located with the 13th International Semantic Web Conference ISWC (2014)
4. Verborgh, R., Steiner, T., de Walle, R.V., Gabarro, J.: Linked data and linked APIs: similarities, differences, and challenges. In: Simperl, E., Norton, B., Mladenic, D., Valle, E.D., Fundulaki, I., Passant, A., Troncy, R. (eds.) ESWC 2012 Satellite Events. LNCS, vol. 7540, pp. 272–284. Springer, Heidelberg (2015)
5. Lanthaler, M., Gtl, C.: On using JSON-LD to create evolvable RESTful services. In: Third International Workshop on RESTful Design, WS-REST 2012, Lyon, France, April 16, 2012, pp. 25–32 (2012)
6. Lanthaler, M.: Creating 3rd generation web APIs with hydra. In: 22nd International World Wide Web Conference, WWW 2013, Rio de Janeiro, Brazil, May 13–17, pp. 35–38 (2013)
7. Alarcn, R., Wilde, E.: RESTler: crawling RESTful services. In: Proceedings of the 19th International Conference on World Wide Web, WWW 2010, pp. 1051–1052 (2010)
8. Bianchini, D., De Antonellis, V., Melchiori, M.: Link-based viewing of multiple web API repositories. In: Decker, H., Lhotská, L., Link, S., Spies, M., Wagner, R.R. (eds.) DEXA 2014, Part I. LNCS, vol. 8644, pp. 362–376. Springer, Heidelberg (2014)
9. Lyu, S., Liu, J., Tang, M., Kang, G., Duan, Y.: Three-level views of the web service network: an empirical study based on programmable web. In: IEEE International Congress on Big Data, pp. 374–381 (2014)
10. Bennara, M., Mrissa, M., Amghar, Y.: An approach for composing RESTful linked services on the Web. In: 23rd International World Wide Web Conference, WWW 2014, pp. 977–982 (2014)
11. Chen, W., Paik, I.: Improving efficiency of service discovery using Linked data-based service publication. Inf. Syst. Front. **15**(4), 613–625 (2013)
12. Holzschuher, F., Peinl, R.: Performance of graph query languages: comparison of cypher, gremlin and native access in Neo4j. In: Workshop Proceedings Joint 2013 EDBT/ICDT Conferences, EDBT/ICDT 2013, Genoa, Italy, pp. 195–204 (2013)

Crowdsourcing for Web Service Discovery

Fatma Slaimi[1,2]([✉]), Sana Sellami[2], Omar Boucelma[2],
and Ahlem Ben Hassine[1]

[1] National School of Computer Science (ENSI),
University of Manouba, Manouba, Tunisia
[2] Aix-Marseille Université, CNRS, LSIS UMR 7296, 13397 Marseille, France
{fatma.slaimi,ahlembh}@gmail.com,
{fatma.slaimi,sana.sellami,omar.boucelma}@univ-amu.fr

Abstract. Over last decade, research in Web service discovery has brought a variety of techniques to find out responses for a Web service request. While the accuracy of matchmaking approaches has continuously improved, human contributions remain a key ingredient of the process. In this paper, we propose an approach called Crowd4WS (Crowdsourcing for Web service discovery) to complement and refine matchmaking approaches by using crowdsourcing techniques. We describe our approach and present the results of experiments on a known collection of RESTful services described with hRESTS.

Keywords: Web services discovery · Matchmaking · Crowdsourcing

1 Introduction

Web services discovery has been considered as one of the key challenges for achieving efficient service oriented computing. During the last decade, the advent of the semantic Web has led to the development of several semantic matchmaking techniques and systems [1–5]. Matchmaking process aims to discover the most relevant services for a user request. Services are ranked according the similarity scores (a service versus a query). Previous works [6] have shown that matchmaking remains a semi-automatic process, that leading to some false positive results and still may require some form of human assistance.

More recently, with the rapidly growing of Social Web, Crowdsourcing has gained momentum and proved useful in many practical applications. In a nutshell, crowdsourcing [7] [8] can be considered as a model in which a problem is divided into sub-problems and distributed among a group of people (called the crowd or workers). Each sub-problem may result in one or several microtask(s), performed by several workers on behalf of some organizations. Tasks are performed individually or in a collaborative way. Crowdsourcing domains applications examples are: content classification, objects ranking, image annotation, etc.

In this paper we describe Crowd4WS (Crowdsourcing for Web service discovery), a crowdsourcing approach and implementation. Given a subset of relevant precomputed Web services (candidate returned by a matchmaker), and a Web

© Springer International Publishing Switzerland 2015
C. Debruyne et al. (Eds.): OTM 2015 Conferences, LNCS 9415, pp. 451–464, 2015.
DOI: 10.1007/978-3-319-26148-5_30

service request, Crowd4WS asks the crowd to assess the relevance of the services candidates. The outcome of the system is a set of Web service(s) that are the most relevant to a service request. For the experimentation described in this paper, Crowd4WS takes as an input a subset of relevant Web services generated by SR-REST, an hybrid matchmaker described in a previous work [9].

Despite a reasonable number of crowdsourcing applications and platforms, to the best of our knowledge, the crowdsourcing computational paradigm has not been used in the context of the Web services discovery domain: One of the main reasons being the lack of expertise (experts) in such domain. Given this context, we believe the contributions of the work described in this paper are as follows:

(1) we proposed to leverage existing matchmaking techniques/systems with the involvement of the crowd;

(2) we came up with an approach that can use different models such as, for example, a probabilistic model to detect faulty workers;

(3) we used real datasets (Web services descriptions) with a real (although small) set of workers, while many crowdsourcing related work use synthetic data.

The remainder of the paper is organized as follows. Section 2 surveys some related works on matchmaking approaches and crowdsourcing. In section 3, we describe a motivating example. Section 4 presents our approach based on crowdsourcing for Web service discovery (Crowd4WS). In section 5, we describe the system architecture and detail the experimental settings and results in section 6. Section 7 concludes the paper.

2   Related Work

Matchmaking. To leverage semantic descriptions of Web services, several matchmaking approaches have been proposed, most of them exploiting SAWSDL [1] [10] or OWL-S annotated services [3]. These matchmakers can be logic-based, non-logic-based or hybrid, i.e., combining of logic and non-logic similarity functions. Recently, RESTful matchmaking approaches and systems have also been proposed in the literature [9][4]. Such systems, like XAM4SWS [2] for instance, compare service operations, inputs, outputs and similarities. In [4] a graph-theoretic approach called semantic flow matching is proposed: the approach matches REST Web services, specified in WADL (Web Application Description Language) and uses linguistic knowledge and domain-specific heuristics. In [9], we developed a matchmaking approach based on several similarity measure functions that exploits different elements of RESTful descriptions.

As studied in [6] matchmaking solutions came back with false positive and negative results and most of them fail to discover all the relevant services according to the user request. Existing matchmakers have to use and combine several similarity measures and deal with aggregating methods of matching scores to resolve discovery issues. For example, in [6][11] authors show that many matchmakers do not consider semantic similarity between services (e.g., synonym relations) and an improvement of semantic similarity is still needed.

Crowdsourcing. Crowdsourcing has gained momentum to overcome computational tasks that require human assistance. Crowdsourcing has been recently
proposed as a solution to a variety of research problems such as ontology alignment, schemas matching or images annotation to cite a few. For example, in
[12] authors used crowdsourcing techniques to validate correspondences between
schemas: they designed questions with contextual information that may help
workers to answer. Crowdmap [8] is a system that collects human contributions via crowdsourced microtasks. For a pair of ontologies, Crowdmap splits
the alignment problem into individual microtasks, publishes them on labor market online, collects results and aggregates them. This process has improved the
precision of results returned by an automatic ontology alignment process. In [13],
crowdsourcing has been used to validate the results of automated images search
on mobile devices. Crowdsourcing techniques have also been successfully applied
for several data management problems leading to systems such as CrowdSearch
[14] or CrowdScreen [13]. In [10] Shen et al. deployed crowdsourcing methods for
schema matching. More recently, approaches that use crowdsourcing to assess
entities extracted form Web pages (text) to URIs was proposed in the literature:
ZenCrowd [15] combines probabilistic reasoning with crowdsourcing to exhibit
correspondences from text entities to linked object data.

To summarize, Matchmaking works have shown that there is no ideal matching and matchmaking may still require some form of human assistance. Crowdsourcing has gained momentum and proved useful in many practical applications
e.g objects ranking, semantic Web, Linked data, ontology engineering etc. Systems such as ZenCrowd demonstrate how crowdsourcing can contribute to the
Semantic Web. All these studies have shown the crowdsourcing benefits and
underline the need of human intelligence to effectively handle difficult tasks.

3   Motivating Example

To motivate our approach, let's consider a simple example, described in [9],
where a user is looking for a Web service that provides information about car
prices. The car price request is described as follow: User request (*name:* car_price,
operation: get_price, *input:* car, *output:* price).

The process can be summarized as follows:

1. First, we apply SR-REST, an hybrid matchmaker on the car prices example.
   This yields a set $S = \{$*Toyota car price, auto price color, bicycle price, car
   year, car report and car recommended price*$\}$, S being considered as the most
   relevant services;
2. Looking carefully at S, it is obvious that *bicycle price* service (*name:* bicy-
   cle_price, *operation:* get_price, *input:* bicycle, *output:* price) is a false positive
   (a bicycle is not a car), although this service proves highly similar to a car
   price service, mainly because the matchmaking algorithm does not require a
   total mapping between the inputs/inputs of user's request and a service [6];
3. When submitting S to the crowd, services that obviously do not match the
   user request, are simply removed, although returned by the matchmaker.

Fig. 1 below illustrates our crowdsourcing process. People, called *workers* are asked to perform a specific work, usually decomposed into a set of elementary tasks called *microtasks*. A microtask represents a task that could be handled by a worker in a reasonable amount of time. A single microtask may be performed by many workers in order to limit the bias of an individual work. In adopting a crowdsourcing approach, we aim (1) at assessing the results returned by the matchmaking, and (2) returning a set of ranked Web services.

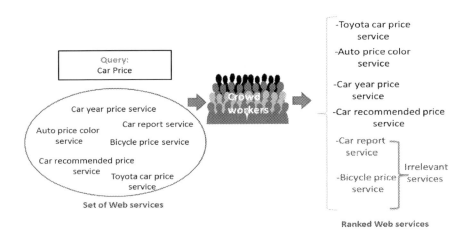

Fig. 1. Illustration of the Crowdsourcing Process

4   Crowd4WS: Crowdsourcing for Web Service Discovery

Crowd4WS, consists of two main steps (microtasks): (1) Validation step, where the crowd checks whether a service matches a request, and hence discard irrelevant services and (2) Ranking step , where the services are ranked by the crowd accordingly with an order of preference (relevance).

Validation. Given a user's query R, a set S of n Web services, $S = \{s_1, s_2,..., s_n\}$, and a set W of k workers ($\{w_1,...,w_k\}$), the validation step returns a set RS of relevant services accordingly to three relevance levels RL = {relevant, possibly relevant, irrelevant}. Each worker assigns a relevance score to a s_i expressing how relevant is the returned service s_i to the query R.

Ranking. The crowd will perform a microtask pairwise comparison between Web services. Each worker has to order the set of services. The symbol > is used to define the order; for example a > b means that the worker prefers the object a to the object b (if we consider a and b as two services, a > b means that a is more relevant then b). This is a preliminary step for inferring a ranking (total ordering) among the results (Web services). We use also an aggregation mechanism to aggregate answers collected from crowd. For each microtask we will apply a set of aggregation functions as described below.

Definition 1 (Results Aggregation): The aggregation process takes as input the set of all answers collected among the workers. More formally, this is represented by a matrix A where a_{ij} represents the answer of a worker w_i for a service s_j.

$$A = \begin{pmatrix} a_{11} & \cdots & a_{1n} \\ \vdots & \vdots & \vdots \\ a_{k1} & \cdots & a_{kn} \end{pmatrix}$$

The result of aggregation process is a set of aggregated values representing the relevance level assigned for the service s_i.

Several aggregation techniques are proposed in the literature to compute the aggregated value such as, majority voting [16] and expectation maximization (EM) [17]. While majority voting aggregates responses for each service independently, the EM method aggregates simultaneously all responses. The majority voting collects and aggregates worker answers for each service.

In our work, a ranked list of services would be generated; our aim is to compute a relevance score for each service. For this reason we will apply an aggregation method based on the majority voting approach. We define a numerical equivalent for each alternative in order to compute a global score per service, then services will be ordered according to these scores.

Definition 2 (Aggregation Score): We denote $Sc(S)$ as the aggregation function applied to compute the score of each candidate Web services from the worker's answers. This function is defined as follow:

$$Sc(s_i) = \frac{\sum_{i=1}^{k}(r_i)}{k}. \tag{1}$$

Where k is the number of workers who have validated service s_i ; and r_i is a relevance number accordingly to the level chosen by the worker such that:

$$\begin{cases} r_i = 1, & \text{if answer=relevant} \\ r_i = 0.5, & \text{if answer=possibly relevant} \\ r_i = 0, & \text{if answer=irrelevant.} \end{cases}$$

After aggregating all answers, an ordered list of Web services will be generated. This list will be submitted to the crowd to rank the services in this list from the best to the worst one. This ranking microtask implies both pairwise comparison between the services and an aggregation of the different results (see Definition 3).

Definition 3 (Ranking Aggregation): The "total" ordering of relevant Web services is given by the aggregation of orders supplied by the workers. The ordering of a worker w_k is denoted by:$\phi_l = \{(i,j), s_i \succcurlyeq s_j\}$ l=$\{1,..,k\}$.

After collecting the answers of all k workers that performed pairwise comparisons, we obtain a set ϕ of ranked Web services, where ϕ represents the set of orders given by the k workers and ϕ_l represents the order given by a worker l.

$$\phi = \cup \phi_l. \tag{2}$$

Results collected from the crowd must be aggregated in order to find a total order. We are using the the the Bradley-Terry model [18] [5] that, given two objects x and y, evaluates the probability that x is preferred to y. More precisely, if $\alpha, \beta \geqslant 0$ respectively denote the relevance scores of x and y, this probability is computed as:

$$Pr(x \succcurlyeq y) = \frac{\alpha}{\alpha + \beta} \tag{3}$$

We assume that there are n candidate services $\{s_1, .., s_n\}$ and a pool of k workers $\{w_1, .., w_k\}$. The set of (pairs of) services evaluated by a worker w_k is denoted by $S_k = \{(i,j) : s_i \succcurlyeq s_j\}$, where $s_i \succcurlyeq s_j$ represents that the worker prefers s_i to s_j , we apply the Bradley-Terry, we have:

$$Pr(s_i \succcurlyeq s_j) = \frac{\alpha_i}{(\alpha_i + \alpha_j)} \tag{4}$$

Where α_i is the relevance score of the service s_i. The score of each service can be estimated in using maximum likelihood method.

A global ranking over n candidates services can be obtained by sorting the vector of scores $= (\alpha_1, \cdots, \alpha_n)$ where α_i is the score of the service s_i.

Example. We consider the previous example of car price service (see section 3). Table 1 represents the pairwise comparison list (see definition 3) submitted for ranking to 5 workers. We computed the number of times a service s_i was preferred to s_j. Then we applied the Bradley and Terry model in using XLSTAT[1], to obtain a final ordering.

A matrix M can be obtained where M_{ij} represents the number of time a service i is considered as better than a service j.

$$M = \begin{pmatrix} - & 3 & 4 & 3 \\ 2 & - & 4 & 1 \\ 1 & 1 & - & 2 \\ 2 & 4 & 3 & - \end{pmatrix} \tag{5}$$

---

[1] www.xlstat.com

Table 1. Pairwise Comparison Results

service 1	service 2	service 1 wins	service 2 wins
Auto color price car (s_1)	Car year price (s_2)	3	2
Auto color price car (s_1)	Toyota car price (s_3)	4	1
Auto color price car (s_1)	Car recommended price (s_4)	3	2
Car year price (s_2)	Auto color price car (s_1)	2	3
Car year price (s_2)	Toyota car price (s_3)	4	1
Car year price (s_2)	Car recommended price (s_4)	1	4
Toyota car price (s_3)	Auto color price car (s_1)	1	4
Toyota car price (s_3)	Car year price (s_2)	1	4
Toyota car price (s_3)	Car recommended price (s_4)	2	3
Car recommended price (s_4)	Auto color price car (s_1)	2	3
Car recommended price (s_4)	Car year price (s_2)	4	1
Car recommended price (s_4)	Toyota car price (s_3)	3	2

The choice of the symbol - for the diagonal entries is arbitrary. This matrix will be used as input to the Bradley and terry model (Definition 3). Results are presented by table 2 below.

Table 2. Bradely and Terry Aggregation Results

test	number of wins	number of losses	percentage of wins	percentage of losses
s_1	20	10	66.67	33.33
s_2	15	15	50.00	50.00
s_3	7	23	23.33	76.67
s_4	18	12	60.00	40.00

Based on the percentage of wins, a simple ordering may be obtained: the "best service" is the one with the best percentage.

5   Crowd4WS Architecture

As depicted in Fig. 2, Crowd4WS takes as inputs a set of Web services generated by a matchmaker and a user query and submit them to the crowd for validation and ranking. The output of this crowdsourcing process is a collection of ranked services corresponding to the user query.

The crowdsourcing workflow consists mainly on: generating microtasks, publishing microtasks, collecting and aggregating workers' answers.

Microtask Generator: generates two kinds of microtask: 1) a validation microtask and 2) a ranking microtask. The validation microtask is used to verify the similarities between the Web services and the user query. While the second microtask performs a ranking as described above.

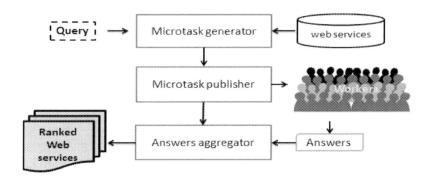

Fig. 2. System Architecture

Microtask Publisher: posts microtasks to the crowd.

Answers Aggregator: collects and aggregates the answers from different workers/microtasks. Answers returned by the crowd might be incorrect for several reasons, such as tasks misunderstanding, leading to errors or even not to finding the right answer. To solve this problem, we need aggregation mechanisms, applied in the Answer Aggregation component.

5.1   Microtask User Interface

Workers are provided with two micro task user interfaces.

Validation Microtask. Recall that during the validation phase, workers have to decide how relevant is a service to a query. As illustrated in Fig. 3, a microtask consists mainly of a question (How relevant is a service?), relevance being expressed as relevant, possibly relevant or irrelevant. The information about the query, the candidate Web service and the alternatives are also displayed to assist the workers (i.e with a simple click on the More Info field).

Ranking Microtask. The goal of the ranking microtask (Fig. 4) is to collect workers preferences on a pairwise comparison basis. The relevant services resulted from the Validation microtask are ranked by the crowd accordingly with an order of preference (relevance). For each pair of services and a request, workers assign a preference order 1 (being the best) or 2 to indicate that a service is more relevant than another.

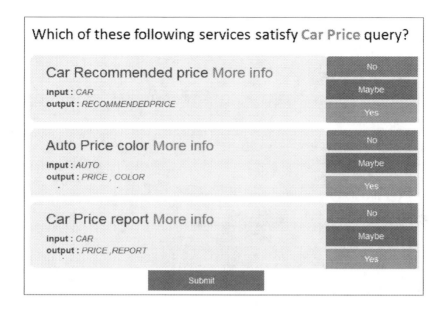

Fig. 3. Validation Microtask UI

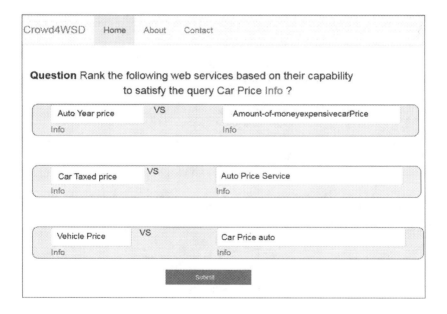

Fig. 4. Ranking Microtask UI

6   Experimentation

Many crowdsourcing research prototypes use commercial platforms [19], such as Amazon Mechanical Turk. We find it easier to implement our own system: a video illustrating the system is accessible[2].

Regarding the workers, we relied on our academic network which is composed mainly staff (lab members) and students at our university. We implemented a Web application that generates microtasks questions from the test collection hREST-TC1[3]. This collection is derived from SAWSDL-TC1 collection and is composed of 25 queries (from different domains: communication, food, economy, medical, travel and education), 895 services and 24 ontologies used to semantically annotate the inputs and outputs parameters of Web services. For each query a relevant set is provided.

The experimental results are detailed below.

6.1   Experimentation Setup

Configuration Parameters for Crowdsourcing. In the crowdsourcing environment, each microtask should be executed by a number of workers. Based on common practices in the crowdsourcing context for similar tasks[20] [8], the number of workers assigned to each task is limited to 5. As microtasks are simple to accomplish and require only few minutes to be performed, each worker is asked to fulfill a set of validation (or ranking) tasks.

Experimental results show that it takes between few minutes to receive answers from each worker (depending on the number of microtasks that should be attributed). In order to evaluate the number of tasks to be assigned to each worker, we measured the time required to perform a set of microtasks by these workers. We will pay attention to the time consumed by worker's to fulfil a set of grouped microtasks. We varied the number of micro tasks per groups between 1 and 30 microtasks. Fig. 5 illustrates the obtained results. In this figure, we show that the time consumed increased when we have more than 10 microtasks.

Then the user interface design and the time required to execute a microtask influenced the crowdsourcing results. Our concern is how to improve the user interface to make more easily the user interaction. Based on these results, we limited the number of microtasks per group to 6 in order to get the maximum number of answers.

6.2   Evaluation Results

Worker's Expertise. To evaluate our approach, first we addressed the problem of the lack of expertise of workers. We have implemented a simple model based on a quiz as illustrated in Fig. 6 to check the expertise of the worker.

---

[2] http://www.lsis.org/sellamis/Projects.html
[3] http://semwebcentral.org/projects/hRESTS-tc/

Time (minutes)
50
45
40
35
30
25
20
15
10
5
0
2 7 10 20 22 25 30 35 40 45
Number of microtaks

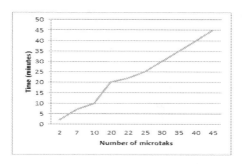

Fig. 5. Time per Set of microtasks

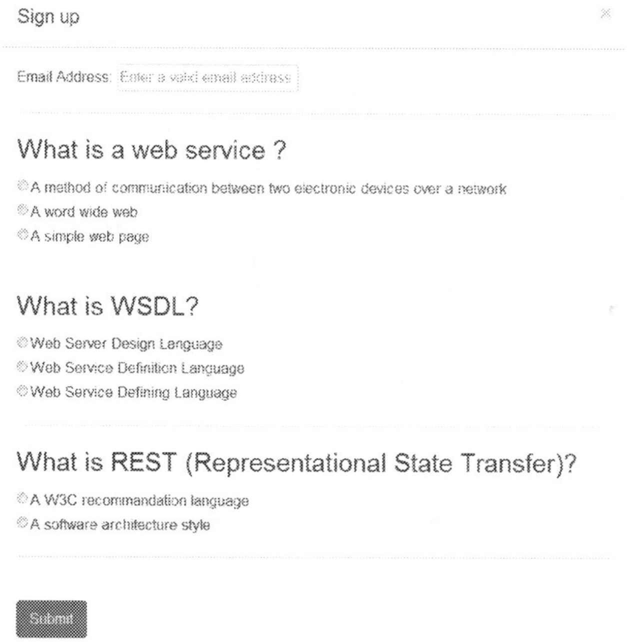

Sign up
Email Address: Enter a valid email address
What is a web service ?
A method of communication between two electronic devices over a network
A word wide web
A simple web page
What is WSDL?
Web Server Design Language
Web Service Definition Language
Web Service Defining Language
What is REST (Representational State Transfer)?
A W3C recommandation language
A software architecture style
Submit

Fig. 6. Worker's Quiz

Workers are asked to answer a set of questions about Web services before executing validation and ranking microtasks. The results of theirs answers will be used to measure a degree of expertise. If the worker makes more than one mistake, he is considered as non expert and the system does not consider her answers.

Crowdsourcing Evaluation. We conducted a series of tests to evaluate the impact of both validation and ranking processes. We measured the average precision of the validation process and then the average precision of both validation and ranking process. For our evaluation, we use precision and recall measures

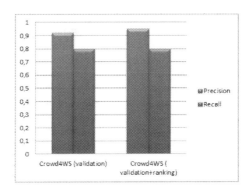

Fig. 7. Crowd4WS Precision and Recall (validation and ranking)

to evaluate the effectiveness of our approach. These measures are described as follows: Precision= $\frac{|A \cap B|}{B}$, and Recall= $\frac{|A \cap B|}{A}$ Where A is the set of all relevant services for a request and B the set of all retrieved services for a request. We then compute the average precision and recall.

As shown in Fig. 7, Ranking microtask has positive impact on the returned list of services. In fact we note that irrelevant services are at the end of the list while the most relevant services are at the top of the list. Ranking microtask improves the precision but gives the same recall as does the validation step. Based on the definition of recall (i.e the number of relevant services that are retrieved by the workers) we conclude that crowdsourced ranking discards false positives but has no impact on the number of relevant retrieved Web services (the same set approved by the validation microtasks).

Crowdsourcing vs Matchmaking. Finally, we compared Crowd4WS with our previously proposed matchamker SR-REST by measuring their average precisions and recalls. Fig. 8 shows the obtained results. We noticed that the use of the crowd to validate services obtained through the matchmaking process leads to a noteworthy precision improvement. This is due to the fact that irrelevant Web services will be discarded as they are judged as impertinent to the user's research. The pruning of these services from the set of returned pertinent services vindicates the recall improvement.

To summarize, our experiments involved 25 different workers. Overall, they confirmed our first hypothesis: human intelligence could be used to enhance precision of automatic Web services discovery approaches. The crowd is able to detect false positive results given by the matchmaker and discards them from the set of returned results.

7   Conclusion

The work described in this paper demonstrates that crowdsourcing may complement and refine matchmaking approaches. The experimental numbers, expressed

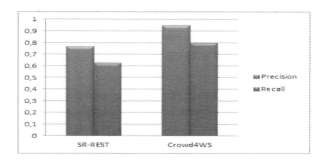

Fig. 8. Crowd4WS vs SR-REST precision and recall

in terms of precision, show a worthy improvement with respect to the number of candidates services provided by the matchmaking process: hence this leaves hope for further investigation in order to come up with an efficient service discovery platform that combines both matchmaking and crowdsourcing. This work can be considered as a first step towards hybrid human-automatic Web service discovery.

As mentioned earlier, we did not use a commercial platform such as AMT, because we need to rely on a "service-aware" crowd. Indeed, tagging a Flickr picture, or recognizing a landmark in a city, are examples of easy tasks; while deciding whether a Web service matches a user request is a harder task because one needs to have some expertise in the service oriented computing area. This remark raises several challenges that need to be tackled such as user's credibility (level of expertise), quality of results, etc.

References

1. Klusch, M., Kapahnke, P., Zinnikus, I.: Adaptive Hybrid Semantic Selection of SAWSDL Services with SAWSDL-MX2. Int. J. Semantic Web Inf. Syst. **6**(4), 1–26 (2010)
2. Lampe, U., Schulte, S., Siebenhaar, M., Schuller, D., Steinmetz, R.: Adaptive matchmaking for RESTful services based on hrests and microwsmo. In: Binder, W., Schuldt, H., (eds.) ACM International Conference Proceeding Series, WEWST, pp. 10–17. ACM (2010)
3. Klusch, M., Kapahnke, P.: The iSeM matchmaker: A flexible approach for adaptive hybrid semantic service selection. J. Web Sem. **15**, 1–14 (2012)
4. Khorasgani, R.R., Stroulia, E., Zaane, O.R.: Web service matching for restful web services. In: Kienle, H.M., Bolchini, D., Tramontana, P., (eds.) WSE, pp. 115–124. IEEE (2011)
5. Chen, X., Bennett, P.N., Collins-Thompson, K., Horvitz, E.: Pairwise ranking aggregation in a crowdsourced setting. In: Leonardi, S., Panconesi, A., Ferragina, P., Gionis, A., (eds.) WSDM, pp. 193–202. ACM (2013)
6. Klusch, M., Fries, B.: Hybrid owl-s service retrieval with owls-mx: benefits and pitfalls. In: SMRR (2007)

7. Brabham, D.C.: Crowdsourcing. The MIT Press essential knowledge series. MIT Press (2013)
8. Sarasua, C., Simperl, E., Noy, N.F.: Crowdmap: crowdsourcing ontology alignment with microtasks. In: Cudré-Mauroux, P., et al. (eds.) ISWC 2012. LNCS, vol. 7649, pp. 525–541. Springer, Heidelberg (2012)
9. Slaimi, F., Sellami, S., Boucelma, O., Ben Hassine, A.: Flexible matchmaking for RESTful web services. In: Meersman, R., Panetto, H., Dillon, T., Eder, J., Bellahsene, Z., Ritter, N., De Leenheer, P., Dou, D. (eds.) ODBASE 2013. LNCS, vol. 8185, pp. 542–554. Springer, Heidelberg (2013)
10. McCann, R., Shen, W., Doan, A.: Matching schemas in online communities: a web 2.0 approach. In: Alonso, G., Blakeley, J.A., Chen, A.L.P., (eds.) ICDE, pp. 110–119. IEEE (2008)
11. Klusch, M.: Service discovery. In: Alhajj, R., Rokne, J. (eds.) Encyclopedia of Social Networks and Mining (ESNAM). Springer (2014)
12. Hung, N.Q.V., Tam, N.T., Miklós, Z., Aberer, K.: On leveraging crowdsourcing techniques for schema matching networks. In: Meng, W., Feng, L., Bressan, S., Winiwarter, W., Song, W. (eds.) DASFAA 2013, Part II. LNCS, vol. 7826, pp. 139–154. Springer, Heidelberg (2013)
13. Parameswaran, A.G., Garcia-Molina, H., Park, H., Polyzotis, N., Ramesh, A., Widom, J.: Crowdscreen: algorithms for filtering data with humans. In: Candan, K.S., Chen, Y., Snodgrass, R.T., Gravano, L., Fuxman, A., (eds.) SIGMOD Conference, pp. 361–372. ACM (2012)
14. Yan, T., Kumar, V., Ganesan, D.: Crowdsearch: exploiting crowds for accurate real-time image search on mobile phones. In: Banerjee, S., Keshav, S., Wolman, A., (eds.) MobiSys, pp. 77–90. ACM (2010)
15. Demartini, G., Difallah, D.E., Cudr-Mauroux, P.: Zencrowd: leveraging probabilistic reasoning and crowdsourcing techniques for large-scale entity linking. In: Mille, A., Gandon, F.L., Misselis, J., Rabinovich, M., Staab, S., (eds.) WWW, pp. 469–478. ACM (2012)
16. von Ahn, L.: Human Computation. Ph.D. thesis, School of Computer Science, Carnegie Mellon University (2005)
17. Dawid, A.P., Skene, A.M.: Maximum likelihood estimation of observer error-rates using the em algorithm. Applied Statistics **28**(1), 20–28 (1979)
18. Bradley, R.A., Terry, M.E.: The rank analysis of incomplete block designs – I. The method of paired comparisons. Biometrika **39**, 324–345 (1952)
19. Yuen, M.C., King, I., Leung, K.S.: A survey of crowdsourcing systems. In: 2011 IEEE Third International Conference on and 2011 IEEE Third International Conference on Social Computing (socialcom) Privacy, Security, Risk and Trust (passat), pp. 766–773. IEEE (2011)
20. Zhao, Y., Zhu, Q.: Evaluation on crowdsourcing research: Current status and future direction. Information Systems Frontiers, 1–18 (2012)

Web Services Discovery Based on Semantic Tag

Sana Sellami[✉] and Hanane Becha

Aix-Marseille University, CNRS, LSIS UMR 7296, 13397 Marseille, France
sana.sellami@lsis.org, hbecha@gmail.com

Abstract. Recently tagging has been employed to improve the performance of service discovery. Two main challenges have to be addressed when tags are used in Web service discovery: tag relevancy and tag sense disambiguation. In this paper, we present our Web service tagging approach that addresses these problems and describe the results of experiments on a collection of real Web services.

Keywords: Web service discovery · Tag · Semantic

1 Introduction

Nowadays, many software applications are developed by invoking different loosely-coupled services, residing in the network and accessible via standardized protocols. The quality of these applications is highly dependent on the quality of the selected Web services from which they are built; hence, the crucial importance of service discovery mechanisms. Generally, service discovery is performed based on matching the input, output, preconditions and effects of Web services descriptions available in the Universal Description Discovery and Integration (UDDI). Recently, tagging was employed to improve the performance of service discovery. However, the rich semantic information included in the user-contributed tags has many issues that have to be addressed; thus, service discovery techniques can take full advantage of the tagging mechanisms. We address in this paper two main challenges when tags are used in Web service discovery : tag relevancy and tag sense disambiguation. First, to address the tag relevancy issue, we recommend the addition of three parameters to each tag: score, popularity, and occurrence. A score is assigned to each tag to denote the relevance of that tag from the user's perspective. Popularity denotes the relevance of a given tag according to the user's expertise. More weight is given for the most experienced users' tags. Occurrence is the number of times that a given tag was added to the same service. Second, to address the tag sense disambiguation, we use the WordNet dictionary to take into account the synonyms of the tags in the service search.

The remainder of the paper is organized as follows. Section 2 presents our approach. Section 3 is devoted to the experimental results. Section 4 surveys some related works and section 5 concludes the paper.

H. Becha—Please note that the LNCS Editorial assumes that all authors have used the western naming convention, with given names preceding surnames. This determines the structure of the names in the running heads and the author index.

© Springer International Publishing Switzerland 2015
C. Debruyne et al. (Eds.): OTM 2015 Conferences, LNCS 9415, pp. 465–472, 2015.
DOI: 10.1007/978-3-319-26148-5_31

2   Web Services Tagging Approach

The main goal of our approach is to prompt tagging that enables unlimited number of ways to classify Web services. Web services that have several different tags enhance the reusability of services in different contexts and business domains. Ideally, users are encouraged to tag a maximum number of Web services using as many relevant tags as possible. Our approach consists of three main processes: Web services tagging, semantic search of tagged Web services and ranking processes.

2.1   Web Services Tagging

Web service Tagging is the process of describing a resource by assigning some relevant key-words (tags) to it. Users can add a set of tags to each Web service and have the ability to request and select a service by specifying a set of tags.

Users can improve the tag-based service discovery mechanism by assigning new tags to each Web service that they have invoked. The user is empowered to perform service discovery by defining a search request using tags and their associated scores only. A Tagging-based request allows users to describe in a simple and specific manner precisely which services correspond best to their needs by specifying tags. Tagging-based request and tagged services are the two key parameters (i.e., services and request tags) which empower users to select the most relevant services for their request based on tag relevance (i.e., between the tags assigned to services and the tags specified in the user's requests and services). However, one of the tag use limits is the tag relevance. To avoid imprecise tags, users can assign tags only to the services that they have actually invoked. Even though, one can argue that there are no wrong tags, still some tags could be more meaningful or relevant than others with respect to a given service. In order to address the tag relevance problem, users are requested to add a score value to each tag that they add (see Definition 1).

Definition 1 (Tag definition): A tag denoted as Tag(S) is a couple of name and a score: Tag $(S) = (name_{Tag}, score_{Tag})$

where $name_{Tag}$ and $score_{Tag}$ are respectively the name and the score of the tag $score_{Tag} \in [0, 100]$. We define the scores values as described in Table 1.

Table 1. Score values of the tags

Tag label	Tag significance	Score range
Strong	Most relevant Tag	[90-100]
Secondary	Relevant Tag	[60-90]
Weak	The tag is partially relevant	[30-60]
Fail	The tag may be irrelevant	[0-30]

A service could have an unlimited number of tags. Whenever, the same tag has been added more than once, the average of scores is calculated.

2.2 Semantic Search of Web Service

The semantic search process locates the most relevant services according to the user's request by performing a similarity search function. This search function takes a set of tags and their score relevance as inputs to calculate the similarity between tags and their scores (see below Definition 2). Each similarity has a weight assigned to it. The sum of the assigned weight of both similarities is equal to one. During the tag search, sense disambiguation techniques based on the WordNet[1] lexical thesaurus are also applied. In WordNet each term (tag) is a synset and it has a set of synonyms. Once the search is performed, a list of the most relevant services is returned to the user.

Definition 2 (Semantic Tag Similarity): The tag similarity denoted as $Sim_{Tag}(R, S)$, where R is a user request and S a service, is defined as follow:
$$Sim_{Tag}(R, S) = Sim_{score}(TagR, TagS) * W_{score} + Sim_{sem}(TagR, TagS) * W_{sem} \in [0, 1] \text{ Where}$$

- Sim_{score} (TagR, TagS) is a tag similarity between the user's score request and services:
$$Sim_{score}(TagR, TagS) = \frac{|min(Score(|TagR \cap TagSi|))|}{\sum Score(TagR)} \in [0, 1]$$

- Sim_{sem} (TagR, TagS) is semantic similarity between tags. This similarity considers synonym relationships based on WordNet Thesaurus.

$$Sim_{sem}(TagR, TagS) = \frac{|Tag(R) \cap Tag(S)|}{|Tag(R)|} \in [0, 1]$$

- W_{score} and W_{sem} are weight set of the tag score and the semantic similarity, respectively and $W_{score} + W_{sem} = 1$.

2.3 Tagged Web Services Ranking

Semantic similar services are sorted based on users' votes to find the most relevant services. The ranking is based on both the tag similarity and the user's vote (Ve) which considers the user's expertise via a simple quiz to give more weight for tags assigned by most experienced users. The user's vote (Ve) is defined as follows:
$$Ve = \begin{cases} 2 & \text{if user responds correctly to the quiz questions} \\ 1 & \text{if the user makes one mistake} \\ 0 & \text{if mistake} > 1 \end{cases}$$

---

[1] https://wordnet.princeton.edu

Based on user's vote and the occurrence of tag, we can define the most popular tags as follow:

Definition 3 (Tag popularity): Popularity evaluates the relevance of the tag according to the user's expertise. It is the ratio of the number of times that a service was tagged relative (Ve(Si)) to the sum of all the number of the services Votes (Ve(S)).

$$TagPopularity(Si) = \frac{|Ve(Si)|}{\sum Ve(S)}$$

3   Preliminary Evaluation

3.1   Experimental Setup

We performed an evaluation on the precision of the semantic search and Web services ranking in our proposed framework for tagging Web Services called WSTP[2](Web Services Tagging Platform). We considered a collection of 151 Web services from different categories including Stock, Tourism, Weather, Telecommunication, Economy and Finance. This dataset[3] [1] is the one used in the Titan[4] search engine. First, we tag all these Web services with the same tags provided by the Titan search engine. We evaluate the precision of the service retrieval (e.g., the number relevant services among all the retrieved ones) and recall (number of relevant services that are retrieved) measures.

3.2   Experimental Results

Tagged Web Services Search Evaluation: We performed an initial evaluation on the precision of WSTP in retrieving relevant Web services. We focused on two categories: Tourism which includes several tagged services and Stock which contains a few tagged services, viz.23% of services (see Table 2). We performed two different query searches: a simple tag (stock:100) and a combination of most frequent tags (e.g., stock:100 company:100).

As illustrated in Fig. 1, precision values are the same regardless of the query tag searches. WSTP returned only tagged Web services which contain the queried tag. We notice the increasing of recall values when we use a combination of tags. The more tags associated to a service, the greater the probability to retrieve relevant services, this validates our assumption.

We performed the precision and recall evaluation of WSTP according to two categories (Fig. 2). We can observe that the recall value is higher for the search on the Tourism category than for the Stock category. The reason for this was that the Tourism category has 79% of Web services tagged whereas only 23% were tagged in the Stock category.

---

[2] http://www.lsis.org/sellamis/Projects.html
[3] http://www.zjujason.com/data.html
[4] http://ccnt.zju.edu.cn:8080/

Table 2. Tagged Web services characteristics

Categories	Number of services	Number of tagged Web services	Ratio
Tourism	39	31	79%
Stock	39	9	23%

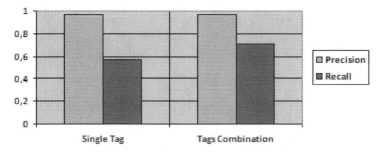

Fig. 1. Precision and Recall of WSTP according to the tag queries

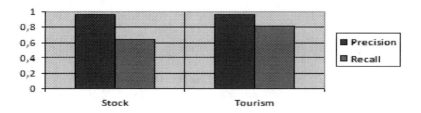

Fig. 2. Precision and Recall of WSTP according to the domains

Search Engine Ranking: We compared the WSTP results with those of the Titan Search engine to evaluate ranking procedure. Our hypothesis is that the first returned services are the most relevant ones according to the user request. Then, we executed the same request in both the WSTP and Titan search engines and we compared the obtained results by using the Normalized Discounted Cumulative Gain (NDCG) as defined below: Given the ideal search ranking (used as baseline) and a predicted search ranking, the NDCG value of Top-k search services can be calculated by:

$$NDCG@k= \frac{DCG@k}{IDCG@k'}$$

Where DCG@k and IDCG@k are the discounted cumulative gain (DCG) values of the top-k services of the predicted ranking and ideal ranking, respectively. The discounted CG (DCG) accumulated is defined as:

$$DCG@k=rel1+ \sum_{i=2}^{p} \frac{reli}{log_2(i)}$$

Where rel_i is the graded relevance of the result at position i.

Experimental results (see Table 3) showed that our system produced the same search results for the Tourism category that were obtained by Titan. However, for the Stock category WSTP does not perform as well. This occurs because only 23% of the Web services are tagged in the Stock category. Moreover, it is interesting to underline that, if we change the search tag tourism with touristy (which is the synonym of tourism); WSTP returns all the results corresponding to the tourism, while Titan does not return any results for this query. Compared to Titan, WSTP offers a semantic search service based on the WordNet thesaurus and thus, it provides a better visualization and browsing of services based on links. Moreover, WSTP displays better results than Titan when we combine different tags of services. However, WSTP could be improved to better process queries by considering n-gram, prefix and suffix techniques, etc.

4   Related Work

Several Web services tagging approaches have been proposed in the literature. We discuss those that rely on tag identification and tag relevance. Mining approaches clustering algorithms have been applied to assign tags to Web services [3], [4],[5], [6]. For example, the authors in [3] applied clustering techniques to extract tags from WSDL documents and consider both structural and lexical information of text segments. Tags are then generated automatically. However, their approach highly depends on the WSDL description of Web services and does not consider other description languages. The approach in [5] uses a clustering technique based on Carrot search clustering and K-means to group similar services to generate tags. The authors also proposed the use of naive bayes algorithm to rank Web services and recommend WSDL services based on tags. The second category of approaches is those that deal with tag relevance. The approach proposed in [2] handles the problem of imprecise, irrelevant and malicious tags and it considers the tag relevance for Web service mining. This approach is based on a mechanism called WS-TRM to measure the relevance of user tag. It considers both semantic tag relevance and the relationship in Service Tag Network (STNet). The tag relevance is computed by evaluating the semantic relevance between each tag and the WSDL document of the corresponding service. Semantic relevance considers both syntactic and structural relations between

Table 3. NDCG@K performance of tagged Web services ranking

NDCG@K	Tool	Stock	Tourism
K=3	WSTP	0.70	0.87
	Titan	0.74	0.87
K=5	WSTP	0.68	0.85
	Titan	0.72	0.85

tags and WSDL elements. In [7] the authors propose a system for semantic collaborative tagging APIs to be deployed in a ProgrammableWeb[5]. The approach addresses the polysemy and homonyms problems and takes into account a social characterization of Web APIs that considers the past experiences of Web designers. However, in ProgrammableWeb, tags are only assigned to the source code of APIs and the APIs themselves are not tagged. Moreover, most of the published APIs do not contain code source support and tags are assigned according to the second category of the service. Service search is then based on category traversal search which is expensive when there are thousands of services. To handle the problem of limited tags, Azmeh et al. [8] propose to employ machine learning technology and WordNet synsets to automatically assign tags to Web services. In this paper, the authors propose an approach that automatically generates a set of relevant tags from a WSDL service description. Similar to our approach, authors in [9] propose a collaborative tagging system for Web service discovery. Tags are labels that a user can associate to a specific Web service and for each tag, a tag weight is assigned. A tag weight is the count of number of occurrences of a specific tag associated to a Web service. Unlike existing approaches, our approach is technology agnostic and it is not tied to the Web Service description language WSDL. Moreover, our approach has been implemented, evaluated on a real collection of Web services, and demonstrated to perform better results.

5   Conclusion and Future Works

In this paper, we described a Web services discovery approach based on a semantic tag that addresses tag relevancy and tag sense disambiguation. The approach has been implemented and tested against a collection of real Web services. In the future, we plan to enhance the semantic services search by enabling querying of LOD (Linked Open Data) like DBpedia[6] and interacting with the Programmable Web to retrieve information on Web APIs from the repository. With this enhancement we will be able to provide a platform for linked services based not only on tag similarities but also on mashups and category links.

References

1. Chen, L., Wang, Y., Yu, Q., Zheng, Z., Wu, J.: WT-LDA: User tagging augmented LDA for web service clustering. In: Basu, S., Pautasso, C., Zhang, L., Fu, X. (eds.) ICSOC 2013. LNCS, vol. 8274, pp. 162–176. Springer, Heidelberg (2013)
2. Chen, L., Wu, J., Zheng, Z., Lyu, M.R., Wu, Z.: Modeling and exploiting tag relevance for Web service mining. Knowl. Inf. Syst. **39**, 153–173 (2014)
3. Fang, L., Wang, L., Li, M., Zhao, J., Zou, Y., Shao, L.: Towards automatic tagging for web services. In: 2012 IEEE 19th International Conference on Web Service, pp. 528–535 (2012)

---

[5] http://www.programmableweb.com/

[6] http://wiki.dbpedia.org/

4. Kapitsaki, G.M.: Annotating web service sections with combined classification. In: Proceedings of the 21th IEEE International Conference on Web Services (ICWS), pp. 622–629 (2014)
5. Lin, M., Cheung, D.W.: Automatic tagging web services using machine learning techniques. In: International Joint Conferences on Web Intelligence (WI) and Intelligent Agent Technologies (IAT), pp. 258–265 (2014)
6. Pan, W., Chen, S., Feng, Z.: Automatic Clustering of Social Tag using Community Detection. Applied Mathematics & Information Sciences **7**(2), 675 (2013)
7. Bianchini, D., De Antonellis, V., Melchiori, M.: Semantic collaborative tagging for web APIs sharing and reuse. In: Brambilla, M., Tokuda, T., Tolksdorf, R. (eds.) ICWE 2012. LNCS, vol. 7387, pp. 76–90. Springer, Heidelberg (2012)
8. Azmeh, Z., Falleri, J.-R., Huchard, M., Tibermacine, C.: Automatic web service tagging using machine learning and wordNet synsets. In: Filipe, J., Cordeiro, J. (eds.) WEBIST 2010. LNBIP, vol. 75, pp. 46–59. Springer, Heidelberg (2011)
9. Chukmol, U., Benharkat, A., Amghar, Y.: An approach for web service discovery based on collaborative structured tagging. In: Proceedings of the 12th International Conference on Enterprise Information Systems ICEIS, pp. 47–56 (2010)

A Model for Identifying Misinformation in Online Social Networks

Sotirios Antoniadis[1], Iouliana Litou[2(✉)], and Vana Kalogeraki[2]

[1] Nokia Solutions and Networks Hellas A.E., Athens, Greece
sotiris.antoniadis@nsn.com
[2] Deptartment of Informatics,
Athens University of Economics and Business, Athens, Greece
{litou,vana}@aueb.gr

Abstract. Online Social Networks (OSNs) have become increasingly popular means of information sharing among users. The spread of news regarding emergency events is common in OSNs and so is the spread of misinformation related to the event. We define as misinformation any false or inaccurate information that is spread either intentionally or unintentionally. In this paper we study the problem of misinformation identification in OSNs, and we focus in particular on the Twitter social network. Based on user and tweets characteristics, we build a misinformation detection model that identifies suspicious behavioral patterns and exploits supervised learning techniques to detect misinformation. Our extensive experimental results on 80294 unique tweets and 59660 users illustrate that our approach effectively identifies misinformation during emergencies. Furthermore, our model manages to timely identify misinformation, a feature that can be used to limit the spread of the misinformation.

1 Introduction

Online Social Networks (OSNs) have evolved into major means of communication and information spreading. They enumerate over 1.61 billion users, which corresponds to 22% of the world's population. However, one major challenge is that the information communicated through the network is not always credible. Previous studies confirm the existence of *spam campaigns* in OSNs [1][2]. Spam campaigns are organized attempts towards spreading false or malicious content through the coordination of accounts or other illicit means in the network. It is estimated that, among the messages published on Twitter, 1% of the messages is spam while 5% of the accounts are spammers[1].

Twitter[2] has evolved as one of the most popular microblogging services. Users publish short messages (*tweets*) of at most 140 characters and follow any other

---

S. Antoniadis—Part of this work was performed when this author was at Athens University of Economics and Business.

[1] http://digital.cs.usu.edu/ kyumin/tutorial/www-tutorial.pdf
[2] https://twitter.com/

© Springer International Publishing Switzerland 2015
C. Debruyne et al. (Eds.): OTM 2015 Conferences, LNCS 9415, pp. 473–482, 2015.
DOI: 10.1007/978-3-319-26148-5_32

registered users to receive status updates. Twitter offers to users the opportunity to report a tweet as *spam, compromised* or *abusive*. Other filters to detect spam (e.g the number of followers in regard to followees, random favorites and retweets etc.) are also used. Still, tweets containing misinformation regarding an emergency event may not be identified based solely on the aforementioned mechanisms.

The credibility of images propagated in the network has been the focus of recent work. Zubiaga and Ji [3] and Gupta et al. [4] focus on the credibility of images propagated in the network during emergency events but not in the content of the information. The works closest to ours is that of Castillo et al. [5] and Xia et al. [6]. Both works use supervised learning and Bayesian Network classification to identify credible information propagated in the network. Castillo et al. [5] cluster the instances to newsworthy or chats and later perform credibility analysis on the newsworthy clusters. Xia et al. [6] propose a model to detect an emergency event and identify credible tweets. As we illustrate in our experimental evaluation, our approach performs better than both approaches in identifying misinformative tweets with over 14% higher accuracy.

In this work we suggest a methodology for identifying and limiting misinformation spread in OSNs during emergency events by identifying tweets that are most likely to be inaccurate or irrelevant to an event. Our work makes the following contributions:

- We present a novel filtering process for identifying misinformation during emergencies that is fast and effective. The filters are identified based on an extensive analysis conducted on a large dataset of users and tweets related to the emergency event of Hurricane Sandy. As our experimental results illustrate, the filtering process extracts over 81% of the misinformative tweets, while identifying over 23% of the tweets that contain misinformation.
- We employ a number of supervised learning algorithms that very effectively classify credible or misinformative tweets. Based on the features we propose, classification techniques achieve weighted average accuracy of 77%.
- Our experiments suggest that without considering propagation of tweets, our classification methodology achieves 77.8% weighted average accuracy, offering the ability to timely limit the spread of false news before cascading. Furthermore, the filtering process and the classification algorithms perform in less than 2 seconds, making our methodology appropriate for real-time applications.

2   Problem Description, Parameters and Methodology

Several studies reveal that news spread faster in the network of Twitter compared to traditional news media [7,8]. Yet, a fundamental challenge is the quality of content published in OSNs. Distinguishing between credible and inaccurate information regarding emergency events is important, since misguidance or inability to timely detect useful information may have critical effects.

Fig. 1. Example of misinformation for Hurricane Sandy.

Objective: The objective of our work is to detect misinformation related to emergency events in the Twitter social network. We define as *misinformation* any false or inaccurate information that is spread either intentionally or unintentionally. An example of misinformation concerning the event of Sandy hurricane is presented in Figure 1.

Our Approach: Our approach for solving the problem of misinformation identification follows 3 discrete steps: (i) Given a set of tweets T related to an event and a set of users U that published at least one tweet $t \in T$, we conduct an extensive analysis on characteristics of tweets and users who published them. Our analysis focuses on a number of features and combinations of them and assists in identifying abnormal behaviors of users and characteristics of tweets. (ii) Based on the findings of the analysis, we extract extreme or suspicious behaviors and exploit them to filter tweets that are more likely to constitute misinformation. (iii) We then apply a series of learning algorithms implemented on Weka [9] to identify misinformative tweets, using supervised learning techniques.

2.1   Parameters

Tweet Features: Each tweet $t \in T$ is represented as a feature vector I_t that includes information about the tweet and the user who published it. Thus, each tweet $t \in T$ is characterized by the following information: **(i)** *Number of characters - words:* Short messages may not contain useful information, while long messages may cover unrelated topics. **(ii)** *Number of favorites - retweets - replies:* The popularity of a tweet may be an indication of its content. We expect that tweets of interest will be cascaded in the network and thus be more retweeted or favorited. **(iv)** *Number of mentions - hashtags - URLs - media:* Features related to the structure of the tweet are considered to draw conclusions about the quality of the tweet.

User Features: For each user $u \in U$ that published at least one tweet $t \in T$ we consider the following characteristics: **(i)** *Number of followers - followees:* Trustworthy users such as news agencies are expected to have many followers [7], while spammers may have more followees. We define as followees the number of users an account follows. **(ii)** *Followers-Followees Ratio (FF-Ratio):* We compute the FF-Ratio of a user u as $FF\_Ratio = followers(u)/(followers(u) + followees(u))$. **(iii)** *Total tweets - Tweets during the event:* We suspect illegitimate users may be more active for a short time (e.g. the time of the event), thus we also consider the number of tweets users publish. **(iv)** *Days Registered:* The days the user is registered in the network before publishing a tweet. Recent users have greater chances of being spammers in contrast to older ones.

Additional Features: Finally, for each tweet we extract the following set of features: **(i)** *URLs to Tweets (UtT) - Media to Tweets (MtT):* For tweets published by a user we compute the ratio of tweets containing URLs and Media separately. We suspect that users frequently publishing URLs are candidate spammers, while media may be irrelevant to the event. **(ii)** *Followers to Replies (FtR) - Retweets (FtRt) - Favorited (FtFav):* Less popular tweets may indicate disapproval from followers. Therefore we consider the ratio of followers to the features indicating the popularity. **(iii)** *Average Tweets per Day (ATpD):* The average number of tweets published by user u that is registered $d\_a(u)$ days in the network is computed as $ATpD = t(u)/d\_a(u)$, where $t(u)$ is the total number tweets u published. **(iv)** *Positive / Negative / Average Sentiment:* We use SentiStrength [10] to extract the positive and negative sentiment rate of the tweet text and compute the average sentiment.

3   Data Analysis

In order to evaluate the performance of our approach for detecting misinformation during emergency events we used a dataset of tweets related to the Sandy Hurricane, a major emergency event that unfolded in 2012, from October 22 to November 2, and severely affected the area of New York City [3]. Tweets related to the event were collected based on the keywords "sandy" and "hurricane", as described in [3]. We then use the findings of the analysis to decide which values constitute a possible indication of misinformation.

Analysis of User Characteristics: In Figures 2 and 3 we present the number of tweets published by users, both total and during the event. We split the number of tweets in buckets of 100, i.e., bucket 0 contains the number of users that published 1 to 99 tweets in total. The Power Low distribution shown in the Figures is in accordance to findings of Bagrow *et al.* in [7]. Most of the users

---

[3] http://en.wikipedia.org/wiki/Hurricane_Sandy

published tweets related to the event with a frequency of 60 to 1000 seconds, while there are users that published more than one tweet per minute. The number of users' followers and followees are presented in Figures 4 and 5 respectively. The trend is similar for both connection types, with the majority of users having few followers and followees. The peak in the number of users that have up to 2000 followees is due to Twitter policy that limits the users to follow up to 2000 users and is later differentiated based on the followers to followees fraction. In Figure 6 we also present the FF-Ratio. The FF-Ratio approaches a Gaussian distribution with most users having an average ratio of around 0.5, meaning that they have equal amount of followers and followees, although we can observe another peak from 0.9 to 1.

Analysis of Tweet Characteristics: In Figure 7 we present an analysis of the number of words contained in a tweet. The majority of the tweets include 20 to 120 characters and 5 to 20 words. We further consider retweets, favorites and replies of a tweet to determine its popularity. As observed in Figures 8 and 9, the number of retweets and favorites follows a power law distribution. Finally, most of the tweets have fewer than 20 replies, but after a point the tweets containing more than

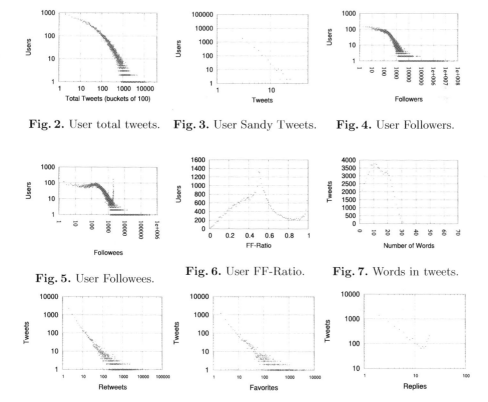

Fig. 2. User total tweets.   **Fig. 3.** User Sandy Tweets.   **Fig. 4.** User Followers.

Fig. 5. User Followees.   **Fig. 6.** User FF-Ratio.   **Fig. 7.** Words in tweets.

Fig. 8. Retweets received by tweets.   **Fig. 9.** Favorites received by tweets.   **Fig. 10.** Replies received by tweets.

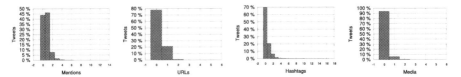

Fig. 11. Tweets with mentions. **Fig. 12.** Tweets with URLs. **Fig. 13.** Tweets with hashtags. **Fig. 14.** Tweets with media.

20 replies rises (Figure 10). Figures 11 through 14 depict the number of mentions, URLs, hastags and media presented in a tweet. Most of the tweets contain at most one mentions and the majority of the tweets related to the event contain no link, while there are tweets with over two links. 70% of the tweets contain no hashtags, while the number of tweets containing a media is restricted to less than 10%.

4   Experimental Evaluation

We evaluated the performance of our approach on 80294 tweets related to hurricane Sandy from 59660 users. In the first set of experiments we focus on estimating the performance of the filtering process. By applying the filters of Table 1, 12955 tweets are returned. We manually annotate a sample of 4000 randomly selected tweets among them. Humorous, irrelevant and deleted tweets and accounts are considered as misinformation (assuming they are reported or deleted due to violations [11]). For 176 of the tweets we could not draw conclusions. Out of the remaining 3824 tweets, 898 constitute misinformation. Since tweets are randomly selected, we conclude that over 23% of the filtered tweets are indeed misinformation. We also annotated 4000 random tweets among those that did not meet the filtering criteria. For the 3559 tweets that could be classified, 212 are identified as misinformation, i.e., less than 6%. Overall, 1110 out the total 7383 labelled tweets constitute misinformation. The filtering process captures 898, yielding recall values of over 81%.

Supervised Learning: We exploited a set of different supervised learning algorithms implemented on Weka [9] to evaluate the performance of information identification on the set of features we considered. We use 10-fold cross validation for evaluating the classification results. The labelled dataset of the 3824 filtered tweets is used as input to Weka. In Table 2 we present the classification results. Weighted Average F1 measure indicates that Bootstrap Aggregating has the best performance. Regarding average precision, Random Forest achieves better results, with 0.792 average precision.

Table 1. Filters applied during the filtering process.

Words ≥ 30	Characters $== 140$	Favorites $(\geq 2 \ \&\& \ \leq 10) \ \| \ (\geq 1100)$
Hashtags ≥ 4	Mentions ≥ 4	Retweets $((\geq 2 \ \&\& \ \leq 10) \ \| \ (\geq 1000))$
Media ≥ 2	Followees $(\leq 10 \ \| \ \geq 100000)$	Followers $(\leq 10 \ \| \ \geq 200000)$
Replies ≥ 11	URLs ≥ 3	Followers/Followees ≥ 30000
Event tweets ≥ 7	Total Tweets ≥ 500000	Interval $(\leq 300sec \ \| \ \geq 70000sec)$

Table 2. Summary of Classification using Supervised Learning Algorithms.

	Precision	Recall	F-Measure	Precision	Recall	F-Measure
	Bayes Network			**J48**		
Credible	0,845	0,834	0,839	0,825	0,889	0,856
Misinformation	0,480	0,500	0,490	0,516	0,385	0,44
Weighted Avg.	0,759	0,755	0,757	0,752	0,771	0,758
	k-Nearest Neighbors			**Random Forest**		
Credible	0,800	0,951	0,869	0,821	0,958	0,884
Misinformation	0,586	0,225	0,325	0,699	0,318	0,438
Weighted Avg.	0,750	0,781	0,741	0,792	0,808	0,779
	Adaptive Boosting			**Bootstrap Aggregating**		
Credible	0,839	0,888	0,863	0,828	0,931	0,877
Misinformation	0,549	0,447	0,493	0,622	0,372	0,466
Weighted Avg.	0,771	0,784	0,776	0,780	0,799	0,780

Real-Time Misinformation Identification: The values of retweets, favorites and replies are unknown at the time the tweet is published. Thus, to evaluate the performance of our approach in timely detecting misinformation we conducted another set of experiments ignoring the above attributes and features related to them. The results for Bootstrap Aggregating and Random Forest are presented in Table 3. The table shows that precision and recall drop slightly. Still, weighted average precision is over 0.77, indicating the approach is appropriate for real time misinformation identification. The filtering process requires just 963ms and adding the execution times of the algorithms, less than 2 seconds are needed to efficiently extract tweets containing misinformation, proving that the method is efficient under real-time constraints.

Table 3. Classification with features known at run time.

	Precision	Recall	F-Measure	Precision	Recall	F-Measure
	Random Forest			**Bootstrap Aggregating**		
Credible	0,812	0,949	0,875	0,816	0,951	0,879
Misinformation	0,631	0,286	0,394	0,655	0,301	0,412
Weighted Avg.	0,770	0,793	0,762	0,778	0,799	0,769
Execution time:	0.41 sec			0.89 sec		

5   Related Work

Castillo et al. [5] aim at automatically detecting credibility of information in the network of Twitter. They use a number of features related to tweets and supervised learning to distinguish between newsworthy or false news and later perform credibility analysis. Gupta et al. [12] present TweetCred, an extension of the previous work that enables users feedback. Xia et al. [6] also study the problem of information credibility on Twitter after the event is detected and relevant tweets are retrieved. Bosma et el. [13] suggest a framework for spam detection using unsupervised learning. Anagnostopoulos et al. [14] study the role of homophily in misinformation spread. McCord and Chuah [15] are using traditional classifiers to detect spams on Twitter. Stringhini et al. in [11] aim at identifying spammers in social networks. Identifying spammers on the network of Twitter is also the objective of Benevenuto et al. in [16]. They extract features of the account that may be indication of spamming behavior and use SVM learning model to verify their approach. Zubiaga and Ji in [3] and Gupta et al. [4] focus on the credibility of images propagated in the network during emergency events. They consider a number of features related to the image and the tweet. Budak et al. [17] address the problem of misinformation spread limitation by performing an extensive study on influence limitation. Faloutsos [18] developed a botnet-detection method and a Facebook application, called MyPageKeeper, that quantifies the presence of malware on Facebook and protects end-users. Ghosh et al. [19] examine suspended accounts on Twitter and investigate link farming and finally discourage spammers to acquire large number of following links. Thomas et al. [1] identify the behaviors of spammers by analyzing tweets of suspended users in retrospect. Mendoza et al. [20] focus on cascades of tweets during emergency events and study the propagation of rumours. They conclude that this defers from the propagation of news tweets and it is possible to detect rumors by aggregating analysis on the tweets. Liu et al. [21] propose a hybrid model that utilizes user behavior information, network attributes and text content to identify spams.

6   Conclusions

In this work we presented a methodology for identifying misinformation on social networks during emergency events. As we illustrate in our experiments our approach manages to correctly identify misinformation achieving accuracy of up to 77%. The filtering process suggested in this work identifies over 81% of misinformative tweets. Our approach is fast and effective and timely identifies misinformation, offering the ability to limit the spread in the network.

Acknowledgment. This research has been co-financed by the European Union (European Social Fund ESF) and Greek national funds through the Operational Program "Education and Lifelong Learning" of the National Strategic Reference Framework (NSRF) - Research Funding Program:Thalis-DISFER, Aristeia-MMD, Investing in knowledge society through the European Social Fund, the FP7 INSIGHT project and the ERC IDEAS NGHCS project.

References

1. Thomas, K., Grier, C., Song, D., Paxson, V.: Suspended accounts in retrospect: an analysis of twitter spam. In: Internet Measurement Conference, pp. 243–258 (2011)
2. Gao, H., Hu, J., Wilson, C., Li, Z., Chen, Y., Zhao, B.Y.: Detecting and characterizing social spam campaigns. In: ACM Conference on Computer and Communications Security, pp. 681–683 (2010)
3. Zubiaga, A., Ji, H.: Tweet, but verify: Epistemic study of information verification on twitter (2013). CoRR, vol. abs/1312.5297
4. Gupta, A., Lamba, H., Kumaraguru, P., Joshi, A.: Faking sandy: characterizing and identifying fake images on twitter during hurricane sandy. In: Ser. WWW 2013 Companion (2013)
5. Castillo, C., Mendoza, M., Poblete, B.: Predicting information credibility in time-sensitive social media. Internet Research **23**(5), 560–588 (2013)
6. Xia, X., Yang, X., Wu, C., Li, S., Bao, L.: Information credibility on twitter in emergency situation. In: Chau, M., Wang, G.A., Yue, W.T., Chen, H. (eds.) PAISI 2012. LNCS, vol. 7299, pp. 45–59. Springer, Heidelberg (2012)
7. Bagrow, J.P., Wang, D., Barabasi, A.-L.: Collective response of human populations to large-scale emergencies (2011). CoRR, vol. abs/1106.0560
8. Guy, M., Earle, P., Ostrum, C., Gruchalla, K., Horvath, S.: Integration and dissemination of citizen reported and seismically derived earthquake information via social network technologies. In: Cohen, P.R., Adams, N.M., Berthold, M.R. (eds.) IDA 2010. LNCS, vol. 6065, pp. 42–53. Springer, Heidelberg (2010)
9. Weka. http://www.cs.waikato.ac.nz/ml/weka/
10. Thelwall, M., Buckley, K., Paltoglou, G., Cai, D., Kappas, A.: Sentiment in short strength detection informal text. J. Am. Soc. Inf. Sci. Technol. **61**(12), 2544–2558 (2010)
11. Stringhini, G., Kruegel, C., Vigna, G.: Detecting spammers on social networks. In: ACSAC, pp. 1–9 (2010)
12. Gupta, A., Kumaraguru, P., Castillo, C., Meier, P.: Tweetcred: real-time credibility assessment of content on twitter. In: Aiello, L.M., McFarland, D. (eds.) SocInfo 2014. LNCS, vol. 8851, pp. 228–243. Springer, Heidelberg (2014)
13. Bosma, M., Meij, E., Weerkamp, W.: A framework for unsupervised spam detection in social networking sites. In: Baeza-Yates, R., de Vries, A.P., Zaragoza, H., Cambazoglu, B.B., Murdock, V., Lempel, R., Silvestri, F. (eds.) ECIR 2012. LNCS, vol. 7224, pp. 364–375. Springer, Heidelberg (2012)
14. Anagnostopoulos, A., Bessi, A., Caldarelli, G., Vicario, M.D., Petroni, F., Scala, A., Zollo, F., Quattrociocchi, W.: Viral misinformation: The role of homophily and polarization (2014). CoRR, vol. abs/1411.2893
15. McCord, M., Chuah, M.: Spam detection on twitter using traditional classifiers. In: Calero, J.M.A., Yang, L.T., Mármol, F.G., García Villalba, L.J., Li, A.X., Wang, Y. (eds.) ATC 2011. LNCS, vol. 6906, pp. 175–186. Springer, Heidelberg (2011)
16. Benevenuto, F., Magno, G., Rodrigues, T., Almeida, V.: Detecting spammers on twitter. In: CEAS (2010)
17. Budak, C., Agrawal, D.: Abbadi, A.E.: Limiting the spread of misinformation in social networks. In: WWW, pp. 665–674 (2011)
18. Faloutsos, M.: Detecting malware with graph-based methods: traffic classification, botnets, and facebook scams. In: WWW (Companion Volume), pp. 495–496 (2013)

19. Ghosh, S., Viswanath, B., Kooti, F., Sharma, N.K., Korlam, G., Benevenuto, F., Ganguly, N., Gummadi, P.K.: Understanding and combating link farming in the twitter social network. In: WWW, pp. 61–70 (2012)
20. Mendoza, M., Poblete, B., Castillo, C.: Twitter under crisis: can we trust what we rt? In: Proceedings of the First Workshop on Social Media Analytics, ser. SOMA 2010, pp. 71–79. ACM, New York (2010)
21. Liu, Y., Wu, B., Wang, B., Li, G.: Sdhm: a hybrid model for spammer detection in weibo. In: 2014 IEEE/ACM International Conference on ASONAM, pp. 942–947, August 2014

Traceability of Tightly Coupled Phases of Semantic Data Warehouse Design

Selma Khouri[1,2]([⊠]) and Ladjel Bellatreche[2]

[1] National Computer Science Engineering School (ESI), Algeria, France
selma.khouri@ensma.fr
[2] LIAS/ISAE-ENSMA – Poitiers University, Poitiers, France
bellatreche@ensma.fr

Abstract. Ontologies have largely contributed in designing and exploiting decision systems. This is due to their ability to capture the semantics of design artifacts. Note that the design process of Data warehouses ($\mathcal{DW}$) projects involves several important and *tightly coupled* steps, where each step is permanently changing and evolving to satisfy the new requirements offered by the technology progress. Passing from one phase to another requires important and heavy processes and decisions made by design actors. These decisions are usually lost once the warehouse is built. Tracing these decisions is a challenging issue. In this paper, we propose to study the tractability management in the context of semantic data warehouses. We claim that the presence of ontologies can be an asset for the traceability, since the ontology can semantically define the design artifacts and their transformations during the whole cycle. To do so, we propose an approach for semantic data warehouse tractability that requires: (i) the formalization of each design phase and (ii) the identification and storage of horizontal interactions (inside the phase) and vertical interactions (between phases). The approach is illustrated using LUBM benchmark. It is implemented in a case tool assisting the designer for managing the $\mathcal{DW}$ traceability.

Keywords: $\mathcal{DW}$ traceability · Ontology-based approach · Design life-cycle

1 Introduction

Data warehouses ($\mathcal{DW}$) are central repositories used for supporting decisional analysis in companies and organizations. Designing a $\mathcal{DW}$ system is a complex task which requires various *resources, actors, software applications* and *design artifacts*. As any database application software, $\mathcal{DW}$s have a well identified life cycle including five main phases [10]: requirements definition, conceptual design, Extract-Transform-Load (ETL), logical design, deployment and physical design. Three main particularities characterize these phases: (i) each phase is complex, time consuming and it uses its own modeling languages, tools, etc. For instance, in the conceptual phase, the designer may choose UML as her/his favorite modeling language, and Rational Rose as her/his tool. As a consequence, a $\mathcal{DW}$

C. Debruyne et al. (Eds.): OTM 2015 Conferences, LNCS 9415, pp. 483–500, 2015.
DOI: 10.1007/978-3-319-26148-5_33

product can be seen as a chain of phase's instances. (ii) The inputs of one phase are the outputs to another, this phenomenon is called *sequential cohesive*. (iii) Different dependencies are present between the phases, this situation is called *tightly coupling of the phases*. Actually, many recent studies demonstrate this tight coupling by indicating the importance of expliciting hidden links between adjacent and nonadjacent design phases [2,4,12,20]. The fact that these steps are sequential cohesive and tightly coupled requires important and heavy processes and decisions to pass from one phase to another. To reduce the complexity of these phases and to leverage their semantics at conceptual and exploitation levels, several research studies proposed the use of ontologies. Contrary to traditional databases, where ontologies have mainly contributed in the conceptual phase, in the $\mathcal{DW}$ context, they contributed in the majority of the steps [1]. More concretely, ontologies have been used to assign semantic to data sources [7], to formalize requirements definition [17], to identify multidimensional concepts [16] and to automate the ETL process [19]. The strong presence of ontologies in the life cycle of the $\mathcal{DW}$ construction gives raise a new type of warehouse called semantic $\mathcal{DW}$, denoted by $\mathcal{SDW}$.

The $\mathcal{DW}$ technology is ever evolving to deal with changes and pressures for BI today[1]. These evolutions are motivated by two aspects: (i) the new requirements of today's BI environments for managing: the data deluge, the augmentation of $\mathcal{DW}$ users, the diversity of data and of data sources, the presence of complex and dynamic queries and the presence of mixed workloads. (ii) The diversity of design alternatives including many storage layouts (Row Store, Column Store, Hybrid, etc.), deployment platforms (Cloud infrastructures, HPC clusters, etc.) and emerging hardwares (GPU, APU, FPGA). This situation motivates companies and organizations owning $\mathcal{DW}$ technology to tune one instance or several instances of phases to obtain a new implementation of the warehouse, in order to migrate from one $\mathcal{DW}$ configuration to another one. To facilitate this migration, tracing the life of design artifacts is one of the issue that has to be explored [21]. Managing traceability is an important challenge for $\mathcal{DW}$ design, mainly for: the validation of requirements, the management of source and requirements evolution, the support of change propagation, decision support about alternative implementations and more generally for supporting the quality management of the $\mathcal{DW}$ system [15,21]. Actually, many quality standards such as IEEE Std. 1219, ISO 9000ff, ISO 15504 (SPICE), and SEI CMM/CMMI, recommend traceability as an attribute of software quality [21]. Due to the special idiosyncrasy of semantic $\mathcal{DW}$ development, a traceability approach specifically tailored to face several challenges is required [14,15]. We claim that the presence of ontologies can be an asset for the traceability, since the ontology can semantically define the design artifacts and their transformations during the whole cycle. Studying traceability in the context of $\mathcal{SDW}$s needs an understanding of whole phases of the life cycle. Figure 1 illustrates the design process of a typical $\mathcal{SDW}$. A consensual domain ontology schema (supposed existing) defining the domain of interest is used. A set of sources

---

[1] ftp://ftp.software.ibm.com/software/uk/itsolutions/leveraginginformation/ ever_evolving_data_warehouse.pdf

and a set of users' requirements are considered as inputs. The sources (traditional and semantic[2].) are linked to the domain ontology using defined mappings. The requirements definition phase analyzes the requirements from data sources and from users' requirements. The conceptual design phase defines an implementation-independent and expressive conceptual schema for the warehouse according to a conceptual design model. This schema is usually defined as a fragment of the domain ontology after matching sources and requirements to this ontology. The obtained ontology is called the $\mathcal{DW}$ ontology ($\mathcal{DWO}$). Its schema is defined using a multidimensional view that identifies the *Fact* concepts, which are central concepts to analyze and the *Dimension* concepts representing perspectives of analyzing the facts. The ETL phase includes three steps: the extraction of data from operational sources, their transformation and their loading into the target $\mathcal{DWO}$ schema. This process is based on the mappings assertions defined between sources and the target schema. The logical design phase includes the matching between the conceptual and logical model using some translation rules, and the derivation of a corresponding logical schema. The logical schema can be defined using different layouts like relational, object, Nosql, etc. The deployment phase includes the choice of the platform managing the final warehouse (centralized machine, cloud, database cluster, etc.). The physical design phase includes the implementation of the $\mathcal{DW}$ schema and the selection of relevant optimization techniques such as index schemes. Passing from one phase to another requires important and heavy processes and decisions. This passage is usually performed using rules/mappings. To establish a rule, we need to know the instance of the current and next phases. The traceability process has to store the instances of phases and their corresponding mappings. In the literature, traceability in the context of $\mathcal{DW}$s has been studied by considering at most two phases. These studies ignore the tight coupling of the design life cycle phases. Additionally, the traced links are not explicitly defined in existing approaches. The availability of the ontology is priceless for managing traceability because the ontology can define semantically and consensually (by domain experts) the design artifacts and their transformations during the whole life-cycle.

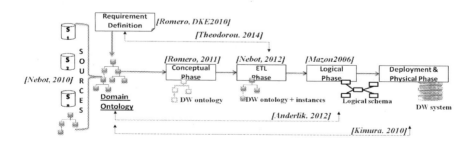

Fig. 1. Semantic $\mathcal{DW}$ design process

---

[2] A semantic source is a source having its own ontology.

This paper is organized as follows: section 2 presents a motivating example. Section 3 presents the main concepts related to traceability in software products in general, then in $\mathcal{DW}$ context. Section 4 presents the $\mathcal{SDW}$ design cycle formalization framework. Section 5 illustrates the proposed traceability approach. Section 6 presents the implementation of the approach. Section 7 concludes the paper and sketches some future works.

2 Motivating Example

In order to illustrate our proposal, let us define the following example that will be used in the implementation section. The study uses LUBM benchmark, which consists of a university domain ontology (named Univ-Bench ontology[3]), customizable and repeatable synthetic data and a set of test queries. We consider the test queries as the set of user's requirements. These requirements have been adapted in order to illustrate decisional requirements. The benchmark provides the Data Generator tool (UBA) used to create OWL data over the Univ-Bench ontology. Semantic sources are populated locally with data using UBA tool. We chose Oracle semantic database system to implement the sources and the DW. Each source schema is defined as a fragment of Univ-Bench ontology schema. The $\mathcal{DW}$ ontology is populated using a defined ETL process, based on some defined mappings. The consistency of these mappings must be managed by the designer. ETL processes are defined in literature as workflows. Each ETL workflow defines an ordered sequence of ETL operations that are applied to some input elements. Figure 2 presents an example of the ETL workflow used to populate the $\mathcal{DW}$ Lecturer concept from Lecturer concepts of Sources S1 and S2.

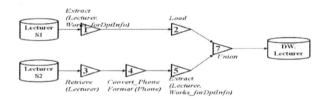

Fig. 2. ETL Workflows example

The target $\mathcal{DW}$ ontology is then translated to a logical schema. As instance, Figure 3 illustrates the ontology concept "Lecturer" and its translation to a logical schema using the three known relational layouts: vertical, binary and horizontal. In the three cases, the obtained schema is very different from the initial one. The logical schema is then implemented using a semantic DBMS.

A traceability approach should, as instance, define the information given by the following requirement: *"this requirement identifies the number of publications of lecturers working for Computer Science department"*. This requirement

---

[3] http://swat.cse.lehigh.edu/projects/lubm/profile.htm

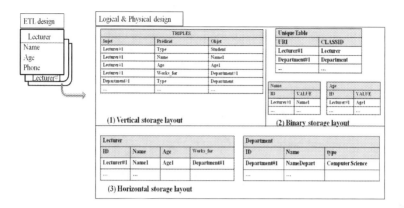

Fig. 3. Semantic $\mathcal{DW}$ design process: example

has identified the following concepts in the conceptual schema: *Lecturer, Department, Publication* and all their properties. The concept *Publication* is identified as a fact and the concepts *Lecturer* and *Department* are identified as dimensions. The ETL workflow presented in the figure is used to populate the target Lecturer concept. The source elements that populated the concept are *Lecturer.S1* and   *Lecturer.S2*. The $\mathcal{DW}$ concepts are transformed into relations then into tables in the physical level (using corresponding translation rules). The backward path can also be identified. As instance, the *Department.DW* table is a translation of the *Department.DW* concept. The requirements that are related to the *Department.DW* Concept are Requirements 1, 2, 3, 5, 7, 8, 10 and 12 (in LUBM benchmark).

3   Related Work

This section presents the main concepts related to traceability in software product in general, then in semantic $\mathcal{DW}$ context.

3.1   Traceability: Definition and Related Concepts

Traceability has emerged in Requirements Engineering area. It has then been used in model-driven development area [21]. Traceability is defined in the IEEE Standard Glossary of Software Engineering Terminology [18] as: (1) the degree to which a relationship can be established between two or more products of the development process. (2) The degree to which each element (like documents, models, or code) in a software development product establishes its reason for existing. A *trace* is defined in the same standard glossary as a relationship between two or more products of the development process. Ontologies have proven their effectiveness for managing traceability for software products [22]. Basically, there are four activities for managing traceability [21]: planning for traceability, recording traces, using them, and maintaining them. These activities are performed as part of the software development process. Storing the traces allows an easy forward and backward navigation between design elements. As defined by the ANSI/IEEE Std 830-1993, backward traceability refers to the ability to follow the traceability links from a specific artifact back to its sources from which it has been derived. Forward traceability stands for following the traceability links to the artifacts that have been derived from the artifact under consideration.

Traceability Meta-Model. A traceability model is the basic component of a traceability approach. It allows identifying the traces and recording them. Different ad hoc traceability meta-models have been proposed in the literature. These models share the same core conception. Currently there is no single standardized traceability meta-model. We thus use the traceability model proposed in [21], which presents the common features of the meta-models found in literature. The model is presented in figure 4.

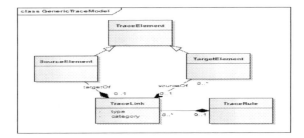

Fig. 4. Generic Traceability Model

The model defines a context used to define the trace links, which can contain metadata defining which rule or operation created the trace. The most important feature of a trace is the links to the model elements or artifacts, which are connected via the trace (source and target elements). Two *types* of traceability links are identified [15]: horizontal traceability that links elements belonging to the same project phase or level of abstraction, and vertical traceability links elements belonging to different ones.

3.2 𝒟𝒲 Traceability: Related Works

Different studies pointed out that there is only little to no guidance for practitioners for applying traceability approaches into standard procedures [21]. The lack of a "generic" approach has pushed to the proposition of specific approaches dedicated to 𝒟𝒲 systems. However, these approaches focus on some aspects of 𝒟𝒲 design, and do not cover the whole design life-cycle. Among these studies, *Chui et al.* [8] provide an algorithm for tracing the lineage of tuples in set-based aggregate-select-project-join (ASPJ) views in relational DWs. This study aims to trace instances of data by means of queries. However it studies traceability from source perspective, it does not support modeling and ignores the impact of user's requirements and the translations between the design phases. *Marotta et al.* [13] propose a $\mathcal{DW}$ design approach using a schema transformation approach. The approach identifies the traces as the links (or the path) providing the information about the sequences of primitives that were applied to each $\mathcal{DW}$ element starting from a source element. The approach focuses on the traces between the target $\mathcal{DW}$ schema and the sources schemas only, and the process providing the traces is not detailed. *Trujillo et al.* [14,15] proposed a trace meta model and an approach used for expliciting the traces between the conceptual $\mathcal{DW}$ schema obtained from the mapping between sources and requirements. The ETL, logical and physical models are ignored in this study. Additionally, these frameworks focus on traceability of model elements through consecutive transformation steps, which is not the case of all $\mathcal{DW}$ design steps. As instance, the ETL phase does not transform the $\mathcal{DW}$ schema but just populates it.

These studies do not define the traces semantically. Most of the approaches are dedicated to relational $\mathcal{DW}$ systems. Additionally, these studies ignore the *tight coupling* of the $\mathcal{DW}$ life-cycle steps. Many studies demonstrate the strong coupling between nonadjacent design phases. As instance, Bellatreche et al. [4] present a personalization framework for OLAP queries and analyzes the impact of preferences on physical $\mathcal{DW}$ design (in particular for data partitioning, index and materialized view selection). Theodorou et al. [20] clarify and exploit the implicit links between the ETL model and the $\mathcal{DW}$ collected requirements. Many studies exploit concepts correlations for multidimensional OLAP annotation and hierarchical OLAP normalization. For example, Anderlik et al. [2] exploit subsumption levels between ontological concepts in the definition of Roll-up hierarchies used for OLAP data aggregation. Other studies exploit correlations of type soft dependencies, inclusion dependencies or integrity constraints in the definition of physical design structures. For example, Kimura et al. [12] exploit the correlations linking the attributes (that can be detected from the conceptual phase) in the definition and recommendation process of materialized views and indexes. We believe that the recent consensus established around the cited design life-cycle including the five phases, allows us to define a global traceability approach covering this cycle. The traceability approach is first based on a traceability model, instantiating the meta model (presented previously, cf. section 3.1) for semantic $\mathcal{DW}$ design context. This study requires the formalization of the design life-cycle, that is presented in the next section.

4 $\mathcal{SDW}$ Design Life-Cycle: Formalization

The $\mathcal{SDW}$ life-cycle formalization that we propose is based on a thorough study of semantic $\mathcal{DW}$ design that we conducted in [11]. Note that the framework formalization must contain the model-based and the process-based facets.

4.1   Model-Based Formalization

We start by the presentation of the model-based aspect, which is formally defined
as follows: $< RM, CM, ETL, LM, PM >$, such as :

Requirements Model (RM) is formalized as follows: <Req, Relationship,
Formalism>, such as:

- Req : is the set of requirements collected from users and validated.
- Relationship: define different types of relationships between requirements,
  such as and/or, conflicts, equivalents, requires, etc.
- Formalism : is the formalism used for analyzing the set of requirements (like
  textual, UML, etc)

For the **Conceptual Model (CM)**, our goal was to find a high level formalism that covers the most important existing static conceptual models like
UML class diagram, ER models and OWL ontological models. We chose Description Logic (DL) formalism. DL formalism is defined as the formalism used to
define logics specifically designed to represent structured knowledge and to reason upon. DL is able to capture the most popular data *class-based modeling*
formalisms presently used in *databases* and *Information system* analysis [3].
Ontology Web Language (OWL), the language standardized by W3C to define
ontologies, is also based on DL formalism. A knowledge base in DL is composed
of two components: the *TBOX* (Terminological Box) stating the *intensional*
knowledge and the *ABOX* (Assertion Box) stating the *extensional* knowledge or
the instances. In our context, the domain ontology is defined by its TBOX, the
instances are stored in the local ontologies of the sources.

The conceptual model is formally defined as follows CM: <C, R, Ref (C),
Ref'(R), Formalism, Multidim> (We assume the reader is already familiar with
DL formalism [3])

- C: denotes *Concepts* of the model (atomic concepts and concept descriptions).
- R: denotes *Roles* (relationships) of the model. Roles can be relationships
  relating concepts to other concepts, or relationships relating concepts to
  data-values (like Integers, Floats, etc).
- $Ref : C \rightarrow$ (Operator, Exp(C,R)). Ref is a *function* defining terminological axioms of a DL TBOX. Operators can be inclusion ($\sqsubseteq$) or equality ($\equiv$).
  Exp(C,R) is an expression over concepts and roles of CM using construc-
  tors of description logics such as union, intersection, restriction, etc. (e.g.,
  Ref(Student)$\rightarrow$($\sqsubseteq$, Person $\sqcap$ $\forall$takesCourse(Person, Course))).
- $Ref' : R \rightarrow$ (Operator, Exp(C,R)). Ref' is a similar function as Ref, but is
  defined for roles.
- Formalism is the *formalism* followed by the global ontology model like RDF,
  OWL, etc.
- $Multidim : C \cup R \rightarrow$ Role. $Multidim$ is a function that denotes the multidimensional role (fact, dimension, measure, attribute dimension) of concepts
  and roles. Not all concepts and roles have to be annotated by their multidimensional role.

The **ETL model** defines the extract-transform-load process, by which data from heterogeneous sources are integrated and duplicated in $\mathcal{DW}$ system, after applying an ETL algorithm. A data integration system is formally defined as follows $< G, S, M >$. In semantic $\mathcal{DW}$ design, G is defined as the domain ontology, S are defined by their local ontologies that reference the domain ontology using defined mappings.

The global schema (G) is defined by its conceptual model, as defined previously: CM_G :<C, R, Ref (C), Ref'(R) Formalism>. (*Multidimim* function is not required)

The sources (S) Each local source S_i is defined as follows:
$S_i :< O_i, I_i, Pop_i >$, with:

- O_i :$< C_i, R_i, Ref_i, Ref_i', formalism_i >$ is the ontology defining the source.
- I_i: presents the set of *instances* of the source.
- Pop_i: $C_i \rightarrow 2^{I_i}$ is a *function* that relates each concept to its instances from the set I_i.

The mappings (M) The mappings are defined between global and local schemes as follows M :<*MapSchemaG, MapSchemaS, InputSet, OutputSet, Interpretation*>. This formalization is based on the meta-model proposed in [6], defined for conceptual mappings.

- *MapSchemaG* and *MapSchemaS*: present respectively the *mappable schema* of the global schema (domain ontology) and of the local schema (local ontology).
- *InputSet* and *OutputSet*: the *OutputSet* is an element (usually a class) of *MapSchemaG*, and *InputSet* is an expression over source ontological schemas. This expression is built using a set of ETL operators. Skoutas et al. [19] defined ten generic operators typically encountered in an ETL process, which are: Extract, Retrieve, Merge, Union, Join, Store, Detecte-Duplicate, Filter, Convert, Aggregate.
- *Interpretation*: presents the *Intentional* interpretation or *Extensional* (instances) interpretation of the mapping. The intentional interpretation is often used since it reduces the number of mappings.

LM designates the $\mathcal{DW}$ **logical model** $\mathcal{LM}$: $< LM_{Element}, Formalism_{LM} >$ is formally defined as follows:

- $LM_{Element}$: the constructs of the logical data schema. For the relational model, it would be the relations and their attributes.
- $Formalism_{LM}$: the used formalism in logical phase (E.g. Relational, Object, etc)

PM designates the $\mathcal{DW}$ **physical model**. The formalization of this component is as follows $< PM_{Element}, I, Pop, SM_{CM}, SM_I, Ar, Platform >$:

- $PM_{Element}$: the constructs of the physical data schema. For the relational model, it would be the tables and their columns.
- I: presents the set of *instances* (individuals) of the $\mathcal{DW}$ system.
- $Pop : PM_{Element} \rightarrow 2^I$ is a *function* that relates each physical element to its instances. Note that I and Pop function are obtained by the ETL algorithm, which aliments each class by its corresponding instances according to the defined mappings.
- SM_{CM}: represents the *Storage Model* chosen for the CM.
- SM_I: represents the *Storage Model* chosen for the instances part I_i, which can be the same as SM_{CM} (like in *Oracle* semantic DBMS) or different from SM_{CM} (like in *IBM Sor* semantic DBMS). In this case, two types of translation rules are used.
- Ar_i: is the *architecture* type of the storage system. As instance, three main semantic DBMS architectures are provided (type I, type II or type III) [9].
- *Platform*: is the *platform* type of the $\mathcal{DW}$ (centralized, parallel, etc). This item must includes the different physical components and the nodes they are deployed in. We focus in our approach on the centralized platform.

4.2   Process-Based Formalization

The process-based formalization concerns the different algorithms used during the design process. These algorithms are dependent of the design approach. Whatever the algorithms used, we just need to identify the correspondences (matching, translation, merging) between design phases (vertical traces) and inside the phases (horizontal traces). According to the traceability meta-model proposed, we have to identify for each trace element: the source element, the target element and the trace link between them. In semantic $\mathcal{DW}$ design, four main **vertical traces** are identified:

(1) The conceptual schema is defined after the matching between sources schemas and users' requirements. The set of concepts used by requirements or by source mappings are projected on the global ontology (G) in order to unify the used vocabulary and to eliminate ambiguities between used terms. Requirements definition phase allows the designer to identify the set of relevant concepts (the *dictionary*) used by the target system. As the ontology model describes all concepts and properties of the concerned domain, the connection between the requirements model and the ontology model is feasible (the G model). This connection allows identifying the set of relevant concepts that should be stored in the DW: the $\mathcal{DW}$ ontology (DWO). The DWO can be the same ontology as the domain ontology or one fragment of the domain ontology. We defined a connection between each requirement and the resources (*concepts* and *roles*) of the domain ontology. Figure 6 presents the $\mathcal{SDW}$ traceability model and illustrates these trace links. In the figure, the *Requirement* and $CM_{Element}$ classes are linked to the *OntologyResource* class.

(2) The ETL process uses the set of mappings M in order to populate the $\mathcal{DW}$ ontology with data from sources. The mappings identifies an ETL workflow

(composed of ETL operators) that takes some InputSets (expression over source ontological schemas), to populate each OutputSet (a class in the $\mathcal{DW}$ ontology). In figure 6, the *InputSet* and *OutputSet* classes are linked to the *OntologyResource* class.

(3) The logical schema is derived from the conceptual schema using some defined rules ($CM_{Element}$, $LM_{Element}$ and *Translation* classes in figure 6).

(4) The physical schema is derived from the logical schema using some defined rules ($LM_{Element}$, $PM_{Element}$ and *Translation* classes in figure 6).

The main ***horizontal traces*** identified are:

(1) The correspondence between the requirements schema and the sources schemas if their concepts use the same ontological resource (Class *SourceReq* in figure 6).

(2) The matching between the domain ontology and the DWO ontology (*DO_DWO* relationship in figure 6).

(3) The link between the DWO concept and the conceptual element, defining its multidimensional role: fact, dimension, measure, dimension attribute or hierarchy level (*defines* relationship between *OntologyResource* and $CM_{Element}$ in the figure).

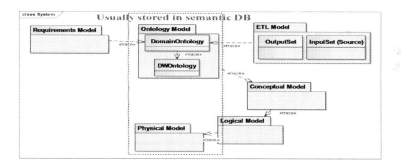

Fig. 5. Vertical Trace links

Figure 5 illustrates the vertical trace links. Figure 6 illustrates the $\mathcal{SDW}$ trace model that we propose. As defined in the traceability meta model, the trace links are presented in the model using the stereotype $<< TraceLink >>$. The source and target trace elements are defined in the model for each design phase. The class *OntologyResource* in the model designates resources of the domain ontology, the local ontology and the DWO. Each ontology has a unique identifier (the URI), which is associated to each resource name, composing the resource identifier.

5   Proposal: Semantic $\mathcal{DW}$ Traceability Approach

This section proposes a traceability approach including the four recommended activities [21]:

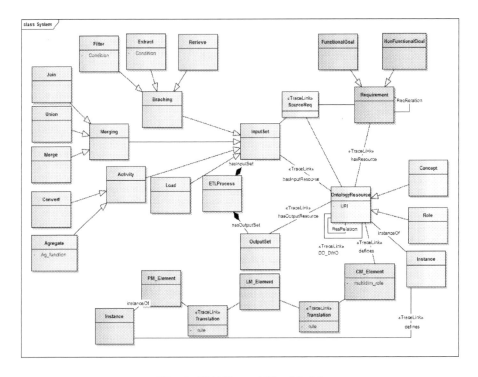

Fig. 6. $\mathcal{DW}$ Traceability Model

1. Planing: the outcome of this activity is a traceability model, which is described in the previous section.

2. Recording: this activity leaves traces on the artifacts and makes them persistent. This can be done during the design process or after the actual design process has been finished. It is recommended that traces are recorded immediately to avoid recording imprecise traces. The recording activity is achieved in our approach using the ontology model. In a semantic $\mathcal{DW}$ design, we notice that the ontology model is used as an intermediary model defining and linking design artifacts of different design levels. Since the ontology is the "natural" component used for recording $\mathcal{DW}$ information, we propose to use it in order to record the traceability model. In a conventional design process, two main components are recorded in a semantic DBMS: (1) the ontology model defining the schema and its instances and (2) the ontology meta-model defining the ontology model. Since information about the traces are considered as meta-data, the ontology meta-model can be extended to store the traceability model proposed. This process can be easily achieved using an ontology editor like Protégé[4]. Figure 7 illustrates this process. The meta-concepts are first made visible. As instance, the requirements model extends this meta-schema by the creation of new meta-concepts (*Requirement, FunctionalRequirement* and *NonFunctionalRequirement*). Each requirement is defined by ontological resources

---

[4] http://protege.stanford.edu/

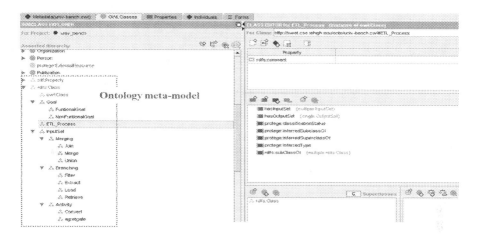

Fig. 7. Extending the ontology meta-model (using Protégé editor)

of the domain ontology. The ETL model extends the ontology model, using *ETL-Process*, *InputSet* and *OutputSet* meta-concepts. Note that in the ontology repository, Protégé can store different ontology models. Each ontology has a unique URI (source ontology URIs, $\mathcal{DW}$ ontology URI and the domain ontology URI). This process is done for the whole traceability model proposed.

During the $\mathcal{DW}$ implementation stage, a semantic DBMS system is used in order to record information about data and meta-data. Two components are recorded: (1) the meta-base which contains the ontology meta-model (and thus the traceability model) and (2) the ontology model, which contains the ontology schema and its instances. The traceability concepts are consequently made persistent in the $\mathcal{DW}$ repository. This process is automatically achieved by existing semantic DBMSs which provide mechanisms for creating a semantic database and loading a given ontology inside this database (Eg. SQL*Loader for Oracle semantic DBMS).

The traces can be stored in the trace model *manually* by the designer, as instances of the traceability model. A better scenario would be to store *automatically* the traces during the design process. In a conventional design process, some design tasks are achieved manually (like requirements analysis process) or using some tools (like ETL tools which are used to define the ETL workflows), and the traces are usually lost once the $\mathcal{DW}$ developed. Ideally, the storage of the traces in the trace model should be "triggered" automatically for each design phase during the design process. Since there is no consensual semantic $\mathcal{DW}$ design tool, we have proposed our own case-tool (presented in the next section) which allows the designer validating each design phase, and then stores the traces as *instances* in the trace model. Following database triggers syntax, a trigger is defined as a rule having three main components: the *event* that triggers the rule, the *condition* that determines whether the rule action should be executed and the *action* to achieve. These triggers are defined as rules updating the trace model:

Rule1:

- *Event*: Source mappings validated
- *Condition*: mapping defined following a specific syntax defined in the formalization framework (i.e. each mapping links an ontology concept to a expression over local ontologies).
- *Actions*: store the set of mappings between the local ontologies and the domain ontology as instances of the ETL part of Traceability Model. Each mapping links a source resource to a domain ontology resource using *InputSet* and *OutputSet* concepts and defined ETL operators.

Rule2:

- *Event*: Requirements analysis validated
- *Condition*: No conflicts between requirements.
- *Actions*: store the set of requirements validated and their ontological resources as instances of the Requirement part of the Traceability Model.

Rule3:

- *Event*: Conceptual design validated
- *Condition*: Multidimensional annotations defined (manually or automatically) and the ETL algorithm defined.
- *Actions*:
  - Generate the $\mathcal{DW}$ ontology (DWO) : this ontology is extracted from the domain ontology (DO). This process is possible in ontology engineering and is referred to ontology modularization, and is achieved based on a signature of terms. In our approach, the signature includes the set of concepts participating in the requirements and in the source mappings. What we are concerned with here is, the output of the process (the DWO) and not the process itself.
  - Populate the DWO concepts using the ETL algorithm.
  - Store the set of conceptual elements composing the $\mathcal{DW}$ conceptual model (fact, dimension, attribute, measure, etc) as instances of the Conceptual model part of the Traceability Model. The link between the DO and the DWO is usually ensured by the modularity approach.

Rule4:

- *Event*: Logical design validated
- *Condition*: Translation rules defined
- *Action*: the traceability information are stored as instances of $LM_{Element}$, $CM_{Element}$ and *Translation* classes.

Rule5:

- *Event*: physical design validated
- *Actions*: Load the ontology in the selected semantic DBMS. The link between the physical concept and its ontological concept is already stored in the database. Semantic Database architectures are composed of two main layers: the meta-base layer and the model layer. The first layer will be extended by the Traceability Requirement Model, Traceability ETL Model, Traceability Conceptual Model and the Traceability Logical Model. The model layer stores the traces.

3. Using: this activity retrieves data describing the traces in order to find relevant information. Since the recording activity is achieved using the ontology repository, the access to data is done using a dedicated query language. For example, we defined a set of Sparql[5] queries in order to retrieve traceability data and trace links. Various examples of queries are given in the next section.

4. Maintaining: the traces must be maintained in case of a structural change of the design process, or if errors in the trace data has been detected. Note that if most evolutions that may occur are managed by the ontology editor. As instance, the deletion of a class in the *DWO* implies its deletion from the traceability model where it is stored. However, this activity requires a detailed maintenance strategy. This issue is out of the scope of this study.

6   Implementation

In order to illustrate the feasibility of our approach, we use the case study presented in section 2. The first three activities of the traceability approach have been implemented: (1) *Planing*: the implementation of the traceability model in Protégé Editor and in Oracle semantic database by extending the Ontology meta-model as illustrated in Figure 7. (2) *Recording*: which is achieved by the implementation of the traceability rules defined previously. (3) *Using*: the retrieval of the traceability data is achieved using Sparql queries over the ontology meta model (from an ontology editor like Protégé or from the semantic DBMS). These queries can be defined by the designer, or hidden in a case tool as proposed. Many examples can be given. As instance, the following query retrieves the ETL workflow used to populate the concept DW.Lecturer, as illustrated in the motivating example section.

```
PREFIX onto: <http://swat.cse.lehigh.edu/onto/univ-bench.owl#>
SELECT  ?r
 WHERE { ?p onto:hasOutputSet ?q.
?q onto:hasResource onto:Lecturer.
?p onto:hasInputSet ?r
}
```

The second query retrieves the set of sources involved in each task of the previous ETL workflow (figure 8). The result of the query in the figure illustrates the traces retrieved.

```
PREFIX onto: <http://swat.cse.lehigh.edu/onto/univ-bench.owl#>
SELECT  ?r ?t
 WHERE { ?p onto:hasOutputSet ?q.
?q onto:hasResource onto:Lecturer.
?p onto:hasInputSet ?r.
?r onto:hasResourcep ?t
}
```

---

[5] http://www.w3.org/TR/rdf-sparql-query/

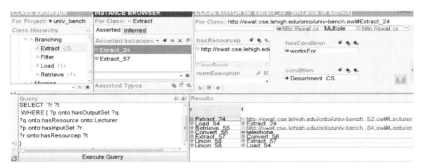

Fig. 8. traceability data retrieval (sources schemas)

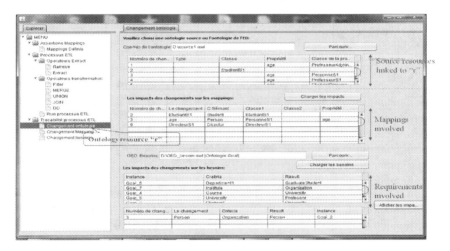

Fig. 9. Traceability data retrieval

The retrieval of traces can be done at the data level. As instance, the following query retrieves the sources that provided *Lecturer6* instance. The set of source instances that are involved in the process is indicated in each ETL operation.

```
PREFIX onto: <http://swat.cse.lehigh.edu/onto/univ-bench.owl#>
PREFIX ontoS: <http://www.Department0.University0.edu/>
PREFIX rdf: <http://www.w3.org/1999/02/22-rdf-syntax-ns#>
SELECT  ?r ?t
 WHERE { ?p onto:hasOutputSet ?q.
ontoS:Lecturer6 rdf:type ?u.
?q onto:hasResource ?u.
?p onto:hasInputSet ?r.
?r onto:hasResourcep ?t.
FILTER regex(str(?t), "http://swat.cse.lehigh.edu/onto/univ-bench_S") .
}
```

Furthermore, reasoning mechanisms offered by the ontology can be used, as instance to relate artifacts (eg. requirements) that use the same concepts in a hierarchy or concepts related by a property.

For the implementation of activities 2 and 3, we have developed a case tool implementing a semantic design process that we have proposed in [5], we have added modules for the implementation of the recording and using activities.

The tool takes as input a set of Oracle semantic sources and a set of requirements. The designer defines specific mappings between these inputs and the selected domain ontology. The tool is developed in Java language, following the MVC architecture which defines three main layers: (1) View Layer: defining the user interfaces. (2) Controller Layer: the design process and the traceability activities (*recording* and *using*) are implemented in this layer. The tool provides a semantic $\mathcal{DW}$ populated from ontological instances. The traceability recording rules defined in the previous section are implemented in this layer after the validation of each design phase by the designer. The retrieval of trace data is implemented using Sparql queries. The result of the queries is directly displayed through interfaces. As instance, figures 9 illustrates the retrieval of the all the concepts in different design levels (sources, mappings, requirements) linked to one given domain ontology resource. (3) Model Layer: represents the classes that define the access to the ontologies (meta-model, model and instances). This access is implemented using OWL API.

7 Conclusion

We have presented in this paper a semantic $\mathcal{DW}$ traceability approach. Two main facts motivated this study: the recent consensus around the design lifecycle including tight coupling aspects and the availability of the ontology, which naturally links the different design artifacts. To the best of our knowledge, it is the first time that these aspects are considered in studies dealing with traceability in the context of $\mathcal{DW}$s. The approach is based on the cycle formalization and includes four activities. The approach is illustrated using LUBM benchmark. A case tool implementing a design process and extending it by the traceability approach, has been proposed. The current challenges involve the automation of the last activity for maintaining the traces when evolutions occur, the definition of an ontological reasoning strategy for managing the traces efficiently, the proposition of a $\mathcal{DW}$ evolution strategy based on the traceability approach which will be used to facilitate the change propagation process and the extension of the case tool in order to provide a detailed visual support for trace links.

References

1. Abelló, A., Romero, O., Pedersen, T.B., Llavori, R.B., Nebot, V., Cabo, M.J.A., Simitsis, A.: Using semantic web technologies for exploratory OLAP: A survey. IEEE Trans. Knowl. Data Eng. **27**(2), 571–588 (2015)
2. Anderlik, S., Neumayr, B., Schrefl, M.: Using domain ontologies as semantic dimensions in data warehouses. In: Atzeni, P., Cheung, D., Ram, S. (eds.) ER 2012 Main Conference 2012. LNCS, vol. 7532, pp. 88–101. Springer, Heidelberg (2012)
3. Baader, F., Calvanese, D., McGuinness, D., Nardi, D., Patel-Schneider, P., eds.: The Description Logic Handbook: Theory, Implementation, and Applications. Cambridge University Press (2003)
4. Bellatreche, L., Giacometti, A., Marcel, A., Mouloudi, H., Laurent, D.: A personalization framework for olap queries. In: Proc. of DOLAP05, pp. 9–18 (2005)

5. Bellatreche, L., Khouri, S., Berkani, N.: Semantic data warehouse design: from etl to deployment à la carte. In: Meng, W., Feng, L., Bressan, S., Winiwarter, W., Song, W. (eds.) DASFAA 2013, Part II. LNCS, vol. 7826, pp. 64–83. Springer, Heidelberg (2013)

6. Brockmans, S., Haase, P., Serafini, L., Stuckenschmidt, H.: Formal and conceptual comparison of ontology mapping languages. In: Stuckenschmidt, H., Parent, C., Spaccapietra, S. (eds.) Modular Ontologies. LNCS, vol. 5445, pp. 267–291. Springer, Heidelberg (2009)

7. Calvanese, D., DeGiacomo, G., Lenzerini, M., Nardi, D., Rosati, R.: Data integration in data warehousing. International Journal of Cooperative Information Systems 10(03), 237–271 (2001)

8. Cui, Y., Widom, J.: Lineage tracing for general data warehouse transformations. The VLDB Journal -The International Journal on Very Large Data Bases 12(1), 41–58 (2003)

9. Fankam, C.: OntoDB2: un systeme flexible et efficient de Base de Donnees à Base Ontologique pour le Web semantique et les donnees techniques. PhD thesis, ENSMA, Decembre 2009

10. Golfarelli, M.: From user requirements to conceptual design in data warehousedesign a survey. In: Data Warehousing Design and Advanced Engineering ApplicationsMethods for Complex Construction, pp. 1–16 (2010)

11. Khouri, S.: Cycle de vie smantique de conception de systmes de stockage et de manipulation de donnes. PhD thesis, ENSMA & ESI, October 2013

12. Kimura, H., Huo, G., Rasin, A., Madden, S., Zdonik, S.B.: Coradd: Correlation aware database designer for materialized views and indexes. Proceedings of the VLDB Endowment 3(1–2), 1103–1113 (2010)

13. Marotta, A., Ruggia, R.: Data warehouse design: a schema-transformation approach. In: Proceedings. 22nd International Conference of the Chilean Computer Science Society, SCCC, pp. 153–161. IEEE (2002)

14. Maté, A., Trujillo, J.: A trace metamodel proposal based on the model driven architecture framework for the traceability of user requirements in data warehouses. Information Systems 37(8), 753–766 (2012)

15. Maté, A., Trujillo, J.: Tracing conceptual models evolution in data warehouses. Computer Standards & Interfaces 36(5), 831–843 (2014)

16. Mazón, J.-N., Trujillo, J.: Enriching data warehouse dimension hierarchies by using semantic relations. In: Bell, D.A., Hong, J. (eds.) BNCOD 2006. LNCS, vol. 4042, pp. 278–281. Springer, Heidelberg (2006)

17. Nebot, V., Berlanga, R.: Building data warehouses with semantic web data. Decision Support Systems (2012)

18. Jane, A.G.R., Katki, F.: IEEE standard glossary of software engineering terminology. Std 610.12-1990, 1–84, December 1990

19. Skoutas, D., Simitsis, A.: Ontology-based conceptual design of etl processes for both structured and semi-structured data. International Journal on Semantic Web and Information Systems (IJSWIS) 3(4), 1–24 (2007)

20. Theodorou, V., Abelló, A., Thiele, M., Lehner, W.: A framework for user-centered declarative etl. In: Proceedings of the 17th International Workshop on Data Warehousing and OLAP, pp. 67–70. ACM (2014)

21. Winkler, S., Pilgrim, J.V.: A survey of traceability in requirements engineering and model-driven development. Software & Systems Modeling 9(4), 529–565 (2010)

22. Zhang, Y., Witte, R., Rilling, J., Haarslev, V.: Ontological approach for the semantic recovery of traceability links between software artefacts. IET software 2(3), 185–203 (2008)

Aggregation Operators in Geospatial Queries for Open Street Map

Jesús M. Almendros-Jiménez, Antonio Becerra-Terón[✉], and Manuel Torres

Information Systems Group, University of Almería, 04120 Almería, Spain
{jalmen,abecerra,mtorres}@ual.es

Abstract. One of the most stablished Volunteered Geographic Information (VGI) systems is Open Street Map (OSM) offering data from the earth of urban and rural maps. Recently [1], we have presented a library for querying OSM data with the XML query language XQuery. This library is based on the well-known spatial operators defined by Clementini and Egenhofer, providing a repertoire of XQuery functions which encapsulates the search on the XML document representing a layer of OSM, and makes the definition and composition of queries on top of OSM layers easier. This paper goes towards the incorporation in the library of aggregation operators in order to be able to express queries involving data summarization and ranking. A rich repertoire of aggregation operators has been defined which, in combination with the previously proposed library, makes possible to easily formulate aggregation-based queries. Also we present a Web-based tool, called *XOSM (XQuery for Open Street Map)*, developed in our group, that uses the proposed library to query and visualize OSM data.

1 Introduction

Volunteered Geographic Information (VGI) is a term introduced by Goodchild [12] to describe geographic information systems based on crowdsourcing, in which users collaborate to a collection of spatial data of urban and rural areas of the earth. VGI makes available a very large resource of geographic data. The exploitation of data coming from such resources requires an additional effort in the form of tools and effective processing techniques. *Open Street Map* (OSM) [5] is one of the most relevant VGI systems, with almost two millions of registered users. OSM data can be visualized from the OSM web site[1], and many applications[2] have also built for the handling of maps.

In spite of the growing interest in OSM and the fact many tools have been developed, the main tasks tools are able to carry out are edition, export, rendering, conversion, analysis, routing and navigation, but less attention has been

This work was funded by the EU ERDF and the Spanish Ministry of Economy and Competitiveness (MINECO) under Project TIN2013-44742-C4-4-R, and by the Andalusian Regional Government (Spain) under Project P10-TIC-6114.

[1] http://www.openstreetmap.org
[2] http://wiki.openstreetmap.org/wiki/Software

© Springer International Publishing Switzerland 2015
C. Debruyne et al. (Eds.): OTM 2015 Conferences, LNCS 9415, pp. 501–518, 2015.
DOI: 10.1007/978-3-319-26148-5_34

paid for querying. Urban areas are considerably more contributed by users, existing a wide coverage of towns and cities in OSM. Querying urban maps can be seen from many points of view. One of the most popular querying mechanism is the so-called *routing* or *navigation*, which gives the most suitable route to go from one point to another of the city. In this case, the input of the query are two points (or streets) and the output is a sequence of instructions to be followed in order to reach the destination. Nevertheless, querying an urban map can also be interesting for city sightseeing. In fact, the places of interests around a given geo-localized point are the major goal. In this case, the input of the query is a point and a city area, close to the point, and the output is a set of points. The tourist would also like to query streets and buildings close to a given street when he/she is looking for a hotel, or to query parking areas, restaurants, high ways, etc. In such queries, the input is a given point (or street) and the output is a number of streets, parking areas, restaurants, high ways, etc. Additionally, in a city sightseeing, keyword based searching is useful. Let us suppose that the tourist is looking for leisure and shopping places, restaurants areas, as well as a pharmacy. In this case, the input of the query is a keyword, and the output is a set of points, streets, areas, etc.

XQuery [2,20] is a programming language proposed by the W3C as standard for the handing of XML documents. It is a functional language in which *for-let-orderby-where-return (FLOWR)* expressions are able to traverse XML documents. It can express Boolean conditions and provides format to output documents. XQuery has a sublanguage, called *XPath* [6], whose role is to address nodes on the XML tree. XPath is properly a query language equipped with Boolean conditions and many path-based operators. XQuery adds expressivity to XPath by providing mechanisms to join several XML documents.

Recently [1], we have presented a library for querying OSM with the XML query language XQuery. This library is based on the well-known spatial operators defined by Clementini and Egenhofer [7,9], providing a repertoire of XQuery functions which encapsulates the search on the XML document representing a layer of OSM. In essence, the library provides a repertoire of *OSM operators*, for nodes and ways which, in combination with *higher order* facilities of XQuery, makes easy the definition and composition of *spatial* and *keyword search* based queries. OSM data are indexed by (1) an *R-tree* structure [15] for spatial data, where nodes and ways are enclosed by *Minimum Bounding Rectangles (MBRs)*, as well as by (2) an *XML indexing* structure for textual data. Indexing enables shorter answer time.

In this paper we extend the library with aggregation operators. We have incorporated a rich repertoire of aggregation operators which, in combination with the previously proposed library, makes possible to formulate aggregation based queries easily. Data summarization and ranking is crucial in database systems and query languages have to be equipped with aggregation operators. In the special case of spatial databases, aggregation is required to summarize both spatial and non-spatial data. Several proposals of aggregation operators for spatial data have been proposed in the literature (see [8,21] among others).

They have been studied in the context of *Spatial Data Warehouses* and the *OLAP* model. The term *SOLAP* was coined in this framework, and extensions to the well-known OLAP model have been proposed. Additionally, R-tree based structures have been proposed to deal with spatial indexing and aggregation (see [19] for an example). Our proposal, even when cannot be properly considered a SOLAP approach, is inspired by this framework.

Basically, the library makes possible to compute the *maximum* and *minimum*, the *mode*, etc., of non-spatial data associated to OSM elements occurring in an OSM layer, and also, to retrieve the OSM elements to which these values correspond to. The library enables the retrieval of objects of a given OSM layer according to a certain *ranking*. The ranking can be defined for measures like distance, area, perimeter, etc., but other measures can also be used. The ranking operators have a parameter indicating the measure to be ranked. For instance, we can get the hotels with the maximum number of stars, the restaurants with the most typical cuisine, etc. Additionally, the library provides functions like *sum*, *count*, *average*, etc., enabling data *summarization*. Moreover, XQuery makes possible the composition of queries, that is, the result of a query can be the input of another one, and thus several rankings can be combined. Thus, the library permits to count hotels with the highest number of stars, compute distance averages of monuments to a certain city point, etc.

We have developed a Web-based tool[3], called XOSM, for querying and visualization of OSM maps. In XOSM the user can select an area of the OSM map, and after an indexing process, to query the area using the XQuery library. Results are highlighted in the map. The XOSM tool is based on a client-server architecture, in which the Web page sends requests to the API Rest server of *BaseX* XQuery interpreter [14]. The XOSM is equipped with three main modules. (1) *Indexing*: an XML-based R-tree is generated from the select area of the map; (2) *Query Engine*: Parsing and execution of queries making use of the XQuery library; (3) *Result Layout*: Visualization of results with *LeafLet* and *jQuery*.

The rest of this article is organized as follows. Section 2 will present the basic elements of OSM, it will summarize the OSM indexing process and describe the main OSM operators. Section 3 will define the OSM aggregation operators and Section 4 will present the XOSM tool, showing examples and benchmarks for several datasets. Section 5 will compare with related work and finally, Section 6 will conclude and present future work.

2   Open Street Map Querying

2.1   Open Street Map Basic Elements

OpenStreetMap uses a topological data structure which includes the following core elements: (1) *Nodes* which are points with a geographic position, stored as coordinates (pairs of a latitude and a longitude) according to WGS84. They are used in ways, and allow to describe map features without a size, like points of

---

[3] http://indalog.ual.es/XOSM

interest and mountain peaks. (2) *Ways* are ordered lists of nodes, representing
a poly-line, or possibly a polygon if they form a closed loop. They are used to
represent streets, rivers, among others, as well as areas; for instance, forests,
parks, parkings and lakes. (3) *Relations* are ordered lists nodes, ways and relations. Relations are used for representing the relationship of existing nodes and
ways. (4) *Tags* are key-value pairs (both arbitrary strings). They are used to
store *metadata* about the map objects (such as their type, name and physical
features). Tags are attached to a node, a way, a relation, or to a member of a
relation. For instance, the street *"Calzada de Castro"* of the Almería city (Spain)
is represented by a way as follows:

```
<way id='-3731'>
    <nd ref='-3625' />
    <nd ref='-3623' />
    <nd ref='-3621' />
    <tag k='highway' v='residential' />
    <tag k='name' v='Calle Calzada de Castro' />
    <tag k='oneway' v='yes' />
</way>
```

wherein the representation includes the set of node identifiers as well as the
tags for expressing that *"Calzada de Castro"* is a residential oneway. In spite
of the simplicity of the XML representation of OSM, many features[4] in a OSM
layer can be described.

2.2   Open Street Map Indexing Process and Functions

In order to handle large city maps, in which the layer can include many objects,
an R-tree structure to index spatial objects has been implemented. The R-tree
structure is based as usual on MBRs to hierarchically organize the content of
an OSM map, and they are also used to enclose OSM nodes and ways in leaves.
The R-tree structure has been implemented as an XML document as follows:

```
<node x="-2.4574724" y="36.8305714" z="-2.4473768" t="36.849285">
<node x="-2.4565026" y="36.8319462" z="-2.4476476" t="36.849285">
<node x="-2.4557511" y="36.8319462" z="-2.4491401" t="36.8414807">
<leaf x="-2.4557511" y="36.8347249" z="-2.4522051" t="36.8396123">
<mbr x="-2.4533564" y="36.8383646" z="-2.452359" t="36.8384662">
<way id="-11215" visible="true">
....
</way>
<node id="-10263" visible="true" lat="36.8384662" lon="-2.452359"/>
<node id="-10833" visible="true" lat="36.8383646" lon="-2.4533564"/>
</mbr>
...
</node>
```

The tag based structure of XML is used to represent the R-tree with two
main tags called *node* and *leaf*. A tag *node* represents an inner node, while a
tag *leaf* represents the leaves. Leaves store OSM ways and nodes. In addition,
the tag *mbr* is used in order to represent MBRs. The root element of the XML
document is the root node of the R-tree, and the children can be (inner) nodes or
leaves. x, y, z and t attributes of nodes are the left (x, y) and right (z, t) corners

---

[4] http://wiki.openstreetmap.org/wiki/Map_Features

Table 1. Index-based Functions

Name	Definition
getLayerByName(rt,n,d)	Nodes and ways of *rt* at distance *d* to an OSM element with name *n*
getLayerByElement(rt,e,d)	Nodes and ways of *rt* at distance *d* to an OSM element *e*
getElementByName(rt,n)	OSM representation in *rt* of an OSM element with name *n*
getElementsByKeyword(rt,k)	Nodes and ways of *rt* annotated with the keyword *k*

of the MBRs. MBRs are also represented by left and right corners. A function of the our library called *load_file* is used to transform a given OSM layer to an R-tree. OSM to R-tree transformation is called indexing process. The functions of the library to query OSM layers work with R-trees instead of OSM layers. In the XOSM tool, the first step consists in the selection of an OSM map area and the indexing of the area.

We have implemented in XQuery a set of *index-based functions*, shown in Table 1, to handle the R-tree of an OSM layer. From them, the function *getLayerByName* obtains, given the name of an OSM element (node or way), the nodes or ways of the OSM layer close to the given element. With this aim, a *distance* value has to be provided. Closeness means that the shortest distance between the MBRs associated to the returned elements (i.e., nodes and ways) and the MBR of the given element is smaller than the given distance value. *getLayerByElement* is similar to *getLayerByName*, but the OSM representation of a node or way is given as input instead of the name. Additionally, we provide two functions: *getElementByName* to retrieve the OSM representation of a given name, and *getElementsByKeyword* to retrieve the set of nodes and ways annotated with a keyword. The query language under the proposed library allows (1) geo-localized queries, using *getLayerByName* or *getLayerByElement* as basis, in the sense that, queries are focused on a certain area of interest; and (2) keyword-based queries, using *getElementsByKeyword* as basis, for the retrieval of a set of nodes/ways annotated with a given keyword. A particular element can be retrieved by *getElementByName*.

2.3   Open Street Map Operators

Additionally, a repertoire of OSM operators has been designed in order to express (a) spatial and (b) keyword queries over OSM layers. With respect to (a), two kinds of operators are considered: *Coordinate based OSM operators*, shown in Table 2 and *Clementini based OSM operators*, shown in Table 3. With respect to (b), the *Keyword based OSM operators* shown in Table 4 are considered.

On the other hand, XQuery 3.0 is equipped with higher order facilities. It makes possible to define functions in which arguments can also be functions.

Table 2. (Spatial) Coordinate Based OSM Operators

Name	Definition	Spatial Operation
isIn(s1,s2), isNext(s1,s2) and isAway(s1,s2)	true whenever the shortest distance between $s1$ and $s2$ is smaller (in central angel degrees) than 0.0001, 0.001 and 0.01, respectively	Distance
furtherNorthNodes(p_1,p_2) and furtherNorthWays(s_1,s_2)	true whenever p_1 (resp. s_1) is further north than p_2 (resp. s_2)	Using latitudes of in north and south hemispheres
furtherSouthNodes(p_1,p_2) and furtherSouthWays(s_1,s_2)	true whenever p_1 (resp. s_1) is further south than p_2 (resp. s_2)	furtherNorthNodes and furtherNorthWays negation
furtherEastNodes(p_1,p_2) and furtherEastWays(s_1,s_2)	true whenever p_1 (resp. s_1) is further east than p_2 (resp. s_2)	Using latitudes of in west and east hemispheres
furtherWestNodes(p_1,p_2) and furtherWestWays(s_1,s_2)	true whenever p_1 (resp. s_1) is further west than p_2 (resp. s_2)	furtherEastNodes and furtherEastWays negation

Table 3. (Spatial) Clementini Based OSM Operators

Name	Definition	Clementini's Operator [7]
inWay(p,s)	true whenever p (point) is in s (street)	Contains
inSameWay(p_1,p_2,m)	true whenever p_1 (point) and p_2 (point) are in the same street of the OSM map m	inWay and Equals
intersectionPoint(s_1,s_2)	the intersection point of s_1 (street) and s_2 (street)	Intersection
isCrossing(s_1,s_2)	true whenever s_1 (street) crosses s_2 (street)	Crosses
isNotCrossing(s_1,s_2)	true whenever s_1 is not crossing s_2	Negation of isCrossing
isEndingTo(s_1,s_2)	true whenever s_1 ends to s_2	Intersection and Equals
isContinuationOf(s_1,s_2)	true whenever s_2 is a continuation of s_1	Equals

Table 4. Keyword Based OSM Operators

Name	Definition
searchKeyword(e,kv)	true whenever the OSM element e has some k or v equal to kv
searchKeywordSet(e,($kv_1,\ldots,kv_n$))	true whenever the OSM element e has some k or v equal to some kv_i of ($kv_1,\ldots,kv_n$)
searchTag(e,k_0,v_0)	true whenever the OSM element e has some k and v equal to k_0 and v_0, respectively
getTagValue(e,k_0)	the value v of k equal to k_0 in the OSM element e

Table 5. Higher order functions of XQuery

Name	Definition
fn:for-each(s,f)	Applies the function f to every element of the sequence s
fn:filter(s,p)	Selects the elements of the sequence s for which p is true
fn:sort(s,f)	Sort the elements of the sequence s with respect to the value of the function f

In fact, XQuery provides a library of built-in higher order functions (see Table 5). Making use of this capability, our library makes possible to combine higher order functions with Coordinate and Clementini Based OSM Operators, and Keyword

Based OSM Operators in order to express (a) Spatial and (b) Keyword Based Queries, respectively.

For instance, with respect to (a), the higher order function *filter* combined with the spatial OSM operator *isCrossing* can be used to retrieve all the streets that cross a given street (for instance, the street *"Calzada de Castro"* in Almería city, Spain) as follows:

```
let $layer  := rt:getLayerByName(.,"Calle Calzada de Castro",0.001),
    $street := rt:getElementByName(.,"Calle Calzada de Castro")
return
    fn:filter($layer,xosm_sp:isCrossing(?, $street))
```

Here *getLayerByName* obtains, from the indexed OSM layer (represented by '.'), all the elements close, i.e. with MBRs at distance 110 meters (0.001 in central angel degrees), to the street *"Calzada de Castro"*[5], and *getElementByName* retrieves the OSM way representing the street *"Calzada de Castro"*. The symbol '?' indicates the *isCrossing* argument to be filtered.

With respect to (b) (i.e., Keyword Based Queries), the keyword operator *searchKeyword* (i.e. true whenever an OMS element has the given keyword) in combination with the higher order function *filter* can be used to retrieve, from the indexed OSM layer, all the schools close to the street *"Calzada de Castro"*. In this case, the search is restricted to vicinity of the street *"Calzada de Castro"*.

```
let $layer  := rt:getLayerByName(.,"Calle Calzada de Castro",0.001)
return
    fn:filter($layer,xosm_kw:searchKeyword(?,"school"))
```

Let us remark that we have required a distance of *0.001* (i.e., 110 meters) to *"Calzada de Castro"*, which means MBRs of schools are at distance *0.001* from the MBR of *"Calzada de Castro"*. Increasing distance, farther away schools are retrieved.

3   Aggregation Operators

Now, we show the proposed operators for expressing aggregation queries (see Table 6). The aggregation operators are inspired by SOLAP operators. In [21], a taxonomy of operators has been stablished of the so-called *numeric operators* whose result is numeric[6]. They consider two levels of operators. The first level includes *numeric-spatial* and *numeric-multidimensional* operators. Numeric-spatial operators can be topological (Boolean (i.e., one-zero) Clementini's operators), and metric (*area*, *length*, *perimeter* and *distance*), while numeric-multidimensional operators are *max*, *min*, *sum*, *count* and *distinct count*, among others. A second level is defined as combinations of operators of the first level.

---

[5] "Calle" means street in spanish.

[6] In [21] they also consider *spatial operators* whose result is spatial (*ConvexHull, Envelope, Centroid, Boundary, Intersection, Union, Difference* and *Buffer*). They also consider navigation and temporal operators.

Table 6. Aggregation Based OMS Operators

Type	Name
Distributive	*topologicalCount(sq,e,b)*, *metricMin(sq,m)*, *metricMax(sq,m)*, *metricSum(sq,m)*, *minDistance(sq,e)* and *maxDistance(sq,e)*
Algebraic	*metricAvg(sq,m)*, *metricStdev(sq,m)*, *avgDistance(sq)*, *metricTopCount(sq,k,m)*, *metricBottomCount(sq,k,m)*, *topCountDistance(sq,k)* and *bottomCountDistance(sq,k)*
Holistic	*metricMedian(sq,m)*, *metricMode(sq,m)* and *metricRank(sq,m,k)*

Numeric-multidimensional operators can be classified by *distributive, algebraic* or *holistic* [13]. An aggregate function is *distributive* if it can be computed in a distributed manner, that is, the result derived by applying the function to the n aggregate values is the same as that derived by applying the function to the entire data set (without partitioning). An aggregate function is *algebraic* if it can be computed by an algebraic function with m arguments (where m is a bounded positive integer), each of which is obtained by applying a distributive aggregate function. Finally, an aggregate function is *holistic* when there does not exist an algebraic function with m arguments that characterizes the computation.

Let us now introduce the proposed aggregation operators. With respect to the first level, numeric spatial operators (both topological and metric), they are derived from the Boolean spatial operators defined in Section 2.3, and from the JTS library in the case of metric operators (i.e., *area, length, perimeter* and *distance*). Numeric multidimensional operators of the first level are taken from the built-in XQuery functions.

With respect to the second level, they are summarized in Table 6. *Distributive* operators are defined as follows: (1) *topologicalCount(sq,e,b)* returns the number of objects of a sequence of objects *sq* that meet a given Boolean spatial relation *b* with the OSM element *e* (i.e., *isIn, isNext, furtherNorthNodes, isCrossing*, and so on); (2) *metricMin(sq,m)*, resp. (3) *metrixMax(sq,m)*, returns the objects of *sq* having the minimum, resp. maximum, value of a given metric operator *m*; (4) *metricSum(sq,m)* returns the result of adding the values of *sq* of a given metric operator *m*; and, finally, (5) *minDistance(sq,e)*, resp. (6) *maxDistance(sq,e)*, returns the object of *sq* with the minimum, resp. maximum, distance with respect to the OSM element *e*.

In the case of *algebraic* operators, we have defined the following operators: (1) *metricAvg(sq,m)* returns the average value of a given metric operator *m* in *sq*; (2) *avgDistance(sq)*, the same as *metricAvg* but for *distance*; (3) *metricStdev(sq,m)* returns the standard deviation of a given metric operator *m* in *sq*; (4) *metricTopCount(sq,k,m)* (resp. (5) *metricBottomCount(sq,k,m)*) returns the k elements with the highest (resp. the lowest) values of a given metric operator *m*; and, finally, (6) *topCountDistance(sq,k)* and (7) *bottomCountDistance(sq,k)* are similar to the last ones but for *distance*.

Finally, with regard to *holistic* operators, we have considered the following ones: (1) *metricMedian(sq,m)* and (2) *metricMode(sq,m)* returning the median and mode value of a given metric operator *m*, respectively, and (3) *metricRank(sq,m,e)* which returns the position of an element *e* in the ranking of the metric operator *m*.

We would like to remark that our proposal of aggregation operators is richer than the proposed in [21]. In all the cases of metric operators, functions passed as arguments can be one of *area, perimeter, length* and *distance,* as well as any function which computes numeric values from OSM elements. This is the case of *metricMin, metricMax, metricSum, metricAvg, metricStdev, metricTopCount, metricBottomCount, metricMedian, metricMode* and *metricRank.* Additionally, operators *metricMin* and *metricMax* which return an unique value in [21], can here return more than one value. There *metricMin* and *metricMax* are used for area, perimeter and length which rarely are equal for more than one value. Here, *metricMin* and *metricMax* can be applied to any operator returning a numeric value, for instance, number of stars of hotels, which can be the same for several hotels. Finally, *metricMode* can be applied to any operator, not only numeric.

Now, let us see the implementation of the operators in our framework. Let us start with the distributive operators. For instance, *topologicalCount* is defined as follows:

```
declare function xosm_ag:topologicalCount($sq as node()*,$e as node(),$b as
    xs:string)
{
 count(fn:filter($sq,function($o){xosm_sp:booleanQuery($o, $e, $b)}))
};
```

Due to the XQuery higher order facilities, *topologicalCount,* in our approach, has an input parameter (i.e., *$b*) representing the name of the spatial operator. *topologicalCount* is defined in terms of *count* (built-in XQuery function), *filter* (higher-order function) and *booleanQuery. booleanQuery* is a function of our library for checking a given boolean relation (for instance, topological) between two OSM elements. *metricMax* is also defined using the higher order facility as follows:

```
declare function xosm_ag:metricMax($sq as node()*, $m as xs:string)
{
 let $l := xosm_ag:metricList($sq,$m),
     $max := fn:max(data($l/tag[@k=$m]/@v))
 return
     fn:filter($l, function($o){xosm_kw:searchTag($o,$m,$max)})
};
```

metricMax uses the built-in XQuery function *max, filter,* the keyword operator *searchTag* (i.e. true whenever the OSM element has a tag with the given values), and an auxiliary function *metricList* of our library. *metricList* annotates the computed values from the metric operator (represented by the input parameter *$m,* i.e. area, perimeter, etc) in each OSM element. These values are added as a tag in each element.

With regard to algebraic operators, *metricBottomCount* is defined as follows:

```
declare function xosm_ag:metricBottomCount($sq as node()*,$m as xs:string,$k
    as xs:integer)
{
 let $l := xosm_ag:metricList($sq,$m)
 return
 fn:subsequence(fn:sort($l,function($o){xosm_kw:getTagValue($o,$m)}),1,$k)
};
```

which is defined in terms of *metricList*, the higher order function *sort*, the built-in XQuery function *subsequence* and the keyword operator *getTagValue*. *topCountDistance* is similarly defined as follows:

```
declare function xosm_ag:topCountDistance($sq as node()*, $k as xs:integer)
{
 fn:subsequence(fn:sort($sq,
                function($o){-(xosm_kw:getTagValue($o,"distance"))}),1,$k)
};
```

topCountDistance can be easily implemented because distances have been annotated in the R-tree to each OSM element. Finally, we have also implemented the holistic ones; for instance *metricMedian* is defined as follows:

```
declare function xosm_ag:metricMedian($sq as node()*, $m as xs:string)
{
  let $1 := xosm_ag:metricList($sq,$m),
      $ol := fn:sort($1/*,function($o){xosm_kw:getTagValue($o,$m)}),
      $c := count($ol)
  return
    if ($c mod 2 != 0) then $ol[xs:integer($c div 2)+1]
    else
    ($ol[$c div 2]/tag[@k=$m]/@v + $ol[($c div 2) + 1]/tag[@k=$m]/@v) div 2
};
```

metricMedian is defined in terms of *metricList*, *sort* and *count*. Finally, *metricRank* is defined in terms if *metricList*, *sort* and the keyword operator *getTagValue*, as follows:

```
declare function xosm_ag:metricRank($sq as node()*,$m as xs:string, $k as xs:
    integer)
{
  let $1 := xosm_ag:metricList($sq,$m)
  return fn:sort($1,function($o){xosm_kw:getTagValue($o,$m)})[$k]
};
```

4 XOSM Tool

In this section, we will show the XOSM (XQuery for Open Street Map) tool, developed by our group. The Web-based tool facilitates map querying, enabling the selection of an area of the OSM map and the creation of an index (see Figure 1). Once the index has been created, queries can be executed from the XQuery shell (see Figure 2). Additionally, the tool is equipped with a batch of pre-defined spatial, keyword and aggregation queries (among them, the included in this paper). XOSM visualizes the answer highlighting ways in a different color and with an icon in the case of nodes (see Figure 2). In case the result is a value (integer, real, etc.,) XOSM visualizes the result in a pop-up window.

4.1 Examples of Queries

Now, we show some examples of queries. Figures 3 and 4 show the results of the queries in the XOSM tool.

Example 1. The first query requests the size of park areas close to the "Paseo de Almería" street. The query is expressed as follows:

OpenStreetMap Spatial Indexing Wizard

Selection of Map and Zoom Level for Indexing

OpenStreetMap Spatial Indexing Wizard

Specification of Spatial Index Name

OpenStreetMap Spatial Indexing Wizard

Spatial Index Creation

Fig. 1. Select Area, Index Name and Create Index

Fig. 2. Execution of Queries

```
let $layer := rt:getLayerByName(.,"Paseo de Almeria",0.003),
    $parkAreas := fn:filter($layer,xosm_kw:searchKeyword(?,"park"))
return
    xosm_ag:metricSum($parkAreas,"area")
```

Here, *getLayerByName* allows us to retrieve all the OSM elements at a distance of 330 meters from "Paseo de Almería". Next, *filter* and *searchKeyword* select those OSM elements labeled with the tag "park", and finally, *metricSum* is used to sum sizes of park areas.

Example 2. The second example requests the hotels with most frequent star rating close to "Paseo de Almería". The query is expressed as follows:

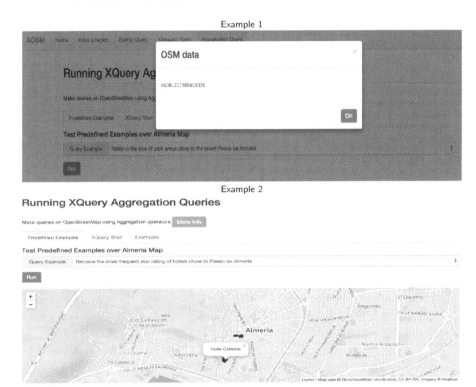

Fig. 3. Results of Examples 1 and 2 in XOSM

```
let $layer := rt:getLayerByName(.,"Paseo de Almeria",0.003),
    $hotels := fn:filter($layer,xosm_kw:searchKeyword(?,"hotel"))
return
    xosm_ag:metricMode($hotels,"stars")
```

In this query the searched tag with the functions *filter* and *searchKeyword* is "hotel", and the holistic operator *metricMode* is used.

Example 3. The third example requests the biggest hotels of top star ratings close to "Paseo de Almería". The query is expressed as follows:

```
let $layer := rt:getLayerByName(.,"Paseo de Almeria",0.003),
    $hotels := fn:filter($layer,xosm_kw:searchKeyword(?,"hotel"))
return
    xosm_ag:metricMax(xosm_ag:metricMax($hotels,"stars"), "area")
```

In this case the functions *filter* and *searchKeyword* are used to search the tag "hotel", and after the distributive function *metricMax* is used twice. Thus this example shows how to compose queries. The first result (i.e., the hotels with the maximum number of stars) is used to compute the second result (i.e., the maximum of sizes).

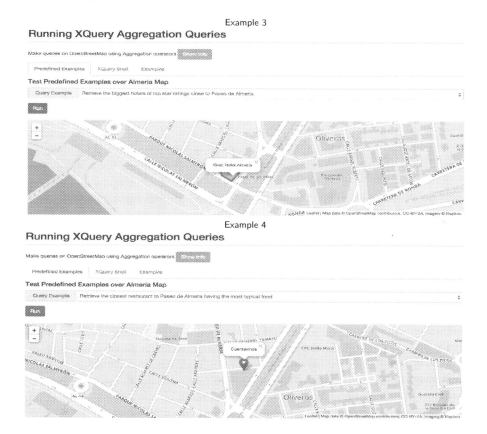

Fig. 4. Results of Examples 3 and 4 in XOSM

Example 4. The last example requests the closest restaurant to "Paseo de Almería" having the most typical food. The query can be expressed as follows:

```
let $layer := rt:getLayerByName(.,"Paseo de Almeria",0.003),
    $restaurants := fn:filter($layer,xosm_kw:searchKeyword(?,"restaurant"))
return
    xosm_ag:metricMin(xosm_ag:metricMode($restaurants,"cuisine"),"distance")
```

Again, *filter* is combined with *searchKeyword* for the keyword "restaurant". Now, the distributive operator *metricMin* is composed with the holistic one *metricMode*. *metricMin* is used for the retrieval of the closest restaurant to "Paseo de Almería", while *metricMode* is used for the retrieval of the most typical food.

4.2 Benchmarks

Now, we show the benchmarks with aggregation queries. We have taken response times for the previous examples, varying size of layers. Layers range from 1353 to 19929 objects (i.e., from 5km to 10km). We have used the *BaseX Query* processor

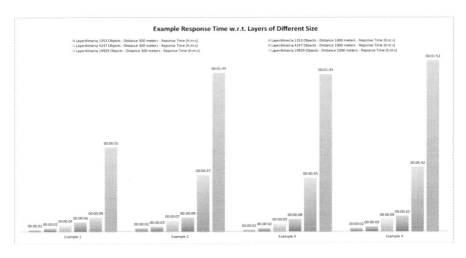

Fig. 5. Time for Query Execution

in a HP Proliant (two processors and 16 MB RAM Memory) with Windows
Server 2008 R2. The results are shown in Figure 5. We can see that costly
queries are those involving composition, but all of them exhibit a good behavior
(from several seconds to two minutes). The layers used can be considered of
medium-size. For getting reasonable times in big cities, is crucial to be focused
on a medium-size city area. Even when the whole layer of big cities can be
handled in our approach, the XOSM queries are focused on an smaller sublayer
(of a certain area of the city). For this reason, we have tested the examples with
the Almería layers, which have a size similar to big areas of big cities. XOSM
limits the size of OSM layers to be indexed and queried.

5   Related Work

Most tools are able to query OSM with very simple commands: searching by
tag and relation names. This is the case of *JOSM*[7] and *Xapiviewer*[8]. The *OSM
Extended API (or XAPI)*[9] is an extended API that offers search queries in OSM
with a XPath flavoring. The *Overpass API (or OSM3S)*[10] is an extension to
select parts of the OSM layer. Both XAPI and OSM3S act as a database over
the web: the client sends a query to the API and gets back the dataset that corresponds to the query. OSM3S has a proper query language which can be encoded
by an XML template. OSM3S offers more sophisticated queries than XAPI,
but it is equipped with a rather limited query language. OSM3S is specifically
designed for search criteria like location, types of objects, tag values, proximity or combinations of them. OSM3S has the query languages *Overpass XML*

---

[7] https://josm.openstreetmap.de/
[8] http://osm.dumoulin63.net/xapiviewer/
[9] http://wiki.openstreetmap.org/wiki/Xapi
[10] http://overpass-api.de/

and *Overpass QL*. Both languages are equivalent. They handle OSM objects ((a) standalone queries) and set of OSM objects ((b) query composition and filtering). With respect to (a), the query language permits to express queries for searching a particular object, and it is equipped with forward or backward recursion to retrieve links from an object (for instance, it enables to retrieve the nodes of a way). With respect to (b), the query language permits to express queries using several search criteria. Among others, it can express: to find all data in a bounding box (i.e., positioning), to find all data near something else (i.e., proximity), to find all data by tag value (exact value, non-exact value and regular expressions), negation, union, difference, intersection, and filtering, with a rich set of selectors, and by polygon, by area pivot, and so on. However, OSM3S facilities (i.e., query composition and filtering) cannot be combined with spatial operators such as Clementini's crosses or touches. In OSM3S, only one type of spatial intersection is considered (proximity 0 by using across selector). For instance, the query (allowed in our library) *"Retrieve the streets crossing Calzada de Castro street and ending to Avenida de Montserrat street"* is not allowed in OSM3S. On the other hand, OSM3S has a rich query language for keyword search based queries. Aggregation operators are not covered by OSM3S, and thus our proposal can be considered richer than the existent OSM specific query languages.

PostGreSQL is a well-known RDBMS with a spatial extension called Post-GIS. PostGIS adds datatypes and spatial operators to PostGreSQL. Indexing of spatial data is carried out by the R-Tree-over-GiST scheme. Open Street Map can be handled by PostGIS with the following tools: (1) osmosis[11]: a Java-based library for OSM loading, writing and ordering; (2) Osm2pgsql[12] on top of osmosis, to transform OSM; (3) Imposm[13] a Python-based tool to import OSM in XML and PBF ("Protocolbuffer Binary Format") formats. We have implemented our own R-tree structure to store XML-based OSM data. However, we plan to adopt PostGIS indexing in the future versions of the XOSM tool.

In the context of RDF and SPARQL, there are several proposals of languages and tools for working with spatial data. GeoSPARQL[3] (standard of the Open Geospatial Consortium) and stSPARQL[17] are the most relevant contributions to this area. Both are very similar. GeoSPARQL provides a vocabulary to express spatial data in RDF, and defines an extension of SPARQL for querying. The vocabulary includes a set of topological operations based on Egenhofer and Region Connection Calculus (RCC8). Parliament[4] is an implementation of the GeoSPARQL using Jena as RDF system. uSeekM also uses the Sesame RDF store as well as PostGIS, and implements GeoSPARQL features. Omitting aggregate functions and updates from stSPARQL, stSPARQL is a subset of GeoSPARQL. stSPARQL is supported by Strabon[18], which extends the RDF store Sesame with spatial data stored in PostGIS. stSPARQL uses SELECT, FILTER and HAVING clauses of SPARQL in combination with spatial

---

[11] https://github.com/openstreetmap/osmosis
[12] https://github.com/openstreetmap/osm2pgsql
[13] http://www.imposm.org/

predicates to query RDF spatial data. The "OpenGIS Simple Feature Access" standard (OGC-SFA)[14], Egenhofer and RCC-8, are used as languages for topological spatial relations. FILTER can be combined with them to define spatial selections and joins. These can be also used in the SELECT and HAVING clauses. Aggregation is present in stSPARQL in the form of union, intersection and extent (i.e., minimum bounding box of a set of geometries). stSPARQL uses a B-tree to index non spatial data, while R-Tree-over-GiST is used is used for spatial indexing (provided by PostGIS). stSPARQL is mapped to SQL queries executed under PostGreSQL. Virtuoso, OWLIM and AllegroGraph are RDF-based engine supporting geometries of points. Open Street Map has been integrated in the RDF area thanks to the OSM Semantic Network, in which OSM data resources are available in RDF format.

While the context is different (RDF/SPARQL versus XML/XQuery) we found analogies with the existent approaches. With regard to topological operators, our library is built on top of JTS, and thus providing similar expressivity. Indexing is based in all the cases on R-tree like structures. With regard to expressivity of the query language, RDF/SPARQL based languages can be considered similar to our proposal, except for aggregation operators. The only case of language equipped with aggregation is stSPARQL, including union, intersection and extent. Thus our library provides a richer set of aggregation operators.

Unfortunately, we cannot compare our benchmarks with existent implementations of similar tools due to the following reasons. Even when OSM has been used for providing benchmarks in a recent work [10], they use OSM as dataset for Description Logic based reasoners rather than to evaluate spatial queries. There are some proposals [11,16] for Spatial RDF benchmarking, but none of the queries involve the same kind of aggregation we propose. Benchmarks of RDF/SPARQL tools are generally concerned with execution times of large RDF resources, that most of cases are built from several RDF namespaces.

Our goal is less ambitious, focused on the development of a tool (XOSM) for map querying and visualization. XOSM limits the size of maps to be indexed and queried. This is also the case of other OSM APIs. In any case, XOSM has to answer in short time, and the efficiency of XOSM has been one of our main concerns during the development of our work.

6   Conclusion and Future Work

In this paper, we have presented an extension of a previously defined library for querying Open Street Map, and a Web-based tool for the visualization and querying of OSM maps. The extension incorporates aggregation operators which makes possible to rank and summarize data from OSM maps. We have shown how to work with this kind of queries using the developed XOSM tool. As future work, we would like to extend our work as follows. Firstly, we would like to use an R-tree based structure to improve performance of aggregation operators. The idea would be to annotate each MBR of the R-tree with a pre-defined

---

[14] http://www.opengeospatial.org/standards/sfs

set of aggregation values (maximum, minimum, mode, etc.,) of each area. It would make possible to implement more efficient algorithms which discard those MBRs of upper (or lower) values. Secondly, and related to the first goal, top-k algorithms will be implemented making use of the new R-tree structure.

References

1. Almendros-Jiménez, J.M., Becerra-Terón, A.: Querying open street map with xquery. In: Proceedings of the 1st International Conference on Geographical Information Systems Theory, Applications and Management, pp. 61–71 (2015)
2. Bamford, R., Borkar, V., Brantner, M., Fischer, P.M., Florescu, D., Graf, D., Kossmann, D., Kraska, T., Muresan, D., Nasoi, S., et al.: XQuery reloaded. Proceedings of the VLDB Endowment **2**(2), 1342–1353 (2009)
3. Battle, R., Kolas, D.: Geosparql: enabling a geospatial semantic web. Semantic Web Journal **3**(4), 355–370 (2011)
4. Battle, R., Kolas, D.: Enabling the geospatial semantic web with Parliament and GeoSPARQL. Semantic Web **3**(4), 355–370 (2012)
5. Bennett, J.: OpenStreetMap - Be your own cartographer. Packt Publishing Ltd (2010)
6. Berglund, A., Boag, S., Chamberlin, D., Fernández, M.F., Kay, M., Robie, J., Siméon, J.: XML Path Language (XPath) 2.0. Technical report (2010)
7. Clementini, E., Di Felice, P.: Spatial operators. ACM SIGMOD Record **29**(3), 31–38 (2000)
8. da Silva, J., de Oliveira, A.G., Fidalgo, R.N., Salgado, A.C., Times, V.C.: Modelling and querying geographical data warehouses. Information Systems **35**(5), 592–614 (2010)
9. Egenhofer, M.J.: Spatial SQL: A Query and Presentation Language. IEEE Trans. Knowl. Data Eng. **6**(1), 86–95 (1994)
10. Eiter, T., Schneider, P., Šimkus, M., Xiao, G.: Using openstreetmap data to create benchmarks for description logic reasoners. In: Proceedings of the 3rd International Workshop on OWL Reasoner Evaluation (ORE 2014), vol. 1207, pp. 51–57. CEUR Workshop Proceedings (2014)
11. Garbis, G., Kyzirakos, K., Koubarakis, M.: Geographica: a benchmark for geospatial RDF stores (long version). In: Alani, H., et al. (eds.) ISWC 2013, Part II. LNCS, vol. 8219, pp. 343–359. Springer, Heidelberg (2013)
12. Goodchild, M.F.: Citizens as sensors: the world of volunteered geography. GeoJournal **69**(4), 211–221 (2007)
13. Gray, J., Chaudhuri, S., Bosworth, A., Layman, A., Reichart, D., Venkatrao, M., Pellow, F., Pirahesh, H.: Data cube: A relational aggregation operator generalizing group-by, cross-tab, and sub-totals. Data Mining and Knowledge Discovery **1**(1), 29–53 (1997)
14. Grun, C.: BaseX. The XML Database (2014). http://basex.org
15. Hadjieleftheriou, M., Manolopoulos, Y., Theodoridis, Y., Tsotras, V.J.: R-trees-a dynamic index structure for spatial searching. In: Encyclopedia of GIS, pp. 993–1002. Springer (2008)
16. Kolas, D.: A benchmark for spatial semantic web systems. In: International Workshop on Scalable Semantic Web Knowledge Base Systems (2008)

17. Koubarakis, M., Kyzirakos, K.: Modeling and querying metadata in the semantic sensor web: the model stRDF and the query language stSPARQL. In: Aroyo, L., Antoniou, G., Hyvönen, E., ten Teije, A., Stuckenschmidt, H., Cabral, L., Tudorache, T. (eds.) ESWC 2010, Part I. LNCS, vol. 6088, pp. 425–439. Springer, Heidelberg (2010)
18. Kyzirakos, K., Karpathiotakis, M., Koubarakis, M.: Strabon: a semantic geospatial DBMS. In: Cudré-Mauroux, P., et al. (eds.) ISWC 2012, Part I. LNCS, vol. 7649, pp. 295–311. Springer, Heidelberg (2012)
19. Papadias, D., Kalnis, P., Zhang, J., Tao, Y.: Efficient OLAP operations in spatial data warehouses. In: Jensen, C.S., Schneider, M., Seeger, B., Tsotras, V.J. (eds.) SSTD 2001. LNCS, vol. 2121, pp. 443–459. Springer, Heidelberg (2001)
20. Robie, J., Chamberlin, D., Dyck, M., Snelson, J.: XQuery 3.0: An XML query language. W3C Proposed Recommendation (2014)
21. Ruiz, C.V., Times, V.C.: A taxonomy of SOLAP operators. In: SBBD, pp. 151–165 (2009)

Provalets

OSGi-Based Prova Agents for Rule-Based Data Access

Adrian Paschke[✉]

Freie Universitaet Berlin, Berlin, Germany
paschke@inf.fu-berlin.de

Abstract. Rule-based Data Access (RBDA) has become an active R&D topic in the recent years. In this paper we propose an easy to use agent-based rule programming model and a general component architecture for RBDA. The programming model supports rapid prototyping and reuse of existing Prova rule agents/components which are published and managed in OntoMaven repositories. We name these components Provalets. We propose a declarative component description language that is powerful enough to represent different types of Provalets, including the representation of their functional interfaces and their semantics as well as their non-functional collaboration aspects and quality of service attributes.

1 Introduction

In this publication we propose the concept of ***Provalets***, specifically for use in the context of for Rule-based Data Access (RBDA). Provalets use ideas from (mobile) software agents, automated Maven repository and build management (OntoMaven [6,7]), trusted OSGi component runtime environments and cloud infrastructures to encapsulate data intensive routines and rule-based decision and reaction logic in Prova agents [9][1]. In this paper we describe the principles of Provalets (section 2), the declarative description language for Provalets (section 3) and the OSGi-based reference implementation of Provalets (section 4). We conclude our work in section 5.

2 Principles of Provalets

Provalets are (mobile) rule-based software agents [9] that act as inference component providing rule-based data access and rule-based data processing using Prova. Prova (Prolog + Java) is both a declarative rule-based programming language and a Java-based rule engine which can be used in Prova agents. Prova provides various built-ins for rule-based data access[2]. For instance, the following example defines a rule-based data access rule which selects with the SPARQL query built-in of Prova all luxury car manufacturers from DBpedia.

---

[1] http://prova.ws

[2] Prova has various built-ins for rule-based data access such as Java object access, file access, XML (DOM), SQL, RDF triples, XQuery, SPARQL.

© Springer International Publishing Switzerland 2015
C. Debruyne et al. (Eds.): OTM 2015 Conferences, LNCS 9415, pp. 519–526, 2015.
DOI: 10.1007/978-3-319-26148-5_35

```
luxuryCar(Manufacturer) :-
 sparql_connect(Connection, "http://dbpedia.org/sparql"),
 Query="SELECT ?manufacturer ?name ?car   % SPARQL RDF Query
        WHERE {?car <http://purl.org/dc/terms/subject>
          <http://dbpedia.org/resource/Category:Luxury_vehicles> .
            ?car dbo:manufacturer ?man .
            ?man foaf:name ?manufacturer.   } ORDER by ?manufacturer",
 sparql_select(Connection, Query, QueryID),
 sparql_results(QueryID, Manufacturer).
```

Provalets have a clear REST input and output interface, specifically an input URI and an output URI. They run in a controlled and secure runtime environment that guarantees that Provalets can only read data from input resources and write data to output resources. Provalets describe their functionality in terms of pre- and post-conditions on the sets of input and output data (section 3 defines the declarative interface description of Provalets).

Provalets describe themselves using the Linked Data principles: Each Provalet has a unique URI that is resolvable via HTTP. The description contains metadata about the Provalet including runtime dependencies and permissions required on the runtime platform as well as the description of the functionality it provides in the form of statements about pre- and post-conditions over the sets of input and output data.

2.1   Input and Output Interface of Provalets

Each Provalet is configured with one input URI that it is allowed to read from and one output URI that it is allowed to write to. The runtime environment of a Provalets should not allow the Provalet to cause any other side effects. The runtime environment controls which types of data and which KB sources of data are accessible by the Provalet.

This restriction of the Provalet side effects allows to describe their functionality in a more formal way than is possible with todays web services. Provalets can be described as algebraic operators on sets of RDF data. For example, a Provalet may describe the output data as a subset or superset of the input data, assertions borrowed from set theory. A Provalet may as well restrict itself to produce only specific kinds of data as semantically defined result sets. Provalets make no other assumption about the input and output sources other than they provide and accept data.

2.2   Permissions of Provalets

Provalets described permissions they require as metadata that is read by the runtime environment during deployment. By default Provalets are solely allowed to see the data which are directly served by the configured input URI. Provalets may define additional required permission. For example to access additional static URIs or crawl URIs that are visible in the set of input data. The sources of data may be restricted by subnets, domains, protocols or even types of data a Provalets is allowed to see. Provalet may provide HTTP access credentials to the input and output resources upon request.

Provalets must request permission to use additional computing resources on the machine they are executed. A Provalet may request harddisk space to store intermediate results. Other resources include memory, CPU time, account information, access to other web services. The latter can be used by Provalet to enforce license models through trusted providers. It is the task of the runtime container of a Provalet to grant required permissions and allow access to requested resources.

2.3   Runtime Environment of Provalets

Not only the the permissions for Provalets are enforced by the runtime environment. Essentially Provalets are shielded from any platform details. By default Provalets are not allowed to access any resource on the host system. For example Provalets should not even be allowed read information about the systems time or memory consumption. Basically Provalets should only be allowed to manipulate data without making any assumptions of the system nor to collect information about it.

Container Resource. The container resource acts like a knowledge base resource and describes itself with metadata in RDF. A user or agent receives information about a container resource by sending an HTTP request to the container URI. For example the container resource describes which permissions it can grant.

To use a container resource to execute a Provalet the user sends an HTTP request adding three parameters to the container URI: the Provalet URI, the input URI and the output URI. This way it is straight forward to execute a Provalet and lookup the results afterwards, by receiving the HTTP response of the output URI.

2.4   Lifecycle of Provalets

The life cycle of a Provalet is as follows:

1. Activation request: the Provalet's URI is passed as a parameter to a container resource together with the URI of the input and the output resource.
2. Reading the Provalet's description: the resource container makes an HTTP request to the URI of the Provalet and fetches data describing the it.
3. Permission enforcement: the runtime container is configured with the requested permissions for the Provalet. If the requirements do not match the containers restrictions the request is answered with HTTP status code 200.
4. Resolving Provalet dependencies: the fetched description contains metadata that allows to compute all runtime-dependencies of a Provalet. See section 4 for technical details of our reference implementation.
5. Downloading runtime dependencies: the container resource fetches all required libraries and constructs the classpath for executing it.

6. Provalet execution: the Provalet bundle is deployed in a secured local runtime environment and the Provalet bundle is started.

7. Provalet response: the user request is answered with an HTTP status code 200 (asynchronous container), or the agent is redirected to the output URI (synchronous container).

8. Writing the result set, the data that form the result are written to the output URI.

9. Finalizing Provalet, all additionally requested resources such as file and memory are released.

10. Undeploy, this step is optional, if configured so the runtime container may erase all libraries from the system. Which will require to download them for the next call.

Our reference implementation is written in Java and is based on web standards and open source libraries.

3   Provalet Description Language

Provalets are described by a semantic component description language that is powerful enough to represent their functional interfaces and their semantics as well as their non-functional collaboration aspects and quality of service attributes. These component descriptions are based on a plug-able semantic vocabulary to model the Provalets component descriptions in a platform-independent manner. The Provalet component description follows the classification of component contracts from Beugnards et al. [4] into four layers:

1. Basic syntactic Provalet component description layer expressing the Provalet artifact characteristics and functional interfaces.

2. Behavioural Provalet description specifying Provalet component semantics.

3. Synchronisation Provalet description describing dependencies between Provalets.

4. Quality of service and licensing Provalet description describing requirements with respect to response times, quality of results etc., as well as rights and obligations with respect to security, trust and licensing (e.g. metering and accounting).

A Provalet description contains

- A set of defined types (URIs) contributed by the Provalet.
- A set of defined properties (URIs) contributed by the Provalet.
- A set of defined constraint relationships (URIs) contributed by the Provalet.
- A function (URI Rest) to load a Provalet resource given a reference and a resource type.
- A function (URI Rest) that can be used to check the properties and relationships contributed by the Provalet component.

A Provalet component description has four parts:

1. In the Provalet component section the Provalet interfaces and necessary artifact characteristics are described, such as the groupId, artifactId, version and the optionally repository dependencies of the Provalet.
2. In the input data section the input resources of the Provalet are defined. The resources defined are constants identified by name and type. The types are defined in an (external) ontology and represented by URIs. This information can be used by the Provalet component to query the RDF data resources if needed.
3. In the output data section, the resources of the Provalet are defined. This is where a Provalet component provides (computed) data resources to be consumed by a consumer. These resources are also typed.
4. In the constraints part, the pre- and post conditions, rights and obligations are specified. The semantics supports the use of standard logical connectives such as AND, OR and XOR to define complex conditions. In addition to the conditions, value properties and existence conditions are supported as well.

Types, properties and relationships are defined in plugable ontologies. The resource types are defined using the web ontology language OWL or RDFS. The component semantics is described by relations between pre- and post-conditions of the Provalet method invocations. Test cases are used for this purpose by using JUnit as the Java standard. The Provalet descriptions provide test suites as part of specifications. Furthermore, Java annotations are used in order to stipulate in the description that a Provalet has to use annotations provided by additional components. Annotations are useful if the Provalet is to take advantage of injected services.

property	semantics	verification
usesAnnotation	classes use the annotations defined	JVM, ASTanalyser
implements	classes implement the interface or extend the abstract class	JVM
extends	classes extend other classes (transitive)	JVM
isVerifiedBy	a class is verified by a test suite	JUnit test runner
tests	a test suite provides tests for an abstract type	JVM

Rule-based conditions in Provalet descriptions can be either atomic or complex. To build complex conditions, the usual rule-based logical connectives with their standard semantics can be used. Three types of atomic conditions are supported: relationships between resources, resource properties, and conditions that a resource must exist. Based on these we can now define rules describing the validity constraints, rights and obligations of a Provalet. For instance, consider the following rule:

```
extends(?x, xp1 : ProvaletInstance) :-
parser(?x : ProvaletInterface, ?c : JavaInstantiableClass),
implements(?c, i : JavaAbstractType),
tests(?s : TestSuite, i),
isVerifiedBy(?c, ?s).
```

The Provalet component has to supply an implementation class of the Provalet interface that must pass a test suite. In order to run the tests, the test runner must instantiate the implementation class, and bind the variable in the test cases within the test suite to this instance. Then the test cases are executed.

4   Implementation

As execution environment for Provalets we applied a framework implementing the OSGI standards [5]. It allows us to dynamically install, update, and uninstall a Provalet and its dependencies, in a running system. Furthermore the OSGI specification provides a security model that is capable of offering a secure execution environment. Our current implementation deploys Apache Felix [1] as OSGi framework, but can be exchanged with another one as well.

Provalets themselves are Maven OSGi artifacts deployed in an OntoMaven artifact repository using OntoMaven [6,7] for the automated management. To automatically generate a new Provalet a Maven archetype can be used. An OntoMaven generated Provalet project provides all necessary dependencies and mechanism. The included *Provalet* class extends the *AbstractProvalet* from our ProvaletCore API and must be filled with the Provalet functionalities. The *ProvaletActivator* class extending the *AbstractProvaletActivator* serves as an OSGi entrance point to the Provalet. During the Provalet development the developer has to keep attention to only specify dependencies to APIs being OSGi capable. The artifact specification can be found in the Provalet description.

To execute the Provalet on a selected input resource the user needs to call the URI of a container resource (*containerURI*) via an HTTP GET request providing the URI of the Provalet (*ProvaletURI*), the input (*inputURI*) and the output URI (*outputURI*) as parameters:

```
<containerURI>?Provalet=<ProvaletURI>&input=<inputURI>&output=<outputURI>
```

The container resource is a special resource with an assigned OSGi environment for the execution of Provalets. It handles the Provalet call and answers the HTTP request with an HTTP response message. First it resolves the Provalet characteristics by calling the *ProvaletURI* and reading the Provalet description which also includes the necessary artifact characteristics (groupId, artifactId, version and optionally the repository). With OntoMaven's dependency resolution mechanism [3,7] the Provalet artifact and all its dependencies are resolved and downloaded to a local temporary repository using the integrated Aether library [11]. The downloaded artifacts are then deployed into the OSGi framework of the container resource and the RDF representation of the *inputURI* is passed as an object to the working method of the Provalet. Finally the container resource starts the installed Provalet bundle. After execution of the working method the Provalet passed its resulting data back to the container. The container checks the contend and enforces restrictions on the Provalet execution and the output and writes the RDF representation to the `outputURI`.

Once an instantiated Provalet exists, verification of the Provalet constraints and rules can be performed using Prova's inference mechanisms. The OSGi bundle classloader is used to load the resources and instantiate a Provalet instance as OSGi component with the translated Provalet rules and ontologies describing the Provalet conditions and constraints. Furthermore, OSGi features (see RFC 125 OSGi) are used to make Provalet licensing information part of the machine readable component meta-data. This enables the Provalet execution applications to reason about this.

Finally, the container resource is responsible for uninstalling all bundles and optionally removing all the locally installed dependencies.

Two working modes of container resources are defined. Asynchronously working containers immediately response with an HTTP response code indicating that the Provalet working method was successfully started. The user of an asynchronously started Provalet has in principal two possibilities to work with the results: (1) an agent polls the output URI after a defined time and (2) the agent uses a subscription mechanism to be informed about updates in the output URI. In the synchronous working mode of a Provalet container the agent is redirected to the output URI once the results have been successfully written to the output URI. In this working mode the user can read the result immediately after receiving the HTTP response. However if the execution of the Provalet is taking too long the server may return with a timeout.

5   Conclusions

We conclude by summarizing the advantages of the Provalet concept.

- Provalets have functional properties with a logic/rule-based semantics. They are guaranteed to produce the same output for the same input.
- Provalets can be formally described with pre- and post conditions over input and output data. This allows formalizing their functionality.
- Provalets can be formally described by their functionality, which allows for automated test generation and automated service consumption. This guarantees their quality.
- Provalets are standardized OSGi components, which execute on a local desktop, in the cloud or on a database system without the need of changing the code or the configuration.
- Provalets cannot violate data privacy constraints. Because they can move to the data and are then not allowed to communicate to the outside.
- Provalets allow simple development and testing independently of the platform they execute on. Provalets support REST protocols.
- No configuration is necessary to execute a Provalet. All steps from selection, download, deployment and execution of a Provalet is packaged in one REST URL call.
- Provalets support reuse of mobile software agents and thereby reduce cost for developing and testing software.
- Provalets dynamically benefit from scaling-out resources. Provalets may spawn themselves to more nodes and split the workload by partitioning.
- Provalets dynamically benefit from scaling-up resources. By adding more resources to a server more Provalets can run on this machine. This reduces network traffic between Provalets.

Future work on the Provalet concept include the use of the new OMG API4KP standard [2,8] for the Provalet interface descriptions and the support of aspects in the automated Aspect OntoMaven [10] deployment of Provalets.

Acknowledgments. This work has been partially supported by the "InnoProfile-Corporate Smart Content" project funded by the German Federal Ministry of Education and Research (BMBF) and the BMBF Innovation Initiative for the New German Länder - Entrepreneurial Regions.

References

1. Apache Software Foundation. Apache felix project. http://felix.apache.org/
2. Athan, T., Bell, R., Kendall, E., Paschke, A., Sottara, D.: API4KP metamodel: a meta-api for heterogeneous knowledge platforms. In: Bassiliades, N., Gottlob, G., Sadri, F., Paschke, A., Roman, D. (eds.) RuleML 2015. LNCS, vol. 9202, pp. 144–160. Springer, Heidelberg (2015)
3. Athan, T., Schäfermeier, R., Paschke, A.: An algorithm for resolution of common logic (edition 2) importation implemented in ontomaven. In: Proceedings of the 8th International Workshop on Modular Ontologies Co-located with the 8th International Conference on Formal Ontology in Information Systems (FOIS 2014), September 22, 2014, Rio de Janeiro (2014)
4. Beugnard, A., Jézéquel, J.-M., Plouzeau, N.: Making components contract aware. IEEE Computer **32**(7), 38–45 (1999)
5. OSGI Alliance. OSGi Service Platform, Core Specification, Release 4, Version 4.2. Technical report, OSGI Alliance, September 2009
6. Paschke, A.: Ontomaven API4KB - a maven-based API for knowledge bases. In: Proceedings of the 6th International Workshop on Semantic Web Applications and Tools for Life Sciences, December 10, 2013, Edinburgh (2013)
7. Paschke, A.: Ontomaven: maven-based ontology development and management of distributed ontology repositories (2013). CoRR, abs/1309.7341
8. Paschke, A., Athan, T., Sottara, D., Kendall, E., Bell, R.: A representational analysis of the API4KP metamodel. In: Cuel, R., Young, R. (eds.) FOMI 2015. LNBIP, vol. 225, pp. 1–12. Springer, Heidelberg (2015)
9. Paschke, A., Boley, H.: Rule Responder: Rule-Based Agents for the Semantic-Pragmatic Web. International Journal on Artificial Intelligence Tools **20**(6), 1043–1081 (2011)
10. Paschke, A., Schäfermeier, R.: Aspect ontomaven - aspect-oriented ontology development and configuration with ontomaven (2015). CoRR, abs/1507.00212
11. Sonatype. Aether, June 2011. http://aether.sonatype.org/

Light-Weight Cross-Lingual Ontology Matching with LYAM++

Abdel Nasser Tigrine[✉], Zohra Bellahsene, and Konstantin Todorov

LIRMM / University of Montpellier, Montpellier, France
{Tigrine,Bellahsene,Todorov}@lirmm.fr

Abstract. During the last decade, several automatic ontology matching systems were developed to address the problem of ontology heterogeneity. Aligning cross-lingual ontologies is among the current challenging issues in the field of ontology matching. The majority of the existing approaches rely on machine translation to deal with this problem. However, inherent problems of machine translation are imprecision and ambiguity. In this paper, we propose a novel approach to the cross-lingual ontology matching task, relying on the large multilingual semantic network BabelNet as a source of background knowledge to assist the matching process. We have designed and tested a novel orchestration of the components of the matching workflow. Our approach is implemented under the form of a prototype named LYAM++ (Yet Another Matcher–Light)—a fully automatic cross-lingual ontology matching system that does not rely on machine translation. We report the results of our experiments that show that LYAM++ outperforms considerably the best techniques in the state-of-the-art according to the obtained results on the MultiFarm datasets of the Ontology Alignment Evaluation Initiative 2014.

Keywords: Ontology matching · Background knowledge · Cross-lingualisme

1 Introduction

Ontologies have become key elements in a variety of knowledge-based applications. However, they are continuously confronted with the problem of heterogeneity – syntactic, terminological, conceptual or semantic. Ontology matching techniques propose solutions to the heterogeneity problem by automatically discovering correspondences between the elements of two different ontologies and thus enabling interoperability [1,2].

In spite of the considerable progress that has been made in the field of ontology matching recently, many questions still remain open and many challenges to face — a complete overview can be found in [3]. The current work addresses the challenge of using explicit reference knowledge in order to make up for the missing background knowledge in the matching process. We apply this solution to a particular ontology matching problem — aligning cross-lingual ontologies, i.e., ontologies that are defined in different natural languages.

© Springer International Publishing Switzerland 2015
C. Debruyne et al. (Eds.): OTM 2015 Conferences, LNCS 9415, pp. 527–544, 2015.
DOI: 10.1007/978-3-319-26148-5_36

Indeed, considering multilingual and cross-lingual information is becoming more and more important, in view particularly of the growing number of content-creating non-English users and the clear demand of cross-language interoperability leading to the need of bringing multilingual semantic information and knowledge together in an explicit manner. In the context of the web of data, it is important to propose procedures for linking vocabularies across natural languages. Ontology matching techniques are also largely applied for data linking, or instance matching, where the problem of multilingualism appears even more often. Cross-lingual data and ontology matching is therefore a crucial task in order to foster the creation of a global information network, instead of a set of linguistically isolated data islands. However, as observed by Spohr et al. [4], most of the ontology alignment algorithms assume that the ontologies to be aligned are defined in a single natural language.

The methods that have been proposed to deal with cross-lingual ontology matching most commonly rely on automatic translation of labels to a single target language [5]. However, machine translation tolerates low precision levels and there is often a lack of exact one-to-one correspondence between the terms in different natural languages. Other approaches apply machine learning techniques [4] that usually require large training corpora that are rarely available in an ontology matching scenario.

We present LYAM++ (Yet Another Matcher - Light), a fully automatic cross-lingual ontology matching system making use of background knowledge to assist the matching process and to recreate the missing semantic context. Since we focus on the cross-lingual ontology matching problem, we rely on the multi-lingual semantic network BabelNet[1], which has the advantages of being openly available, large and general-purpose. Note that an alignment system is composed by a number of components, comprising usually a terminological matcher and a structural matcher, as well as certain filtering and verification modules [6]. The background knowledge provided by BabelNet is used in our approach within two of these components. In the first place, it is applied to evaluate the terminological similarities between the names of the ontological elements by reconstituting in a semantically coherent manner the label of a source entity in the language of the target ontology. In the second place, BabelNet is called upon within the structural matching component of the matching procedure. Note that the explicit background knowledge helps to reduce significantly the complexity of the similarity computation algorithms (wherefrom the word "light" in the name of our tool). Another original feature of our approach is the choice of orchestration of the components of the alignment workflow. Our experiments on the MultiFarm[2] benchmark data show that (1) our method outperforms the best cross-lingual matching approaches in the current state-of-the-art and (2) the novel workflow orchestration provides better results compared to the one that is commonly used by the established alignment systems.

---

[1] http://babelnet.org/
[2] http://web.informatik.uni-mannheim.de/multifarm/

In the following section, we focus on the technical aspects of our approach (Section 2). The experiments that have been conducted and their results are discussed afterwards (Section 3), followed by an overview of related approaches (Section 4) and a conclusion (Section 5).

2   Overview of the Approach

LYAM++ is a matching system specialized in dealing with cross-lingual ontology heterogeneity. LYAM++ makes use of several matching modules of YAM++ (an established and highly-performant tool [2], also developed by our research group), adding a reference knowledge component that aims to (1) provide the missing semantic context in the matching process and (2) lighten the alignment pipeline used in the original system. Particularly, LYAM++ makes use of the natural language processing module from YAM++ as well as several similarities measures. Indeed, one of our working hypotheses is that background knowledge, when used appropriately, can help to reduce the effort of matcher selection and tuning and can considerably shorten the chain of similarity measures that is commonly applied within the alignment processing workflow [6].

The workflow of LYAM++ is shown in Fig. 1. Let S and T be two input ontologies. Our goal is to align the former (*source*) to the latter (*target*). Additionally, we assume that S is given in a natural language l_S and T – in a language l_T. We have chosen BabelNet as a source of background knowledge and our processing pipeline uses two matchers: a multilingual terminological matcher (the main matcher), making use of only two similarity measures, and a structural matcher. In addition, we apply a mapping verification and selection filter.

2.1   A Novel Orchestration of the Workflow Components

In the following sections, we will describe each of the components mentioned above in details. Here, we draw the reader's attention to the first original contribution of our approach, which lies in the choice of orchestration of these components (Fig. 1). Note that most of the alignment tools perform terminological and structural matching before mapping selection and verification [6]. We reversed this order in an attempt to ensure that we "feed" only good quality mappings to the structural matcher. In that, LYAM++ filters the discovered correspondences right after producing the initial terminological alignment. The viability of this decision is supported experimentally in Section 3.

2.2   Preprocessing

As every ontology matching system, LYAM++ transforms the source and the target ontologies before applying the alignment procedure. The first preprocessing step performed by LYAM++ consists in splitting the elements of each ontology into three groups: labels of *classes*, labels of *object properties* and labels of *data object properties*, since these groups of elements are to be aligned separately.

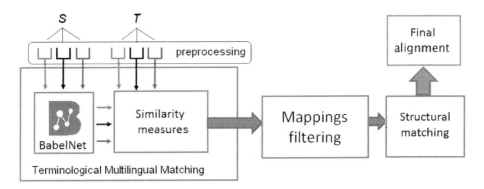

Fig. 1. The processing pipeline of LYAM++.

The labels of ontological elements are seen as strings of characters. In order to improve the result of comparing two strings, we apply a standard set of preprocessing procedures: normalization of characters and spaces, removing diacritics or accents, deleting numbers, punctuations and stop words, tokenization and lemmatization.

2.3   Background Knowledge: BabelNet

As stated above, our system makes use of multilingual background knowledge and our choice has fallen on BabelNet for several reasons. BabelNet is a multilingual semantic network and ontology that has been built by merging different encyclopedic and linguistic resources, such as the English and the multilingual WordNet, Wikipedia, the linked database Wikidata, and the multilingual dictionaries Wiktionary and OmegaWiki. The integration of these resources has been conducted automatically. BabelNet is openly available, large in scale and general-purpose resource, covering 271 languages. For these reasons, it appears to be an appropriate choice of background knowledge for cross-lingual ontology matching, although potentially our system is not restricted to this particular choice and could make use of any other multilingual reference knowledge base.

2.4   Terminological Similarity Measures

The main matching component of an alignment system (see following subsection) produces an intermediate alignment based on terminological similarities between the labels by calling on a string-based similarity measure. The ontology matching literature is rich in definitions of measures computing the degree of similarity between two labels. An exhaustive overview can be found in [7]. Our system makes use of only two similarity measures – a simple token similarity and a compound label similarity. The former is applied for measuring similarities between single-token strings while the latter is suited for labels composed of several tokens (like for example "Conference_Dinner", "ConferenceDinner", "Conference-Dinner"). We will denote by s and t – two labels (strings of characters) to be compared, by s_i and t_j – tokens belonging to s and t, respectively, and by $|s|$ – the number of tokens in s.

Single-Token Similarity Measures. An ontology matching system designer can choose among a large set of single-token similarity measures. Our choice has fallen on the Jaccard coefficient, which is based on the simple idea of estimating the relative overlap of two sets of objects. In our case, two tokens are seen as two strings of characters, s_i and t_j and the Jaccard coefficient is given as $sim(s_i, t_j) = \frac{|s_i \cap t_j|}{|s_i \cup t_j|}$, where the numerator represents the number of common symbols of the two strings and the denominator – the total number of symbols. Note that we have carried out experiments with edit-distance based measures, such as Levenshtein, but we retained the Jaccard coefficient because it showed to perform best in our experiments.

Similarity Measures for Compound Labels. This group of measures is based on first splitting the labels into the tokens that compose them, then applying a simple token similarity function (such as Levenshtein or Jaccard, denoted by sim in the following) internally before evaluating the overall label similarity. Our choice has fallen on three of the most common measures of this type.

(1) The **SoftTFIDF** measure is defined as a modification of the well-known cosine measure by using the TF/IDF weights [8]. We refer the reader to [7] for a formal definition. The TF/IDF weighting scheme is used to measure the relevance of a term with respect to a document and within a given corpus. In an ontology matching scenario, given a label composed by several tokens and an ontology composed of several labels, this scheme is applied by considering a token as a term, a label — as a document and the collection of labels in an ontology — as a corpus.

(2) The **Monge-Elkan** measure is defined as follows:

$$MongeElkan(s, t) = \frac{1}{|s|} \sum_{i=1}^{|s|} \max_{i=1}^{|t|} sim(s_i, t_j)$$

(3) The **Extended Jaccard** measure, as its name suggests, is based on the Jaccard similarity [7] given as follows:

$$ExtJaccard(s, t) = \frac{|C|}{|C| + |UniqueToken(s)| + |UniqueToken(t)|},$$

where $token(s)$ is a function returning the set of tokens composing a string s, $C = \{(s_i, t_j) | s_i \in token(s) \wedge t_j \in token(t) : sim(s_i, t_j) > \theta\}$ and $UniqueToken(s) = \{s_i | s_i \in token(s) \wedge t_j \in token(t) \wedge (s_i, t_j) \notin C\}$.

2.5   Main Multilingual Terminological Matching Using BabelNet

The main matcher is responsible for producing an initial *terminological* (i.e., based on the labels of the ontology elements) alignment that will be further on improved by the filtering modules and the structural matcher. This matcher uses in its algorithm the tools described in the previous subsections (BabelNet and two similarity measures). The multilingual matching is performed in two steps: (1) the labels of the source ontology are transformed into the language of the target ontology by using BabelNet and then (2) a monolingual label similarity computation is performed. In this process, two similarity measures are used – a simple similarity measure applied on single-token strings (in step 1) and a similarity function applied on compound labels composed by multiple tokens (in step 2). Our main contribution within this matching module lies in (1) a procedure for transforming the source labels into the language of the target ontology by using BebelNet and (2) a method for the semantic expansion of the transformed labels aiming to improve the final similarity values.

Transforming the Source Labels into the Target Language. In order to overpass the cross-lingual barrier, the tokens of the elements of T are transformed and enhanced by the help of BabelNet. At first, every token of a given label s in S is enriched by related terms and synonyms from BabelNet in the language l_T, which makes these terms comparable to the tokens of the labels in T. A simple similarity evaluation by the help of the Jaccard coefficient selects the term in each set of related terms corresponding to a given token from s that has the highest score with respect to every token in each label of T. This helps to re-constitute the label s in the language l_T. This procedure is presented in Algorithm 1. Finally, the labels in each group of S and T, seen as sets of tokens *in the same language (l_T)*, are compared to one another by using one of the measures described above (Soft TFIDF, Extended Jaccard or Monge-Elkan).

Example. We accompany the algorithm by an example given in Fig. 2. We look at the source label $s=\{$"chair of program committee"$\}$ given in English and the target label $t=\{$"président du comité de programme"$\}$, given in French. After tokenization of s, the function *getSources*() is called for each of its tokens. This function queries BabelNet and returns a set of terms in the target language (French) related to the token it takes in its argument. In our example, we have

- *getSources*("chair", "EN", "FR")=\{Chair_acrobatics, maître_de_cérémonie, **président**, Fixation_des_rails_aux_traverses, professeur, fauteuil, Chaise_électrique, plomb, chaise\}
- *getSources*("program", "EN", "FR")=\{Animatrix, logiciel, mission, plan, Programme_électoral, **programme**, programmer\}
- *getSources*("committee","EN", "FR")=\{**comité**, Committee_(comics)\}.

The resulting tokens are compared to the tokens of t pairwise by using the Jaccard measure, denoted by *sim* in the algorithm and in the figure. In order to

Algorithm 1. Transforming a label from its source language into a target language by using BabelNet.

Input: s, t: two labels
  $s_i \in s, t_j \in t$: two tokens
  l_S : language of s , l_T : language of t
  $sim(s_i, t_j)$: a basic token similarity measure (e.g., Jaccard, Levensthein, or other)
Output: *BabelLabel*: the transformed label of s in the language l_T, as an outcome of
  BabelNet
 1: **for each** $s_i \in s$ **do**
 2:    $babelsource \leftarrow getSources(s_i, l_S, l_T)$
 3:    **for each** $t_j \in t$ **do**
 4:      **for each** $b \in babelsource$ **do**
 5:        $score \leftarrow sim(b, t_j)$
 6:        **if** $score > maxScore$ **then**
 7:          $maxScore \leftarrow score$
 8:          $source \leftarrow b$
 9:        **end if**
10:      **end for**
11:      $add(BabelLabel, source)$
12:    **end for**
13: **end for**

---

constitute the French version of the source label s, denoted by $s_{"FR"}$, we replace each source token by the token returned by *getSources* that has scored best with respect to the target tokens (in bold in the example above). As a result, the transformed version of the source label takes the form $s_{"FR"} = \{$ "président", "programme", "comité"$\}$. The final similarity score between s and t is an outcome of a compound label similarity function, like for example, the SoftTFIDF, computed for the labels $s_{"FR"}$ and t, that are now both in the same language (French, in our example).

Semantically Enhancing the Transformed Source Label Terms. In the case when the final similarity value produced by the softTFIDF measure for a given pair of labels is not satisfactory (i.e., is under a given threshold), Alg. 1 is called again by each of the tokens of the source label in its transformed form (an outcome of Alg.1), this time taking as an argument the token and two times the language l_T in order to enhance semantically the input information by looking for more related terms in BabelNet that might be better matching candidates. This process can be called upon as many times as desired, but in order to avoid complexity problems, we have limited the number of these iterations to two.

Example. Let us take a look at the source token $s_i = $ "bid", and let $l_S = $ "EN" and $l_T = $ "FR", where "EN" stands for English and "FR" – for French. In this case, $getSources(s_i, l_S, l_T) = \{$Prixbid, souhaiter, offre, commande, offrir, Bid-TV, inviter, implorer, appeler$\}$. However, the right term for "bid" is "proposition" and it is not on the list. This results in flawed values of the final similarity

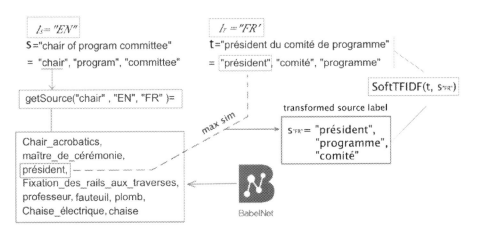

Fig. 2. Applying Alg. 1 – a transformation of a source label into the language of a target label by using BabelNet. An example with the token "chair".

between the source label, of which "bid" is part and any target label. To make up for that, since the terms in BabelNet are linked, we can map from the term "offre" to the term "proposition" by applying $getSources($"offre"$, l_T, l_T)$.

Unlike most matching systems, which translate the labels of source and target ontology into English, LYAM++ transforms the labels of S from the language of S into the language of T. Note again that only one similarity measure is used on label level and one – on token level, which makes LYAM++ a light-weight ontology matching system.

2.6   Mapping Verification and Mapping Selection

The mapping verification step aims to remove correspondences that are less likely to be satisfiable based on the information present in the ontologies. This component filters out the trustworthy pairs of aligned concepts by looking at the similarity values produced for their parents and their children in the ontology hierarchies.

In an ontology matching system, mapping selection is an important task used as a filter to select high quality mapping candidates before producing the final alignment. This module transforms the initial 1 to many alignment (a source element possibly corresponding to multiple target elements) to a 1:1 alignment (a source element corresponds to exactly one target element) based on the principle of iteratively retaining the pairs of concepts with maximal value of similarity.

2.7   Structural Matching with BabelNet

Structural methods exploit the relations between entities, relying often on the hierarchical structure of the ontologies defined by the subsumption relation.

The basic idea is that if two entities are similar, their "relatives" could also be in one way or another similar. Two entities are considered similar if either of the following heuristics is true: (i) their direct super-entities (or all super-entities) are similar, (ii) all their sisters, who are the entities with the same super entity directly with the entities in question are similar, (iii) all of their sub-entities are similar, (iv) their descendants are similar, (v) all their leaves are similar.

In order to cope with the cross-lingual character of the input ontologies in the process of structural matching, we call upon BabelNet again. Note that the structural information is language independent, but a similarity measure is needed to verify the heuristics given above, and this similarity measure is most commonly language dependent, since it is based on similarity of strings. Our cross-lingual structural matching procedure is presented in Algorithm 2. Similarly to Algorithm 1, we query BabelNet to construct language transformations of the labels of the source ontology. Before computing similarity between the transformed source labels and the labels of the target ontology we check their structural information using the $MatchExist()$ function. The function $GetStructure()$ returns all structural information of an entity such as its super-entities and sub-entities. $MatchExist()$ returns true if any structural informations of the two entities are similar. It reduces the number comparisons between entities and thus optimizes considerably the matching process.

Algorithm 2. Structural matching with BabelNet

Input: e_1, e_2: two entities
    s: label of e_1, t: label of e_2
    $s_i \in s, t_j \in t$: tow tokens
    $- l_S$: language of s , l_T : language of t
Output: $BabelLabel$: outcome of BabelNet
 1: **for each** $s_i \in s$ **do**
 2:    **if** $MatchExist(IA, getStructure(e_1), getStructure(e_2))$ **then**
 3:       $babelsource \leftarrow getSources(s_i, l_S, l_T)$
 4:       **for each** $t_j \in t$ **do**
 5:          **for each** $b \in babelsource$ **do**
 6:             $score \leftarrow sim(b, t_j)$
 7:             **if** $score > maxScore$ **then**
 8:                $maxScore \leftarrow score$
 9:                $source \leftarrow b$
10:             **end if**
11:          **end for**
12:          $add(BabelLabel, source)$
13:       **end for**
14:    **end if**
15: **end for**

---

3   Evaluation and Results

We have evaluated LYAM++ on data coming from the ontology alignment evaluation initiative (OAEI)[3] of year 2014 and particularly Multifarm—a benchmark designed for evaluating cross-lingual ontology matching systems. Multifarm data consist of a set of 7 ontologies originally coming from the *Conference* benchmark of OAEI, translated into 8 languages. Two evaluation tasks are defined: *task 1* consists in matching two different ontologies given in different languages, while *task 2* aims to align different language versions of one single ontology.

We used the Alignment API[4] in order to compute precision, recall, and F-measures. We use BabelNet 3.0 API to query online BabelNet.

We have performed experiments on both tasks by using several MultiFarm datasets (the ontologies *CMT, conference, confOf, iasted* and *sigkdd*). We have conducted three experiments. In the first one, we compare LYAM++ to Agreement Maker Light (AML) [5] on both tasks and all pairs of languages. The choice of AML is motivated by the fact that, according to the reports of the OAEI 2014, this system performs best on the Multifarm track. In the second experiment, we evaluate the standard orchestration of the ontology matching workflow and the novel orchestration proposed in this paper. Finally, the third experiment compares the resuts obtained by each of the three similarity measures introduced in the previous section (TF/IDF, Extended Jaccard and Monge-Elkan) and shows that the performance of LYAM++ does not depend on the choice of measure, but is due to the use of background knowledge and the novel orchestration of the matching workflow.

3.1   Comparing LYAM++ to AML

The mapping threshold determines the value of the similarity function, above with a pair of labels can be considered as a potential mapping. It can also be seen as a confidence value of the produced alignment – the higher the mapping threshold, the more conservative we are in filtering out mappings and therefore the more confident we are in the final result. The F-measure depends strongly on this value and therefore, commonly, ontology matching results are presented in the form of an F-measure curve as a function of the mapping threshold.

Within this experiment, the SoftTFIDF similarity measure has been used to produce the initial terminological similarities. The Jaccard coefficient has been applied for the source label reconstitution in the target language (the measure *sim* within Alg. 1).

Table 1 shows the average F-measures over all threshold values per language pair for tasks 1 and 2. As it can be seen, LYAM++ outperforms AML systematically for all pairs of languages on both tasks, even for more difficult to handle languages like Russian. The high average F-measure values over all threshold values provide evidence of the stability of LYAM++ in terms of confidence value.

---

[3] http://oaei.ontologymatching.org/
[4] http://alignapi.gforge.inria.fr/

Table 1. Comparing LYAM++ to AML

Lang. pair	FR-RU	FR-PT	FR-NL	ES-FR	ES-RU	ES-PT	ES-NL	EN-PT	EN-RU	EN-FR
LYAM++	0.54	0.58	0.62	0.60	0.60	0.60	0.63	0.67	0.53	0.59
AML	0.48	0.51	0.47	0.53	0.47	0.51	0.52	0.53	0.51	0.49

Average F-measures over all threshold values per language pair for task 1.

Lang. pair	FR-RU	FR-PT	FR-NL	ES-FR	ES-RU	ES-PT	ES-NL	EN-PT	EN-RU	EN-FR
LYAM++	0.58	0.72	0.67	0.77	0.64	0.70	0.68	0.74	0.59	0.85
AML	0.44	0.64	0.57	0.66	0.51	0.66	0.61	0.68	0.48	0.70

Average F-measures over all threshold values per language pair for task 2.

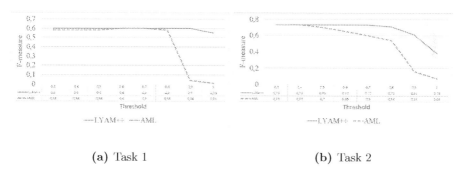

(a) Task 1   (b) Task 2

Fig. 3. Average F-measures over all language pairs per threshold value and task.

Figure 3 shows the average F-measures over all language-pairs per threshold value and task. On task 1, both systems have similar and stable behavior for threshold values lower than 0.8. When this value is surpassed, however, one can see a clear advantage of LYAM++, which remains on more or less the same F-measure level, while the performance of AML drastically decreases reaching almost a 0 F-measure for a threshold values close to 1.

On task 2, the divergence in the performance of the two systems is observed at a much lower value—0.4—of the mapping threshold. For threshold values greater than 0.4, the values of the F-measure for AML start to decrease while LYAM++ remains stable until the threshold value reaches 0.8.

We explain the good results of our system by the appropriate use of a specific background knowledge source (BabelNet), particularly suited for cross-lingual ontology matching, as well as by the novel composition of the matching modules (see results of the experiment in the following subsection). We underline the fact that LYAM++ remains stable and outperforms AML for even high threshold values (close to or equaling 1), which demonstrates the capacity of the system to produce quality cross-lingual alignments with a very high level of confidence.

Table 2. Comparing the standard and the novel orchestrations

Langauge pair	FR-RU	FR-PT	FR-NL	ES-FR	ES-RU	ES-PT	ES-NL	EN-PT	EN-RU	EN-FR
Novel	0.58	0.72	0.67	0.77	0.64	0.70	0.68	0.74	0.59	0.85
Standard	0.50	0.58	0.60	0.39	0.54	0.57	0.58	0.50	0.32	0.39

Average F-measures over all threshold values per language pair for task 2.

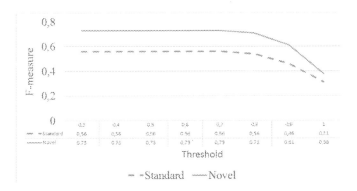

Fig. 4. Average F-measures over all language-pairs per threshold value of task 2 for the novel and the standard orchestrations.

3.2 Comparing the Standard and the Novel Orchestrations

This experiment aims to demonstrate the advantage of the novel orchestration of the components within the matching workflow as compared to the standard one. Again, the two similarity measures that are used are SoftTFIDF for the intermediate terminological alignment and Jaccard for the label reconstitution (Alg. 1). Following the same presentation pattern as the one in the subsection above, Table 2 shows the average F-measures over all threshold values per language pair, while Figure 4 shows the average F-measures over all language-pairs per threshold value. We have presented the results on task 2 only for reasons of space limitation. Similar results were obtained on task 1.

As we can see, the novel orchestration largely outperforms the classical one. This is due to the fact that the mappings resulting from the mapping selection module have high precision and these mappings are passed to the structural matcher, responsible for the final alignment.

3.3 Impact of the Choice of Similarity Measure

This experiment evaluates the impact of the choice of a similarity measure for comparing compound labels on the quality of the alignment produced with LYAM++. Fig. 5 shows the average F-measures over all language-pairs per threshold value again for task 2. It can be seen that the F-measures obtained by the three evaluated similarity measures are not significantly different and are all of good quality.

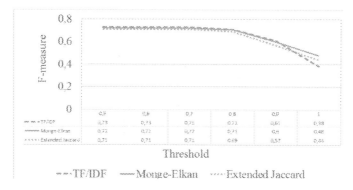

Fig. 5. Comparing the similarities measures.

This comes to show that our system is robust to the choice of similarity measure, its high performance being mainly due to the novel orchestration and the use of suitable background knowledge in the alignment process.

4 Related Work

The current section introduces related approaches to ontology matching with regard to two aspects: (1) the use of background knowledge and (2) handling cross-lingual heterogeneity.

4.1 Ontology Matching Using Background Knowledge

Using background knowledge (BK) for enhancing ontology matching is an idea that has been realized in several matching approaches in the literature. Sabou *et al.* [9] motivate the use of BK by the observation that two ontologies are always inherently different in terms of intention. Background knowledge comes to bridge the inherent semantic gap between them. We provide an overview of some of the relevant groups of techniques, categorized in terms of the type of background knowledge that is used, following the introduction found in [3].

Reusing Existing Mappings. Stored mappings can be used to discover new ones. Several approaches [10–12] follow this paradigm by reusing existing mappings to efficiently match two ontologies. The weak point of this group of approaches is the fact that they depend heavily on the quality of the re-used mappings, therefore on the performance of the ontology matching techniques that have been used to produce the initial mappings.

Using Domain Specific Corpus. A corpus can be seen as a collection of elements (e.g., relation and attribute names) and their data types, relationships between elements, sample data instances, and other knowledge that can be used to discover mappings between entities [13,14]. Since a corpus is specific to a domain, it can only be used in specific matching cases. For example, a corpus in the field of anatomy can only be used for matching anatomy ontologies.

Using Domain Specific Ontologies. Domain specific ontologies are often seen as quality sources of background knowledge. In [15,16], the alignment process takes place in two steps: *anchoring* and *driving relations*. Anchoring consists in matching the concepts of the source and target ontologies to the concepts of the reference knowledge using standard ontology matching techniques. In this step, each concept from the source and the target ontologies is mapped, or *anchored*, to a concept from the reference ontology. Driving relations is the process of finding relations between source and target concepts by checking if their corresponding anchored concepts are related.

Using the Semantic Web. This group of approaches is based on harvesting the semantic web in order to discover and explore multiple heterogeneous on-line knowledge sources [9]. The originality of the proposal is the use of the web in order to discover (by crawling) automatically appropriate BK sources (instead of using a single fixed source). Thus, the question of the availability and the coverage of the BK is addressed. This is particularly useful when the needed background knowledge is spread among different available sources.

Discussion. Due to the nature of the background knowledge that is used in our system, it is difficult to situate our approach in one of these families. Indeed, BabelNet can be seen as a corpus of existing mappings, since the terms are related semantically, but it can be also seen as an ontology. In contrast to the cited approaches, in our case the BK is used to enrich the semantic information contained in the source ontology in order to make it more "compatible" and easer to compare to the target ontology.

4.2   Cross-Lingual Ontology Matching

Gracia *et al.* [17] present a global *vision of a multilingual semantic web* together with several challenges to the multilingual semantic web community. According to the authors, multilingualism has to be seen as an extension of the semantic web– a group of techniques which will be added to the existing semantic technologies in order to resolve linguistic heterogeneity where it appears. The semantic web is seen as language-independent, because semantic information is given in formal languages. The main gap is, therefore, between language specific needs of users and the language-independent semantic content. The authors prognosticate that monolingual non-English linked data will increase in years creating "islands" of unconnected monolingual linked data. The challenge is to connect these islands by interconnecting the language-specific information. The authors outline the development of systems for establishing relations between ontology terms or semantic data with labels and instances in different languages as a main direction of future research. We proceed to discuss different cross-lingual approaches grouped in four main categories depending on the underlying technique.

Machine Translation (MT). The majority of approaches rely on MT techniques. Fu *et al.* [18] follow a standard paradigm of using monolingual matching techniques enhanced with an MT module. As a result of an analysis of the effect of the quality of the MT, the authors propose a noise-minimization method to reduce the flaw in the performance introduced by the translation. Trojahn *et al.* [19] have implemented an API for multilingual OM applying two strategies: a direct matching by a direct translation of one ontology to the other prior to the matching process and indirect matching, based on a composition of alignments. The latter approach is originally proposed by Jung *et al.* [20] and it is based on first establishing manual alignment between cross-lingual ontologies and then using these alignments in order to infer new ones. Paulheim *et al.* [21] apply web-search-based techniques for computing concept similarities by using MT for cross-lingual ontologies. Several well-established ontology matching systems propose to take cross-lingual ontologies as input by using machine translation in the alignment process, two of them being YAM++ [2] and AML [5].

Machine Learning (ML). Spohr *et al.* [4] present an approach applying ML techniques. They use a small amount of manually produced cross-lingual alignments in order to learn a matching function for two cross-lingual ontologies. The paper introduces a clear distinction between a multilingual ontology (that which contains annotations given in different languages) and cross-lingual ontologies (two or more monolingual ontologies given in different natural languages).

Use of Background Knowledge. On the edge of the OM approaches that use background knowledge, Rinser *et al.* [22] propose a method for entity matching by using the info-boxes of Wikipedia. Entities given in different languages are aligned by the help of the explicit relations between Wikipedia pages in different languages. The matching relies mainly on the values of each property, since the actual labels are in different languages (e.g., "population" and "Einwohner" have approximately the same values (3,4M) in the info-boxes of the English and the German Wikipedia pages of Berlin). A very important and useful contribution of this paper is an analysis of the structure of the Wikipedia interlanguage links. Todorov *et al.* [23] [24] propose an ontology alignment framework based on background knowledge (the multilingual YAGO ontology) and fuzzy sets and logics to deal with imprecision in the cross-lingual matching process.

Natural Language Processing (NLP). Outside of the context of ontology matching, in the NLP field, research has been carried on the topic of measuring semantic distance between cross-lingual terms or concept labels. Mohammad *et al.* [25] and Eger *et al.* [26] propose measures of semantic distance between cross-lingual concept labels based on the use of bilingual lexicons. Explicit Semantic Analysis (ESA) applied with Wikipedia has been proposed as a framework for measuring cross-lingual semantic relatedness of terms, first in a paper by Gabrilovich *et al.* [27] and then in an extended proposal by Hassan *et al.* [28]. It is suggested to rely on the multiple language versions of Wikipedia in order to measure semantic relatedness between terms. The authors use an ESA framework in order to model a concept as a vector in a space defined by a set of "encyclopedic concepts" in which the concept appears.

Discussion. The methods that have been proposed to deal with multilingualism in ontology matching, with few exceptions, rely on automatic translation of labels to a single target language. As noted in the introduction, MT tolerates low precision levels and often external sources are needed in order to achieve good performance. An inherent problem of translation as such is that there is often a lack of exact one-to-one correspondence between the terms across natural languages. Our approach is therefore closer in spirit to the approaches comping the NLP domain, the main idea being to use a bilingual reference vocabulary in order to link related terms across languages.

5   Conclusion

The moment to pay attention to cross-lingual ontology matching appears to be appropriate for several reasons. On the one hand, an important factor is the historical moment of the development of the Web community. As mentioned at the start, although originally predominantly English-speaking the Web, and consequently the Semantic Web, has the tendency of comprising more and more non-English active users, i.e., users that both consume *and* create Web content in languages other than English. In the current state of affairs there is only little above 30 percent of English Internet users[5] and the number of other language speaking users is constantly growing. In order to fully unlock the potential of the Web of Data project, the web community needs to be provided tools for the automatic integration of web knowledge—vocabularies and data— given in different natural languages.

In this paper, we have addressed this problem by proposing a novel cross-ontology matching approach implemented in the system LYAM++. In order to make up for the disadvantages of the currently existing cross-lingual matching systems, we do not rely on machine translation, but make use of background knowledge in the form of a large multilingual lexical network (BabelNet). In addition, we have proposed a novel orchestration of the matching components that form the ontology matching processing pipeline. We have shown experimentally by using data from the Multifarm benchmark, that our matching technique outperforms the best systems in the current state-of-the-art and that the novel workflow orchestration provides better results than the standard one.

In the future, we plan to explore the use of different kinds of background knowledge and the impact of this choice on the matching task. We will also apply our technique to the monolingual matching problem by exploiting the rich semantic information contained in a background knowledge source.

Acknowledgments. This work has been partially supported by the French National Research Agency (ANR) within the DOREMUS Project, under grant number ANR-14-CE24-0020 and the Ministry of Higher Education and Research of Algeria.

---

[5] http://www.internetworldstats.com/

References

1. Euzenat, J., Shvaiko, P.: Ontology Matching. Springer-Verlag, Heidelberg (DE) (2007)
2. Ngo, D.H., Bellahsene, Z.: YAM++ : a multi-strategy based approach for ontology matching task. In: ten Teije, A., Völker, J., Handschuh, S., Stuckenschmidt, H., d'Acquin, M., Nikolov, A., Aussenac-Gilles, N., Hernandez, N. (eds.) EKAW 2012. LNCS, vol. 7603, pp. 421–425. Springer, Heidelberg (2012)
3. Shvaiko, P., Euzenat, J.: Ontology matching: state of the art and future challenges. IEEE Transactions on Knowledge and Data Engineering **25**(1), 158–176 (2013)
4. Spohr, D., Hollink, L., Cimiano, P.: A machine learning approach to multilingual and cross-lingual ontology matching. In: Aroyo, L., Welty, C., Alani, H., Taylor, J., Bernstein, A., Kagal, L., Noy, N., Blomqvist, E. (eds.) ISWC 2011, Part I. LNCS, vol. 7031, pp. 665–680. Springer, Heidelberg (2011)
5. Faria, D., Pesquita, C., Santos, E., Palmonari, M., Cruz, I.F., Couto, F.M.: The agreementmakerlight ontology matching system. In: Meersman, R., Panetto, H., Dillon, T., Eder, J., Bellahsene, Z., Ritter, N., De Leenheer, P., Dou, D. (eds.) ODBASE 2013. LNCS, vol. 8185, pp. 527–541. Springer, Heidelberg (2013)
6. Ngo, D.H., Bellahsene, Z., Todorov, K.: Opening the black box of ontology matching. In: Cimiano, P., Corcho, O., Presutti, V., Hollink, L., Rudolph, S. (eds.) ESWC 2013. LNCS, vol. 7882, pp. 16–30. Springer, Heidelberg (2013)
7. Ngo, D.H., Bellahsene, Z., Todorov, K.: Extended tversky similarity for resolving terminological heterogeneities across ontologies. In: Meersman, R., Panetto, H., Dillon, T., Eder, J., Bellahsene, Z., Ritter, N., De Leenheer, P., Dou, D. (eds.) ODBASE 2013. LNCS, vol. 8185, pp. 711–718. Springer, Heidelberg (2013)
8. Cohen, W.W., Ravikumar, P.D., Fienberg, S.E.: A comparison of string distance metrics for name-matching tasks. In: IIWeb, pp. 73–78 (2003)
9. Sabou, M., d'Aquin, M., Motta, E.: Exploring the semantic web as background knowledge for ontology matching. J. Data Semantics **11**, 156–190 (2008)
10. Do, H.H., Rahm, E.: COMA - a system for flexible combination of schema matching approaches. In: VLDB 2002, Proceedings of 28th International Conference on Very Large Data Bases, August 20–23, 2002, pp. 610–621, Hong Kong (2002)
11. Groß, A., Hartung, M., Kirsten, T., Rahm, E.: GOMMA results for OAEI 2012. In: Proceedings of the 7th International Workshop on Ontology Matching, November 11, 2012, Boston (2012)
12. Saha, B., Stanoi, I., Clarkson, K.L.: Schema covering: a step towards enabling reuse in information integration. In: Proceedings of the 26th International Conference on Data Engineering, ICDE 2010, March 1–6, 2010, pp. 285–296, Long Beach (2010)
13. Madhavan, J., Bernstein, P.A., Chen, K., Halevy, A.Y., Shenoy, P.: Corpus-based schema matching. In: Proceedings of IJCAI 2003 Workshop on Information Integration on the Web (IIWeb 2003), August 9–10, 2003, pp. 59–63, Acapulco (2003)
14. Madhavan, J., Bernstein, P.A., Doan, A., Halevy, A.Y.: Corpus-based schema matching. In: Proceedings of the 21st International Conference on Data Engineering, ICDE 2005, April 5–8 2005, pp. 57–68, Tokyo (2005)
15. Aleksovski, Z., Klein, M., ten Kate, W., van Harmelen, F.: Matching unstructured vocabularies using a background ontology. In: Staab, S., Svátek, V. (eds.) EKAW 2006. LNCS (LNAI), vol. 4248, pp. 182–197. Springer, Heidelberg (2006)

16. Aleksovski, Z., ten Kate, W., van Harmelen, F.: Exploiting the structure of background knowledge used in ontology matching. In: Proceedings of the 1st International Workshop on Ontology Matching (OM-2006) Collocated with the 5th International Semantic Web Conference (ISWC-2006), November 5, 2006, Athens (2006)

17. Gracia, J., Montiel-Ponsoda, E., Cimiano, P., Gomez-Perez, A., Buitelaar, P., McCrae, J.: Challenges to the multilingual web of data. Web Semantics: Science, Services and Agents on the World Wide Web (2011)

18. Fu, B., Brennan, R., O'Sullivan, D.: Cross-Lingual ontology mapping – an investigation of the impact of machine translation. In: Gómez-Pérez, A., Yu, Y., Ding, Y. (eds.) ASWC 2009. LNCS, vol. 5926, pp. 1–15. Springer, Heidelberg (2009)

19. dos Santos, C.T., Quaresma, P., Vieira, R.: An api for multi-lingual ontology matching. In: Procs of LREC (2010)

20. Jung, J.J., Håkansson, A., Hartung, R.: Indirect alignment between multilingual ontologies: a case study of korean and swedish ontologies. In: Håkansson, A., Nguyen, N.T., Hartung, R.L., Howlett, R.J., Jain, L.C. (eds.) KES-AMSTA 2009. LNCS, vol. 5559, pp. 233–241. Springer, Heidelberg (2009)

21. Paulheim, H., Hertling, S.: Wesee-match results for oaei 2013. Ontology Matching, p. 197 (2013)

22. Rinser, D., Lange, D., Naumann, F.: Cross-lingual entity matching and infobox alignment in wikipedia. Inf. Syst. **38**(6), 887–907 (2013)

23. Todorov, K., Hudelot, C., Geibel, P.: Fuzzy and cross-lingual ontology matching mediated by background knowledge. In: Bobillo, F., Carvalho, R.N., Costa, P.C.G., d'Amato, C., Fanizzi, N., Laskey, K.B., Laskey, K.J., Lukasiewicz, T., Nickles, M., Pool, M. (eds.) URSW 2011-2013. LNCS, vol. 8816, pp. 142–162. Springer, Heidelberg (2014)

24. Todorov, K., Hudelot, C., Popescu, A., Geibel, P.: Fuzzy ontology alignment using background knowledge. International Journal of Uncertainty, Fuzziness and Knowledge-Based Systems **22**(1), 75–112 (2014)

25. Mohammad, S., Gurevych, I., Hirst, G., Zesch, T.: Cross-lingual distributional profiles of concepts for measuring semantic distance. In: EMNLP-CoNLL, pp. 571–580 (2007)

26. Eger, S., Sejane, I.: Computing semantic similarity from bilingual dictionaries. In: Procs of the 10th International Conference on the Statistical Analysis of Textual Data (JADT-2010), pp. 1217–1225 (2010)

27. Gabrilovich, E., Markovitch, S.: Computing semantic relatedness using wikipedia-based esa. In: IJCAI, vol. 7, pp. 1606–1611 (2007)

28. Hassan, S., Mihalcea, R.: Cross-lingual semantic relatedness using encyclopedic knowledge. In: Proceedings of the 2009 Conference on Empirical Methods in Natural Language Processing: Volume 3-Volume 3, pp. 1192–1201. Association for Computational Linguistics (2009)

ABOM and ADOM: Arabic Datasets for the Ontology Alignment Evaluation Campaign

Abderrahmane Khiat[1(✉)], Gayo Diallo[2], Beyza Yaman[3],
Ernesto Jiménez-Ruiz[4], and Moussa Benaissa[1]

[1] LITIO Laboratory, University of Oran1 Ahmed Ben Bella, Oran, Algeria
abderrahmane_Khiat@yahoo.com
[2] University Bordeaux, ISPED, Centre INSERM U897, 33000 Bordeaux, France
[3] DIBRIS, University of Genoa, Genoa, Italy
[4] Department of Computer Science, University of Oxford, Oxford, UK

Abstract. In this paper we present two test sets in the Arabic language, ABOM and ADOM, to evaluate ontology alignment systems. The purpose of these test sets is to evaluate not only the behavior of ontology alignment systems specially designed for Arabic language but also those designed for multilingual ontologies. We have tested the ABOM and ADOM with two ontology alignment systems, namely the LogMap and AOT systems, which have participated in the OAEI evaluation campaign. The experiment shows that the ABOM and ADOM datasets are suitable to evaluate ontology alignment systems.

Keywords: Arabic ontologies · Multilingual ontologies · Ontology alignment · Ontology matching · OAEI · Semantic interoperability · Semantic web

1 Introduction

The Semantic Web relies on ontologies to describe the content of different information sources in order to overcome the heterogeneity issue and achieve their semantic interoperability [1]. However, these ontologies are heterogeneous, distributed and even they are described in different languages. A solution to this heterogeneity is to use ontology alignment to bridge the semantic gap between these ontologies [1,2]. The ontology alignment system receives as input two or more ontologies and generates as output a set of semantic correspondences between the entities of the ontologies that are being processed [1,7]. Indeed, these semantic correspondences are the bridges that hold the heterogeneous ontologies together and ensure their semantic interoperability. Moreover, with the enormous volume of ontologies already available on the web and their constant evolution, manual identification of semantic correspondences is not feasible [2]. Therefore, ontology alignment tools are required to have the ability of identifying semantic correspondences between entities of different ontologies in an automated way.

© Springer International Publishing Switzerland 2015
C. Debruyne et al. (Eds.): OTM 2015 Conferences, LNCS 9415, pp. 545–553, 2015.
DOI: 10.1007/978-3-319-26148-5_37

However, the automatic identification of semantic correspondences is not a trivial task due to the conceptual diversity between the ontologies [6]. In the literature, several overall methods based on the lexical similarity of the entity labels have been used to align ontologies automatically (e.g. [1,12,13]). Even more elaborated approaches have been developed, such as, similarity aggregation and alignment extraction [1,2]. For a more complete review of ontology alignment systems, we refer the reader to [7]. The labels that are used to express the entities of an ontology can be in different languages to reflect the diversity of the world. Performing an ontology alignment task between ontologies described in Western languages such as English is challenging, however, the task is even more challenging when dealing with the Arabic language due to some special features of this language. Five characteristics could be emphasized as follows [5]:

1. The scripts of Arabic language e.g. no short vowels and no capitalization.
2. Ambiguity problem (in average, 2.3 per word in other languages to 19.2 in Arabic [4]).
3. Complex word structure, for example the sentence "رأوه بالمدينة" can be translated in English language as "they saw him in the city".
4. Normalization problem e.g. آ ، إ ، أ ، ا → ا i.e. losing distinction آن ، إن ، أن.
5. The Arabic language is one of the pro-drop languages, i.e. languages that allow speakers to omit certain classes of pronouns.

As far as we know, such characteristics are not usually taken into account by current ontology matching systems due to their specifications. In addition, the available standard benchmarks, such as those provided by the Ontology Alignment Evaluation Initiative (OAEI) campaign [12,13] do not provide a suitable dataset for evaluating the performance of systems that are able to address the specifications of the Arabic language.

In this paper, we present two test sets in the Arabic language describing the bibliography and conference domains: ABOM and ADOM, respectively. We have created these datasets by translating and improving the ontologies of the *biblio* [20] and the *multifarm* [8] tracks of the OAEI campaign.

ABOM and ADOM aims at providing an answer to the following questions when it comes to evaluate ontology matching systems: *(i)* are the evaluated systems able to handle ontologies described in the Arabic language efficiently? *(ii)* are external knowledge resources, such as WordNet[1] [18] and Wikipedia[2], available for the Arabic language?

The rest of the paper is organized as follows. First, we describe the ABOM and ADOM datasets in Section 2. The Section 3 contains the experimental results obtained via ABOM and ADOM datasets. Finally, some concluding remarks and future directions are presented in Section 4.

---

[1] http://wordnet.princeton.edu/
[2] www.wikipedia.org

2   Arabic Datasets for Evaluating Ontology Matching Systems

In this section we describe two datasets in Arabic language, namely ABOM and ADOM, to evaluate Arabic and cross-lingual ontology alignment systems. We justify the proposal of these datasets by the following points: *(i)* to the best of our knowledge, no such dataset exists yet in Arabic language;[3] *(ii)* the OAEI campaign, which is the most recognized and well-known evaluation campaign for testing the performance of ontology matching systems, lacks so far a test case involving ontologies in the Arabic language which penalizes the evaluation of ontology alignment systems dedicated to align ontologies described in Arabic; and *(iii)* there are several contexts, such as, Web information retrieval where the ontology matching systems are needed both in inter-multilingual ontologies and intra-Arabic ontologies. In order to employ these ontology matching systems, we need to test their performance first. These situations bring us to develop such datasets.

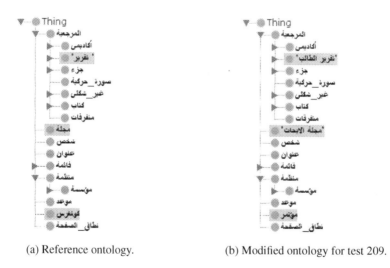

(a) Reference ontology.   (b) Modified ontology for test 209.

Fig. 1. Example of two ontologies of the ABOM dataset.

2.1   The ABOM Dataset

The ABOM dataset is constituted of 45 tests in Arabic language describing the bibliography domain. These tests are based on the (English) ontologies of the *biblio* track of the OAEI campaign [20]. Each test contains the reference ontology, a modified version of the reference ontology, and a reference alignment.

---

[3] Note that, in the literature one can find datasets in Arabic language applied to other domains different from Ontology Matching (e.g. [15,16]).

(a) Conference (French)   (b) Iasted (Arabic)   (c) Cmt (Arabic)

Fig. 2. Example of ontologies involved in the ADOM dataset.

The reference ontology is modified in various ways, including:[4] (i) change of entities' names such as the ontology of the test 266, (ii) synonym of entities such as the ontology of the test 209 (see Figure 1), and (iii) modification of the hierarchy: flattened such as the test 206, expanded such as the test 223 and suppressed such as the test 265, etc. The purpose of these modifications is to analyze the strong and weak points of ontology matchers. For instance, the modified ontology of test 209 has been created by replacing the entities of the reference ontology by synonyms. This will require ontology alignment systems to use an Arabic dictionary to overcome this lexical mismatch.

2.2 The ADOM Dataset

The ADOM dataset [17] contains seven ontologies in Arabic language (Cmt, Conference, ConfOf, Edas, Ekaw, Iasted, Sigkdd). These ontologies describe the conference domain and they are based on the ontologies of the OAEI *conference* track [14]. The ADOM dataset has been integrated within the multilingual dataset of the OAEI 2015 *multifarm* track[5] [8]. The purpose of the ADOM dataset in particular and the *multifarm* in general is to evaluate the ability of matching systems to deal with ontologies described in different languages including Arabic. The multifarm track also includes other nine languages: English, Chinese, Czech, Dutch, French, German, Portuguese, Russian, and Spanish. Thus, the pairwise combination of those seven ontologies in those nine languages leads to 225 tests, with their corresponding reference alignment, in the ADOM dataset. Figure 2 shows an example of three ontologies involved in the ADOM dataset. Note that French version of the Conference ontology belong to original *multifarm* dataset.

---

[4] The characteristics of each modified ontology of each test can be found in the OAEI website: http://oaei.ontologymatching.org/tests/

[5] http://oaei.ontologymatching.org/2015/multifarm/index.html

2.3   Methodology

In order to develop the Arabic ontologies and reference alignments for the ABOM and ADOM datasets, we have proceeded as follows.

Step1: Translation of Ontology Entities. In this step, we have identified the concepts, object and data-type properties of the ontologies for both datasets. For example regarding the ABOM dataset, we can list the class "كتاب (Book)", the object property "الناشر (Publisher)" and data-type property "نشرت لأول مرة (First Published)", etc. For the ADOM dataset, we can list the concept "البحث (paper)", data-type property "لديه اسم (has name) and object property "لديه موقع على رابط (has website at URL), etc.

We have semi-automatically translated the ontologies from English and French (if available) to Arabic. The translation phase was performed manually and the generation phase of the ontologies was achieved automatically using regular expression with the regex API. We have proceeded the translation manually by considering the context of bibliography i.e., the bibliography domain (for ABOM) and conference context (for ADOM) in order to avoid false meaning of the entities. For instance, if we translate simply the concept Journal, we get "صحيفة (newspaper)" in Arabic language, but "صحيفة (newspaper) is not the correct meaning of the concept "Journal". For that reason, we have considered the context of bibliography. In this case, the correct meaning of the class "Journal" is "مجلة .".

Step 2: Generation of Reference Alignments. In this step, we have reused the available reference alignments among the ontologies in the *biblio* and *multifarm* tracks to generate the new reference alignments for ABOM and ADOM respectively. For example, in the reference alignment for ABOM dataset, we can list the concept "كونغرس (Congress)" of the ontology the test 209 is equivalent to the concept "مؤتمر (Conference)" of the reference ontology (see Figure 1). In the reference alignment for ADOM dataset (see Figure 2), we can list for instance, the concept "الحدث (event)" of the ontology Confof is equivalent to the concept "نشاط (activity)" of the ontology Iasted (see Figure 2b). In the reference alignment for ontologies in Arabic and French languages, we can list the concept "éditeur (Editor)" of the ontology conference (see Figure 2a) is equivalent to the concept "مشرف" of the ontology Cmt (see Figure 2c).

Note that we can also generate reference alignments between ABOM which contains Arabic ontologies and *biblio* which contains English ontologies. For example, in the reference alignment for ontologies in Arabic and English languages, we can list the concept "كونغرس" of the ontology test 209 of the ABOM dataset which is equivalent to the concept "Conference" of the reference ontology of *biblio* track. This could potentially add a multilingual variant to the original *biblio* track test cases.

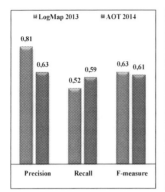

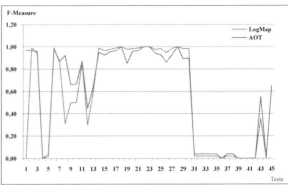

(a) Average results

(b) Detailed results

Fig. 3. LogMap 2013 and AOT results on ABOM Dataset.

Step 3: Validation by a Linguistic Expert. Our two datasets was validated by a linguistic expert with regard to the translation of concepts and properties. Furthermore, we also checked the correctness of the new reference alignments.

3   Experimentation

In order to perform a preliminary evaluation of the ABOM and ADOM datasets we have tested two ontology alignment systems, namely the LogMap [3,11,19] and AOT [10] systems. The purpose of this evaluation is to show that the ABOM and ADOM datasets are suitable to evaluate state-of-the-art ontology matching systems.

The LogMap system [3] is a highly scalable ontology matching system with built-in reasoning and inconsistency repair capabilities. LogMap extracts mappings between classes, properties and instances.

The AOT system [10] (Ontology Alignment at Terminological level) consists in combining different terminological matchers with the average aggregation strategy after local filtering. The AOT system shows also good results in terms of F-measure on different tracks of OAEI 2014, especially in the OAEI Benchmark series [20].

We have tested LogMap (version 2013) [11] and AOT on ABOM dataset, and the 2014 [3] and 2015 [19] versions of LogMap on ADOM dataset. Note that LogMap 2013 does not implement a multilingual module; while LogMap 2014 uses a multilingual module based on Google translate, and LogMap 2015 uses both Microsoft and Google translator APIs [19].

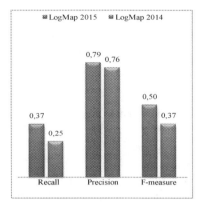

(a) LogMap results on ADOM dataset

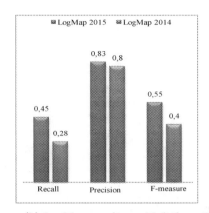

(b) LogMap results on Multifarm Track

Fig. 4. LogMap 2014 and 2015 results on ADOM and in all multifarm dataset.

3.1   Experiment Results on ABOM Dataset

The main purpose of this experiment is not to compare the performance of LogMap and AOT, but to show that the ABOM dataset is suitable to evaluate ontology matching systems in practice.

Figure 3 summarizes the results obtained by LogMap and AOT. Figure 3a provides the average results in terms of standard precision, recall and F-measure, while Figure 3b provides the detailed results in terms of F-measure for each of the tests in ABOM.

The results show that LogMap and AOT systems give good results in terms of F-measure for the tests 101, 222, ... , 246 (see Fig. 3b) since the modified ontologies of these tests did not alter the terminological information of the reference ontology. On the contrary, the tests 248, 249, ..., 266 (see Fig. 3b) did contain important transformations affecting the terminological information of the reference ontology which was reflected in the results obtained by both LogMap and AOT.

3.2   Experiment Results on ADOM Dataset

Figure 4 summarizes the average results, in terms of precision, recall and F-measure, obtained by LogMap on the ADOM dataset (Figure 4a) and on all multifarm tests (Figure 4b). We can appreciate that the combination of Google translate and Microsoft translator (LogMap 2015) significantly improves the results of LogMap 2014 both in the ADOM dataset and in the multifarm track. We can also appreciate that, on average, the ADOM dataset brings an additional complexity to the multifarm track, with regard the results obtained by LogMap. Note that, we aim at obtaining a more comprehensive evaluation during the OAEI 2015 evaluation campaign to confirm this fact.

4   Conclusion and Perspectives

In this paper we have presented ABOM and ADOM, two new test sets in Arabic language describing the bibliography and conference domains, respectively. To the best of our knowledge there is not any other dataset in Arabic language to evaluate ontology alignment systems.

The purpose of ABOM dataset is to study, develop and evaluate ontology alignment systems dedicated to the Arabic language. On the other hand, the main target of the ADOM dataset is to evaluate cross-lingual ontology alignment systems. The experimental study shows that ABOM and ADOM datasets are suitable for the task of evaluating ontology alignment systems. Furthermore, ADOM has already been integrated within the multifarm dataset and it will be evaluated in the OAEI 2015 campaign.

As future challenges, we aim at *(i)* integrating ABOM within the OAEI evaluation campaign, *(ii)* populating the concepts with instances in order to evaluate the instance-based matchers, *(iii)* providing ABOM in different languages, *(iv)* adding some very important feature of the Arabic language such as the vowel marks "حَرَكَات", and *(v)* exploiting state-of-the art Arabic ontologies (e.g. [15,16]) to generate new datasets for ontology matching.

Acknowledgments. This work was partially funded by the EU project Optique (FP7-ICT-318338), and the EPSRC projects MaSI[3], Score! and DBOnto.

References

1. Euzenat, J., Shvaiko, P.: Ontology Matching. Springer-Verlag, Heidelberg (2013)
2. Ehrig, M.: Ontology Alignment: Bridging the Semantic Gap. Springer (2007)
3. Jiménez-Ruiz, E., Grau, B.C., Horrocks, I.: LogMap and LogMapLt results for OAEI 2013. In: Proceedings of the 8th International Workshop on Ontology Matching ISWC (2013)
4. Buckwalter, T.: Arabic Morphological Analyzer Version 2.0. LDC catalog number LDC2004L02 (2004)
5. Farghaly, A.: Arabic NLP: Overview, state of the art, challenges and opportunities. In: The International Arab Conference on Information Technology, ACIT 2008, Tunisia (2008)
6. Bouquet, P., Euzenat, J., Franconi, E., Serafini, L., Stamou, G., Tessaris, S.: Specification of a Common Framework for Characterizing Alignment, Deliverable 2.2.1, Knowledge Web NoE, Technical Report, Italy (2004)
7. Shvaiko, P., Euzenat, J.: Ontology Matching: State of the Art and Future Challenges. IEEE Transactions on Knowledge and Data Engineering **25**(1), 158–176 (2013)
8. Meilicke, C., Garca-Castro, R., Freitas, F., Van Hage, W.R., Montiel-Ponsoda, E., De Azevedo, R.R., Stuckenschmidt, H., vb-Zamazal, O., Svtek, V., Tamilin, A., Trojahn, C., Wang, S.: MultiFarm: A benchmark for multilingual ontology matching. Web Semant. Sci. Serv. Agents World Wide Web **15**, 62–68 (2012)
9. Euzenat, J.: Semantic precision and recall for ontology alignment evaluation. In: The Proceedings of the 20th IJCAI, pp. 348–353, Hyderabad (2007)

10. Khiat, A., Benaissa, M.: AOT / AOTL results for OAEI 2014. In: Proceedings of the 9th International Workshop on Ontology Matching with ISWC 2014, pp. 113–119. CEUR-WS.org, Trentino (2014)
11. Jiménez-Ruiz, E., Grau, B.C., Zhou, Y., Horrocks, I.: Large-scale interactive ontology matching: algorithms and implementation. In: The 20th European Conference on Artificial Intelligence (ECAI), pp. 444–449 (2012)
12. Dragisic, Z., Eckert, K., Euzenat, J., Faria, D., Ferrara, A., Granada, R., Ivanova, V., Jiménez-Ruiz, E., Kempf, A.O., Lambrix, P., Montanelli, S., Paulheim, H., Ritze, D., Shvaiko, P., Solimando, A., Trojahn-dos-Santos, C., Zamazal, O., Grau, B.C.: Results of the ontology alignment evaluation initiative 2014. In: 9th Workshop on Ontology Matching (2014)
13. Grau, B.C., Dragisic, Z., Eckert, K., Euzenat, J., Ferrara, A., Granada, R., Ivanova, V., Jiménez-Ruiz, E., Kempf, A.O., Lambrix, P., Nikolov, A., Paulheim, H., Ritze, D., Scharffe, F., Shvaiko, P., dos Santos, C.T., Zamazal, O.: Results of the ontology alignment evaluation initiative 2013. In: 8th Workshop on Ontology Matching (2013)
14. Svab, O., Svatek, V., Berka, P., Rak, D., Tomasek, P.: OntoFarm: Towards an experimental collection of parallel ontologies. In: Poster Track of ISWC 2005, Galway (2005)
15. Bounhas, I., Elayeb, B., Evrard, F., Slimani, Y.: ArabOnto: Experimenting a new distributional approach for Building Arabic Ontological Resources. International Journal of Metadata, Semantics and Ontologies, Inder-science **6**(2), 81–95 (2011)
16. Ben Khiroun, O., Ayed, R., Elayeb, B., Bounhas, I., Ben Saoud, N.B., Evrard, F.: Towards a new standard arabic test collection for mono- and cross-language information retrieval. In: Métais, E., Roche, M., Teisseire, M. (eds.) NLDB 2014. LNCS, vol. 8455, pp. 168–171. Springer, Heidelberg (2014)
17. Khiat, A., Benaissa, M., Jiménez-Ruiz, E.: ADOM: arabic dataset for evaluating arabic and cross-lingual ontology alignment systems. In: Proceedings of the 10th International Workshop on Ontology Matching ISWC 2015, USA (2015)
18. Fellbaum, C.: WordNet. An Electronic Lexical Database, pp. 1–7. The MIT Press (1998)
19. Jiménez-Ruiz, E., et al.: LogMap family results for OAEI 2015. In: Proceedings of the 10th Workshop on Ontology Matching ISWC 2015, USA (2015)
20. Euzenat, J., Rosoiu, M.E., Trojahn dos Santos, C.: Ontology matching benchmarks: Generation, stability, and discriminability. J. Web Sem. **21**, 30–48 (2013)

Cloud and Trusted Computing 2015 (C&TC) 2015

C&TC 2015 PC Co-Chairs' Message

Welcome to the Cloud and Trusted Computing 2015 (C&TC2015), the 5th International Symposium on Cloud Computing, Trusted Computing, and Secure Virtual Infrastructures, held in Rhodes, Greece, as part of the OnTheMove Federated Conferences & Workshops 2015.

Continuing the successful events of previous years, the C&TC 2015 edition fostered the establishment of a strong and focused research community for its main topics. C&TC2015 addressed challenges from four different research domains: i) trust, security, privacy and risk management in cloud computing; ii) cloud data management; iii) cloud computing infrastructures and architectures; and iv) cloud computing applications.

In this scope, a multitude of specific challenges have been addressed by our authors. Ranging from improved defense architectures for the cloud via virtual machine modeling approaches to a broad set of advances on the topics of trust and trust enhancement, the excellence of contributions in this year's edition of C&TC was remarkable. All submitted papers passed through a rigorous selection process. Each submission has been evaluated on the basis of its significance, novelty, and technical quality, and reviewed by at least three members of the Program Committee. In the end, we decided to accept 6 regular papers and 2 short papers, reflecting a selection of the best among the excellent. In addition to the technical program composed of the papers in the proceedings, the conference included a keynote by Michele Bezzi.

Organizing a conference like C&TC is a team effort, and many people need to be acknowledged. First, we would like to thank everyone who submitted their contributions to this event for having chosen C&TC to present and discuss their work. Their contributions were the basis for the success of the conference. Second, we would like to acknowledge the hard work of all our colleagues from the Program Committee, experts in the research domains of the conference, for performing the extremely valuable tasks of reviewing and discussing the many excellent contributions. Third, we would like to thank everyone at the OTM organizers team for their exceptional support and, in particular, the OTM Conferences & Workshops General Chairs Robert Meersman, Tharam Dillon, Hervé Panetto, and Ernesto Damiani. Finally, a special thanks to the keynote speaker, Michele Bezzi, for delivering the keynote talk at the conference.

All of these people contributed to these Proceedings of the 5th International Conference on Cloud and Trusted Computing, and all of them deserve our highest gratitude. Thank you!

September 2015

Claudio A. Ardagna
Meiko Jensen

All You Need is Trust – An Analysis of Trust Measures Communicated by Cloud Providers

Julian Gantner, Lukas Demetz[✉], and Ronald Maier

Department of Information Systems, Production and Logistics Management,
University of Innsbruck, Innsbruck, Austria
julian.gantner11@gmail.com,
{lukas.demetz,ronald.maier}@uibk.ac.at

Abstract. Cloud computing represents an information technology (IT) provisioning model in which IT resources are consumed as a service. They are no longer installed and run on premises of consuming organizations, but at cloud providers. Cloud computing poses unique security and privacy challenges because of its architectural features and because cloud providers are separate legal entities serving multiple customers. Trusting a cloud provider represents a critical barrier to adopt cloud computing. Although trust is difficult to assess, customers need to be assured that cloud services are provided as promised. This article describes what measures selected cloud providers communicate to increase their customers' trust in their organization and services. We conducted a document analysis of whitepapers and Web sites of four globally operating cloud providers, described and categorized trust measures, which we discussed with four Swiss cloud providers. The results show a list of 28 trust measures assigned to 14 focus areas.

Keywords: Cloud computing · Cloud provider · Document analysis · Privacy · Security · Trust measure

1 Introduction

Over the last years, we saw a change in the form how information technology (IT) is provided. Computing is transformed from running software on individual computers owned by the consuming organization towards software for millions to consume as a service, sometimes described as similar to traditional utilities such as water, electricity, and telephony [1]. Cloud computing is a computing model that allows ubiquitous and on-demand access via the Internet to a shared pool of computing resources that can be rapidly provided by a cloud provider [2]. The shared pool of resources can be offered via the three service models Software as a Service (SaaS), Platform as a Service (PaaS), and Infrastructure as a Service (IaaS).

Organizations have started to adopt cloud computing hoping to increase their flexibility, reduce costs, and to be more focused on their main business [3]. The rising number of organizations using cloud services shows the increasing importance and acceptance of cloud computing [4]. The cloud market is projected to reach $ 191 billion by 2020 growing from $ 58 billion in 2013 [5].

© Springer International Publishing Switzerland 2015
C. Debruyne et al. (Eds.): OTM 2015 Conferences, LNCS 9415, pp. 557–574, 2015.
DOI: 10.1007/978-3-319-26148-5_38

Cloud computing's architectural features raise several security and privacy concerns [6] and risks, including inappropriate use of data due to a lack of control, and the uncertainty if the contractual partner fulfills service level agreements [3]. As potential customers are aware of these concerns and risks, trust in a cloud provider is one of the most critical barriers to adopt cloud computing [7]. Cloud customers require a certain level of trust in the cloud provider [8], its technical competence and economic stability [3].

Trust as well as security and privacy are, however, difficult to assess. Nevertheless, customers need to be assured in some way that cloud services are provided as promised [3]. Applying security and privacy-related measures and communicating such measures to increase a customer's trust is assumedly crucial for adopting cloud computing and for forming long-term relationships with cloud providers.

The goal of this article is to explore what measures cloud providers communicate to positively influence their customers' trust. We refer to trust measures as comprising all actions and (automated) procedures as means to an end [9] used by a cloud provider to increase the trust of its customers. For this purpose, we conducted a qualitative content analysis of data collected from whitepapers and Web sites offered by cloud providers. Additionally, we discussed the identified trust measures with employees of four Swiss cloud providers. The results indicate that measures regarding security and privacy are the most critical for increasing trust in a cloud provider.

2   Background

Trust is a multidimensional concept that has been studied from the viewpoint of many disciplines, including social psychology [10], sociology [11], and marketing [12]. Trust plays also a main role in the context of information systems [13], in the use of third-parties [14], in privacy protection [15] as well as in online situations [16]. It is a complex, context-dependent, social phenomenon people understand in different ways [17]. Trust is a belief in the competence and expertise of others, such that one can feel that one can reasonably rely on them to care for their valuable assets [18]. Mayer et al. [19] define trust as the willingness of a trusting party to be vulnerable to the actions of another party, for instance, people, organizations, as well as computing systems [20]. Trust is the willingness of an individual to behave in a manner that assumes another party will behave according to expectations in a risky situation [21]. Trust is therefore especially relevant in risky situations where one cannot control in advance what is to happen [22].

The possibility of risk and negative consequences makes trust important, but problematic, especially in unfamiliar or uncertain environments like the Internet [23]. Corritore et al. [16] define online trust as "an attitude of confident expectation in an online situation of risk that one's vulnerabilities will not be exploited."

Those aspects apply to all kinds of Internet business where end-users are supposed to trust an online organization, especially in e-commerce. Kim et al. [24] define online consumer's trust as a "consumer's subjective belief that the selling party or entity will fulfill its transactional obligations as the consumer understands them." Thus, to be willing to buy online, a customer has to trust the web vendor [25, 26]. Web vendors can provide trust by influencing the perceived quality of information provided to the customers, perceived privacy, perceived security protection, presence of third party seals, and positive reputation [24]. When end-users trust the parties they are dealing with, they believe they will receive long-term benefits if they maintain that relationship [12].

An important area in information systems that has not yet received much attention by researchers is trust in cloud computing. Since e-commerce has already been established in the mid-nineties, there exists more research on trust in e-commerce than in cloud computing. As in e-commerce, a cloud customer is more likely to cooperate, if he trusts another party. Although the idea of cloud computing should allow customers to easily swap from one provider to another, proprietary interfaces of cloud providers restrict changing the cloud providers [1]. As changing cloud providers is not as easy as expected, cloud providers and their customers form long-term relationships [27, 28]. For forming such long-term relationships, trust plays a key role [29]. As in e-commerce, cloud customers are more likely to cooperate, if they trust another party. Cloud providers thus have to create and maintain trust to acquire and retain customers and in further consequence build competitive advantages [30]. Previous research showed that trust in a cloud provider can be facilitated, for instance by authentication and identity management, secure service composition, and trust management frameworks [3] such as the Trust Cloud framework [7]. To increase trust, cloud providers thus need to communicate how they create, implement and maintain trustworthy cloud services. Cloud providers communicate trust measures to inform their customers accordingly.

While there has been research on challenges in achieving customer trust in cloud computing [7, 31] as well as approaches to identify trust areas in cloud computing [32, 33], there is a gap in research with respect to how cloud providers communicate trust measures. To address this research gap, we conducted a qualitative document analysis of whitepapers and Web sites offered by cloud providers to identify trust measures communicated by cloud providers. We discussed these trust measures in interviews with employees of Swiss cloud providers.

3   Study Design

We conducted a qualitative document analysis of major cloud providers using whitepapers and Web sites publicly available on the Internet in October 2014. We coded the selected documents and identified trust measures communicated by cloud providers. Subsequently we interviewed representatives of four Swiss cloud providers to rate the trust measures identified in the document analysis. In the following, we present (1) the process applied for identifying major cloud providers, (2) the sampling and coding process, and (3) the interview process.

3.1   Cloud Provider Selection Process

As a first step, we selected cloud providers for the latter analysis. For this purpose, we queried Google Scholar using the term "cloud service provider" for articles published between 2011 and 2014. We selected the first accessible 25 English language articles from the result set that had been published in journals or conference proceedings.

Subsequently, we scanned the articles for cloud providers independent of their service models and added them to our list. We extracted a cloud provider whether or not the article mentioned a specific service of a cloud provider. Additionally, we counted the number of articles mentioning a certain cloud provider. We received a list of 17 cloud providers. Table 1 shows the list of identified cloud providers.

Table 1. Identified cloud providers, the terms to identify them, the number of articles mentioning them in the 25 collected articles, and the number of selected resources included in the document analysis

Cloud provider	Term	Occurrences	Whitepapers	Websites
Amazon	("Amazon Cloud", "Amazon Elastic Compute Cloud (EC2)", "Amazon Web Services (AWS)")	16	1	2
Google	("Google App Engine", "Google Cloud", "Google Apps")	9	2	2
Microsoft	("Microsoft Cloud", "Windows Azure")	8	3	2
Salesforce	("Salesforce.com", "Salesforce", "Force.com")	8	3	2
Further Cloud Providers				
Rackspace	("Rackspace")	5		
IBM	("IBM Cloud", "IBM Smart Cloud")	4		
Verizon	("CloudSwitch from Verizon", "Verizon Business", "Verizon Terremark")	3		
VMWare	("VMWare")	3		
GoGrid	("GoGrid")	2		
Joynet	("Joynet", "Joyent Smart Data Center")	2		
Akamai	("Akamai")	1		
Animoto	("Animoto")	1		
Cisco	("Cisco")	1		
Compiere	("Compiere ERP")	1		
NEC	("NEC")	1		
NetSuite	("NetSuite")	1		
Sun Parascale	("Sun Parascale")	1		

Besides relying on scholarly journals and conference proceedings as the basis for our sampling, we used a recent market survey [34] to select cloud providers for our analysis. This market survey is based on metrics such as annual cloud services revenue growth, revenue per employee, and types of cloud services offered by the cloud providers. We extracted the ten highest ranked cloud providers from the list. Subsequently, we considered all cloud providers appearing in both sets for the analysis. The first four cloud providers in Table 1 were present in both lists. The reason for these two data sets was to identify cloud providers from an academic as well as a practitioners' perspective.

3.2   Selective Sampling and Coding Procedure

We used the selective sampling approach of [35] for collecting data. We used the categories of a trust impact model [24] as an initial code set, consisting of trust antecedents that influence consumer trust. These codes served as categories in an initial code set and were meant to be modified during the coding process.

We sampled appropriate data to be analyzed from data available online of the Web site of the first cloud provider on the list of identified cloud providers. We searched the cloud provider's Web site for data to be analyzed using keywords defined in the initial code set described above. During the search process, whitepapers had the highest priority, followed by Web sites. While searching for new data, the Web domain of the currently examined cloud provider was never left. Once appropriate data had been found, we instantly analyzed the data for concepts, that is, we coded it using, revising, and extending the initial code set. Based on the analysis of the data, we collected and instantly analyzed further data. This continued until no further concepts (codes) could be identified on the respective cloud provider's Web site. Then, we moved on to the next provider on the list, where the concept analysis and the sampling process continued. The code set changed over time as new concepts were found or better structures emerged from the coding process. Once there emerged no further codes from data sets of two consecutive cloud providers, we considered the code set to be saturated and final, and ended the data sampling. Finally, we coded all data anew using the final code set.

A second member of the author team coded about 10% of the data and we calculated an inter-coder reliability [36] of 0.87 to check for reliability of the content analysis. The calculated value is above the threshold of 0.80 for an acceptable inter-coder reliability [37]. In contrast to repositories of trust measures, such as the Cloud Security Alliance's Cloud Controls Matrix and its STAR repository that provide possible measures to assess the security risk of a certain cloud provider, the goal of our research was to identify trust measures that are communicated by a cloud provider to its customers.

3.3   Interviews

In December 2014, we contacted five public cloud providers headquartered in Switzerland via e-mail asking for interviews taking approximately 30 minutes. The group of cloud providers we selected for the cold mailings consisted of five Swiss organizations offering cloud computing services.

We received a positive answer from four Swiss cloud providers who were represented by interview partners with a complete understanding of the services offered by the respective cloud provider. In total, we interviewed four employees representing four Swiss cloud providers. Table 2 shows the demographics of the interviewees as well as of their respective employer.

All interviews were conducted via Skype in January 2015. The conversations were recorded and transcribed. Two interviews were conducted by one interviewer, and two interviews by two interviewers. The interviews were conducted as guideline based semi-structured interviews, which took between 25 and 60 minutes and consisted of two parts. In the first part we asked the interviewee about their company and position and about the role of trust for cloud computing. In the second part, we discussed the 14 focus areas of trust identified in the qualitative document analysis.

In this part, we asked the interviewees to rate the importance of these focus areas. In particular, we asked the interviewees to assign one of the following three categories to each trust focus area according to their expert opinion: 1 for being communicated, 2 for partly being communicated, and 3 for hardly/not being communicated.

Table 2. Interview participants

ID	Role	Number of employees	Customer base	Number of customers	Years in market
CMO1	Chief Marketing Officer	17	B2B	15	2
HCPM1	Head of Cloud Product Management	30	B2B	30	6
CEO1	Chief Executive Officer	12	B2B + B2C	150	2
HCD1	Head of Customer Development	21,000	B2B + B2C	3,000,000	7

4   Results

This section describes the results of our analysis. Specifically, we present a structured list of trust measures (section 4.1). Additionally, we present the results of our interview study rating the trust measures and discussing the role of trust in cloud computing by employees of cloud providers (section 4.2).

4.1   Trust Measures

We describe trust measures that cloud providers communicate to their customers, structured according to focus areas detailing the six antecedents of trust affected by these trust measures. The first five antecedents are based on [24]. We extended this model by the antecedent of appropriate human resources adapting their model to cloud computing. For each antecedent, we give an introduction followed by a description of the associated focus areas plus a short description of the trust measures we identified. Quotes serve as examples and may not apply for all cloud providers. However, each trust measure reported has been described by at least two cloud providers. The 14 focus areas are indicated with FA, the 28 trust measures with TM.

Information Quality (IQ). In the interest of customers, cloud providers want to assure high quality of information. They seek to have proper communication channels in place, to provide detailed information to their customers and to keep this information up-to-date.

FA1 Communication Channels to Customer. Cloud providers notify customers automatically if their data are moved geographically, about service interruptions, incidents affecting the confidentiality, integrity, and availability of their data. Google says they "[…] will notify the affected customers of incidents that affect the confidentiality, integrity or availability of their data. Once an initial notification is made, follow-up notifications and calls are possible as needed for the affected parties to understand the incident" [38]. Moreover, cloud providers might maintain an online trust center, where they publish reports about law enforcement requests on a regular basis. For example, Microsoft "[...] publishes a Law Enforcement Requests Report that provides insight into the scope of requests, as well as information from Microsoft's General Counsel about how the company responds to national security requests" [39]. Further examples for measures include bulletin boards, blogs, participation in academic conferences, and vulnerability reporting.

Measure: TM1 Notify on incidents - Establish features to keep the customer notified of any incidents or legal data requests.

FA 2 Supportive/Supplementary Information. We found that cloud providers issue compact information in their whitepapers. We also collected links to other Web resources, like codes of conduct, data center video tours, academic research articles, service organization controls (SOC 3) reports, external reports, subcontractors, or certifications (e.g., ISO, safe harbor). For instance, salesforce.com states that on their trust site "[...] anyone can find live data on system performance, current and recent phishing and malware attempts, and tips on best security practices" [40].

Measure: TM2 Inform on policies - Provide in-depth information about processes and policies.

FA 3 Currency of Information. Cloud providers notify customers in advance of any change of service offerings, and of service fees. Security and privacy policies, as well as the Code of Conduct are periodically reviewed and updated to include customer feedback. For example, Microsoft "[...] will occasionally update our privacy statements to reflect customer feedback and changes in our Services" [41]. Information about the last update time may be added to statements to clearly state their currency.

Measures: TM3 Notify on changes - Customer notification in case of changes to services or fees; TM4 Update policies - Periodically update policies.

Privacy Protection (PP). Cloud customers might be interested in how their personal and payment data are handled in terms of privacy protection. To address this issue, cloud providers detail privacy policies declaring what data they collect, who has access to the data, who owns the data, and where the data are geographically located.

FA 4 Collection and Use of Personal Information. Customers' data are used by cloud providers to help customers completing future transactions. Microsoft, for instance, says, "When you [as the customer] provide Payment Data while authenticated, we will store that data to help you complete future transactions without you having to provide the information again. We do not, however, retain the security code associated with your Payment instrument (e.g., the CSV) in this manner" [41]. Third parties are not authorized to collect customer information and all investigated cloud providers abide by the EU- and Swiss Safe Harbor frameworks regarding the collection and retention of data. Salesforce.com, for instance, "[...] abides by the U.S.-EU Safe Harbor Framework and the U.S.-Swiss Safe Harbor Framework as set forth by the U.S. Department of Commerce and the European Union" [42].

Measure: TM 5 Secure payment - Make payment processes easier for the customer, without disclosing customer information to third parties.

FA 5 Data Access Policy. Customers' cloud data are only accessed by the cloud provider to provide service offerings and in strict compliance with privacy policies and customer agreements. Access for employees is only granted with a legitimate business

564   J. Gantner et al.

need and revoked, as soon as it is no longer needed. Amazon says, "AWS only provides data center access and information to employees and contractors who have a legitimate business need for such privileges" [43]. Moreover, all access to customer data is logged. Requests for additional access require approval of executives and the system owner. However, storing data in a particular country does not necessarily protect the data from access by foreign governments. Legal requests for customer data access are reviewed and checked, if they satisfy legal requirements. Microsoft states, "Should a third party contact us with a demand for Customer Data, we will attempt to redirect the third party to request it directly from our customers. [...] We require a court order or warrant before we will consider disclosing content to law enforcement" [44].

Measures: TM 6 Restrict internal access - Allow employees only access as long as they need it; TM 7 Document access - Log all accesses to data; TM 8 Restrict external access - Prevent governmental institutions from data access.

FA 6 Data Ownership Policy. All investigated cloud providers outline that customers own their data and data will not be sold to third parties. For instance, Amazon says, "[cloud customers] are solely responsible for the development, content, operation, maintenance, and use of [their] content" [45]. Moreover, subcontractors of the cloud provider are contractually obliged to follow the same data ownership policy. Microsoft states, "[w]e contractually obligate subcontractors that work in facilities or on equipment controlled by Microsoft to follow our privacy standards. All other subcontractors are contractually obligated to follow privacy standards equivalent to our own" [44].

Measure: TM 9 Leave rights - Leave all contents, rights, titles, and property rights of customer's cloud data to the customer.

FA 7 Data Storing and Processing Location. Customer data are distributed among a shared infrastructure composed of homogeneous machines and located across multiple data centers. These measures are intended to ensure that customer data remain resilient in the face of most failure modes, including natural disasters or system failures. For instance, "Google operates a geographically distributed set of data centers that is designed to maintain service continuity in the event of a disaster or other incident in a single region" [46]. Customers may specify the geographical regions to let them decide where their data are stored. Microsoft says, "With Windows Azure, customers can specify the geographic area(s) [...] of the Microsoft datacenters in which their Customer Data will be stored" [44].

Measures: TM 10 Replicate data - Store data on several data centers worldwide; TM 11 Select region - Let customers specify the data storage and processing region.

Security Protection (SP). Cloud providers assure their customers that their data are safe concerning confidentiality, integrity, and availability. For this purpose, cloud providers publish information about their logical and physical security measures.

FA 8 Logical Security. Cloud providers follow a least privilege access policy, where employees are granted access to customer data only when needed. As soon as the access is no longer needed, or employees leave the company, access rights are removed. Amazon says, "When an employee no longer has a business need for these privileges, his or her access is immediately revoked, even if they continue to be an employee of Amazon or Amazon Web Services" [43]. All system access activity is logged, except passwords. Cloud providers use firewalls, encryption technologies, and data isolation techniques to logically separate the cloud tenants of different cloud customers with the aim to defend against unauthorized access and intruders. Salsforce.com states, "User passwords are stored using a salted hash format for encryption" [47]. Microsoft claims, "Azure uses logical isolation to segregate each customer's data from that of others" [48]. A limited number of cloud access points, capacity warning alarms, security monitoring tools and a full time information security team are in place for purposes of monitoring. For instance, "AWS has strategically placed a limited number of access points to the cloud to allow for a more comprehensive monitoring of inbound and outbound communications and network traffic" [43]. Passwords for cloud access have to have a minimum level of complexity, and must be changed on a regular basis. Data are chunked and replicated over multiple systems to prevent a single point of failure. In case of incidents, post mortem investigations are performed to determine the root cause of the incidents. Google says, "[...] engineers conduct post-mortem investigations when necessary to determine the root cause for single events, trends spanning multiple events over time, and to develop new strategies to help prevent recurrence of similar incidents" [46]. Vulnerability scans and system penetration tests are performed periodically, and security patches are installed if necessary. After a user deletes a message, account, user, or domain, the respective hard drives are overwritten, followed by a full read of the drive to ensure it is blank.

Measures: TM 12 Prevent intrusion - Prevent from unauthorized access, malware and intrusion; TM 13 Monitor - Perform constant monitoring of all access activities; TM 14 Check vulnerabilities - Check for possible vulnerabilities and eradicate weak spots; TM 15 Manage incidents - Have sophisticated policies for the handling of incidents of all kinds; TM 16 Authenticate - Maintain secure authentication practices; TM17 Authorize - Maintain strict authorization policies.

FA 9 Physical Security. Data centers of cloud providers are housed in nondescript facilities and have strictly controlled physical access policies. We identified interior and exterior video surveillance, security guards, perimeter fences with concrete vehicle barriers, access logging, and biometric access controls as intrusion prevention measures. For instance, "[t]he standard physical security controls implemented at each Google data center include the following: custom designed electronic card access control systems, alarm systems, interior and exterior cameras, and security guards" [46]. Security officers are qualified with training to protect high security enterprises with mission-critical infrastructures. Moreover, all employees and visitors have to have a legitimate business need to enter a data center, where all visitors are permanently escorted. At Amazon, "all visitors and contractors are required to present identification and are signed in and continually escorted by authorized staff" [43]. Automatic fire detection and suppression systems, automatic climate controls, and back-up power generators for the entire facility are in place to avoid physical damage and service outages. Microsoft says, "Microsoft datacenters are physically constructed, managed, and monitored 24 hours a day to shelter data and services from unauthorized access as well as environmental threats" [48]. For major incidents, disaster recovery programs are in place at the data centers and tested periodically.

Measures: TM 18 Defend data centers - Defend against unauthorized access of data centers; TM 19 Avoid damage - Avoid physical damage/failure to storage devices.

Third Party Seal (TPS). Displaying that a cloud provider and its services and processes have been checked or approved by an independent third party might as well help to increase trust in a cloud provider. For this purpose, cloud providers display seals of third parties on their websites.

FA10 Third Party Seal. We found certifications and standards that cloud providers communicate. For instance, "Google Apps and Google Cloud Platform are certified for SSAE 16/ISAE 3402 Type II, received the SOC2 audit and ISO 27001 certification" [38]. Moreover, third party seals also indicate best practices applied by the cloud provider (e.g., NIST 800-88 Guidelines for Media Sanitization) and memberships in cloud computing associations. Microsoft says, "Microsoft Azure [...] participate[s] in the Cloud Security Alliance (CSA) STAR Registry program, which allows cloud customers to compare the compliance posture of participating cloud services" [39].

Measures: TM 20 Get certificates - Obtain third-party certifications; TM 21 Apply best practices - Design practices compliant to standard collections of best practices; TM 22 Team up - Form alliance with fellow cloud providers to establish standards.

Positive Reputation (REP). Showing that customers have already successfully implemented the service of a cloud provider, can be a way to increase the reputation and trust in the cloud provider. For this, cloud providers present success stories on their websites.

FA 11 Positive Reputation. Cloud providers display a number of examples for successful implementations of their cloud services of customers. Those customer success stories comprise information about the customers' business, the challenges they faced before the implementation, the description of the cloud solution used, and the benefits the customers received from the cloud solution. Amazon says, "[The HTC Connected Services Division] decided that Amazon Web Services (AWS) offered the breadth and depth of services required, and came with the support services the division needed in order to be successful" [49]. Additionally, customer quotes or videos are provided. For instance, salesforce.com quotes the Global President of Stanley Black & Decker's Industrial and Automotive Repair Division, saying "With the help of the Salesforce1 Customer Platform we're building smart tools that are really genius ones" [50].

Measure: TM 23 Present success stories - Describe how customers have benefited from cloud services.

Appropriate Human Resources (HR). Cloud customers usually do not know the persons who handle their data. To assure that those persons are reliable and trustworthy, cloud providers publish information about policies, rules, and guidelines their employees have to follow. This includes information about the recruitment routines, security training, education and awareness (SETA), and the code of conduct.

FA 12 Recruitment. Cloud providers use background checks, as permitted by law, before hiring new personnel. Those checks are conducted to receive information about criminal records, financial situation, immigration background, education, previous employment and references of the job applicants. Amazon says, "AWS conducts criminal background checks, as permitted by law, as part of pre-employment screening practices for employees [...]" [43]. Similarly salesforce.com states, that "before being granted access, every employee and contractor must pass a thorough background check" [40].

Measure: TM 24 Check applicants - Conduct background checks of job applicants.

FA 13 Security Education, Training and Awareness. After being employed, employees have to go through initial security orientation and training. During the rest of their employment, employees are required to undergo training on different security topics (e.g., emerging security techniques and policies). At Google, "Training concerning customer data outlines the appropriate use of data in conjunction with business processes as well as the consequences of violations" [46]. The regularity and extent of security training depends on the employee's job role. Salesforce states, "All employees receive regular information security and privacy training. Employees in data handling positions receive additional training specific to their roles" [40]. Thus, software engineers may receive better training in service design, coding practices, and vulnerability testing, while data center technicians may get training in fire prevention and extinction.

Measures: TM 25 Perform logical security training - Educate personnel in terms of logical security incident prevention and response; TM 26 Perform physical security training - Educate personnel in terms of physical security.

FA 14 Code of Conduct. The code of conduct of cloud providers covers topics like security, business ethics, appropriate system usage, and professional standards. Our analysis showed that employees are required to know and understand the company's code of conduct, and might have to sign a confidentiality agreement. For instance, Google says that each of their employees is "required to read, understand, and take a training course on the company's Code of Conduct" [46]. If an employee observes any violation of the code of conduct, they can report this anonymously. Most companies publish their code of conduct and review it periodically to fulfill consumer's changing requirements. Microsoft assures that they "[…] update [the Code of Conduct] periodically if changes are needed to address customers' evolving needs and expectations" [39].

Measures: TM 27 Define a code of conduct - Determine basic rules for ethical behavior of employees; TM 28 Enforce the code of conduct - Take actions to make sure that employees apply the code of conduct.

4.2   Rating of Focus Areas

Table 3 depicts the list of focus areas from the content analysis (section 4.1), ordered by the mean value of their rated importance to be communicated. Additionally, the respective antecedents of trust are enclosed to the focus areas. The list is organized in ascending order of mean values, starting with the mean value to be most important for customer trust (1.00) and ending with the mean value to be least important (2.75).

While rating the focus areas, the interviewees seemed not to agree unanimously on the importance of one single focus area. Based on the statements of the interviewees, this could have multiple reasons. First, customer trust might hold a different level of importance, depending on the industry sector of the cloud provider and the kind of services provided. Moreover, the importance of customer trust in cloud computing may differ depending on the service and deployment models of the cloud provider. The evaluation of focus areas additionally depends on the size of the customer organization.

Table 3. Focus areas ordered by expert evaluations' mean

Focus Area	Mean	Focus Area	Mean
Data ownership policy (PP)	1.00	Positive reputation (REP)	1.63
Logical security (SP)	1.00	Communication channels to customer (IQ)	1.75
Physical security (SP)	1.00	Collection and use of personal information (PP)	1.75
Data storing and processing location (PP)	1.13	Supportive/supplementary information (IQ)	2.25
Data access policy (PP)	1.25	Code of conduct (HR)	2.50
Presence of a third party seal (TPS)	1.50	Recruitment (HR)	2.50
Currency of information (IQ)	1.50	Security education, training & awareness (HR)	2.75

The small sample size, as well as the fact that the interviewees represent different positions in various types of cloud provider organizations, prevent any accuracy for a profound statistical analysis. However, when it comes to customer trust, Table 3 indicates that the interviewees tend to attach the most importance to the two antecedents privacy protection and security protection. Moreover, the appropriate human resource antecedent seems to be perceived as less important in this regard, since its three focus areas received the highest mean values.

Right after the discussion of the 14 focus areas, we asked the interviewees about further focus areas or trust measures, which they deemed important, but were not included in our list. In total, the interviewees mentioned six additional focus areas to reinforce customer trust. Those additional focus areas are: clear SLAs (clear SLAs defining, for instance, maximum downtime and financial remuneration), existing customer fields (promote business fields in which the cloud provider is already active), independence from other vendors and producers, physical and logical segregation of data centers (operate physically and logically segregated data centers such that a failure in one data center does not lead to a failure in another data center), tradition (long tradition ensures that services will be available in the long term), and visibility (explain the processes and methods used).

All interviewees agreed on trust being essentially important to acquire and maintain customers in cloud computing. The increasing number of cloud providers makes it hard to determine which providers can be trusted. CEO1 stated, "Trust and security are among the highest decision points for customers." However, from the experience of HCD1, in most cases trust is more important for central European cloud customers.

When it comes to boosting customer trust in cloud computing, the interviewees came up with a large number of aspects. One important point is transparency for the customer. Several interviewees emphasized that their organization wants their customers to have profound information on their processes, so customers know how their data is handled and thus develop trust. For instance, if a customer desires, he or she can visit the data center in which their data is stored (CMO1). Trust is also facilitated by assigning a specific contact person to customers whom they can approach in case of any issues with the cloud system (HCD1). Being in the market for a long time and having received name recognition are also perceived to boost trust (HCPM1). The size of a cloud computing organization and the ability to maintain a long-term relationship to the customer are also mentioned as an important criterion for customer trust (HCPM1). According to HCPM1, especially large companies, having 500 to 1000 employees, tend to reach out for a big cloud provider who can assure long-term business continuity. In contrast, small providers are perceived to have a higher risk of dropping out of the market and thus, to have a more insecure future. This especially applies for private clouds which customers want to maintain for at least 5 years before, because of the high effort to establish and configure them (HCPM1). Strict service level agreements (SLAs), as well as having certificates are assumed as key facets of customer trust in cloud computing (CEO1). HCPM1 said that there are obligatory certificates (e.g., ISO 27001) which are considered as entry criteria, especially for enterprise customers, but also "nice-to-have" certificates, like Green-IT and energy management certificates are considered as important. Those are intended to show efforts towards a sophisticated enterprise culture and, in further consequence, to raise customer trust in the organization (HCPM1). Moreover, having data centers within the national borders demonstrates control and also may raise customer trust (CMO1). If the cloud provider owns data centers and the infrastructure themselves, this can constitute a major trust booster (HCPM1).

Our interviewees also stressed the Swiss privacy protection of cloud computing data. Switzerland with its history and data privacy laws is seen as a well demanded site for cloud computing businesses (CEO1, CMO1, HCD1, HCPM1). Swiss cloud alternatives accommodate customers' needs by having a strict data protection law (CEO1, CMO1). Where the data is located, the respective data protection law is applicable and Switzerland has stricter data privacy laws, making many customers favor Switzerland to store their data (CEO1).This privacy law is not only applicable to individuals, but also to other entities (companies) and their data. That makes it a unique jurisdiction almost worldwide (CEO1). All of the interviewees agreed that having data stored in data centers within Switzerland is a major trust booster for their customers, being an essential part of their business model. Furthermore, all interviewees of Swiss cloud providers emphasized the term "Swissness", equivalent to the Swiss business attitude of setting great value on customer service, integrity and innovation.

5   Discussion and Limitations

Our research reveals several organizational and technical trust measures. Organizational measures usually include manually implemented procedures, whereas technical measures include automated procedures [9]. We found rules, processes, guidelines, and the assignment of responsibility as organizational trust measures. Notifications, detection, authentication, and monitoring are technical trust measures. The majority of antecedents of trust we found in our two samples contain organizational measures. Solely security protection contains mostly technical trust measures. The antecedents information quality and privacy protection consist mainly of organizational measures, however, we identified technical information quality measures as well, for instance, notify on incidents, secure payment, and document access.

When it comes to auditability, customers cannot check most of the communicated trust measures. Only the trust measures associated with the antecedents information quality, third party seal and positive reputation can be checked by customers. For all other measures, customers cannot have complete assurance that the communicated trust measures are indeed in place.

Trust is unanimously approved by all interviewees to be one of the most important aspects to enable the business model of cloud computing. The discussion of the focus areas from the content analysis implies that especially measures addressing privacy and security protection have a high priority for cloud providers to be communicated to gain customer trust. Beyond the results of the content analysis, the interviewees came up with five additional aspects affecting customer trust: being independent of other vendors and producers, clear SLAs, highlighting existing customer fields, physical and logical segregation of data centers, tradition and transparency.

The results are in line with previous research on cloud computing. Trusting a cloud provider is one of the most critical barriers for adopting cloud computing [7]. Our results supports this, as the interviewees rated all of the identified trust measures as important. As the trust measures related to privacy and security protection were ranked the most important by the interviewees seems to support that cloud computing's architectural features raise security and privacy concerns [6].

Compared to the e-commerce trust model of Kim et al. [24], we came across a sixth antecedent of trust for cloud computing - appropriate human resources, even though our interviewees rated the communication of human resources policies as least important of all six trust antecedents. Unlike e-commerce, cloud computing involves the vulnerability from inside and outside the cloud [27]. Cloud providers communicate measures to confirm that their employees are trustworthy to increase the customers' perceived security from inside the cloud. Thus, we extend current literature on trust by the additional antecedent of trust appropriate human resources. With this additional trust antecedent, we showed that to trust a cloud provider a customer also has to trust a provider's employees.

Additionally, we extend the current academic knowledge base by providing a list of trust measures assigned to focus areas. With these lists we lay the foundation for further research regarding the role of trust measures in cloud computing.

Cloud providers can use our results to improve the communication of trust measures and thus to increase their customers' trust. They can use the list of focus areas and trust measures as a guideline to check which trust measures they already communicate and where they should improve their communication.

This research is not free of limitations. First, whitepapers and Web sites by cloud providers served as the basis for the content analysis. These data sources, however, are occasionally updated. In updated documents, new or changed trust measures may be documented. Thus, the results of the content analysis should be understood as a snapshot of trust measures communicated at the time of our data collection (i.e., October 2014).

Second, the analysis approach used in the content analysis is not complete. That is, we used data provided by a subset of the identified cloud providers. Thus, there is the chance that the cloud providers not considered in our research communicate additional trust measures. However, we used a saturation criterion for stopping the identification of trust measures. As soon as the coding of two consecutive cloud providers did not reveal any new trust measures, we considered the trust measures as matured.

Three of the interviews were conducted and transcribed in German, as it is the native language of both the interviewees and the interviewers. There is the possibility of translation errors during the result interpretation of those interview transcripts. One of the interviews was conducted in English, not being the native language of both interview partners. This includes possible misinterpretations on both sides.

Additionally, we only interviewed four employees representing four Swiss cloud providers. However, the profiles of the interviewees' organizations show a high degree of diversity regarding, for instance, number of employees, customer base and time of market entry (see Table 3). Thus, the results cover a broad and diverse set of cloud providers and incorporate diverse points of view.

The basis for identifying and categorizing the trust measures was a trust model for Business-to-Customer e-commerce [24]. As cloud computing can be both Business-to-Customer and Business-to-Business, we did not explicitly distinguish between these two types of relationships in our research. However, the used trust model served only as a starting point and was adapted accordingly.

6 Conclusion and Outlook

Cloud computing is an IT provisioning model in which software is consumed as a service and no longer installed on individual computers owned by the consuming organization. Organizations adopt cloud computing hoping to increase their flexibility, reduce costs, and to be more focused on their main business [3]. In this article, we conducted a document analysis of whitepapers and Web sites offered by cloud providers to examine measures aimed at gaining customers' trust.

In total, we identified 28 trust measures (TM 1 to TM 28) assigned to 14 focus areas (FA 1 to FA 14). The trust measures affect the six antecedents of trust information quality, privacy protection, security protection, third party seal, positive reputation, and appropriate human resources. In interviews with four employees representing four Swiss cloud providers we discussed these trust measures and focus areas and checked their importance. The interviews revealed that the interviewees tend to attach the most importance to the two antecedents privacy protection and security protection.

The majority of the identified trust measures are organizational measures (i.e., manually implemented procedures). Most of the trust measures and their effectiveness can be checked by an auditing organization. In contrast, a customer can only check trust measures focusing on information quality, presence of a third party seal and positive reputation. The customer is without directly accessible supporting evidence that the communicated trust measures are indeed implemented for all other trust measures.

Summing up, this article explored trust measures currently communicated by cloud providers and contributes to the academic knowledge base (1) by extending the list of trust antecedents by the additional trust antecedent human resources and (2) by providing a structured list of trust measures communicated by cloud providers.

Possible future research in this area can extend the data set of the document analysis to include all cloud providers in the list we identified during the cloud provider selection process. An interesting question that remains is what trust measures have the highest impact on a cloud provider's customers' trust and what measures are the most important in this respect. Interviews with cloud customers and with representatives of organizations that deliberately avoid cloud services could be conducted to analyze the customer perspective regarding trust in cloud computing and contrast it with the offerings by cloud providers. Future work could also look at the impact of delivery models on trust measures. That is, depending on the delivery model used what trust measures does a customer want to be implemented.

References

1. Buyya, R., Yeo, C.S., Venugopal, S., Broberg, J., Brandic, I.: Cloud Computing and Emerging IT Platforms: Vision, Hype, and Reality for Delivering Computing as the 5th Utility. Future Generation Computer Systems **25**, 17 (2009)
2. Mell, P., Grance, T.: The NIST Definition of Cloud Computing. National Institute of Standards and Technology (2011)
3. Takabi, H., Joshi, J.B.D., Ahn, G.-J.: Security and Privacy Challenges in Cloud Computing Environments. IEEE Security & Privacy Magazine **8**, 24–31 (2010)
4. Forbes (2014). http://www.forbes.com/sites/tjmccue/2014/01/29/cloud-computing-united-states-businesses-will-spend-13-billion-on-it/
5. Bartels, A., Rymer, J.R., Staten, J., Kark, K., Clark, J., Whittaker, D.: The Public Cloud Market Is Now In Hypergrowth (2014).
   https://www.forrester.com/The+Public+Cloud+Market+Is+Now+In+Hypergrowth/fulltext/-/E-RES113365?intcmp=blog:forrlink
6. Nofer, M., Hinz, O., Muntermann, J., Roßnagel, H.: The Economic Impact of Privacy Violations and Security Breaches. Business & Information Systems Engineering **6**, 339–348 (2014)
7. Ko, R.K.L., Jagadpramana, P., Mowbray, M., Pearson, S., Kirchberg, M., Liang, Q., Lee, B.S.: Trustcloud: a framework for accountability and trust in cloud computing. In: Proceedings of the 2011 IEEE World Congress on Services (SERVICES), pp. 584–588 (2011)
8. Kaufman, L.M.: Data Security in the World of Cloud Computing. IEEE Security and Privacy **7**, 61–64 (2009)
9. Bachlechner, D., Thalmann, S., Maier, R.: Security and Compliance Challenges in Complex IT Outsourcing Arrangements: A Multi-stakeholder Perspective. Computers and Security **40**, 38–59 (2014)
10. Robinson, S.L.: Trust and Breach of the Psychological Contract. Administrative Science Quarterly **41**, 574–599 (1996)
11. Rotter, J.B.: Interpersonal Trust, Trustworthiness, and Gullibility. American Psychologist **35**, 1–7 (1980)
12. Morgan, R.M., Hunt, S.D.: The Commitment-Trust Theory of Relationship Marketing. Journal of Marketing **58**, 20–38 (1994)
13. Kong, W.C., Hung, Y.T.C.: Modeling initial and repeat online trust in B2C e-commerce. In: Proceedings of the 39th Annual Hawaii International Conference on System Sciences (HICSS 2006) (2006)

14. Durkan, P., Durkin, M., Gillen, J.: Exploring Efforts to Engender On-line Trust. Entrepreneurial Behaviour and Research **9**, 93–110 (2003)
15. Walters, G.J.: Privacy and Security: An Ethical Analysis. Computers and Society **31**, 8–23 (2001)
16. Corritore, C.L., Kracher, B., Wiedenbeck, S.: On-line Trust: Concepts, Evolving Themes, a Model. International Journal of Human Computer Studies **58**, 737–758 (2003)
17. Huang, J., Nicol, D.: A Formal-Semantics-based Calculus of Trust. IEEE Internet Computing **14**, 38–46 (2010)
18. Gambetta, D.: Can We Trust Trust? In: Gambetta, D. (ed.) Trust: Making and Breaking Cooperative Relations 213–237 (2000)
19. Mayer, R.C., Davis, J.H., Schoorman, F.D.: An Integrative Model of Organizational Trust. Academy of Management Review **20**, 709–734 (1995)
20. Lee, M.K.O., Turban, E.: A Trust Model for Consumer Internet Shopping. International Journal of Electronic Commerce **6**, 75–91 (2001)
21. Deutsch, M.: The Effect of Motivational Orientation upon Trust and Suspicion. Human Relations **13**, 123–139 (1960)
22. Ratnasingham, P.: The Importance of Trust in Electronic Commerce. Internet Research **8**, 313–321 (1998)
23. McKnight, D.H., Chervany, N.L.: Conceptualizing trust: a typology and e-commerce customer relationships model. In: Proceedings of the 34th Annual Hawaii International Conference on System Sciences (HICSS 2001) (2001)
24. Kim, D.J., Ferrin, D.L., Rao, H.R.: A Trust-Based Consumer Decision-Making Model in Electronic Commerce: The Role of Trust, Perceived Risk, and their Antecedents. Decision Support Systems **44**, 544–564 (2008)
25. Bhattacherjee, A.: Individual Trust in Online Firms: Scale Development and Initial Test. Journal of Management Information Systems **19**, 211–241 (2002)
26. Gefen, D.: Reflections on the Dimensions of Trust and Trustworthiness among Online Consumers. ACM SIGMIS Database **33**, 38–53 (2002)
27. Armbrust, B., Griffith, R., Joseph, A.D., Katz, R., Konwinski, A., Lee, G., Patterson, D., Rabkin, A.: A View of Cloud Computing. Communications of the ACM **53**, 50–58 (2010)
28. Durkee, D.: Why Cloud Computing will never be Free. Communications of the ACM **53**, 62–69 (2010)
29. Ganesan, S.: Determinants of Long-term Orientation in Buyer-Seller Relationships. Journal of Marketing **58**, 1–19 (1994)
30. Urban, G.L., Amyx, C., Lorenzon, A.: Online Trust: State of the Art, New Frontiers, and Research Potential. Journal of Interactive Marketing **23**, 179–190 (2009)
31. Khan, K.M., Malluhi, Q.: Establishing Trust in Cloud Computing. IT Professional **12**, 20–27 (2010)
32. Firdhous, M., Ghazali, O., Hassan, S.: Trust Management in Cloud Computing: A Critical Review. International Journal on Advances in ICT for Emerging Regions **4**, 24–36 (2012)
33. Zissis, D., Lekkas, D.: Addressing Cloud Computing Security Issues. Future Generation Computer Systems **28**, 583–592 (2012)
34. Talkin'Cloud (2014). http://talkincloud.com/TC100/talkin-cloud-100-2014-edition-ranked-1-25
35. Sandelowski, M., Holditch-David, D., Harris, B.G.: Using Qualitative and Quantitative Methods: The Transition to Parenthood of Infertile Couples, pp. 301–323. Sage Publications, London (1992)
36. Holsti, O.R.: Content Analysis for the Social Sciences and Humanities. Addison-Wesley Pub. Co. (1969)

37. Klenke, K.: Qualitative Research in the Study of Leadership. Emerald Group Publishing, Bingley (2008)
38. Google: How Google handles your data (2014). https://support.google.com/googleforwork/answer/6057301?hl=us
39. Microsoft: Protecting Data and Privacy in the Cloud (2014). http://azure.microsoft.com/en-us/support/trust-center/resources/
40. salesforce.com: Secure, private, and trustworthy: enterprise cloud computing with Force.com (2010). http://www.salesforce.com/assets/pdf/misc/WP_Forcedotcom-Security.pdf
41. Microsoft: Microsoft Azure Privacy Statement (2014). http://www.microsoft.compPrivacy/principles.aspx
42. salesforce.com: Salesforce Privacy Statement (2014). http://www.salesforce.com/company/privacy/full_privacy.jsp
43. Amazon.com: Amazon Web Services: Overview of Security Processes (2014). http://media.amazonwebservices.com/pdf/AWS_Security_Whitepaper.pdf
44. Microsoft: Windows Azure Privacy Overview (2014). http://azure.microsoft.com/en-us/support/trust-center/resources/
45. Amazon.com: AWS Customer Agreement (2012). http://aws.amazon.com/de/agreement/
46. Google: Google's Approach to IT Security - A Google Whitepaper (2012). https://cloud.google.com/files/Google-CommonSecurity-WhitePaper-v1.4.pdf
47. salesforce.com: Salesforce Security, Privacy and Architecture Documentation (2014). https://help.salesforce.com/apex/HTViewSolution?urlname=Salesforce-Services-Trust-and-Compliance-Documentation&language=en_US
48. Microsoft: Security, Privacy, and Compliance in Microsoft Azure (2014). http://azure.microsoft.com/en-us/support/trust-center/resources/
49. Amazon.com: AWS Case Study: HTC (2014). http://aws.amazon.com/solutions/case-studies/htc/
50. salesforce.com: Salesforce Case Study: Stanley Black and Decker (2014). http://www.salesforce.com/customers/

Modelling the Live Migration Time of Virtual Machines

Kateryna Rybina$^{(\boxtimes)}$, Waltenegus Dargie, Subramanya Umashankar, and Alexander Schill

Computer Networks Group, Technical University of Dresden, Nöthnitzer Str. 46, 01187 Dresden, Germany
{kateryna.rybina,waltenegus.dargie,alexander.schill}@tu-dresden.de

Abstract. Dynamic server consolidation in data centres enables the efficient usage of resources, because it aims to minimise the underutilisation or overloading of physical servers, both of which produce a disproportional amount of energy consumption. Server consolidation takes place by migrating virtual machines from one server to another while the virtual machines are still executing. However, live migration comes with corresponding costs in terms of execution latency and additional resource and power consumption. Whether or not these costs are significant depends on how long a migration lasts. In this paper we propose models to estimate the time it takes to live migrate virtual machines at runtime. Our models are built using simple and multiple linear regressions. The paper reveals useful insights into the most important parameters which are strongly correlated with the migration time. These are: Instructions retired, last level cache line misses, and dirtying memory pages.

Keywords: Virtual machines · Live migration · Service consolidation · Migration time · Linear regression model

1 Introduction

The advent of server virtualisation and cloud computing has enabled great flexibility in managing computing resources. It is now possible to create an abstract partitioning of a single physical server into multiple, non-overlapping, and non-interfering computing environments (virtual machines), so that they can be used by multiple independent users. The portion of these partitions can be dynamically adapted (or resized) to the need of the individual users. The physical servers themselves can also be managed by dynamically (live) migrating virtual machines from one server to another without actually stopping or suspending the virtual machines.

One of the advantages of virtual machine migration is dynamic consolidation of servers in a cloud infrastructure or data centre. Due to the fluctuation of incoming workloads, resources may not be utilised uniformly across all servers.

© Springer International Publishing Switzerland 2015
C. Debruyne et al. (Eds.): OTM 2015 Conferences, LNCS 9415, pp. 575–593, 2015.
DOI: 10.1007/978-3-319-26148-5_39

Some of them may be overloaded while others are underutilised or even idle. This imbalance not only creates dissimilar quality of service for different users but it is also inefficient because the power consumption of idle and underutilised servers exceeds 50% of their peak power consumption [1], [2]. By aggregating the virtual machines of data centres on a few number of machines, the rest can be switched off. Similarly, when servers are overloaded, additional servers can be switched on and virtual machines from overloaded servers can be migrated to them, thus seamlessly balancing the load of the data centres.

Aggregating virtual machines, however, introduces some costs. To begin with, a background process should continuously or at a regular interval estimate the size of the incoming workloads and the amount of resources required to handle them. Secondly, the live migration of virtual machines requires additional resources to iteratively transfer the content of the virtual machines and to coordinate the migration. Thirdly, the quality of service execution within the migrated virtual machines may degrade, since the virtual machines should now share resources (such as CPU and network bandwidth) with the migration process. Of all these costs, the third is the most significant one because it directly affects the service level agreement between the computing platform provider and the platform users. The cost is more pronounced if the migration takes a long time and the deterioration of service quality is perceived by the platform users (for example, in terms of increased response time and jitter).

Migration time depends on many factors including the activity and RAM utilisation of the virtual machines, the available CPU cycles and network bandwidth during migration, and the activity of co-located virtual machines. Several studies have been made in the past to estimate migration time and to determine the conditions that initiate VM migration. The model of Strunk [7] estimates the migration time of an idle virtual machine using a simple linear regression with an independent variable expressing the ratio of the active memory occupied by the VM to the available network bandwidth during migration. Clark et al. [6] and Liu et al. [4] investigate the impact of VM memory size, memory page dirtying rate, and network bandwidth on migration time. Akoush et al. [3] investigate the upper and lower bounds of migration time and the runtime parameters that influence migration time. Similar to Clark et al. they too investigate the impact of network bandwidth, memory page dirtying rate, VM memory size, and pre- and post-migration overheads on migration time. Moreover, they experimentally show that (1) network bandwidth is inversely proportional to migration time; (2) a non-linear dependency exists between memory page dirtying rate and migration time due to a stop conditions defined by pre-copy migration strategies; and (3) migration time linearly increases with the VM RAM size. Wu et al. [5] investigate the relationship between migration time and the amount of CPU resources available for migration. The authors propose separate models for different types of workloads (CPU intensive, memory read and write intensive, disk I/O intensive, and network I/O (send-receive) intensive workloads). Likewise, Verma et al. [8] propose an application-aware model to estimate migration time. The model accounts for CPU resource contention on the source server by co-located virtual machines and by the migration process itself.

In this paper we experimentally investigate the scope and usefulness of several resource utilisation metrics to estimate migration time. Unlike previous approaches, (1) we provide adequate and quantitative justification for the selection of the relevant metrics; (2) the metrics we identify estimate the migration time of different virtual machines with comparable accuracy regardless of the workload they process, and (3) the models we propose are all lightweight, linear models that are easy to comprehend.

The remaining part of this paper is organised as follows: In Section 2 we provide a brief background regarding virtual machine migration and linear regression. In Section 3 we introduce our experiment setting, the selection strategy of resource utilisation metrics and benchmarks, and the training and testing datasets. In Section 4 we introduce our approach and provide quantitative justification to the models we propose. We also provide experiment results and discus the results. Finally, in Section 5, we point out concluding remarks and outline future work.

2 Background

2.1 Virtual Machine Migration

In order to estimate the migration time of a virtual machine, it is essential to understand how migration takes place. During the live migration of a virtual machine, its RAM content is copied from the source to the destination server without stopping the execution of the virtual machine. Since the virtual machine is active, its memory content on the source server can change any time (i.e., the memory pages can be dirtied) and this change has to be synchronised with the content of the destination server. This is done by iteratively copying the dirty pages to the destination server. The iteration, however, does not go on indefinitely. Upon reaching a pre-defined threshold (stop-condition) by the migration algorithm, the VM is briefly stopped, all the updated pages are copied to the destination server for one final time; and the VM is started on the destination machine. The total VM migration time referred to as migration time is the time interval between the initialisation of the VM migration at the source server and the starting of the VM at the destination server. Obviously, this time is a function of the memory size of the virtual machine, the available network bandwidth, the memory update rate of the applications or services the virtual machine hosts, the CPU load, and the additional resources the virtual machine monitors on the two servers require to coordinate migration. Consequently, a model that estimates the migration time of a virtual machine should take these parameters into consideration.

2.2 Estimation Error

We begin our investigation on migration time by assuming that a linear dependency can be established between migration time and resource utilisation during migration. In other words, migration time can be expressed as a linear combination of independent parameters that describe resource utilisation. The strength of this expression can be tested by examining such useful metrics as residual standard error, prediction error, mean absolute percentage error, and coefficient of determination (R^2).

Given two random variables X and Y, we wish to express one of them (Y) in terms of the other (X). A linear regression assumes that a conditional expectation $\mathbf{E}\{Y \mid X = x\}$ is a linear function of x [14]:

$$Y = G(x) = \mathbf{E}\{Y \mid X = x\} = \beta_0 + \beta_1 x . \tag{1}$$

where β_0 and β_1 are intercept and slope, respectively. Because Y is related to a single independent variable (predictor), the relation is said to be Simple Linear Regression (SLR). A Multiple Linear Regression (MLR) relates the dependent variable with more than one independent variables and assumes that the conditional expectation of the dependent variable is a linear function of the independent variables (predictors) $x_{1i}, ..., x_{ki}$ [13], [14]:

$$Y_i = G(x) = \beta_0 + \beta_1 x_{1i} + ... + \beta_k x_{ki} \quad i = 1...n . \tag{2}$$

where n is the number of observations (samples), k is the number of independent variables, β_0 is an intercept, β_j is the regression coefficient for the j-th independent variable, showing the expected change of the dependent (response) variable when the corresponding predictor changes by a unite value while all the other predictors remain constant; and x_{ji} is the j-th independent variable's value for the i-th observation. The linear regression model minimises the sum of squared residuals. In other words, the model parameters are so selected that the sum of squared differences between the actual values of the dependent variable and the fitted values by the model (which lie on the fitted regression line or plane) are minimised.

The model's error is a measure of how well the model fits the measured data. The residual standard error of the linear regression model (as calculated in R statistical tool [15]) is defined as:

$$Res_{st.err} = \sqrt{\frac{\sum_{i=1}^{n}(y_i - \hat{y}_i)^2}{n - k - 1}} = \sqrt{\frac{\sum_{i=1}^{n} r_i^2}{n - k - 1}} . \tag{3}$$

where y_i is the actual (measured) value of the dependent variable and $\hat{y}_i$ is the fitted by the model value; n is the sample size, k is the number of independent variables, minus 1 accounts for the estimated intercept, and r_i^2 denotes the squared residual for the i-th observation. The residual standard error of the model is calculated on the training data. The model's standard error of estimate from a sample (prediction error) is calculated on the testing data. It quantifies the departure of the predicted (estimated) by the trained model value $\ddot{y}_i$ of the dependent variable from the actual (or measured) value:[1]

---

[1] Available at http://onlinestatbook.com/2/regression/accuracy.html

$$Pred_{st.err} = \sqrt{\frac{\sum_{i=1}^{n}(y_i - \ddot{y}_i)^2}{n - k - 1}} . \tag{4}$$

The percentage error[2] is another metric that analyses how close the predicted value $\ddot{y}_i$ is to the true (measured) value y_i and it gives the difference between the predicted and the true value as a percentage of the true value. It is calculated as follows:

$$Perc = \frac{\ddot{y}_i - y_i}{y_i} * 100\% . \tag{5}$$

In case of n observations the mean absolute percentage error of the model (its prediction accuracy) will be calculated as a mean of the absolute values of the percentage errors of these n observations as shown in equation below:

$$Perc_m = \frac{\sum_{i=1}^{n}\left|\frac{\ddot{y}_i - y_i}{y_i}\right|}{n} * 100\% . \tag{6}$$

3   Experiment

3.1   Experiment Settings

The hardware setup of our experiments consists of two (source and destination) homogeneous servers which are interconnected via a 1 Gbps Ethernet switch, a client server used to trigger the experiments, a network attached storage (NAS), and two power analysers. Both servers consist of two Intel 15-680 Dual Core 3.6 GHz processors, 4 GB DDR3-1333 SDRAM and a 1 Gbit/s Ethernet NIC. The NAS employs an Intel Xeon E5620 Quad-Core 2.4 GHz processor, 10 GB DDR3-1333 SDRAM memory, and 1 Gbps Ethernet NIC. Fedora (Linux kernel v. 2.6.38, x86 64) was installed as the host operating system on both physical servers. KVM[3] was used as a hypervisor and libvirt[4], as a toolkit to manage virtual machines. As a NAS we employed FreeNAS[5], which is a FreeBSD-based operating system (v. 8.0.1, AMD 64). In our experiments each time one VM was running in isolation on the source server and migrated between the source and the destination physical servers. For different experiments we varied the network bandwidth from 70 MBps to 100 MBps in steps of 10 MBps. The VM was allocated 4 GB RAM, 4 virtual CPUs and 20 GB disc space on the NAS. Ubuntu 14.04.2 LTS (Linux kernel 3.16.0-30-generic) was the operating system installed on the VM.

Inside the migrated virtual machine we executed benchmarks from the SPEC CPU2006 benchmark suite [9] (more information is given in Subsection 3.4). While a benchmark is still executed we migrated the virtual machine back

---

[2] Available at http://mathworld.wolfram.com/PercentageError.html
[3] http://www.linux-kvm.org/page/Main_Page
[4] Libvirt: The virtualization API. http://libvirt.org/
[5] FreeNAS: FreeBSD-based operating system. http://www.freenas.org/

and forth 20 times each time with the same network bandwidth. We carefully recorded the beginning and end of a migration time and the values of the resource utilisation parameters of the servers as well as the VM. The data analysis were realised with R statistical tool [15].

3.2 Selection of Parameters

The complete list of parameters (independent variables) we examined to model and estimate the migration time (the dependent variable) is shown in Table 1. We employed *dstat* to record the CPU and RAM utilisation of the servers as well as the VM (CPU_{util_server}, CPU_{util_vm}, MEM_{server}, and MEM_{vm}). Likewise, we employed the *Intel PCM* tool (Intel Performance Monitoring Counters) [10] to monitor last level cache line misses ($L3_{miss}$) and the total number of instructions retired $INST$ [12]. We also recorded the total amount of "dirty memory" (in kilobytes) waiting to be written back to the disk [11]. From these statistics we derived two additional parameters, namely, the total number of "dirty" pages of the source server during migration ($DirtyPages_{server}$) and the number of "dirty" pages in the source server per second per migration ($DirtyPages_{server\_per\_sec}$). The former was derived as follows: Using timestamps we extracted the $Dirty$ statistics of the source server in KB which corresponded to the migration duration; then we calculated the positive increase in the number of $Dirty$ memory in KB, summed it and divided the sum by the page-size. The page-size in our system was 4 KB. The latter was derived by dividing the number of "dirty" pages during migration by the migration duration (in seconds). Finally, we adopted an additional parameter from Poellabauer et al. [16] (memory access rate (MAR)), which is derived as the ratio of data cache misses to the instructions executed:

$$MAR = \frac{L3_{miss}}{INST} \ . \tag{7}$$

where $L3_{miss}$ refers to the total number of last level cache line misses during migration and $INST$ refers to the total number of instructions retired during migration. Memory access rate is proportional to the last level cache line misses. Consequently, if a benchmark modifies a memory page during migration, this page will have to be resent, resulting in an increase in the migration time. Thus, it is of interest to examine the strength of correlation between the migration time, on the one hand, and the $L3_{miss}$ and MAR parameters, on the other. The total number of instructions retired $INST$ is another parameter which potentially correlates well with the migration time.

3.3 Dataset

Our complete dataset consists of 880 observations containing 13 variables (12 of which are the independent variables and one, t_{mig}, the dependent variable). These correspond to 11 benchmarks × 4 different network bandwidths × 20 migrations per a configuration. One of our tasks was selecting from the long list of independent variables a handful of those which are strongly correlated

Table 1. Resource utilisation parameters (independent variables) used for modelling the VM migration time (t_{mig}).

Name of variable	Description
t_{mig}	Total VM migration time in seconds
BW	Network bandwidth available for migration in MBps
$L3_{miss}$ [12]	Total number of L3 cache line misses during VM migration
$INST$ [12]	Total number of instructions retired during migration
MAR [16]	Ratio of total number of L3 cache line misses to the total number of instructions retired during migration
CPU_{util_server}	Mean total CPU utilisation of the source server during the VM migration
CPU_{util_vm}	Mean total CPU utilisation of the VM during the migration process
MEM_{server}	Mean active memory utilisation of the source server during the VM migration in MB
MEM_{vm}	Mean active memory utilisation of the VM during the migration process in MB
$MEMtoBW_{server}$	Ratio of active memory utilised by the source server to the network bandwidth available for migration
$MEMtoBW_{vm}$	Ratio of active memory utilised by the VM to the network bandwidth available for migration
$DirtyPages_{server}$	Number of "dirty" pages observed in the source server during the migration process
$DirtyPages_{server\_per\_sec}$	Number of "dirty" pages observed in the source server per second during the migration process

with the migration time. We divided the dataset into **training dataset** and **testing dataset**. The training data are used to build relationship between the dependent and independent variables whereas the test data are used for testing the estimation accuracy of our models. As a rule three fourth of the dataset is used for setting up (training) the model and one fourth is used for testing. We randomly divided the dataset thus: The measurements pertaining to the network bandwidth of 70 MBps, 80 MBps, and 100 MBps belong to the **training data** and the measurements pertaining to the network bandwidth of 90 MBps belong to the **testing data**.

3.4 Benchmarks

Jaleel et al. [17] made an extensive analysis of the benchmarks from the SPEC CPU2006 benchmark suite with regard to their resource utilisation characteristics. Based on this study we selected eleven benchmarks, six of which are predominantly CPU intensive (even though they also utilise a sizeable memory); and the other five are memory intensive. The CPU intensive benchmarks used the maximum CPU time, keeping the CPU busy most of the time during the benchmarks execution. A benchmark is considered to be memory intensive if it has a large number of reads/writes operations from/to the memory subsystem. Hence: **libquantum**, **gromacs**, **h264ref**, **namd**, **sphinx3**, and **soplex** belong to the *CPU intensive* benchmarks; and **bzip2**, **astar**, **mcf**, **gcc**, and **perlbench** belong to the *memory intensive* benchmarks.

4   Modelling Migration Time

Fig. 1 displays the VM migration time for different *CPU* intensive benchmarks for 20 migrations realised at a fixed network bandwidth of 70 MBps. As can be seen, the migration time for different benchmarks and migrations was different. The shortest migration time was 26.25 seconds (for **sphinx3**) and the longest was 69.4 seconds (for **libquantum**). The migration time of **sphinx3** exhibited low variation (variance = 0.14) while the migration time of **libquantum** exhibited the largest variation (variance = 36.26). Similarly, Fig. 2 shows the VM migration time for the *memory* intensive benchmarks, which were migrated with a network bandwidth of 80 MBps. Unlike the previous case, the migration times were significantly longer and the variances between the different migrations for some of the benchmarks were considerably larger than the variances we observed in the *CPU* intensive benchmarks. For example, the variances of **astar**, **mcf**, and **perlbench** were 8400.3, 2799.7, and 100.8, respectively. From this it can be concluded that the migration time is strongly influenced by the operating point at which the migration starts and the specific operations the benchmarks execute during migration.

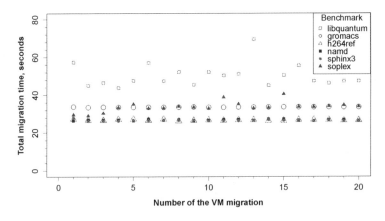

Fig. 1. The migration time of *CPU* intensive benchmarks from the SPEC CPU2006 benchmark suite. The migration bandwidth was 70 MBps.

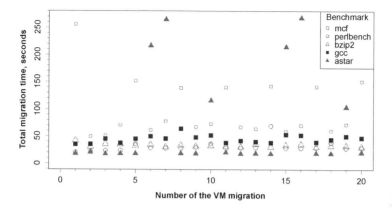

Fig. 2. The migration time of *memory* intensive benchmarks from SPEC CPU2006 benchmark suite. The migration bandwidth was 80 MBps.

4.1   Linear Dependency

To determine the existence of linear dependencies between the independent variables and the migration time, it suffices to calculate the Pearson's correlation coefficient [14] for each independent variable. Table 2 displays the results of our calculation using the training dataset which includes all the measurements we took for different network bandwidths: 70 MBps, 80 MBps and 100 MBps.

Table 2. Pearson correlation coefficients between the migration time and the resource utilisation parameters described in Table 1.

Pearson's correlation, ρ	Value
$cor(t_{mig}, INST)$	0.8604983
$cor(t_{mig}, L3_{miss})$	0.8106588
$cor(t_{mig}, DirtyPages_{server})$	0.8442557
$cor(t_{mig}, MAR)$	0.3986198
$cor(t_{mig}, MEM_{server})$	0.1925516
$cor(t_{mig}, MEMtoBW_{server})$	0.2797072
$cor(t_{mig}, DirtyPages_{server\_per\_sec})$	-0.2659009
$cor(t_{mig}, CPU_{util\_server})$	-0.08078284
$cor(t_{mig}, BW)$	-0.1088528
$cor(t_{mig}, CPU_{util\_vm})$	0.09879503
$cor(t_{mig}, MEM_{vm})$	0.4579728
$cor(t_{mig}, MEMtoBW_{vm})$	0.4950578

As can be seen from Table 2, some of the independent variables, namely, $INST$, $L3_{miss}$, and $DirtyPages_{server}$, display strong linear dependencies while some of the remaining parameters such as $MEMtoBW_{server}$, $MEMtoBW_{vm}$, and MAR are moderately correlated with the migration time. The strong correlations can be logically explained. The number of retired CPU instructions corresponds with the CPU activity level during migration. A large number of retired instructions signifies a high level of CPU activity, which in turn implies a longer migration time. If the data required by a benchmark execution are not available in the cache during VM migration, they have to be fetched from, in case of write access modified, and rewritten back to the main memory. These data have to be resent to the destination server, as they are no longer in sync with the memory content of the destination server. This process prolongs the migration time. Similarly, as the number of dirty pages $DirtyPages_{server}$ increases during migration, the size of data that have to be updated at the destination server increases, which in turn increases the migration time. From our dependency analysis, we concluded that most of the resource utilisation parameters are linearly correlated with the migration time and indeed a few of them show strong linear dependencies. Hence, it is possible to employ linear regression to express migration time in terms of these variables. The question: "How many of these independent variables are sufficient to estimate migration time?" can be answered by considering different combinations of the independent variables and by analysing:

1. the R^2 values and the residual standard error $Res_{st.err}$ (Equation 3) to test how well the models fit the training data; and,
2. the prediction error (Equation 4) and the mean absolute percentage error (Equation 6) of the models using the testing dataset. The latter is the prediction accuracy of the models, as it expresses their accuracy as a percentage.

4.2 Simple Linear Regression Models

The simplest approach is to setup a linear regression model consisting of a single independent variable. The strength of the model and the appropriateness of the independent variable can be judged by analysing R^2 which, for a single independent variable, is simply the square of the sample correlation coefficient (ρ^2) given in Table 2 [14]. R^2 expresses the portion of the total variance of the dependent variable (migration time) that can be captured and explained by the independent variable. A value of 1 implies the regression line perfectly fits the measured data. The adjusted R-square R^2_{Adj} is a more useful measure of goodness-of-fit when a model consists of more than one independent variable, as it includes the notion of number of degrees of freedom and penalises when irrelevant or insignificant independent variables are added into the model. Table 3 summarises the simple linear regression models (SLR) we constructed and tested using our independent variables. The independent variables BW, CPU_{util_server}, and CPU_{util_vm} have p-values equal to 0.005, 0.038 and 0.011, respectively, which are lower than the significance level of 0.05. All the other parameters are significant with the p-value lower than the smallest significance level (0.001) which indicates that these independent variables are appropriate for estimating the migration time.

The model that relates migration time with the total number of instructions retired ($INST$) during migration resulted in the highest R^2 value (0.74).

Table 3. Summary of the Simple linear regression models (SLR).

SLR: lm ($t_{mig} \sim Predictor$)	R^2	R^2_{Adj}	$Res_{st.err}$ on 658 df	$Pred_{st.err}$	$Perc_m$
$INST$	0.7405	0.7401	17.05	15.35	30.79
$L3_{miss}$	0.6572	0.6566	19.6	12.07	20.6
$DirtyPages_{server}$	0.7128	0.7123	17.94	16.89	20.51
MAR	0.1589	0.1576	30.7	30.96	29.21
CPU_{util_server}	0.0065	0.005	33.36	34.15	37.06
MEM_{server}	0.03708	0.03561	32.85	33.68	39.35
$MEMtoBW_{server}$	0.07824	0.07684	32.14	33.41	29.21
$DirtyPages_{server\_per\_sec}$	0.0707	0.06929	32.27	31.74	31.22
BW	0.01185	0.01035	33.27	33.94	31.14
CPU_{util_vm}	0.0098	0.0083	33.31	34.03	37.8
MEM_{vm}	0.2097	0.2085	29.76	29.23	26.23
$MEMtoBW_{vm}$	0.2451	0.2439	29.08	29.33	25.46

Fig. 3 displays the linear dependence of migration time on $INST$. The black line is the best fit regression line (trained model) that regresses t_{mig} on $INST$. The expression for the SLR model is:

$$t_{mig} = -11.1 + 2.9 \times 10^{-4} \times INST . \tag{8}$$

where the intercept of -11.1 is just an adjustment constant; the regression coefficient 2.9×10^{-4} implies the expected increase of 2.9×10^{-4} seconds in migration time for a unit increase in the instructions retired. Thus, when the number of CPU instructions retired increases during migration by 100000, the total migration time is expected to increase by 29 seconds. The residual standard error $Res_{st.err}$ of the model on 658 degrees of freedom equals to 17.05 seconds. The prediction error of the trained model on the testing data (standard error of the estimate from a sample of 220 observations) equals to 15.35 seconds. But its prediction accuracy (the mean absolute percentage error) on the testing data is still quite low and equals to 30.79%.

The linear regression model which produced the second highest R^2 value (0.71) is the one that relates migration time with the number of "dirty" pages observed in the source server during migration ($DirtyPages_{server}$). The residual standard error and the prediction error of the model are 17.94 and 16.89 seconds, respectively. Though, its prediction accuracy on the testing dataset is better ($Perc_m = 20.51\%$). Fig. 4 shows the linear dependency of the total migration time on the total number of "dirty" pages observed at the source server during migration. The relationship is expressed as follows:

$$t_{mig} = -0.78 + 0.94 \times DirtyPages_{server} . \tag{9}$$

Consequently, migration time increases by 0.94 seconds when the number of dirty pages increases by a unit value (which corresponds to an update of 4 KB of memory at the source host). The model that relates migration time with the

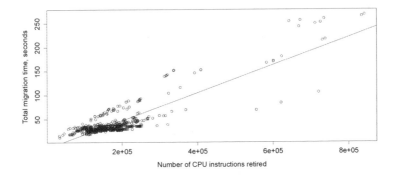

Fig. 3. Dependence of the total migration time on the total number of instructions retired during migration process. Regression line: $t_{mig} = -11.1 + 2.9 \times 10^{-4} \times INST$

total number of last level (L3) cache line misses resulted in the third highest R^2 value (0.65). The residual standard error and the prediction error of the model are 19.6 seconds and 12.07 seconds, respectively. Its mean absolute percentage error equals to 20.6%. Fig. 5 shows the dependency between the total migration time and the last level (L3) cache line misses. Accordingly, the dependence of t_{mig} on $L3_{miss}$ can be described by:

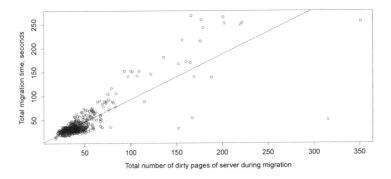

Fig. 4. Dependence of the total migration time on the "dirty" pages observed in the source server during migration. Regression line: $t_{mig} = -0.78 + 0.94 \times DirtyPages_{server}$.

$$t_{mig} = 25.2 + 8 \times 10^{-8} L3_{miss} \, . \tag{10}$$

The R^2 of models with all the other independent variables is so small that they cannot be considered alone to estimate migration time. In fact, the residual and prediction errors of the SLR models with even the best predictors are considerably high and their prediction accuracy is low ($Perc_m$ exceeds 20%) that none of the SLR models is adequate to estimate migration time.

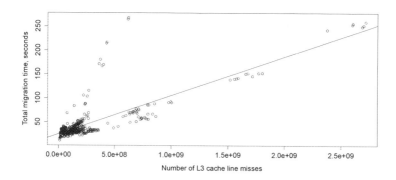

Fig. 5. Dependence of the total migration time on the last level (L3) cache line misses observed during the VM migration. Regression line: $t_{mig} = 25.2 + 8 \times 10^{-8} L3_{miss}$.

When CPU instructions retired and the last level cache line misses are considered in combination, they captured 92% of the variance of t_{mig}. Fig. 6 shows the dependency of the total migration time on the two independent variables. The dashed plane is the regression plane which fits the measured data best and thus, minimises the sum of squared residuals. The expression that describes the multiple regression model with two independent variables is given as:

$$t_{mig} = -5.1 + 2.03 \times 10^{-4} INST + 4.98 \times 10^{-8} L3_{miss} \ . \tag{11}$$

The residual standard and prediction errors of the model are 9.17 seconds and 8.02 seconds, respectively. Its prediction accuracy is significantly improved as well ($Perc_m$ equals to 15.18%). However, combining other independent variables in the same way does not always produce the same remarkable improvement. For example, a combination of $MEMtoBW_{vm} + DirtyPages_{server}$ did not significantly improve R^2 that was achieved by $DirtyPages_{server}$ alone, though its prediction accuracy was still improved by 1.58%. Table 4 provides a summary of the estimation improvements we observed with multiple regression for these two cases. Each of the parameters in all presented MLR models are significant with p-value lower than the smallest significance level (0.001).

Table 4. Simple vs. Multiple linear regression models with two predictors.

SLR versus MLR: lm ($t_{mig} \sim$ Predictor(s))	R^2	R^2_{Adj}	$Res_{st.err}$	$Pred_{st.err}$	$Perc_m$
$INST$	0.741	0.7401	17.05	15.35	30.79
$L3_{miss}$	0.657	0.6566	19.6	12.07	20.6
$INST + L3_{miss}$	**0.925**	**0.9248**	**9.171**	**8.02**	**15.18**
$MEMtoBW_{vm}$	0.245	0.2439	29.08	29.33	25.46
$DirtyPages_{server}$	0.713	0.7123	17.94	16.89	20.51
$MEMtoBW_{vm}$ $+DirtyPages_{server}$	**0.744**	**0.7436**	**16.94**	**16.25**	**18.93**

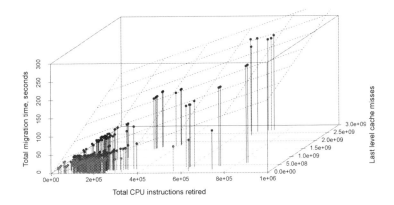

Fig. 6. 3D scatter plot with regression plane showing the dependence of the total VM migration time on CPU instructions retired and last level cache line misses. Multiple linear regression model: $t_{mig} = -5.1 + 2.03 \times 10^{-4} INST + 4.98 \times 10^{-8} L3_{miss}$.

4.3   Multiple Linear Regression Models

As the number of independent variables in a linear regression model increases, the strength of the model in accounting for the variance in migration time increases. Understandably, the model's complexity increases too. It is also possible that the model gets over-fitted and, as a result, looses its prediction power. Therefore, care must be taken to strike the right balance between expressiveness, complexity, and potential over-fitting. For this purpose, we identified the five most significant independent variables that can be combined together. These are: (1) Instructions retired, (2) last level cache line misses, (3) total "dirty" pages at the source server, (4) ratio of active memory used by the source server to network bandwidth, and (5) average CPU utilisation of the source server during migration.

We employed *all subsets regression* [13] in order to identify the best multiple linear regression model that balanced estimation accuracy with complexity. The method examines all possible models and compares the gain in the adjusted R-square. Since we have five independent variables, the *all subsets regression* considers all possibles models with one, two, three, four, and five independent variables which corresponds to 31 possible models. Fig. 7 depicts one best model for each subset size (one, two, three, four, and five independent variables) with respect to adjusted R-square measure.

As we already mentioned above, the best SLR model with respect to R^2_{Adj} is the one using $INST$ (depicted here as TI); the best MLR model consisting of two independent variables is the one using $INST$ and $L3_{miss}$ (depicted here as TL-TI); the best MLR model consisting of three independent variables is the one using $INST$, $L3_{miss}$, and $DirtyPages_{server}$ (depicted here as TL-TI-TD). Its R^2_{Adj} is 0.935 and $Perc_m$ equals to 13.39%. The adjusted R-square of the best model with four independent variables is 0.943 and it consists of $INST$, $L3_{miss}$, $DirtyPages_{server}$ and CPU_{util_server} as independent variables.

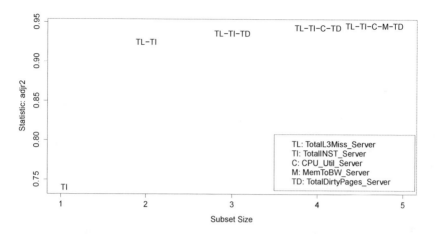

Fig. 7. Defining the best models with all subsets regression method.

Its prediction accuracy is also improved ($Perc_m = 12.12\%$). The model with all the five independent variables has R^2_{Adj} which is equal to 0.946. Its mean absolute percentage error is the lowest and equals to 10.14%. The residual standard error of the model on the 654 degrees of freedom is 7.8 seconds and the standard error of estimate on the testing data is comparatively low, namely, 5.4 seconds. The linear equation for the model consisting of all the five independent variables is given as:

$$t_{mig} = 32.5 + 4.52 \times 10^{-8} L3_{miss} + 1.8 \times 10^{-4} INST - 0.9 \times CPU_{util\_server} +$$
$$+ 0.17 \times DirtyPages_{server} - 0.29 \times MEMtoBW_{server} .$$
$$(12)$$

Table 5 summarises the adjusted R-square values, the residual standard errors, the standard errors of estimate for a dataset of 220 observations, and the mean absolute percentage errors of the best models with three, four, and five independent variables.

Table 5. The best Multiple linear regression models with three, four, and five independent variables.

The best Multiple linear regression models lm ($t_{mig} \sim Predictors$)	R^2	R^2_{Adj}	$Res_{st.err}$	$Pred_{st.err}$	$Perc_m$
$L3_{miss} + INST + DirtyPages_{server}$	0.936	0.9356	8.487	7.028	13.39
$L3_{miss} + INST + CPU_{util\_server} + DirtyPages_{server}$	0.943	0.943	7.984	5.811	12.12
$L3_{miss} + INST + DirtyPages_{server} + CPU_{util\_server} + MEMtoBW_{server}$	**0.946**	**0.9456**	**7.802**	**5.379**	**10.14**

To further assess the generalisability of the best model with five independent variables we realised a *10-fold cross-validation* of R^2 [15]. It allows us to see how well the model will perform on the unseen (testing) data. This method divides the training data into 10 sub-samples each of which serves as a testing group and the remaining 9 sub-samples (training group) are used to train the model. The performance (R^2) for each of the 10 prediction equations applied to the 10 testing groups is recorded and averaged, which gives us a new metric, namely *10-fold* cross-validated R^2 [13]. The results of the *10-fold cross-validation* of the best model with five independent variables are as follows: original R^2 equals to 0.946, 10-fold cross-validated R^2 is equal to 0.937. Thus, the difference is very small (0.009) and the model is performing well on the unseen data.

Adding a sixth independent variable (for instance, the ratio of active memory used by the VM to network bandwidth ($MEMtoBW_{VM}$) or the average CPU utilisation of the VM did not improve the adjusted R-square appreciably. Fig. 8 compares the relative importance (relative weights) of the independent variables in producing $R^2 = 0.94$ in the best MLR model with five independent variables – The CPU instructions retired (depicted in the plot as *TotalINST_Server*) contributed 37.8%, the last level cache misses contributed 31.4%, number of "dirty" pages contributed 27.6%. The CPU utilisation of the source server and the ratio of active memory to network bandwidth contributed 0.7% and 2.3%, respectively. Thus, we can see that *TotalINST_Server* is the most important independent variable in estimating the migration time. The code for calculating the relative weights was adapted from Kabacoff [13].

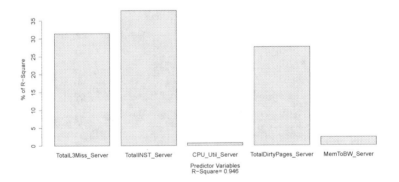

Fig. 8. Relative importance of independent (predictor) variables.

The distributions of the errors of the model built using training dataset and the distribution of its prediction errors on the testing dataset are displayed in Fig. 9 and Fig. 10, respectively. Both distributions tend to form a normal distribution curve with 0 mean. The prediction errors depicted in Fig. 10 are obtained by subtracting from the real values of the migration time of the testing dataset the values predicted by the model. Hence, the error is measured

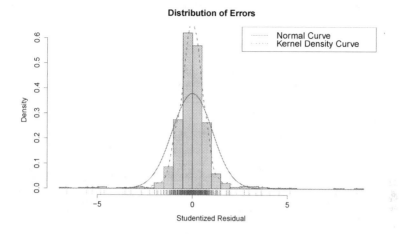

Fig. 9. Normality test of the trained model.

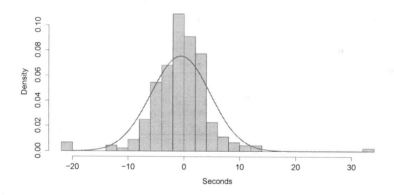

Fig. 10. Distribution of the prediction errors of the model.

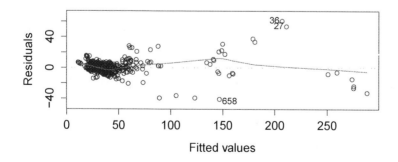

Fig. 11. Diagnostic plot of the linearity assumption.

in seconds. Finally, Fig. 11 illustrates the assumption pertaining to the existence of linearity between the dependent and independent variables for the best MLR model with five independent variables. If a model satisfies the linearity assumption, there will be no systematic relationship between the residuals and the fitted values [13]. It can be shown from the figure that our model satisfies this requirement. Though, due to high variances in migration time introduced mainly by *mcf* and *astar* memory intensive benchmarks the model faces the problem of non-constant variance which is often the case in practice. Nevertheless, the non-constant variance is not substantial in this case because the model behaves well on the testing data and its prediction accuracy equals to 10.12%. In order to satisfy additionally constant variance assumption in our future work we are planning to 1) build separate MLR models for CPU intensive benchmarks only and 2) investigate additional techniques such as weighted least squares.

5   Conclusion and Future Work

This paper extensively discussed migration time as a consequence of dynamic server consolidation in data centres and virtualised environments. We experimentally demonstrated that migration time can be adequately expressed as a linear combination of a few number of resource utilisation parameters, particularly, in terms of the total number of retired CPU instructions, the total number of L3 cache line misses, and the number of "dirty" pages observed in the source server during migration. By employing various simple and multiple linear regression models we closely and quantitatively examined the significance of these parameters in reducing residual and prediction errors as well as in improving R^2 and R^2_{Adj}. Furthermore, we experimentally showed that the expressive power and the complexity of the models depended on the number of independent variables they include. However, we also showed that increasing the number of independent variable beyond five could not appreciably increase the strength of the models.

This paper mainly focused on migration time. In future we will be considering other costs introduced by virtual machine migration, such as the energy overhead and how these costs can be estimated using a single unifying model.

Acknowledgments. This work is supported in a part by the German Research Foundation (DFG) in the Collaborative Research Center 912 Highly Adaptive Energy-Efficient Computing.

References

1. Barroso, L.A., Holzle, U.: The Case for Energy-Proportional Computing. IEEE Computer **40**(12), 33–37 (2007)
2. Dargie, W.: Analysis of the power consumption of a multimedia server under different DVFS policies. In: Fifth International Conference on Cloud Computing, Honolulu, HI, USA, pp. 779–785 (2012)

3. Akoush, S., Sohan, R., Rice, A., Moore, A.W., Hopper, A.: Predicting the performance of virtual machine migration. In: 2010 IEEE International Symposium on Modelling, Analysis and Simulation of Computer and Telecommunication Systems (MASCOTS), pp. 37–46 (2010)

4. Liu, H., Xu, C., Jin, H., Gong, J., Liao, X.: Performance and energy modeling for live migration of virtual machines. In: Proceedings of the 20th International Symposium on High Performance Distributed Computing, pp. 171–182. ACM, New York (2011)

5. Wu, Y., Zhao, M.: Performance modeling of virtual machine live migration. In: 2011 IEEE International Conference on Cloud Computing (CLOUD), pp. 492–499 (2011)

6. Clark, C., Fraser, K., Hand, S., Hansen, J.G., Jul, E., Limpach, C., Pratt, I., Warfield, A.: Live migration of virtual machines. In: Proceedings of the 2nd Conference on Symposium on Networked Systems Design and Implementation, Vol. 2, pp. 273–286. USENIX Association, Berkeley (2005)

7. Strunk, A.: A lightweight model for estimating energy cost of live migration of virtual machines. In: 2013 IEEE Sixth International Conference on Cloud Computing (CLOUD), pp. 510–517 (2013)

8. Verma, A., Kumar, G., Koller, R., Sen, A.: CosMig: modeling the impact of reconfiguration in a cloud. In: 19th International Symposium on Modeling, Analysis and Simulation of Computer and Telecommunication Systems (MASCOTS) 2011, pp. 3–11. IEEE (2011)

9. SPEC CPU2006 Benchmark Descriptions. https://www.spec.org/cpu2006/publications/CPU2006benchmarks.pdf

10. Intel performance monitoring counters. https://software.intel.com/en-us/blogs/2014/07/24/developer-api-documentation-for-intel-performance-counter-monitor

11. Linux Dirty statistic from proc/meminfo/. http://www.centos.org/docs/5/html/5.2/Deployment_Guide/s2-proc-meminfo.html

12. Intel PCM column names. https://software.intel.com/en-us/blogs/2014/07/18/intel-pcm-column-names-decoder-ring

13. Kabacoff, R.I.: R in Action: Data Analysis and Graphics with R. MANNING Shelter Island (2011)

14. Baron, M.: Probability and Statistics for Computer Scientists, 2nd edn. CRC Press Taylor and Francis Group, New York (2014)

15. Core Team, R.: R: A language and environment for statistical computing. R Foundation for Statistical Computing, Vienna (2014). http://www.R-project.org/

16. Poellabauer, C., Singleton, L., Schwan, K.: Feedback-based dynamic voltage and frequency scaling for memory-bound real-time applications. In: 11th IEEE Symposium on Real Time and Embedded Technology and Applications, RTAS 2005, pp. 234–243 (2005)

17. Jaleel, A.: Memory characterization of workloads using instrumentation-driven simulation. http://www.jaleels.org/ajaleel/publications/SPECanalysis.pdf

CloudIDEA: A Malware Defense Architecture for Cloud Data Centers

Andreas Fischer[3], Thomas Kittel[1], Bojan Kolosnjaji[1], Tamas K. Lengyel[1],
Waseem Mandarawi[3], Hermann de Meer[3], Tilo Müller[2], Mykola Protsenko[2],
Hans P. Reiser[3], Benjamin Taubmann[3(✉)], and Eva Weishäupl[4]

[1] Technische Universität München, München, Germany
{kittel,kolosnjaji,tklengyel}@sec.in.tum.de
[2] University of Erlangen-Nürnberg, Erlangen, Germany
tilo.mueller@cs.fau.de, mykola.protsenko@fau.de
[3] University of Passau, Passau, Germany
{andreas.fischer,waseem.mandarawi,hermann.demeer,hans.reiser,
benjamin.taubmann}@uni-passau.de
[4] University of Regensburg, Regensburg, Germany
eva.weishaeupl@wiwi.uni-regensburg.de

Abstract. Due to the proliferation of cloud computing, cloud-based systems are becoming an increasingly attractive target for malware. In an Infrastructure-as-a-Service (IaaS) cloud, malware located in a customer's virtual machine (VM) affects not only this customer, but may also attack the cloud infrastructure and other co-hosted customers directly. This paper presents CloudIDEA, an architecture that provides a security service for malware defens in cloud environments. It combines lightweight intrusion monitoring with on-demand isolation, evidence collection, and in-depth analysis of VMs on dedicated analysis hosts. A dynamic decision engine makes on-demand decisions on how to handle suspicious events considering cost-efficiency and quality-of-service constraints.

1 Introduction

Cloud computing has become a dominant computing paradigm over the past years. The flexibility and scalability offered by cloud providers lead to more and more services to be outsourced to the cloud. In this paper, we address security challenges that arise in an Infrastructure-as-a-Service (IaaS) cloud environment.

Detecting, analyzing and preserving evidence about attacks against customers' virtual machines (VMs) in the cloud is more complex than handling similar attacks on a local infrastructure controlled by the customer: the customer on the one hand has detailed knowledge about his own VMs, but lacks direct access to the cloud infrastructure. On the other hand, the cloud provider has full control over the cloud infrastructure and is potentially in a good position for analyzing abnormal activities, but lacks the contextual knowledge about the hosted VMs.

This difficulty limits the applicability of intrusion detection systems (IDSs) by the cloud operator. Using a heuristics-based IDS incurs the danger of false

© Springer International Publishing Switzerland 2015
C. Debruyne et al. (Eds.): OTM 2015 Conferences, LNCS 9415, pp. 594–611, 2015.
DOI: 10.1007/978-3-319-26148-5_40

positives, i.e., classifying normal behavior of a VM as an attack. If an IDS suspicious activities alarm is used to automatically terminate the affected VM, false alarms will inhibit a legitimate service. If the only reaction to the alarm is a notification of the cloud customer, a delayed manual reaction to the alarm puts the cloud provider and other customers' VMs at risk.

The accuracy of attack detection, the comprehensiveness of malware analysis and the conclusiveness of evidence depend on the selection of information sources and monitoring mechanisms. Typically, more detailed information gathering incurs higher runtime cost. A non-trivial tradeoff to be made is between performance impact on a production system, analysis costs and quality of the collected data. Collecting data within a VM is susceptible to manipulation by the attacker. Acquiring conclusive evidence requires data collection at a place where an adversary is not able to alter it.

There are many existing approaches that address partial aspects of the outlined problem. To our best knowledge, however, there is no solution that combines stealthy intrusion detection, comprehensive evidence collection and in-depth automated malware analysis in a joint architecture for cloud-based environments. In this paper, we address the following core research questions:

- How can both cloud providers and customers take advantage of state-of-the-art malware defense mechanisms based on virtual machine introspection?
- What introspection-based techniques are sufficiently lightweight in order to be used continuously on a production system?
- What introspection-based techniques – possibly heavy-weight – can be activated on demand to yield additional information and a detailed understanding of malicious attacks and malware behavior?

In this paper, we present CloudIDEA, a system that monitors the activity of VMs using lightweight detection mechanisms with low overhead on the production environment. Upon observing abnormal symptoms, these mechanisms will trigger events that a decision engine (DE) will combine with quality of service (QoS) parameters and the current virtual resources allocation to take appropriate actions such as isolating the VM to a dedicated analysis environment.

2   Threat Model

As illustrated by Figure 1, there are three basic attack targets in a cloud environment: the cloud management system, the hypervisor and node management, and the VMs executed in the cloud.

The *cloud management system*, as any other software, potentially contains exploitable security flaws [39]. Avoiding or detecting such attacks is currently not in the main focus of our work. The *hypervisor/node management* subsystem manages VMs and is controlled by the cloud management system. We assume that the management interface is not accessible by external attackers, as it is

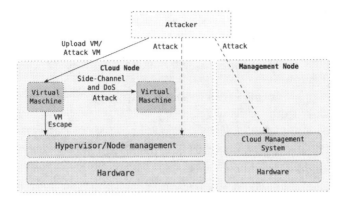

Fig. 1. IaaS cloud threat model; arrows with solid lines are attacks considered in this paper

typically hidden within a dedicated management VLAN, and thus do not consider direct external attacks against this subsystem. If the attacker controls a VM, the hypercall interface of the VM is a potential attack vector [31].

The customer VMs can be both a target and a potential source of attacks. As a target, an attacker can directly exploit vulnerabilities of software running within the virtual machine. Such attacks cause immediate harm for the affected cloud customer, and a core focus of our work is supporting the cloud customer in the defense against such attacks. Furthermore, an adversary can simply upload any malicious VM in a public cloud. In both cases, a malicious VM can perform two attacks against other VMs: denial of service (DoS) attacks and cross-VM side channel attacks. DoS attacks can be performed by overloading physical resources of a cloud node or through the virtual network [38]. Cross-VM side channel attacks can be performed by examining the behavior of virtual or physical hardware modules, such as the L2 cache [53], and deducing information about the state of other VMs. Additionally, an infected VM might try to escape the hypervisor using different mechanisms such as privilege escalation or memory brute force attacks. In this case, the attacker gains control of other VMs, the hypervisor, or the cloud node completely [40].

We assume that, in the future, the biggest threats to IaaS based clouds are network based attacks against VMs, internal cross-VM side channel attacks and VM escapes. Thus, the main focus of CloudIDEA is to detect those attacks by monitoring and tracing VMs.

3   Architecture

The CloudIDEA architecture enhances the security of IaaS cloud data centers by improving the capability to detect, analyze in depth, and preserve evidence about the attacks described in Section 2. The architecture aims to satisfy the following design goals:

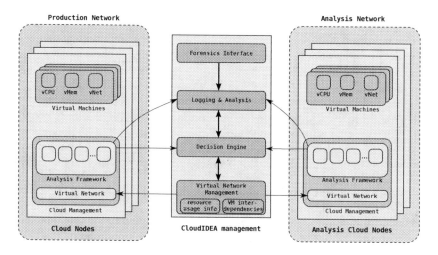

Fig. 2. The CloudIDEA architecture

- *Security-as-a-Service*: Enable a cloud customer to use advanced detection, analysis and evidence preservation techniques, such as transparent virtual machine introspection (VMI).
- *Security for the provider*: Support the cloud provider in dealing with malicious behavior originating from virtual machines, targeting the cloud infrastructure, other customers, or external targets.
- *Running in production systems*: Be well-suited to be used in a production system. This means that we need to support mechanisms that are sufficiently lightweight to cause only negligible overhead. Also, the system needs to be tailored to the specific needs of both cloud provider and cloud customer.
- *In-depth analysis and evidence preservation*: Provide detailed information and conclusive evidence about attacks.

3.1   Overview

The CloudIDEA architecture is shown in Fig. 2. This architecture contains a decentralized, modular, and scalable analysis framework, which supports both lightweight monitoring and heavyweight in-depth analysis, controlled by a central CloudIDEA management component. For isolating potentially infected VMs and for analysing them with resource-intensive mechanisms, the suspicious VMs can be migrated to a dedicated analysis environment.

Every VM is monitored by a decentralized *analysis framework*, which is part of every physical cloud node. It includes plug-ins for tracing and introspection of VMs, e.g. , network traffic monitoring and hypercall tracing. Those plug-ins can be activated and deactivated at runtime on demand, in order to minimize the overhead in a production environment and tailor the monitoring mechanisms to the observed current threat level.

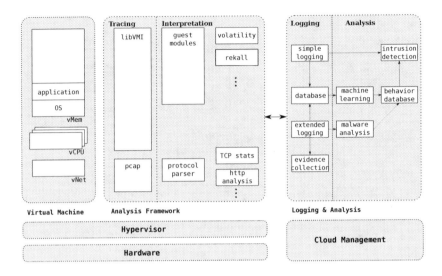

Fig. 3. Analysis Framework and Cloud Management

The traces are processed in a central *CloudIDEA management* component. It incorporates all components that are responsible for attack detection, mitigation and evidence collection in a central place in order to learn and compare common patterns for all VMs in a cloud data center. This information is used, for example, to detect distributed attacks against several targets. If suspicious behaviour is observed, further processing, such as deeper analysis or restarting, is computed by the DE. The components of the *CloudIDEA management* are: *the forensics interface, logging & analysis, DE and the virtual network management*.

The *logging & analysis* component is responsible for storing the traces of VMs to provide that information for intrusion detection and evidence collection (see Figure 3). The *behavior database* contains a model for each VM which is deduced with machine learning algorithms from the traces of the analysis framework. These models serve as a basis for *intrusion detection* to recognize deviant behavior. The *forensics interface* provides customers access to this data and enables customers to execute forensics analysis on their VMs. Whenever an anomaly is detected, the *DE* is informed and determines how to react, e.g., by isolating or restarting the corresponding VM. The decision is influenced by the customer (e.g., predefined configurations and service level agreements (SLAs)) and cloud internal information (e.g., available resources and VM interdependencies). If a VM shows a suspicious behavior, which needs to be analyzed more intensely, it is migrated to an analysis host. Therefore, the *virtual network management* reconfigures the virtual network infrastructure and ensures that resources are still available and SLA compliances can still be guaranteed.

3.2   Intrusion Detection and Analysis

Monitoring and tracing the state of VMs is an important feature of the analysis framework in order to detect possible intrusions. In this section we will discuss the applied techniques.

VM Introspection for Intrusion Detection and Prevention. Over the last decade, there has been a significant push to move the security stack from VMs into regions protected by the hypervisor [23,30]. With the proliferation of kernel-mode rootkits, this elevated protection has become ever more important [3,13]. While running external to the context of the VM being protected, such security software inherently had to tackle the *semantic gap problem*: reconstructing high-level state information from low-level data-sources [14]. This problem has been a main motivation for a significant portion of research over the last decade. However, with recent advances in forensics tools, the semantic gap problem can be considered a solved engineering problem [21].

In recent years, open-source forensics memory analysis frameworks such as Volatility[1] and Rekall[2] have achieved an unparalleled view into the execution of modern operating systems, such as Windows, Linux and MacOS X. Further-more, as the underlying use-case for these frameworks has been extracting evidence of compromise, the inclusion of various methods to side-step obfuscation and rootkit techniques has significantly raised the bar for malware to achieve effective stealth [9]. Further combined with active monitoring systems, such as utilizing the CPUs two-stage paging mechanism (Intel EPT) to monitor memory accesses [47] or via stealthy breakpoint-injection [7], external security software are now capable of not just extracting state-information of running VMs but also interposing on the execution to deliver additional protection mechanisms [8,26].

Ongoing research thus has not been focusing on how to gain access to the required information but rather how to utilize it to deliver additional security services: intrusion detection and intrusion prevention [15]. Furthermore, it is essential for such systems to exert limited overhead on production systems. Research has shown that system call interception [19] and heap-tracing [34] are a viable approach to detect intrusions; however, the exerted overhead may be prohibitive on production systems. While upcoming next-generation virtualization extensions such as Intel #VE may be capable of mitigating some of that overhead, there is a clear need for lightweight detection mechanisms as well [11].

Lightweight Malware Detection. Compared to classical antivirus (AV) engines, VMI based detection systems have the advantage of being able to monitor and alter the execution of the operating systems they protect from an elevated CPU mode [5]. While static signature based malware detection mechanisms can be ported to use VMI for data-access, additional protection mechanisms can also be implemented. For example, buffer-overflow and heap-spray attacks inherently rely on placing code into memory regions normally used

---

[1] The volatility framework - https://www.volatilesystems.com/default/volatility
[2] Rekall: Memory forensics analysis framework - http://www.rekall-forensic.com

only for data: the stack and the heap [41]. While modern OS's provide counter-measures to these types of attacks, such as data execution protection (DEP) and address space layout randomization (ASLR), they are known to be easily circumvented. However, if DEP is implemented by the hypervisor as well, it can act as a low-overhead indicator of compromise (IoC). Recent extensions to open-source hypervisor technologies, such as Xen[3], now actively support such protection schemes, where the shell-code can further be turned into a NOP-sled via the use of emulators [2].

Rootkit mechanisms also notoriously rely on placing *hooks* into the OS execution [50]. The behavior is well documented in several malware families, and the immediate target of such hooks are core tables, for example, holding the addresses for system call handlers and interrupts [27]. By replacing members of these tables, rootkits can actively interpose on the execution of the OS, thus being able to log and mangle the output of any such event. Stealthier versions place *inline-hooks* [4] directly into the target function entry points, which have the advantage of allowing a wider set of combination of placing the hooks, thus detection can be complicated on systems that allow dynamic run-time kernel patching and updates to be deployed [25]. Other hardware events may also act as low-overhead indicators of compromise, such as the rapid querying of the Time Stamp Counter (TSC) counter. Such behavior usually indicates an in-guest agent attempting to detect the presence of out-of-guest monitors [8]. Furthermore, the rapid querying of the TSC has also been used during side-channel attacks [53]. Given that the RDTSC instruction can be configured to be trapped into the hypervisor, an external frequency analysis would easily reveal such malicicous behaviors.

These malware behaviors naturally lend themselves to lightweight detection: under normal operation of the operating system well-behaved application would never exhibit such behaviors. Furthermore, as the overhead added by the protection only applies when a malicious behavior is triggered, it would arguably be negligible.

Heavyweight Malware Detection. While the lightweight detection mechanisms apply to a potentially wide-range of malware, it is by no means exhaustive. A lot of malware operates without exhibiting the behaviors previously discussed. Therefore, our lightweight detection is not a replacement for existing security solutions, such as in-VM antivirus engines and network IDS solutions, rather an augmentation on the existing stack. While ideally lightweight detection would be possible for all malware instances, we need to collect additional artifacts for systems which exhibit *suspicious* but unidentifiable malicious behavior.

Growing number of malware instances and families create significant difficulties for traditional signature-based detection systems to correctly detect and classify malware samples. A recent trend of malware having properties of multiple families further complicates the detection and classification. An attempt to solve this is using statistical machine learning methods. These methods leverage

---

[3] Xen - http://www.xenproject.org

gathered behavioral data about malware to generate statistically confident knowledge. This has been attempted in the past with various data sources that characterize program behaviour: system calls [45], registry accesses [18], network packets [42]. These event sequences are analyzed using unsupervised (clustering) or supervised learning (classification) methods. The used methods can be further divided into one-class anomaly detection and multiclass learning.

For the heavyweight detection mechanism it is crucial to maintain the sample set from different malware families and their behavioral patterns to be able to properly classify the suspicious applications. Furthermore, in the case of sequential data, automatic methods for extraction of semantically relevant features must be used to cope with the possibly noisy and high-dimensional data. An example of this is given by recent application of topic modeling approaches to the classification of system call sequences [49]. This approach can be extended by including memory allocation patterns and other traceable operations. The standard methods for direct classification of sequential data are Hidden Markov Models (HMM) and Recurrent Neural Networks (RNN). Support vector machines (SVM) with string kernels give another approach, where a standard classification scheme is augmented to work with sequences of variable length [32]. Network traffic produced by the analyzed samples can be classified by taking into account the frequency and length of different type of packets or generating n-gram features out of packet payloads.

Results of the heavyweight detection mechanisms can be structured to form a significant knowledge base. The knowledge acquired after executing the heavyweight detection mechanisms can be fed back to the lightweight detection as behavioral signatures, to further decrease the necessary resource usage. Also, malware samples that do not belong to the previously defined families can be added as prototypes to the clustering or classification schemes. This method has shown success in the previously published work [35].

In case of suspicious activity, our architecture enables extensive data collection using tools for VMI and network traffic analysis. This data is an input for the machine learning-based malware detection mechanism. The machine learning engine contains two main parts: extraction of relevant, preferably semantically interpretable features from raw data and classification based on those features. Different feature extraction methods are applied based on the type of data. Based on these features, a suspicious application is either classified into known families, as benign, or as a malware of unknown family. In the last case, the behavioral signature of this application is used to form a new class. Ensemble learning enables the usage of different classifiers and averaging out of their results. The classification results are fed back to the DE. Feature values and the classification results of the analyzed sample are saved to the behavior database for further reference.

3.3   Decision Engine

The task of the DE is to orchestrate the decentralized analysis frameworks. A main mechanism of the architecture is to isolate suspicious VMs by migrating them to a dedicated analysis environment. This environment provides an infrastructure with smaller attack surface and with the required features and resources for the analysis, which may not be available in the production environment. The main challenge of the migration is keeping the service requirements and dependencies between VMs satisfied. The approaches for resource allocation in virtual environments try to optimally allocate VMs according to certain requirements such as to minimize energy consumption [22]. An optimized reconfiguration process is required to determine the minimum set of VM migrations that can reconfigure the virtual network in a way that allows for a detailed analysis and at the same time adhere to the QoS requirements.

Economical Aspects. The distribution of specialized investigation hosts plays a main role in the decision process. Finding an efficient distribution of these hosts is also an economical challenge of the proposed architecture. This requires a detailed analysis of the target environments and expected attack scenarios. The trade-off between protection costs and attack costs will be a major output of this analysis. Another economic aspect is the minimization of the VM's downtime during the migration to prevent a monetary [48] and a reputational loss [16] for the cloud provider. The service provider commits to a certain level of service, which is described by a SLA. Usually, the SLA expresses the VM availability. For example, 99.999% guaranteed availability means 5 minutes downtime per year. Non-compliance to such SLAs can lead to (monetary) penalties for the providers and can harm their reputation [44]. Reputational damage leads to economical long-term consequences, because the consumer's trust in the service might be lost and fewer customers might use the provider's services in future. Therefore, the downtime and migration time of the VM need to be minimized. Although live migration usually causes only a short downtime to a VM, small interruptions ranging from 60 milliseconds to 3 seconds are inevitable [1]. In order to guarantee a certain QoS it is, therefore, essential to predict the worst case downtime as precisely as possible [36]. Based on the model presented by Salfner et al. [36] and the characteristics of our architecture, the migration time and downtime will be predicted and measured. Voorsluys et al. [44] performed experiments to evaluate the cost of migration of VMs considering service disruptions and violations of SLAs. They concluded that most SLAs can still be met when migrations are performed, so that the reputational harm is within limits.

Inputs. The DE depicted in Figure 4 is the central component of the proposed architecture. It has communication interfaces with the cloud management system, detection mechanisms deployed in cloud nodes, a set of databases, and the cloud administrator and customer. The main role of this engine is to react to alarms received from the detection mechanisms when certain behavior patterns are detected. The reaction can be a certain reconfiguration action in the cloud environment, or raising an alarm to the cloud administrator or customer. To perform this task, the DE needs four main inputs.

The first input is the configuration and monitoring data that is acquired from the cloud management system and contains four data sets. The physical

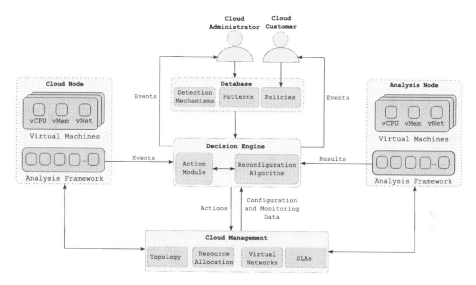

Fig. 4. Decision Engine Interfaces

network defines the cloud hosts and analysis nodes and detection mechanisms deployed in them, the resource capacities and usage, and the network topology. The virtual networks deployed in the environment define the topology, resource demands, and constraints of the virtual networks. An example constraint is the maximum communication latency between two VMs. The resource allocation defines how resources are allocated to the virtual networks in the cloud environment. The SLAs define the QoS requirements of the virtual networks such as service availability. This availability could modeled as a downtime budget for each VM.

The second input comes from three databases. The *behavior patterns* database is maintained by the cloud administrator and by the analysis nodes that update the information about possible attacks based on the results of the analysis. This database includes pre-defined behavior patterns that refer to a probability of a certain attack. This database consists of records of the form: {*Pattern, Parameter ranges, Suspected malware, Possible attacks, Suspicion level*}. An example of such a record is: {*Network traffic spike, Period > 5 seconds, Unknown, DoS, 50%*}. The *policy* database is maintained by both the cloud administrator and customer. It specifies a list of actions that should be executed by the DE when an event from a detection mechanism or an analysis result from an analysis node is received for a specified VM. This database consists of records of the form: {*Pattern, VM ID, Actions*}. An example of such a record is: {*Network traffic spike, VM 100, block*}. The *detection mechanisms* database is maintained by the cloud administrator. It is used by the DE mainly to find the estimated resource requirements of each mechanism. The structure of this database can only be determined after an extensive evaluation of the resource utilization by the required detection mechanisms.

The third input of the DE is the events received from detection mechanisms. The detection mechanisms running in cloud nodes should have access to the behavior patterns database. When a certain behavior is detected, an event is reported to the DE. The event includes the following information: { *VM ID, node ID, pattern, Parameters*}. An example of such an event is: { *VM 100, Node 1, Memory usage spike, Period:5 seconds*}.

The last input is the analysis results received from analysis nodes. When a suspicious VM is migrated to an analysis node, the node sends the analysis results to the decision engine that executes further actions defined in the policy.

Actions. The DE includes an action module that receives the events from the detection mechanism, reads the behavior and policy database, and determines the required list of actions to respond to this event. Possible simple cloud actions are blocking the network connections of a VM when the VM is suspected to be performing a network attack, restarting a VM when facing a transient attack, and shutting down the VM immediately when an attack is highly probable and the damage that might be caused to the environment cannot be easily recovered. A significant action is activating additional detection mechanisms in the cloud node to perform a more detailed analysis on the VM if the required resources for running these mechanisms are available in the node. The most important action in the DE is migrating the VM to a dedicated analysis node where an extensive analysis can be performed without interrupting the functionality of this VM. A similar action is cloning the VM and moving the copy to an analysis node when service interruption is not feasible and the suspicion level is low. One important action after receiving an analysis result of a migrated or cloned VM is recovering the VM in case the analysis identifies the VM as harmless.

Reconfiguration Algorithm. To perform the cloning and migration actions, the DE uses a reconfiguration algorithm that reads the configuration and monitoring data for the affected virtual network and finds the available analysis nodes. In the cloning action, the algorithm has only to find an analysis node that has enough resource capacities to host the VM and perform a detailed analysis. In the migration action, the algorithm is more complex, and three main factors should be considered in the decision making. The first factor is the migration downtime. The live migration of VMs usually causes a small downtime. However, a maximum downtime should be estimated before the migration is performed. The migration downtime mainly depends on the memory usage of the VM, the network bandwidth, and migration strategy. This downtime should be then compared with the downtime budget of the VM. The second factor is the resource capacities of the analysis nodes that have to match the requirements of the VM. The last factor is VMs dependencies in the virtual network. A typical example of these dependencies is the communication delay among virtual machines [20]. The dependencies might require a full or partial reconfiguration of the virtual network when a VM is migrated to an analysis node. The reconfiguration might need to migrate other VMs to keep the constraints of the virtual network satisfied. The migration downtime and resource requirements of the these VMs should also be considered.

The decision engine waits for the events or analysis results from the production environment and the analysis environment respectively. On one hand, when an event is received, the appropriate action will be performed according to the event parameters, detected behavior, and security policies. The migration action needs to adhere to the service requirements of the VM. It might also require a reconfiguration of the virtual network according to its dependencies. On the other hand, when an analysis result is received, the appropriate action is performed depending on the VM state by either recovering the original configuration of the virtual network if no attack is identified, or performing a certain action according to the policies if an attack is identified.

4   Evaluation and Future Work

Performance. In order to illustrate the classification of monitoring tools as lightweight or heavyweight, we have implemented a framework for monitoring system calls of VMs, which supports four different monitoring configurations: (1) without any tracing system calls (**none**), (2) tracing **execve** system calls, (3) tracing **open** system calls and (4) tracing **all** system calls of the virtual machine. The system call tracing is implemented by inserting software breakpoints into the guest system and by handling the corresponding interrupts using libVMI[4]. The overhead depends not only on the monitoring mechanism, but also on the software running within the virtual machines. For this reason, we measured the overhead for four different use cases executed within the VM: (1) the extraction of a Linux Kernel archive, (2) the compilation of the Linux kernel, (3) writing of 1.2 GB file with zero bytes and (4) the computation of 5000 digits of the number pi. Figure 5 presents the results of the measurements.

Based on these results we can do a very basic classification: By tracing only the execve or open system call, the additional overhead is still acceptable and can be further decreased by a faster implementation. Tracing the execve system call is for example useful for forensics purposes, e.g., to log the executed commands of an attacker or to perform intrusion detection. Hence, tracing a small set of system calls can be classified as lightweight.

The overhead which is required to monitor all system calls is obviously higher but it also allows to get a better insight of the processes in a VM, e.g., in order to do malware analysis. Thus, tracing all system calls can be classified as heavyweight analysis. Another example for a heavyweight analysis is the tracing of library calls, e.g., malloc in the libc library. The decision about which tracing strategy to apply depends on the current threat level of a VM. However, the computation of the threat level and the corresponding action needs to be investigated in more detail in future work.

---

[4] libVMI - http://libvmi.com/

Usecase		#syscalls	$t_{real}(s)$	overhead	$t_{user}(s)$	overhead	$t_{sys}(s)$	overhead
extract	none	0	11.350		6.508		1.664	
	execve	5	13.038	14.8%	6.560	0.80%	1.692	16.8%
	open	54	11.810	4.05%	6.532	0.37%	2.384	43.3%
	all	65.7k	116.664	928%	6.940	6.64%	108.936	655%
compile	none	0	657.508		595.704		24.116	
	execve	33k	849.250	29.2%	635.556	6.69%	176.404	631%
	open	4022k	1663.985	153%	651.360	9.34%	651.360	270%
	all	13539k	2987.852	354%	660.120	10.8%	2248.744	922%
write	none	0	10.008		0.028		0.924	
	execve	1	10.729	7.20%	0.044	57.1%	0.972	5.19%
	open	12	10.081	0.73%	0.036	28.6%	0.928	4.32%
	all	602k	94.324	842%	0.220	686%	93.220	1000%
compute	none	0	20.413		20.408		0.004	
	execve	1	20.437	0.61%	20.428	0.1%	0.004	0%
	open	5	20.460	0.23%	20.448	0.2%	0.004	0%
	all	1080	20.767	1.73%	20.450	0.2%	0.100	250%

Fig. 5. Overhead generated by tracing system calls of a virtual machine. t_{real} is the total execution time, t_{user} is the time where the programming was running in user space and t_{sys} is the time spent in system calls (times measured with the Linux tool `time`). The overhead is computed in relation to the case when no tracing is active.

Security. Currently, the analysis framework runs in the XEN Dom0. Thus, if an intruder is able to exploit it he gets full control over all other VMs. To improve the security level and in order to increase the trustworthiness of the forensics data we plan to start the analysis framework in a separate and very minimal monitoring VM for each production VM. Thereby each monitoring VM shall be restricted to access only one production VM, e.g., by applying XSM flask policies [6].

Limitations of VMI. In order to execute VMI, a priori knowledge about the guest operating system is required in order to bridge the semantic gap and interpret the guest memory. We assume that a cloud customer who wants to benefit from CloudIDEA makes this information available to analysis framework. In future work we will discuss whether malware can fool the interpretation of the analysis framework.

5   Related Work

Several researchers have addressed the problem of *evidence collection in the cloud*. Zafarullah et al. [51] propose a centralized approach to analyze log files in an IaaS environment, in which the cloud provider is responsible for forensic investigations. Martini and Choo describe an integrated conceptual digital forensic framework for cloud computing [29]. Dykstra and Sherman [12] present FROST, a digital forensics tool for the OpenStack cloud platform that enables the acquisition of virtual disk snapshots, API logs, and guest firewall logs. While these approaches focus on enabling interactive forensic data collection, our proposed architecture enhances evidence collection by providing a analysis framework on each host of a production system and by automatically deciding which detector module to activate in suspicious situations. Poisel et al. [33] they discuss the possibility of acquiring evidence at the hypervisor level using virtual machine introspection, and identify the need for extending such approaches from evidence collection on a single host to a larger setup with multiple cloud nodes.

A second area related to CloudIDEA is the *detection of malware in the cloud*. Harrison et al. [17] define a framework for detecting malware in the cloud by identifying the symptoms of malicious behaviour. Small "Forensic Virtual Machines" (FVMs) monitor customer VMs for specific malware symptoms using VMI and collaborate with each other by exchanging messages via secure channels. Examples for detectable symptoms are missing processes such as sysclean and tcpview, modification of in-memory code such winlogon, absence of antivirus software from the process table, and snippets of program code that has been obfuscated or uses certain cryptographic algorithms. FVMs report to a command & control module that collects and correlates the information so that suitable remedial actions can take place in real-time. For mitigating the cost of monitoring, the authors propose a mobility algorithm in which FVMs monitor only a small subset of all VMs that changes in time in an unpredictable way. While the proposed framework shares some similarities with our approach, it lacks means for evidence preservation and it is not intended for continuous lightweight monitoring of all VMs. Also, we propose a DE that automatically decides taking appropriate actions in a more flexible way.

Schmidt et al. [37] present an architecture for malware detection and kernel rootkit prevention in cloud environments. In this approach, all running binaries are intercepted by a small in-kernel agent and submitted to one or more backend units where the actual classification process happens. The in-kernel agent can be deployed by the cloud provider by replacing the OS kernel within the customer's VM image. In contrast, CloudIDEA aims at detecting and analyzing malware in the cloud without depending on modifications of the guest system.

Many researchers addressed the *behavior study* of both traditional malware and virtual environment specific malware in cloud environments. For example, Dolgikh et al. [10] propose an efficient behavioral modeling scheme to detect suspicious processes in client VMs by monitoring system calls. Manerides et al. [28] describe how to detect the traditional Kelihos malware in virtual machines by monitoring the memory usage and number of processes. According to the authors, Kelihos malware causes a memory explosion for few seconds, which is not a normal behavior for traditional applications. Zhang et al. [52] use machine learning to deploy a lightweight mechanism in a VM to detect the behavior of L2 cache side channel attacks performed by other VMs.

Another aspect that influences the quality of a cloud malware detection and analysis environment is the *stealthiness of analysis*, i.e., the question whether malware can detect if it is being analysed. Cobra, a framework by Vasudevan and Yerraballi [43], is known to be one of the first malware dynamic analysis frameworks with an explicit emphasis on stealth as a design goal, also providing support for self-modifying, self-checking code, and any form of code obfuscation. A somewhat stronger solution was proposed by Dinaburg et al. [8]. Their framework, Ether, is based on hardware virtualization extensions, e.g., Intel VT. The analysis functionality is facilitated by the Xen hypervisor and therefore resides completely outside the target OS. Ether is capable of monitoring single instruction executions, memory writes, and system calls. Since it does not have any presence in the guest OS, it is immune against the most of detection methods, except some timing attacks. Spider [7] is another tool based on hardware virtualization and provides stealth binary instrumentation and debugging capabilities. Drakvuf by Lengyel et al. [26], also based on hardware virtualization, is able to track behavior of both user- and kernel-level malware. Willems et al. [46] proposed an approach to stealth dynamic malware analysis based on the *branch tracing* feature of modern CPUs. The use of this feature can provide full execution traces, and could only be detected by ring-0 programs or by means of timing attacks. However, with this approach neither the process memory state nor CPU registers can be revealed. Kirat et al. [24] proposed a method of detecting Malware with analysis-evasion capabilities by executing it within different environments, for which they have used Anubis, based on emulation, Ether, based on Xen hypervisor, Cuckoo sandbox based on virtualization, and on "bare metal" devices. By considering the hierarchical similarity of the obtained behavior profiles, they were able to successfully detect evasive malware.

6   Conclusion

CloudIDEA enables cloud customers to benefit from advanced techniques for attack detection, analysis, and evidence preservation in case of malicious attacks against VMs running on IaaS infrastructures. CloudIDEA combines continuous monitoring on production systems with in-depth analysis, including the possibility to migrate VMs to a dedicated analysis environment.

The low-level analysis framework allows using a configurable set of tracing and introspection plug-ins, which include lightweight techniques that are suitable for continuous monitoring as well as heavyweight techniques that have a significant run-time overhead and can be activated on demand. Measurements on our prototype system illustrate the run-time cost of several monitoring techniques.

The high-level decision engine automates the dynamic selection of monitoring plug-ins and reconfigurations of the virtual machine and virtual network deployments. Within constraints regarding quality of service (as defined in SLAs) and security requirements (policies defined by cloud customer and cloud provider) it takes decision about actions such as terminating a VM or isolating it in a dedicated analysis environment.

In summary, the CloudIDEA architecture is a step forward in defending against malware in cloud infrastructures.

References

1. Akoush, S., Sohan, R., Rice, A., Moore, A., Hopper, A.: Predicting the performance of virtual machine migration. In: IEEE Int. Symp. on Modeling, Analysis Simulation of Comp. and Telecomm. Systems (MASCOTS), pp. 37–46 (2010)
2. Bitdefender: Xen: Emulate with no writes (2014). http://lists.xen.org/archives/html/xen-devel/2014-08/msg00264.html
3. Butler, J.: DKOM (direct kernel object manipulation). Black Hat Windows Security (2004)
4. Butler, J., Silberman, P.: Raide: Rootkit analysis identification elimination. Black Hat USA **47** (2006)
5. Chen, P.M., Noble, B.D.: When virtual is better than real. In: Proc. of the 8th Workshop on Hot Topics in Operating Systems, pp. 133–138. IEEE (2001)
6. Coker, G.: Xen security modules (xsm), March 24, 2015. http://mail.xen.org/files/summit_3/coker-xsm-summit-090706.pdf
7. Deng, Z., Zhang, X., Xu, D.: SPIDER: stealthy binary program instrumentation and debugging via hardware virtualization. In: Proc. of the 29th Annual Computer Security Applications Conference, ACSAC 2013, pp. 289–298. ACM (2013)
8. Dinaburg, A., Royal, P., Sharif, M., Lee, W.: Ether: malware analysis via hardware virtualization extensions. In: Proceedings of the 15th ACM Conference on Computer and Communications Security, CCS 2008, pp. 51–62. ACM (2008)
9. Dolan-Gavitt, B., Srivastava, A., Traynor, P., Giffin, J.: Robust signatures for kernel data structures. In: Proceedings of the 16th ACM Conference on Computer and Communications Security, pp. 566–577. ACM (2009)
10. Dolgikh, A., Birnbaum, Z., Chen, Y., Skormin, V.: Behavioral modeling for suspicious process detection in cloud computing environments. In: IEEE 14th Int. Conf. on Mobile Data Management (MDM), vol. 2, pp. 177–181, June 2013
11. Dontu, M., Sahita, R.: Zero-footprint guest memory introspection from xen, January 15, 2015. http://www.xenproject.org/component/allvideoshare/video/xpds14-introspection.html
12. Dykstra, J., Sherman, A.T.: Design and implementation of FROST: Digital forensic tools for the OpenStack cloud computing platform. Digit. Investig. **10**, 87–95 (2013)
13. Florio, E.: When malware meets rootkits. Virus Bulletin (2005)
14. Garfinkel, T., Rosenblum, M.: A virtual machine introspection based architecture for intrusion detection. In: Proc. Network and Distributed Systems Security Symposium, pp. 191–206 (2003)
15. Gionta, J., Azab, A., Enck, W., Ning, P., Zhang, X.: Seer: practical memory virus scanning as a service. In: Proceedings of the 30th Annual Computer Security Applications Conference, pp. 186–195. ACM (2014)
16. Gonzalez, N., Miers, C., Redigolo, F., Carvalho, T., Simplicio, M., Naslund, M., Pourzandi, M.: A quantitative analysis of current security concerns and solutions for cloud computing. In: Proc. of the 2011 IEEE 3rd Int. Conf. on Cloud Computing Technology and Science, CLOUDCOM 2011, pp. 231–238. IEEE CS (2011)
17. Harrison, K., Bordbar, B., Ali, S., Dalton, C., Norman, A.: A framework for detecting malware in cloud by identifying symptoms. In: IEEE 16th Int. Enterprise Distributed Object Computing Conference (EDOC), pp. 164–172, September 2012
18. Heller, K., Svore, K., Keromytis, A.D., Stolfo, S.: One class support vector machines for detecting anomalous windows registry accesses. In: Workshop on Data Mining for Computer Security (DMSEC), pp. 2–9 (2003)

19. Hofmeyr, S.A., Somayaji, A., Forrest, S.: Intrusion detection using sequences of system calls. Journal of Computer Security **6**, 151–180 (1998)
20. Ivaturi, K., Wolf, T.: Mapping of delay-sensitive virtual networks. In: Int. Conf. on Computing, Networking and Communications (ICNC), pp. 341–347 (2014)
21. Jain, B., Baig, M.B., Zhang, D., Porter, D.E., Sion, R.: Sok: Introspections on trust and the semantic gap. In: Proc. of the 2014 IEEE Symp. on Security and Privacy, SP 2014, pp. 605–620. IEEE CS (2014)
22. Jansen, R., Brenner, P.: Energy efficient virtual machine allocation in the cloud. In: Int. Green Computing Conference and Workshops (IGCC), pp. 1–8, July 2011
23. Jiang, X., Wang, X., Xu, D.: Stealthy malware detection through vmm-based "out-of-the-box" semantic view reconstruction. In: Proc. of the 14th ACM Conference on Computer and Communications Security, CCS 2007, pp. 128–138. ACM (2007)
24. Kirat, D., Vigna, G., Kruegel, C.: Barecloud: bare-metal analysis-based evasive malware detection. In: Proc. of the 23rd USENIX Conference on Security Symposium, SEC 2014, pp. 287–301. USENIX Association, Berkeley (2014)
25. Kittel, T., Vogl, S., Lengyel, T.K., Pfoh, J., Eckert, C.: Code validation for modern os kernels. In: Workshop on Malware Memory Forensics (MMF), December 2014
26. Lengyel, T.K., Maresca, S., Payne, B.D., Webster, G.D., Vogl, S., Kiayias, A.: Scalability, fidelity and stealth in the drakvuf dynamic malware analysis system. In: Proc. of the 30th Annual Computer Security Applications Conference (2014)
27. Lobo, D., Watters, P., Wu, X., Sun, L., et al.: Windows rootkits: attacks and countermeasures. In: 2010 Second Cybercrime and Trustworthy Computing Workshop, pp. 69–78. IEEE (2010)
28. Marnerides, A., Watson, M., Shirazi, N., Mauthe, A., Hutchison, D.: Malware analysis in cloud computing: network and system characteristics. In: 2013 IEEE Globecom Workshops (GC Wkshps), pp. 482–487, December 2013
29. Martini, B., Choo, K.R.: An integrated conceptual digital forensic framework for cloud computing. Digital Investigation **9**(2), 71–80 (2012)
30. Payne, B.D., Carbone, M., Sharif, M., Lee, W.: Lares: An architecture for secure active monitoring using virtualization. In: IEEE Symposium on Security and Privacy, SP 2008, pp. 233–247. IEEE (2008)
31. Perez-Botero, D., Szefer, J., Lee, R.B.: Characterizing hypervisor vulnerabilities in cloud computing servers. In: Proc. of the 2013 Int. Workshop on Security in Cloud Computing. Cloud Computing 2013, pp. 3–10. ACM (2013)
32. Pfoh, J., Schneider, C., Eckert, C.: Leveraging string kernels for malware detection. In: Lopez, J., Huang, X., Sandhu, R. (eds.) NSS 2013. LNCS, vol. 7873, pp. 206–219. Springer, Heidelberg (2013)
33. Poisel, R., Malzer, E., Tjoa, S.: Evidence and cloud computing: The virtual machine introspection approach. Journal of Wireless Mobile Networks, Ubiquitous Computing, and Dependable Applications (JoWUA) **4**(1), 135–152 (2013)
34. Rhee, J., Riley, R., Xu, D., Jiang, X.: Kernel malware analysis with untampered and temporal views of dynamic kernel memory. In: Jha, S., Sommer, R., Kreibich, C. (eds.) RAID 2010. LNCS, vol. 6307, pp. 178–197. Springer, Heidelberg (2010)
35. Rieck, K., Trinius, P., Willems, C., Holz, T.: Automatic analysis of malware behavior using machine learning. Journal of Computer Security **19**(4), 639–668 (2011)
36. Salfner, F., Tröger, P., Richly, M.: Dependable Estimation of Downtime for Virtual Machine Live Migration. Int. J. on Advances in Systems and Measurements **5** (2012)

37. Schmidt, M., Baumgartner, L., Graubner, P., Bock, D., Freisleben, B.: Malware detection and kernel rootkit prevention in cloud computing environments. In: 2011 19th Euromicro International Conference on Parallel, Distributed and Network-Based Processing (PDP), pp. 603–610, February 2011

38. Shea, R., Liu, J.: Performance of virtual machines under networked denial of service attacks: Experiments and analysis. IEEE Systems Journal 7(2), 335–345 (2013)

39. Somorovsky, J., Heiderich, M., Jensen, M., Schwenk, J., Gruschka, N., Lo Iacono, L.: All your clouds are belong to us: security analysis of cloud management interfaces. In: Proc. of the 3rd ACM Workshop on Cloud Computing Security, CCSW 2011, pp. 3–14. ACM, New York (2011)

40. Studnia, I., Alata, E., Deswarte, Y., Kaaniche, M., Nicomette, V.: Survey of security problems in cloud computing virtual machines. Tech. rep., CNRS, LAAS, 7 Avenue du colonel Roche, F-31400 Toulouse, France (2012)

41. Szekeres, L., Payer, M., Wei, T., Song, D.: Sok: Eternal war in memory. In: IEEE Symp. on Security and Privacy, pp. 48–62. IEEE (2013)

42. Tegeler, F., Fu, X., Vigna, G., Kruegel, C.: Botfinder: finding bots in network traffic without deep packet inspection. In: Proc. of the 8th Int. Conf. on Emerging Networking Experiments and Technologies, pp. 349–360. ACM (2012)

43. Vasudevan, A., Yerraballi, R.: Cobra: fine-grained malware analysis using stealth localized-executions. In: IEEE Symp. on Security and Privacy, pp. 15–279 (2006)

44. Voorsluys, W., Broberg, J., Venugopal, S., Buyya, R.: Cost of virtual machine live migration in clouds: a performance evaluation. In: Jaatun, M.G., Zhao, G., Rong, C. (eds.) Cloud Computing. LNCS, vol. 5931, pp. 254–265. Springer, Heidelberg (2009)

45. Warrender, C., Forrest, S., Pearlmutter, B.: Detecting intrusions using system calls: alternative data models. In: Proc. of the IEEE Symp. on Security and Privacy, pp. 133–145. IEEE (1999)

46. Willems, C., Hund, R., Fobian, A., Felsch, D., Holz, T., Vasudevan, A.: Down to the bare metal: using processor features for binary analysis. In: Proc. of the 28th Ann. Computer Security Applications Conf. (ACSAC), pp. 189–198. ACM (2012)

47. Willems, C., Hund, R., Holz, T.: Cxpinspector: Hypervisor-based, hardware-assisted system monitoring. Ruhr-Universitat Bochum, Tech. rep. (2013)

48. Wood, T., Cecchet, E., Ramakrishnan, K.K., Shenoy, P., van der Merwe, J., Venkataramani, A.: Disaster recovery as a cloud service: economic benefits & deployment challenges. In: Proc. of the 2nd USENIX Conf. on Hot Topics in Cloud Computing. HotCloud 2010, p. 8. USENIX Association (2010)

49. Xiao, H., Stibor, T.: A supervised topic transition model for detecting malicious system call sequences. In: Proceedings of the 2011 Workshop on Knowledge Discovery, Modeling and Simulation, pp. 23–30. ACM (2011)

50. Yin, H., Poosankam, P., Hanna, S., Song, D.: Hookscout: proactive binary-centric hook detection. In: Kreibich, C., Jahnke, M. (eds.) DIMVA 2010. LNCS, vol. 6201, pp. 1–20. Springer, Heidelberg (2010)

51. Zafarullah, Anwar, F., Anwar, Z.: Digital forensics for eucalyptus. In: Proc. of the 2011 Frontiers of Information Technology, FIT 2011, pp. 110–116. IEEE CS (2011)

52. Zhang, Y., Juels, A., Oprea, A., Reiter, M.: Homealone: co-residency detection in the cloud via side-channel analysis. In: IEEE Sympl. on Security and Privacy, pp. 313–328, May 2011

53. Zhang, Y., Juels, A., Reiter, M.K., Ristenpart, T.: Cross-vm side channels and their use to extract private keys. In: Proc. of the 2012 ACM Conf. on Computer and Communications Security, CCS 2012, pp. 305–316. ACM (2012)

S-Test: A Framework for Services Testing

Nabil El Ioini[(✉)]

Free University of Bozen, Bolzano, Italy
nabil.elioini@unibz.it

Abstract. The advance in Cloud services development has led to a paradigm shift in which different heterogeneous components and platforms can connect and collaborate to solve business problems. This advancement adds a new level of abstraction to the existing stack of technologies and development methodologies, but it adds also new challenges. One such a big challenge is testing. From the consumers prospective, a service is a black box that needs to be tested before being used, mainly to confirm service providers claims concerning the quality of their services. By calling a service, we delegate part of our business logic to an external provider to do it for us. Thus, we have no control over what could happen during the execution of that part of the system. To this end, many testing approaches and techniques have been proposed in the literature to address this issue. In this paper, we propose a framework to help integrate the different testing techniques. The main idea is that depending on the consumers context, one testing technique could be more helpful than another; therefore, providing a framework in which all the techniques could be integrated would help the consumers decide which one is more effective for their particular cases.

Keywords: Cloud services · Testing

1 Introduction

Testing services from the consumer prospective brings mainly two challenges. The first one is that the only type of testing we consider in a realistic scenario is black box testing. This is mainly due to the fact that it is very unlikely that service providers give access to their consumers to check the services' code. The second issue is that service consumers do not own services; instead, they can only invoke them, which makes it very difficult to create a controlled environment for testing. The current state of services testing suggests that there are still many challenges to be addressed [6]. However, several solutions have been already proposed. Furthermore, due to the dynamic nature of services, building a general solution to satisfy all the testing needs is highly infeasible. Consequently, each of the existing approaches tries to focus on solving a specific problem. Looking at the big picture, we find that while more and more techniques are developed and implemented, there is a need to integrate them as part of a framework to make it easy for consumers to use. The main reason for this is that consumers have

© Springer International Publishing Switzerland 2015
C. Debruyne et al. (Eds.): OTM 2015 Conferences, LNCS 9415, pp. 612–619, 2015.
DOI: 10.1007/978-3-319-26148-5_41

different scenarios for which different testing techniques could be applied. To this end, we think that it would be useful to provide a framework that manages different testing techniques, allowing consumers to select or add new ones to the framework. The rest of this paper is organized as follows. Section 2 presents our approach for integrating the different testing techniques. Section 3 discusses the implementation of the framework. Section 4 describes our evaluation method. Finally, section 5 presents our conclusions.

2   Approach

The proposed framework takes advantage of the existing testing techniques by integrating them in a way that hides all the complexity of generating and executing tests from the consumer. This idea is based on the fact that consumers need to know how services behave before using them; however, it is not always easy to decide which testing technique to use in order to find the information they need. Furthermore, there is the overhead generated by applying each testing technique independently. The framework addresses these concerns by proposing an architecture that provides the basic blocks to integrate various testing techniques and generate a report that summarizes the test results, which is an extension of an early work we did in [7]. Figure 1 shows the overall structure of the framework. It is composed of two main blocks. The TestCases Manager, which is responsible for generating, executing and collecting the results of the test cases, and the report Manager, which takes the test results as input and generates a document called S-Report, in which the test scores of the service under test are reported.

2.1   Testing

As there are many test cases generation techniques reported in the literature, a general pattern has been repeatedly used in many of the studies such as [4] [8] [9]. There are mainly five steps that most of the techniques have in common.

1. *Data extraction.* Extracting all necessary information from the used specification such as: operations parameters, data types, operations dependencies;
2. *Test data generation.* Generating test data based on the extracted information. Additionally, data could be provided manually by testers;
3. *Test cases generation.* It is a straight forward task consisting of generating services calls;
4. *Test cases execution.* Executing the service calls manually or automatically by making http requests to the services under test;
5. *Results analysis.* Validating the responses coming back from the service. It is one of the hardest task to automate and, in many approaches, it has been done manually or using some heuristics [8].

To address these five steps in the design, an interface has been defined for each step. Each time a new testing technique is implemented, to be part of

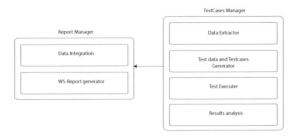

Fig. 1. Overall structure of the framework.

the framework, it needs to implement this interface. Each testing technique is referred to as a policy inside the framework. Furthermore, the framework provides a set of libraries to help developers create new policies easily. The main libraries are:

1. *Data extraction classes:* help developer extracting the information they need from specifications. For now, the framework supports WSDL specification, however, new specifications could be added easily. Information such as operation signature, data types could be extracted;

2. *Test data classes:* we provide supporting classes to help developers generate some types of test data. For example, there are classes that given a data type and the range of values, different combinations of those values could be generated. The provided classes could be extended and more features could be added;

3. *Test cases classes:* to facilitate the test cases generation, a set of classes handles all the request messages construction. Currently, we support SOAP/REST messages;

4. *Test cases execution classes:* sending request messages and receiving the responses is also handled by the framework;

To illustrate with more concrete examples how to use the framework, we identified two techniques that use Web Service Definition Language (WSDL) as a base to generate test cases, which can be added as policies into the framework. Adding a new policy requires the developer to develop such a policy within the framework and adds it to the test cases manager engine. The three test cases generation techniques are Boundary values testing, invalid inputs and persistency [5], [10], [13]. The examples are presented in the evaluation.

In order to add support to the existing technologies, we have integrated our framework into a registry server. This way each time a new service is registered/updated, it can be tested using our framework. The TestCases Manager performs its task as follows (Figure 2):

1. The registry server (e.g, UDDI) receives a request to register a new service from a service provider;

2. The registry server registers the service and passes its WSDL to the TestCase Manager;

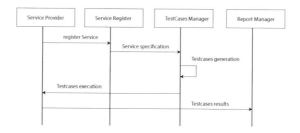

Fig. 2. Service registration sequence diagram.

3. The TestCase Manager generates a suite of test cases based on the WSDL specification and execute them against the new registered service;
4. The results of the tests are passed to the Report Manager.

2.2 Report Manager

The main job of the Report Manager is to receive as input the incoming data (test results), and generate S-Reports. A S-Report is a simple XML file that presents the testing scores of services under test. A S-Report can be used by consumers to decide whether to use a service or not. It can be used also as a selection criterion to compare the quality of services providing the same functionality.

3 Implementation

To implement the Testcases Manager component we have used three existing components: TestGen4J, WSDL4J, and SoapUI library. TestGen4J is a collection of open-source tools and libraries that automatically generates unit test cases [11]. WSDL4J instead is set of libraries that allow the manipulation of WSDL documents [3]. SoapUI library is a set of components for testing services [2].

We have used part of TestGen4J to generate test data used for services testing. In particular, the class TestDatageneration takes a method signature and generates test data based on a configuration file. The configuration file assigns the values that each data type could assume. For example, in case of boundary values test data an Integer data type could be configured to have the following values (2147483647, 2147483648, 2147483649, 0, -2147483647, -2147483648, -2147483649). The WSDL4J is used to manipulate WSDL documents and extract all the types of information that is needed to generate test data and test cases. SoapUI is used for services invocation and capturing the response messages. The three components interact with each other in the following way:

- The WSDL is parsed and the needed information is extracted (e.g., methods names, parameter types).
- Test data is generated
- Test cases are generated using the test data
- Tests are executed and the results are reported

4   Evaluation

The framework has been evaluated by performing different tests and analyzing the impact of the changes on the final report. In the following, the scenarios of our test and the results are described. In these scenarios we assume that the registry server is populated with a set of services. When adding a new service the framework will generate and execute a set of test cases, which will constitute the first S-Report.

4.1   Services Under Test

Two services were used to experiment the framework:

1. The first one is a simple service to calculate the triangle volume [12]. It takes three parameters one for each side of the triangle and returns the triangle volume
2. The second service is a GuidGenerator [1], it does not take any parameter but every time it is called a Globally Unique Identifier (GUID) is generated.
3. Two other services have been developed internally to be used in one of the scenarios discussed later. The two services take a simple integer n as input and return a random string with length n. The difference between the two services is the response time and the throughput. These two services are used to show how consumers can decide which service to use if the services perform the same exact task with different execution time.

4.2   Used Policies

For testing purposes three policies were developed to use and illustrate how the framework operates.

1. The boundary values policy: This policy takes the operations extracted from the WSDL file as input and generates test cases based on the boundary values of the operations' parameters data types. All the combinations of parameters are used as test cases. The drawback of this policy is that the number of generated test cases grows exponentially with the number of parameters. In the boundary values, we only considered the values above the boundaries, which means that if the service is working correctly all the boundary values test cases should fail.
2. Invalid types policy: In the random policy we generate invalid type for each parameter. The advantage of this policy is that it violates the data types specified, so we can send strings instead of integers, for instance. The expected results are errors stating incompatible types.
3. The persistency policy: This policy uses random values from the domain specified by the operations parameters. For instance, if an operation takes a string as parameter, this policy generates a ten characters length string. The goal of this policy is to execute the same test cases more than once

and checks if the services send back the same response. This policy is useful in cases where the response of a service does not depend only on the input parameters but also on the internal state of the service. For instance, in a hotel booking system, by calling the booking service twice. it is very likely that we receive different responses, since the first call might change the state of the system (e.g. no more rooms available). If the service does not take any parameter values, ten calls are made to check if the service responses are similar.

4.3   First Scenario

In the first scenario the Triangle service is used. Once the service is added to the registry, each of the policies generates and executes its test cases. Table 1 shows the results of the tests.

Table 1. Results of testing the Triangle web service

Policy	Generated tests	Passed tests
Boundary Values	125	125
Invalid input	2	0
Persistency	10	10

In the experiment, it has been found that the way the policies are implemented need to be scrutinized and analyzed. This is because sometimes the results could be misleading such as in the example of boundary values policy we implemented. As we mentioned earlier, we have considered in the boundary values policy that if an error message is returned. then the test is considered failed. However, in the case of the Triangle service, the provider does not send back the typical error message using soap:Fault, instead a normal response is returned with the string INF, which has mislead our policy, so all the tests that have passed the Boundary values policy in reality they have failed, because as long as we do not see the soap:Fault in the returned response, we consider the response to be correct. For the Invalid input policy, the tests did not pass because we used strings instead of double values, which is the data type required by the Triangle web service. Finally, the Persistency was irrelevant in this scenario since no matter how many times we call the Triangle service with the same parameters we always receive back the same response. For the experiments, WSDL was used as the main source of information to generate test data and test cases, however, WSDL does not give enough information about the expected values when testing its operations. For this reason, when test cases are executed, the test is consider to have passed if no error messages or exceptions are returned. The policies however, do not detect if there are any semantical errors. The generated report is shown in Figure 3.

```
<S-report>
  <testing dateTime="">
    <policy name="persistenctpolicy">
      <operation name="OperationName">
        <numberOfTests>10</numberOfTests>
        <percentPass>100</percentPass>
      </operation>
    </policy>
    <policy name="boundaryValues">
      <operation name="OperationName">
        <numberOfTests>25</numberOfTests>
        <percentPass>100</percentPass>
      </operation>
    </policy>
    <policy name="invalidInput">
      <operation name="OperationName">
        <numberOfTests>2</numberOfTests>
        <percentPass>0</percentPass>
      </operation>
    </policy>
  </testing>
</S-report>
```

Fig. 3. S-Report.

4.4   Second Scenario

In the second scenario, we have used a similar configuration but we tested the second service. When submitting the GuidGenerator service to the registry server, test cases have been generated and the results are reported in Table 2.

Table 2. Results of testing the GuidGenerator web service

Policy	Generated tests	Passed tests
Boundary Values	0	0
Invalid input	0	0
Persistency	10	0

In this scenario. the only policy that is relevant is the persistency policy. Since the service does not take any input parameters, we could not apply any of the other policies. However, for the persistency policy, although it does not generate any input parameters, ten service calls have been generated to check if the service responses are similar. However, non of them passed the tests. This information suggests that the services responses depend on information other than the input parameters.

5   Conclusions

While existing tools provide different strategies for assessing services quality, still many of them focus only on looking at the quality from one prospective (e.g., testing, monitoring). Additionally, services impose new challenges that did not exist before such as run-time discovery and run-time binding. These challenges require new ways of looking at the quality assessment. In the long term. new techniques and methodologies that are specific to this new paradigm need to be created, but in the short term extending the existing techniques help having more understanding of what we need to build in the future. In the presented framework. we have shown how to integrate some of the existing techniques used for services testing to help consumers assess services before using them. Our future work focuses on extending the implementation of the framework and evaluate its results with real examples.

References

1. Aspalliance.com GetGuid (2014). http://authors.aspalliance.com/nothingmn/guid.asmx?wsdl (retrieved 2014)
2. Eviware. soapui (2014). http://www.soapui.org/ (retrieved 2014)
3. WSDL4J (2014). http://sourceforge.net/projects/wsdl4j/ (retrieved 2014)
4. de Almeida, L., Vergilio, S.: Exploring perturbation based testing for web services. In: International Conference on Web Services, ICWS 2006, pp. 717–726, September 2006
5. Bartolini, C., Bertolino, A., Marchetti, E., Polini, A.: Towards automated wsdl-based testing of web services. In: Bouguettaya, A., Krueger, I., Margaria, T. (eds.) ICSOC 2008. LNCS, vol. 5364, pp. 524–529. Springer, Heidelberg (2008)
6. Canfora, G., Di Penta, M.: Testing services and service-centric systems: challenges and opportunities. IT Professional 8(2), 10–17 (2006)
7. Damiani, E., El Ioini, N., Sillitti, A., Succi, G.: Ws-certificate. In: 2009 World Conference on Services - I, pp. 637–644, July 2009
8. Martin, E.: Automated testing and response analysis of web services. In: IEEE International Conference on Web Services, ICWS 2007, pp. 647–654, July 2007
9. Noikajana, S., Suwannasart, T.: An improved test case generation method for web service testing from wsdl-s and ocl with pair-wise testing technique. In: 33rd Annual IEEE International Conference on Computer Software and Applications, COMPSAC 2009, vol. 1, pp. 115–123, July 2009
10. Offutt, J., Xu, W.: Generating test cases for web services using data perturbation. SIGSOFT Softw. Eng. Notes 29(5), 1–10 (2004)
11. TestGen4J (2014). http://sourceforge.net/projects/spike-test-gen (retrieved 2014)
12. Triangle. Areas And Volumes (2011). http://hooch.cis.gsu.edu/bgates/MathStuff/Mathservice.asmx?wsdl (retrieved 2011)
13. Xu, W., Offutt, J., Luo, J.: Testing web services by xml perturbation. In: 16th IEEE International Symposium on Software Reliability Engineering, ISSRE 2005, p. 10, pp. 257–266, November 2005

Design and Implementation of a Trust Service for the Cloud

Julien Lacroix and Omar Boucelma$^{(\boxtimes)}$

Aix-Marseille Université, CNRS, ENSAM, Université de Toulon, LSIS UMR 7296,
13397 Marseille, France
{j.lacroix,omar.boucelma}@univ-amu.fr

Abstract. Cloud computing is probably one of the most promising and appealing technologies since it supplies access to an unlimited number of virtualized resources. However, due to its distributed and opaque nature, the Cloud raises many issues such as security, and integrity to cite a few. As a result, these issues inhibit a more general migration of workloads into the Cloud.

In this paper we discuss the design and implementation of a system that may help users trust the cloud. The system combines provenance, access control and reasoning models.

Keywords: Cloud · Access control · RBAC · Provenance · PROV-DM

1 Introduction

After witnessing a wealth of hype around Cloud computing, this technology, slowly but surely, is becoming a reality as more companies are putting a large number of applications into the Cloud. However, despite this increasing interest, we are still far away from a wide adoption, mainly because of the fear of security breaches, leading to a lack of trust in the Cloud.

Access control models and policies are the most known approaches to enforce protection on data and resources in a system. In a cloud environment, as stated in [1], provenance may bring an added value to cloud providers and should be treated as a first-class citizen. Simply stated, provenance consists in recording entities and activities involved in producing or transforming an object (more generally a piece of data) or a thing. Provenance may help answering questions such as: Who created this data product and when? When was it modified and by whom? What was the process used to create the data product? Were two data products derived from the same raw data? etc. Behind these questions, several (hidden) issues may arise, such as data integrity, privacy, security and access control, to cite a few. In a distributed context (e.g.; the Cloud), components/activities used during each step can locate on different sites in different countries and each may have specific management policies in compliance with local regulations. Hence combing provenance with access controls may lead to

© Springer International Publishing Switzerland 2015
C. Debruyne et al. (Eds.): OTM 2015 Conferences, LNCS 9415, pp. 620–638, 2015.
DOI: 10.1007/978-3-319-26148-5_42

an efficient system for enforcing trust in the cloud: this is the credo of the work described in this paper.

Provenance based access control for the Cloud (PBAC^2 for short) is the system we describe in this paper. With respect to the state of the art, as discussed in Section 5 below, the contribution of this paper are:

1. We capture and model provenance in using PROV-DM, "the conceptual data model that forms a basis for the W3C provenance (PROV) family of specifications" [5];
2. we extend well known Role Based Access mechanisms (RBAC) with a set of (policy) rules encoded *à la* Datalog, and processed with a basic inference engine that acts as a mediator between different cloud stakeholders;
3. we provide an implementation (prototype) on top of proven and non proprietary technologies.

The paper is organized as follows. Section 2 introduces PROV-DM and PBAC^2, i.e.; the background that is mandatory for the comprehension of the work; Section 3 presents a real-world scenario; Section 4 sketches the design and implementation of the prototype. Related work is discussed in Section 5. A short conclusion is presented in Section 6 while a step by step description of a running example (demo) is provided in Appendix.

2   Background

2.1   Modeling Provenance with PROV-DM

2.1.1   PROV-DM Concepts

The PROV Data Model (PROV-DM) [2] is "the conceptual provenance data model that forms a basis for the W3C provenance (PROV) family of specifications". It allows the description of different types of objects (such as data) and permits the expression of causal dependencies (links). PROV-DM is a W3C Recommendation for provenance expression. It allows to represent all types of objects such as data and allows the expression of causal dependencies (links) among objects. The model consists of three core object types (vertices) and seven core relations (dependencies between objects), that can be represented as a directed acyclic graph (DAG) $G = (V, E)$ where V denotes the set of vertices (nodes), and E is the set of edges.

A PROV-DM object type (graph node) can be either:

1. an *entity* (immutable object state), or
2. an *activity* (process), or
3. an *agent* (process invoker).

There are 4 PROV-DM relations (defined in the model as *Generation, Usage, Association, Delegation*) that express direct dependencies among object types, and 3 relations (*Communication, Derivation, Attribution*) that may model indirect dependencies between object types. Table 1 illustrates direct relations (with their abbreviations used in this paper), while the other 3 relations, that can be expressed as regular expressions over direct ones, are depicted in Table 2.

Table 1. Representation of edge types with their abbreviations

Edge type	Abbreviation
used	*use*
wasGeneratedBy	*gen*
wasAssociatedWith	*assoc*
actedOnBehalfOf	*del*

Table 2. Indirect dependencies as regular expressions

Edge type	Abbreviation	Regular Expression
wasInformedBy	*inf*	*use.gen*
wasDerivedFrom	*der*	*gen.use*
wasAttributedTo	*att*	*gen.assoc*

2.1.2   PROV-DM Informal Semantics

In PROV-DM, dependencies between elements (the DAG) are read from "effect-to-cause". Fig. 1 shows an example of dependencies that are interpreted as follows:

- activity *Activity*1 used entity *Entity*1,
- *Entity*2 was generated by *Activity*2,
- *Activity*3 was associated with the agent *Agent*1 (controller),
- agent *Agent*2 acted on behalf of agent *Agent*3 (delegator), while executing *Activity*4,
- *Activity*5 was informed (triggered) by *Activity*6,
- *Entity*4 was derived from *Entity*5,
- *Entity*6 was attributed to *Agent*4 (creator/generator).

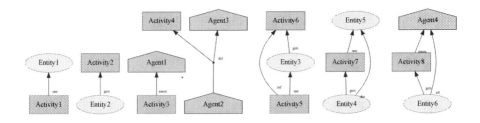

Fig. 1. A sample of PROV-DM graphs

2.2   PBAC^2: Provenance-Based Access Control for the Cloud

In this section, we highlight the main concepts and usage of our provenance-based access control model for the cloud (PBAC^2 for short).

The motivation behind PBAC^2 is threefold:

(1) to augment a provenance graph with access control activities in order to make cloud systems more trusted, knowing that any malicious user can try to execute any activity inside a cloud system,

(2) to apply a set of rules that comply with security policies. Rules are expressed in a Datalog style, and allow the system to handle various security policies: the system has been experimented with two security policies that are *Regimentation* and *Regulation* as defined in [8];

(3) to design a cloud oriented architecture, where a central component called a mediator will be in charge of monitoring the activities and controlling the execution of the rules.

The inception work on PBAC^2 originated from [3], while the design of PBAC^2 was highly influenced by PBAC [4] from which it borrows concepts described in subsection 2.2.1. Note also that PBAC is neither cloud-oriented, nor it does rely on PROV-DM.

2.2.1   Object Dependency List and Rules

In this section, we recall two main concepts borrowed from PBAC [4], that are: an object dependency list and access control rules.

An object dependency (OD for short) is an expression of the form
$$< DNAME, DPATH >$$
where:
- $< DNAME >$ represents a dependency name or abstraction, and
- $< DPATH >$ represents a dependency path or regular expression.

The set of ODs, denoted DL_O, allows the expression of indirect relationships between provenance subgraphs. As an example, below is a list with 2 ODs for a *Search* activity: dependencies expressed here have the same meaning as *att* and *der* indirect dependencies represented in Table 2 above.

$$< wasSearchedBy, gen_{search}.assoc > \text{(att)}$$

$$< wasSearchOf, gen_{search}.use > \text{(der)}$$

As defined in [4], a generic access control rule is an expression of the form:

$$allow(agent, activity, entities) \Rightarrow UAuth \wedge AVal.$$

The head of the rule takes at least two input parameters: an activity and the user (agent) who started the activity. An additional (third) input parameter may represent the list of entities that will be used during the activity execution. The body of the rule contains two predicates $UAuth$ (user authorization) and $AVal$ (action validation):

1. $UAuth$ specifies that the user controlling the activity is the one being authorized to use the data. Table 3 recaps the generic types of rules that can be combined in $UAuth$.

Table 3. $UAuth$ Rule Types

$UAuth$ Rule	Meaning
$agent = {'Bob'}$	the agent is 'Bob'
${'T1'} \in typeOf(agent)$	the agent is of type 'T1'
$agent \in (entity,\ wasOtherActedBy)$	the agent already ran an other activity on the entity

2. $AVal$, the action validation, defines specific conditions that must hold when activities are performed against the data.
   Table 4 enumerates the $AVal$ possible instances of rules.

Table 4. $AVal$ Rule Types

$AVal$ Rule	Meaning
$\mid (entity,\ wasOtherActedBy)\mid \neq 0$	the entity has already been altered by an other activity
$\mid (entity,\ wasOtherActedBy)\mid = 0$	the entity has never been altered by any activity

2.2.2   PBAC² Mediator

As stated above, the PBAC model is not cloud-oriented. In addition, it does not provide any implementation. Our concern is to provide both a model and design for a system dedicated to the cloud.

Besides adopting W3C PROV recommendations for modeling the provenance, we suggest to design a mediator that will be in charge of orchestrating the activities, and controlling the compliance with security policies (rule verification). From a design (and implementation) point of view, the mediator could be a simple web service or a complex business process hosted by a private or public cloud.

In that way, no rules are stored inside the cloud systems or instances: there is no way for an attacker to know why an activity he tried to execute was forbidden. Here only the mediator knows and stores the rules. The administrator of the security service that the mediator enforces via the rules is the only one who can define and modify these rules. This can be seen as a pessimistic approach (Regimentation).

Fig. 2 depicts PBAC^2 workflow execution. Each time an activity *Activity* is invoked by an *Agent* inside a cloud, the following steps occur:

1. a *CheckAuthorization* activity is triggered and processes the input parameters of *Activity*, denoted *ActivityInputParameters*: entities that will be used (*EntityUsed1*, ..., *EntityUsedN*) and invoking agent (*Agent*),
2. *CheckAuthorization* constructs and passes to the mediator a PBAC^2 *Subgraph*, which contains rule firing conditions.
3. The *CheckRules* activity is designed to verify all the rules that are specific to this activity. Depending on the validation (resp. refutation) of all (resp. one of) the *Activity*'s authorization rules by the *CheckRules* activity inside the mediator, the following actions are triggered:
   (a) a confirmation (resp. refutation) is sent to the *ReceiveAuthorization* activity in the appropriate cloud,
   (b) thus, allowing (resp. disallowing) the execution of the initial *Activity*. In the case of allowance, the entities (*EntityGenerated1*, ..., *EntityGeneratedN*) that are generated by the activity *Activity* are integrated to the provenance graph.

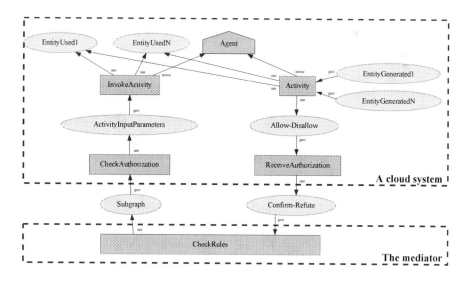

Fig. 2. PBAC workflow at each activity invocation

Algorithm 1 builds PBAC^2 *Subgraph*, that is passed to the mediator, and propagates rules' triggering conditions. For each parameter $\in$ *ActivityInputParameters*, every object is reachable by any OD path, so when the mediator's rules are checked, the dependencies name and path inferred by the rules can be verified.

Algorithm 1 CreateSubGraphPBAC^2

Input: (1) PROV-DM graph $G = (V, E)$, where each vertex is either an *entity*, an *agent* or an *activity*, and each arc label $\in \{use, gen, assoc, del\}$; (2) *ActivityInputParameters* input parameters of the *activity* invocation that triggered the *CheckAuthorization* activity, which is responsible for sending the subgraph; (3) object dependency list (DL_O)

Output: PBAC^2 subgraph $SG = (V', E')$ with $V' \subseteq V$

$V' \leftarrow \emptyset$

$E' \leftarrow \emptyset$

foreach *input parameter* $Zi_{activity}$ *in ActivityInputParameters* **do**

$\quad$ $V' = V' \cup Zi_{activity}$

$\quad$ **foreach** $< DNAME, DPATH >$ *of* DL_O **do**

$\quad\quad$ **foreach** *object directly accessible through DPATH from* $Zi_{activity}$, *i.e.; for each object (entity, activity, agent) such that object* $\leftarrow DPATH \leftarrow Zi_{activity}$

$\quad\quad$ **do**

$\quad\quad\quad$ **if** *object* $\notin V'$ **then**

$\quad\quad\quad\quad$ $|$ $V' = V' \cup \{object\}$

$\quad\quad\quad$ **end**

$\quad\quad\quad$ $E' = E' \cup \{object \leftarrow DNAME \leftarrow Zi_{activity}\}$

$\quad\quad$ **end**

$\quad$ **end**

end

return $SG = (V', E')$

Each input parameter $Zi_{activity}$ of *ActivityInputParameters* sent by an *InvokeActivity* that triggers a *CheckAuthorization* is added to the subgraph in order to allow rule execution/verification. Moreover, for each *object* reachable from $Zi_{activity}$ (and for each $Zi_{activity}$) using DL_O ($< DNAME, DPATH >$), we add $DNAME$ to the subgraph with the *object* on which the dependency from $Zi_{activity}$ is derived. In doing so, we guarantee completeness and minimality of the subgraph (only useful objects and dependencies). Since the Cloud doesn't know the rules, the subgraph couldn't be smaller since we still must add all accessible objects and dependencies from each $Zi_{activity}$. Note that the edges of subgraph returned by Algorithm 1 are slightly different from those of the provenance graph: they represent abstract regular expressions ($DPATH$) over (direct) edges of the provenance graph.

3   Motivating Example

3.1   Description

In this section, we describe a simple but yet real-world example with multiple activity executions and security rules. Cloud Computing is not just about storing data online, like in Amazon S3, with simple queries to create, update and delete files. We will here present a more generic case of Cloud usage with generic process executions that could be replaced by any other use case, like Amazon S3 queries or any Amazon EC2 computation.

A user denoted $User1$ attempts to execute a list of command-lines (denoted cmd in the sequel) on a given system:

#1. `echo random>random-file.txt`

$User1$ writes the text "random" on a random-file.txt file after creating it (the process will be called $echo1$ to be user-friendly everywhere except in the provenance graphs: $echo >$),

#2. `echo random-again>>random-file.txt`

$User1$ writes "random-again" on an existing random-file.txt file (called $echo2$ except in the provenance graphs: $echo >>$),

#3. `echo random-again>>random-file.txt`

same as cmd #2,

#4. `zip -u -r random-file.zip random-file.txt`

$User1$ compresses an existing random-file.txt file into a random-file.zip file,

#5. `unzip -u random-file.zip -d random-dir`

$User1$ uncompresses an existing random-file.zip file into a random-dir folder,

#6. `unzip -u random-file.zip -d random-dir`

same as cmd #5,

#7. `zip -u -r random-file.zip random-dir`

$User1$ compresses an existing random-dir folder into a random-file.zip file.

3.2   PBAC^2 Formalization

The main concepts that need to be represented are: the object dependency list DL_O, the PBAC mediator's rules, and the provenance graph.

3.2.1   DL$_O$ As depicted in Fig. 3, the list of dependencies DL_O allows an easy manipulation of entities and their related activities: from any entity e, we have direct access to both entities from which e derived and to which e was derived, and the agent controlling the activity that generated e.

3.2.2   Rules Rules described in Fig. 4 can be interpreted as follows:

- $echo1$ activity can be executed on some data only if that data has never been used by this activity before ($AVal$),

- $echo2$ activity can be executed on some data only if that data was previously directly generated by the $echo1$ activity and the same agent ($UAuth$) and if it has never been used by this activity before ($AVal$),

- zip activity can be executed on some data only if that data has never been used by this activity before ($AVal$),

- $unzip$ activity can be executed on some data only if that data was previously directly generated by the zip activity and the same agent ($UAuth$) and if it has never been used by this activity before ($AVal$).

Stated otherwise:

- a user can create a file but never recreate it with the same name,

- a user can write to a file only if it has previously been created (by $echo1$ activity) but he never could write to it again then,

$$< wasEcho1edBy,\ gen_{echo1}.assoc >$$
$$< wasEcho1edOf,\ gen_{echo1}.use >$$
$$< wasEcho1edOriginBy,\ wasEcho1edOf^{-1}.wasEcho1edBy >$$

$$< wasEcho2edBy,\ gen_{echo2}.assoc >$$
$$< wasEcho2edOf,\ gen_{echo2}.use >$$
$$< wasEcho2edOriginBy,\ wasEcho2edOf^{-1}.wasEcho2edBy >$$

$$< wasZipedBy,\ gen_{zip}.assoc >$$
$$< wasZipedOf,\ gen_{zip}.use >$$
$$< wasZipedOriginBy,\ wasZipedOf^{-1}.wasZipedBy >$$

$$< wasUnzipedBy,\ gen_{unzip}.assoc >$$
$$< wasUnzipedOf,\ gen_{unzip}.use >$$
$$< wasUnzipedOriginBy,\ wasUnzipedOf^{-1}.wasUnzipedBy >$$

Fig. 3. DL_O of the motivation example

- a user can compress a file/folder but never compress it again,
- a user can uncompress a ZIP file only if it has previously been zipped (only if it appears like that in the provenance graph, in fact), but he never will be able to uncompress it again.

$$allow(au,\ echo1,\ o)\ \Rightarrow\ |\ (o,\ wasEcho1edOriginBy)\ |= 0.$$

$$allow(au,\ echo2,\ o)\ \Rightarrow\ au\ \in\ (o,\ wasEcho1edBy)\ \wedge\ |\ (o,\ wasEcho2edOriginBy)\ |= 0.$$

$$allow(au,\ zip,\ o)\ \Rightarrow\ |\ (o,\ wasZipedOriginBy)\ |= 0.$$

$$allow(au,\ unzip,\ o)\ \Rightarrow\ au\ \in\ (o,\ wasZipedBy)\ \wedge\ |\ (o,\ wasUnzipedOriginBy)\ |= 0.$$

Fig. 4. Mediator's rules

3.2.3   Provenance Graph Fig. 5 illustrates the provenance graph related to the example described above. This figure represents an SVG representation of the internal provenance graph.

4   PBAC^2 Prototype

4.1   Functional Architecture

The PBAC^2 Prototype has been designed in adopting basic principles such as: simplicity to use, portability, reusability of existing (open source) software whenever possible, etc. These principles led us to a simple software architecture illustrated in Fig. 6.

The main software components of the system are:

1. PBAC -Cloud: a Node.js [8] App with a HTML5 / Java-Script / CSS3 client UI (Node.js modules: ejs, express, socket.io, xmlhttprequest). One can:
   * Import and export provenance graph to PROV-JSON,
   * Reset provenance graph,
   * Execute a *cmd*,
   * Execute a *cmd* list, step-by-step, by importing from JSON,
   * Export history of all *cmds* to JSON,
   * View near-real-time provenance as SVG thanks to Luc Moreau's Prov-Translator API [9],
   * Export displayed provenance graph to SVG,
   * View provenance graph history as snapshots via a timeline.
2. PBAC -Mediator: a Node.js REST API (Node.js modules: restify). This API is the mediator of the PBAC architecture, which can decide the executions of multiple cloud instances' activities based on PBAC rules defined in advance by an administrator. These PBAC rules are specified and automatically verified in JavaScript: the head of each rule corresponds to the header of a function, while the body is implemented in the body of the function. The return value of the function is *true* or *false*, accordingly to the confirmation or refutation given by the rule.Here are the inputs and outputs:
   * Input: provenance (sub)graph, entities that will be used, activity that will be executed, entities that will be generated and agent associated with the activity execution,
   * Output: HTTP 202 status if the activity execution is authorized, HTTP 203 else.

Each time an activity execution is invoked on an instance of PBAC -Cloud, the PBAC -Mediator REST API is called via a POST request with a minimized provenance subgraph that contains all the information needed to check the activity execution authorization. Our solution automatically detects entities (files) that will be used, activity that will be executed and the agent associated with each activity execution and entities that are generated. Provenance is represented in PROV-JSON [10].

Distributed systems such as the Cloud imply many features that are elasticity (scalability) and multi-tenancy. Our simple software architecture and implementation use only one mediator system as a service, that is only a necessary condition (not sufficient) to support cloud computing. While it is perfectly adapted to

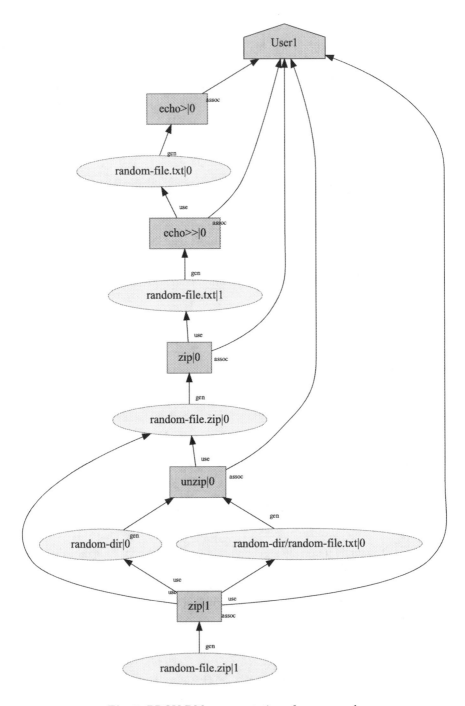

Fig. 5. PROV-DM representation of our example

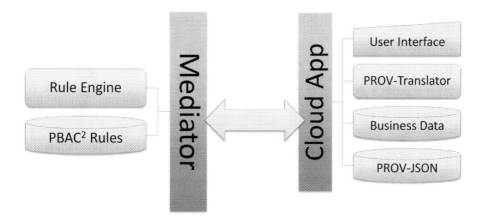

Fig. 6. PBAC^2 Software Components

our motivating example with simple systems, our prototype could be extended to fully support cloud systems.

In order to support (1) elasticity and (2) multi-tenancy, a fully-oriented cloud architecture would have to be implemented the following ways:

1. The cloud systems' elasticity aspect consists in automatically adapt themselves (their resources) to the actual workload. If a given cloud system workload increases (resp. decreases), the resources must grow bigger (resp. diminish). Thus, access controls must adapt themselves to that feature that can be viewed as scalability: if the mediator is implemented as a Web Service, multiple mediator systems must be available (with the same set of rules) and managed by a super-mediator ; else, if the mediator is implemented as a cloud system, that cloud system must be elastic, too, in order to be able to manage the access controls when the workload increases.
2. Regarding multi-tenancy aspects of cloud systems (multiple application or usage types per one system), here two solutions can be implemented too. One could keep the same mediator system to control accesses to the data thanks to a set of rules that can manage all types of applications and usages, but it might be difficult for the administrator to make the set of rules consistent (i.e. without any logical conflict). On the other hand, a better solution would be to provide a different mediator for each usage or application type.

4.2 Experimentation

In the following we will execute our motivating example on our Node.js application, and provide screenshots of the UI all along. Our machine for this experimentation was running Microsoft Windows 7 Professional as the operating system and Google Chrome as our browser to access client UI. PBAC -Cloud was running through localhost:8080 and PBAC -Mediator on localhost:8081. The demonstration video is available at:

https://www.dropbox.com/s/093pcw1nr7jscc5/PBAC2.mp4

A full description of the video demo is in Appendix.

5   Related Work

In this Section we review both research and demo papers that are relevant to provenance and access control policies.

Park *et al* [4] proposed PBAC, a model that allows the expressions of object dependency lists and access control rules that use the provenance graph to decide process executions. PBAC relies on OPM (Open Provenance Model) [11], the precursor of W3C PROV family of specifications. No implementation is provided.

In [3] a diagnosis approach is presented. Threats and security breaches can be identified after activity executions. This is not a real-time threat detection. Provenance is specified in OPM, and the provenance graph is translated to a Colored Petri Net analyzed with CPN Tools.

In [5], in addition to ensuring completeness of the object dependency lists on top of the provenance graph, we compared PROV-DM and PROV-O [16] models in terms of efficiency and expressiveness regarding provenance graphs. We showed that while PROV-O allows us to get rid of any completeness algorithms, the graph to be sent to the mediator might potentially be very large, hence raising inference engine efficiency and (large) management.

In [6], a new provenance model (cProv) and policy language named cProvl are proposed. The former is based on PROV extended with 10 dependencies and 5 node types. The latter is based on a restricted version of PROV-CONSTRAINTS [14], mapped then to XACML. The rules are generic and some of them are actually activity-oriented, very close to the RBAC model, but less expressive than Datalog rules.

A PROV validator is described in [15]. Based on PROV-CONSTRAINTS [14], the system allows the validation of a PROV-DM instance, that is a provenance graph specified in PROV-DM. The system is published as a REST service and takes as input a provenance object for validation.

ProvTranslator [9] is an API that allows the conversion of a PROV instance into other formats such as Trig, PROV-JSON, PROV-N [16], PROVX, and Turtle.

Git2PROV [17] is a simple a useful application that allows provenance capturing from a Github repository; outputs may be in PROV-JSON, PROV-N, PROV-O and SVG.

In [18], provenance-aware access control policies are discussed, including PAC (Provenance Access Control, i.e., the control of accesses to the provenance itself) and PBAC (access control to the data using the provenance graph). An abstract provenance model TPM (Type Provenance Model) is proposed and expressed with OPM, the Open Provenance Model. TPM allows the expression of complex dependencies using regular expressions in a similar way as it is done in PBAC [4] with object dependency lists. Based on TPM, authors illustrate their access control policy enforcement: they identify workflows, activities, agents and the needs of access control in the system.

Access control (RBAC) and trust are the main contribution of [19]. Authors propose a formal model that assigns a trust degree to each entity in the cloud. Trust degrees are evaluated from provenance of the derived entities, and various degrees exist depending on which cloud domain/system entities come from. They compare the success rates between RBAC and their Trust-based Access Control model which, sometimes, proves more successful than RBAC regarding entity accessibility. Even if the access control approaches based on trust are interesting, the PBAC approach seems to be more secure because of strict authorization rules, instead of trust values granted to a particular type of activity per user.

6 Conclusion

In this paper we described the design and implementation of PBAC², a Provenance-Based Access Control model for the Cloud. The system relies on PROV-DM and RBAC to control access in the Cloud via a rule-based mediator, and implements natively the Regimentation security approach. We implemented a fully-functional prototype[1] that can serve as a basis for a more robust software. The main components of the software are: a Node.js Web Service acting as the mediator and a JavaScript UI with a Node.js user application that allow execution and traceability of set of command lines. Visualization of provenance graphs is done in real time, hence, as a side-effect, the system acts also as a PROV editor.

For the future, we would like to test the prototype with an industrial use case, and to extend the model in order to cope with other security policies.

References

1. Muniswamy-Reddy, K.-K., Seltzer, M.I.: Provenance as first class cloud data. Operating Systems Review **43**(4), 11–16 (2009)
2. Moreau, L., Missier, P. (eds.): PROV-DM: The PROV Data Model. W3C Recommendation (2013)
3. Li, Y., Boucelma, O.: A CPN provenance model of workflow: towards diagnosis in the cloud. In: ADBIS (2), pp. 55-64 (2011)
4. Park, J., Nguyen, D., Sandhu, R.: A provenance-based access control model. In: Proceedings of the 10th Annual International Conference on Privacy, Security and Trust (PST 2012) (2012)
5. Lacroix, J., Boucelma, O.: Trusting the cloud: a PROV + RBAC approach. In: Proceedings of the 7th IEEE International Conference on Cloud Computing (CLOUD 2014) (2014)

---

[1] We are planning to make the prototype available to the community.

6. Ali, M., Moreau, L.: A provenance-aware policy language (cProvl) and a data traceability model (cProv) for the cloud. In: Proceedings of the 2013 IEEE 3rd International Conference on Cloud and Green Computing (CGC 2013) (2013)

7. Singh, M.P.: Towards a science of security. In: Presented keynote 4 at the 7th IEEE International Conference on Cloud Computing (CLOUD 2014) (2014)

8. Dahl, R.L., et al.: Node.js (2010). https://nodejs.org/

9. Moreau, L.: ProvTranslator REST API (2013). https://provenance.ecs.soton.ac.uk/validator/view/api.html

10. Jewell, M.O., Keshavarz, A.S., Michaelides, D.T., Yang, H., Moreau, L.: The PROV-JSON Serialization - W3C Member Submission (2014). https://provenance.ecs.soton.ac.uk/prov-json/

11. Moreau, L., Clifford, B., Freire, J., Futrelle, J., Gil, Y., Groth, P., Kwasnikowska, N., Miles, S., Missier, P., Myers, J., Plale, B., Simmhan, Y., Stephan, E., den Bussche, J.V.: The open provenance model core specification (v1.1). Future Generation Computer Systems (2010)

12. Lebo, T., Sahoo, S., McGuinness, D., (eds.): PROV-O: The PROV Ontology. W3C Recommendation (2013)

13. Goble, C., et al.: Taverna (2009). http://www.taverna.org.uk

14. Cheney, J., Missier, P., Moreau, L., (eds.): Constraints of the PROV Data Model. W3C Recommendation (2013)

15. Moreau, L., Huynh, T.D., Michaelides, D.: An online validator for provenance: algorithmic design, testing, and API. In: Gnesi, S., Rensink, A. (eds.) FASE 2014 (ETAPS). LNCS, vol. 8411, pp. 291–305. Springer, Heidelberg (2014)

16. Cheney, J., Soiland-Reyes, S.: PROV-N: The Provenance Notation. W3C Recommendation (2013)

17. De Nies, T., Magliacane, S., Verborgh, R., Coppens, S., Groth, P., Mannens, E., Van de Walle, R.: Git2PROV: exposing version control system content as W3C PROV. In: Poster and Demo Proceedings of the 12th International Semantic Web Conference (2013)

18. Sun, L., Park, J., Sandhu, R.: Engineering access control policies for provenance-aware systems. In: Proceedings of the third ACM conference on Data and application security and privacy (CODASPY 2013) (2013)

19. Lin, G., Bie, Y., Lei, M.: Trust Based Access Control Policy in Multi-domain of Cloud Computing. Journal of Computers **8**(5), 1357 (2013)

Appendix - Running Example

In this section we provide a step-by-step description of the running example [2] described in 3. In particular, we show detailed versions of the 7 subgraphs (states) passed to the mediator to allow the verification of PBAC^2 rules (described in Fig. 4). Please note that each file modification or file alteration creates a new version (entity — version_number) of the file in the provenance graph. Each file creation leads to a version denoted (entity — 0) of the file entity in the graph.

1. Fig. 7 depicts the first provenance subgraph sending before in cmd #1 execution. It consists of $User1$ only, because there is one input parameter of $echo1$ activity, that is $User1$. No objects are accessible from it with any dependency

---

[2] Recall that a demo is accessible at https://www.dropbox.com/s/093pcw1nr7jscc5/PBAC2.mp4

Fig. 7. Subgraph State Before Executing *cmd* #1

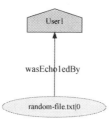

Fig. 8. Subgraph State Before Executing *cmd* #2

path. The rule below is validated because no *wasEcho1edOriginBy* dependencies are present from any *entity*: the user can create this file only once. *random − file.txt* is created.

2. In Fig. 8, the input parameters of *echo2* are *User*1 and *random − file.txt* (before execution of *cmd* #2). A dependency named *wasEcho1edBy* from *random − file.txt* to *User*1 is generated. *echo2* rule is checked and validated: *User*1 that issued *echo2* activity is the same agent who executed *echo1* previously, generating *random − file.txt*. Since *random − file.txt* was never used by *echo2* before (no *wasEcho2edOriginBy* dependencies from *random − file.txt*), *User*1 thus produces a new version of *random − file.txt* (version 1).

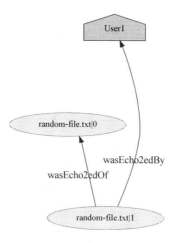

Fig. 9. Subgraph State Before Executing *cmd* #3 (idem for *cmd* #4)

3. Fig. 9 depicts the subgraph sent to the mediator before the execution of *cmd* #3, with the following input parameters: *User*1 and *random − file.txt* (version 1). Knowing that this new version was generated by *echo*2, the older version becomes accessible through *wasEcho*2*edOf*. In addition, *random − file.txt* (version 1) has a dependency to *User*1 named *wasEcho*2*edBy*. With this subgraph, *echo*2 rule is refuted because *User*1 has no *wasEcho*1*edBy* dependency originating from *random − file.txt* (version 1). This rule ensures that *echo*2 executes only once: in this case, *AVal* is useless because *echo*2 generates the same files as the one used, so it will never be tested. The *cmd* #3 (*echo*2) is not executed.

4. The same figure (Fig. 9) depicts the subgraph sent before *cmd* #4 execution too, because *cmd* #4 (*zip*) has the same input parameters as *cmd* #3: *User*1 and *random − file.txt* (version 1); and also because no activities that could have altered the value of those parameters were executed since the last subgraph sending. The *zip*'s rule only allows zipping once for a given file. In the subgraph, no dependencies named *wasZipedOriginBy* originating from *random − file.txt* (version 1) are present, so the rule will be validated, zipping *random − file.txt* into *random − file.zip*.

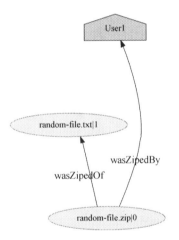

Fig. 10. Subgraph State Before Executing *cmd* #5

5. Fig. 10 depicts the subgraph state before *cmd* #5 executes. We may notice that input parameters of *unzip* are *random − file.zip* and *User*1, and also the fact that *random − file.zip* has a dependency named *wasZipedOf* to *random − file.txt* (version 1) and one named *wasZipedBy* to *User*1 agent. The rule for *unzip* allows unzipping of a zip file only if it was zipped by the same agent and if it has never been unzipped before. Here *User*1 is the agent that zipped *random − file.zip* (*UAuth*) and no dependencies named *wasUnzipedOriginBy* are accessible from *random − file.zip*, because it

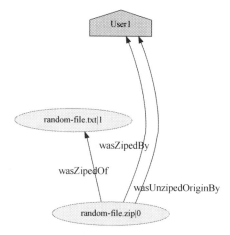

Fig. 11. Subgraph State Before Executing *cmd* #6

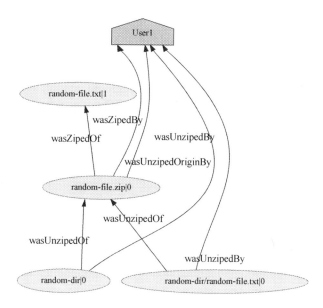

Fig. 12. Subgraph sent to the mediator before executing *cmd* #7

has never been unzipped before. Hence *unzip* is allowed to execute and
random − file.zip is unzipped into *random − dir* directory that contains
random − dir/random − file.txt.

6. Fig. 11 differentiates from Fig. 10 by means of an additional
   wasUnzipedOriginBy arc (from *random − file.zip* to *User*1). Indeed, *cmd*
   #6 is the same as *cmd* #5, so the input parameters are the same. So the

$AVal$ part of $unzip$ rule will be refuted and the cmd will not be executed and no unzipping will be done again on $random - file.zip$.

7. Fig. 12 illustrates the final subgraph sent before cmd #7 execution. Input parameters of zip are: $User1$, $random - file.zip$ (to be updated), $random - dir$ (to add into the zip file with $random - dir/random - file.txt$). The subgraph reflects the $unzip$ activity execution (performed by #5) plus the previous zip execution of #4 (containing the subgraph of cmd #6). Here both $UAuth$ and $AVal$ are validated since no input parameters have a $wasZipedOriginBy$ dependency originating from them.

Security Aspects of De-materialized Local Public Administration Processes

Giancarlo Ballauco[1], Paolo Ceravolo[2], Ernesto Damiani[3],
Fulvio Frati[2(✉)], and Francesco Zavatarelli[2]

[1] I-Conn, Trento, Italy
giancarlo.ballauco@nitidaimmagine.it
[2] Computer Science Department, Università Degli Studi Di Milano, Milan, Italy
{paolo.ceravolo,fulvio.frati,francesco.zavatarelli}@unimi.it
[3] Etisalat British Telecom Innovation Center/Khalifa University, Abu Dhabi, UAE
ernesto.damiani@kustar.ac.ae

Abstract. De-materialization processes and services of local public administration processes are becoming of paramount importance in the context of Italian and European public administrations. An important aspect of these frameworks is the possibility of providing remote assistance by human operators when needed, in order to ease the access to services for citizens and reduce costs for organizations. In this paper we describe our framework, which is in an advanced state of development and will be tested in several municipalities of the province of Trento (Italy), and focus on the enforcement of security aspects.

Keywords: BPMN · Adaptive business processes · Local Public Administration

1   Introduction

Like many other European countries, Italy is undergoing the process of merging several little municipalities into districts, to allow local administrations to streamline local services, re-organize staff, and thus reduce indirect costs [4]. In particular in rural and mountain areas, local services are relocated to municipalities chosen as district leaders, forcing citizens to face longer trips and increased inconvenience in accessing services. This situation has triggered research [1,2] on technologies and platforms for the de-materialization of Local Public Administration (LPA) processes, in order to provide remote access to such services via smartphones or special-purpose access points located in supervised places like schools, post offices, and shops.

   Our solution [6] relies on a platform that executes all LPA process steps remotely, calling in a human operator for assistance only when necessary. The level of assistance is context-dependent, i.e. takes into account the task at hand, the logistics of the point of access, the age, hearing and eyesight capabilities of the user as well as the current state of the Internet connection and access devices. If the user looks uncertain or confused, the remote assistance gets activated automatically without waiting for a specific request. Experience has shown that citizens used to have face-to-face interactions in fulfilling LPA processes find hard to access LPA services via Web sites.

© Springer International Publishing Switzerland 2015
C. Debruyne et al. (Eds.): OTM 2015 Conferences, LNCS 9415, pp. 639–643, 2015.
DOI: 10.1007/978-3-319-26148-5_43

In the i-Conn infrastructure, business processes are started and accessed via remote kiosks equipped with all the I/O devices needed to fulfil common LPA processes: monitors, touch screen, printer, scanner, smart card readers, etc. When needed, our kiosks are able to contact process experts that are connected via an operator workstation. Experts can interact with citizens through high quality audio-video connections, and take direct control of the kiosk to help them if they get stuck on specific activities like filling in forms. Whenever process tasks involve choices that may generate a penalty (for instance, paying a local tax, where even an error in good faith can trigger a fine for the taxpayer), users may request the assistance of a human expert [3,4]. The i-Conn framework does not allow connections coming from mobile devices or through the Net, to make sure users access processes via the kiosk and can be provided with remote human assistance when needed.

In this paper we discuss some security-by-design aspects that need to be considered and the way implemented them, in order to keep the system usable and limit the implementation effort of new processes.

1.1   Custom Extension to BPMN Language

In our system, LPA processes are described using the BPMN standard model and language (www.bpmn.org). We extended the standard BPMN palette with specific design widgets, which in turn are associated to scripts capable to detect and activate the right assistance level and send direct commands to I/O devices (printer, scanner ...). Widgets are available also to handle security features. By inserting such widgets in process definitions, i-Conn process designers can handle the level of interactivity by inserting specific scripts.

We defined a set of heuristic rules [5] that evaluate environment variables in the process context (for instance *ConnectionQualityLevel* > 3) and decide the action to deal with it, e.g. *StartAudioCall*. Our rules are written as annotations to the BPMN diagram used in process design. Figure 1 shows an extended BPMN diagram, where icons in the upper left corner of each activity determine the type of rule implemented in the activity.

2   Security Aspects

The overall i-Conn architecture has been designed in order to ensure a double level of security enforcement:

- At **network level**, satisfying security requirements implemented to secure the communication between kiosks, server, and operators;
- At **process level**, providing *widgets* to allow the process designer to determine, differentiate, and apply security properties (i.e., strong authentication based on biometrics) directly during the process design.

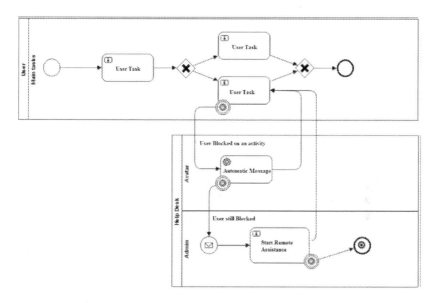

Fig. 1. Example of enriched BPMN diagram.

2.1   Network-Level Security

Figure 2 shows an example of the i-Conn network architecture. The whole architecture is based on a cloud-based virtual server that *(i)* provides document management services, *(ii)* acts as a proxy between remote kiosk and operators, and *(iii)* manages the overall network. I-Conn kiosks (and the operator's workbench) are equipped with a workstation and a set of devices connected to the network, including printers, scanners, digital cameras, and smart card readers.

The cloud server that provides document and process management services acts as a proxy between remote kiosk and operators, and manages the overall network. Kiosks and operators are equipped with a workstation and a set of devices connected to the network, including printers, scanners, digital cameras, and smart card readers. Each devices is assigned an IP address that belongs to a private subnetwork that is dedicate to the i-Conn system.

Special agreements have been signed with the cloud provider in order *(i)* to locate all elements on the same virtual local network *(ii)* to keep the virtual local network fully insulated from other tenants' networks and from the public Net, avoiding any possible contact with (or intrusions by) malicious users. Each LPA's i-Conn system is thus fully de-coupled from the others. The virtual server hosting the document and process management services can be deployed according to two patterns: *partitioned/multi-tenant* and *replicated/single-tenant* deployment.

In the partitioned pattern, a single instance of the i-Conn process/document management engine handles LPAs as individual users.

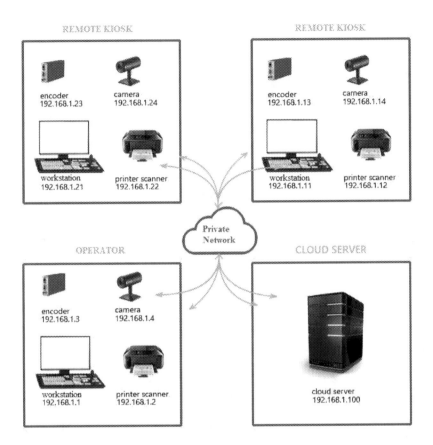

Fig. 2. Example of network architecture.

The single Virtual Machine (VM) hosting the process server is multi-homed on the multiple virtual networks corresponding to different LPAs. In the replicated pattern, the server is replicated on a separate VM for each LPA, and each VM is single-homed on the virtual network of the corresponding LPA, for improved de-coupling and security. Of course, the replicated pattern involves higher hosting costs.

Communications between all the components of the virtual local network is secured using HTTPS and TLS/SSL. In the partitioned pattern, securing data-in-transit aims to avoid possible man-in-the-middle attacks on the part of co-tenants.

Whatever the deployment pattern, the availability of a private local network for each LPA makes the i-Conn system highly scalable in terms of the number of connected kiosks, devices, and operators. The number of kiosks is bounded by the maximum number of remote kiosks that an assistance operator can effectively follow simultaneously (usually 6), and the number of available operators.

2.2   Process-Level Security

In computing, the term *widget* is often used to denote small applications with limited functionality that can be installed and executed within a web page by an end user. A widget has the role of a transient or auxiliary application. I-Conn custom extension to BPMN allows the process designer to use i-Conn widgets to add the actions needed to establish simple security properties, including confidentiality, integrity and authenticity of the information exchanged between the process actors (user, operator and process management engine). I-Conn security widgets incorporate specific controls and scripts to raise the security level. For instance, assume that the first activity of a process should be executed only if the process has already performed a simple username-password authentication of the user. Then, if the following tasks require stronger authentication levels (e.g., strong authentication via smart card), the i-Conn process designer will include an activity widget with the strong authentication flag, and the process will continue if and only if a correct authentication has been executed via the i-Conn script. The i-Conn process editor will assist process designers to select the right widgets for achieving the desired security level, showing specific flags and switches in the editor for the configuration of the activity. Furthermore, before starting a process the system will verify that all the devices used by process-level security components are available. If not, the process will not be started.

3   Conclusions and Future Work

Our solution for de-materializing LPA processes preserves human assistance to users. I-Conn BPMN extension can activate specific features for each activity in the process directly at design time, like for instance expressing the interaction level with the citizen, or requesting specific security feature.

References

1. Armenia, S., Canini, D., Casalino, N.: A system dynamics approach to the paper demateria-lization process in the italian public administration. In: Interdisciplinary Aspects of Information Systems Studies. Springer (2008)
2. Mirabella, N., Rigamonti, L., Scalbi, S.: Life cycle assessment of Information and Communication Technology application: a case study of dematerialization in the Italian Public Administration. Journal of Cleaner Production **44**, 115–122 (2013)
3. Becker, J., Niehaves, B., Bergener, P., Räckers, M.: Digital divide in egovernment: the eInclusion gap model. In: Wimmer, M.A., Scholl, H.J., Ferro, E. (eds.) EGOV 2008. LNCS, vol. 5184, pp. 231–242. Springer, Heidelberg (2008)
4. Goldsmith, M.J., Page, E.C. (eds.): Changing Government Relations in Europe. From Localism to Intergovernmentalism. Routledge, Oxon (2010)
5. Sakurai, Y., Takada, K., Anisetti, M., Bellandi, V., Ceravolo, P., Damiani, E., Tsuruta, S.: Toward sensor-based context aware systems. Sensors **12**(1), 632–649 (2012)
6. Ballauco, G., Ceravolo, P., Damiani, E., Frati, F., Zavatarelli, F.: De-Materializing Local Public Administration Processes. PNSE @ Petri Nets 2015, pp. 311–312 (2015)

Monitoring-Based Certification of Cloud Service Security

Maria Krotsiani[✉], George Spanoudakis, and Christos Kloukinas

Department of Computer Science, City University London, London, UK
{Maria.Krotsiani.1,G.E.Spanoudakis,C.Kloukinas}@city.ac.uk

Abstract. In this paper, we present a novel approach to cloud service security certification. This approach could be used to: (a) define and execute automatically certification models, which can continuously and incrementally acquire and analyse evidence regarding the provision of services on cloud infrastructures through continuous monitoring; (b) use this evidence to assess whether the provision is compliant with required security properties; and (c) generate and manage digital certificates confirming the compliance of services if the acquired evidence supports this. We also present the results of an initial experimental evaluation of our approach based on the MySQL server and RUBiS benchmark.

1   Introduction

Cloud technology offers a powerful approach to the provision of infrastructure, platform and software services without incurring a considerable cost of owning, operating and maintaining the computational infrastructures required for this purpose. However, despite being cost effective, this technology has raised concerns regarding the security, privacy, governance and compliance of the data and software services offered through it. This is due to the fact that the internals of service provision are not visible to service consumers, and service providers are reluctant to take full responsibility for the security of services that they offer through clouds, and accept liability for security breaches [2]. In such circumstances, there is a trust deficit that needs to be addressed.

The potential of certification as a means of addressing the lack of trust regarding the security of different types of software (and hardware) systems, including the cloud, has been widely recognised [19]. However, the recognition of this potential has not led to as a wide adoption as it was expected originally. The reason for this is that certification has traditionally been carried out through standards and certification schemes (e.g., ISO27001 [19], ISO27002 [19] and Common Criteria [7]), which involve predominantly manual systems security auditing, testing and inspection processes. Such processes tend to be lengthy and have a significant financial cost, which often prevents new and smaller technology vendors from adopting it [11].

The certification of cloud services is not an exception to this overall trend. On the contrary, most of the existing certification schemes (e.g., STAR [27] and OCF [8]) are not fit-for-purpose for the certification of cloud services. This is due to several reasons. Firstly, current schemes offer no automation and can only support certification at distinct time points without considering the continuum of service provision between these points. Secondly, they produce certificates based on testing without incorporating real and continuous cloud service monitoring. Finally, they cannot support dynamic changes in the structure, deployment and configuration of the systems

© Springer International Publishing Switzerland 2015
C. Debruyne et al. (Eds.): OTM 2015 Conferences, LNCS 9415, pp. 644–659, 2015.
DOI: 10.1007/978-3-319-26148-5_44

and data that underpin the provision of cloud services as, for example, the dynamic migration of data and software components across different computational nodes within a cloud infrastructure or a cloud federation.

In this paper, we present a novel approach to cloud service certification. This approach can be used to: (a) define and execute automatically certification models, which can continuously and incrementally acquire and analyse evidence regarding the provision of services on cloud infrastructures through continuous monitoring; (b) use this evidence to assess whether the provision is compliant with required security properties; and (c) generate and manage digital certificates confirming the compliance of services if the acquired evidence supports this. Our approach has been developed as part of the EU R&D project CUMULUS and has been implemented as part of the prototype certification infrastructure of it [10]. An early account of our approach was introduced in [18] and examples of different types of certification models based on it have been presented in [17] and [16]. In this paper, we present an advanced version of our approach, incorporating an elaborated scheme for: (i) assessing the sufficiency of evidence for producing certificates and (ii) executing certification processes according to precisely defined models of them. We also present the results of an initial experimental evaluation of our approach.

The rest of this paper is organized as follows. Section 2 gives an overview of the CUMULUS approach to certification. Section 3, 4 and 5 describe three key ingredients of the certification models that drive the certification process in CUMULUS, i.e., the specification of security properties, the specification of the evidence assessment scheme in such models and the specification of the certification process model, respectively. Section 6 discusses the results of an initial experimental evaluation of our approach. Finally, Section 7 reviews related work and Section 6 summarizes our approach and provides directions for future work.

2   Overview of CUMULUS

CUMULUS has developed an infrastructure supporting the collection and analysis of different types of evidence, including for example test and monitoring data for cloud service provision, as well as data gathered from trusted platform modules [10]. The developed infrastructure can be used by certification authorities to generate and manage digital security certificates for cloud services. It can also be used by cloud service providers operating at different levels of the cloud stack, i.e., cloud infrastructure, platform and/or software service providers for self-certification.

The use of this CUMULUS infrastructure for different types of cloud services and security properties and by different types of cloud service providers is enabled through the specification of appropriate *certification models*. These models describe the process of collecting and analysing evidence in order to assess security properties and the process of creating and managing digital certificates asserting the outcomes of this process. More specifically, a certification model specifies:

(i)   the cloud service to be certified (i.e., the target of certification (TOC));
(ii)   the security property to be certified for TOC;
(iii) the certification authority that will sign the certificates generated by the model;

(iv)   an assessment scheme that defines general conditions regarding the evidence that must be collected for being able to issue a certificate;

(v)   additional validity tests regarding the configuration of the cloud provider that must be satisfied prior to issuing certificates;

(vi)   the configurations of the agents that will be used in order to collect the evidence required for generating certificates;

(vii)   the way in which the collected evidence will be aggregated in certificates (evidence aggregation); and

(viii) a life cycle model that defines the overall process of issuing certificates.

Our monitoring-based approach for certification has been developed as part of the CUMULUS infrastructure and is based on monitoring-based certification models (MBCM) in order to specify and drive the execution of the certification process. Such models incorporate the items (i)-(viii) listed above and are specified in an XML-based language whose top-level structure is shown in Fig. 1.

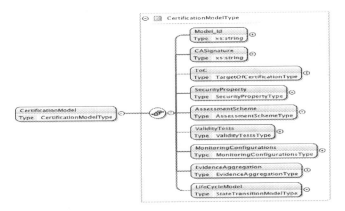

Fig. 1. Monitoring-based Certification Model schema elements

In the following, we introduce the elements in MBCMs, which are essential for understanding the realization of our approach, namely the specification of security properties, evidence assessment schemes and the process of certification (also known as *life cycle model*).

3   Specification and Monitoring of Security Properties

In MBCMs, a TOC is specified as a concrete endpoint with a set of service interfaces that are offered by it to external parties (*provided interfaces*), and a set of interfaces required of external parties (*required interfaces*).

The security property to be certified for TOC is specified by one monitoring rule and zero or more assumptions:

Security-property:= MonitoringRule ["," MonitoringAssumption]*

In a security property specification, monitoring rules are assertions expressing conditions that must be satisfied during the monitoring of TOC, whilst monitoring assumptions are assertions, which are used to record and update state variables indicating the state of TOC during monitoring. Both monitoring rules and assumptions are expressed as *assertions* in *EC-Assertion+*. *EC-Assertion+* is an extension of *EC-Assertion*, i.e., the language for expressing monitoring conditions in the EVEREST monitoring system [26], which is part of the CUMULUS framework. *EC-Assertion+* is based on Event Calculus [25]. Within it, assertions are formulas of the form:

$$\textit{Assertion} ::= \textit{[precondition]}* \text{ ``}\Rightarrow\text{''} \textit{postcondition}$$

The (optional) *precondition* element in an assertion determines the conditions under which the assertion should be checked. The meaning of the *postcondition* element depends on whether the assertion is a monitoring rule or an assumption. In assertions expressing monitoring rules, *postcondition* determines the conditions that are guaranteed to hold (i.e., should be true if the preconditions are true). In assertions expressing monitoring assumptions, *postcondition* determines the states of the system that can be inferred to be true if the preconditions are true.

Both monitoring rules and assumptions are defined in terms of *events* and *fluents*. An event is something that occurs at a specific instance of time and has instantaneous duration. Fluents represent system states and are initiated and terminated by events. The basic predicates used by *EC-Assertion+* are:

- *Happens(e,t,[L, U])* – This predicate denotes that an event *e* of instantaneous duration occurs at some time point *t* within the time range *[L, U]*. An event *e* is specified as *e(_id, _snd, _rcv, TP, _sig, _src)* where *_id* is its unique id of it, *_snd* is its sender, *_rcv* is its receiver, *_sig* is its signature, and *_src* is the source where *e* was captured from. *TP* denotes the type of the event. *EC-Assertion+* supports three event types: (a) captured operation calls (REQ), (b) captured operation responses (RES) and (c) forced operation execution events (EXC), i.e., operation executions triggered by the monitor itself. EXC events constitute one of the extensions of *EC-Assertion+* over its predecessor *EC-Assertion*. When such events are encountered in a formula, EVEREST attempts to execute the operation defined by *_sig* (by invoking an external service) and, if successful, it replaces any output parameters of the operation with the values produced by it and considers the relevant *Happens* predicate to be true. If the call to the external operation fails, the *Happens* predicate is considered to be false. EXC events are used to execute external computations (e.g., online tests) during monitoring.
- *Initiates(e,f,t)* – This predicate denotes that a fluent *f* is initiated by an event *e* at time *t*. fluents are expressed as n-ary relations of the form $relation(arg_1, ..., arg_n)$, where arg_i can be constant values or variables of basic data types.
- *Terminates(e,f,t)* – This predicate denotes that a fluent *f* is terminated by an event *e* at time *t*.
- *HoldsAt(f,t)* – This is a derived predicate denoting that a fluent *f* holds at time *t*. *HoldsAt(f,t)* is true if *f* has been initiated by some event at some time point *t'* before *t* and has not been terminated by any event within *[t',t]*.
- *<rel>(x,y)* – These are relational predicates (<rel>::= $= | < | > | \leq | \geq | \neq$) enabling comparisons between variables of basic data types, or between such variables and constant values.

To demonstrate the use of *EC-Assertion+* in specifying security properties, consider an example showing how it may be used to specify a security property included in the Protection Profile for Database Management Systems developed by Oracle [DBMS PP, 2000] (i.e., a Common Criteria (CC) profile developed for the certification of relational database management systems). This security property (also known as *security functional requirement* or SFR in the context of CC [7]) is about the timing of user identification and is expressed as follows within the protection profile:

> **FIA_UID.1.2:** *The TSF shall require each DATABASE user to be successfully identified before allowing any other TSF-mediated actions on behalf of that DATABASE user.*

The certification model for monitoring and certifying FIA_UID.1.2 consists of three assertions: two assumptions and one monitoring rule. The two assumptions in the MBCM are used to initialise and terminate a fluent indicating whether a user is connected to the DBMS following successful authentication. The fluent is expressed by the relation *Connected(_thread-id, _user)*. The meaning of the relation is that the user indicated by the variable _user has been connected to the DBMS through the thread indicated by the variable _thread-id. The fluent *Connected(.)* is initiated when an event showing the successful connection of _user to the DBMS occurs. The assumption that is used to initiate the fluent is expressed as[1]:

FIA UID.1.2.A1

```
Happens(e(_eId,_thread-id,_host,REQ,o(_thread-id,_query-id,
_queryType,_user),_SRC),_t1,R(_t1,_t1)) ∧ (_queryType = Connect) ⇒
Initiates(e(_eId,    _thread-id,    _host,    REQ,    o(_thread-id,_query-id,
_queryType,_user),_SRC), Connected(_thread-id, _user),_t1)
```

The above assertion monitors events of the form *o(_thread-id, _query-id, _queryType, _user)*. When an event of this form occurs during the operation of the DBMS and the type of the query captured by the event (i.e., _queryType) is "Connect", the state *Connected(.)* is initiated. The events *o(_thread-id, _query-id, _queryType, _user)* required in order to operate the certification model of this example are captured during the operation of the DBMS to be certified and are passed to the CUMULUS framework by an event translator that we have developed for this purpose (see Sect 4). The state *Connected(.)* may also be terminated during the operation of a DBMS if a given user disconnects from the DBMS. The assumption that captures such disconnection events and updates the fluent *Connected(.)* is expressed as:

FIA UID.1.2.A2

```
Happens(e(_eId,_thread-id,_host,REQ,o(_thread-id,_query-id,
_queryType,_user),_SRC), _t1, R(_t1, _t1)) ∧ (_queryType = Quit) ∧
HoldsAt(Connected(_thread-id, _user), _t1) ⇒
Terminates(e(_eId,    _thread-id,    _host,    REQ,    o(_thread-id,    _query-id,
_queryType, _user), _SRC), Connected("thread-id", "user"), _t1)
```

---

[1] For readability, we provide the specification of assertions in the high level syntax of *EC-Assertion+*. *EC-Assertion+* has also an XML schema used in actual monitoring.

According to above assertion, the fluent *Connected(.)* is terminated, when a "Quit" event occurs for a user, provided that at the time when the "Quit" event the particular user is connected. This is checked in the formula by the *HoldsAt(Connected(_thread-id, _user), _t1)* condition.

The monitoring rule assertion that is used to check if a DBMS satisfies FIA_UID.1.2 is expressed as:

FIA UID.1.2.MR1

```
Happens(e(_eId, _thread-id, _host, REQ, o(_thread-id, _query-id,
_queryType, _user), _SRC), _t1, R(_t1, _t1)) ∧
not (_queryType = Connect) ⇒
HoldsAt(Connected(_thread-id, _user), _t1)
```

The above rule monitors if at each time (_t1) when a user executes queries at the DB server, which are not of type "*Connect*", he/she must have been successfully connected to the server. Thus, the monitoring rule checks that when queries of a type other than "*Connect*" occur, the fluent *Connected(_thread-id, _user),* which indicates that the user has already established a connection to the server through the specific thread, holds.

3.1   Specification and Verification of Assessment Scheme

The assessment scheme in a MBCM defines conditions regarding the sufficiency of evidence that must be collected in order to be able to issue a certificate. These conditions are related to: (i) the sufficiency of the extent of the collected evidence, and (ii) anomalies and conflicts that should be monitored during the certification process. In this paper we do not discuss anomalies and conflicts but an account of them is available in [17].

Evidence sufficiency conditions may be specified as: (a) the minimum period of monitoring TOC, (b) the minimum number of monitoring events, and/or (c) the representativeness of the monitoring events with respect to the expected behaviour of TOC that should be seen by the monitor before a certificate can be issued. Whilst the specification of (a) and (b) is straightforward, to enable checks of the representativeness of monitoring events, the certification model should include a specification of a model of the *expected behaviour* of TOC (i.e., an ETOCB model). This model is specified as a deterministic automaton with expected relative event frequencies of the form:

$$\text{ETOCB} = \text{<States, Events, } s_{init}, \text{ PTrans, FinalStates>}$$

In the ETOCB specification: *States* is the (finite) set of TOC states that are critical for the monitoring process; *Events* is the set of all possible events the TOC may produce that are of interest to certification; s_{init} is the initial TOC state; *PTrans* is a finite set of labelled transitions between two states; and *FinalStates* is the set of states where the certification automaton terminates. *PTrans* includes elements of the form *(os, ds, e, R(lpr, upr))* where *os* is the origin state of the transition, *ds* is the destination state of the transition, *e* is the signature of the event triggering the transition, and *R(lpr,upr)* is the range of the expected relative frequence of undertaking this transition whilst the system is in *os* (*R(lpr, upr)* can be: *(lpr, upr)*, *[lpr, upr)*, *(lpr, upr]* or *[lpr, upr]²*) The ETOCB model must satisfy some constraints. In particular: (i) *e* must be an element of *Events*, i.e., an event denoting the invocation (or the response produced following an invocation) of an operation in the *provided* interface of TOC; (ii) the boundaries *lpr, upr* should satisfy the conditions: $0 \leq lpr$, $upr \leq 1$, and $lpr \leq upr$; and (iii) ETOCB must be a deterministic model.

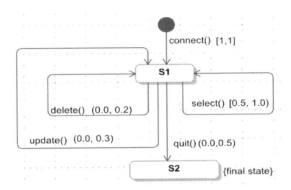

Fig. 2. Expected System Operation Model for Monitoring-Based Certification Model

ETOCB defines events that should be seen at different states during the operation of TOC (i.e., executed operations of the ToC) for the monitoring evidence to be sufficient. For certifying MySQL server, for example, this evidence should include executions of select, update, delete, and quit MySQL commands with specific frequencies. ETOCB is not required to be a complete model of TOC's behaviour; it only needs to define the states and events of importance for the property to be certified.

Fig. 2 gives an example of the ETOCB model for a relational DB server. This model expresses a view about the typical range of the server usage that should be taken into account in the certification of the server. According to it:

- The first interaction with the TOC should be a *connect* call to it (see event of transition from *InitialState* to *S1*) since a connection to the server should be established before any other query occurs. Also, according to the frequency range of this transition (i.e., [1,1]), *connect* calls should be the only initial event in any monitoring event trace, for the trace to be considered valid for the purposes of certification.
- Once a connection to the server is established, interactions with it may be requests for the execution of *select()*, *update()*, *delete()* or *quit()* operations (i.e., SQL queries) with expected frequency ranges [0.5, 1.0), (0.0, 0.3), (0.0, 0.2), and (0.0, 0.5), respectively, as indicated by the relevant transitions from S1 to S1 and S2. These expected frequency ranges require that data retrieval events (*select()* queries) will constitute at least half of the interactions with the server but data *update()* and *delete()* queries should also be seen. The model also expresses that: (a) it will be sufficient for certification purposes to see an event trace with update queries up to

---

[2] "[" and "]" denote a closed range at the lower and upper boundary respectively, and "(" and ")" denote an open range at the lower and upper boundary respectively.

below 30% and delete queries up to below 20% of all interactions, and (b) whilst at S1, the user may decide to *quit()* (see transition from S1 to S2). Also, the *lpr* of the latter transition (i.e., *lpr > 0*) reflects that an event trace must always end with a *quit()* request for it to be a valid event trace for certification.

Table 1. Algorithm for checking compliance of event traces with ETOCB

```
CheckEvent(e, state, nstate, CountES[e,state], CountS[state], valid) {
// CountES[e,state] is the total number of occurrences of e in state
// CountS[state] is the total number of occurrences of any event in state
  if there is t in state.transitions such that t.event = e then {
    CountES[e,state] = CountES[e,state] + 1;
    CountS[state] = CountS[state] + 1; nstate = t.ds; valid = true }
  else
    {valid = false}
}
Boolean UpdateCounts(trace){
/* ValidPR[e,s] indicates the satisfaction of expected frequency range of
   all events of all state transitions */
Set CountES[e,s] to 0 for all states s and events e of its transitions;
Set CountS[s] to 0 for all states s;
Set ValidPR[e,s] to false for all states s and events e of its transitions;
CST = ETOCB.s0; //CST is the current state
NST = nil;
validTrace = true;
While not end of event trace and validTrace do {
  e = next non processed event in trace;
  CheckEvent(e, CST, NST, CountES[e,CST], CountS[CST], validTrace);
  if validTrace {
    for each t in CST.transitions do {
      if (CountES[t.e,CST]/CountS[CST] in R(t.e.lpr, t.e.upr)) {
        ValidPR[t.e,CST] = true}
    }
  CST = NST
  }
  return (validTrace)
}
```

The existence of the ETOCB model enables the CUMULUS infrastructure to check if a representative sample of the behaviour of TOC has been considered before a certificate can be issued. The check of the coverage of ETOCB by the stream of TOC events that has been processed by CUMULUS is carried according to the algorithm of Table 1. The algorithm *UpdateCounts()* in the figure checks if each next event in the event trace is consistent with the ordering of events in ETOCB. If it is not, *UpdateCounts()* reports the trace as invalid (as relative frequencies would not matter). If an encountered event is valid, *UpdateCounts()* updates the relative frequency of it in the current state (see array *CountES[e,state]*). It also updates the array *ValidPR[e,s]*, which indicates if the expected frequency range of the current event *e* in state *s* is preserved by the current relative frequencies of events. *ValidPR[e,s]* can be checked once all other sufficiency conditions (e.g., period of monitoring) are established to check if the coverage sufficiency conditions w.r.t. ETOCB are also satisfied.

3.2   Specification and Execution of Life Cycle Model

The life cycle model (LCM) in a certification model defines the process by which certificates can be generated and managed (e.g., monitored, issued, suspended, revoked). LCM is a compulsory element of a certification model as it enables a certification authority to specify with full precision the certification process, by defining the different states of certificates that can be generated by the certification model and which events should change it. During the operation of the CUMULUS framework, the LCM is used to monitor on-going certification processes, determine the state at which they are (e.g., collecting monitoring evidence, checking validity conditions prior to issuing a certificate) and, depending on it, update the state of the certificate that may be generated by the process.

A life cycle model (LCM) is defined as a state transition model of the form

$$\mathtt{LCM} = \mathtt{<S_{init},\ States,\ Trans>}$$

In an LCM, (i) *States* is the finite set of states of it (a state may be an atomic state or a composite state specified by another embedded LCM); (ii) s_{init} is the initial state of the process; and (iii) *Trans* is a finite set of transitions between two states. *Trans* includes elements of the form $(s_i,\ s_j,\ e,\ g,\ a)$ where s_i is the origin state of the transition; s_j is the destination state of the transition; e is the signature of the event triggering the transition; g is guard condition that must be satisfied for the transition to take place; and a is a set of actions that should be executed if the transition takes place. In an LCM, e must be an element of the *provided* interface of CUMULUS (e.g., the operation enabling the notification of monitoring events, the operation to be executed if the user of the framework wishes to suspend or revoke a certificate).

An example of an LCM is shown in Fig. 3. The LCM in the figure has an initial state called *Activated* and the states *InsufficientEvidence*, *Pre-Issued*, *Issued*, and *Revoked*. It also has two composite states: *Continuous Monitoring* and *Issuing*.

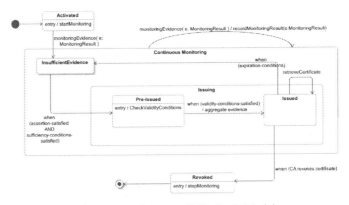

Fig. 3. UML diagram of Life-Cycle Model

According to the model, after a certificate is activated, it moves to the *InsufficientE-vidence* state, at which the monitoring evidence that is relevant to it starts getting accumulated. When the accumulated evidence becomes sufficient according to the *EvidenceSufficiencyConditions* specified in the MBCM, and there have been no violations of the monitoring rule that defines the security property (i.e., the security property of the MBCM is satisfied), the certificate moves to the state *Pre-Issued*. At this state, the certification infrastructure will check if the extra validity conditions for the certificate type (if any) are satisfied and, if they are, the certificate will move to the state *Issued*. In this state, any interested party with appropriate authority can retrieve the issued certificate from the CUMULUS infrastructure. Whilst a certificate is at the *Issuing* state, monitoring continues and if a violation of the monitoring rule of the MBCM is detected, the certificate moves to the *Revoked* state at which it will no longer be valid and available. It should be noted, that for readability purposes, in Fig. 3, we have used condition labels that indicate the meaning of the relevant conditions. In the actual specification of LCM, however, conditions are declared by their unique XML level IDs, which enable condition elements to be retrieved and checked against the evidence database of the CUMULUS infrastructure.

The LCM of a certification model is used by the CUMULUS framework to monitor the overall certification process and update the status of certificates that may be generated according to it. More specifically, starting from the initial state of the LCM the framework will process all events according to the model. This processing is based on the algorithm of Table 2. The events received/generated by the framework during the certification process are placed in a queue. An event can be a condition that is met (e.g., *EvidenceSufficiencyCondition*, aggregation period, expiration condition etc.). The algorithm checks if there is an event in the queue that matches an event of a listed transition of the current state of the LCM and if the guard condition of it (if any) is satisfied. When these conditions are satisfied for the specific transition, the algorithm executes the actions for the transition, and sets the status of the certificate that is being handled by the process, to the state that the transition leads to. To check the conditions associated with the transitions of an LCM, the algorithm pulls regularly data from the database storing the monitoring evidence gathered, and checks the conditions against it (e.g., see condition *assertion-satisfied* in the LCM of Fig. 3).

Table 2. Algorithm of the Life Cycle Manager component

```
State ChooseTransition(State curstate, EventQueue queue){
  top = queue.head(); //returns null when queue is empty
  trev = {t ∈ transitions(curstate): top≠null && t.event()=top};
  //trans matching events
  trem = {t ∈ transitions(curstate): t.event() = ""}; //trans with no events
  enev = {t ∈ trev: satisfied(guard(t))}; //trans with True guard & match event
  enem = {t ∈ trem: satisfied(guard(t))}; //trans with True guard but no event
  t = null;
  if (enev = 0 && enem = 0){
    if (top≠null) throw invalidEvent; //non matching event from the queue
    else return(curstate);
  } else if (enev ≠ 0) { //select transition with event
    t = select (enev);
    queue.pop();
  } else { //select transition with True guard but no event
    t = select (enem);
  }
  for (a : retrieveActions(t)) { //retrieve transition actions
    execute(a); //execute actions
  }
  return t.nextState(); //return the new state
}
```

4   Evaluation

In order to evaluate the performance of our monitoring-based certification approach, we have conducted an experiment based on a case study involving the certification of a real system. The system that we selected was the open source MySQL server [21]. Our choice was influenced by: (a) the complexity of this system, (b) the existence of a Protection Profile generated by Oracle that specifies security properties for such systems based on Common Criteria [9] (aka *Security Functional Requirements (SFR)*), and (c) the existence of benchmarks for creating realistic workloads for the MySQL server that would enable us evaluate our automated certification process in realistic conditions. Moreover, since our approach does not support interventions with the purpose of addressing or restoring security violations, we focus only on the evaluation criteria of the MySQL server, based on the selected Protection Profile.

The experiment that we set up to evaluate our approach realised a certification process for the security functional requirement FIA_UID.1.2 for the MySQL Server, based on a certification model including the assertions as described in Sect. 3. We also used the RUBiS benchmark [24] to produce realistic workloads of events for the MySQL server and monitor the server for certification purposes during the execution of these workloads. RUBiS is an auction site prototype, similar to eBay, which implements the core functionality of an auction site, i.e., selling, browsing and bidding. To capture events (i.e., logs of queries) from the operation of the server, we used the MySQL AUDIT Plugin developed by McAfee [20]. This plugin captured the logs created during the execution of the RUBiS workloads against the server. The events logged by the plugin were initially exported as *.json* files and subsequently parsed and converted into events, in the .xml format required by the CUMULUS infrastructure. All the different systems used in our experiment, including RUBiS, MySQL, EVEREST and CUMULUS were deployed on a cloud cluster involving a test-bed Cloud cluster equipped with four 4-core server machines each running at 2.20GHz, with 8GM of main memory, 450GB of disk space under Ubuntu 3.8.0.

The basic measure that we used in order to evaluate the performance of the certification process was the average time for making a decision about the monitoring assertion formulas in the model, called decision delay or *d-delay*. d-delay measures the difference between the time point when the latest event that is needed in order to make a decision about the satisfaction or otherwise of a monitoring formula occurs (t_c) and the time when following the capture and processing of the event, the monitor makes a decision on whether the formula is satisfied (t_p), i.e., $d = t_p - t_c$. Based on d-delay measures for individual instances of monitoring formulas, we calculated the average delay in the monitoring process using following formula $ave(d) = \Sigma d/N$ where: (i) d is the d-delay of each monitoring rule instance, and (ii) N is the total number of monitoring rule instances for which a decision was made.

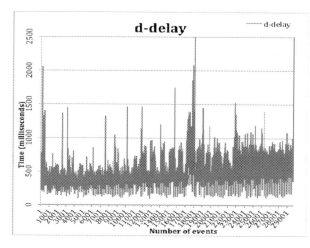

Events	Ave(d)
[1-5000]	326.02
[5001-10000]	324.47
[10001-15000]	357.59
[15001-20000]	443.31
[20001-25000]	413.87
[25001-29746]	443.83

Fig. 4. d-delay in execution of the database certification model

The graph in Fig. 4 shows the d values for the different events of the RUBiS benchmark that caused monitoring rule checks in the certification model, and the moving average of *d-delay* (*Ave(d)*) calculated over a window of 1000 events. The average value of d-delay across the whole RUBiS benchmark was 384.33 milliseconds (standard deviation = 118.92 milliseconds). As shown in the figure, *ave(d)* remained relatively stable throughout the execution of the benchmark, showing that certification results can be produced quickly following the actual events.

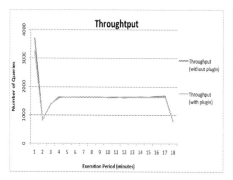
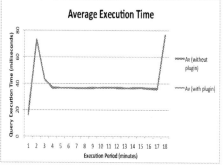

Fig. 5. Average throughput (i) and query processing time (ii) in executing the RUBIS benchmark on MySQL server with and without the MySQL AUDIT plugin

Table 2. Average throughput and query execution time with and without the AUDIT plugin

Min	Throughput		Average Query Processing Time (msecs)	
	No Plugin	*With plugin*	*No plugin*	*With plugin*
1	3688.9	3245	16.27	18.49
2	819.9	824.7	73.18	72.75
3	1390.9	1386.1	43.14	43.29
4	1615	1651.1	37.15	36.34
5	1630.4	1629.7	36.8	36.82
6	1638.2	1636.5	36.63	36.66
7	1630.7	1645.9	36.79	36.45
8	1633.9	1643.9	36.72	36.5
9	1624.4	1648.5	36.94	36.4
10	1630.2	1619.9	36.81	37.04
11	1630.9	1611.8	36.79	37.23
12	1617	1646.9	37.11	36.43
13	1638.8	1648.5	36.61	36.4
14	1651.5	1627.3	36.33	36.87
15	1631.3	1628	36.78	36.86
16	1665.5	1635.4	36.03	36.69
17	1677.4	1649.8	35.77	36.37
18	788.2	779.6	76.12	76.96

In addition to the time needed to generate certification results, the execution of a CUMULUS monitoring-based certification model may have an impact on the operation of TOC as it is necessary to instrument and/or configure the TOC in order to produce the events needed for the monitoring process that underpins certification. To evaluate this overhead in the case of the MySQL server, we executed the RUBiS benchmark without using the MySQL audit plugin in the server (*case (a)*) and with the use of the MySQL audit plugin in the server (*case (b)*). The overhead was estimated by calculating the average throughout (i.e., the number of queries executed per minute) of the server in 10 different executions of case (a) and 10 different executions of case (b). Each of these 20 executions involved the execution of the same number of RUBIS queries against the server (~30,000 queries) but the queries executed in each execution were selected randomly by the RUBIS system. The completion of the execution of the different query sets took on average 18 minutes.

The average throughput for cases (a) and (b) was measured per minute and the result is shown in the *Throughput* graph of Fig. 5. As shown in this graph the use of the MySQL AUDIT plugin had almost a very minor effect on the performance of the server. The same is evident from *Average Execution Time* graph in Fig. 5, which shows the average execution time per RUBIS query (in milliseconds), for every minute during the execution period. The absence of any significant effect is also evident from which shows the actual throughput and average query execution times for (a) and (b). The main difference in query execution time was observed only in the initial stage of the execution of each query set, when RUBiS sent queries to establish the connection to MySQL for each transaction thread.

5   Related Work

Research related to our approach includes work for service certification, cloud security and cloud monitoring. In this section we give an overview of this work.

Similar approaches in the field of security certification schemes focus mostly on concrete software components and provide self-assessed, human-readable certificates. As a result, these approaches cannot be integrated into dynamic service processes that require machine-readable certificates. Significant work on the representation and use of digital certificates in SOA systems was done in the FP7 Project ASSERT4SOA. This project developed a test-based certification of software services and a framework for representing and using machine-readable certificates, known as ASSERTS.

Research on the certification of cloud services is still in an early stage. The work of Grobauer et al. [12], assess some vulnerabilities of cloud computing, and outlines the main reason of the existence of such vulnerabilities as the lack of certification schemes and security metrics. Heiser and Nicolett [13] have evaluated the cloud security risks and proposed an IT risks sharing scheme. Furthermore, Anisetti et al [1] presented a trusted model for certifying cloud services, by delegating different dynamic testing mechanisms.

A commonly used framework for cloud certification is CSA's Cloud Controls Matrix (CCM) [5]. CCM contains a comprehensive set of baseline controls to assess the information security assurance level of cloud providers and maps these controls to existing frameworks such as ISO/IEC 27001-2013, PCI DSS Cloud Guideline [23], COBIT [6], NIST [15], or IT Baseline Protection Catalogues [16].

The Cloud Security Alliance has also developed and launched in 2011 the CSA Security, Trust and Assurance Registry (STAR) Program [27], which is a third party independent assessment of the security of a cloud service provider. STAR is based on a multi-layered structure defined by Open Certification Framework (OCF) Working Group [8] and on the requirements of the ISO/IEC 27001 management system standard together with the CSA CCM. STAR approach consists of three different levels of certification. Our approach is similar to the third level of STAR, which is the CSA STAR Continuous Monitoring, which is meant to enable automation of auditing, assessment, monitoring and certification of security practices of cloud providers.

Cloud monitoring has been supported by several monitoring systems. Most of them, however, focus on monitoring performance and SLAs monitoring rather than security properties (e.g., [15][3]) and do not support security certification.

6   Conclusion

In this paper, we have presented an automated certification approach for cloud services based on continuous monitoring. We have described the core mechanisms of our approach that can be used to specify and realise a certification process for the security of cloud services. We have also given an example showing how the approach can be used to realise, in an automated manner, the certification of a security property defined in a Common Criteria protection profile for database systems.

The certification model underpinning this example has been used to evaluate our approach as part of an experiment in which we used the MySQL server. The results of this evaluation showed that the certification process that we proposed can produce results in an automated manner, fast and without interfering significantly with the performance of the system that is certified. The average time complexity of the monitoring algorithm is N*M, where N is the average number of events and M is the average number of rule instances, at different time periods during the monitoring process. M depends on the number of different events in assertions and the time constraints between them. The average delay in checking assertions is experimentally shown not to be significant. Basic security properties (integrity, availability, confidentiality) can be expressed by assertions of such complexity as shown in the literature. Hence, our approach is feasible for large numbers of events. A video of a demo of the implementation of our approach is available from: *http://youtu.be/HWb_dA2UCxM*.

Our on-going work focuses on a further evaluation of our approach for different types security properties and cloud services. We are also investigating the use of model checking techniques to verify statically properties of certification models.

Acknowledgment. The work presented in this paper has been partially funded by the EU FP7 project CUMULUS (grant no 318580).

References

1. Anisetti, M., Ardagna, C. A. and Damiani, E.: A certification-based trust model for autonomic cloud computing systems. In: Int. Conf. on Cloud and Autonomic Computing (CAC 2014), London, UK (2014)
2. Ardagna, C.A., Asal, R., Damiani, E., Vu, Q.V.: From Security to Assurance in the Cloud: A Survey. ACM Computing Surveys (CSUR) **48**(1), Article 2, July 2015
3. Barham, P., et al.: Xen and the art of virtualization. ACM SIGOPS Operating Systems Review **37**(5) (2003). ACM
4. Bezzi, M., Sabetta, A., Spanoudakis, G.: An architecture for certification-aware service discovery. In: 1st Int. IEEE Workshop on Securing Services on the Cloud, pp. 14–21 (2011)
5. Cloud Security Alliance, Cloud Controls Matrix. https://cloudsecurityalliance.org/research/ccm/
6. COBIT, IT Assurance Guide: Using COBIT, Control Objectives for Information and related Technology. Information Systems Audit and Control Association (2007)
7. Common Criteria (CC) for Information Technology Security Evaluation, CCDB USB Working Group, 2012, part 1-3. http://www.commoncriteriaportal.org
8. CSA: Open Certification Framework. https://cloudsecurityalliance.org/research/ocf/
9. Database Management System Protection Profile, Issue 2.1, May 2000. http://www.commoncriteriaportal.org/files/ppfiles/T129%20-%20PP%20v2.1%20%28dbms.pp%5B1%5D%29.pdf
10. Egea, M., Mahbub, K., Spanoudakis, G., Vieira, M.R.: A certification framework for cloud security properties: the monitoring path. In: Felici, M., Fernández-Gago, C. (eds.) A4Cloud 2014. LNCS, vol. 8937, pp. 63–77. Springer, Heidelberg (2015)

11. ENISA, Security Certification Practice in the EU: Information Security Management Systems– A Case Study, v1, October 2013. https://www.enisa.europa.eu/

12. Grobauer, B., Walloschek, T., Stocker, E.: Understanding Cloud Computing Vulnerabilities. Security & Privacy, IEEE **9**(2), 50–57 (2011)

13. Heiser, J., Nicolett, M.: Assessing the Security Risks of Cloud Computing. Gartner TR (2008)

14. Heiser, J., Nicolett, M.: Assessing the security risks of cloud computing, 1–6 (2008)

15. IT Baseline Protection Catalogs. http://www.bsi.de/gshb/index.htm

16. Katopodis, S., Spanoudakis, G., Mahbub, K.: Towards hybrid cloud service certification models. In: 2014 IEEE International Conference on Services Computing, pp. 394–399

17. Krotsiani, M., Spanoudakis, G.: Continuous certification of non-repudiation in cloud storage services. In: 4th IEEE Int. Symp. on rust and Security in Cloud Computing (2014)

18. Krotsiani, M., Spanoudakis, G., Mahbub, K.: Incremental certification of cloud services. In: 7th Int. Conf. on Emerging Security Information, Systems and Technologies (2013)

19. Lagazio, M., Barnard-Wills, D., Rodrigues, R., Wright, D.: Certification Schemes for Cloud Computing. EU Commission Report, ISBN 978-92-79-39392-1, doi:10.2759/64404

20. McAfee MySQL AUDIT Plugin. https://github.com/mcafee/mysql-audit

21. MySQL server. http://www.mysql.com/

22. National Institute of Standards and Technology: Information Security Handbook: A Guide for Managers. NIST Special Publication 800-100, October 2006

23. Payment Card Industry Data Security Standard (PCI DSS). https://www.pcisecuritystandards.org/security_standards/documents.php?document=dss_cloud_computing_guidelines

24. RUBiS Benchmark. http://rubis.ow2.org/

25. Shanahan, M.: The event calculus explained. In: Veloso, M.M., Wooldridge, M.J. (eds.) Artificial Intelligence Today. LNCS (LNAI), vol. 1600, pp. 409–430. Springer, Heidelberg (1999)

26. Spanoudakis, G., Kloukinas C., Mahbub K.: The serenity runtime monitoring framework. In: Security and Dependability for Ambient Intelligence, pp. 213–237. Springer (2009)

27. STAR Certification, Cloud Security Alliance. https://cloudsecurityalliance.org/star/

28. Emeakaroha, V.C., et al.: DeSVi: an architecture for detecting SLA violations in cloud computing infrastructures. In: 2nd Int. ICST Conference on Cloud Computing (2010)

Balancing Trust and Risk in Access Control

Alessandro Armando[1,2], Michele Bezzi[3($\boxtimes$)], Francesco Di Cerbo[3],
and Nadia Metoui[1,4]

[1] Security & Trust Unit, FBK-Irst, Trento, Italy
[2] DIBRIS, University of Genova, Genoa, Italy
[3] SAP Product Security Research, Sophia Antipolis, France
[4] DISI, University of Trento, Trento, Italy

Abstract. The increasing availability of large and diverse datasets (*big data*) calls for increased flexibility in access control so to improve the exploitation of the data. Risk-aware access control systems offer a natural approach to the problem. We propose a novel access control framework that combines trust with risk and supports access control in dynamic contexts through trust enhancement mechanisms and risk mitigation strategies. This allows to strike a balance between the risk associated with a data request and the trustworthiness of the requester. If the risk is too large compared to the trust level, then the framework can identify adaptive strategies leading to a decrease of the risk (e.g., by removing/obfuscation part of the data through anonymization) or to increase the trust level (e.g., by asking for additional obligations to the requester). We outline a modular architecture to realize our model, and we describe how these strategies can be actually realized in a realistic use case.

Keywords: Trust · Privacy · Risk

1 Introduction

The increasing availability of large and diverse datasets (*big data*) calls for increased flexibility in access control so to improve the exploitation of the data. Indeed, organizations are now in the position to exploit these diverse datasets to create new data-based businesses or optimizing existing processes (real-time customization, predictive analytics, etc.). Yet, they are often unable to fully leverage this potential due to the lack of appropriate data release mechanisms ensuring that sensitive information is not disclosed. As a consequence, most organizations still strongly limit (even internally) the sharing and dissemination of data making most of the information unavailable to decision-makers, and thus they do not fully exploit the power of these new data sources.

To overcome the problem, access control systems must weigh the risks against the trustworthiness of the incoming requests. In other words, access control decisions must be based on an estimation of expected cost and benefits, and not (as in traditional access control systems) on a predefined policy that statically defines

© Springer International Publishing Switzerland 2015
C. Debruyne et al. (Eds.): OTM 2015 Conferences, LNCS 9415, pp. 660–676, 2015.
DOI: 10.1007/978-3-319-26148-5_45

what accesses are allowed and denied. In other words, in Risk-based Access control for each access request, the corresponding risk is estimated and if the risk is less than a threshold then access is guaranteed, otherwise it is denied. The aim is to be more permissive than in traditional access control system by allowing for a better exploitation of data. Although existing risk-based access control models provide an important step towards a better management and exploitation of data, they have a number of drawbacks which limit their effectiveness. In particular, most of the existing risk-based systems only support binary access decisions: the outcome is *allowed* or *denied*, whereas in real-life we often have exceptions based on additional conditions (e.g., *"I cannot provide this information, unless you sign the following non-disclosure agreement."* or *"I cannot disclose these data, because they contain personal identifiable information, but I can disclose an anonymized version of the data."*). In other words, if the system can propose appropriate risk mitigation measures, and they are accepted by the requester, a relevant part of additional information can be shared.

In this paper we propose a novel access control framework that combines trust with risk and supports access control in dynamic contexts through trust enhancement mechanisms and risk mitigation strategies. This allows us to strike a balance between the risk and the trustworthiness of the data request. If the risk is too large compared to the trust level, then the framework can identify adaptive strategies that can decrease the risk (e.g., by removing/obfuscating part of the data through anonymization) and/or increase the trust level (e.g., by asking for additional obligation to the requester).

Our framework enjoys a number of features:

1. it explicitly models trust and risk, which are the key factors of any business decision;
2. it increases the flexibility of existing risk-aware access control, by introducing trust;
3. it supports complex authorization scenarios by simply changing the configuration (trust and risk configuration modules, and corresponding mitigation/enhancement strategies).

In the next section we provide a motivating use case. The use case illustrates how the framework can work in practice, addressing access control requirements in a natural way, that would otherwise need complex authorization structure and calibration. In Section 3 we introduce our risk- and trust-based access control model. In Section 4 we provide an architectural view of our access control framework. With the reference to our use case, in Section 5 and, in Section 6, we discuss approaches to risk evaluation and mitigation that can be supported by our framework. In Section 8, we discuss the related work and in Section 9 we conclude with some final remarks.

2   Use Case

Consider a company with an ERP system with a Human Resource (HR) Management module, enabled with the proposed Trust and Risk-aware access control

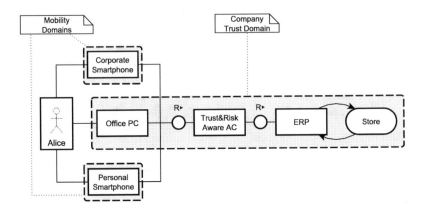

Fig. 1. Use Case: Alice accessing an HR report with personal data covered by EU Directive on Data Protection 95/46/EC.

system (see Fig. 1). By using the ERP functionalities corporate user Alice can generate an HR report containing a list of employees with their location and salaries. The report contains sensitive information and personal data, and the company has strict rules for accessing the data such as security measures to minimize the disclosure risk when data are moved outside the company. The risk scenario considered is the leakage of the the salary information associated to a specific employee (re-identification risk). To ensure compliance with EU data protection laws, additional restrictions must be applied if data are accessed outside EU.

In her daily business, Alice may access the report using multiple devices: her office PC at corporate premises, a corporate smartphone and her own smartphone. Access in mobility suffers from a high level of risk, since it is more exposed to external attacks and, depending on the geographical location, different rules may apply. A conservative approach, easily implementable with traditional access control systems, would imply a security policy like that:

- if Alice is on premises, then access is granted
- if Alice is in mobility, access is denied as the security and compliance risks could be too high

Basically, access is limited to corporate premises, where full data can viewed whereas outside no information is available and no reports can be produced. Even though this approach could seem simplistic, many real-life access control systems offer a similar level of functionality [1].

Ideally, Alice would like to get a wider access to the data, and perform her business tasks (e.g., reporting) also in mobility, using different devices in multiple locations, but still keeping security risk under control, as summarized in Table 1.

In the next sections, we will show how these scenarios can be realized in our framework.

Table 1. Possible usage scenarios, comprising different devices and locations, and expected utility (i.e., type of reports needed) and security levels

	Scenario			Expected	
#	Device	Location	Administration	Utility	Security
1	PC	on premises	corporate	full access	no restriction
2	Smartphone	EU	corporate	grouped by country	medium risk
3	Smartphone	EU	personal	grouped by region	minimal risk
4	Smartphone	no EU	-	no access	no access

3 Model

At an abstract level, a risk- and trust-based access control framework can be represented by a function $Auth(Obj, u, p)$ defined as follows. User u is granted permission p on object obj iff the trustworthiness of the incoming request is larger or equal to the risk, i.e.,

$$Auth(Obj, u, p) = \begin{cases} \textbf{Allow}, & \text{if } (T(u, C) - R(obj, p, C)) \geq 0 \\ \textbf{Deny}, & \text{otherwise} \end{cases} \quad (1)$$

where $T(u, C)$ is the trustworthiness of the request, which depends on user u and context information C (e.g., location of the requester) and $R(obj, p, C)$ is the risk, which depends on the requested object obj (e.g. a file) to the permission p (e.g., read or write)[1] and context C.

If access is denied, then there are two possible methods for improving the accessibility to the resource: *(i)* applying risk mitigation strategies to decrease R, or *(ii)* increase the trustworthiness T, until the condition condition $T > R$ is granted. We will discuss how risk and trust can be modeled, and possible mechanisms to reduce/increase their values in the next subsections.

3.1 Modeling Trust

Trust is a wide concept, and different definitions have been proposed in literature [4]. To our scope we can use the definition by McKnight and Chervany [5], which better related to the concepts of utility and risk attitude.[2]

> *Trust is the extent to which one party is willing to depend on something or somebody in a given situation with a feeling of relative security, even though negative consequences are possible.*

---

[1] In most cases the dependency of risk from permission is mediated by roles. For the sake of simplicity, we do not consider here roles, for an extension of this model including roles, we can follow the lines of the models described in [2,3].

[2] A popular used definition is from Gambetta [6], which stresses the *reliability* aspects of trust. For a discussion see [4].

In our case, we consider trust expressing the level of confidence the resource controller has on the user u not misusing the resource he wants to access. We expect this level to depend on the user u (identity, role, and previous behavior) and on the given context C (e.g., the device or system environment he is using).

Trust values are assigned in various ways depending on the specific use cases. For example in reputation models, trust assessments from other entities are combined to compose a trust evaluation, or in behavioral trust a value is assigned based on the historical records of transactions [4]. Trust can be also derived from assessing a set of *trust indicators* such as security metrics (e.g., level of authentication) and from trust assertions (e.g. stamp of approval) issued by trusted entities (i.e., certification authorities).

From the risk-based system point of view, the identity of the requester heavily depends on the effectiveness of the authentication mechanism employed. To take into account this, the trustworthiness of user u in context C, say $T_{eff}(u, C)$, should take into account the possibility that the authentication is not carried out correctly (e.g., an identity theft scenario). This situation can be modeled in our framework by replacing $T(u, C)$ with $T_{eff}(u, C)$ in (1), where

$$T_{eff}(u) = T(u)(1 - P_{it}) + T(u' \neq u)P_{it}$$

where $T(u' \neq u)$ is the Trust associated to any, not specified, other user that is not u, in practice it should be zero or negligible and P_{it} is the probability of an identity theft. P_{it} represents the strength of the authentication mechanisms.

3.2   Modeling Risk

Risk is defined by the likelihood and the impact of the occurrence of one or more a series of failure scenarios $s \in S$ (also called risk scenarios). Although different quantitative risk methodologies exist, see [7] and references therein, for independent scenarios as risk can be computed by:

$$R(obj, p) = \sum_{s \in S(C)} P(s)I(s)$$

where S is the set of possible failure scenarios related to the access of p in the context C, $P(s)$ is the probability of occurrence of the failure scenario s, and $I(s)$ the associated impact (often measured as monetary cost).

The risk exposure can be decreased implementing a set of controls and mechanisms, and in this case we refer it as residual risk. In addition, temporary risk mitigation strategies can be applied to further reduce the risk. In case of access control, they include for example, decreasing the probability of failure, by obfuscating (part of) the data (e.g., anonymization) or imposing usage control restrictions (e.g., data retention period); or decreasing the impact, by insurance. Eq. 1 implies that trust and risk are measured in the same units. Ideally, risk should be measured in monetary units (since the impact is the cost of occurrence of a certain scenario), and, accordingly, trust should have the same units, as in the previous example for financial transactions. Unfortunately, estimating risk in information systems is much less consolidated practice, due to: i) the limited availability of historical data on failure scenarios, which makes difficult to estimate the corresponding probabilities. ii) the difficulty to estimate the impact of a failure to protect an intangible digital assets.[3]

To overcome these problems, existing risk based access control systems use various approaches: they estimate these values from the parameters of traditional (non-risk based) access control models (e.g., see [9] for multi-level security models), they use relative measures for both trust and risk (in practice they normalize these quantities in the interval $[0, 1]$, see [3]), or they use heuristics for estimating these numbers from qualitative risk assessments [7].

In the sequel, to demonstrate our approach, we will consider a single risk factor related to data privacy (re-identification risk). This allows us to compare trust, normalized in the interval $[0, 1]$, directly with the probability of the risk scenario. The model can clearly include any other security risk factors, as far as a quantitative risk estimation is possible, for example, deriving risk values from the rating of the Common Vulnerability Scoring System (CVSS) [10].

4   Architecture

In this section we present an abstract architecture for our Trust and Risk-aware Access Control Framework. The architecture, depicted in Figure 2, is composed of four main modules that are described in the remaining part of the section. To better illustrate their functionalities, we will use the use case as running example, i.e., we focus on re-identification risk and anonymization as risk mitigation strategies, and obligation as a means for trust enhancement. This architecture, however, is conceived to deal with arbitrary strategies and trust/risk functions.

Risk-Aware Access Control Module is the entry point to our system, through which users can submit requests to retrieve data from the underlying database. The module evaluates the access authorizations of the data requester and grants or denies access. To do so, the Risk-Aware Access Control module will call the Risk Estimation Module to determine the risk level of the request and the Trust Estimation Module to determine the requester's and context trust. Trust and Risk Mitigation Module enters into play to increase trust and reduce risk if necessary.

---

[3] For these reasons, so far, most of the risk assessments for information system are qualitative, where probability and impacts are classified in broad categories and no explicit numerical values are assigned (e.g., in many application of ISO 27005:2011 [8]).

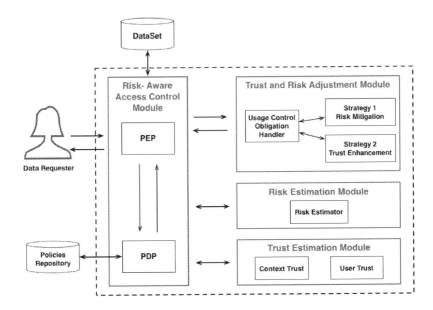

Fig. 2. Architecture of the Trust and Risk-aware Access Control framework

This module is realized internally with a PEP-PDP[4] pair (a Policy Enforcement Point and Policy Decision Point respectively). A PIP[5] (Policy Information Point) is used to provide additional attributes for the requester and the context.

Risk Estimation Module. It is used to determine the level of risk, based on the data requested, context and on the criteria defined in the risk estimator configuration. For example, for re-identification risk, this configuration includes the metrics respect to domain-specific knowledge about what information is to be considered critical or not. Besides the evaluation of the risk, this module produces an estimation of the minimal anonymization level to be applied in order to meet the required risk level. (i.e., in case of k-anonymity metric, the risk estimation module computes the minimal value of k that respects the risk threshold constraint, see Section 5).

Trust Estimation Module. It is used to compute the trust aspects of a request. In particular, it can take into account user attributes like role, organizational units, age for instance; as well as context attributes, like the geo-

---

[4] In the XACML (eXtensible Access Control Markup Language) standard [11] the PDP is the component that evaluates an access request against an authorisation policy, and issues an access decision. PEP Policy Enforcement Point is the point that intercept user's request, calls the PDP for an access decision, and then it enforces this decision by allowing or denying the access.

[5] The PIP (in XACML) is the module that can be called to provide additional information about resource, requester or environment.

graphic location where a request was created, the software used to issue it as well as the characteristics of a network connection.

Trust and Risk Adjustment Module. This module is activated by the Risk-Based Access Control module in order to mitigate risk and/or to increase the trust level for the request, when the access risk to the requested resource exceeds the trust level, in such a case, two possible options are available:
- *Decrease Risk* by applying optimal risk mitigation strategies (e.g., anonymization operations, which decrease risk but minimise the information loss).
- *Enhance Trust* by complementing an authorization decision with access and usage control obligations (explained in the following Sect. 6). These obligations can condition the acceptance of a request to the execution of operations at the moment of the request or when specific events occur; for example, an usage control obligation may prescribe the deletion of a resource after that a retention period expires. If such obligation is guaranteed to be enforced, then the trust estimation can be increased.

The usage control obligations Handler will enforce the selected risk adjustment strategy.

5   Risk Evaluation and Mitigation

The risk of privacy violations is often associated with the concept of *individual identifiability*, used in most privacy laws e.g. EU data protection directive [12], Health Insurance Portability and Accountability Act (HIPAA) [13], etc.). Immunity against individual identifiability can be interpreted as taking measures to prevent the identification or learning of private information about any individual in a dataset with probability or confidence greater than a certain threshold [14], or, in other terms, ensuring a certain level of anonymity to each individual in the dataset. In this section we will discuss how re-identification risk can be measured and how anonymization can be used to mitigate the risk associated with a tabular-data extraction request while querying a privacy-sensitive dataset, as in our use case.

From a privacy perspective, attributes (or columns) in a dataset can be classified as follows:

- *Identifiers.* These are data attributes that can uniquely identify individuals. Examples of identifiers are Name/Last Name, the Social Security Number, and the passport number.
- *Quasi-identifiers (QIs) or key attributes* [15]. These are the attributes that, when combined, can be used to identify an individual. Examples of QIs are the postal code, age, job function, location, and gender.
- *Sensitive attributes.* These attributes contain intrinsically sensitive information about an individual (e.g., diseases, political or religious views, income) or business (e.g., salary figures, restricted financial data or sensitive survey answers).

Table 2. Re-identification risk for different anonymization methods

Risk	Anonymization Method
Full risk	$k = 1$ $(P = 1.0)$
Medium risk	$k = 2$ $(P = 0.5)$
Minimal risk	$k = 10$ $(P = 0.1)$

In presence of identifiers the re-identification risk is clearly maximum (i.e., probability of re-identification $P = 1$), but even if identifiers are removed, combining QIs individuals can be singled out and this implies a high risk. To measure this risk various privacy metrics have been proposed in the literature. These metrics differ in a number of ways, but they all express the risk of disclosing personal-identifiable information when releasing a given dataset (see [16,14] for a review). In the context of re-identification, the most popular one is k-anonymity [17][6]. The k-anonymity condition requires that *every* combination of QIs is shared by at least k records in the dataset. A large k value indicates that the dataset has a low re-identification risk, because, at best, an attacker has a probability $P = 1/k$ to re-identify a record (i.e., associate the sensitive attribute of a record to the identity of a respondent). For example, the (unaltered) table in Table 4, has clearly $k = 1$ (name/lastname are unique identifiers), and $P = 1$ for ri-identification risk (for the sake of simplicity we do not consider impact here).

A possible way to decrease the disclosure risk is anonymization. Anonymization is a commonly used practice to reduce privacy risk, consisting in obfuscating, in part or completely, the personal identifiable information in a dataset. Anonymization methods include [19]:

- *Suppression:* Removal of certain records or part of these records (columns, tuples, etc., such name/last name column);
- *Generalization:* Recoding data into broader classes (e.g., releasing only the first two digits of the zip code or replacing towns with country or regions) or by rounding/clustering numerical data;

Traditionally, anonymization is run offline, but more recently risk-based access control models, which use in-the-fly anonymization as mitigation strategy have been proposed [20]. In practice, to minimize the risk to a certain level (compared to the trust threshold), anonymization methods are applied to decrease the probability of re-identification (or, in other words, by increasing k), common values for k in anonymized data are in range between 2 and 30 [21], depending on the use cases.

In our example, we can take $k = 2$ $(P = 0.5)$ as *medium* risk (see the 'expected security' column in Table 1) and $k = 10$ $(P = 0.1)$ for *minimal* risk. Table 2 summarizes the values for k in relation with the different risk expectations.

---

[6] Other privacy metrics exist (for example, ℓ-diversity, and t-closeness, see [18] for a review), but k-anonymity is still a *de-facto* standard in real applications.

Table 3. Trust values in different contexts C

Context	$T(u, C)$
On premise	1.0
Mobility (secure)	0.5
Mobility (standard)	0.1
Mobility (outside EU)	0.0

6   Trust Enhancement by Obligations

Obligations are actions or operations that must be carried out as result of an authorization decision. In the standard XACML architecture [11], obligations are defined as parts of policies and included in authorization responses created by the PDP; they are enforced by the PEP on behalf of the subject issuing the authorization request. Besides their application as outcome of authorization decisions, obligations may also be applied during or after the consumption of a requested resource or the execution of a requested operation [22,23]: for example, a policy may state a specific retention period for any copy of a resource whose access was granted to the requester. In these cases a trusted component must exist that is able to operate in real time as a PEP. This situation is generally referred as *Usage Control* (UC) [24]. UC models and mechanisms have been proposed to address privacy requirements [25], and applied to both the cloud and the mobile environments [26,27].

AC/UC policy definitions may comprise a broader set of directives, regulating runtime aspects originated from an authorized access; for example, a policy may prescribe to monitor the location where a mobile user consumes a resource and to react with a deletion obligation in case the user leaves the country. Such capabilities are particularly useful to achieve compliance with directives (law requirements or corporate policies): for example, data privacy regulations introduced in Section 5 impose the application of certain principles and UC can enforce automatically some aspects [28].

Therefore, the usage of obligations, when their enforcement is guaranteed, can be considered as a means to enhance a request's trust estimation in our proposed system. In fact, it can be assumed that prescriptions specified by a security policy are applied and that they can regulate how resources or operations are used, thus ensuring their compliance. For instance, in our use case the trust level could change with the context as shown in Table 3. For the sake of simplicity we assume that trust is independent from the specific user, i.e., $T(u, C) = T(u', C)$ for all contexts C and users u and u'. Therefore, for the most trusted environment (On premise) we have $T(u, C) = 1$, whereas for requests coming from outside the EU that cannot be trusted and we set $T(u, C) = 0$.

Table 4. HR report: original view

Name	Job	Location	**Salary**
Timothy Lulic	Senior Developer	London	46200
Alice Salamon	Support	London	45000
Perry Coda	Junior Developer	London	32000
Tom Torreira	Admin	Milan	28000
Ron Savic	Senior Developer	Rome	56000
Omer Regini	Senior Developer	Shanghai	47000
Bob Eramo	Support	Macau	18000
Amber Mesb	Admin	Bangalore	30000
Elise Moisander	Admin	Bangalore	31000

7   Application to the Use Case

We now show how our framework can support the scenarios introduced in Section 2 and achieve the expected utility and security levels. In all scenarios considered, we assume user Alice requests access to the data listed in Table 4.

Scenario #1: Access from Business Environment. The Risk Estimation module is called to estimate the re-identification risk associated to the dataset: $R(obj, p, C) = 1$, since the report contains personal data with an elevate re-identification risk. The Trust Estimation module in turn computes the trust associated to the context where the request is originated: $T(u, C) = 1$, since Alice is in her office. Therefore, $Auth(Obj, u, p) = $ **Allow** and therefore access is granted.

Scenario #2: Access in Mobility from EU Using Corporate Smartphone. Since the request is performed in mobility $T(u, C) = 0.1$ and while $R(obj, p, C) = 1$. The Trust and Risk Adjustment module then triggers the trust enhancement and risk mitigation strategies. Specific AC/UC obligations are thus assigned to the report (e.g., do not share, delete after 2 hours, only usable in EU) to be enforced by an obligation enforcement engine deployed on the corporate smartphone. The application of these measures increases the trust in the context to $T(u, C) = 0.5$. To decrease risk, k-anonymity with $k = 2$ allows to reduce the re-identification risk to 0.5. Therefore, $Auth(Obj, u, p) = $ **Allow** and Alice receives the anonymized view of Table 5.

Scenario #3: Access in Mobility from EU Using Personal Smartphone. This scenario is similar to the previous one, with the notable exception that now no trust enhancing measures can be enforced on the mobile phone. Therefore, the Trust and Risk Adjustment module can only apply the risk mitigation strategy, by using k-anonymity with an greater value of k, i.e. $k = 10$, that will result in a re-identification risk of 0.1. Thus, $T(u, C) = 0.1$ (access though personal smartphone), $R(obj, p, C) = 0.1$ (after applying k-anonymity with $k = 10$), and

Table 5. HR report: anonymized view with $k = 2$.

Name	Job	Location	**Salary**
***	***	UK	46200
***	***	UK	45000
***	***	Italy	32000
***	***	Italy	28000
***	***	Italy	56000
***	***	China	47000
***	***	China	18000
***	***	India	30000
***	***	India	31000

Table 6. HR report: anonymized with $k = 4$.

Name	Job	Location	**Salary**
***	***	EMEA	46200
***	***	EMEA	45000
***	***	EMEA	32000
***	***	EMEA	28000
***	***	EMEA	56000
***	***	APAC	47000
***	***	APAC	18000
***	***	APAC	30000
***	***	APAC	31000

thus $Auth(Obj, u, p) =$ **Allow**. The report received by Alice in this scenario is given in Table 6[7].

Scenario #4: Access in Mobility from Outside EU with Personal Smartphone. In this case, the risk of violating the regulations is maximum. This means that the trust in the environment is 0, no mitigation strategies may be adopted and therefore $T(u, C) = 0$ (request from outside EU), $R(obj, p, C) = 1$, and thus $Auth(Obj, u, p) =$ **Deny**.

8 Related Work

Several approaches has been recently proposed to address the limitations of traditional access control models in terms of lack of flexibility, inability to handle contextual information, evaluation of the trustworthiness of users and in managing access risk.

---

[7] Table 6 is just included as exemplification and depicts the result of k-anonymity for $k = 4$.

Context-aware access control models propose the use of contextual information to determine access to resources, e.g. determining the decision based on temporal[29], or more general, environmental conditions [30], also in combination with risk models [31]. However these models, mostly, define in a static manner the context parameters with which the access to resources will be granted or denied.

A more dynamic approach is taken in risk and trust based access control models (e.g. [2,33,34,35,36]), where for each access request or permission activation, the corresponding risk is estimated and if the risk is less than a threshold (often associated with trust) then access is guaranteed, otherwise it is denied. Cheng et al. [33], following the multi-level-security paradigm, compute risk and trust thresholds from the sensitivity labels of the resource and clearance level of the users. They also consider what we define a trust enhancement mechanism (the authors call it risk mitigation strategy in their paper) that provides users with a limited amount of *tokens*, which allow them to access resources with risk higher than their trust level. The details on how this mechanism can be applied in real cases are not provided.

In another work, Chen et al. [2] introduced an abstract model which allows role activation based on a risk evaluation compared to predefined risk thresholds. Trust values are considered, and they impact (decreasing) risk calculation. If risk is too high, the model includes mitigation strategies, indicated as (system) obligations. The paper does not specify how to compute the risk thresholds, trust, and the structure and impact of obligations. In a derived model [32], mitigation strategies have been explicitly defined in terms of user obligations in addition to system obligation. An user obligation describes some actions that have to be fulfilled by the user to get access. Although the model does not consider explicitly trust, it introduces the concept of *diligence score*, which measured the diligence of the user to fulfill the obligations (as in behavioral trust model), and impact the risk estimation. An extension of the model proposed by Chen et al. [2] has been recently proposed [20,36], such work focuses on re-identification risk and anonymization is used as mitigation strategy (as in our paper).

Following the original Chen et al. [2] model, these papers consider trust as part of the risk value. As a consequence: *i)* trust enhancement and risk mitigation strategies are mixed, and it becomes difficult to find an optimal set of strategies to increase access, keeping risk under control, *ii)* trust thresholds become dependent on the risk scenario, decreasing the flexibility in presence of multiple risk factors. Our model solves these issues, clearly separating trust aspects from risk.

The impact of obligations on trust is also considered in other studies. We can distinguish between two categories of obligations: *provisions* or *pre-obligations* [37] are actions that must be executed as a pre-condition for authorization decision; *post-obligations* are actions that must be fulfilled after the authorization decision is made. In [38], the trust value of an user is impacted by his previous history of fulfilling or not post-obligations, also considering their level of criticality.

Other approaches have also incorporated user trust in privilege assignment Dimmock et al. [39] propose a framework where users are assigned to roles according to their trust level. Baracaldo et al. extended this idea in [3] and propose to mitigate access risk by lowering the trust level of misbehaving users in order to (temporarily) revoke critical privileges. This model includes separation of duties constraints in risk computation (which we do not consider in our), particularity relevant for addressing insider attack risk scenarios.

These models can be incorporated in the computation of the trust values in our model. Indeed in the scenario we proposed in Sect. 6, obligations increases the trust value, however we do not consider the history of previous obligation fulfillment, since we rely on the secure environment for assuring their enforcement.

9   Future Work and Conclusions

Motivated by the need to balance the advantages of big data availability, and stringent security and privacy requirements, novel access control paradigms are emerging. Risk plays a central role, and access control decisions can mimic the business decision process, where risk is assessed relatively to trust. We have proposed an access control framework based on these two factors (trust and risk) and showed that it can address complex authorization requirements by dynamically applying strategies for risk mitigation and trust enhancement. The possibility to play with both risk and trust at the same time and its application to a real use case are the main novelties of our work. Our framework can also be combined with more classical (policy-based) approach, as described in [20] for risk-based access control.

Although promising, our approach presents a number of open issues to be solved for a practical usage. In particular, the overall approach (as for any quantitative risk model) relies on the numerical estimation of risk and trust. These quantities are difficult to compute. Indeed, the diversity of risk scenarios, the intangible nature of trust, and the limited amount of historical data for incidents make an accurate quantitative assessment extremely difficult. As also shown in our paper, using some heuristics it is possible to derive sound relative estimation (i.e., using dimensionless units) for trust and risk, in some specific usage scenarios, but a general approach applicable to multiple use cases is missing. Ideally, we should estimate trust and risk in terms of monetary value, which has several advantages: 1) it provides a common *unit of measure* to combine risk and trust factors of very different nature (e.g., security risk, compliance risk, privacy risk or trust from reputation systems, trust-factors, behavioral analysis), 2) it is easy to understand for non-technical experts 3) it can be easily combined with risk mitigation and trust enhancement strategies that have a clear monetary value (e.g., insurance, certifications, legal contracts, trusted devices). In this respect, it is particularly interesting the emergence of new cyber-insurance models (building on techniques derived by the financial sector, e.g. Value-at-risk, Monte-Carlo simulations) to compute the values of cyber-risk and hence the cost of insurance premiums. [40].

In the short term, we want to validate our model on other use cases, where some quantitative methods are, even partially, available (either using dimensionless units or monetary values). We will also investigate the impact of authentication mechanisms on trust (as hinted in Section 3), and based on estimated probability of authentication success [41], to devise optimal strategies which combine multiple authentication methods according the risk associated to the request.

Acknowledgments. The research leading to these results has received funding from the FP7 EU-funded project Coco Cloud (grant No. 610853) and SECENTIS (FP7-PEOPLE-2012-ITN, grant no. 317387).

References

1. Trabelsi, S., Ecuyer, A., Alvarez, P.C.Y., Di Cerbo, F.: Optimizing access control performance for the cloud. In: Helfert, M., Desprez, F., Ferguson, D., Leymann, F., Muñoz, V.M. (eds.): CLOSER 2014 - Proceedings of the 4th International Conference on Cloud Computing and Services Science, Barcelona, Spain, April 3–5, 2014, 551–558. SciTePress (2014)
2. Chen, L., Crampton, J.: Risk-aware role-based access control. In: Meadows, C., Fernandez-Gago, C. (eds.) STM 2011. LNCS, vol. 7170, pp. 140–156. Springer, Heidelberg (2012)
3. Baracaldo, N., Joshi, J.: An adaptive risk management and access control framework to mitigate insider threats. Computers and Security **39**, 237–254 (2013)
4. Josang, A., Ismail, R., Boyd, C.: A survey of trust and reputation systems for online service provision. Decision Support Systems **43**(2), 618–644 (2007). Emerging Issues in Collaborative Commerce
5. Mcknight, D.H., Chervany, N.L.: The meanings of trust. Technical report (1996)
6. Gambetta, D.: Can we trust trust? In: Trust: Making and Breaking Cooperative Relations 213–237. Basil Blackwell (1988)
7. Celikel, E., Kantarcioglu, M., Thuraisingham, B., Bertino, E.: A risk management approach to RBAC. Risk Decis. Anal. **1**(1), 21–33 (2009)
8. ISO: Iec 27005: 2011 (en) information technology-security techniques-information security risk management switzerland. ISO/IEC (2011)
9. Cheng, P.C., Rohatgi, P., Keser, C., Karger, P.A., Wagner, G.M., Reninger, A.S.: Fuzzy multi-level security: An experiment on quantified risk-adaptive access control. In: Proceedings of the 2007 IEEE Symposium on Security and Privacy, SP 2007, pp. 222–230 (2007)
10. Houmb, S.H., Franqueira, V.N.L., Engum, E.A.: Quantifying security risk level from cvss estimates of frequency and impact. J. Syst. Softw. **83**(9), 1622–1634 (2010)
11. Moses, T., et al.: extensible access control markup language (xacml) version 2.0. Oasis Standard **200502** (2005)
12. Council of Europe: Handbook on european data protection law. Technical report (2014)
13. Scholl, M.A., Stine, K.M., Hash, J., Bowen, P., Johnson, L.A., Smith, C.D., Steinberg, D.I.: Sp 800–66 rev. 1. an introductory resource guide for implementing the health insurance portability and accountability act (HIPAA) security rule. Technical report (2008)

14. Clifton, C., Tassa, T.: On syntactic anonymity and differential privacy. Trans. Data Privacy **6**(2), 161–183 (2013)
15. Dalenius, T.: Finding a needle in a haystack-or identifying anonymous census record. Journal of official statistics **2**(3) (1986)
16. Bezzi, M.: An information theoretic approach for privacy metrics. Transactions on Data Privacy **3**(3), 199–215 (2010)
17. Samarati, P.: Protecting respondents' identities in microdata release. IEEE Trans. Knowl. Data Eng. **13**(6), 1010–1027 (2001)
18. Fung, B.C.M., Wang, K., Chen, R., Yu, P.S.: Privacy-preserving data publishing: A survey of recent developments. ACM Comput. Surv. **42**(4), 1–53 (2010)
19. Ciriani, V., De Capitani di Vimercati, S., Foresti, S., Samarati, P.: Theory of privacy and anonymity. In: Atallah, M., Blanton, M. (eds.) Algorithms and Theory of Computation Handbook (2nd edn). CRC Press (2009)
20. Armando, A., Bezzi, M., Metoui, N., Sabetta, A.: Risk-aware information disclosure. In: Garcia-Alfaro, J., Herrera-Joancomartí, J., Lupu, E., Posegga, J., Aldini, A., Martinelli, F., Suri, N. (eds.) DPM/SETOP/QASA 2014. LNCS, vol. 8872, pp. 266–276. Springer, Heidelberg (2015)
21. Committee on Strategies for Responsible Sharing of Clinical Trial Data: Sharing Clinical Trial Data: Maximizing Benefits, Minimizing Risk. National Academies Press (US), Washington (DC) (2015)
22. Mont, M.C., Beato, F.: On parametric obligation policies: enabling privacy-aware information lifecycle management in enterprises. In: Eighth IEEE International Workshop on Policies for Distributed Systems and Networks, POLICY 2007, pp. 51–55. IEEE (2007)
23. Ali, M., Bussard, L., Pinsdorf, U.: Obligation language for access control and privacy policies (2010)
24. Sandhu, R., Park, J.: Usage control: a vision for next generation access control. In: Gorodetsky, V., Popyack, L.J., Skormin, V.A. (eds.) MMM-ACNS 2003. LNCS, vol. 2776, pp. 17–31. Springer, Heidelberg (2003)
25. Ardagna, C.A., Cremonini, M., Capitani di Vimercati, S., Samarati, P.: A privacy-aware access control system. Journal of Computer Security **16**(4), 369–397 (2008)
26. Pretschner, A., Hilty, M., Basin, D.: Distributed usage control. Communications of the ACM **49**(9), 39–44 (2006)
27. Di Cerbo, F., Doliere, F., Gomez, L., Trabelsi, S.: Ppl v2.0: uniform data access and usage control on cloud and mobile. In: Proceedings of the 1st International Workshop on TEchnical and LEgal aspects of data pRIvacy and SEcurity, IEEE (2015)
28. Trabelsi, S., Sendor, J., Reinicke, S.: Ppl: primelife privacy policy engine. In: 2011 IEEE International Symposium on Policies for Distributed Systems and Networks (POLICY), pp. 184–185, June 2011
29. Bertino, E., Bonatti, P.A., Ferrari, E.: Trbac: A temporal role-based access control model. ACM Trans. Inf. Syst. Secur. **4**(3), 191–233 (2001)
30. Bonatti, P., Galdi, C., Torres, D.: Erbac: event-driven rbac. In: Proceedings of the 18th ACM Symposium on Access Control Models and Technologies. SACMAT 2013. ACM NY (2013)
31. Ahmed, A., Zhang, N.: A context-risk-aware access control model for ubiquitous environments. In: IMCSIT. IEEE (2008)
32. Chen, L., Crampton, J., Kollingbaum, M.J., Norman, T.J.: Obligations in risk-aware access control. In: Cuppens-Boulahia, N., Fong, P., García-Alfaro, J., Marsh, S., Steghöfer, J. (eds.) PST, pp. 145–152. IEEE (2012)

33. Cheng, P.C., Rohatgi, P., Keser, C., Karger, P.A., Wagner, G.M., Reninger, A.S.: Fuzzy multi-level security: an experiment on quantified risk-adaptive access control. In: IEEE Symposium on Security and Privacy, pp. 222–230. IEEE Computer Society (2007)
34. Dickens, L., Russo, A., Cheng, P.C., Lobo, J.: Towards learning risk estimation functions for access control. In: In Snowbird Learning Workshop (2010)
35. Shaikh, R.A., Adi, K., Logrippo, L.: Dynamic risk-based decision methods for access control systems **31**, 447–464 (2012)
36. Armando, A., Bezzi, M., Metoui, N., Sabetta, A.: Risk-based privacy-aware information disclosure. International Journal of Secure Software Engineering (IJSSE) **6**(2), 70–89 (2015)
37. Bettini, C., Jajodia, S., Wang, X.S., Wijesekera, D.: Provisions and obligations in policy management and security applications. In: Proceedings of the 28th International Conference on Very Large Data Bases. VLDB 2002, pp. 502–513. VLDB Endowment (2002)
38. Baracaldo, N., Joshi, J.: Beyond accountability: Using obligations to reduce risk exposure and deter insider attacks. In: Proceedings of the 18th ACM Symposium on Access Control Models and Technologies, SACMAT 2013, pp. 213–224. ACM, New York (2013)
39. Dimmock, N., Belokosztolszki, A., Eyers, D., Bacon, J., Moody, K.: Using trust and risk in role-based access control policies. In: Proceedings of the Ninth ACM Symposium on Access Control Models and Technologies. SACMAT 2004, pp. 156–162. ACM, New York (2004)
40. Shah, A., Dahake, S., J., S.H.H.: Valuing data security and privacy using cyber insurance. SIGCAS Comput. Soc. **45**(1), 38–41 (2015)
41. Kelley, P., Komanduri, S., Mazurek, M., Shay, R., Vidas, T., Bauer, L., Christin, N., Cranor, L., Lopez, J.: Guess again (and again and again): measuring password strength by simulating password-cracking algorithms. In: 2012 IEEE Symposium on Security and Privacy (SP), pp. 523–537 (2012)

Author Index

Aljalbout, Sahar 443
Almendros-Jiménez, Jesús M. 501
Andrikopoulos, Vasilios 337, 348
Antoniadis, Sotirios 473
Armando, Alessandro 660

Bach, Thomas 219
Ballauco, Giancarlo 639
Bauer, Thomas 267
Becerra-Terón, Antonio 501
Becha, Hanane 465
Belaïd, Djamel 3
Belhaj, Nabila 3
Bellahsene, Zohra 527
Bellatreche, Ladjel 483
Ben Hassine, Ahlem 451
Benaissa, Moussa 545
Benammar, Riyadh 397
Bezzi, Michele 660
Böhmer, Kristof 166
Boucelma, Omar 443, 451, 620

Ceravolo, Paolo 639
Charrada, Faouzi Ben 19
Chen, Liu 378
Cuzzocrea, Alfredo 146
Czepa, Christoph 311

Damiani, Ernesto 639
Dargie, Waltenegus 575
De Leone, Renato 423
de Meer, Hermann 594
De Meo, Pasquale 57
Demetz, Lukas 557
Di Cerbo, Francesco 660
Di Noia, Tommaso 405, 423
Diallo, Gayo 545

El Ioini, Nabil 612
Eshuis, Rik 202

Farias, Tarcisio M. 361
Fazzinga, Bettina 320
Fdhila, Walid 90

Fischer, Andreas 594
Flesca, Sergio 320
Folino, Francesco 146
Frati, Fulvio 639
Furfaro, Filippo 320

Galhardas, Helena 237
Gammoudi, Mohamed Mohsen 285
Gantner, Julian 557
Gering, Patrick 303
Grambow, Gregor 127
Grefen, Paul W.P.J. 202
Grossmann, Georg 257
Guarascio, Massimo 146

Hacid, Mohand-Said 285
Hadded, Leila 19
Hahn, Michael 337
Herbst, Joachim 267

Indiono, Conrad 90

Jiménez-Ruiz, Ernesto 545
Jordan, Andreas 257

Kalogeraki, Vana 473
Karastoyanova, Dimka 337
Kathiravelu, Pradeeban 237
Khiat, Abderrahmane 545
Khouri, Selma 483
Kim, Thanh Tran Thi 311
Kitagawa, Hiroyuki 109
Kittel, Thomas 594
Kloukinas, Christos 644
Kolb, Jens 127
Kolosnjaji, Bojan 594
Krotsiani, Maria 644
Küng, Josef 329
Kusters, Rob J. 202

Lacroix, Julien 620
Lahmar, Imen Ben 3
Leite, Letícia Lopes 76
Lengyel, Tamas K. 594

Leymann, Frank   348
Litou, Iouliana   473
Liu, Mengchi   378
Lukasiewicz, Thomas   423

Maier, Ronald   557
Mandarawi, Waseem   594
Maret, Pierre   397
Masciari, Elio   320
Maurino, Andrea   423
Mayer, Christian   219
Mayer, Wolfgang   257
Meissner, Malte   303
Messina, Fabrizio   57
Metoui, Nadia   660
Mohamed, Mohamed   3
Müller, Luana   76
Müller, Tilo   594
Mundbrod, Nicolas   127
Mynarz, Jindřich   405

Nguyen, Benjamin   38
Nicolle, Christophe   361

Onishi, Sei   109

Pappalardo, Giuseppe   57
Paschke, Adrian   519
Pontieri, Luigi   146, 320
Protsenko, Mykola   594
Pucheral, Philippe   38

Rasouli, Mohammad R.   202
Reichert, Manfred   127, 267
Reiser, Hans P.   594
Rinderle-Ma, Stefanie   90, 166, 311
Rosaci, Domenico   57
Rosati, Jessica   423
Rothermel, Kurt   219
Roxin, Ana   361
Ruhsam, Christoph   311
Rybina, Kateryna   575

Sarnè, Giuseppe M.L.   57
Schill, Alexander   575

Schrefl, Michael   257
Sellami, Mokhtar   285
Sellami, Sana   443, 451, 465
Selway, Matt   257
Silveira, Milene Selbach   76
Slaimi, Fatma   451
Spanoudakis, George   644
Stumptner, Markus   257
Sun, Bo   185
Svátek, Vojtěch   405

Tariq, Muhammad Adnan   219
Tata, Samir   19
Taubmann, Benjamin   594
Tiedeken, Julian   267
Tigrine, Abdel Nasser   527
To, Quoc-Cuong   38
Todorov, Konstantin   527
Torres, Manuel   501
Tran, Huy   311
Trémeau, Alain   397
Trienekens, Jos J.M.   202

Umashankar, Subramanya   575

Veiga, Luís   237
Vetschera, Rudolf   90

Wang, Jianmin   185
Wang, Yuquan   185
Wardani, Dewi W.   329
Weiß, Andreas   337
Weishäupl, Eva   594
Weiss, Erhard   311
Wen, Lijie   185
Wettinger, Johannes   348
Wintrich, Nikolaus   303

Yamaguchi, Yuto   109
Yaman, Beyza   545
Yan, Zhiqiang   185
Yu, Ting   378

Zavatarelli, Francesco   639
Zdun, Uwe   311

Printed in the United States
By Bookmasters